Shock City Image and Architecture in Industrial Manchester

Mark Crinson

PAUL MELLON CENTRE
FOR STUDIES IN BRITISH ART
Distributed by Yale University Press
New Haven and London

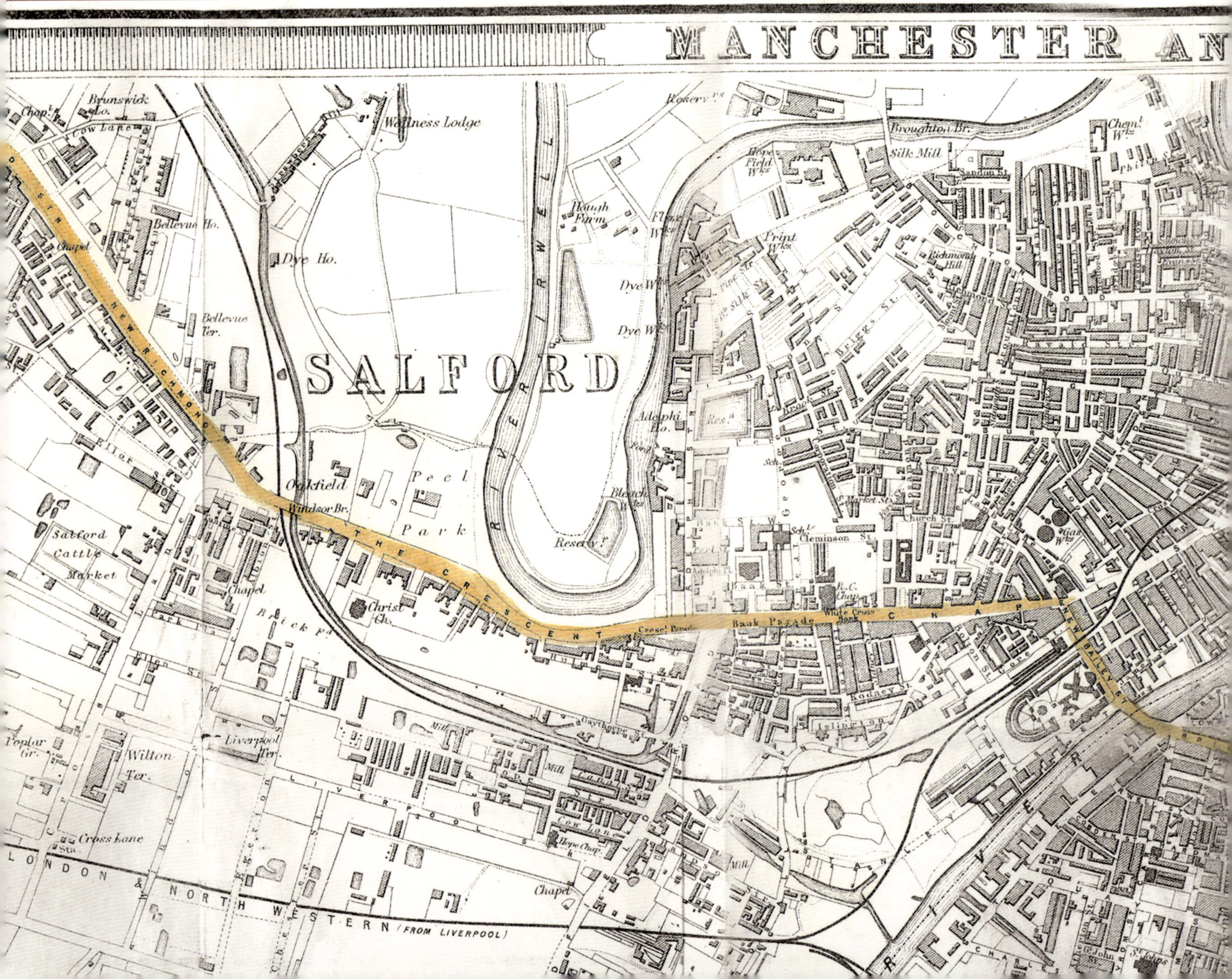

Shock City

Image and Architecture in Industrial Manchester

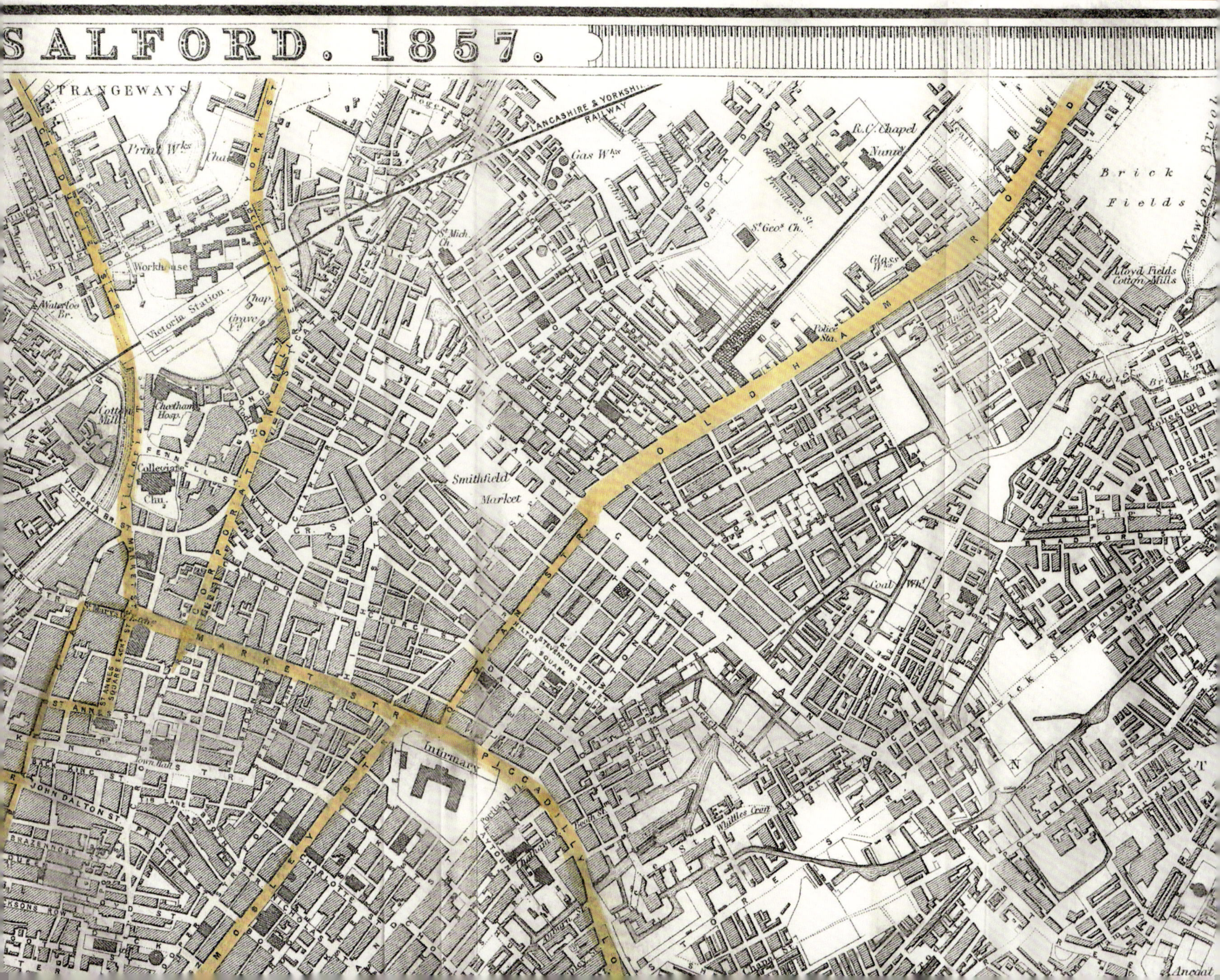

First published in 2022 by the Paul Mellon Centre for Studies in British Art
16 Bedford Square, London, WC1B 3JA
paul-mellon-centre.ac.uk

ISBN 978-1-913107-33-8 HB
Library of Congress Control Number: 2022937499

British Library Cataloguing-in-Publication Data
A catalogue record for this book is available from the British Library

Designed by Dalrymple
Origination by Evergreen Colour Management Ltd
Printed in China through World Print Ltd

MIX
Paper | Supporting responsible forestry
FSC® C014688

Frontispiece: Map of Manchester, 1857. Published by J. T. Cornish (detail of fig. 5).

Contents

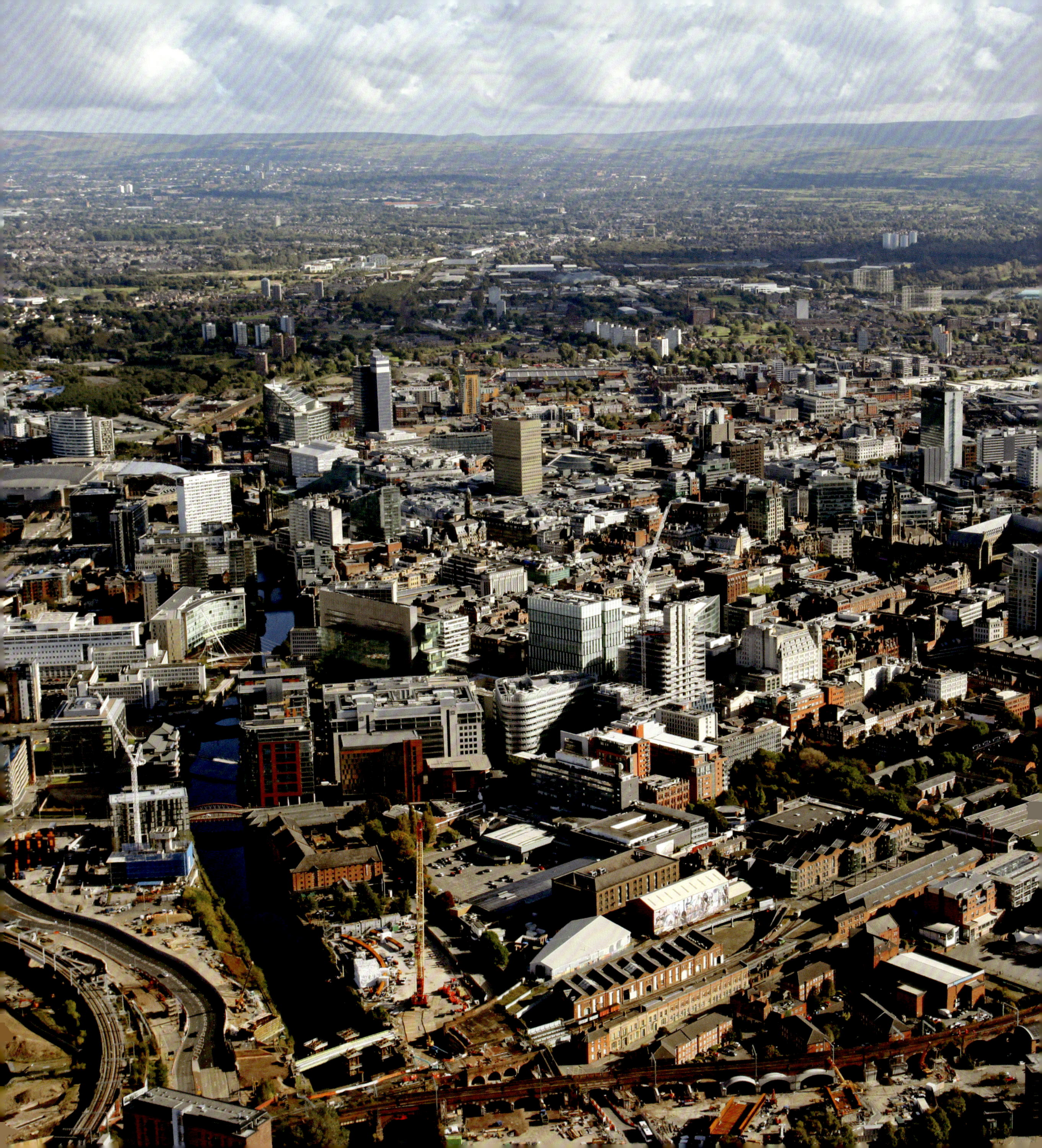

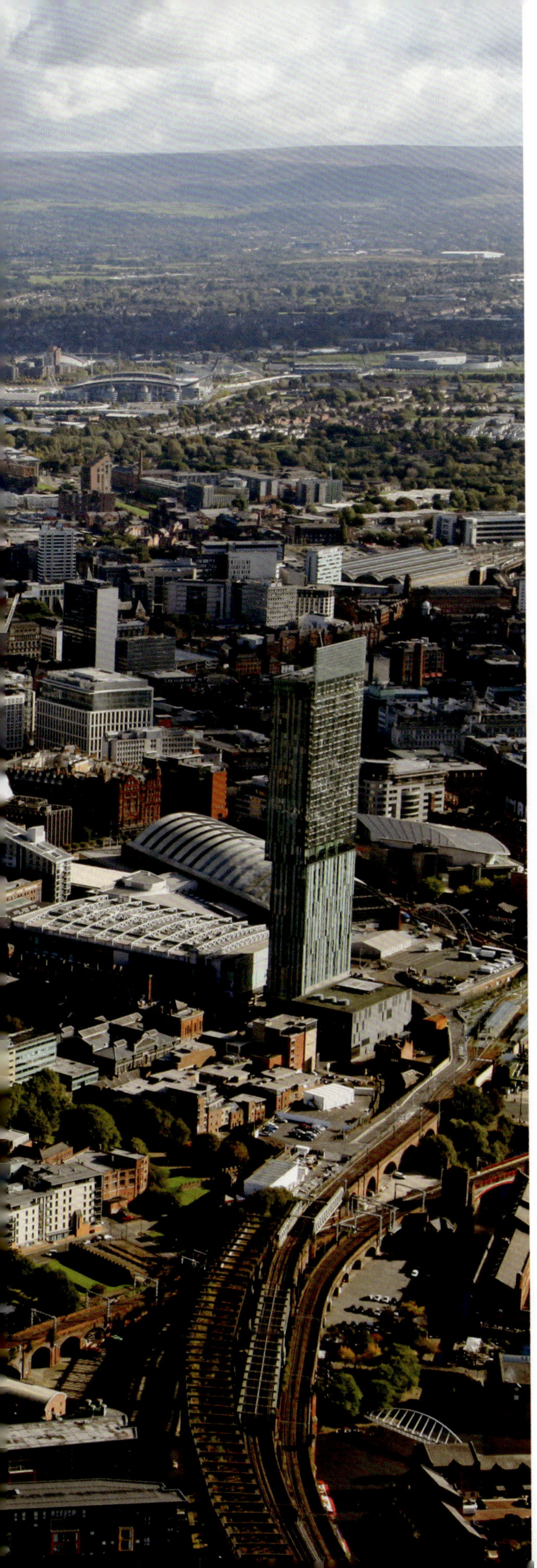

Aerial view of the Manchester skyline in 2016.

Preface and Acknowledgements

MY WAY INTO MANCHESTER WAS AT FIRST OBLIQUE. In the mid-1980s I stayed a few times with my sister on trips back from the United States, where I was then studying. She lived with her partner in Charles Barry Crescent in the inner-city suburb of Hulme. The city was then in the depths of industrial decline – in fact beyond them – and the public housing of the 'crescents', a cut-price systems-built estate of the 1960s, had declined rapidly. Maintenance, as ever, was the main problem, but the estate was asbestos and pest ridden, damp, cold and plagued by casual crime. Another lifestyle had taken over – great for penniless artists, students and musicians, not so good for families or if you were old and infirm. From my sister's flat and the deck outside you could see some of the other curving blocks also named after British architects – Adam, Kent, Nash, Hawksmoor. You also looked down onto the Russell Club, a pent-roof brick community centre where punk and post-punk bands played on the weekly Factory night – Joy Division, The Cure, A Certain Ratio and so on. This was an outlier for the more famous Haçienda club in the city centre, also run by the Manchester music scene's rising promoter Tony Wilson.

Dotted around the crescents were the isolated institutions of a previous age – pubs, a library, churches (Pugin's poverty-scratched St Wilfrid's was nearby) – but almost all the Victorian terraces and the grid of streets they stood alongside had disappeared. It was as if the nineteenth century was shameful and must be expunged. The isolation and anachronism seemed the very image of the much discussed 'English decline' at the time. As you walked from Hulme into Manchester, it felt as if you were going against the older city's grain. You cut eastwards past shapeless empty plots and over a dual carriageway, and arrived suddenly in Chorlton-on-Medlock, once another inner-city town centre around a churchyard which, by the 1980s, had mostly been taken over by the polytechnic (its art school was housed partly in an old department store). On the corner with Oxford Road a snooker club helped to spin out long afternoons; it was later taken over by drug dealers.

It was not the kind of north I'd known before. I was a southerner from the peri-urban flatlands around Heathrow, west of London. As a family, we had taken regular trips up to the north-east to stay with my grandparents in a mining village. That kind of north was still recognisable for what it had been, but Manchester in the north-west was different. The same soot-black spires and chimneys but a different set of industries, a very different relation to landscape and to scale and, as I came to see, an entirely different sense of its significance.

A few years later, in the early 1990s, I got a job as a lecturer at Manchester University, then just stirring from its long identity crisis after its mid-century pre-eminence in the sciences (the Arts dean presided over my interview panel, held in a neo-Gothic committee room, wearing mortar board and academic gown). I'd missed out on a job in the architecture school two years before and instead found one in the art history department. That was a good thing. Every morning, walking to work from Piccadilly station, I crossed empty rectangles of ground on the diagonal, the muddy paths sometimes passing over exposed cobbles or paving stones. Over the next twenty years or so those plots were built over as the city successively levered itself back into some kind of contention, exploiting first the IRA bomb of 1996 for funding, then the Commonwealth Games of 2002, then the expansion and merging of universities and so on. Meanwhile, the crescents were demolished and a neo-Victorian Hulme was created, low-rise and bricky, forgetting its all too brief modernism.

In my subsequent twenty-three years at the university, as I got to know the city better through living there, I began to do bits and pieces of research on it, mostly in the gaps between projects on other subjects and mostly on aspects of the post-industrial city. I hold to an idea, dating back to my days with other doctoral students in Philadelphia, that the city one lives in should be one of the subjects that an architectural historian works on, but Manchester had become more than just an architectural subject. There is some irony for me that the book I came increasingly to want to write has only reached its completion after I relocated to the south.

As a consequence of all this, my debts are stretched across a long period. First of all, thanks to those who have invited me to give presentations about the material: Jeff Cohen (at the Society of Architectural Historians, United States); Gary Boyd (also at the SAH, USA); Matthew Walker (at Oxford University); Hollis Clayson, David Van Zanten and Stephen Eisenman (at Northwestern University); Carla Yanni and Seth Koven (at Rutgers University); Aris Sarafianos and Aristotelis Dimitrakopoulos (at the University of Ioannina); and Claire Zimmerman (at the University of Michigan). With Claire I organised a symposium at Birkbeck on 'Factory Worlds' and benefited immensely from hearing about other speakers' work, in particular Tilo Amhoff, Peter Christensen, Anke Hagemann and Katie Lloyd Thomas, as well as Claire's own work.

Many others have helped with suggestions, conversation and answers to my questions, or with their hospitality. Among them are John Archer, Maria Balshaw, Hannah Barker, Richard Brook, Alistair Cartwright, Penny Crinson, Helen Hills, Pat Kelleher, Mike McCulloch, the late Robina McNeil, the late John Pickstone, Marcia Pointon, Frank Salmon, Aris Sarafianos, Shaun Theobald, Paul Tyrer and Terry Wyke. Both Tony King and Peter Scriver intrigued me with totally separate conversations in Singapore. Jeff Cohen made me look more carefully at Thomas Harrison. David Van Zanten kickstarted several of my lines of thought when he came to Manchester University back in the 1990s – I hope he will be surprised by where they have led.

Although the research for this book has stretched over a considerable period of time, bringing the book to completion would have been impossible without a British Academy / Leverhulme Senior Research Fellowship in 2016–17.

Manchester benefits from a wealth of archives, galleries and libraries, and the work of their expert and dedicated staff, even through the difficulties of local authority (and other) funding cuts and the COVID-19 pandemic. I wish in particular to thank Aoife Larkin and Thom Keep at Portico Library; Elizabeth Gow and Hannah Hillen at John Rylands Library Special Collections; Fergus Wilde at Chetham's Library; James Peters at Manchester University Library; the staff at the Local History Library, Salford Art Gallery and Museum; David Blair at Bolton Central Library; Chris Hyland at Manchester Central Library; and Bev Hogg and John Peel at Manchester Art Gallery.

I have benefited hugely from conversations with colleagues at two universities. Warm thanks go to my colleagues at Birkbeck (especially Leslie Topp, Kate Retford, Lynda Nead, Steve Edwards and Fiona Candlin) and at Manchester (particularly Anthony Gerbino and Ed Wouk). I have also been fortunate with my publisher and especially with Emily Lees as editor and Jacqueline Harvey as copy editor. Two anonymous readers suggested some important changes – their support and perceptions have been greatly valued.

Above all, I want to thank a group of friends and scholars who read earlier drafts of the book and offered me their opinions, insights, encouragement and further references: Steve Edwards, Asia Haut and Richard J. Williams. Steve Edwards, in particular, has been hugely encouraging, providing insights big and small.

The book is dedicated to Marcia Pointon, who has always been a model for me from my first studies at university, through to being my boss and then my colleague, and a friend all along. It was she who really got me stuck on Manchester.

My previous published work on Manchester includes 'Manchester and the "Hypocritical Plan": Architecture, Shopping, and Identity in the Industrial City', in *Thinking Northern: The Formation of Identity in Northern England*, ed. Christoph Ehland, Amsterdam: Rodopi, 2007, pp. 193–216; 'Towards the Beautiful City', in *Fabrications: New Art and Urban Memory in Manchester*, ed. Mark Crinson, Helen Hills and Natalie Rudd, Manchester: UMiM, 2002, pp. 18–23; 'Pictorialism and Industry: Alvin Langdon Coburn in Manchester', *History of Photography* 30, no. 2 (2006), pp. 155–72; 'Explaining Urbanism to Wild Animals', *Mute* 29 (2005), pp. 62–6; 'Urbisville', *Mute* 25 (2002), pp. 20–5; and 'Glass Architecture: A Riotous Mythology', *Mute* 36 (2012), pp. 1–9. My edited book *Urban Memory: History and Amnesia in the Modern City* (London: Routledge, 2005) includes 'Mnemotechny of the Industrial City: Contemporary Art and Urban Memory'; with Paul Tyrer, 'Clocking Off in Ancoats: Time and Remembrance in the Post-industrial City'; and, again with Paul Tyrer, 'Totemic Park: Symbolic Representation in Post-industrial Space'. A short section from the Coburn article is adapted for part of the Coda here, but other than that the only article that appears in this book (considerably revised and updated in Chapter 3) is 'Photography and the Industrial City: Manchester and Salford, Ancient and Modern', *Word and Image* 18, no. 4 (2002), pp. 295–314.

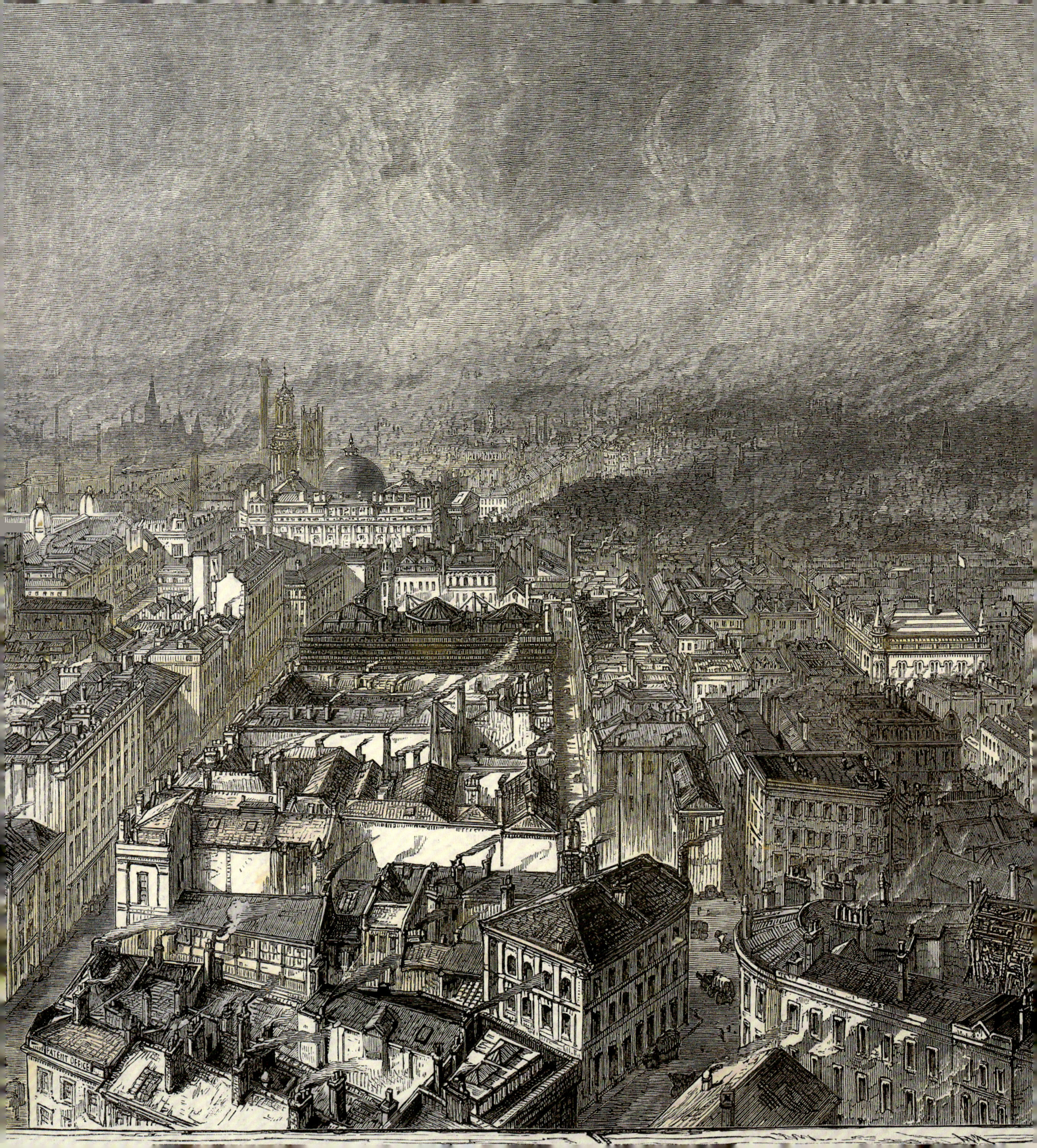
PATENT OFFICE

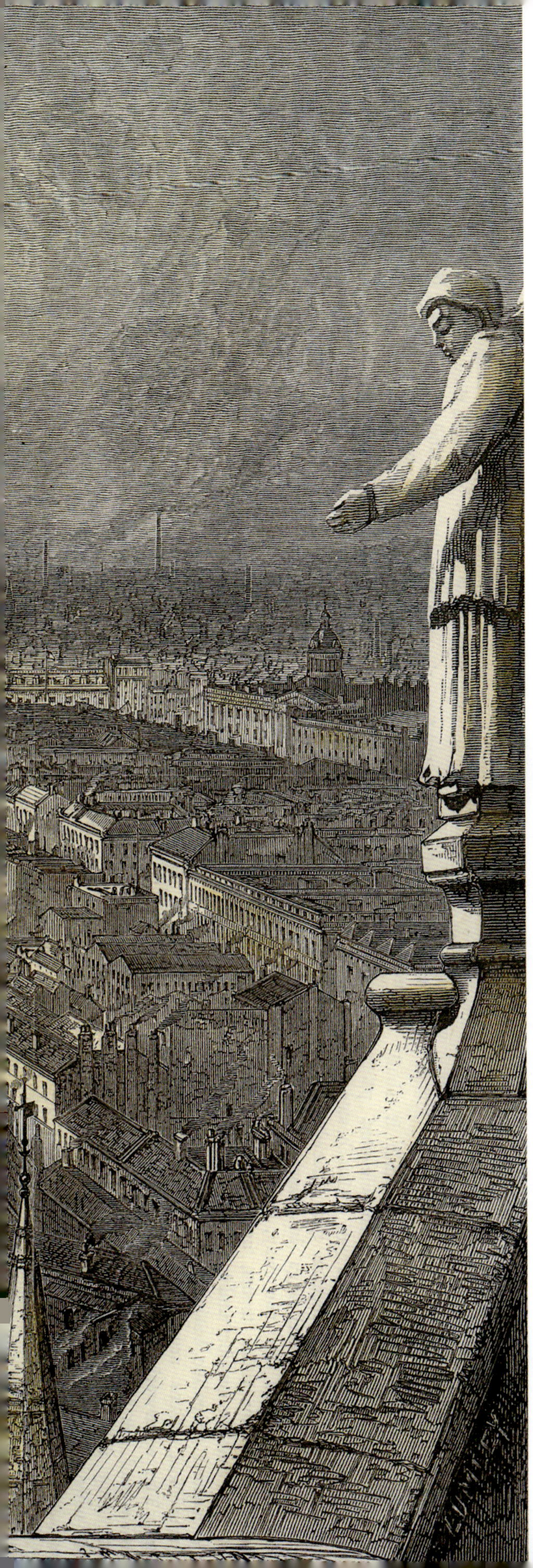

[1] 'Bird's-Eye View of the City from the New Town Hall Tower'. Engraving published in *The Graphic*, 14 October 1876.

Introduction

Shock, Smoke and Charity

HERE IS A VIEW OVER THE CENTRE OF MANCHESTER, a raking fragment or slice of the city (fig. 1).[1] An angled road on one side and an angled parapet on the other suggest a kind of forced containment. And we look from an unexpected height – not Icarian, yet not ordinary – not from a human place. This is the height of roof-level sculpture, set on a tower and far higher than the tallest roof around. We're looking eastwards and northwards from the tower of the newly completed Manchester Town Hall. It's 1876, and this is the shock city of the Industrial Revolution, notorious and famed as much for its pollution and slums as for its new building types, new classes and new technologies. Or perhaps it *was* the shock city and this now shows the dispelling of its chaos, an order newly being achieved. A city in progress.

Let's look a little closer. Near us, on the same ledge, a stone figure gestures to the city below. She is Charity, *Caritas* the giver, the greatest of the theological virtues, the bearer of love's beneficence. And with her stock gesture she tends to the city, perhaps offering what she stands on, what she is a part of in her stoniness. (This may be the moment to acknowledge that, if this sculpted figure looking down on the city seems familiar, we have overlaid onto it Luc-Olivier Merson's much more famous gargoyle-level illustration of 1881 for Victor Hugo's *Notre-Dame de Paris*.[2]) Beyond and beneath her, the city's busyness is expressed both by the short trails of smoke from chimneys in the foreground and by the street corridors carved into the urban mass and leading back into its depths towards certain domes and towers. There's a kind of history laid out, to be found in small contrasts and differences: in a fire-wrecked roof, in a narrow court or cluster of irregular upper storeys, in the repeated windows of newer warehouses and offices, in the heavy cornice and trio of conical roofs of the old town hall, or in the square tower of St Ann's church on the left-hand edge. The sculpted quality in these areas is produced by effects of light and perspective that pick out humdrum as well as grand buildings, and that hint at a pattern emerging beneath the statue's hand. Institutions abound. Beneath Charity, the tall dome of the Royal Infirmary with warehouses around it; towards the centre, the banded roof of the pinnacled Reform Club; to the left the bulbous dome of the Royal Exchange; just beside this the stumpy tower of the restored cathedral; and finally here where we are, the new Town Hall, a Valhalla for Free Trade. Seen this way, the print serves as a kind of ledger, an inventory, of what Manchester's civic and industrial elite had achieved over the previous thirty years.

But this crust of institutions is only just formed over the city's convulsive past, only this side of it. The streets lead to nowhere in particular. Even the Royal Exchange is marginal: there is no culminating point between it and Charity, no great square, no axis or vista or answering facade that fixes the view, that offers completion. And beyond the proud buildings there is no view onto a surrounding landscape: it's not even half-visible – no sunny horizon, no surrounding hills, no such nature–culture boundary. Instead, looming in the mid-distance, and barely intimated by the tame domestic smoke of the foreground, is a formidable billowing curtain, a barrier of lead-coloured smoke – the 'incense of industry', 'devil's darkness', the fossil economy in its first full flood, industrial melanism. Lower in the sky it drifts in rhythmic furls still subject to the prevailing wind, but ominous shapeless plumes have formed above. Long chimneys just visible in the gusting drifts are the only architecture discernible in that background. Perhaps this smoke is Charity's opposite, the vice of Cruelty, and perhaps it intimates the tasks that the city has yet to perform.[3] This, one might presume, is the trope of the chaotic industrial city, seedbed of Manchester's prosperity and source of its shame, of muck and brass, of what it must move on from by the civilising of the city's centre, a process in which the Town Hall was the culminating and most prodigious result. Chaos and civility; murk and sun. Certainly, the contrast between the sharpness of light here, from where we look, the crisply cubic quality of building form and street void, even the vertiginous plunge down to the tiny figures, carriages and horses, and the diffuse greyness, the merging of air and smoke and building, of distance itself, is extreme. If Charity, the embodiment of civic governance, presides over all this, then, and almost despite what surely were the artist's aims, the distance is as much of a threat as a challenge: that background can easily become foreground. Shock city or city of civic order? Either might prevail.

I come back to Charity. What does it mean to identify her with municipal government, to understand her as tending to a city? Where is she standing metaphorically? In other words, does she look to the past or from the past (or even from the future back at this present)? And are we really meant to think that the machinery of bureaucracy beneath her is the answer to the grey barrier beyond? Friedrich Engels, that great critic of the industrial city, understood charity as one of the expressions of the relationship between the idea of Free Trade and the government of modern cities. Government was necessary to hold the proletariat in check but charity was the bourgeois Free Traders' balm; paid for with taxes and subscriptions, it was both the performance of benevolence and the means (guaranteed as much by the municipal police as by the Infirmary) by which the unsightly might be cleared from the city's streets.[4] Not so much, then, shock city *or* city of civic order as both, the one as a means to the other, or the one as screened from the other ('concealed with the cloak of charity', as Engels put it[5]). Although Engels was writing thirty years before this engraving was published, his terms are closely relevant to it. Charity and the new Town Hall – both are products of the city's 'mighty benefactors' and the city is the object of their concern, of their ministrations. Charity's effect is a kind of clearance, a make-over, the expression of a class apartheid, so that what is before us is the city of consumption, exchange (the global marketplace), distribution, good government, and what is beyond, hidden but also signalled by the grey pall, is the place of production. The proletariat may be absent from the streets below, or anonymously tiny, but perhaps that is because they have been identified with that smoke, have taken on its substance.[6] The plumes and furls are the side effects of their labours, perhaps even their etherealised bodies.

It is difficult to imagine a figure of Charity having any role at all on a municipal building a hundred years later, such was the way the twentieth century came to believe that its modernity was complete. Charity on the Manchester Town Hall, like the hints of neo-Gothic paraphernalia around her, instead signals unmodernity to us moderns and postmoderns, or at least imperfectly or not-yet-achieved modernity. Charity seems to belong either to tradition and revivalism, the vestiges of religious convictions, the ornamental margins, or to the now overfamiliar magic of the panoptic view, the seer and the seen. What about smoke – where does it belong? Surely, in its sky-blotting excess, as much as in the technologies and architectures that produced it, smoke must be the modern incarnate. It is an effluent, necessary but unwanted. How could modernity be announced, be celebrated even, by something inexpressive, by a deconstructed and wasted nature, the means and not the ends?

There is, then, a face-off. Charity's hand may hover above the Infirmary but most of her is outlined against that murk. And, of course, both she and it are material products of this city. Indeed, there had been few more startling sites of advanced modernity in the previous decades of that century. Smoke plays into this fame (or infamy) of Manchester as the shock city. Charity, though, is part of another scenario – the city without shock, the city which cures itself and makes itself more recognisably city-like. Does the sum of these two scenarios add up to something that might be claimed as the modern city of its time? Not so much absolute newness, nor absolute rejection, but a constant reverberating, oscillating motion between the two.

THE TERM 'SHOCK CITY' WAS COINED BY THE HISTORIAN Asa Briggs in a short and still illuminating essay originally published in 1963.[7] In a kind of inversion of grand tourists leaving Britain to view the Continent's ancient ruins, European visitors (technologists, economists, journalists, architects and spies) were drawn to Manchester for its lessons as much as its sights. It was a place of advanced technology, they thought, a new territory of the modern. But what they, and visitors from other parts of Britain, found was something viscerally repulsive and awesome, something that was certainly new but also discordant and startling. How could this otherness – the city's scale and its perceived labyrinthine qualities, its noise and murk, its stark facades and forests of tall chimneys – be assimilated to any sense of what a city should be? This is what we read about in Alexis de Tocqueville, Friedrich von Raumer, Hans Caspar Escher, Léon Faucher, Eugène Buret, Johann Georg Kohl and many others.[8] But we could also distinguish another shock from this, and that is the shock that the city itself went through (one might say experienced, as if it were creatural) as a result of unfettered development encouraged by a number of favourable local conditions including, paradoxically, the weakness of Manchester's then archaic local government (a link that continues to be made by historians).[9] And it was this second experience of shock that was the subject of the social reformers, notably James Phillips Kay (later Kay-Shuttleworth), a local surgeon, who wrote *The Moral and Physical Condition of the Working Classes* (1832); Edwin Chadwick, another local man, with the wider remit of his *Report on the Sanitary Condition of the Labouring Population of Great Britain* (1842); and Friedrich Engels, the son of a German industrialist then working as a clerk for his father's firm in the city, Ermen & Engels, who published his investigations as *The Condition of the Working Classes in England* (1845).[10] And here the medico-anthropological concerns move back and forth between the body of the stricken (and often racialised) poor and the fragmented body of the inhuman city.[11]

Faucher gives us a sense of the vividness of the first kind of encounter and its response to the spaces and buildings of the city. A journalist and Free Trader, and within a few years a minister under Louis-Napoléon, Faucher's 1844 account was a relatively late commentary of this kind. As with our engraving, he found that 'labour presents a mysterious activity, somewhat akin to the subterraneous action of a volcano'. Physically, urbanistically, it was the lack of anything like Paris that struck him: 'there are no great boulevards or heights to aid the eye in measuring the vast extent of surface which it occupies ... a want of public squares, fountains, trees, promenades and well-ventilated buildings. In

[2] Locomotive for the Madras Railway in the Beyer Peacock Yard at Gorton, Manchester, *c.*1860. Photograph: James Mudd.

fact there is nothing to compare with this city.' Fantastically (we begin to get the gist), 'you hear nothing but the breathing of the vast machines', and the smoke exhaled by their chimneys '[offers] up to the heavens, as it were in token of homage, the sighs of the Labour which God has imposed upon man'. It seemed both repetitious and perplexing: 'all the houses, all the streets, resemble each other; and yet this uniformity is in the midst of confusion ... everything is alike and everything is new'.[12] Charity had little place in this version of shock; it was about the experience of the incomprehensible, the new, the plumes of smoke. The modern was in the very forms of the city.

The second shock was often expressed as a direct ratio between the same conditions and the state of the classes that laboured under them. For the Benthamite social reformer Edwin Chadwick, epidemic and disease correlate to 'atmospheric impurities produced by decomposing animal and vegetable substances, by damp and filth, and close and overcrowded dwellings'. Each of these had equivalent environmental solutions in forms of cleansing, clearing, draining and ventilating, if only 'scientific ... and structural arrangements' were made, bypassing the 'desuetude' of existing local governance. All of this would in turn reform the 'moral condition of the population'.[13] Here the labouring body is not offstage or intimated by animate objects, as in the first form of shock; it is directly related to the condition of what it lives in and is surrounded by, not as the volcano below the city but as the seismograph of the city's moral and physical state. We could say that in this form of shock the living body of the city is to be saved by Charity from its suffocating, debilitating and self-made ills. The benevolent modern – in the forms of medicine, bureaucracy, legislation and urban 'improvements' (if not just architecture then certainly in areas of an instrumentalised environment) – is the cure for a peculiarly new form of chaos, perceived as malevolent.

It was the combination of the two ideas of shock – the jolt of newly experiencing the modern and the changes that remake the modern – that gave Manchester its symbolic status, its unique representativeness. For better or worse, it was understood as a city that had not been seen or experienced before because its economy, its technologies and the effects of its means of production were unprecedented. In Briggs's shock list, the city was associated with 'size, with industry, with newness, with squalor, and, above all else, with unfamiliar and, on occasion, alarming social relationships'.[14] Some of the items on this list are clearly included in another title often given to Manchester, that of the 'first industrial city'.[15] But it was the social relations that clearly interested Briggs the most: the vast gap between rich and poor; the emerging new heteroclite class of industrialists (the 'cottonocracy') and their awareness of themselves as a class; the proletariat ('called into existence', Engels wrote, 'by the introduction of machinery'[16]), drawn to the city to work in its new mills; the role of the 'shopocracy' or petit bourgeoisie; and the question of the continuing powers of the landed gentry as their world seemed transformed.[17] There were also the struggles between these classes, including riots, machine breaking and brutal acts of suppression such as the Peterloo massacre; the displaced class struggles (or 'social war') that ramify through many other relations and that produce what has been called the 'political unconscious'; the 'repressed and buried reality of this [more] fundamental history' in the cultural productions of the time where each class is defined by its other.[18] Struggle is implicitly there – we can add – in the social effects of the advance of industrial machinery, most especially the steam engine and the subsumption of unruly labour that many hoped for from it.[19] This 'fossil economy' – an economy based on the energy produced by fossil fuels and their growing consumption – was first born in Britain as an essential part of the Industrial Revolution. The most prominent city responsible for this, certainly the one most associated with it by contemporaries, was Manchester.

Two points need making parenthetically before we develop this discussion of shock city, because the notion encompasses more than either the effects of cotton manufacture or of Manchester narrowly conceived. First, it was the cotton trade that had given the town its regional prominence since the beginning of the eighteenth century, and it was the textile industry that then saw many of the extraordinary innovations in technology, labour practices and infrastructure that dramatically scaled up the industry and gave it what might be called its revolutionary cutting edge.[20] The whole conception in the early nineteenth century of a 'mill' or a

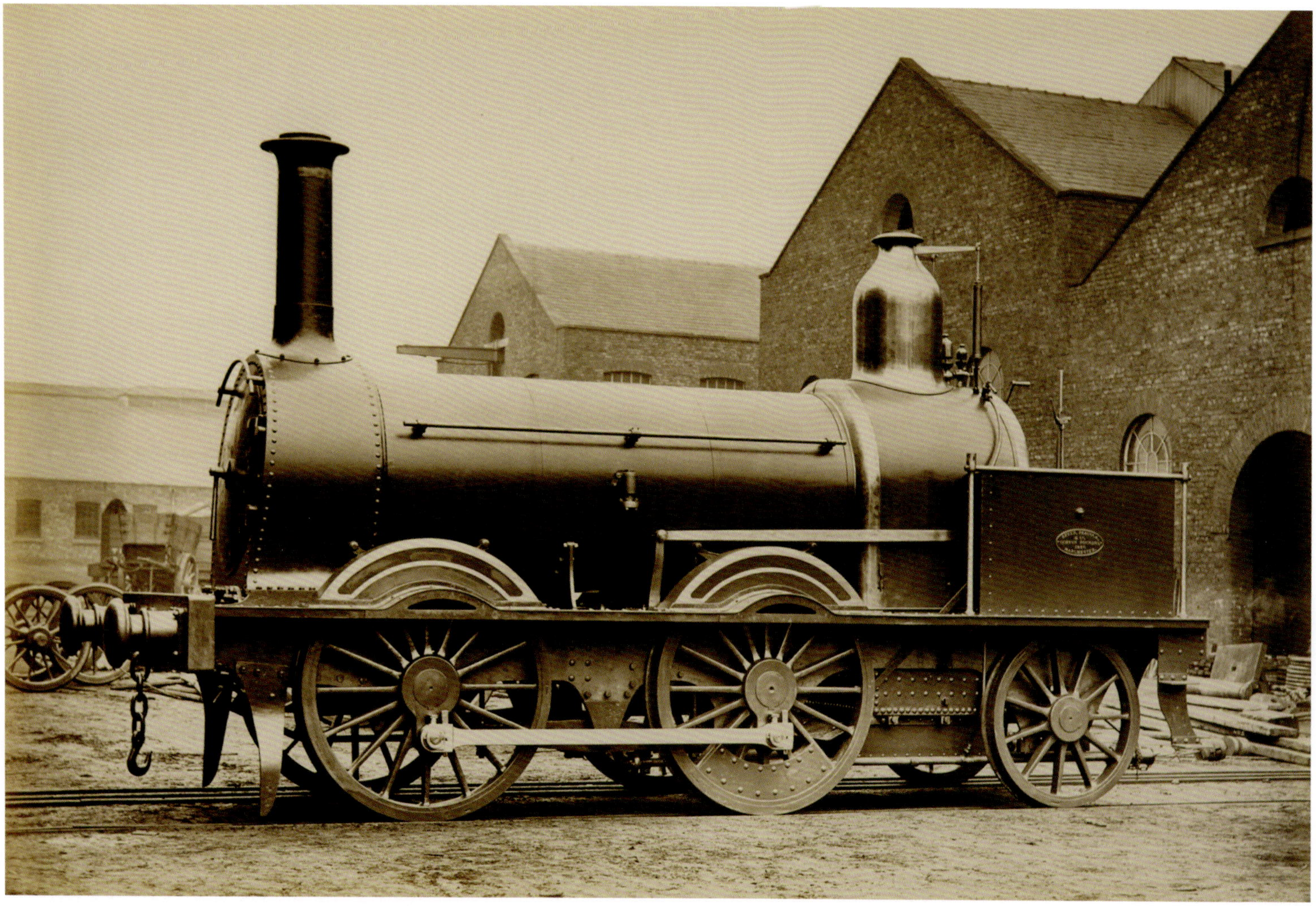

'factory' (the terms will be used interchangeably here as they were in the nineteenth century), even of 'industry' itself, was bound up with cotton and the changes that had been wrought around it.[21] But a host of other industrial and industry-related areas also developed: in chemicals for dyeing and fixing; in machine making and machine tools; in mining, locomotives, warehousing, finance, engineering and so on – all of them tied into international and imperial networks of trade (fig. 2). Second, by 'Manchester' is meant – in this book as well as in Briggs and many others – a whole region: not just the town that became a city in the early nineteenth century, but its cheek-by-jowl sister city Salford, its ring of satellite towns, its suburbanising growth and even the industrialised countryside.[22] It is a convenience (with little appeal to Salfordians) to call all this Manchester but one that has an economic and geographic rationale over and above its brevity.[23] And as a city-region Manchester's significance needs to be understood as a locality whose status was as much or more locked into the global as the national.[24]

The curve of interest in Manchester as shock city started suddenly. It rose in the 1800s, when what had only a few decades before been a regional centre suddenly went through dynamic and chaotic change. It reached a peak in the 1830s and 1840s, and then suddenly fell. Within this there was another narrative, between the two forms of shock described earlier. Here the outsiders' sense of awe early on was replaced by an active desire – often felt by insiders – for palliation, for reform, for what Briggs calls 'new and formative social values'.[25] (The relation between Briggs's ideas of shock city, the welfare state of his time and the accompanying, generally negative, attitudes towards the Victorian city, would reward some analysis.) And then, as a result of this second phenomenon and other factors, a post-shock – even an after-shock – city is understood to have taken over. According to Briggs, even by the time of Queen Victoria's visit in 1851, the city had become more orderly, had 'ceased to excite the emotions' or, as *Chambers's Edinburgh Journal* put it in 1858, tellingly ladling on the clichés, had become 'the very symbol of civilisation, foremost in the march of improvement, a grand incarnation of progress'.[26] A new narrative, a synthesis or movement between shock and post-shock, had quite deliberately been scripted.[27] Progress was not shock, of course, but it could be understood in terms of Charity. If we have not been alerted yet, we must be now. Shock city – both as named by Briggs and as observed without that name in the nineteenth century – is not just a descriptor for a certain kind of city (of its real conditions and experiences of newness). It also has allegorical roles: it plays a part in narratives of improvement; it marks a founding moment of negative values, a ground zero of modernity; and it has powerful aesthetic and political dimensions. Its use also organises the city's temporality, conjuring into being at least two other urban eras: the pre-shock or even un-shock city, and the post- or after-shock city. As we shall see, this kind of epochal thinking – which translates also into the pre-industrial (or 'ancient') and the industrial (or 'modern') as much as into 'Hell' (or pre-municipal power) and the 'civilised' (or municipal order) – runs through much of the material in this book, slipping fluidly between binary and ternary epochal sequences.

What comparisons with other cities were possible? In one sense, none. Manchester quickly came to be seen as the ur-industrial city; there was nothing typical about it (though it would become the measure for a series of subsequent shock cities around the world – Chicago, Ahmedabad, Lodz, Mumbai, Jakarta, Lagos and so on[28]). Faucher had not seen anything of Paris there.[29] Perhaps it had a different kind of representative function. Briggs suggested that it was 'just as difficult to be neutral about [Manchester] ... as it was to be neutral about Chicago in the 1870s or Los Angeles in the 1930s'.[30] What motivated the comparison was not how Chicago and Los Angeles' bubbles of expansive energy were matched by distinct new cultural forms – the skyscraper, Hollywood cinema, the freeway, for example – but instead something more basic. If Manchester was about class, Chicago was about ethnicity. But this doesn't take us very far. More interesting would be a comparison that may at first appear absurd but is worth indulging. If there really are ways in which certain cities can be understood as most representative of certain eras, it is Paris that has usually been taken as the key to the nineteenth century.[31]

THE MOST SUGGESTIVE ARGUMENT FOR PARIS, CERTAINLY that with the most far-reaching implications, is Walter Benjamin's in his essay 'Paris, the Capital of the Nineteenth Century' (1935). Many accounts of the desires and fears represented by urban modernity, most especially in its historical images, have been illuminated by this work. For Benjamin, Paris was so fundamental to the 'primal history [*Urgeschichte*] of the nineteenth century' that only it could be the century's capital.[32] What mattered was the combination of how this modernity was apprehended and the conditions that produced the modern: this was as much about experience as it was about, say, technology – each was implicated in the other. The Paris arcades, for example, were built for certain commercial reasons, they attracted foreign commentators (shades of Manchester), and they depended on innovations in gas lighting, glass and iron.[33] But what made the arcades part of primal history was the way in which their newness was permeated by a deep past, producing what Benjamin called collective 'wish images' of a utopian classless society (they were specifically linked to the building-as-machine of Charles Fourier's phalanstery, the building intended to produce a new yet also primeval psychology in its inhabitants[34]).

Benjamin's was a concise yet complex argument (it was actually a proposal for a book), not at all one based on familiar ideas about the primacy of cities depending on size or innovation. Unlike other claims for Paris, usually based on the post-1848 city, it ranged across the century. And 'capital' had a dual meaning (in English at least – in Benjamin's German it was *Hauptstadt*), not just as the top, the capstone or the centre, but as capitalism, the mode of making and distributing wealth. Among other things, Paris was 'the capital of luxury and fashion' whose rhythms were set by the operetta as 'the ironic utopia of the enduring reign of capital [*Kapitals*]'.[35] The arcades produced a mix of myth and dreaming – even dreaming the future – that was the essence of modernity for Benjamin. His key figure was the poet Charles Baudelaire with his city of chthonic and contemporary elements, the ancient and the novel, the mythic and the ephemeral. But this spliced modernity was always seen as produced in circumstances that were as much political and economic as technological. Even the notion of privacy in the middle-class dwelling was seen as complementary to the commercial world of the office. In fact what Benjamin intended, as Theodor Adorno saw, was to abolish the distinction between material and epistemological questions.[36] So, for instance, the daguerreotype, and photography more widely, brought together in Paris technological and social concerns that produced new conceptions as much of what constituted nature in the city as of what constituted subjectivity (which had implications in turn for painting).[37] Similarly with world exhibitions, seen as festivals of emancipation through distraction, in which the masses are schooled in the commodities from whose consumption they are usually excluded. At the centre of much of this were Haussmann's boulevards, providing the framework for the apotheosis of new bourgeois institutions, underpinned by state-sponsored financial speculation and embellishing the city while distracting its citizens from revolt. Engineering, literature, photography and commercial art were all part of Benjamin's spectrum of material, his 'city-tableau'.[38] But importantly it was architecture that was key to the 'dialectical image' – that eruption of the past into the present, that heterogenous time (like a freeze-frame, a whirlpool, the mythic becoming alive), which he saw as a definitive condition of modernity. Arcades, exhibition halls, interiors and boulevards were all 'residues of a dream world'.[39] Primal history is, in Paris, the phantasmagorias induced by the world of commodities whose 'ventriloqual precision' compensate its citizens for what they have lost – this is the city's claim to be capital of the nineteenth century.[40] But it is a claim based squarely on consumption and the world of the bourgeoisie.[41]

What of the shock city? Was it simply another kind of city – a more direct product of the Industrial Revolution like Manchester – or was it present in Paris too? Of relevance here is Adorno's criticism of Benjamin, specifically that the idea of 'the nineteenth century as hell' did not play into the latter's argument, which therefore lacked necessary contradiction or counterpoint.[42] According to Adorno, for instance, Benjamin understood the dialectical image to be immanent, that it belonged to the structure of consciousness rather than being produced in the consciousness by the contradictions of social experience. Thus the presence of such resonant concepts as 'utopia' and 'dream', tied by Benjamin to an anthropomorphised epoch or a psychologised collectivity, were not shown to be produced out of the conflicts of social reality and so did not do sufficient work in revealing their material conditions – they were part of a 'mirror realism' that represented the dream's content rather than showing the contradictions in the social position of the dreamer.[43] So it was the obverse, a more properly dialectical conception of the nineteenth century, one that included its conceptions and experiences of Hell as much as Golden Age (or, as Adorno put it, 'of underworld and Arcadia'), indeed of Golden Age and Hell as bound into each other, that was effectively left out.[44] Accordingly, the utopia suggested by the arcades was better understood as a 'phantasmagoria of hell', and its effect as 'catastrophe' rather than as dream.[45] Clearly Adorno was not conjuring up Hell here to indicate another kind of city but because he wanted both to sharpen the social dimension and to historicise the development of the commodity form in relation to industrial production.

Adorno's critique and its consequences are important to how we understand any nineteenth-century city, but arguably especially so with Manchester as shock city. The work of Charity, the 'dreaming' of the neo-Gothic Town Hall or the domed Exchange, are not to be understood as Golden Age in some 'mirror realism' relation to the curtain of smoke – effectively, as the negation of its Hell – because that would simply reiterate the myth that is being created. Rather, they might be understood more dialectically in Benjamin's sense of nineteenth-century capitalism as 'a reactivation of mythical forces'.[46] The promise of grace in Charity is only one part of the way she has become commodity. And it is as well to remember, as Adorno insisted, that when we evoke the city or its architecture as 'construction', that concept itself, 'as the alienation *and* the control of material', as he put it (we might say, as what was nature and has become culture; as the illusory image; and as the making of something – something *in* or *under* construction), is eminently dialectical.[47] Does construction play 'the role of the subconscious', as Sigfried Giedion argued, or does it, according to Benjamin, play 'the role of bodily processes around which "artistic" architectures gather, like dreams around the framework of physiological processes'?[48] Subjects are '*dictated* by the built environment',[49] but also they dictate to that environment: they are ventriloquised by it as well as speak through it. The illusion was that the 'forms of construction', as Benjamin put it, could be emancipated by art.[50] What was needed was for modernity to emerge from its cocoon of academic convention.

There is, however, a distinctive concept of shock in Benjamin that is connected with Hell in a different way, one that is explicitly to do with the effects of modern industry but where those effects are felt at some remove. This is expressed as a kind of poetic principle that Benjamin found in his contemporary, Franz Hessel, as well as in Edgar Allan Poe and Charles Baudelaire, and it was related to a distinctively modern experience. Shock, or *Erlebnis*, was the intrusion of technology or its effects into everyday life as felt in a series of punctual, stressful but barely apprehended stimuli. This is experience as a jolting moment with potentially threatening implications that need to be warded off or at least edited out; it is opposed to *Erfahrung* (English doesn't really have equivalent terms), which indicates an older understanding of experience as cumulative, producing wisdom (or ethos) and incorporated habit.[51] *Erlebnis* (shock experience), Benjamin writes, is tied to the 'inhospitable, blinding age of big-scale industrialism'.[52] We hear nothing more about scale, or even inhospitability – both of which will be important issues in any book on Manchester. Instead, Benjamin describes a form of physical and psychological obscuring and distancing, a refracted effect relative to that kind of phenomena; he is concerned, for instance, with the ragpicker who collects refuse 'between the jaws of the goddess of Industry',[53] with the abrupt machine-like movements of sections of crowds in Poe's work and, most of all, with the techniques of detachment practised by the bourgeois figure of the *flâneur* 'botanizing on the asphalt'.[54] He uses Engels's *Condition of the Working Class in England* to relate the idea of the *flâneur* also to the new population masses and traffic of London. Again, the distance from 'big-scale industrialism', from Manchester, is apparent.[55]

Industrialism, then, really comes into Benjamin's account only around his concept of shock (*Erlebnis*). It takes two forms. First, an evocation in the manner of the sociologist Georg Simmel of a traffic-ridden urban environment where the senses are bombarded with stimuli, screened by consciousness. And, second, in terms of a rhythmic pattern that Benjamin equates with assembly line production and 'the great fluidity of the connection between segments in manual labour'.[56] This second form arguably has more of an analogical power than a descriptive one – the instrumentalisation of the worker by the machine undoubtedly led to a coordination of bodily movements with those of the industrial process, and this was imprinted beyond the factory. Benjamin, for instance, described the face as becoming a kind of 'mimetic shock absorber'. Already, with this striking phrase, we have been taken out of the factory and into a generic crowd. In fact, the shocks being absorbed are now more of the first kind (traffic) than the second (the assembly line). The disconnect was actually even greater than this because Benjamin can hardly even be talking about an obscured industrialism. Factories were almost unknown in the Paris of the 1840s, when Baudelaire was composing the poems that would appear in *Les Fleurs du mal* (1857), and its crumbling infrastructure was entirely unsuited to industrial development. Although it was the second biggest city in Europe (to London), its industries were dominated by the production of high-end fashion goods and the provision of specialised services, and these were largely still handmade in workshops only one in ten of which employed more than ten artisans.[57] Marx's description of workers '[coordinating] their movements to the uniform and unceasing motion of an automaton' (that is, in a factory) was an uncommon experience in Baudelaire's Paris.[58] As Benjamin admits, neither Baudelaire nor Poe had any experience of industrial production, and when he writes that 'the shock experience which the passer-by has in the crowd corresponds to what the worker "experiences" at his machine', an entirely analogical weight is placed on that word 'corresponds' (and no particular machine is evoked).[59] The passer-by is clearly the *flâneur*, for whom the crowd is an equivalent of the assembly line – it allegorises for him, or represents to him, the shocks of a fragmented and alienated process. And so, while the initial link to heavy industry remains striking, especially in relation to the 'shock city' idea, just as striking is that Baudelaire's poetry and Poe's stories seem at best to be linked only either to the epiphenomena of this industrialism or to a secondary (detached) psychic experience. The Paris represented in their work is primarily the city of streets, traffic, building sites and random stimulations and only by analogy or within a generalised optic that of factories and other sites of production. Meanwhile, of slums and industrial pollution, of 'vast piles of building full of windows where there was a rattling and a trembling all day long',[60] and other aspects of what is taken to be the industrial city, we hear little or nothing. Put differently, shock as *Erlebnis* is an experience of disassociation from the crowd, not an experience of being part of it, let alone of the crowd as constituted by the new industrial proletariat.

Again, Adorno offers an interesting point of difference. Productivity can be shown to be aesthetic, he suggests, rather than felt only through a chain of mediations. This is in part an issue about the vanguardism of technological change providing a paradigm for the artistic avant-garde. More relevantly, it is also about what he calls 'the reduction in the permissible or the tolerable and the intensification of construction proper'. We must not mistake this: Adorno is writing about a very different kind of artistic reaction, but he does relate it to the 'very fact of industrialization itself as a force in people's daily lives'.[61] We just need to follow the development backwards, Adorno implies, to industrialisation's first forms and experiences.

Paris has other important cases made for its primacy. Among its most interesting analysts (the advocates are infinite), the arguments tend to relate most closely to this idea of *Erlebnis* or some equivalent phenomenon to it that acts as screen or symptom of the epistemic changes of modernity.[62] In T. J. Clark's *The Painting of Modern Life* the idea of the 'spectacle' has this function, the city remade, the product of accumulated capital investment, so that it can be enjoyed as image or screen, 'consumed in the abstract, as one convenient fiction'.[63] The case for Paris's primacy is again based on the city being a distinctive manifestation of capital, combined with (or perhaps producing) the kind of artists whose work was made modern by virtue of how it engaged with this phenomenon (Manet has now taken over from Baudelaire). In fact, so advanced is this manifestation that it derives from Situationist theory of the mid-twentieth century, now shifted to the mid-nineteenth and understood as an 'oscillation' inherent in capitalism from one kind of production to another: here the shift to consumer goods and services and the concurrent dominance of everyday life by 'commercialised forms of leisure ... and their accompanying industries of tourism, recreation, fashion and display'.[64] The areas most conducive to this interpretation have great similarity with Benjamin's: the boulevards, the arcades, the world expositions and the department stores. To these Clark adds the *banlieue*, those half-built, half-ruined edges of the city which were both products of the changes within the centre and places where the spectacle could be seen as if exposed in its droll half-construction. The *banlieue* therefore complements the mythology of the boulevard, that the latter's life really was the epitome of modernity.[65] All of these sites are at an even further remove from the practices and places of production (Clark's Paris is decidedly a later one, but the factories are still at best 'lumpish buildings' in the distance); that, after all, is the point of the spectacle, its work of making things unintelligible.[66]

This is not to say – and nothing in the following chapters will deny this – that Manchester was not also a city that enjoyed, indeed depended on, the new arts of commerce. Kendal Milnes (dating from 1836) has some claim to be the world's first department store, and the city's warehouses and financial institutions will be of particular interest later in this book. But no one was left in any doubt in Manchester, however newly civilised the city was in the century's middle decades, that consumption was always proximate to production. Even as a visitor you could follow the cotton bales as they passed along the canals into the mills; you could see the manufactured cotton loaded on the horse-drawn lurries and wagons, 'incessantly travelling the streets';[67] you

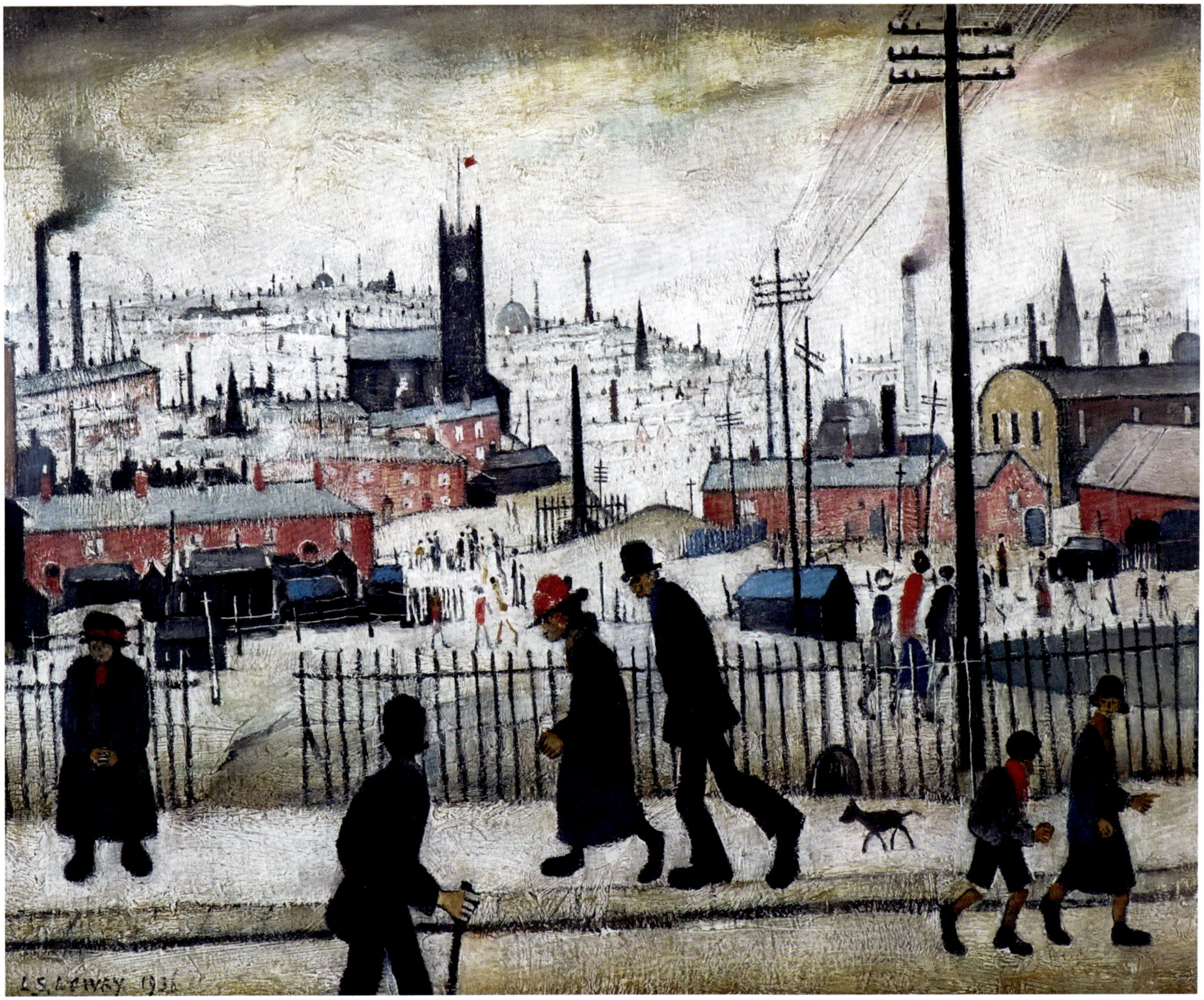

could view and buy the fabric displayed there; you could taste industrial pollution in the air; and you could hear the cacophony of thousands of cotton machines or the sound of clogs on cobbles as workers spilled into the streets at the end of their shifts. And the sight of chimneys and mills was always there, however swathed in smoke. If, to some extent, the city had hidden some of its secondary effects – the culverted rivers, the abandonment of middle-class residences and removal to the suburbs, the 'hypocritical plan' (Engels's term) of shop-lined main streets that screened off the slums of the poor – the fact of production was nevertheless always apparent.[68]

Perhaps as a kind of compensation, but perhaps also because of Paris-formed ideas about modernity, Clark later turned to that inimitable mid-twentieth-century painter of the Manchester industrial scene, L. S. Lowry. The idea of modernity being a disavowal of, or for some other reason at one remove from, the industrial that made it possible is here, in a sense, consciously corrected. The book's title – *Lowry and the Painting of Modern*

[3] L. S. Lowry, *View of a Town*, 1936. Oil on canvas. Usher Gallery, Lincoln.

Life – makes Baudelairean Paris resonate with Lowry's late industrial Manchester. And there are other ironies here, both because Lowry's coming to terms with the industrial city was made by deploying, if a little belatedly, some of the means of French nineteenth-century painting, and because the kind of atmosphere those techniques were used to conjure up was both the terrible environmental and human despoliation that industry had caused, and the obduracy and humour of the life within it.[69] In fact, 'irony' seems the wrong word for this; a sustained dialogue, even argument, between the two cities is much more what is implied. But Lowry remains firmly within the constrictions and non-sublime mysteries, 'world-historical' as Clark puts it, of his industrial subject. Distorted, near-syncopated bodies fill the streets; smoke suffuses every space; the very paint appears as if mixed with soot. Meanwhile Charity has descended from her perch and become another trudging pedestrian, if prideful in her jaunty red hat (fig. 3).

REHEARSING THESE ARGUMENTS HELPS US TO UNDERstand the peculiarities – exemplary and resonant as they may be – of the case made for Paris. Manchester, as it were, had the prior claim on the modern but, seemingly because it did not have the cultural practices to match, it would remain only the shock city of the nineteenth century, never its capital. Even given that Paris is a far older city, long a capital city, steeped in great events and so on, this is still an extraordinary situation only partly explained by shock's necessary (ontological) shortness and sharpness (it's Hell but that will pass to somewhere else). And putting aside the (unbalanced) comparison, putting aside the lack of a Manchester Baudelaire or Manet, or even Haussmann (though what about the importance of Manchester to Marx and Engels? what about its role as the antitype for utopian thought as much for a Robert Owen as a John Ruskin, and so on?), one can still be struck by the symbolic thinness of the way in which Manchester has been given world-historical status while its actual responses to and experiences of shock have been relatively marginal in our cultural histories. But if nothing else, the juxtaposition with Manchester demonstrates the omissions of the Paris argument. If industry is indeed a major part of what we understand by modernity, Paris's response to industry – at least as argued in the ways just adumbrated – is at one remove. Parisian experiences and representations, or at least those that are celebrated, are mostly at second hand in relation to the industrialisation of production and its global, economic, social and urbanistic consequences. And it is these consequences that we still live with and recognise as central to one strong version of modernity. It was Manchester that was the industrial capital of the nineteenth century.[70]

This explains the main motivating questions of this book: not so much why this cultural marginalisation should have happened, but what were the urban and architectural forms of the first industrial city, what can be learned from their representation and how can they be related to the idea of shock city? The interrelation of architecture and its representations, and of images of the city and the 'city itself' (a strange yet productive term), is where the weight of the book's analysis lies. And integral to this is the attempt to understand the cultural relation to shock in the dialectical forms of the post-shock or civic city. What if, putting aside any tendentiousness (and any claims by Paris or even London[71]) and instead of merely claiming Manchester as the capital of the nineteenth century, we were to treat the physical city and its representations as if they might have interesting things to say about newness, about industry, about the modern?[72] David Harvey's idea of the industrial city as an unstable configuration may be useful here. Created by a drive to facilitate production and organise labour, technologies and goods, the industrial city was also beset by the 'social anarchy' caused by these very same conditions: innovation was necessary to it, but innovation was inherently and continually disruptive.[73] And this instability would play out also in the spatial and architectural forms of the industrial city. Is it possible that an alternative modernity lies in this instability, almost unnoticed, a 'bastard birth' at the very heart of the industrial modern, marginalised by the norms and forms of seemingly more alluring ideas of European modernity?[74] Could it be said also that reactions to the industrial city tended to provincialise the commentator? Benjamin pointed out that Engels had come from 'a Germany that was still provincial',[75] and we might add that even those from Berlin

[4] The Royal Manchester Institution, Manchester (now the Manchester Art Gallery), 1824–35. Architect: Charles Barry. Photograph: James Mudd, c.1860. Manchester Libraries, Information and Archives.

like Karl Schinkel (discussed in Chapter 1) were coming from a city that was still pre-industrial and in some ways (if for political reasons) much less developed in its middle-class public discourse (one measure is that, where Berlin had two newspapers in the early 1800s, Manchester had at least three times this number). Manchester's industrialism was in good measure internally produced; those historic European cities 'were subjected to the assault of industrial and capitalist forces that arose externally and often in opposition to them'.[76]

Among the factors that may place Manchester as the capital of the nineteenth century is the machine and the city's new relationship to the world. The ownership of capital meant most obviously the ownership of machines in Manchester, including the factory as a larger machine of machines (see Chapters 1 and 4). (Tellingly, this is not the mere resemblance to machines, or analogy with them, as in Benjamin's reference to Fourier.[77]) It meant what Marx called a 'machinofacture', a striving often among the most acclaimed industrialists for invention and development away from manufacture and towards 'self-acting' machines and the further control of the workforce. It meant a machine consciousness, a machine futurism, but also a projection backwards of the machine onto the past, so that we can think of medievalism itself as imbued with something like an industrial period eye (Chapter 4). This was part of, arguably central to, the culture of the industrial bourgeoisie, whether or not their fortunes were made by it, as they expanded into and beyond the spaces patchily occupied by local landed classes.[78] It invested their intellectual activities – in the work of James Prescott Joule, Peter Mark Roget, John Dalton, Richard Cobden, John Bright, William Fairbairn, James Nasmyth, Joseph Whitworth – and it directed their institutions and the ones they began to influence – whether the Manchester Infirmary, the Literary and Philosophical Society, the Statistical Society, the Mechanics' Institute, Owens College, the Portico Library or the Royal Manchester Institution (fig. 4). And machinofacture is part of what has been called both an 'industrial enlightenment' and a 'crucible of class struggle': it is both liberal and illiberal.[79] All this has an architectural dimension too, both in buildings for machines and in buildings where the machine is more implicit, as well as when built environments are seen as the direct and indirect means of coercion, the thing to be resisted.[80]

As for the world, Manchester's position, as was always evident at the time and has often been acknowledged in global histories since, was the main cog in another machine – that of global cotton.[81] It triggered industrial development in many very distant places, as well as their deindustrialisation to sustain Manchester's eminence; it encouraged both spying and more licit means of technology transfer over national borders; and it led to an influx of economic migrants to Manchester bringing expertise, finance and labour (especially, here, from Britain's first colony, Ireland). One imperative of the industrial city was to be an imperial city; industrialising cotton would be a means to globalise the city's relations of production, distribution and consumption, including the import of 'cheap natures' from slave plantations as much after the abolition of slavery as before it.[82] And another imperative, interdependent with this, was the exploitation of such 'cheap natures' from much more local sources – coal most especially, for whose transport whole infrastructures like canals were predominantly built, and for whose extraction labour forces were mobilised and exploited in a manner that might equally well be called colonial.

Such as it was, the logic of globalism was registered less in obvious urban symbols and toponymic acknowledgements – a Bengal Street or an Asia House – than in the deeper forces that made and broke the city's fabric. Less, then, the phrases painted into the dome above the Royal Exchange's trading room extolling the gentlemanly business of global finance than the sheer increasing scale of global business requiring that building to be built and rebuilt four times, each time hugely enlarged, in just over a century (see Chapter 6).

GIVEN MANCHESTER AS SHOCK CITY, GIVEN THIS machinofacture and this global status, there has been surprisingly little attention paid to the relation between industrial change and the forms and practices of architecture and urban form, including their various visual expressions. The city's surfaces, the ways in which its buildings give shape to voids or give expression to matter – all this vivid particularity, how it is represented and how it

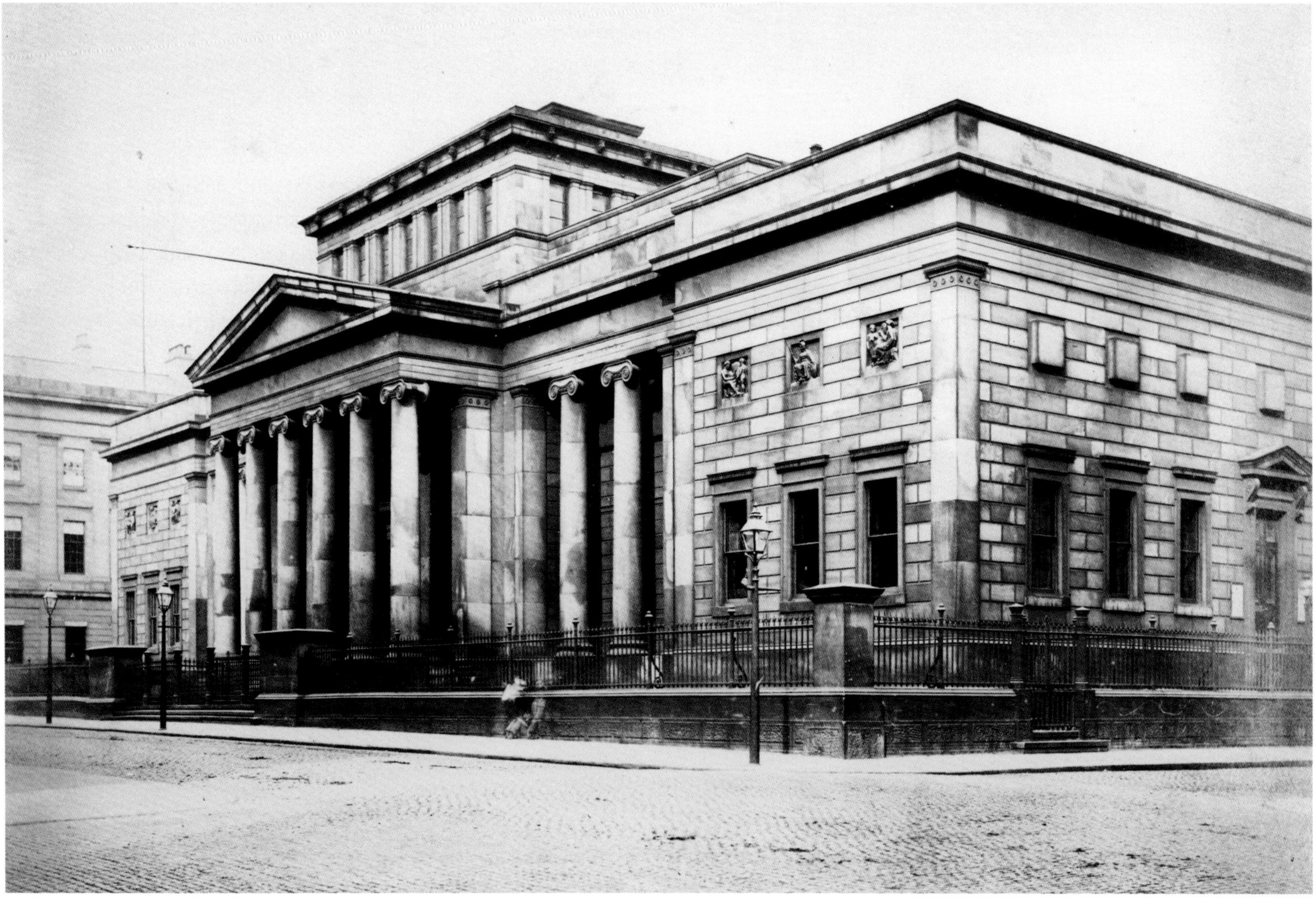

manifests the political unconscious in specific ways – have played little part in our understanding of shock city. This is as much a problem of the writing of history as of the writing of architectural history. There has long been research by historians and debates about matters such as the causes of the Industrial Revolution (and even whether such a concept is viable); the shift from rural-based to urban-based industry; gender and industrial work; the significance of energy sources and systems; what is meant by social class and how it emerges and changes in this period; and industrial change (both cumulative and cataclysmic) and globalisation.[83] In all of these Manchester has often been a key focus, but its architecture and visual culture have featured hardly at all.

More recently these historical debates appear to have been sidelined, their interest in precedence, causation, social change and innovation bypassed by a set of approaches that have often also used Manchester as their focus. Through the influence of Michel Foucault, Bruno Latour and others, the writing of Manchester's history has become marked by concepts such as governmentality and liberalism, and been concerned with the place of experts and surveillance within them; and these in turn have been inflected by ideas about the agency of objects and knowledge as a product of networks.[84] There is the appeal of big horizons of understanding and method to some of this, but – as will become clear – it is largely unhelpful in terms of interpretive strategies, especially in getting at what architecture actually does and what images express about the city. Form and labour are marginal (at best) to the Foucauldians, who prefer 'biopower' and 'human capital'. Yet both form and labour are vital to an understanding of the sensuous materials, images and spaces of art and architectural history.[85] In Foucauldian accounts, moreover, terms like 'power', 'discipline' and 'liberalism' are both abstracted and normalised; lacking any determinate qualities and found everywhere, they lose their difference and unevenness. Liberalism, for instance, is understood as 'not a cohesive body of ideas' and as 'something very broad, multiple and eclectic ... both a political philosophy (formal or inchoate) and a mode of sociotechnical organisation'.[86] This conceptual overreach is why, for instance, I prefer 'Free Trade' and 'industrial bourgeoisie' to 'liberalism'. Free Trade not only was strongly connected with Manchester's industrialists and their urban ideas and schemes (it is what was meant by the 'Manchester School'), but identifies a set of beliefs specifically about the market and therefore brings a new kind of capitalism directly to the foreground rather than, as with Foucault's use of 'liberalism', leaving capitalism in some vague background.[87] Industrial bourgeoisie identifies the forming and formation of a particular group around certain shared practices, identities and ideas and even, I will argue, certain areas and buildings in the city. That these are historically grounded categories means not that they are fixed but that they are complex and inconsistent, especially as they are contested and embattled by other ideas and other groups.

More fundamentally, if not often pointed out, there is a hidden intentionalism in Foucauldian history, a consonance between ideas and ends embedded deep within it. Yet the intentions – mostly statements of purpose by individuals or groups that are instrumental to 'liberalism' – are understood as a kind of drive inherent in the *dispositif* itself (the apparatus or social institution – with its discursive and material technologies – of which the panopticon is the most famous).[88] The alignment of Foucauldian analysis with the putative intentions of the *dispositif* allows no room for contradiction. A *dispositif*, and not the totality of capitalist production – so the argument goes – constitutes its own subjects and such systems of micropower ramify their effects through society, always with an aspect that is positive (creating knowledge), but always strangely unattached to any specific social entity. Agency is thus implanted in the disciplines integral to these *dispositifs* but – as if model and ends were identical – particular outcomes, their experience as much as their failure or success, don't really matter. The norms set by Foucauldian *dispositifs* are irreducible; the truths they produce cannot be refuted, while older and alternative practices and approaches are magicked away or treated as mere survivals or nugatory resistances in the glamorous and categoric sweep of new epistemes.[89] And yet architecture, long treated as an epiphenomenon by most historians and at best a kind of residue of other forces or a scenography, is central to much Foucauldian work. Or it is perhaps better to say that one particular aspect of architecture is central – space. As pervasive a concept as it is as a condition or quality – hugely metaphorical, freighted with epistemic and hegemonic significance, a force of its own – Foucauldian space is the ocularcentric theatre of another hyperbolic abstraction: 'the eye' or 'the gaze'.[90] As is already apparent, this again is not what this book tries to bring to light.

Industrial culture has suffered a deep unfashionability over the last few decades, notably in political and cultural life. In architectural history the problem is particularly acute. The big issues signalled by phrases like 'the condition of England', 'the factory question', 'the machinery question', 'smoke abatement', even 'Free Trade', all of which have contemporary ramifications, have rarely been treated as if they have serious implications for the understanding of architecture – or indeed as if architecture might speak in interesting ways to them. Postmodernist and poststructuralist anti-Marxism still have an effect here, felt of course across the humanities. Specifically for architectural history, the reasons for this lack of interest in substantially coming to terms with industrialism (or its parcelling off into other subdisciplines as an issue of technology) may be similar to those that T. J. Clark argued were behind the dearth of twentieth-century paintings depicting the industrial scene – that industry was the subject not to be spoken of, by comparison with matters like 'the cult of the countryside, the comedy of upper-class manners, the dull decencies and resentments of the new middle classes, the lure of London, the grandeur and ambiguity of Empire' (an architectural equivalent might be found for each of these).[91] However, to connect back to the Paris–Manchester discussion earlier, where was the experience of modernity most sharply felt and where was its greatest challenge to the very idea of the city?

Something needs to be said about the kinds of materials and the claims made about them here. Faucher had written in 1844 that, while the sciences were thriving in Manchester, 'literature and the arts are a dead letter'.[92] Almost contemporary with the engraving celebrating the Town Hall's completion, John Ruskin wrote that, 'Taken as a whole, I perceive that Manchester can produce no good art and no good culture.'[93] Whatever Faucher and Ruskin expected, there are no counterclaims made for Manchester's painters, printmakers or photographers, nor even for a bohemia which, if it existed, has left virtually nothing (contrast that with Paris's bohemia which existed alongside 'the first debris of industrialism').[94] There is also little that is recognisable as modernism in the conventional forms now emerging in Manchester – those would come in a second, later, stage of capitalism. Claims of quality or innovativeness are not what I am interested in, or at least not in supra-historical ways. Instead, there are arguments made for the utility of images in helping us to think through what 'shock city' meant. As with the architecture, some of these images have almost become overfamiliar; their repeated reproduction has remade them into ciphers – mere evidence or illustration. We can best speak of this subject again only if we open up the cipher rather than turn aside to other subjects, and this requires us both to combine images and architecture and to use them to draw out the many-dimensioned aspects of the subject. Architecture and image require a reinvestment, a belief or wager that they are means of imagining, fashioning, experiencing or perceiving that are relatable but not reducible to other means, other 'evidence', and that their makers continue to speak and to shape through them, just as we may speak to and struggle with them.

A MAP INDICATES SOME OF THESE ISSUES AND THE WAY they are encoded in one form of representation of the city (it will also be helpful to identify some of the locations and buildings discussed in later chapters) (fig. 5). It shows the city in 1857 and was printed for a specific purpose – as a guide to visitors who were coming to see the Art Treasures Exhibition of that year. The map tries to make of the city something image-able and usable, to be kept in a pocket as the tourist roamed, and to be unfolded on an omnibus or perhaps in a tea room (it is 50 × 42 cm in size and folds into a handy hardbacked package of 14 × 9 cm). The site of the exhibition buildings, in the Botanic Gardens of Old Trafford, is coloured in brown at the bottom left corner of the map, while certain roads are coloured yellow to indicate the main ways of getting about the city by bus and to the exhibition building. Very much a product of the post-shock city, the map aims to orientate and even to model a new kind of visitor, not the tourist of shock but one arriving in the city specifically to enjoy it as itself a newly arrived centre of the fine arts – post-shock, in our terms.[95]

At first glance the mapped city is formidably knot-like and entangled, its frequent comparisons with a spider's web far from apparent. Like any urban map, it shows the sum of many different agents and factors, of an infinity of decisions, of an improvised incoordination almost as much as a coordination of practices. That it hangs together as something city-like is as much an effect of will and effort as of imagination and representation, but while infrastructure is prominent on any such map it is predominant here. And, as we look, a broad logic of growth becomes apparent: the infrastructure is as much concentric as radial. The yellow roads form a web that touches the other major transport infrastructure of the city – its waterways (canals and rivers) and its railways, with the main stations, the London Road (later Piccadilly) terminus and Victoria station, to the top and right of the centre and Liverpool Road station, which opened in 1830 and was historically the first passenger station in the world but by this time was already little more than an appendix, to the left of centre. The largest river, the Irwell, flows diagonally from upper centre to lower left, dividing Manchester and Salford, while the River Medlock enters more serpentine from the right, coiling east–west. The rivers define a triangular city centre and connect with the canal network (four main canals, built between 1765 and 1804) and its many nodal branches, wharfs and basins, reaching out to the industrial suburb of Ancoats to the top right of the map. Almost all of the city's industry cleaved to this water system.[96] The city's institutions are represented by another code – a darker grey of the shading that denotes buildings – and we can see how these are distributed across the central parts of the city. The Infirmary has a

[5] Map of Manchester, 1857. Published by J. T. Cornish.

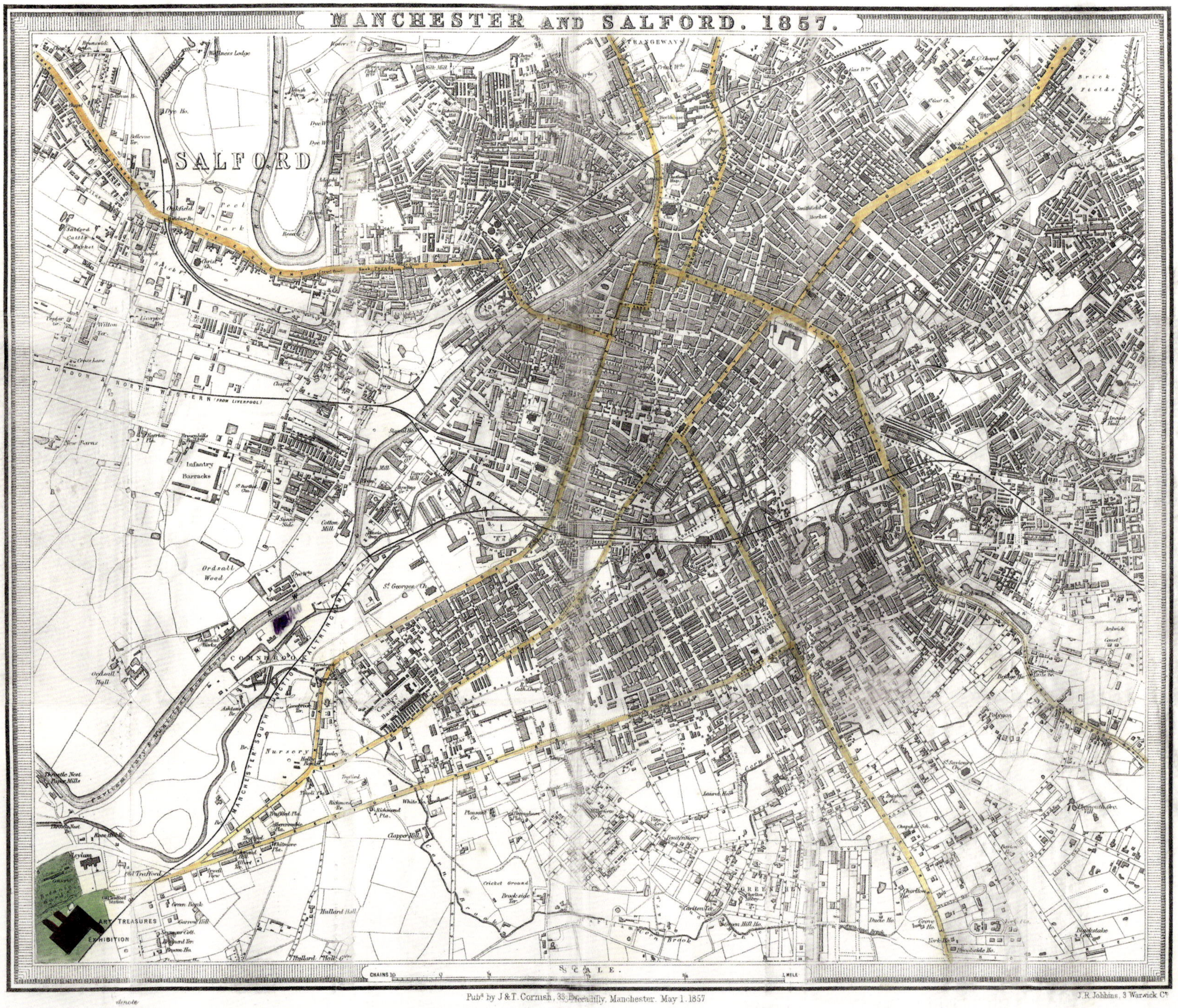

penumbra of open space around it, and there are a number of dark grey buildings in the grid of streets immediately to the south-west of it (this is the Free Trade city of Chapter 2). The older centre is west and north-west of this, around the marketplace and the cathedral where the Irwell forks off into the river Irk near the top centre. On a near axis from the cathedral is the apse-ended shape of the Exchange (newly dignified as the Royal Exchange) and St Ann's church, with the Town Hall nearby on King Street (this is the old town hall seen in our opening engraving, not the place from which we see that view). Industrial structures can be found in a broad triangle around this inner city and most obviously in the gridded streets parallel to canals, in the curves of the Medlock and in the big canted grid in Ancoats. New suburban developments, already beginning to form crescents and roads of villas can be seen to the bottom right. Much more could be said, of course, but of final note are the barracks and penitentiaries: most obviously, a cavalry barracks between the roads leading to Old Trafford and an infantry barracks in open country a little further north of it, both expansive organisations of buildings and land housing substantial garrisons, but also the New Bailey prison, with its semicircular and cruciform blocks between the Irwell and the Salford railway station, and the large workhouse just behind Victoria station.[97] All this too is Charity.

The chapters that follow present differentiated aspects of Manchester, both as shock and as post-shock city, as overlapping yet often non-successive episodes in its existence, arranged roughly according to the broad chronology of their topics. The city as a density of structures, especially its 'planless, knotted chaos' of housing and its 'low modernity' of nondescript buildings,[98] is not going to be well captured here, although this density is a constant presence in every one of these episodes. Likewise, the related issues of rent, land values and building speculation, which also appear on the edges of the discussion.[99]

Each chapter employs a different method of structuring the material, avoiding the despotism of an overall chronological narrative. The city is not a story, at least not if it can be distinguished from its rhetoricians. Instead, the analyses here build up into accounts of certain institutions and certain places, as we might expect, but also of certain ways of understanding change itself, of certain forms of material connectedness that may not be to do with proximity or site. Each chapter also has its reigning mode or figure (successively production, ideology, time, government, culture and exchange) which are embodied by specific images, buildings or areas of the city and by shifting aesthetic modes of materialisation and experience. Chapter 1 uses the year 1826 to explore Ancoats, Manchester's factory suburb and the focus of concerns about shock city; how the factory was conceived and represented is crucial here. Chapter 2 exposes a new conception of the identity of the city – as a cityscape that seems to put shock city behind it and instead is expressive of Free Trade, especially through the new palazzo warehouses and their connections with reformed or emerging institutions. Chapter 3 addresses ideas of before and after shock (industrial change) through one photograph, exploring both how epochal change from the pre-industrial to the industrial city was visualised, and how the medium itself enabled different meanings (associations, memories) and temporalities to be produced out of it. Chapter 4 focuses on one building, the Town Hall, seen both as an expression of the industrial bourgeoisie's sense of good government and as the architectural manifestation of the settlement that was to be found between the machine and history – a steam-powered Gothic for a 'steam aristocracy'.[100] A different tack is taken in Chapter 5, which is organised around the idea that, by following smoke from the places of its industrial use and then into the city and its places of greatest rejection (and apotheosis), the itineraries that normally render significance to architecture can be differently connected. Chapter 6 spans over 150 years in the history of one building (the Royal Exchange) to show how its increasingly global significance came into periodic scalar contest with the local situation of shock city; the space it occupied was increasingly understood as a kind of pressurised capsule between the bodies of those occupying it and the spaces of city and world beyond. The Coda reflects briefly on all this from the perspective of the 1920s.

[6] Karl F. Schinkel, detail of a page from his Travel Diary showing factories in Ancoats, 1826. Staatliche Museen zu Berlin, Zentralarchiv.

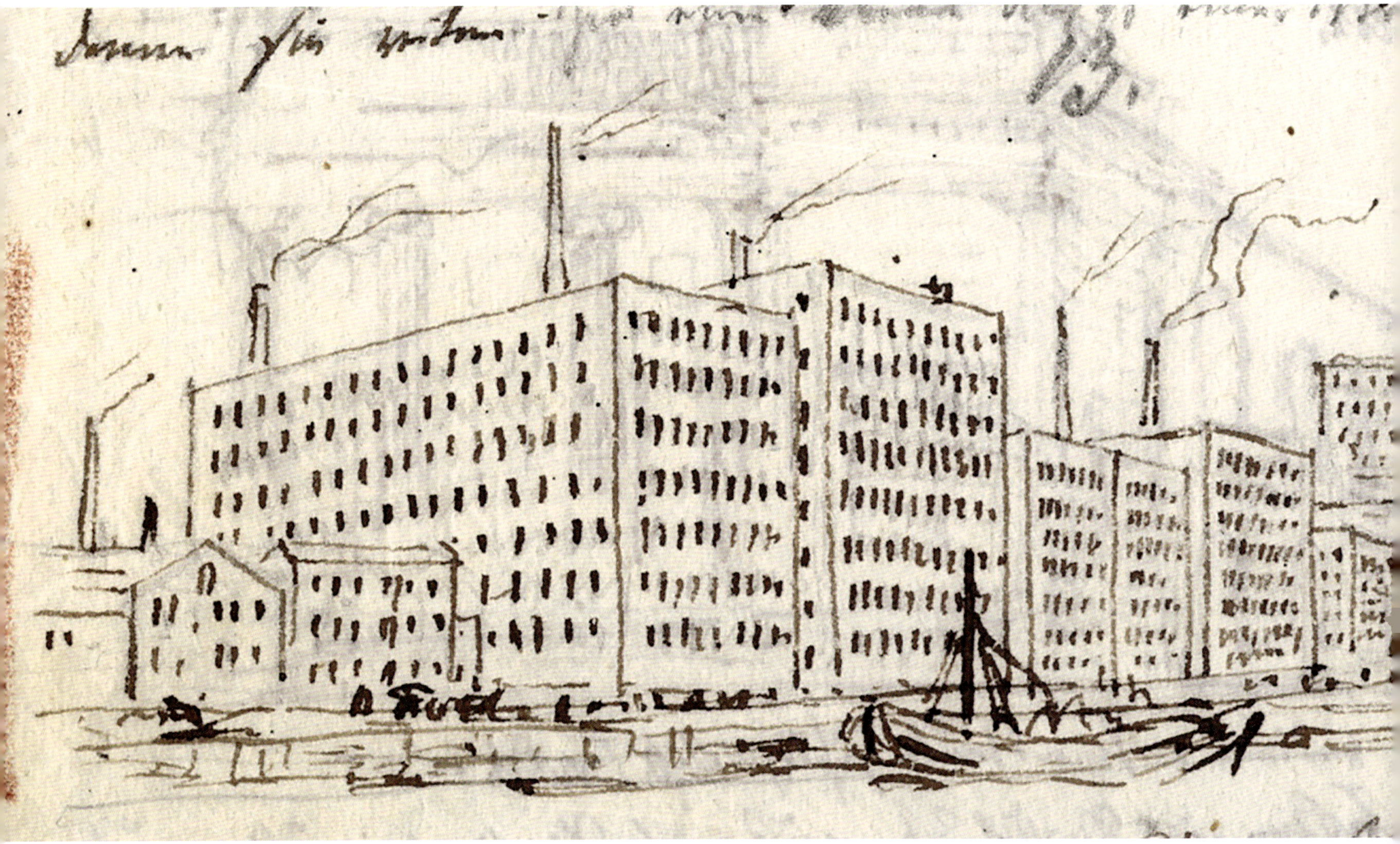

1 Ancoats, 1826

The Shock of the Factory

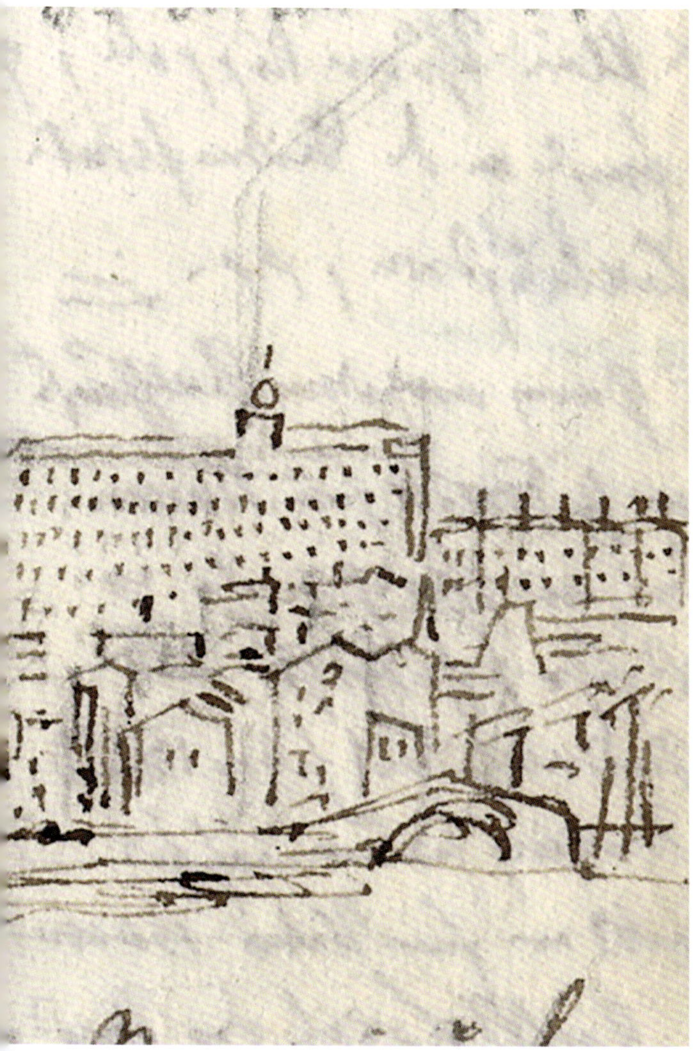

ON MONDAY, 17 JULY 1826, KARL FRIEDRICH SCHINKEL drew a sketch of Ancoats, Manchester's industrial suburb.[1] Tired by several days in Scotland and a whole weekend spent on stage-coaches travelling down through Cumbria and Lancashire, the Prussian architect had rested at the Royal Hotel while his companions went off to look at factories. With his energies restored after an evening meal, he ventured out into the long summer daylight. It was a notably hot and dry midsummer but Ancoats was only half a mile from his town centre hotel.[2] The drawing he made in his notebook, barely 4 centimetres high by 14 centimetres wide, is a view from the level of the Rochdale Canal (fig. 6). In the centre foreground is a canal boat and to the far right a distinctive humpback bridge, the equipment and infrastructure of the new industrialism. But the sketch is dominated by a more disjunctive modernity – a row of massive buildings far taller, far more capacious and more crudely block-like than anything around them. Indeed, for an architect so drawn to nature, there is nothing of the natural here. Above the channelled water of the canal everything bar the wisps of smoke is cubic building matter.

Schinkel used his pen to stab in every window on these buildings. We can count them on the nearest block, seven levels high and nine windows across, and on the taller one beside it, eight windows high and ten across, and then on several lower but still substantial blocks until the diminution of size made marking impossible.[3] Beyond these canal-side buildings several scattered figures ascend a sloping street. The long building commanding the rise again has a careful alignment of pen marks notching up the number of windows. Chimneys rise into the sky. To the right

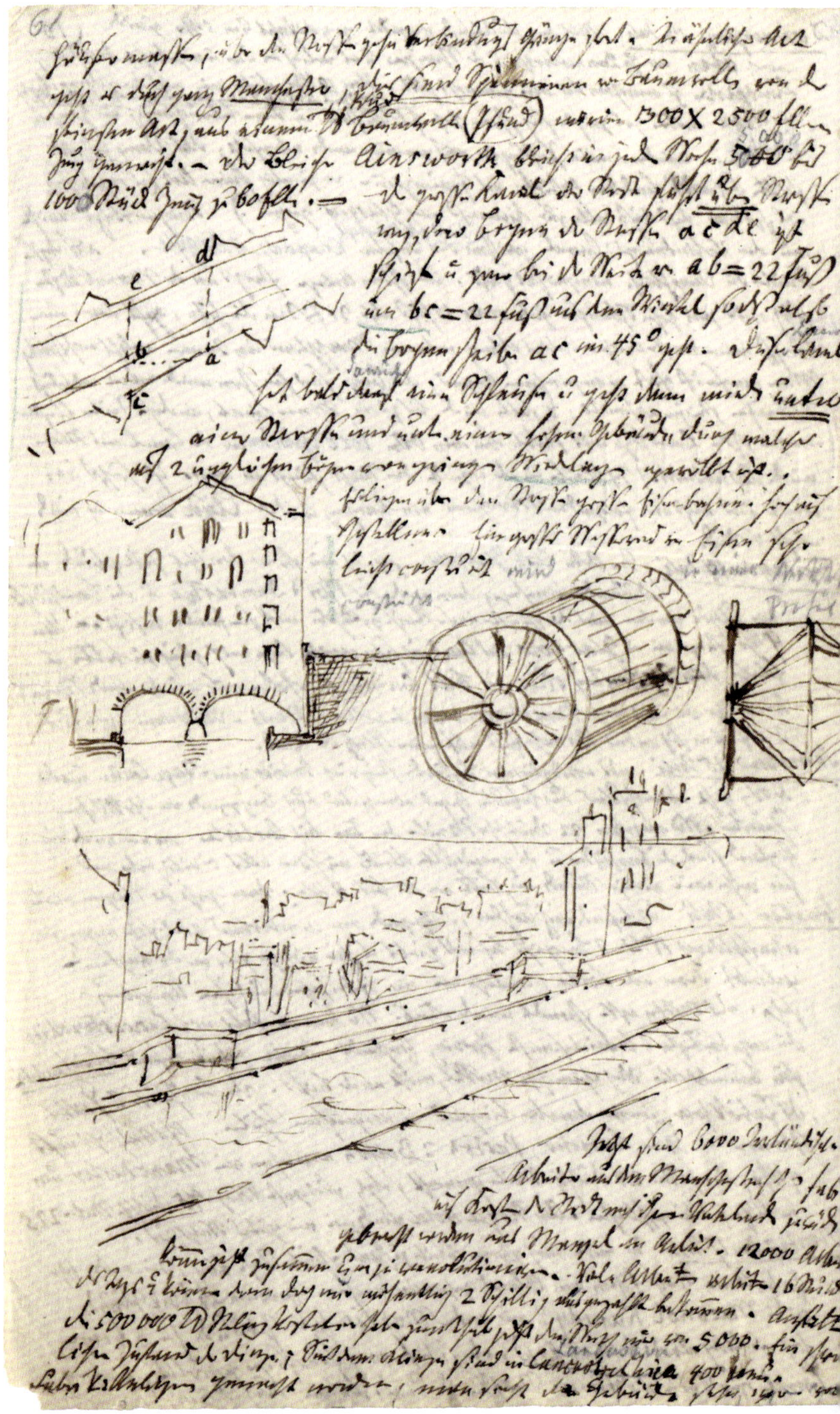

[7] Karl F. Schinkel, a page from his Travel Diary showing various items in Ancoats, 1826. Staatliche Museen zu Berlin, Zentralarchiv.

a cluster of angular buildings – gable ends, lean-to roofs and a spire – complete the scene. It is, for all the page's modest size, a striking image full of Schinkel's sense of *Stimmung* (atmosphere or mood conjured by acute perception), and it seems to go to the heart of at least one idea of what industrial modernity could mean (certainly this is what its frequent reproduction would suggest).[4] This is a place where the combination of brute scale and dauntless repetition has extinguished anything that could stand for nature, its landscapes, trees, diurnal rhythms, perhaps even the very idea of the organic.

More typical of what Schinkel was doing on his journey is the notebook's previous page (fig. 7), on which he made several careful records, probably earlier that same evening: a plan of an aqueduct, a sketch of a canal passing under a mill, a waterwheel in perspective and section, and a view of the same aqueduct with streets and houses below. Most likely he observed these on Store Street, on the way north-eastwards from his hotel. The Store Street aqueduct, built by Benjamin Outram in the later 1790s, enabled the Ashton Canal to pass over the slope at this point; innovatively, it adopted a skewed form as the line of the canal met the different direction of the street below. This kind of ingenuity, which threaded the water system under and above the growing city, impressed Schinkel. He wrote:

> *The great canal of the town goes above the streets. This canal then reaches a lock and goes this time under a street and under a tall building which rests on 2 unequal arches with small abutments. There lie above the streets great iron ways high up on supports. A big iron waterwheel, very lightly constructed.*[5]

His notations typically indicate that Schinkel wanted to learn from what he saw. He wanted to take home a trove of usable observations, records of industrial ingenuity. The canal and waterwheel thus made a different sense here; they at least could be drawn with some investigative purpose, something other than the jabbed, repetitive lines of the mill windows.

It was a curious stay in Manchester, and the Ancoats sketches and notes – barely a page and a half – were a contradictory and ambiguous record of it. Schinkel had left Berlin on 16 April and spent the rest of the spring and most of the summer until 22 August travelling through France, England and Scotland, visiting and studying museums and other architecture, as well as engineering works, factories and new machinery. He travelled with his friend Peter Beuth, the director of Prussia's department of trade and technology, then on his third trip to Britain.[6] As adviser to the department, Schinkel sought out not only the new museums that were the official subject of his trip but also the technologies, new spaces and expanding towns that had given Britain its extraordinary industrial impetus. And yet, curiously, the architect spent only a few hours looking at Manchester's industrial structures, despite Beuth's enthusiastic response to them.[7] Next day, he set off for the coast, filling the rest of the second Ancoats page with details of the structure of a market building in Liverpool. In a trip full of information gathering, of meetings with architects, engineers and industrialists, Schinkel seems to have met no one in Manchester.

Although this most shocking city of the Industrial Revolution occupied only a few hours of his time and its satellite towns none at all, Schinkel brought away powerful impressions, and it is among these that we may find reasons for his short stay. In one of his letters the architect wrote of Ancoats:

> *one sees buildings standing where three years ago there were still fields, but these buildings appear as blackened with smoke as if they had been in use for a hundred years. It makes a dreadful and dismal impression: monstrous shapeless buildings put up only by foremen without architecture, only the least that was necessary and out of red brick.*[8]

This debased architecture – ruddy, begrimed, peremptory and scale-less – itself appeared to have agency. As Schinkel elaborated in a letter two days later:

> *For the last 50 years, for as long as machines have been in operation, England has doubled, and in some places tripled and quadrupled its population, and has become much improved. This is an extraordinary phenomenon which any discriminating traveller must note. But the peak has now been reached, and speculation has now surpassed itself. In Manchester, where we were yesterday, 400 new cotton mills have been erected since the war ... thousands of smoking obelisks from steam-engines around them, whose height of 80 to 180 ft destroys all the impact of the church towers. All these structures have produced such an enormous mass of goods that the world is glutted with them.*[9]

Here is the classic scenario of Manchester as shock city. Drawn to the city by its new reputation, the visitor – part spy, part tourist – looks on it not just for lessons but as something terrifying and exhilarating. Modernity, in all its dread and dream, lies before him as something entirely separated from both nature and what was previously understood as civilisation, something that was not relatable to previous standards, proportions, aesthetics – these are 'monstrous shapeless buildings ... without architecture'. But how can the interests of the tourist and the spy be equally served?[10] How can the unrepresentable be assimilated? This is essentially an issue of representation, then – how to represent but also what architecture represents when it helps to produce such a world, such scale, such repetition. What can be captured and grasped of these places and their buildings? Or, rather, what can be said to have meaning such that other things need not have meaning or need not be comprehended? And behind such matters lurks that other issue of representation, the recognition and non-recognition of political identity and legitimacy. This second representation is bound up in the first: it shapes it and continues to shadow it.

The nature or quality of Ancoats' visibility is what is at stake here; it can be a kind of blind spot or occluded vision, but also something coloured or projected onto. In that regard, this chapter sets itself obliquely to the achievements of empirical research on Ancoats, particularly those of economic and social historians and industrial archaeologists, over the last few decades. This chapter is interested not so much in the factual record of Ancoats' existence as in what could and could not be represented within it (by architecture) and about it (in images) at the time – in effect, the truth limits of its expression and experience. And so, in turn, the chapter discusses a sequence of architecture images: the mill as a view; the mill as analogous to a palace; workers' dwellings and their strange non-relation to the mill; the mill as a model machine; and the mill in its relation to industrial strife. Schinkel's

[8] Map of Manchester, 1793: detail showing Ancoats. Published by C. Laurent.

[9] Map of Manchester, 1794: detail showing Ancoats. Published by William Green.

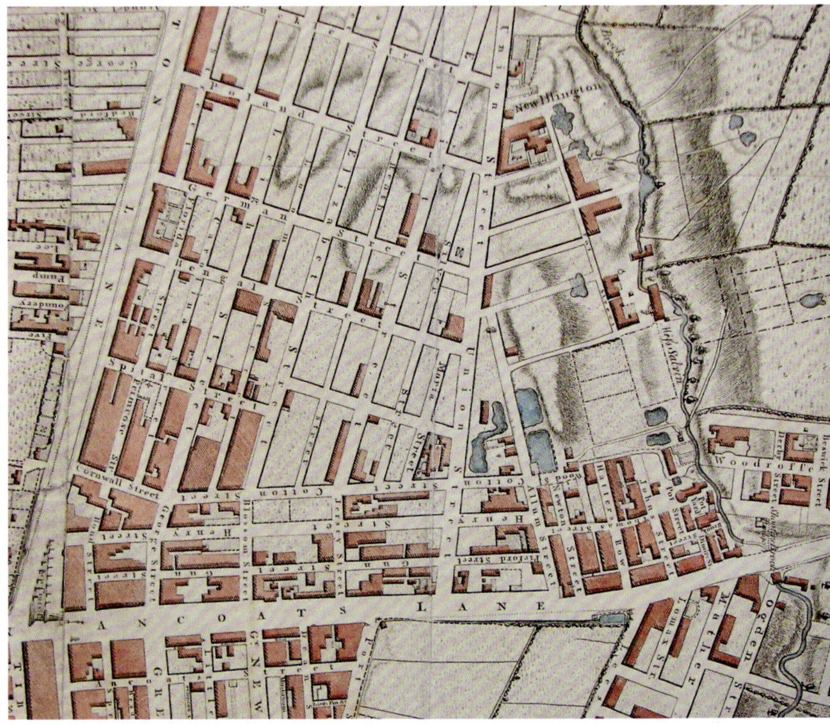

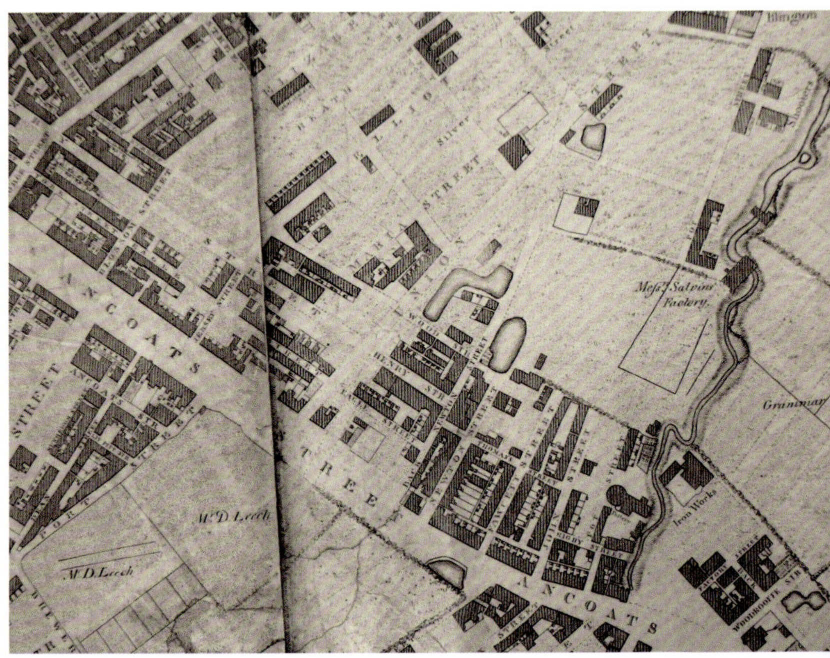

comments and sketch provide a kind of passage into these themes; the chapter is not really about the Prussian architect, nor is it strictly the kind of study that uses one year as a way of treating simultaneity in a synchronic panorama.[11] Rather, insofar as it is a gathering moment, 1826 is rendered as an effect of cumulative developments. And spliced with this are the limits and possibilities of a visualisation of the mill at this time – it is, in a sense, about the construction of shock. First, Ancoats and the mills that Schinkel's pen described.

INDUSTRIAL ENGLAND IN THE 1820S WAS JUSTLY described as a 'fragile and uncertain society'. The effects and uncertainties caused by rapid and successive innovations in industrial machinery were as yet unmatched by political reform – indeed the reverse.[12] Fragility was marked by brutality in the continuing repressions of the immediate post-Waterloo years. Ancoats might be identified as the focal point of all this, with its world-historical status, at this moment of extraordinary change (rather than later in the century when it came to epitomise the problems of housing in the industrial city). The focus of interest was the relation between its open spaces – its still unpaved streets and recently cut waterways – and its factory interiors and the machines they housed. A direct product of the urbanisation of cotton manufacture, Ancoats grew rapidly just to the north-east of the city centre in a squarish area bordered on three sides by Ancoats Lane (which became Great Ancoats Street), Newton Lane (which became Oldham Street) and Shooter's Brook (which became the Ashton Canal), but extending unevenly into country lanes to the north-east (fig. 8). This clear demarcation of the area from the rest of the city was part of the reason for its continued distinctiveness. With the intensity of its gridded industrial development, its dense, increasingly mono-class housing and its lack of institutions and amenities, Ancoats was a kind of Petri dish for industrial modernity.

Cotton spinning and weaving was largely, until the late eighteenth century, domestically based and located in rural areas, where it adopted a number of different kinds of buildings (cottages, barns, outhouses) and used a mixture of power sources and technologies.[13] The work moved more substantially into towns following the invention of steam-powered machinery, with its greater flexibility of location and hence the idea that steam power could lead to a factory system with a more disciplined and more controllable workforce working longer hours.[14] Manchester was already in the mid-eighteenth century a centre for marketing cotton, for dealing in it, and for finishing processes. Inventions like Crompton's spinning mule led to a greater capacity in spinning, with spinners working together on machines in sheds, and, as mill owners appreciated the flexibility of location enabled by steam power, they began to locate mills in towns. This led to the immigration of rural-based and Irish workers, attracted to the towns by higher wages, and some contemporary manufacturers believed that it '[placed] the power amongst the people'.[15] By 1800, Manchester had thirty-two steam engines serving the cotton industry, most of which we can assume were used for powering mules.[16] With this shift came investment not only in machines but also, of course, in buildings to house them: in the last fifteen or so years of the eighteenth century, the capital invested in buildings and machinery in the Lancashire cotton industry increased ninefold.[17]

Ancoats was the exception that became the exemplar. This area, whose land was largely owned by the Grammar School and the Mosley family, and which included a small village of weavers, had already been changing in the eighteenth century, with a scattering of houses and factories. But it was rapidly transformed, made desirable at a different order of scale, by the building of the Rochdale and Ashton canals between 1792 and 1804. Green's map of 1794 (surveyed in 1787) shows the area on the cusp of accelerated industrialisation (fig. 9). Union Street is there, heading into the fields north-eastwards off Great Ancoats Street (previously Ancoats Lane), not yet with the Rochdale Canal beside it but, as it were, pre-empting its impact.[18] A number of other streets have been laid out, some forming a grid, or really two grids, one of large blocks parallel with Great Ancoats Street and the other adjacent to it but canted to follow the angle set by Newton Lane. These are still largely speculative; the only buildings of any density alongside them as yet are at the Manchester side of the area. Rows of houses with backyards are already cheek by jowl with both workshops and larger industrial structures. This pattern of development – of housing and industry together, of different sizes and types, in intimate and jarring lockstep – was to continue and intensify (as was the area as a matter of concern for charitable, philanthropic and medical groups).[19] Architecture in Schinkel's idea of it as measured and historically reassuring, certainly in any notion of it as culturally elevated, was already marginal, and any sense of it belonging properly to a *longue durée*, or at least as a realm separate from that of transient political events, was put at stake.

Things falling apart are things newly mobile. Two entrepreneurs drawn to Manchester by such conditions were the Scots James McConnel and John Kennedy. Both were born in Kirkcudbrightshire in the 1760s to farming families, and both came to England in their mid-teens to be apprenticed as machine makers.[20] In Manchester, where McConnel arrived in 1788 and Kennedy in 1791, they formed a partnership as machine makers and mule spinners with Benjamin and William Sandford in 1791 – as Kennedy explained, 'putting up our own mills in any convenient garrets we could find'.[21] Together they set up in a factory in Canal Street. The Scots broke away four years later to establish their own firm in a rented building in Shooter's Brook, a tributary of the River Medlock on the edge of Ancoats, and they had two rented outliers in Ancoats itself.[22] The firm's progression – by the 1820s they had become the largest firm in the city in terms of the number of workers employed[23] – paralleled that of the brothers Adam and George Murray, who had also travelled down from Kirkcudbrightshire and set up as machine makers in Manchester at this time. The two firms were to be symbiotically linked as friends and rivals when in 1797 McConnel and Kennedy joined the Murrays (who had acquired land there in 1790) on an adjoining site in Ancoats (where Schinkel was to sketch their factories side by side). They, like many other entrepreneurs – Robert Owen, Peter Ewart, Henry Houldsworth and George Lee – all took similar routes into the cotton trade from machine making and renting factory space. The constructing and handling of machines seemed to lead inevitably to the manufacturing of cotton.

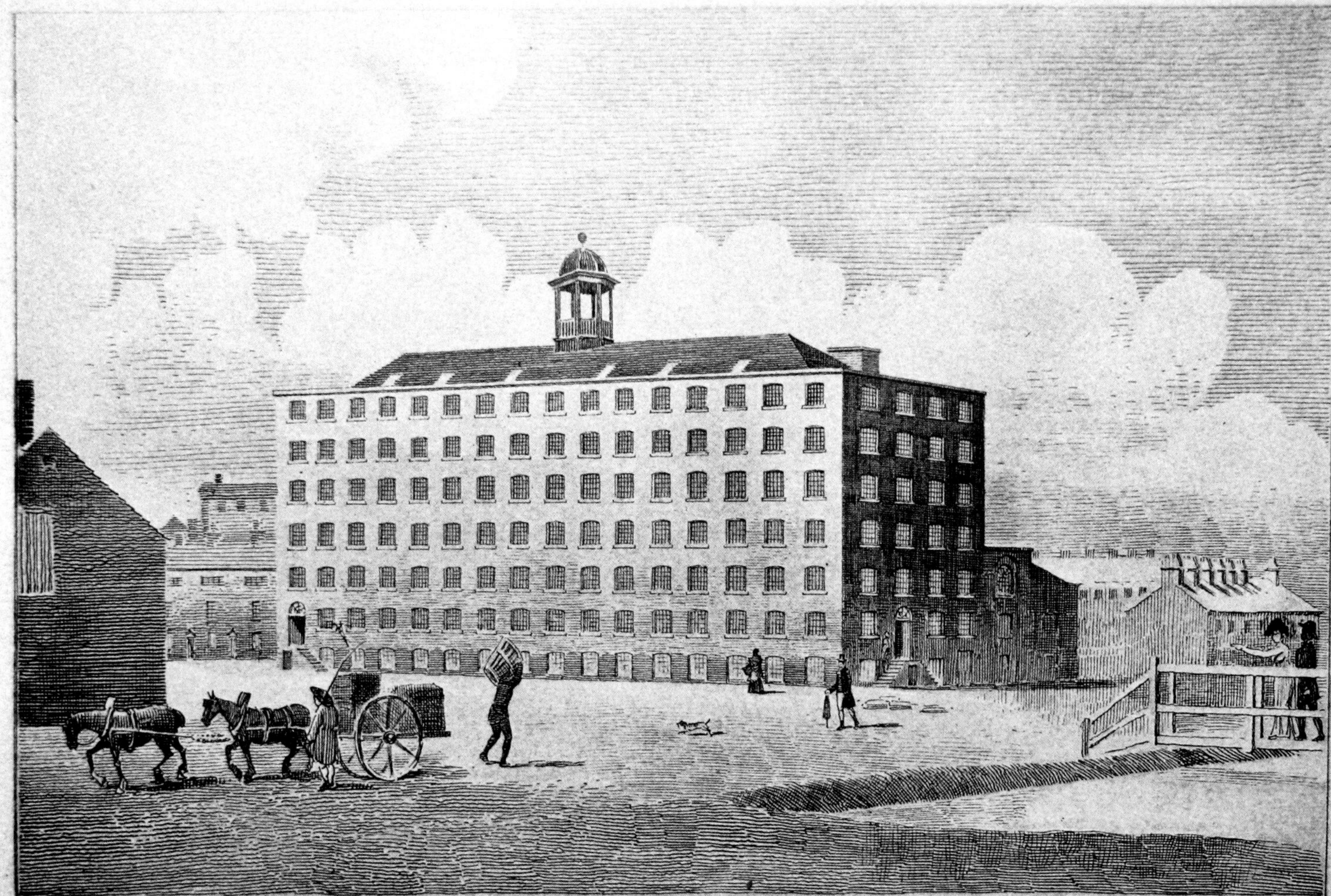

McCONNEL & KENNEDY'S COTTON MILL

From a drawing dated 1800

McConnel & Kennedy's success was based on reinvesting their early profits in new technologies and buildings. They were canny in their timing as well as in their use of what have been called the 'micro-inventions' of the Industrial Revolution – technical improvements and innovations based on local learning that elaborated the better-known 'macro-inventions'.[24] John Kennedy, for example, invented the scutching frame for opening the fibres of raw cotton by means of revolving blades, as well as the process known as 'double speed', by which the spinning mule could make finer yarn.[25] One of the most significant of industrial changes happened in the McConnel & Kennedy mill in 1795 when the Boulton & Watt rotary steam engine was applied to a mule for the first time (Arkwright had, notably, failed to do this in his nearby Miller Street factory).[26] In one move, the costs of steam power were reduced and the potential for locating mills in urban sites opened up. This marked the beginning of the firm's confidence in significant capital investments, and their technological vanguardism would continue until at least the adoption of 600-spindle mules by the early 1830s.[27]

The firm's success in machine making in the years after 1795 – creating larger machines and machines serving different processes in manufacture – led to a need for bigger buildings with space for more steam engines to power the work, and this in turn led to a cycle of obsolescence and change. They were already advising their clients on the size and dimensions of buildings they needed

[10] 'McConnel & Kennedy's Cotton Mill'. Engraving based on drawing dated 1800, from John W. McConnel, *A Century of Fine Cotton Spinning* (1913).

[11] Plan of McConnel & Kennedy mill buildings in 1811. John Rylands Library Special Collections.

[12 A&B] McConnel & Kennedy: plans of (*left to right*) New Mill, Old Mill and Sedgwick mill. From *Plans of all the Spinning Factories Within the Township of Manchester* (1822).

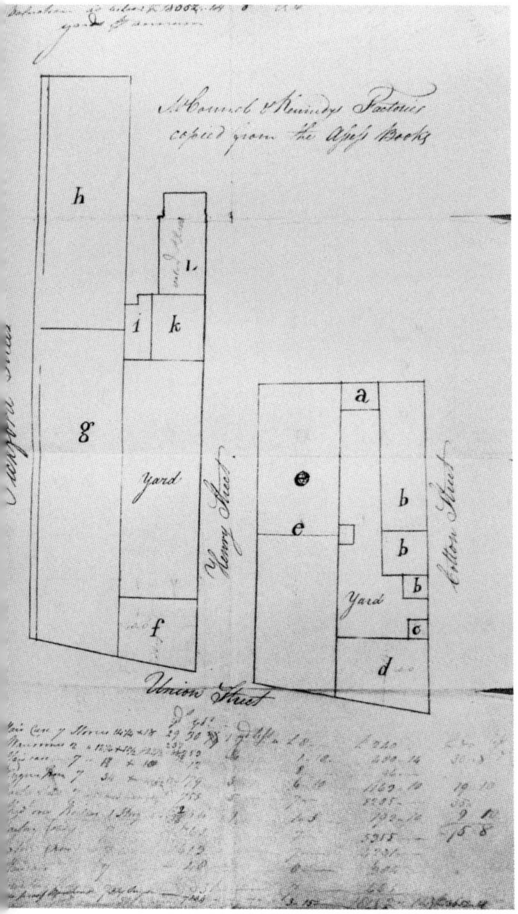

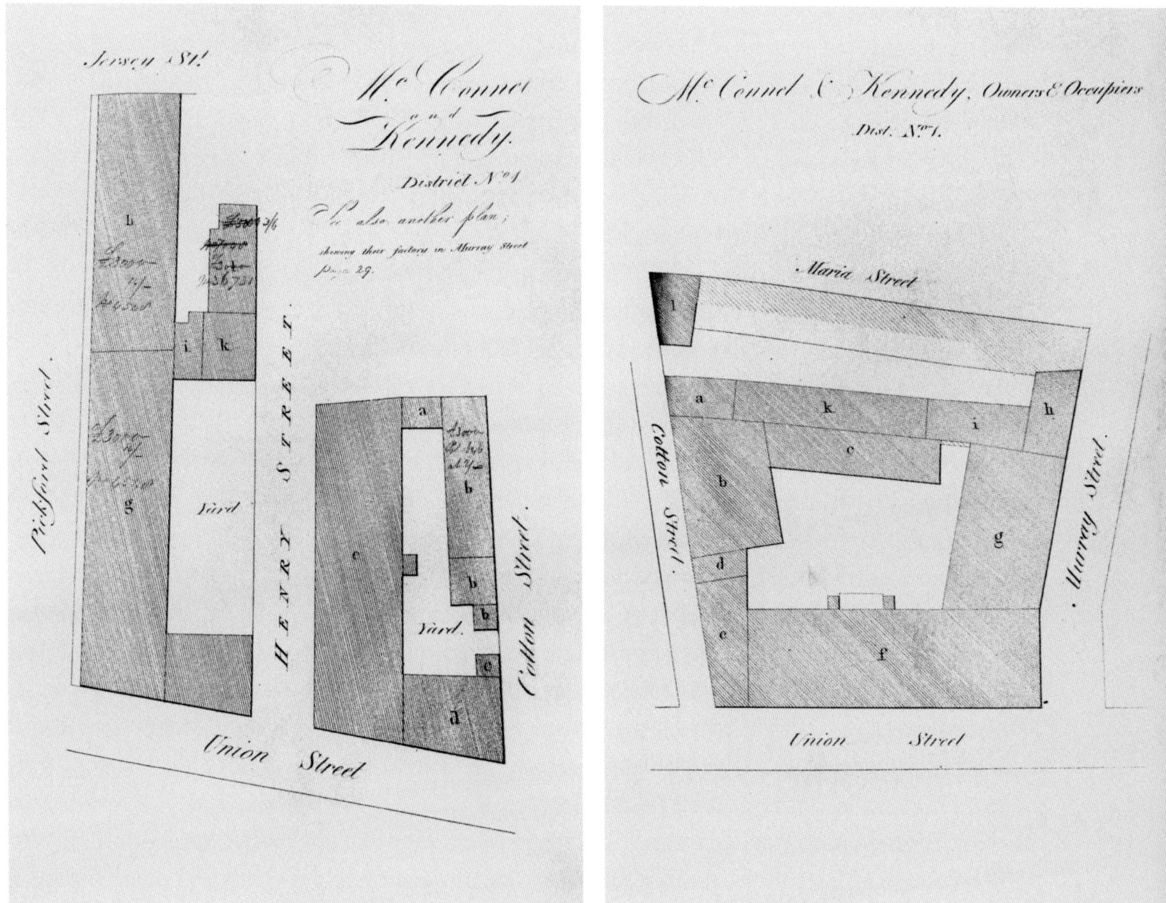

to house McConnel & Kennedy machines. At this time there were clearly no architects capable of understanding this from the perspective of both the innovative machine maker and the manufacturer, or at least none that were interested enough to gain this knowledge (specialist mill architects were not to emerge for at least another thirty years).[28] In 1797 McConnel & Kennedy took the next step and bought land at the junction of Union Street and Henry Street, just beside the excavations for the Rochdale Canal in Ancoats.[29] During the relocation around 1800, the firm shifted definitively away from making machines for sale (but continued to make them for their own use) and instead moved entirely into the spinning trade: they enlarged the customer base for their yarn in Scotland and on the Continent and bought raw cotton largely from a new source, the cotton plantations worked by slaves in the American South.[30] Alongside this, the firm scaled up the power of its Boulton & Watt steam engines.[31] By the time of Schinkel's visit, McConnel & Kennedy were Manchester's largest employer of labour in the cotton industry.[32] As we have seen, for the company there was no significant difference between what Marx called fixed capital as embodied in machines and fixed capital as invested in buildings.[33] Production process and physical framework were interdependent: both needed large outlays, and both involved obsolescence and change. The conjunction of building and machine was intrinsic to the success of cotton manufacture at this time.

[13] Contemporary view of Sedgwick mill, 2019.

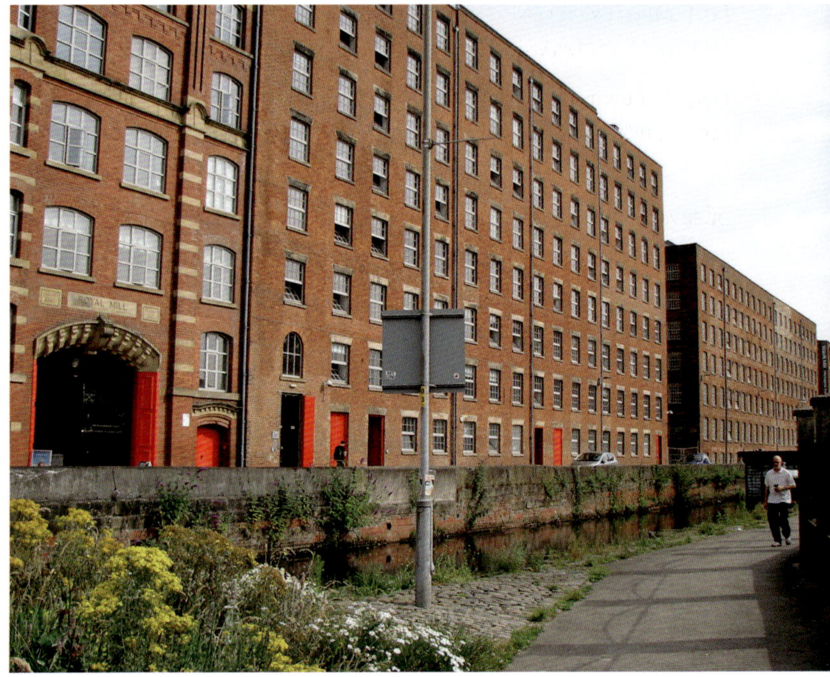

Three huge mill buildings were erected in twenty years, each seven or eight storeys high, each with a main entrance through yards on their long side and an engine house on their short canal-facing side. The firm's first mill, soon called Old Mill, was built between 1798 and 1802. This was a seven-storey block and, if we are to believe a 'drawing dated 1800' reproduced in a later book by the firm, it originally had a domed turret on its roof and elevated entrances on its short side and at one end of its long side[34] (fig. 10). It easily dominated the mix of buildings around it, and the foreground of the engraving shows its relation to the then incomplete canal. A plan of 1811 shows that the actual entrance was on its east side on Cotton Street, with a yard serving all buildings, and that there was an engine house as part of its canal-facing side[35] (fig. 11). Half of the New, or Long Mill, initially seven floors high and 650 square yards in area, was built on the other side of Henry Street from Old Mill in 1801, with the second half added in 1805–6. As with Old Mill, the yard was on its east side, with a main staircase on the north side of the yard. Insofar as there was any theory to guide the plans of mill buildings, it advocated the close proximity of departments of the mill to reduce the movements of workers.[36] (It is also clear that the theory, formulated in retrospect, was geared to a much more modest mill, essentially of one building, than those erected along Union Street in Ancoats.) There was a lower engine house on the south-east side of the site, which again was integral to the canal-facing side, and the offices were located further up Henry Street. Both buildings were early in adopting new technology and were fitted with gas lighting in 1809 (again acquired from Boulton & Watt), with the gas initially made on the premises.[37] A third mill was added to the Union Street frontage between 1818 and 1820, named Sedgwick mill after the site's previous owner, and provided with a 53-horsepower steam engine that supplied energy for seventy-two mules, increasing the company's capacity by 25 per cent[38] (fig. 12 a and b). At least two of these buildings were built on land already occupied by older factories and houses. We also know that the partners were directly involved in contracting out the building work and the supply of brick from a nearby site.

If the aspirant textile barons were effectively the builders of their mills, they were also the coordinators of local and transnational resources. Their use of Ancoats clay is perhaps an underrated aspect of the area's rapid transformation, as is the availability of coal nearby.[39] And, just as this localism mattered, so did the international trade that the firm rapidly built up. They prided themselves on importing the finest sea island cotton from the slave plantations of Charleston and Savannah, and on exporting cotton yarn to Scotland, Ireland, Belgium, France, Germany (Hamburg and Berlin), Italy (Genoa) and Switzerland (St Gallen and Geneva). By the time of Schinkel's visit, they had added buyers in Portugal, Egypt, Poland and India.[40] This was the kind of world that cotton manufacturing was developing.

The buildings assembled beside the canal by the time of Schinkel's visit in 1826, while formidable, were also carefully considered. Old Mill stood in the middle, with the other two mills on either side. In Schinkel's sketch New Mill is the first block on the left; there is the gap of Henry Street between it and Old Mill to its right and slightly higher, while Sedgwick mill is to the right of that. Of the three buildings, only Sedgwick mill survives, and in Schinkel's drawing it appears to project closer to the canal and its eight-storey-high, seventeen-bay front is divided by a vertical line. This last is probably an abbreviation for an architectural refinement, the slight projection of the building's central section

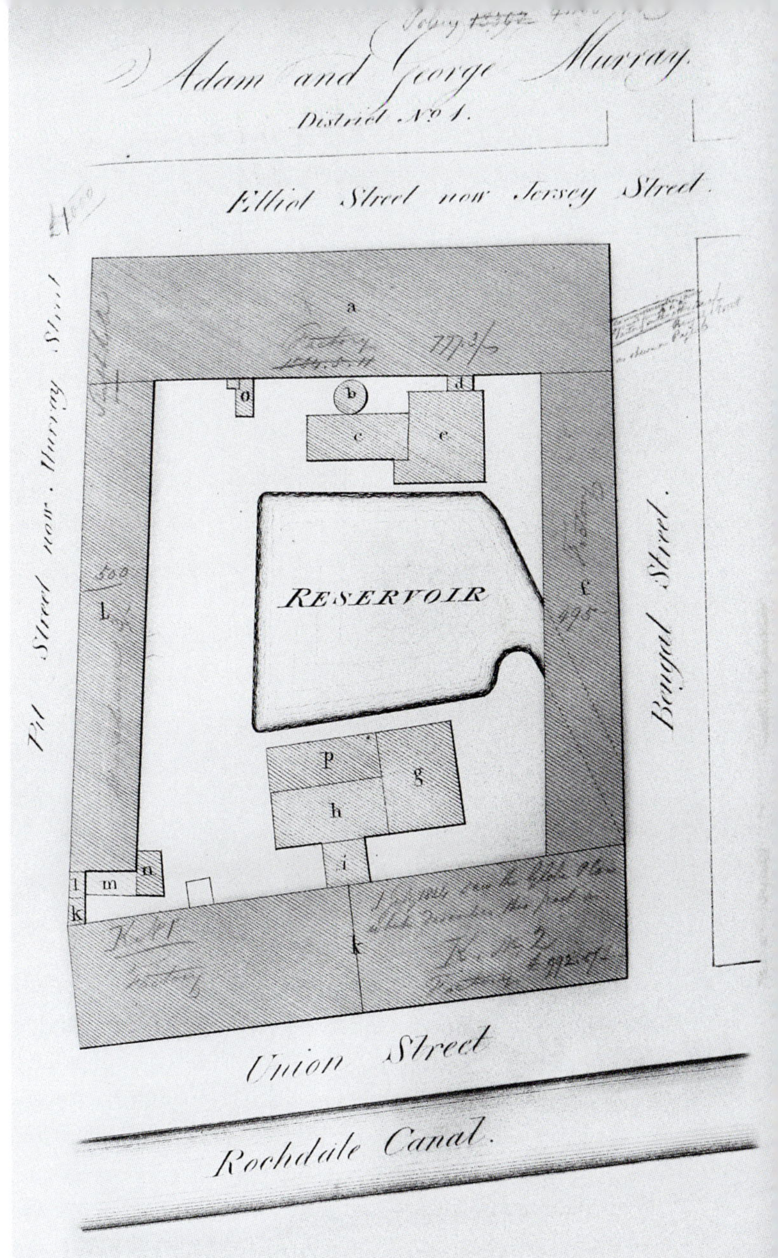

[14] Murray's mills: site plan. From *Plans of all the Spinning Factories Within the Township of Manchester* (1822).

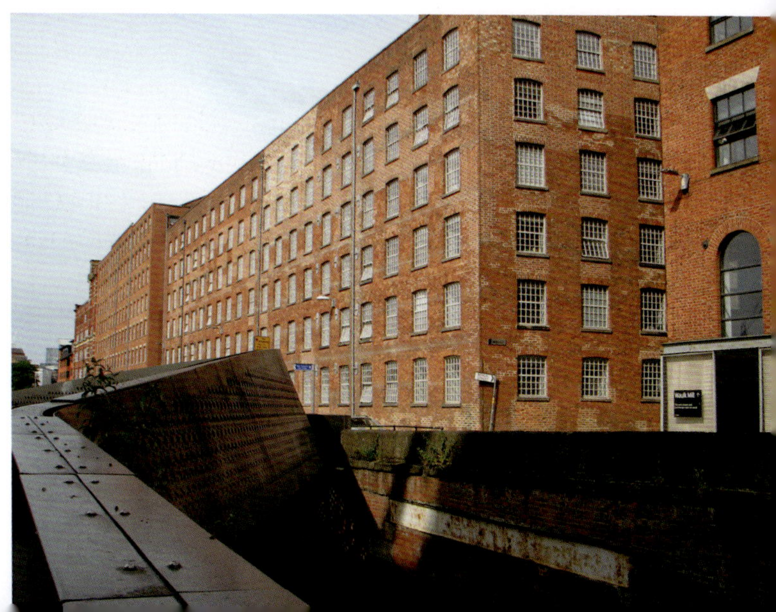

[15] Contemporary view (2019) of Murray's mills (the now blocked tunnel under the road is visible lower right).

of seven bays providing a just sufficient sense of a tripartite frontage (fig. 13). It is a curiously slight concession to the proprieties of architecture, neither enough to provide the kind of building Schinkel would have regarded as having architecture nor making a particular contribution to the performance of the building. A further three blocks, finished by 1820, were also part of Sedgwick mill. These were grouped around a yard, with an engine house attached to the rear of the main block.

The outer appearance of these mills was clearly not fixed from the time of their first building, and this may explain some of the differences between their early representations. Nevertheless, there were clearly some other refinements. In 1809 New Mill had a low wall, about six feet high, extending the full length of the building and providing a barrier between it and Pickford Street (see fig. 11). It continued around the far end of the building but not around the Union Street end. In one sense this was the back of the building, because the working entrance would have been from Henry Street. The wall may have been a security device (including a measure against industrial spying).[41] It would have made it impossible to see anything more than the first few feet of the ceiling of the interior of the lowest mill floor.

Further away, just beyond Sedgwick mill and less visible in Schinkel's sketch, the neighbouring Murray's mill buildings were even larger in capacity than their rivals'.[42] Developed at the same time, between 1798 and 1806, Murray's mills contained a canal basin to which boats could bring coal and cotton via a tunnel under both the road and the eastern building of the complex (figs 14 and 15). The first blocks, Old Mill (1798) and the Decker mill (1801), each eight storeys high and eleven bays wide, were built on the Union Street end of the site. A slightly lower block, New Mill, was built the far side of the courtyard. Engine houses, with Boulton & Watt steam engines, and spiral or square stair towers for all these blocks were situated on their inner sides. The enclosure, which was quite unusual at that time, was completed in 1806 with lower ancillary blocks and with an entrance placed on the south side fronting Murray Street. This framed entrance was the portal for the workforce, opening and closing at the start and end of shifts and providing some form of security in the event

[16] *View of Mills along the Rochdale Canal*, 1820. Watercolour. Manchester Libraries, Information and Archives.

[17] 'Cotton Factories, Union Street, Manchester', 1831. Engraving by Samuel Austin, from Austin et al., *Lancashire Illustrated* (1832).

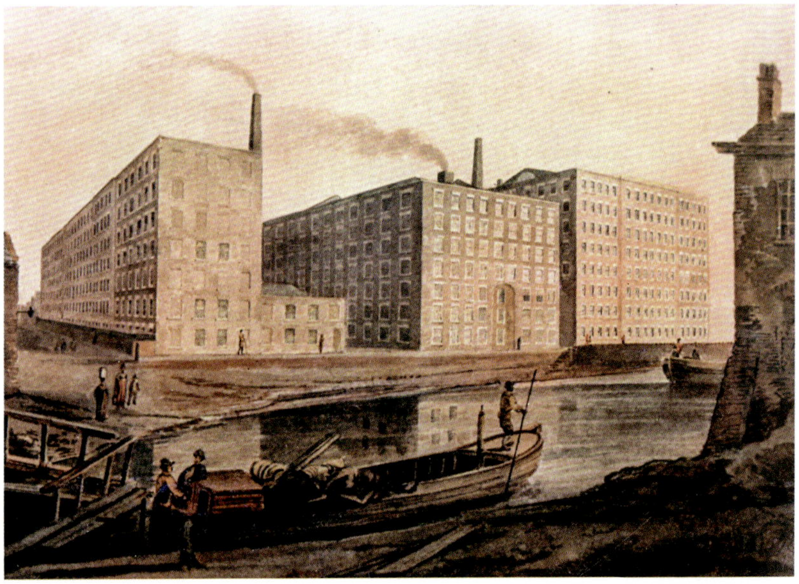

of protest and riot. Within, the mill yard was overlooked by the manager from a bay window. All of this, or course, was invisible from Schinkel's viewpoint.

McConnel & Kennedy's identification with Ancoats gave the area the impetus and concentrated economic activity it needed to become Manchester's (and the world's) first industrial suburb. At the same time McConnel & Kennedy and Murray's were exceptional in their size. Their investment in buildings is sometimes taken as the first and clearest indication of a new stage in the cotton industry, a shift from what has been called the Arkwright era of converting sites and buildings to a substantial ramping up of capital investments on purpose-built mills and mechanical power.[43] The sheer amount of their machinery, which rapidly led to bigger buildings, drew Marx's interest to these large factories, as well as their 'more massive mechanism', 'mightier moving power', 'more complex system of machinery' and, of course, 'the mechanical monster whose body fills whole factories'.[44] But scale, Marx's 'era of machinofacture', can be deceptive when it has no close comparisons. McConnel & Kennedy and Murray's were far bigger than any other cotton firm in Manchester at this time; the next biggest firm in 1815 was less than half their size.[45] And scale can be deceptive also in that these companies' very size, which is also made apparent in their buildings, draws the eye to it and makes the tourist spy complicit in the belief that they must be the best because the biggest expression of the Industrial Revolution. The exceptional becomes a teleology, becomes the exemplary.[46]

SCHINKEL'S AWE AT THE SIZE AND EXTENT OF THE INDUSTRIALISED environment he encountered rings true only in part. It was not just something he expected to see but something he had already seen on his journey. Indeed, perhaps this was and remains a trope in visiting industrial sites in the semi-detached way that Schinkel and others did. As many early twentieth-century visitors felt when they saw Henry Ford's factories, 'the only problem was to find adjectives to fit the marvels ... the wonder was unquestionably heightened by the fact that these were the first manufacturing plants they had seen'.[47] Yet, although Schinkel's language certainly echoes that response it is closer, especially when taken with his sketch and with his reactions to other things recorded in the notebook, to another mode – that of the industrial pastoral. The factory's outer appearance is also an important part of this, but the pastoral makes its claims less insistently.

Schinkel's sketch is familiar but also deceptive. It presents what might be regarded as the exterior, public aspect of the two companies and their mills. This familiarity, which is different from the way he would have appreciated the canal and waterwheel intellectually, comes from the angle of view and the distance, placing the viewer as it does beside the canal with the array of buildings in perspective recession. In this sense it is close to a number of other images of the same mills from this period. An unattributed watercolour view of 1820, possibly commissioned by McConnel & Kennedy, is more idyllic but also even more stark (fig. 16). We have a similar view as Schinkel's, if markedly closer, looking across the canal with a lock gate to the left and a canal boat in the foreground, while another boat enters from the right. The lock gate itself is depicted in such a way as to emphasise the rickety handrail and foot planks – like those on an old bridge over a country stream – rather than the massive weight and precision of its gate. But, while an idyll implies peace and the rural, there is something

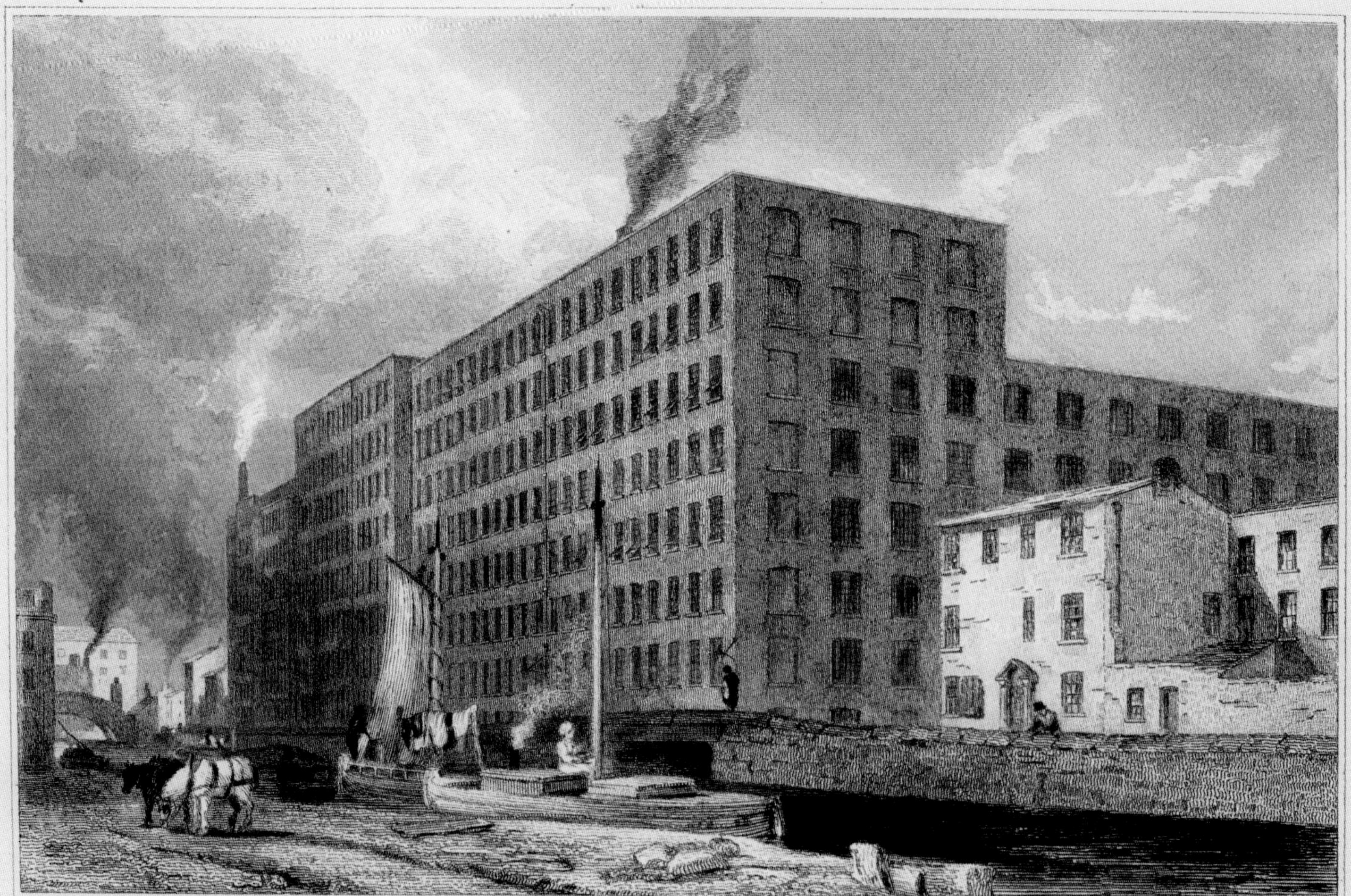

Austin. Mc Gahey.

COTTON FACTORIES, UNION STREET, MANCHESTER.

TO MR MURRAY, AND MR MC CONNEL, THIS PLATE IS RESPECTFULLY INSCRIBED.

flagrantly contrary here; the canal, finished only some fifteen years before, was crucial to Ancoats' transformation. Rather than being a source of water power, the canal supplied water for boilers and steam engines and was the artery for bringing in the mills' coal and raw cotton supplies and transporting much of its cotton goods, as well as the dump for its effluent.[48] It created a world of linkages, connecting Rochdale, the Calder Valley and the east coast of the country with the wharfs, warehouses and other elements of Manchester's new urban infrastructure. Canals energised change: in the words of the contemporary landscape painter John Hassell, they were 'the very heart's blood and soul of commerce'.[49]

There is, then, an ambivalence towards its subject in the watercolour as to how its abrupt angularity and repetition 'without architecture' (in Schinkel's terms) might be conventionalised. On both edges of the painting two smaller and more ramshackle buildings seem to establish either the older Ancoats from which the company's mills had so recently emerged or a more recent, nondescript, modernity: in either case they serve a vernacularising, picturesque purpose.[50] Importantly, they are dark and scraggily flattened things while the mill buildings are cubic entities which catch the light and, doubled by their watery reflections, open up the picture to space and depth. (This contrast between the dark old and the light new will turn up as a marker of epochal change in Chapter 3, where, as we shall see, it's a kind of ideologeme, a tropic package.) Again the image plays up to a certain selective obtuseness. By 1820 mills and housing had filled in the speculative grid of twenty-five years before, yet here McConnel & Kennedy are represented as still high and dry – even Murray's is edited out.[51] It is a view also described by de Tocqueville, though he sees it as if from above: '[the factories'] six stories tower up; their huge enclosures give notice from afar of the centralisation of industry. The wretched dwellings of the poor are scattered haphazard around them.'[52] McConnel & Kennedy's mills dominate the view, the Long Mill to the left providing a sense of great recession into pictorial depth while the two mills to the right present a massive windowed wall seven to eight storeys high along the canal frontage. The Sedgwick mill's engine house, part of its Union Street side, is absorbed into the shape of the building but is given a three-storey-high room.[53] The watercolourist made certain to include the slightly projecting centre of this mill, a slight detail but one not to be missed. (There is also the suggestion – perhaps of a proposed adaptation that was never carried through or temporary – of an arched recess, three storeys high near the centre of Old Mill.)

Through their compositional format and mood, both watercolour and drawing reach for a reassurance about urban industrial space, as if to say that, even if scale and repetition are unavoidable, the dispositions of space and our relation to them are knowable and familiar. This is why what is pictured insists on a certain passivity or slow movement that is associated with the pastoral. Two figures – one poling the canal boat away from the bank, the other carrying a jug on her head – even have something of the georgic about them; they are certainly distinct from the new rhythms and body shapes imposed by industrial modernity. Other figures converse and stroll, their working functions not always clear; there is a tranquillising sense of human presence attempting to be at one with its surroundings, reasserting a benign order. All this despite the very obvious fact to anyone using or passing these buildings that they contained the 'harsh music',[54] the regularised urgency, the rapid regular motions of machinery. But perhaps that which is inherently unsettling – the disjunctive tempos and new productive spaces of modernity – is not entirely reframed and recontained within the visual templates of a pre-modern tradition.

Similar things might be said of an engraving of 1831 that appeared in W. H. Pyne's *Lancashire Illustrated* (fig. 17). This shows the reverse view, looking back along the canal from the north-east, with Murray's mill in the foreground and McConnel & Kennedy's beyond. The accompanying text has little to say: the exterior is noted for its 'great height' while the unshown interior is 'most interesting for its hundreds of works, its different departments, and its regularity of process'.[55] There seems to be a lowering of expectation, a deference that would go along with the original dedication to 'Mr Murray and Mr McConnel'. Some of the same devices are deployed here as in the watercolour: the sharp recession of the mills in perspective, the canal clutter, the smaller building ('Mr Lane's factory') as a foil to the big mills. The light and darkness of old and new are now reversed. The greatest difference is the much less severe effect of the mills: their gauntness is dissipated partly by the smoke and clouds that animate the sky, partly by treating all the mill buildings as one compact block like some oversized terrace. But there is still an impression of extensiveness, repetition and the lack of something that architecture was expected to have and that can be insufficiently suggested by the available conventions.

Surprisingly, we are not looking at the entrance front of buildings in any of these images, including Schinkel's. These are frontages along the canal, but in terms of what happens inside the buildings they are sidelong or even back views. Seen from across the canal, they gave the artists a roomier view of their subjects, establishing a more informal and less imposing relation between street, canal and building. Legislation on land development like the 1794 Rochdale Canal Act, which permitted factories within a short distance to use water from the canal,[56] was no doubt a determinant: sites along the canal were prime and developers made the most of them by positioning the short ends of the grid plots beside the water.[57] Even the most expansive companies could scale up their waterfronts only incrementally. Notions of front, back and sides may not be particularly useful ways to think of these mills. It's a simple point but one worth emphasising. The first two of McConnel & Kennedy's mill buildings were aligned end-on to Union Street, and the third one presented its long side to the street, but with all three, as with Murray's mill, the main yard entrances were from the sides of the complexes where the roads were narrower, and entrances to the individual buildings faced onto these yards. Entrances and their yards were also designed to control and distribute the workforce, and to establish the rhythms and disciplines of the mill. They were less about honorific thresholds between worlds than about establishing the boundary of the mill's rule, less about the palace than the fortress.[58] The image of the factory gate as either the manufacturer's signboard or the point at which workers collectively transitioned into a different temporality – industrial time – would have to wait until much later in the century. For now, the autonomous space of the factory – where labour was 'disconnected from family, community, environment, or any traditional interdependencies or associations'[59] – was unrepresentable.

That the views shown in the watercolour and engraving should be both familiar and deceptive is not unexpected – this was after all the currency of much landscape painting, and the Ancoats mills were seen as a landscape, an abrupt cliff- or ravine-like form. If something approaching the sublime were to transpire, it was a version that was not only abrupt and repetitious but hedged around with equivocations. If the urban mill and its surroundings in Ancoats are to be understood in Schinkel's terms as 'monstrous shapeless buildings ... without architecture', they must still be given some form of visual sense, and this comes from how the viewer is positioned – and the historical viewer was undoubtedly the industrialist and his ilk. Ambivalence, reassurance, familiarity, deception: these are the contradictions that inform such views. This is not to imply that Kennedy, McConnel or their neighbours, the Murrays, bewailed the inadequacies of landscape to capture the new urban realities of their factories. Of course not. These images were perfectly adequate to their purposes, just as they were invisible – simply unavailable – to their workforces.

TO ASSIMILATE THE MILLS WAS OFTEN TO CREATE AN equivalence between them and more familiar structures. Comparing mill buildings to palaces was not uncommon: de Tocqueville twice called them 'huge palaces of industry'; Robert Owen referred to the McConnel & Kennedy mills as 'palace-like buildings'; and in *Coningsby* (1844) Disraeli described Manchester's mills as 'illumined factories with more windows than Italian palaces and smoking chimneys taller than Egyptian obelisks'.[60] Here is Schinkel again:

> *The streets of the town go through these masses of buildings, and over the streets go connecting walkways. We went around: enormous factories, eg MacConnel, Kennedy and another, Morris [he means Murray's], have buildings 7–8 storeys high, as long as the Palace in Berlin and equally wide, with absolutely fire-proof vaulting, a canal at the side and inside.*[61]

The unalloyed bigness of the factories is difficult to come to terms with: Schinkel attempts to understand it within his sense of similar-sized buildings from an entirely different culture of architecture ('as long as the Palace in Berlin'), to which he appends the new technologies of modernity. But his sense of how an urban entity should be organised is put in question by those 'masses of buildings'. The palace analogy is a compensation for both the incoherence of the surroundings and their lack of 'architecture'.

There is something, to cannibalise a concept from literary theory, of a misplaced chronotope about the palace–mill analogy. The chronotope, a term elaborated by the literary theorist Mikhail Bakhtin, is a figure of thought that brings space and time together differently; it situates the subject in a newly politicised way in the here and the now, marking it out as alternatively ordered from the city.[62] The palace-mill is not just a typological conflation, in architectural terms, but also a combined figure juxtaposing time and space, a reflex that adjusts or replaces a hierarchy, if to an ultimately conventionalising effect. There is, as it were, the over there as well as the here, the aristocrat of the past as well as the industrial worker of the present. The new industrialist has old powers of tyranny; the worker is given a glimpse of a different relation to hierarchy. The nature of things is shifted from the present and referred to a different order.[63] To see the mill as a palace is in one sense to deal with the issue of scale through a refusal of the new economic imperatives that demand size over decorum. The palace becomes the measure that enables scalar comparison. This, one might say, is the view borrowed from the old order.

Another version of this is to see the size of the mill itself as part of the drive for social distinction and the accumulation of wealth, a 'palace of infamy' symbiotically linked to the country house or palace.[64] Frances Trollope imagined it this way in her Manchester novel, *The Life and Adventures of Michael Armstrong the Factory Boy* (1840). Embarrassingly, because unavoidably, the mill's presence, 'unpicturesquely visible', is the 'source and headspring' for the pleasures of the house.[65] Here the mill is, crucially, a rural matter. It is not unlike the productive ancillary buildings of the country estate: its six storeys give it 'magnitude'; there are 'principal gates'; a necessary 'ceremony' allows entrance; and all this helps moderate the diabolic tumult within to the niceties without.[66] This may also be connected to a relatively recent history of mills integrated into royal establishments, particularly strong in France, a history that was in turn appropriated by utopian socialists like Charles Fourier.[67] Nevertheless, unlike early mills that had used palatial allusions in their public-facing buildings, the palace analogy is an empty one at Ancoats. None of the Ancoats mills had anything like the Palladian mansion block (let alone its surrounding gardens and pleasure grounds) that Boulton & Watt had built in 1764–5 for their Soho Manufactory in Birmingham, and few had anything equivalent to the Palladian windows Richard Arkwright had built into his mills at Cromford in 1783.[68] So the palace analogy entails discordancy.

To see a mill as a palace was not only the condition of the manufacturer's or architect's sense of ownership, of aggrandisement. One worker in McConnel & Kennedy's mill was prepared to describe his place in the company as a happy one, partly because it was a place dignified by the largeness of the mill edifice:

> *Now see the cotton from the town convey'd*
> *To Manchester, that glorious mart of trade:*
> *Hail splendid scene: the Nurse of every art*
> *That glads the widow's and the orphan's heart!*
> *Thy mills, like gorgeous palaces, arise*
> *And lift their useful turrets to the skies!*
> *See Kennedy's stupendous structure join'd*
> *To thine McConnel – friends of human kind!*
> *Whose ready doors for ever wide expand*
> *To give employment to a numerous band,*
> *Murray's behold! that well deserves a name, –*
> *E'en Lee's and Houldsworth's our attention claim, –*
> *And numerous others, scattered up and down,*
> *The sole supporters of this ample town.*[69]

This is from *The Cotton Mill* by John Jones (1788–1858), an operative spinner known, somewhat predictably, as 'the Welsh bard'. Jones dedicated his poem, written in 1821, to John Kennedy. The poet was later favoured by William Fairbairn, to whom he inscribed his collection *Poems by John Jones* (1856).[70] The rest of the poem is a long and extraordinarily detailed paean to the intricate workings and power of machinery, with industrious spinners and nymph-like weavers under the eye of their frowning yet just master.[71] It would seem that a complete submission to the machine's rhythms was the way in which the operative could gain gratification, poetic as much as physical. While, a few years later, Schinkel would be surprised by what sheer size did to architectural decorum, Jones manages to see both the 'gorgeous' and the 'stupendous' in the mill. It is an anomaly, with the chronotope working as explicit acceptance of the system and as a notably different take on its subject from the hatred of factories and machinery common in what we know of other contemporary working-class responses.[72] There is no mention of the three-month-long strike that had been defeated only three years earlier, or of the bodies deformed by their work, as reported to the House of Lords in 1819, or of the children employed (in 1816 45 per cent of the workforce were under the age of 16),[73] or of the manufacturer as 'ruthless king' and the palace as an utterly different place.[74] Jones actually tells us that the mill is not just the town's pride but its philanthropic support, a kind of palace for the people.

Another aspect of the palace–mill link is that, while the mills' starkness has more to do with the place of production in these workaday surroundings, the analogy with palaces is a kind of placeholder for the house that is not there, that of the mill owner. Initially, mill owners did live near their urban mills. McConnel lived with his wife and young family on Great Ancoats Street from 1799 to 1806. Their residence on the corner of Mill Street was opposite the house where his partner John Kennedy lived at that

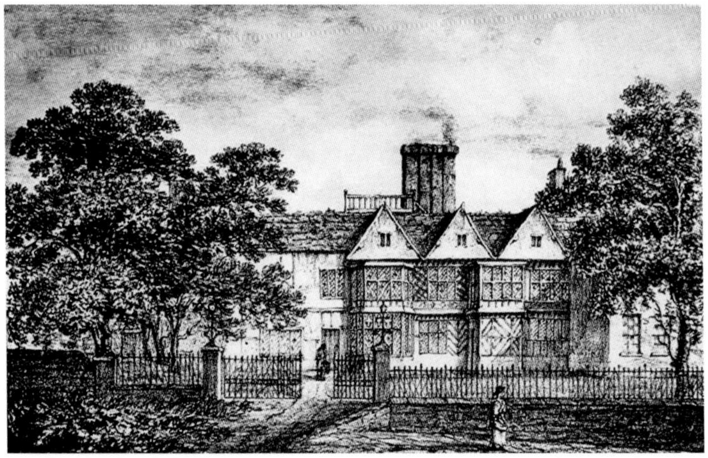

[18] Ancoats Hall in 1825, before its refronting. Lithograph based on an 1825 drawing by James Ralston. From James Croston, *Old Manchester* (1875).

time. In 1806 the McConnels moved a little over a mile away to the new middle-class development known as the Polygon in Ardwick Green, where McConnel had built himself a house. John Kennedy moved into nearby Ardwick Hall at the same time.[75] These are clear markers not just of the firm's financial success but also of these men's aspirations. As Manchester's first residential suburb, Ardwick was described in 1795 as 'principally inhabited by the more opulent classes'.[76]

Similarly, just as the ex-barber Richard Arkwright had built himself a castle, so McConnel sought to give his name greater historical heft by searching out the 'borrowed language' of history, as Marx called it.[77] An invented family coat of arms was one result, created in 1817 at the same time as the firm was about to embark on further expansion on the Ancoats site.[78] McConnel's partner, John Kennedy, was also interested in gaining social distinction within the cotton industry – for instance, he helped mythologise the position of Crompton as a founding and exemplary figure, the new aristocrat of industry.[79] Their neighbour George Murray bought nearby Ancoats Hall in 1813, the family seat of the Mosleys, long the lords of the manor.[80] Located by the River Medlock on the eastern edge of Ancoats, the hall was originally a Tudor house built for the Byrom family in timber and plaster, but in the 1820s Murray had it recast as a stone-fronted mansion (fig. 18). If this was a kind of actual palace, it was also far too close to the mills and their depredated environment, and was to seem increasingly forlorn.

TO TURN FROM THE PALACE-MILL TO CONSIDER THE MILL and its relation to the housing of workers is to move from a realm of the largely imaginary to something all too real. It is also to witness a kind of absence. Workers' housing registered as little in the imaginary of the Ancoats mill as it did in its policy. This may have something in common with the palace–mill analogy – the home as the site of domestic production in rural manufacture had now been bypassed – and with the relinquishing of responsibility by the new urban manufacturers for housing most of their workers. It was a matter of representation too; insofar as the Ancoats manufacturers were not to be identified with housing, the mill image was separated from domestic housing.

This is not to suggest that housing in Ancoats was absent from discourse about the area – that would plainly be absurd given the great concern of social reformers with the notoriously bad conditions there, which was heightened after the cholera outbreak of 1832. Henry Gaulter's *Origins and Progress of the Malignant Cholera* (1833) and James Phillips Kay's *The Moral and Physical Condition of the Labouring Classes of Manchester* (1832) both testify to the interlinked phenomena of extraordinary technological change and, cheek by jowl with it, damp, decrepit and overcrowded housing. Nevertheless, the lack of linkage between the space of the mill and the space of the house remains noteworthy.

By 1815 Ancoats already had the largest number of factories and households of any of Manchester's districts.[81] Houses for some 5,000 to 7,000 people were built over this period, and continued to be built to the 1830s, most of them in blocks of two storeys around the mills and canals. This was the 'template for mixed industrial areas' followed by other cities,[82] the new kind of housing poverty that became a byword for industrial modernity. It was characterised by high densities, housing left to the market (beyond the industrialists), a minimum of public space and the maximising of land use. Such housing provision was nothing if not economical in its use of space. Many of these houses, particularly those built in the 1780s and 1790s were built in rows, with a yard at the back to which direct access could be gained. These might have cellar dwellings and workshops in their attics. Others were back-to-backs, usually one room deep and arranged in small parallel groupings with the rear houses facing a court, an arrangement in which, Engels pointed out, access to ventilation determined the level of rent.[83] Some were the simplest of one-up one-down structures. The housing may not have been quite as flimsy as

[19] A parallelogram, or 'village of unity and mutual cooperation', 1817. Engraving after Robert Owen's scheme, from Owen, *Life of Robert Owen* (1857).

Engels thought, but it was certainly overcrowded: room sizes were notably small, and the structures suffered rapid dilapidation.[84]

Despite the grid, Ancoats housing was developed piecemeal and there was no rush to finish the streets. There was little investment or direction from the textile companies and little or no regulation by local government.[85] Indeed there are few signs that mill owners, unlike many of their rural equivalents, regarded housing provision as their responsibility. Around the time of Schinkel's visit, McConnel & Kennedy owned some eighteen houses in Maria Street, Henry Street and Cotton Street, and Murray's owned fifteen in Gas Street, both in immediate proximity to their mills, though neither company regarded their houses as specifically for cotton spinners, let alone for those in their employment. More likely, they owned them as investments or for the potential of the land for further mill building.[86] De Tocqueville may well have been describing Ancoats in 1835: 'the wretched dwellings for the poor are scattered haphazard around [the mills]. The soil has been taken away, scratched and torn up in a thousand places, but it is not yet covered with the habitations of men.'[87] The incomplete state of Ancoats was a byword, even in Manchester.[88] For James Kay, Ancoats housing was the breeding ground as much of moral corruption as of disease. It was this domestic architecture – or rather the lack of 'architecture' in these dwellings – that had become 'mighty wildernesses of buildings, in which the incurable ills of society rambled, beyond the reach of sanitative interferences'.[89]

One of the most detailed accounts we have of housing in Ancoats was written a little later by the journalist Angus Reach for the *Morning Chronicle* in the 1840s. Reach called this 'the older, worse built, and in all respects inferior quarter of Ancoats':

> *Fancy then, a wide-lying labyrinth of small dingy streets, narrow, unsunned courts terminating in gloomy culs-de-sac, and adorned with a central sloppy gutter. Every score or so of yards you catch sight of one of the second and third class mills, with its cinder-paved courtyard and its steaming engine-house. Shabby-looking chapels, here and there, rise with infinitesimal Gothic arches and ornaments, amid the grimy nakedness of the factories. Now a railroad, upon its understructure of arches, passes over the roofs; anon, you cross a canal, with wharfs and coal-yards and clusters of unmoving barges. In most cases the doors of the houses stand hospitably open, and young children cluster over the thresholds and swarm out upon the pavement: you have thus an easy opportunity of noting the interiors as you pass along. They are, as you will perceive, a series of little rooms, about ten feet by eight, more or less, generally floored with brick or flagstones – materials which are, however, occasionally half-concealed by strips of mats or faded carpeting ... The cellars are, as might be expected, seldom furnished so well. They appear to possess none of the minor comforts, none of the little articles of ornament or fancy furniture which more or less you observe in the parlours. The floors seem damp and unwholesome, you catch a glimpse of a rickety-looking bed in a dark airless corner, and the fire upon the hearth is often cheerlessly small.*[90]

Reach makes Schinkel's sublime Ancoats into something much more everyday, something lived in and liveable, and this is what is unusual about his account. Despite the mythic frame of the labyrinth (also found in de Tocqueville),[91] the description moves easily across the suburb – it is, after all, what the reader can 'fancy', can imagine. The movement is the reader's own as we pass over the depredations of industry and swoop into the house, past its 'sloppy gutter' and repeated arches and into a domestic space where there are 'none of the little articles of ornament'. The passage connects house and engine house, cellar and 'unsunned court', 'rickety-looking bed' and 'third class' mill, and makes them symbiotic. Such symbiosis is rare, so the point needs making. Mills might be compared with the nearby back-to-backs. Umbilically linked to the mills, if disowned by industrialists, Ancoats' housing was the consequence of the new modes of production.[92] Together, mills and housing formed the circuits and limits of working-class architecture. Whereas the houses were shoddily built, essentially short-life structures of small, overcrowded and badly lit spaces, the mills were big, well-lit containers whose structures and construction were good enough in some cases for them to stand to this day. That they were both 'without architecture' makes them the embodiments of shock city.

Housing and the street can also be understood as the negative of the mill. One of the prime examples of this is how the condition of housing, the unregulated courts and the absence of public space

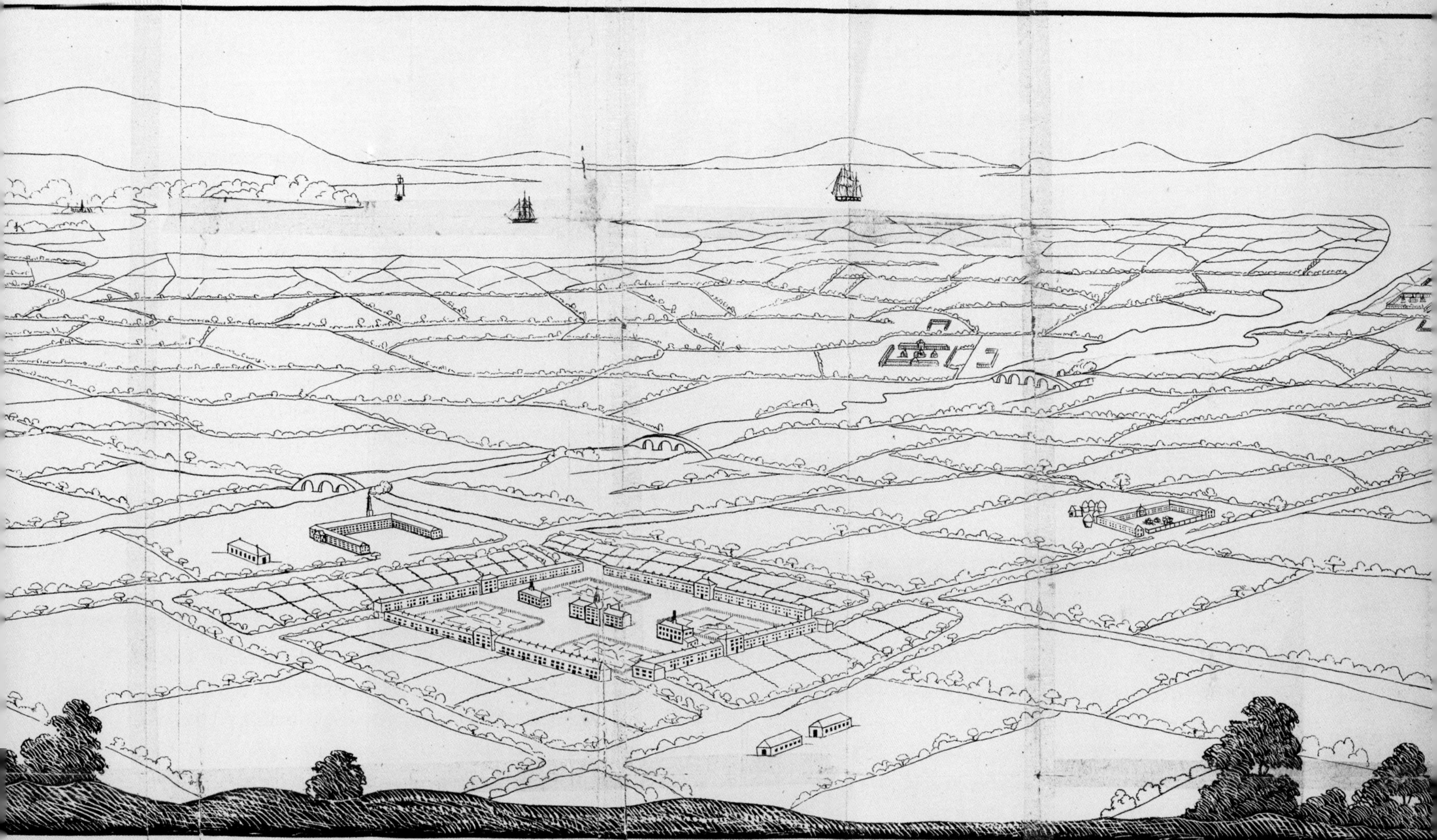

A VIEW & PLAN OF THE VILLAGES OF UNITY & MUTUAL CO-OPERATION.
DESCRIBED IN Mr OWEN'S REPORT ON THE POOR. 1817.

in Ancoats – all detailed in the writing of Engels, Kay and others – constituted the spectre that haunted Robert Owen's utopian socialist projects.[93] A cotton manufacturer in Manchester, renting a mill on Ancoats Lane in the 1790s, Owen came from modest non-English origins, and gained maturity in the same business–technological culture, as McConnel and Kennedy had done.[94] (Like Kennedy, he was also a member of the Manchester Literary and Philosophical Society.) He left his Manchester business in 1799 to move to New Lanark, where he not only created a community around the idea of an efficient, cooperatively organised and humanitarian cotton mill but planned his settlement as the complete obverse of working peoples' experience in industrial Ancoats (while carrying over his sense of environmental determinism).[95] This was indeed, as Lewis Mumford put it, a utopia '[springing] out of the upturned soil of industrialism'.[96] Over the next quarter century Owen embedded his notion of the technology of social reform, first, in the spatial layout of the town and then in his utopian villages spread out over the landscape[97] (fig. 19). In these latter, known as 'parallelograms' (or 'villages of unity and mutual cooperation'), everything is anti-Ancoats. Inside the square

[20] New Mill: plan and section for McConnel & Kennedy by Boulton & Watt, 1809. From Jennifer Tann, *Development of the Factory* (1970).

villages orderly streets are laid out with neat tenements; children and their schools, and communal facilities, are central; industry is extramural and integrated with the landscape; trees are planted and open spaces are laid out for exercise. In his final schemes, the streets and central square are taken over instead by radiating paths centred on a conservatory. The brick and slate environment of Ancoats, with its broken streets, 'surrounded with dirt, enveloped in smoke, and [without] a pleasant object on which to fix their eye', has been made over completely into its other, a pastoral campus dream of a total institution where emotion and dissent are muted while profit and social harmony are both made possible.[98] The vision of a world that defied the destructive division between town and country would stay with Marx and his followers, including William Morris.[99] As the admiring Engels declared, 'the antithesis between town and country no longer exists'.[100] Owen explained: 'as courts, alleys, lanes and streets create many unnecessary conveniences, are injurious to health, and destructive to almost all natural concepts of human life, they will be excluded.'[101]

BUT UTOPIANS DID NOT HAVE TO LEAVE ANCOATS. Another utopia – not a communitarian one like Owen's but a capitalist one – might be imagined within the mill itself. Manufacturers, politicians, political economists, and philosophers were all aware of the so-called machinery question, and the factory was its prime site. The new discipline of political economy emerged out of this and related questions.[102] What were the effects of the machine on society? How would it change the relations between employer and employed? What would be its consequences for skilled workers? And, we might add with Ancoats in mind, how would the machine affect the way that buildings and even cities were shaped and experienced?

John Kennedy himself ventured into these debates, addressing the Manchester Literary and Philosophical Society several times. In one talk he set out a self-serving history of cotton manufacturing, in which early technological advance had caused the 'dissipation' of workers when it led to higher wages. Nevertheless, he argued, the enlightened manufacturer had forged the way, dispelling the 'inveterate prejudices' of the higher as much as of the lower classes. Interestingly, Kennedy also argued that workers had learned 'an activity of mind, and a dexterity of workmanship' from the new technologies.[103] In another talk he argued that machines and the inventiveness that had created them were entirely benevolent; indeed 'those beautiful machines' had made it possible for all family members to be employed, with older men 'set at liberty' to act as the machine overseers.[104] And this in turn led to higher wages, lower costs, better food and clothing, and even 'the more convenient furniture of their humble dwellings'.[105]

Following the arguments of this chapter, we might understand the machinery question as also a mill question or, more widely, as an architecture question. Kennedy certainly thought so. With the coming of the spinning mules, 'larger establishments were erected, and order, system and cleanliness in their arrangement and management, became more necessary and more generally cultivated'. Workers' behaviour would match the mills; like refinements to a machine, they would become 'more regular in their attendance at their work ... more orderly in their conduct ... gradually improving in their domestic comforts and conveniences'[106] – in short, body machines.[107]

The worker in McConnel & Kennedy's mill is to be part of a machine–architecture complex, an assemblage of machines and buildings that interact so closely they cannot be separated into technology and architecture (and bodies). In a move reflecting the company's ambition and shifting from the less prestigious (and usually anonymous) builders of many contemporary mills, the engineer William Fairbairn was brought in to work with Kennedy on the layout and shafting of the Sedgwick mill (following his successful work on this at Murray's mill).[108] One result was a duct under the mill and parallel with Union Street. This contained the horizontal shaft powered by the engine house in the corner of the building, from which vertical shafts conveyed the motive power to the cotton machines on upper floors.[109] This mill work animated the whole, enabling a number of bodies and substances to move in coordination within the building: the cotton machines primarily and, around them, air, water, gas and working bodies.[110]

Spindles were the objects at the end of all this transmission. The Sedgwick mill initially housed 72 mules, each operating 348

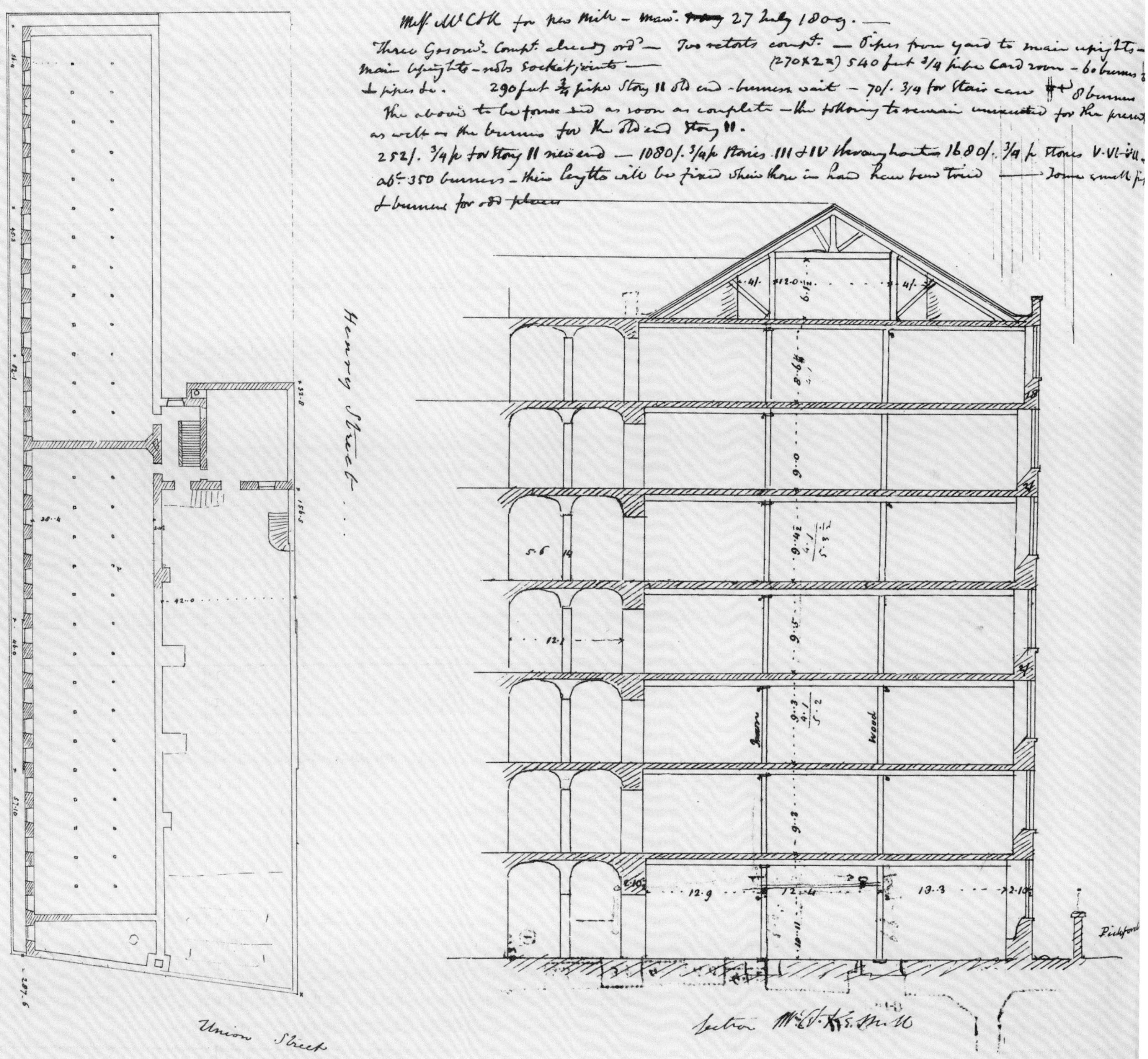
27 July 1809
Three Gasom Compt. already ord.— Two retorts compt. — Pipes from yard to main uprights —
main uprights — socket joints —
(270×2=) 540 feet 3/4 pipe Card room — 60 burners
290 feet 3/4 pipe Story II old end — burners wait — 70/. 3/4 for Stair case — 8 burners
The above to be forwarded as soon as complete — the following to remain unexecuted for the present as well as the burners for the old end Story II.
252/. 3/4 p for Story II new end — 1080/. 3/4 p Stories III & IV throughout — 1680/. 3/4 p Stories V. VI. VII.
ab. 350 burners — their lengths will be fixed when those in hand have been tried — Some small pipes & burners for odd places
Henry Street
Union Street
Iron
Wood
Pickford
Section

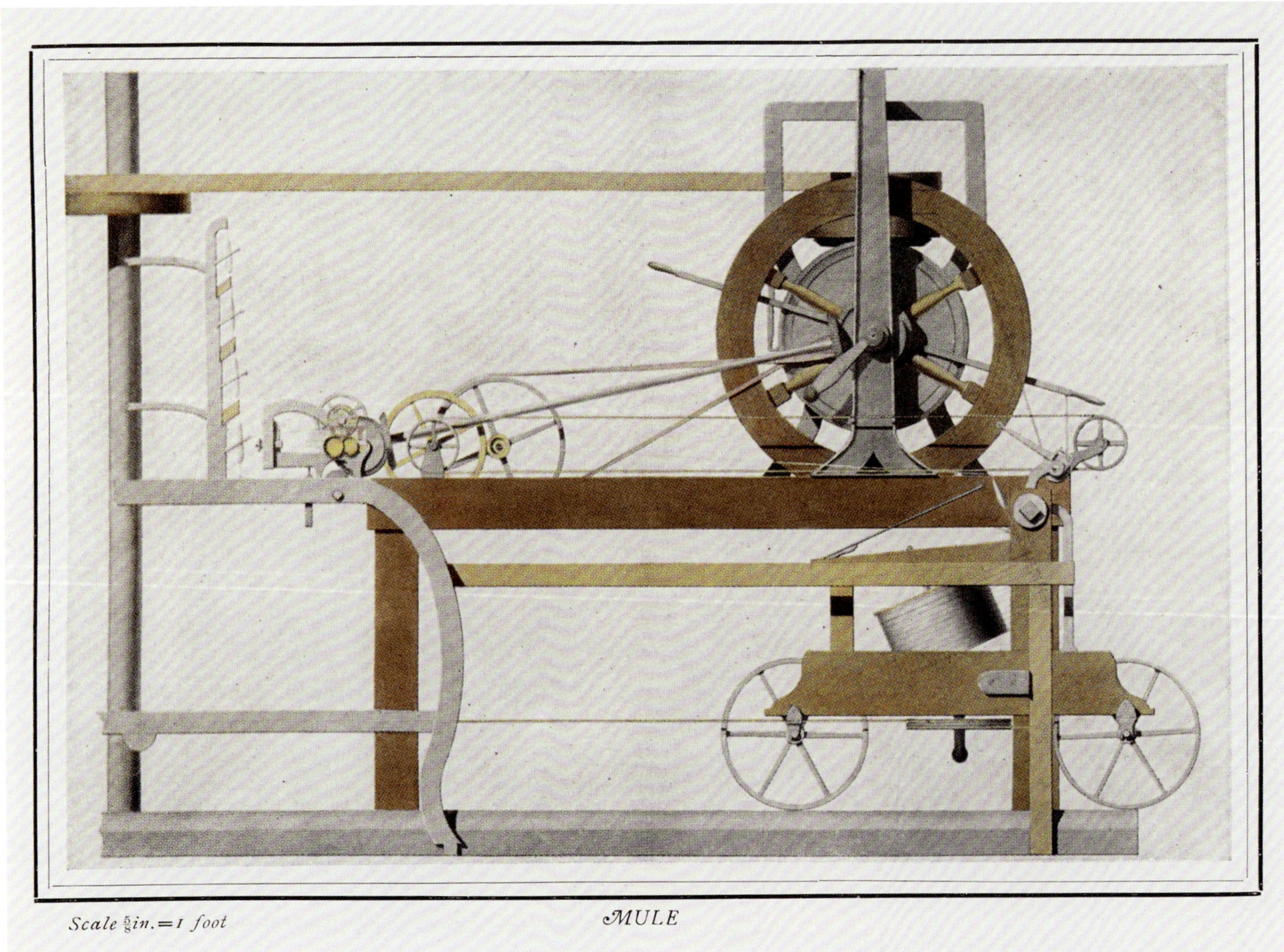

spindles.[111] By the 1820s between 80,000 and 90,000 spindles were at work in the firm's mills (and a similar number in Murray's mills) day and night, producing the finest spun yarn in the world.[112] Rising spindleage had knock-on consequences for mill design. The best position for the mules – as at McConnel & Kennedy – was back to back and transversely across the floors so that window light could illuminate as much of their length as possible. With larger numbers of spindles per machine, the space required for movement of the carriage grew and by the 1820s it was some two metres.[113] And, because this extra space was required longitudinally, the mills themselves grew in width.

The mills built by McConnel & Kennedy and Murray's needed to be flexible containers. Their floor spaces were as well lit as possible so that machines and thread could be examined. Drawings of the New, or Long, Mill in the Boulton & Watt archive, made for the fitting of gas appliances, show the width of the mill floor as over 38 feet with a total length of over 287 feet, with two ranges of pillars running lengthways (fig. 20). There was a slightly greater space between the window front and the first line of pillars (13 feet 3 inches) than between the second line of pillars and the back wall (12 feet 9 inches), while the space between the two lines of pillars was 12 feet 4 inches. Deep window embrasures measuring 2 feet 10 inches further added to the total depth of the building. The heights of these floors varied between 8½ feet on the top floor to nearly 11 feet on the ground floor, with the floors between varying from 9 feet to 9 feet 5 inches.[114] It followed also

[21] 'A Mule', 1826. Drawing possibly by William McConnel. Manchester Libraries, Information and Archives.

[22] 'Mule Spinning'. Engraving, based on drawing by Thomas Allom, from Edward Baines, *History of the Cotton Manufacture in Great Britain* (1835).

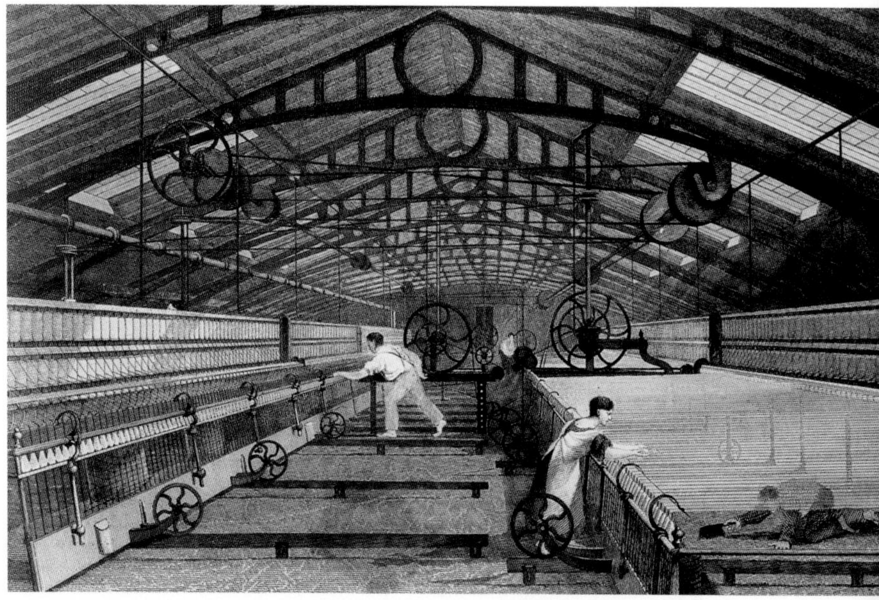

that the floor had to be kept as clear of other obstructions as possible, while the construction had to be relatively fireproof – hence the introduction of slender cast iron columns supporting cast iron beams, with shallow brick arches running transversely between.[115]

We know the kind of mule used in the company's mills from a drawing said to be by James McConnel's son William, and dated 1826 (fig. 21). With its loving attention to working parts, the drawing embodies a particular understanding of such a 'beautiful machine'. It is a pristine image of an unworked if workable machine, less a technical diagram for its construction than a record of achievement and a family icon, both because of who was thought to have made it and because of its importance to the family's fortunes. As a machine portrait, McConnel's mule substitutes technology as a means of production for the human relations and human labour of production.[116] As a combination of 'dead labour' (Marx's term for the past or stored work embodied by machinery) and technical accomplishment, the machine acquires the unquestionable, magical status of an icon, separated from place, time and circumstance – both thingly and sacred. If we can speak of reception with such a drawing, it works as a kind of assurance that the 'capital-relation', as Marx called it, really had been revolutionised.[117]

There are no equivalent interior views of McConnel & Kennedy's mills; indeed, there is a paucity generally of mill interior views from this time. In their absence, historians have often used slightly later images of other mills – they all have a generic feel to them – from J. R. Barfoot's *The Progress of Cotton* (1840) or Edward Baines's *History of the Cotton Manufacture in Great Britain* (1835) as if they were neutral illustrative sources. They are far from that, for Baines was professionally close to Kennedy. Barfoot's images, for instance, depict a kind of life cycle of cotton from the plant to the finished article, in which the dependence on plantation slave labour is taken for granted, despite Britain's supposed abolition of the practice in 1833 (the supply of raw cotton remained dependent on slave plantations for many more decades).[118] One of the most gently protective of human products – cotton – ultimately comes out of one of humanity's most barbaric practices. The textile industry, as Hobsbawm put it, was launched 'like a glider, by the pull of the colonial trade to which it was attached'.[119]

Baines's engraving 'Mule Spinning' manifests the biopolitical function of the images in these books, identifying the life and body of the worker with certain utopian views of the machine and factory (fig. 22). The print accompanies an account of cotton machines, not of mills or their workers and working conditions, so it is presented with technical information and essentially as an exemplary image for the 'man of science and the political philosopher, as well as ... the manufacturer and merchant', to whom the book is addressed.[120] The machines are seen in an attic floor with top lighting, so they extend seemingly to infinity, down the length of the space. As in other interior views, the light, which is shown to have a source, floods the working areas so that all technical detail is illuminated. The mules to the left have their carriages withdrawn so their tracks are exposed on the central area of the floor. Here a male worker demonstratively tends a flywheel to keep the yarn in tension while with his other hand he '[guides] the wire of the faller'.[121] A young female worker checks threads on the mules to the right which have their carriages fully extended into the central space (both mechanical actions, recession and advance, did the job of spinning – hence 'double speed'). Just to her right, and still visible as he crouches under the threads, a male child collects waste with a brush. Each figure exemplifies differentiated and coordinated actions. The working bodies are not so much extensions of the machines as synonymous with them: their working motion, like that of the machines, is perpendicular to the deep space of the attic and, like them, they are organised simply into minor and major parts, heads and bodies. They are harmonised, the unified components of a workforce (evoking Kennedy's manufacturer's utopia of the factory but not, of course, Marx's reflections on the male worker as a 'slave dealer' selling the labour of his wife and children[122]). Between the machines and the roof are located the shafts and gearing (the millwork) that convey motive power. It is not only the boy who is within a machine but anyone who works in this constantly extending and contracting space.

Baines was explicit about the political economy made possible by the self-acting mules visualised here: 'It renders [manufacturers] independent of the working spinners, whose combination and stoppages of work have often been extremely annoying for the masters.'[123] And, if this is a controlled workforce, it is also a social order in epitome. Many of the workers in McConnel & Kennedy's operation were women (as piecers) and children (as scavengers), who were paid by the spinners (largely male until about 1819, when the firm reduced costs by employing more female spinners) responsible for the operation of the mules and for recruiting the workforce under them.[124] Women and children, as well as being cheaper than men, were also regarded as 'more easily moulded to fit the ceaseless rhythm of machine production'.[125]

We observe these scenes, whether interior view or plan, through the eye of capital, which oversees a coordinated and repeated visual field (this may be part of the way the mill retains its status as private property). Barfoot's 'Spinning' has almost the same components as Baines's, with the women and child simply switched to the other mules and working in a different room (fig. 23). The detailed attention to the woman's clothes – the fall of the pleats in her skirt and apron, the details of her collar and puff sleeves – indicate a further level of integration, not just of body and machine but of body, machine and machine product. As before, the idea that the long hours of factory work debilitated the worker's body and led to work-related diseases is entirely beyond the compass of the image.[126]

One of the most beautiful and most baleful of mill images was published in Andrew Ure's *Philosophy of Manufactures* (fig. 24). The author had travelled around northern factories and acted as a consultant for industrialists, many of whom he also taught.[127] His image, a foldaway sheet much bigger than the pages of its book, presents an extraordinary vision of a factory.[128] In Ure's words, the factory was 'a vast automaton, composed of various mechanical and intellectual organs acting in uninterrupted concert for the production of a common object, all of them being subordinate to a self-regulated moving force'.[129] The factory depicted by his artist is a Flaxmanesque fantasy of a barely suppressed, unmanned revelry. It shows what Ure claimed was the interior of a real cotton mill in Stockport, just outside Manchester.[130] Here, the machine room is again spatially lucid – it has minimal shadow and little indication of its lighting bar a few faintly indicated windows to the side – but it is also the scene for a kind of performance. In a clear aisle, a girl is addressed by a male overseer, her flowing dress, in other circumstances, a hazardous affront to the legislators on factory reform.[131] As they recede into the depths, the female workers (mostly just elegantly inclined heads), the mill work and the looms become equivalent linear notations, and the women's 'vigilance and dexterity' a kind of frolicsome inscription upon the rigidities of what is around them. The sense of the women as loosely coordinated across the factory space suggests the association that several contemporary medical commentators made between factories and ballrooms.[132] They may have been concerned by the effects of crowded and overheated spaces, but they may also have been thinking of a brilliantly lit and coordinated animation of movements. The contemporary French historian Jules Michelet was moved to describe well-lit factories as '[having] no shadowy corners in which the imagination can indulge its dreams ... incessantly and mercilessly, it brings us back to reality'.[133] All this is not to make the worker into a machine

[23] 'Spinning', 1840. Lithograph by J. R. Barfoot, from *The Progress of Cotton* (1840).

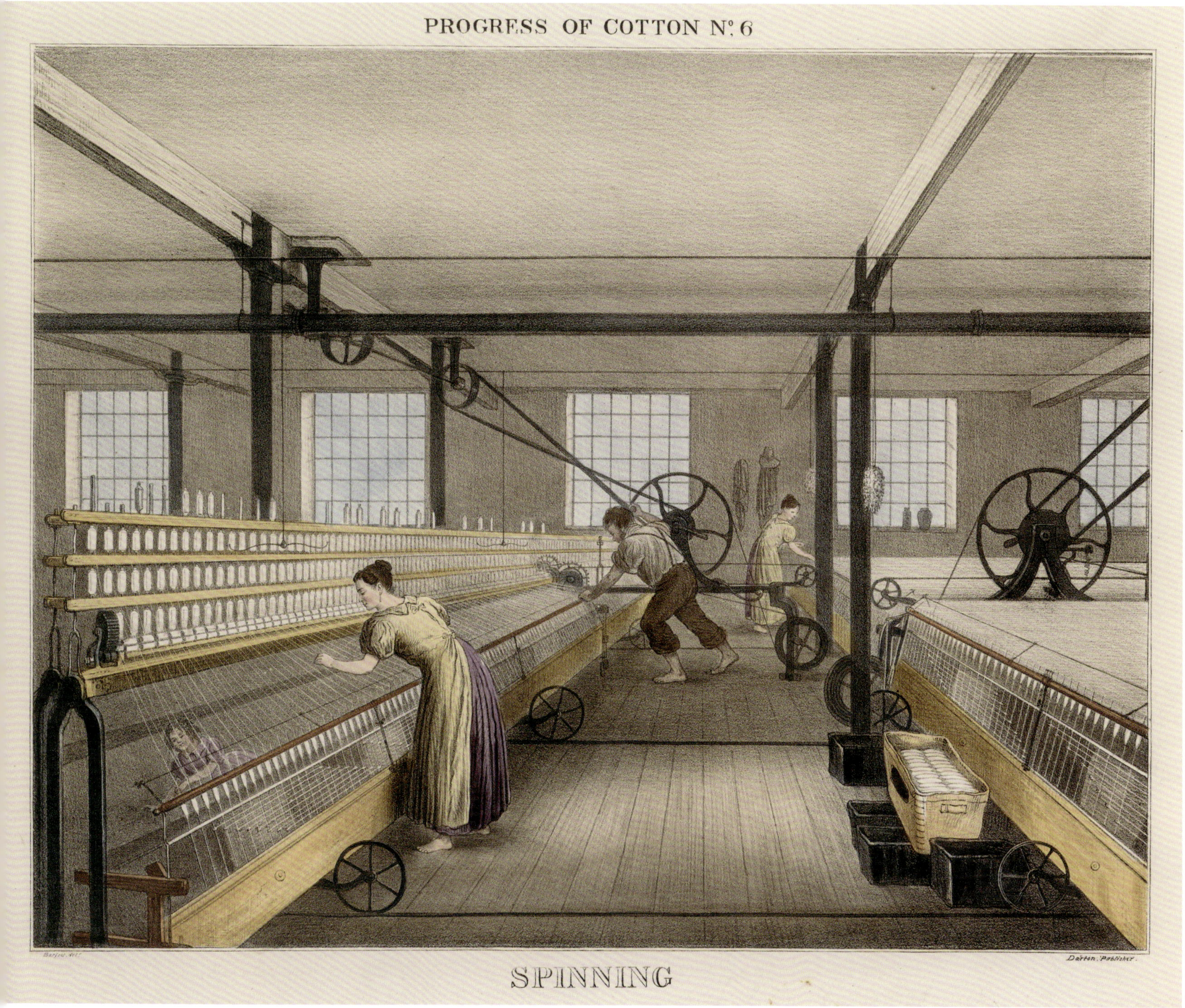

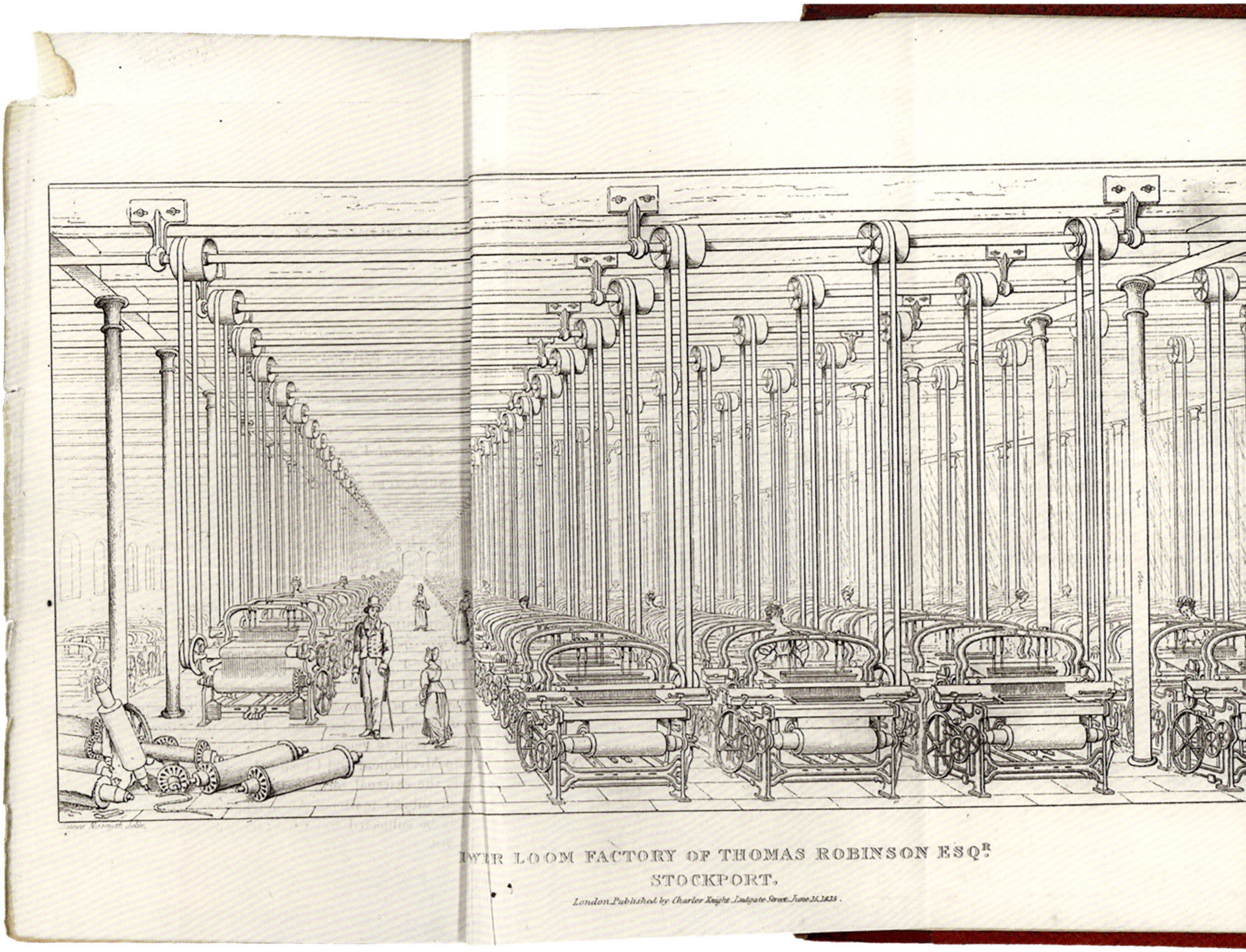

but into its complement, its antithesis.[134] Cotton machines are concatenations of motions: 'complex mechanisms', Ure wrote, 'like the topography of an irregular city'.[135] The whole image represents the factory as a total machine, a machine factory or, in one contemporary definition of a machine, 'a train of pieces connected together in various ways, so that if one be made to move they will all receive a motion, the relation of which to that of the first is governed by the nature of the connexion'.[136]

In the exemplary spaces represented by these images we are given the components of a mill owner's utopia: the machine and its architecture, the supervised space, the time and tempo of the labour process, and the disciplined and divided labour 'identified' with the machine.[137] What other spaces were like these – spaces of inspection of both works and bodies, spaces created by and for private wealth? What other spaces combined to such effect 'dead labour' (both of machines and of factory buildings) and the workers who bring it back to life?[138] We need to look forward about a hundred years to see a related mobilisation of factory space, in the machine buildings and machine humans of Lyubov Popova and Vsevolod Meyerhold at the height of Russian Constructivism.[139] Bodies and machines again come into erotic synchrony, but now as part of a very different political utopia.

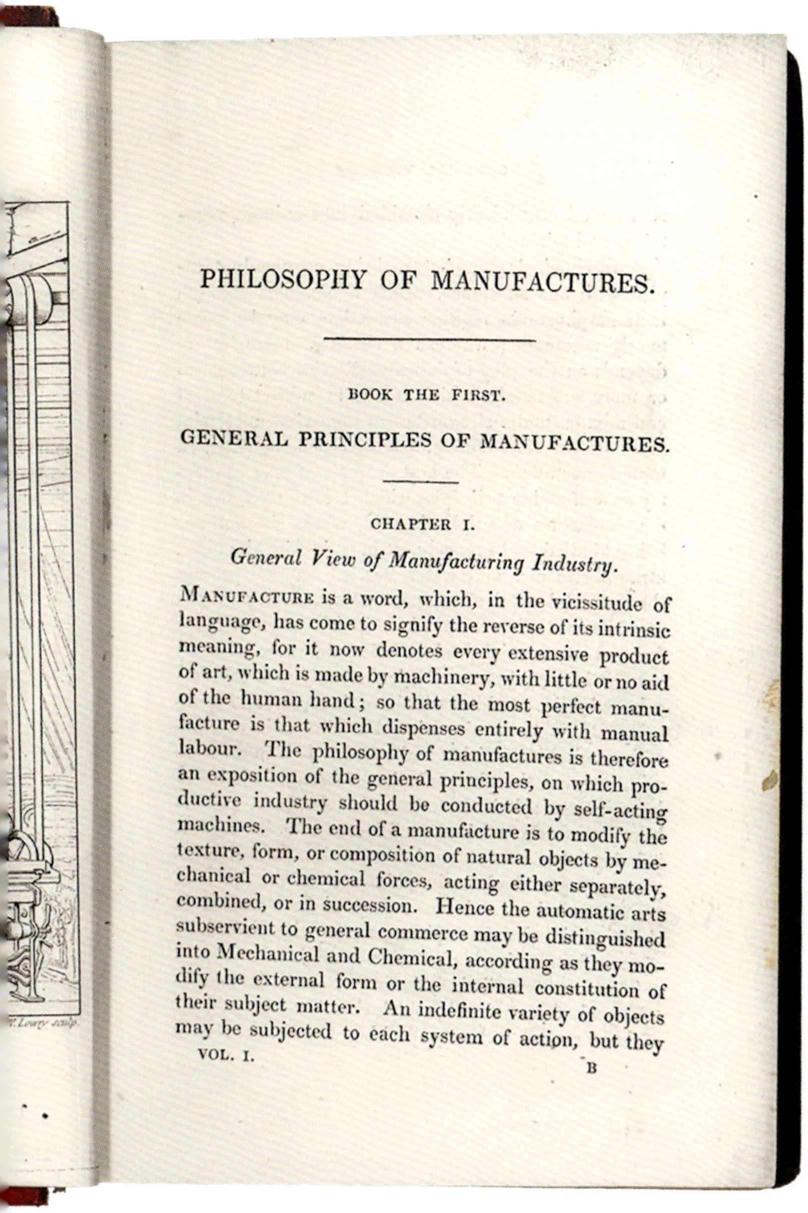

PHILOSOPHY OF MANUFACTURES.

BOOK THE FIRST.

GENERAL PRINCIPLES OF MANUFACTURES.

CHAPTER I.

General View of Manufacturing Industry.

MANUFACTURE is a word, which, in the vicissitude of language, has come to signify the reverse of its intrinsic meaning, for it now denotes every extensive product of art, which is made by machinery, with little or no aid of the human hand; so that the most perfect manufacture is that which dispenses entirely with manual labour. The philosophy of manufactures is therefore an exposition of the general principles, on which productive industry should be conducted by self-acting machines. The end of a manufacture is to modify the texture, form, or composition of natural objects by mechanical or chemical forces, acting either separately, combined, or in succession. Hence the automatic arts subservient to general commerce may be distinguished into Mechanical and Chemical, according as they modify the external form or the internal constitution of their subject matter. An indefinite variety of objects may be subjected to each system of action, but they

VOL. I. B

[24] 'Power Loom Factory of Thomas Robinson Esq., Stockport'. Engraving by James Nasmyth, from Andrew Ure, *Philosophy of Manufactures* (1835).

Mill owners were concerned primarily with capacity and control. How many machines could they have working? How could they increase the number of spindles by replacing wooden frame machinery with stronger iron frames and thus have bigger machines? How could they transfer 'dead labour' to 'ever huger storage facilities',[140] not just to house it but to accommodate it to other technologies? How could they use steam power to ensure more regular productivity and a more controllable human workforce? All these were, of course, facets of the machinery question (and facets of the factory question that developed out of it in the 1830s with the movement to regulate working hours).[141] And they led to further questions. How could they increase their workforce in line with the increase in other aspects of the firm's capacity?[142] And how could mill owners nullify the effect of strikes by using 'self-acting' machinery?[143]

AS SUGGESTED AT THE OUTSET OF THIS CHAPTER, THAT other issue of representation – the recognition or non-recognition of political identity and legitimacy – shadowed the depictions that were made of the industrial city. The year 1826 was critical in this regard. Schinkel's notebook and letters describe the 'dreadful state of affairs' by which the rapid expansion of industry had led to political and economic strife. No one knew what had happened or how to control it, but factories and the factory system seemed to be at the centre of it.[144] The crisis had started the previous year with frenzied speculation, financial disaster and the failure of over forty banks as a result of the collapse of the capital market. Across the country there were already some 1,650 bankruptcies in the first half of 1826.[145] The non-payment of wages and the lack of food supplies sparked protests and disturbances in many industrial areas, including Manchester and its satellite towns, and among the targets of anger were the cotton machines. If the mills could be broached, the machines were highly vulnerable and could be destroyed remarkably quickly.[146] In April and May there were anti-machinery riots in the Lancashire industrial towns, which caused £16,000 worth of damage to over 1,000 power looms in three days. As one contemporary reported, 'by the evening [of 24 April] not a single power-loom was left standing within six miles of Blackburn'.[147] On 27 April the destruction spread to Manchester itself, with a mill on Jersey Street burned down and several other mills unsuccessfully attacked. Attacks on shops and factories continued until at least 3 May, with soldiers brought in and mill owners provided with weapons.[148] The week before Schinkel's arrival, there had been meetings of over a thousand people at St George's Fields, as well as one on waste ground beside the canal in Ancoats involving three or four thousand.[149] Then on the weekend of his arrival a march of several hundred protestors had started from Ancoats Lane, passing along Jersey Street and eventually to Middleton.[150] On all these occasions the soldiers, special constables and cavalry were called out, and the local press preoccupied itself with the perceived senselessness of the actions, the bludgeons wielded, the inflammatory speeches – all of which disorder was contrasted to the authority of the army. Any attempt at objectivity, even explanation, was lost in the concern of the press to dehumanise the protestors.[151]

The state's commitment to the cause of the industrialists was clear.[152] What was also clear was that mills and their machines were perceived by working people to be the cause of distress and were thus made the target of their violence. Ancoats was one of the epicentres of the disturbances and Beaver's mill on nearby Jersey Street was set on fire the following month.[153] In addition, according to neighbouring columns in the same newspapers, there were bankruptcies in the textile industry, as many as seven in the week of Schinkel's visit.[154] His hotel, the Royal, had seen the gathering of special constables the night before his arrival.

Schinkel devoted half of his one and a half pages on Manchester to this industrial strife:

> *6,000 Irish workers from the Manchester factories have recently been transported back to their homeland at the town's expense, because of the shortage of work. 12,000 workers are now coming together to rise up. Many workers work 16 hours a day, and then get a weekly wage of only 2 shillings. Establishments that cost 500,000 pounds sterling are now worth only 5,000. A dreadful state of affairs. Since the war 400 new factories have been built in Lancastershire [sic]; one sees buildings standing where three years ago there were still fields, but these buildings appear as blackened with smoke as if they had been in use for a hundred years ... There is a great English military presence in Manchester to ensure security: fine-looking fellows, men and officers, splendid horses they ride on. – Tremendously wide pavements, 20–30ft, of the finest stone, in undistinguished though wide streets.*[155]

It is an arrestingly vivid observation. Note that the comments on military presence and pavements bookend the intervening sketch of Ancoats (fig. 25). Note too how statistics punctuate the page like exclamation marks, or like the stabs of the pen depicting the mill windows in the sketch. The statistics abstract various crises – workers being transported away, workers rising up, workers being badly paid. And then there is the sense of incomprehensible accelerated change: vast numbers of new buildings, already blackened; fields built upon quickly. Schinkel is of course reporting this, but his position is expressed in that implied parallel between the 'fine-looking fellows' and the 'finest stone' of the pavement – here is some solidity, some architectural order. It may well have been Manchester's unruly state that made him cut short his stay. Through June and July there were reports in the press and rumours about torchlight meetings, workers being armed and drilled, and plans for simultaneous risings in nearby towns.[156]

Architecture – or rather, an insufficient or non-architecture – was implicated in the unrest. A turret, an invisible engine house on a regular frontage, an arched entrance, the minimal projection of a building's centre – none of these was enough to signify architecture, at least to Schinkel's satisfaction. Instead, there was a lack of decorum, a lack of culture – no extravagance, no ornament, no uplift. The 'shapeless' and the 'monstrous' had replaced them. Architecture's insufficiency was linked to the crisis. Too much shock and not yet enough of a city.

For Schinkel there was a feeling of imminent if not actual chaos, certainly a violent face-off. The sense of overreach was closely positioned in relation to a reiterated sense of the loss of decorum and order. From within the terms of the contemporary aesthetic theory of the sublime – the monstrous, dread, the dismal, shapelessness, a vertiginous entropy – it was clear to Schinkel that architecture was at stake as much as society. The philosopher Immanuel Kant may well be behind some of this, with his emphasis on the significance of incomparable scale ('that which is absolutely great') to the idea of the monstrous ('it annihilates the end which its concept constitutes') in the sublime.[157] And, if the aesthetic modality of the sublime (for Kant and Edmund Burke) was typically invoked when objects in the world seemed invested with the threat and promise of capitalist industry, social upheaval and revolution, this was almost an inadvertent admission, an unconscious link (the sublime was, after all, more about the viewer and what they felt than about what was out there). The sublime, its 'unmasterable presence',[158]

[25] Karl F. Schinkel, a page from his Travel Diary showing factories in Ancoats, 1826. Staatliche Museen zu Berlin, Zentralarchiv.

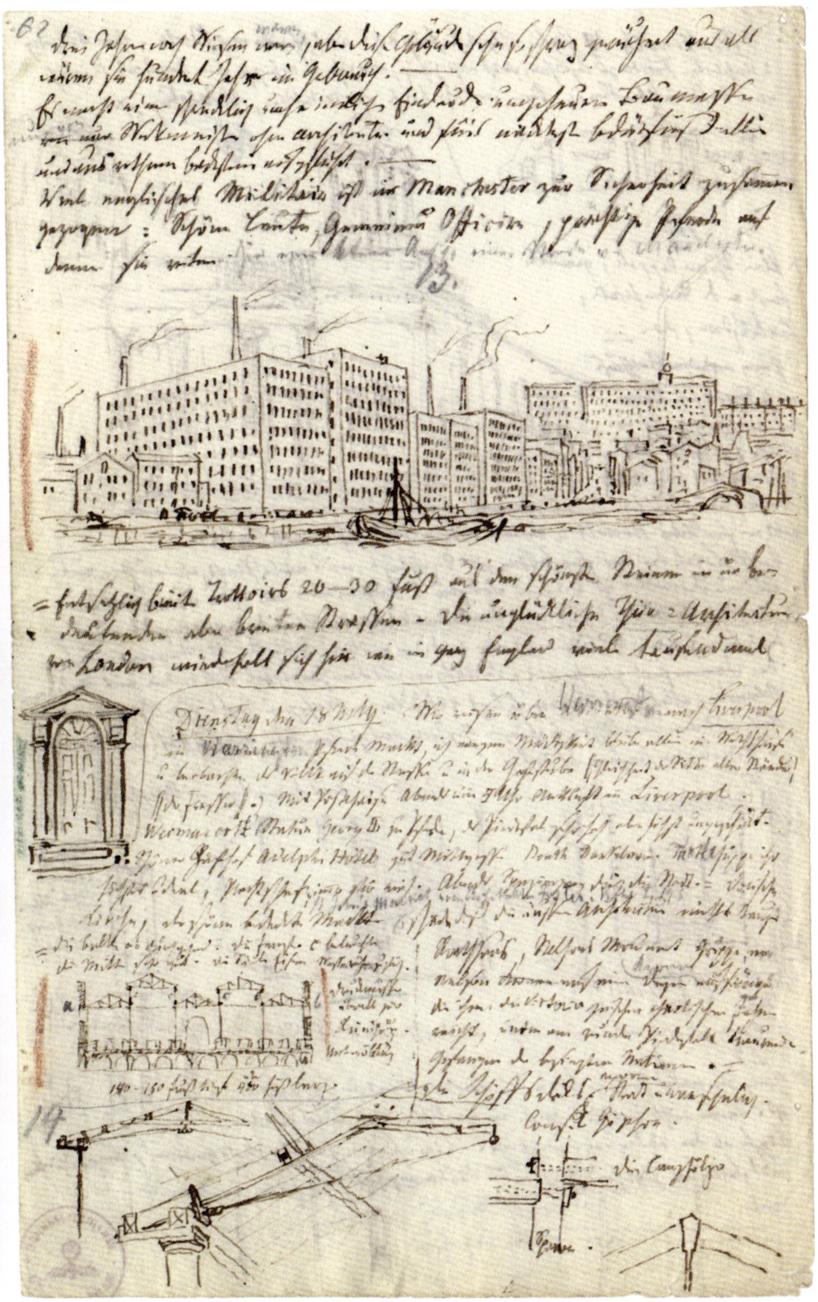

was a way of not counting the bricks on the facades of the mill, of not seeing the labour involved in them, of avoiding the politics of what was seen. The crisis of comprehension worked both ways. Instead, these abrupt and dismal buildings, aged before their time, are a telling contrast to the 'tremendously wide pavements' and the 'fine-looking fellows' and 'splendid horses' that parade on them. If the sublime was the modern, a tearing rupture in one's sense of the world, then Ancoats was its very incarnation.[159]

Protest has its reactions, and they are not only directly repressive. James Kay's *The Moral and Physical Condition of the Working Classes* was at least in part inspired by what he called 'the wild outbreak of popular violence'.[160] The city of Free Trade (see Chapter 2), with its Mechanics' Institute established as early as 1827, expressly in response to machine breaking and the threatened anarchy,[161] was another kind of response. Here architecture would play its part, as the banker Benjamin Heywood put it, in conveying 'the principles in which are to be found the safest guides for individual conduct, and the surest guarantee of public order'.[162] Here the architect would have some chance to act up to Schinkel's transcendent idea of him as 'the ennobler of all human relationships'.[163] But these aspirations were already, in a sense, admissions that the orderly vision of the mill and its machine architecture was always going to fall short. Between its interior and the patrolling soldiers was another world, a world of protesting workers, shoddy houses and broken streets. This was a world that was often at odds and certainly much more difficult to order, even for those with the power to attempt it.

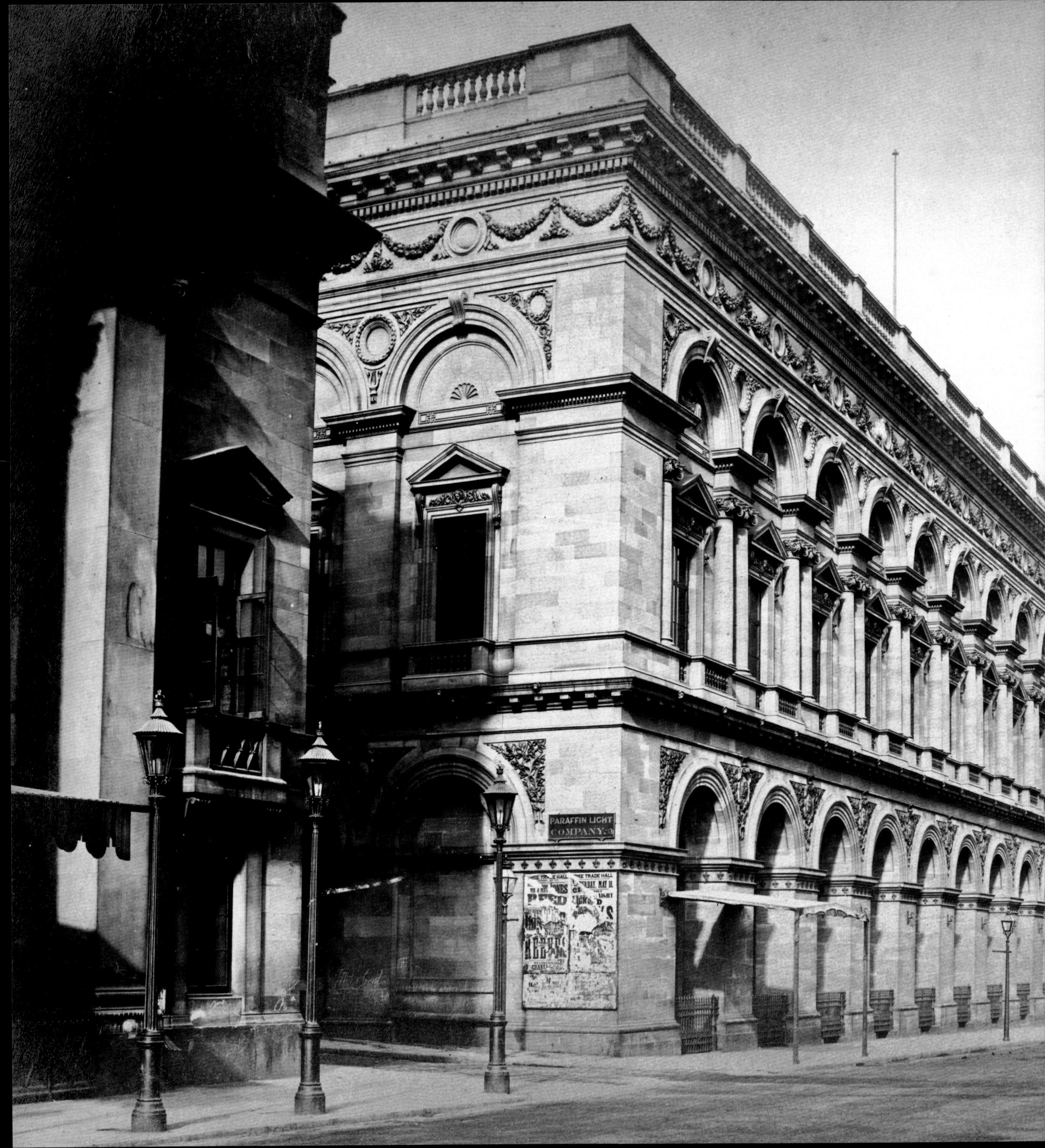
PARAFFIN LIGHT
COMPANY.

[26] Free Trade Hall, Peter Street, 1853–6.
Architect: Edward Walters. Photograph: James Mudd, *c.*1860.
Manchester Libraries, Information and Archives.

2 City of Free Trade

The Urbanism of the Industrial Bourgeoisie

WHAT DOES A FREE TRADE CITY LOOK LIKE – WHAT IS THE character of its forms and spaces? It seems, on the face of it, to be a question that misses the point. Free Trade – the term is capitalised here to indicate its status as practice and theory – is, its supporters claim, an economic and political principle that makes the world a safe and peaceful surface over which goods travel smoothly, freely and without tariffs. Manufacturers make and consumers buy, each unimpeded by the boundaries of nations. Instead, their trade barriers broken, nations enjoy (or suffer) a new interdependence.[1] Why would, and how could, all this be a matter of images and architecture and urban form? And, anyway, haven't we learned from T. J. Clark that capital 'did not need to have a representation of itself laid out upon the ground in bricks and mortar ... capital preferred the city not to be an image'?[2]

We might start by accepting that, as a principle, Free Trade is neither ahistorical nor universal: it has a history and it comes out of a certain place at a certain time. Free Trade was 'a Manchester movement, both locally and essentially' (hence 'Manchester School' or in German *Manchesterthurm*).[3] Advocated by those who represented the new rising classes of industry – such as Manchester's Richard Cobden and John Bright – the Free Trader was as opposed to the protectionist interests of landed, rent-seeking Tories as to the cooperative endeavours of Chartists (though with the latter they often had a more incorporative intent, as if proleptically absorbing 'their arising enemy').[4] In that sense, Free Trade has points of intersection with other beliefs and affiliations in the city: with Unitarian groups or groups of social reformers, for instance, both of whom have also long interested historians.[5]

[27] Map of Manchester, 1793: detail showing Portland Street. Published by C. Laurent.

[28] Map of Manchester, 1794: detail showing Portland Street. Published by William Green.

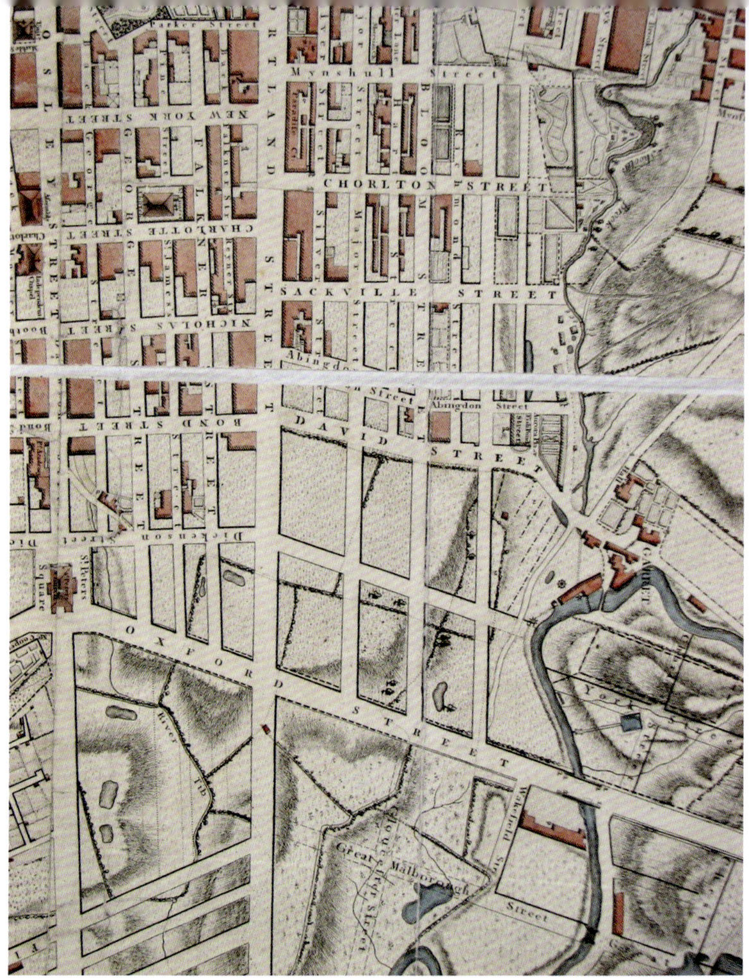

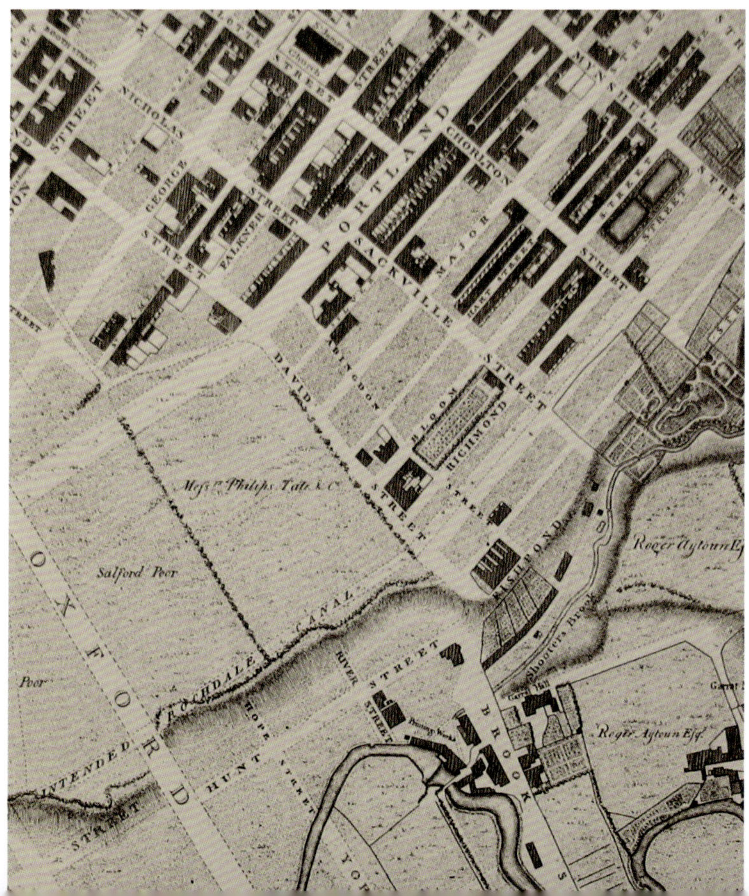

It may also appear to be linked to what Michel Foucault has called the 'liberal project' and even 'governmentality',[6] even if the ways in which these overly abstract concepts are deployed tend to assume too much consensus behind them, to diffuse power into something all-pervasive and to lose a sense of the significance of the specific shapes and spaces of the city. And, with architecture and images, we are at best dealing only partially with the notion of knowledge – typically based on the social disciplines of statistics, public health and map making (or 'numbers, sewers and pipes, maps and markets', as one advocate of this approach puts it[7]) – on which such theories depend. To try to see what Free Trade might have looked like, furthermore, is to enter a much less explored area – Free Trade not as just a principle but as the architectural projection and realisation of one group's interests in the process of their articulation and as part of a narrative of transforming the shock city. In Manchester's case all this requires an effort of documentary archaeology, given the erasures of and changes to this aspect of the city's history.

Several distinctive and interrelated elements of Manchester as the city of Free Trade are examined here: two major buildings (Manchester Infirmary and Free Trade Hall); a new building type – really a subtype (the palazzo warehouse, including the redirection of its achievements in the Watts warehouse); and a small area in and around Piccadilly and Portland Street, which was still on the edge of the city in the early decades of the nineteenth century (see fig. 5). These are all familiar components of Manchester's architectural history, but their interrelation has long been forgotten, especially the way in which, to adopt Marx's description of Free Traders, they manifest 'industrial capital striving to make available its social power as a political power' or the ability of a class to represent and reproduce itself through the architecture and spaces of the city.[8] As these urban elements developed rapidly and simultaneously, they became essential to one class's attempt to make itself identifiable in the city's pell-mell development, remaking this part of Manchester as a civic space for the new 'money aristocracy' of industrialists.[9] This was part of the process described by Engels in 1845 as a 'hypocritical plan', a 'systematic ... shutting out of the working class from the thoroughfares, so tender a concealment of everything that might affront the eye and the nerves of the bourgeoisie'.[10] This was how urban space was diagrammed in Manchester; class was a process of shutting out, a zoning that screened the reality of poverty with the spectacle of commercialism (which is also to evoke T. J. Clark's arguments about Paris[11]). But, while Engels's description is broadly true, it is also far too stark. It tells us little of the complexities of how this was brought about, of the intra-class conflicts involved or of how the industrial city was given modern civic forms. While more modern accounts of the city have sketched how architecture was implicated more broadly in the Industrial Revolution,[12] the symbiosis of other buildings with the evolution of a new building type in this small but crucial area of the city has remained uncovered.

Portland Street, featuring prominently on Engels's schematic map (see fig. 61), epitomises the 'hypocritical plan' he identified (see Chapter 3).[13] Located just outside and south of the pre-industrial town of Manchester, it was a country lane until well into the eighteenth century. Then known as Garratt (or Garret) Lane, it was upgraded into the linked streets of Portland Place and Portland Street at some point in the middle decades of the eighteenth century[14] (fig. 27). Much of this area was part of two estates. First there was the Aytoun estate, which had been advertised for sale in 1772 and was then laid out with a gridiron of streets before being bought by developers and builders. Then there was a package of land belonging to the Mosleys, long-term landowners in the town. Thirty acres of this were laid out in a gridiron in 1783 and sold off by 1794.[15] It is clear from some late eighteenth-century maps that there were plans afoot at this time to extend Portland Street through fields at its south-western end to Oxford Street and beyond, but this (apparently) orderly urban expansion was overtaken by industrial development, specifically the digging of the Rochdale Canal. Any extension was blocked for several decades by the location of light industrial workings of iron, timber and coal situated on branches of the canal at this far end of Portland Street[16] (fig. 28). The very establishment of these industries in this part of Portland Street shows the weakness of any civic improvement project at this time compared to the power of private industrial development; the imbalance was not to be righted for more than half a century. Nevertheless, in 1800 the street, 'nothing more than a third-rate thoroughfare devoted to mean and poor-looking shops', was still marginal to the city's industrialisation.[17] Its development was a response to the chaos caused by industry, and this part of the city was established for large-scale commercial activities rather than being a raw site of production or a place for small and heterogeneous retailers. Such were the changes made in the next few decades that by the end of the nineteenth century Portland Street was to become known as the 'typical street or centre of Manchester trade', the 'essential Manchester ... practically lined throughout with Manchester warehouses'.[18]

One of the arguments of this chapter is that a new building form emerged through the desire to build these warehouses along Portland Street, especially at its north-eastern junction with Piccadilly Gardens. This was the palazzo warehouse, a hybrid of inner-city mansion, shop, office and storage facility given the external form of a Renaissance urban palace. At the same time, and bound up with this, an alternative new centre for Manchester developed, which was particularly expressive of the industrial bourgeoisie and its Free Trade politics.

PORTLAND STREET'S DEVELOPMENT DEPENDED ON A pre-existing and seemingly public-spirited initiative at the north-eastern end of the street where it met Piccadilly. Here the Manchester Infirmary was built in 1754–5, later joined by a Lunatic Hospital (1763–5), public baths (1779) and a dispensary (1792), and with a House of Recovery (England's first specialist fever hospital) established nearby in 1796 (fig. 29). (These are the institutional elements perhaps of 'biopower' but before and at the onset of the industrial city, which would struggle to control the side effects of industry.) One of Manchester's few civic buildings at this time, the Infirmary, was located at what was then still the edge of the town,[19] and its history over the next few decades was to be bound up with both the malaises and the ambitions of Manchester's industry: for instance, typhus, the main cause of fever treated by the House of Recovery, was associated with large cotton mills and the poor-quality dwellings of their workforce.[20]

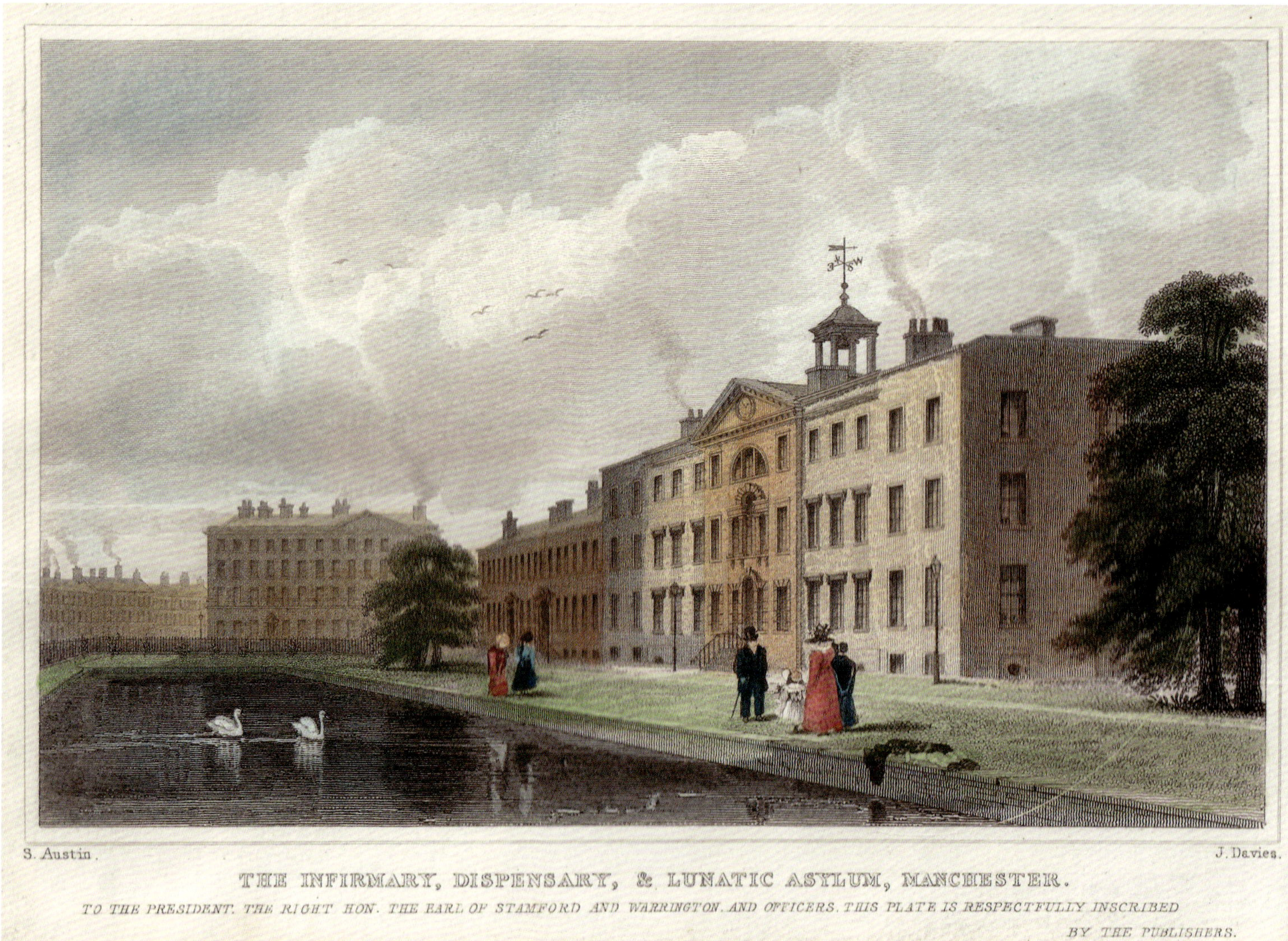

The Infirmary was a philanthropic concern run by a joint stock company. Such companies had similarities with street improvement schemes, each of which had subscribers and a management committee[21] – and more than similarities. There was a great overlap in functions (and often personnel) between such projects as the Infirmary became a hub of urban development. At least to begin with, the Infirmary was also an ostensibly non-political and non-denominational foundation that brought landowners, business and medical men together; as much as a place for the care of the sick, it was a beacon of polite society and a means of patronage and social advancement.[22] Some of these pre-nineteenth-century institutional forms remained well into the new century, and intersected with groups like the Manchester Statistical Society, which contained industrialists, bankers and medical experts.[23] There was a similar continuation in the Infirmary's architecture, specifically how it was seen as part of the same urban development its subscribers and committee members were concerned with in their other activities. But originally, when the first building was finished in 1755, it adopted the established tastes of the landed classes: its external appearance was of a large rural residence with Palladian aspirations, while internally it had rigidly hierarchised spaces for those subject to its philanthropy.

With the town expanding rapidly, the area in front of the Infirmary – previously known as Daub Hole Field because of the extraction of clay (daub) for building purposes and owned by the Mosley family as Lords of the Manor of Manchester – was

[29] 'The Infirmary, Dispensary, & Lunatic Asylum, Manchester', *c.*1829. Coloured engraving by Samuel Austin after James Hey Davies.

[30] Map of Manchester, *c.*1807: detail showing Infirmary and Portland Place, just to the right of centre. Drawn for John Britton, *The Beauties of England and Wales*, vol. 9, *Lancashire, Leicestershire, Lincolnshire* (1807).

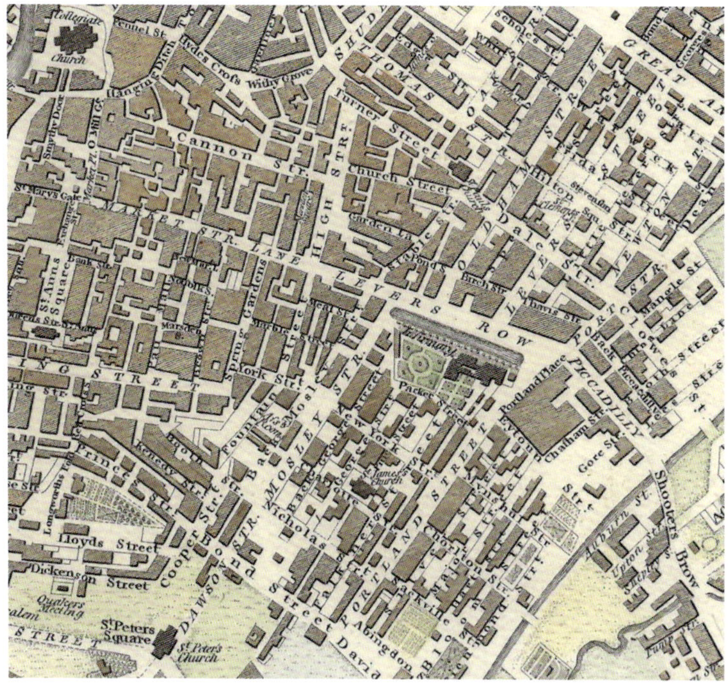

given to the Infirmary in 1808 and became one of the first public spaces created in this new industrial era[24] (fig. 30). The hole was refashioned as a large pond and, with serpentine walks and gardens, this became a space for recuperation and relaxation. Located on one of the higher points in the town, Piccadilly, as the area became known, was emerging as the expression of a new urban identity.[25] But the Infirmary did not just provide a precedent in its civic philanthropy and was not only an architectural embellishment of Manchester's evolving public sphere: it was also a direct generator of urban improvement in creating this alternative centre for the city. Dublin's Lying-in Hospital (later Rotunda Hospital) is a similar contemporary case of a hospital giving rise to a ripple effect of urban and cultural changes well beyond the expansion of medical facilities: the 'very stones of Dublin began to cluster around [it]'.[26] But, as Dublin's hospital helped to form a new urban quarter of elite houses and genteel alfresco leisure, Manchester's Infirmary was also instrumental in redirecting the city's industrial explosion towards more orderly civic ends.

In the late eighteenth and early nineteenth centuries the management of the Infirmary became increasingly politicised through its identification with Dissenting Whigs and Unitarians.[27] Notable features of this period of its history were political divisions between the trustees over expansion of the Infirmary[28] and regular disputes with the Mosley family over land use.[29] By the end of the eighteenth century, the reforming element in the Infirmary had prevailed, and from this time the board of trustees included a mix of medical men and lay members, many of whom were from Manchester's manufacturing and merchant class.[30] The Infirmary was now tied to the fortunes of the cotton trade, from which it also drew most of its subscribers. There is an echo here of the bringing together of medical care and urban reorganisation that had animated the work of James Kay and Edwin Chadwick, and even the utopianism of Robert Owen, but now the interests of the industrial bourgeoisie were central and overt, and focused on the city as an image of that identity.

To the east of the Infirmary was Portland Place, a short block of large houses including the Queen's Hotel, which faced back across Piccadilly. The hotel was the most prestigious in Manchester, and the neighbouring residences reflected some of this glow. As well as senior Infirmary doctors, several of Manchester's prominent industrialists lived here: Thomas Houldsworth, a manufacturer who built his spinning mill nearby; Robert Turner, a calico printer, who owned a warehouse on the High Street; Robert Barbour, a cotton merchant and noted philanthropist; and Richard Ormerod, who ran a machine-shop business.[31] Their continued residence here well into the mid-nineteenth century (Houldsworth remained until his death in 1852) nuances the idea of wholesale middle-class flight to the suburbs.[32] And, when they did eventually leave, their residences were either (in Houldsworth's case) taken over by the hotel or replaced by equally prestigious warehouses.[33] The latter, as will be shown, were intended to maintain – indeed to extend – the respectability of this area, as if to reassure that the shift from house to warehouse, from residence to commerce, which was so abrupt elsewhere in the centre of Manchester,[34] was here managed by a composite of residence and showcase. The co-presence of hospital, major hotel and residents from the industrial elite provided the means and the impulse for the development of this area to counter the chaos and insalubriousness that had overtaken pre-industrial tracts at the core of the city, and to present an alternative of order and responsibility. The presence of civic-minded industrialists was also key to the whole development of Portland

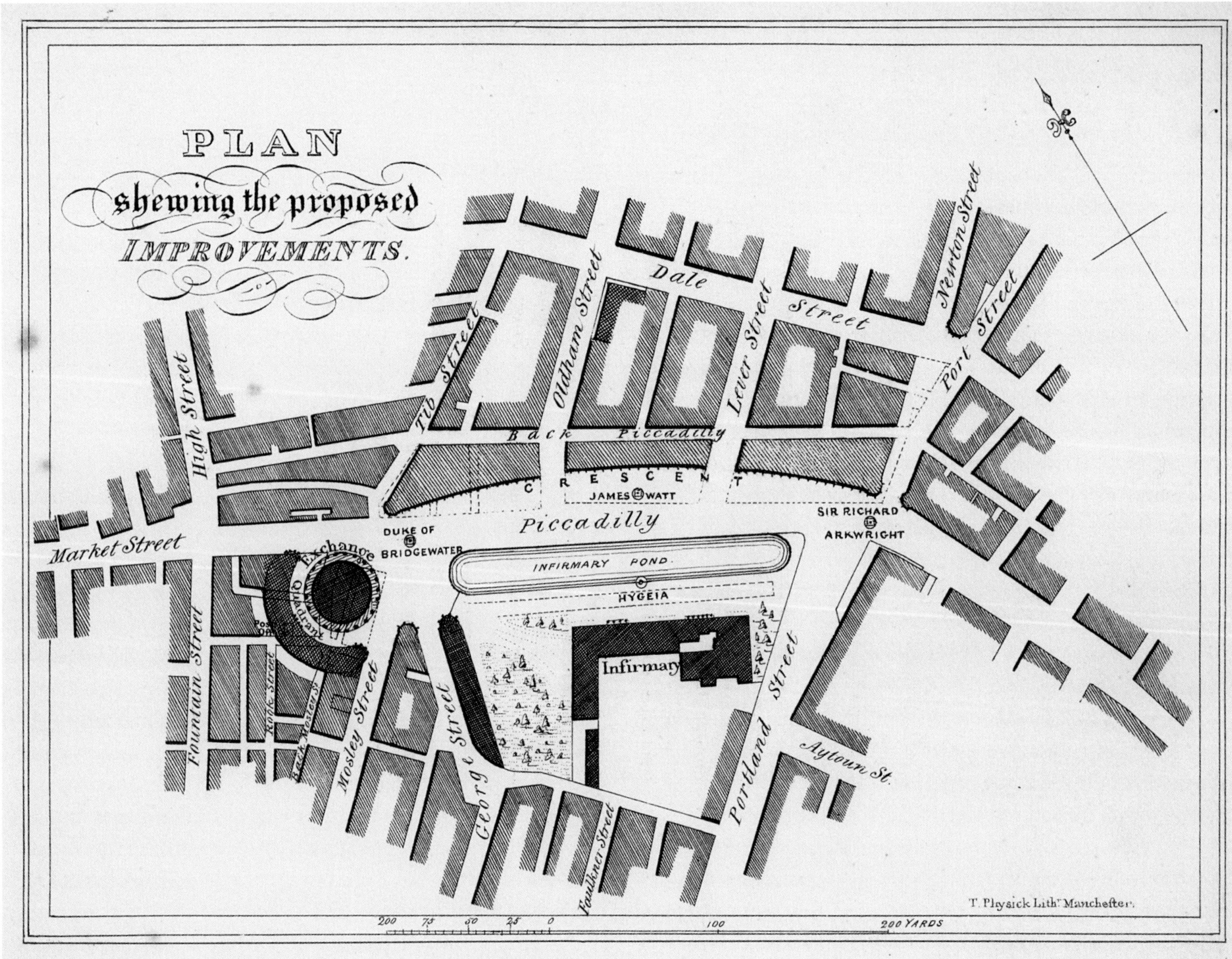

Street. Without understanding this, we cannot get to grips with the architectural genesis of the palazzo-style warehouse, of what it represents in terms of bypassing shock and concretising a new element in the regime of biopolitical linkages.

The Infirmary's further development in the early and mid-nineteenth century was a matter of holding to philanthropic intentions in the face of Manchester's rapid industrialisation – with its vastly increased population and consequent poverty and disease – at the same time as the development of this part of Portland Street earned its civic credentials by welding the booming cotton trade to the Infirmary both financially and urbanistically. One attempt to imagine the Infirmary's potential as a hub of controlled development was William Fairbairn's 1836 pamphlet *Observations on Improvements of the Town of Manchester Particularly as Regards the Importance of Blending in those Improvements, the Chaste and the Beautiful, with the Ornamental and Useful* (fig. 31). (Blending the chaste with the useful was exactly what was to occur by other means.) As one of Manchester's foremost engineers and inventors, Fairbairn (we have already sighted him in Ancoats and he will reappear at several key points in this book) was no mere dreamer. He was helped in his proposal by James Nasmyth, an artist who was then just launching a career that would make him prominent as

[31] 'Plan shewing the proposed improvements': scheme by William Fairbairn. Lithograph based on drawing by James Nasmyth, from Fairbairn, *Observations on Improvements of the Town of Manchester* (1836).

[32] 'Designs for a New Exchange and Quadrant': scheme by William Fairbairn. Lithograph based on drawing by James Nasmyth, from Fairbairn, *Observations on Improvements of the Town of Manchester* (1836).

an engineer. Using the opportunity presented by discussions of public memorials to James Watt and the duke of Bridgewater,[35] Fairbairn projected an image of Piccadilly as both a memory-scape of industrial creativity and a new, grandiose centre for the city. It would 'render Manchester famous', he wrote, 'not only for its manufactures, but also for that architectural good taste, which bespeaks a knowledge of the sublime and the beautiful'.[36] Sweeping away the old as 'inadequate to the refinements of civilisation',[37] the scheme was centred on the pond and the Infirmary (provided with a newly colonnaded front). A crescent of neoclassical buildings crowned with domes would house a bazaar of shops, with a broad pavement for public promenade. The Exchange (or possibly, Fairbairn suggested, a new university) was relocated to the west as a circular colonnaded and domed building with a framing quadrant, and Portland Street to the east would be freshly refaced (fig. 32). The big public space that resulted was to be ornamented with statues not only of Bridgewater and Watt, but also of Richard Arkwright and Hygaeia, goddess of health. Each was placed to command the relevant vistas, signalling the combined values of technological invention and entrepreneurial daring, and so invoking a benevolent modernity. Admitting his inadequacy as an architect, Fairbairn wrote that his scheme had

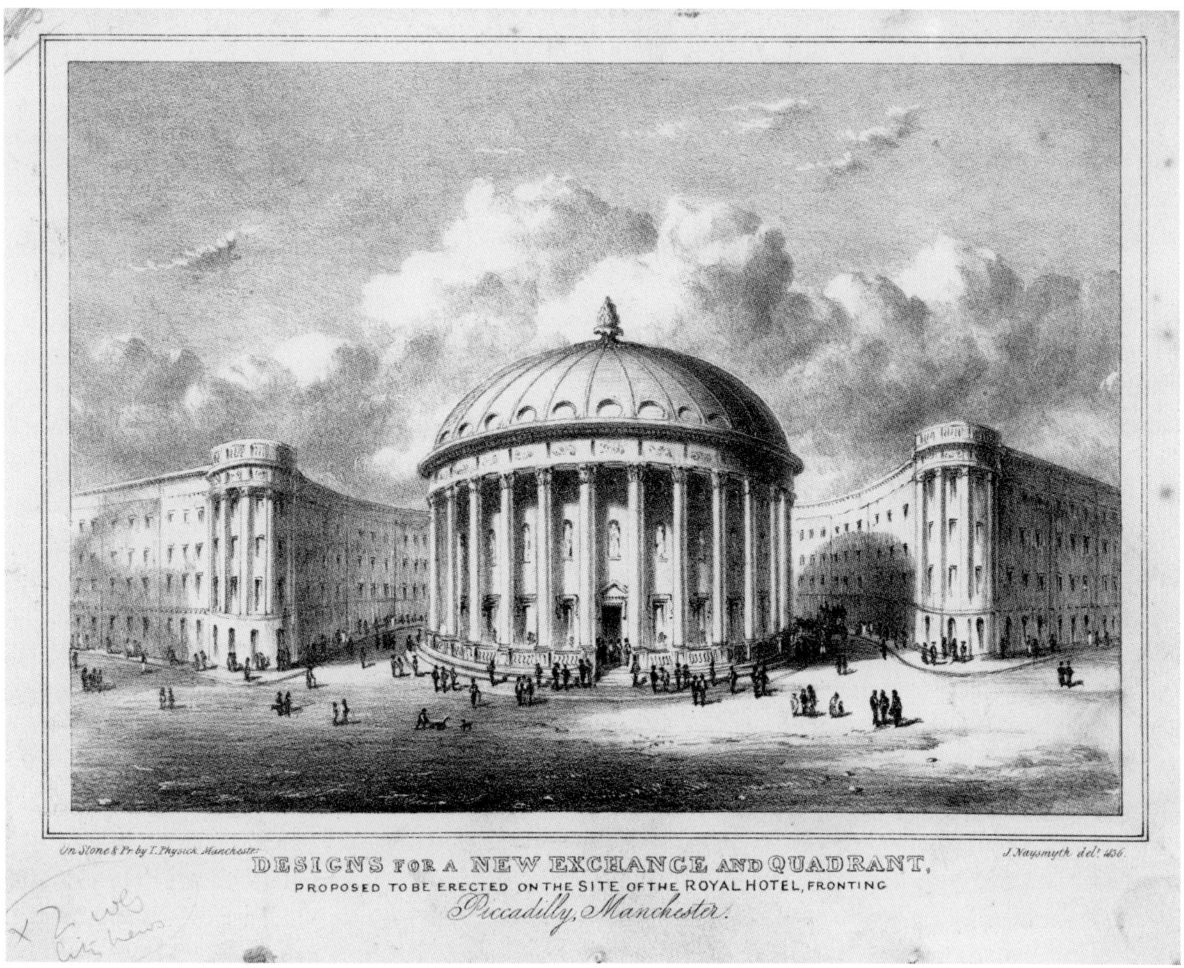

[33] Ordnance Survey map of Manchester, 1851: detail showing Royal Infirmary, Portland Place and Queen's Hotel, with red lines indicating the warehouses on three sides; the Royal Infirmary has only been partially redeveloped, following Richard Lane's designs.

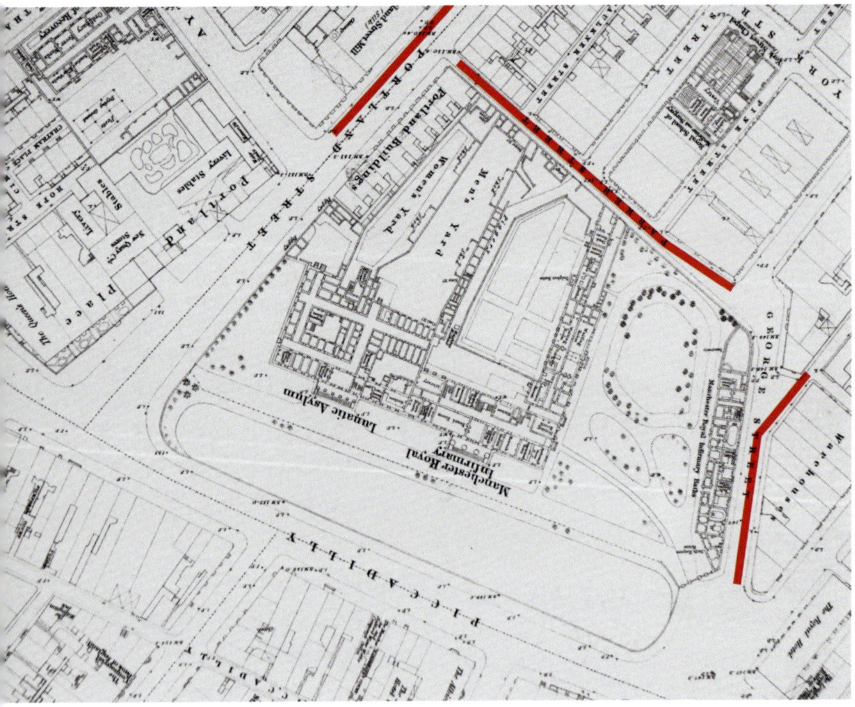

arisen from the indifference of Manchester's wealthier classes – by which he certainly meant its landed classes – to the public realm of the city.[38] Curiously, he did not see a place for commerce, beyond conventional shops, in this public space; given his own affiliations, he could not imagine how the warehouses that already existed in this area could play a part in its civic beautification. His scheme recycled an urbanism that was *retardataire* by 1836, in which the architectural form of unified bourgeois life (in the manner of a previous generation of urbanists such as Nash, Adam and Wood) was to be supplied by a comprehensive scheme. Unincorporated, with only sclerotic landowning interests, and still lacking a unified urban elite, Manchester would take a different course.

While Fairbairn was right in seeing the Infirmary as the likely new hub, development actually took a civic direction by linking the booming cotton trade to the Infirmary. As the expanding city strained the Infirmary's capacities, so the latter was periodically adapted and expanded.[39] A portico with columns was built on the pond side in 1836 and the building was cased in stone (the Lunatic Hospital received much the same treatment).[40] In the 1840s and 1850s it was largely rebuilt, using money raised from the sale of the House of Recovery and by taking over the Lunatic Hospital, whose functions were relocated outside Manchester.[41] First focused on the Infirmary, then piecemeal and on a smaller scale than Fairbairn had initially imagined, several elements of an alternative vision were put in place, now with the manufacturers themselves directly involved (fig. 33). In 1840 two warehouse owners – Samuel Fletcher and George Faulkner, one a trustee of the Infirmary, the other the treasurer of the nearby House of Recovery – organised the widening of Parker Street, immediately behind the Infirmary.[42] But the most important development became possible with the absorption of the Lunatic Hospital in 1845. The Infirmary's front had always faced northwards onto Piccadilly, but with the additions and remodelling that were now possible the building was reconceived as a free-standing building with porticoes facing all four sides, creating what its architect Richard Lane called 'one uniform imposing building ... [affording] eligible points from which its several fronts may be viewed with advantage'[43] (fig. 34).

[34] Manchester Royal Infirmary, *c.*1855. Engraving by W. Morton. Wellcome Collection.

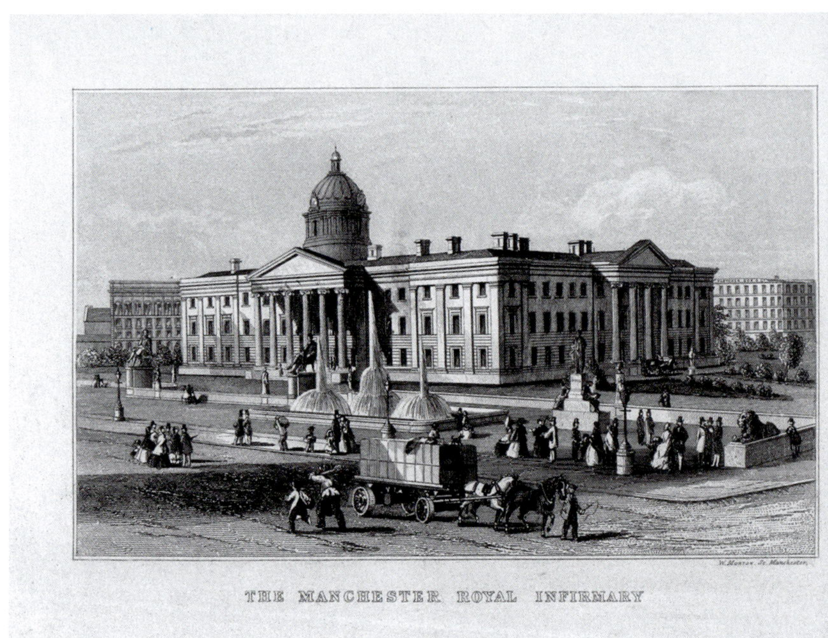

It has been suggested that the taking over of the Lunatic Hospital 'provided a unique opportunity for the expansion of the Infirmary building, long since hemmed in by warehouses and other commercial buildings',[44] but this is to misconceive the relationship between these different types of buildings. The expansion was not at all antagonistic, rather the opposite: there were three areas where the new designs were conceived to have mutual benefit. First, the size of the site for the medical buildings remained the same, and any proposed clearance of buildings around it was not only to enhance the Infirmary site as a civic space but also to increase the value of warehouses nearby.[45] The proposers here were two warehouse-owning trustees of the Infirmary – Samuel Fletcher, again, and Sir Thomas Potter, who had been Manchester's first mayor in 1838 – and part of the arrangement was that, with the increase in value of their neighbouring warehouses, they agreed to make a contribution to the Infirmary funds.[46] Second, Lane deliberately made designs that would both harmonise with the surroundings and, at points, carefully contrast with them. He explained that the result would be

> *[an] improvement to the surrounding streets ... to balance and place in harmony with the noble projections which decorate the front towards Piccadilly; to give that additional importance to the Building as a whole which is rendered desirable by the lofty and massive structures which surround it, and to form a favourable contrast to the flatness which must always pervade warehouse property, however it is attempted to disguise it.*[47]

Attention was even paid to the Parker Street side of the building, at its rear, and to facing the Infirmary with stone to respond to the warehouses and the newly widened street there.[48] Third, a dome was built in 1853. As well as capping the building and emphasising its fully orbicular presence, it also acknowledged Portland Street's new importance and the Infirmary's relation to its warehouse neighbours.[49] Lane, who designed all three of these features, was Manchester's ubiquitous Greek Revivalist and first president of the new Architectural Society set up in 1837. His rise to eminence, and indeed the formation of the new society, inevitably raise the question of how far the incorporation of Manchester stimulated the rise of the professions and professional bodies, rather than these being a ripple effect of changes in the metropolis (the Institute of British Architects had been formed in 1834). Given these conditions, a form of fraternal professionalism – medic speaking to architect, with the latter working on the former's key building – may well have enabled the solidification of the previously insubstantial profession of architects in the city.

Further evidence of the alliance of infirmary and warehouses can be found in the way they were depicted as having a recognisably coordinated effect. This had an aural as well as a visual aspect. The sounding of the Infirmary clock punctuated the working day and its importance to the area was such that the Manchester Corporation helped pay for the new clock on the dome.[50] Throughout this time, photographs and prints showed the hospital with warehouses either harmoniously in the background or in obsequious contrast.[51] This was now a building that clearly enunciated its civic significance, a four-square porticoed mass topped by a significant dome. Without porticoes or dome, the warehouses around mirrored the Infirmary's materials and its classical detailing and could thus be happily included in its representation. If the Infirmary front was the main stage for events like the visit of Queen Victoria in 1857, then the equally bedecked warehouses played a supporting role.[52]

Another manifestation of the alliance between Infirmary and warehouse was an outbreak of statuomania in the 1850s. A wide esplanade and fountains had been designed by Joseph Paxton to replace the pool in front of the Infirmary. The statues on the esplanade were a product of cooperation between city-wide subscription groups and the Infirmary's trustees.[53] Among the four new monuments was the long-discussed monument to Watt (completed in 1857) – again advocated by Fairbairn – and a statue commemorating Sir Robert Peel, the prime minister with local roots (he was the son of a Lancashire textile manufacturer) who finally repealed the protectionist Corn Laws in 1846. They had different associations. Watt was canonised as the inventor of Free Trade's prime energy source, steam power, the means to its class power.[54] According to the mythology, Watt exemplified social change because he had transcended his humble origins, an extraordinary

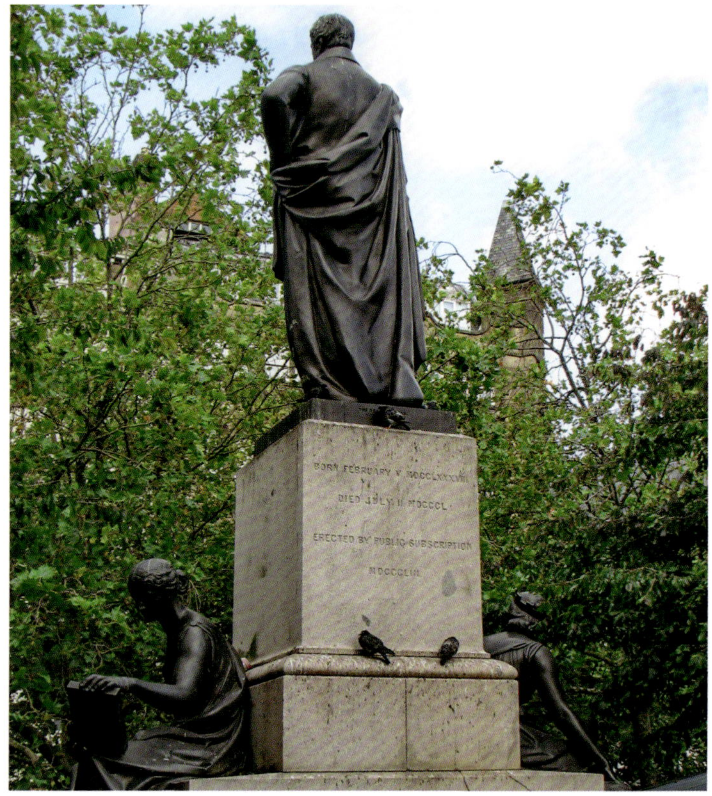

[35] Peel monument, Piccadilly, 1853.
Sculptor: William Calder Marshall.

feat that was possible only for those with 'genius'. But, while he was the 'standard bearer of the rising middle classes', it was more appropriate for lesser beings to follow Watt's moral example than aspire to his genius.[55] The Peel monument, erected in 1853, had particularly acute political connotations: some Tories disdained it as part of Free Trade politics but Manchester's industrialists lauded its subject because he had broken with Conservative protectionism[56] (fig. 35). It was therefore an icon of the industrialists' Free Trade politics, and its placement here, complete with allegories representing 'Manchester, its Trades and Commerce' and 'Art, Learning, Science and Industry', was probably the final and clinching statement of the political coloration of the alliance that had shaped the buildings around Piccadilly Gardens.[57]

The links that Manchester's warehouse owners forged with the Infirmary shows them to have been fully committed to a project of coordinated civic improvement. Portland Street did not develop its warehouse buildings in connection with the coming of the railways in the early 1840s, as might have been assumed, but instead in relation to the Infirmary they formed, as we have seen, a concerted development. Where the nearby London Road railroad station (later renamed Piccadilly station) came into its own was in its supply of clients from London, which helped grant the location a visibility, even a centrality, in this newly emerging part of Manchester. The site conditions for the 'enchantment' of these clients had already been set by the development of the Infirmary and the newly refined exteriors of the warehouses. Importantly, the area was largely outside the melee of competing railway companies that were redeveloping tracts of Manchester through these decades.[58] The working and lower middle classes – whose residences and businesses were pushed out of the area – were the victims here, the collateral casualties of a political battle over space between the landed classes and industrialists.

Should we find it strange that an asylum could face a fashionable warehouse in the heart of Manchester? Like other asylums, its establishment seems to have been motivated by contemporary concerns about private madhouses,[59] but it's hard to find an asylum or hospital – whether in Liverpool, London, Glasgow, Edinburgh or elsewhere – that was quite so closely aligned architecturally with commerce.[60] It is quite possible, however, to see the hospital–warehouse combination as part of a particular conception of the moral city, as contributing to Manchester's emerging civic culture, its lessons and constraints. One newspaper described the warehouses as 'huge stone guardians watching over the morals and health of the city', and another praised 'the humanising, educating influences of stately edifices on the plastic minds of early youth'.[61] To refer to morality here may seem merely rhetorical, but it had important resonances and, as in many Victorian uses of the term, it was aimed in particular at the floating labour force, at the vagabonds and 'street arabs': it was a class concern. It was linked to the opening up of urban space to policing and regulation, and especially to the demolition of pre-industrial areas deemed 'jerry-built', insanitary and 'debased' in contrast to the 'sober, well-considered' warehouses.[62] On a more cultural plane, the perceived 'educating influence' was related to ideas about how certain forms and symbols served to improve or elevate the mind.[63] The new palazzo warehouses on Piccadilly and Portland Street were joined to a discourse that had often contrasted warehouses with factories, the latter sometimes regarded as 'seminaries of vice' and sometimes as well-regulated utopias

[36] Brown's warehouse, 1851–2: detail of the front facing Piccadilly Gardens. Architect: Edward Walters.

[37] Behrens's warehouse, 1860, Portland Street. Architect: P. Nunn.

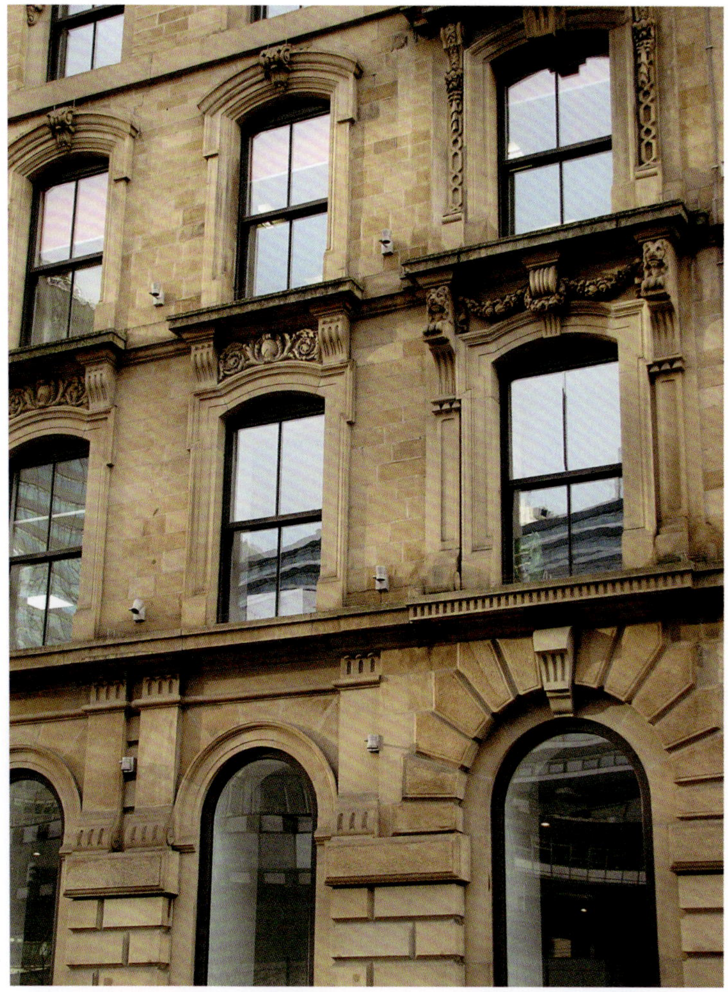

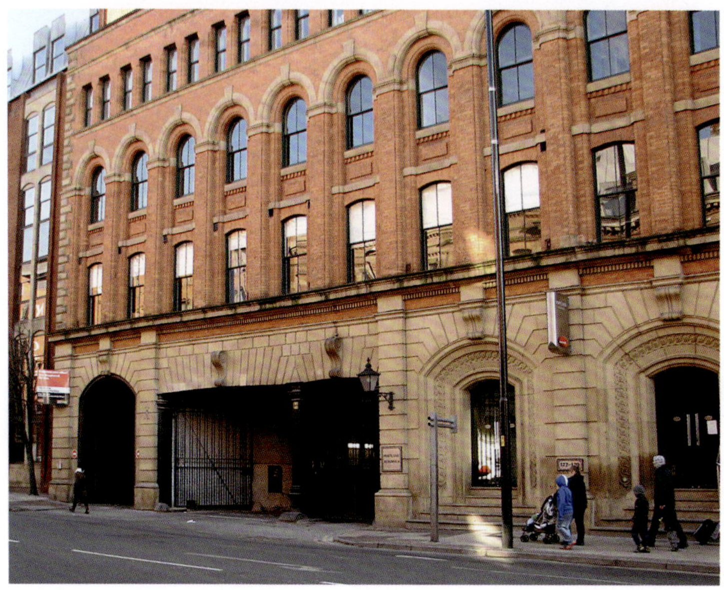

(as with the factory interiors discussed in Chapter 1).[64] Between the low morality of one and the supposed enlightenment of the other, these ideas bound together architecture, commerce, health, morality and urban behaviour, justifying the values and leadership role of the new industrialists.[65] This was still a fragile class formation – barely 15–18% of Manchester's population even in 1861 could be called middle class and above, and business panics such as that in 1857 could easily undermine commercial confidence.[66] As Simon Gunn has suggested, central to the growing role of the middle class in the city was its hunger for public visibility and display.[67] To this might be added the sense of identification with particular tracts of the city as they were remade by the more affluent and civic-minded members of the class; remade not just as backdrop but as manifestations of their sponsorship of a new architectural and spatial decorum.

HOUSE OF DISPLAY AND HOUSE ON SHOW: THE MOST distinctive architectural combination of these was the palazzo warehouse (fig. 36). Although they were dependent on mills as well as other equally essential parts of the urban and extra-urban palaeotechnic economy, warehouses were also quite distinct. They were used for storing and displaying goods, conducting them from producer to consumer and helping to imbue them with the magic of the commodity. They were located mainly in and around the quickly developing centre of Manchester (by 1815 there were, one historian has calculated, 1,500 cotton showrooms in the city[68]), while mills were in the industrial suburb of Ancoats (as seen in Chapter 1) in the city's inner ring or further out in the city's satellite towns. It was mills that inspired the study, awe and revulsion of visitors, while warehouses attracted those who had to do business. Mills intensified production through refinements in power and in manufacturing machinery; warehouses coordinated dispersed production. One was intensive, the other extensive.[69] Warehouses could be wholesale and retail shops, offices, workshops for finishing textile products, department stores and heavy-goods stores all in one.[70] In functional terms, those built along Portland Street from the 1840s, relatively late in terms of warehouses in central Manchester, were mostly for the home trade and dealt with the

[38] 'St Peter's Church and part of Mosley Street, Manchester', 1824. Engraving by John Fethergill. Manchester Art Gallery.

domestic and higher-end cotton products, but there were also some shipping or heavy-goods warehouses.[71] The former were for specialist retailers in the home trade and were often more like shops than storehouses. The latter required only simple storage devices, and barely hid lifting equipment and portals for heavy cartage (several of the Portland Street warehouses – like Behrens – actually have these on their main street frontages with their cavernous iron-framed entrances, though these were at the far end of the street from Piccadilly) (fig. 37). The home-trade warehouses required more light not just from the rear for packing and dispatch purposes but also from as many sides as possible, including from light-wells and glazed courtyards.

Any discussion of the warehouse as an architectural typology has to acknowledge its hybrid and 'imprecise' nature.[72] Functions might blur and change, admitting multiple variations.[73] Great ingenuity was demanded from architects, builders and craftsmen as they struggled to resolve the paradox of a cotton trade that needed damp climatic conditions to lessen cotton dust, yet – in a smoggy, misty locale with short winter days – as much natural light as possible in confined urban spaces.

Within the range of warehouses, the palazzo warehouse had a distinctly heightened purpose. If it was largely a home-trade warehouse, it was no mere nodal point for the showing and distributing of goods; it had heightened symbolic functions as well.[74] It was devised by architects as a specific solution for sites in the expanding city centre and to fulfil the aspirations of clients for expressions of civic-mindedness and their place in a historical lineage beyond Manchester and the Industrial Revolution. The subtypology of the palazzo warehouse exploited the imprecision of warehouse typology to give greater importance to street elevations. Indeed, 'subtypology' may not be an adequate term here – 'extra-' or 'para-typology' might be better – such were the huge differences, especially in elevational treatments, between the palazzo warehouse and more utilitarian warehouses. It is not my aim here to attempt a close definition of the palazzo warehouse in typological terms; even if that were possible, it seems to miss the point that palazzo warehouses were almost as much representational constructs as functional containers. What they helped create and represent was the Manchester industrial middle class. Additionally, the palazzo warehouse was bound up with the construction of a very particular cityscape, one that was not just temporally and geographically specific (and celebrated in many guidebooks at the time)[75] but born out of particular political struggles, local alliances and opportunities.

Contemporaries recognised that palazzo warehouses were the products of 'a new school of architects',[76] and of these the architect most closely identified with them was Edward Walters, but they were also very much the creation of one of the fathers of Free Trade. Walters was brought to Manchester by Richard Cobden, the calico manufacturer, Radical member of parliament, Anti-Corn Law leader and international advocate of Free Trade. Cobden was a major figure in the campaign that eventually established Manchester as a municipal corporation in 1838, wresting the town from its medieval system of local government (this, with the 1832 Reform Act, clearly announced that the industrial bourgeoisie's 'political time had come').[77] For Cobden Free Trade and municipal status were closely linked, as much by his vision of an active polity – a broadening of Liberal support, linking bankers to artisans and mill owners to shopkeepers – as by his idea of the place of a city like industrial Manchester in the nation's culture and economy.[78] And so, although this is unrecognised in his biographies, Cobden was also active in changing the architectural and urban forms of the industrial city.

As we saw in Chapter 1, overproduction and speculation had led, in 1825, to a catastrophic collapse in cotton sales accompanied by a brutal financial crash. In the next few years the chastened industry was slowly refreshed and restructured. Cobden arrived in Manchester in 1828, drawn by 'the openness of its economic system and the small-scale nature of its business units'.[79] In the spring of 1831 he told his brother about a house on Mosley Street – 'exactly opposite to the club house in the best street of the town and a front of five windows' – that he would take over later in the year as a base for his muslin and calico business. Cobden was simultaneously drawn to the house's potential for the commercial lustre of his firm and as a financial investment ('as soon as I fill out the front of my house to make it a warehouse'[80]). Only a decade

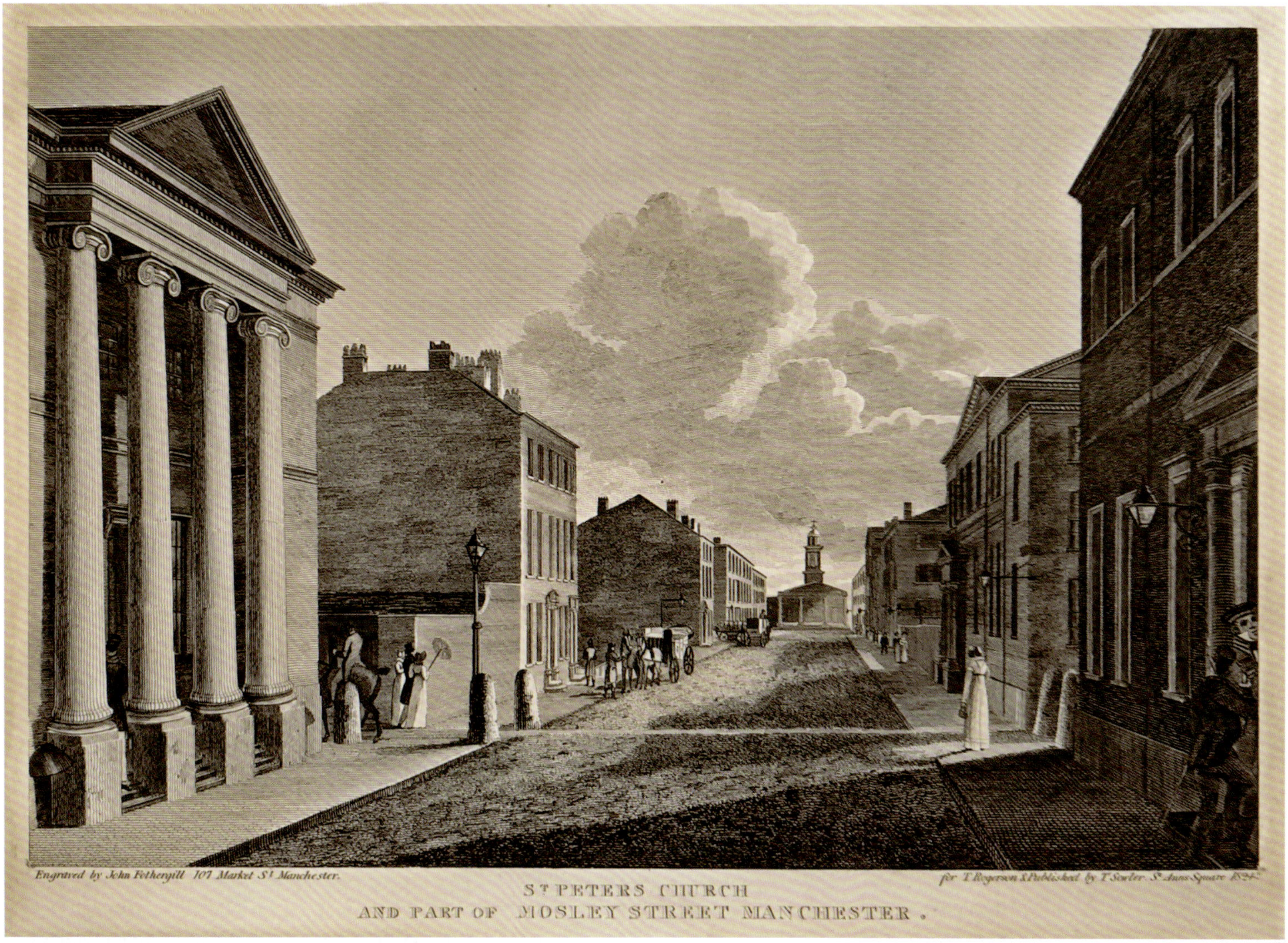

earlier, Mosley Street had been described as 'entirely inhabited by wealthy families'[81] (fig. 38). At the end of the previous century a vista had been created with the building of St Peter's church (James Wyatt, 1788–92), and in the century's first decade its status was affirmed by the temple-fronted Portico Library (Thomas Harrison, 1802–6). But Cobden was riding a very different wave of development:

> *I have given such a start to Mosley Street that all the world will be at my heels soon. My next door neighbour, Brooks, of the firm of Cunliffe and Brooks, bankers, has sold his house to be converted into a warehouse. The owner of the house on the other side has given his tenant notice for the same purpose. The house immediately opposite to me has been announced for sale, and my architect is commissioned by George Hole, the calico-printer, to bid 6000 guineas for it; but they want 8000 for what they paid 4500 only five years ago. The architect assures me if I were to put up my house to-morrow, I might have 6000 guineas for it. So as I gave but 3000, and all the world is talking of the bargain here, and there being but one opinion or criterion of a man's ability – the* making of money *– I am already thought a clever fellow.*[82]

Clearly, Cobden was intensely aware of the profits to be made from the rapid transformation of central Manchester from its pre-industrial gentility, first to a city of enlarged industrial scale and activity, and then from the 1820s increasingly from a manufacturing to a commercial centre. He would also have been aware

[39] Harvest House, Mosley Street, 1839. Architect: Edward Walters.

[40] Salis Schwabe warehouse, Mosley Street, 1845. Architect: Edward Walters. Photograph: J. R. Johnson (*c.*1950). From H.-R. Hitchcock, *Early Victorian Architecture in Britain* (1954).

[41] Athenaeum, Princess Street, 1836–7. Architect: Sir Charles Barry.

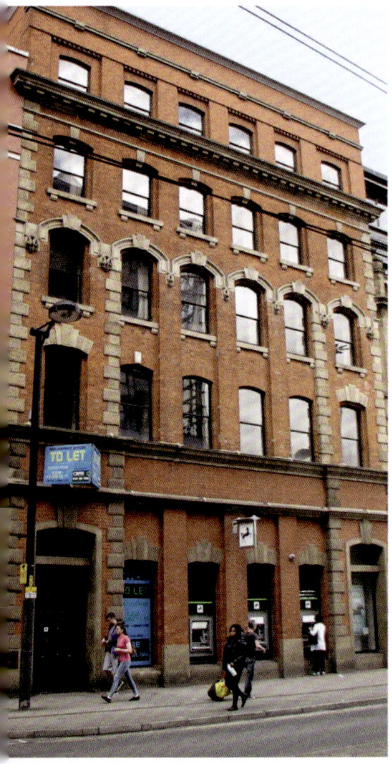

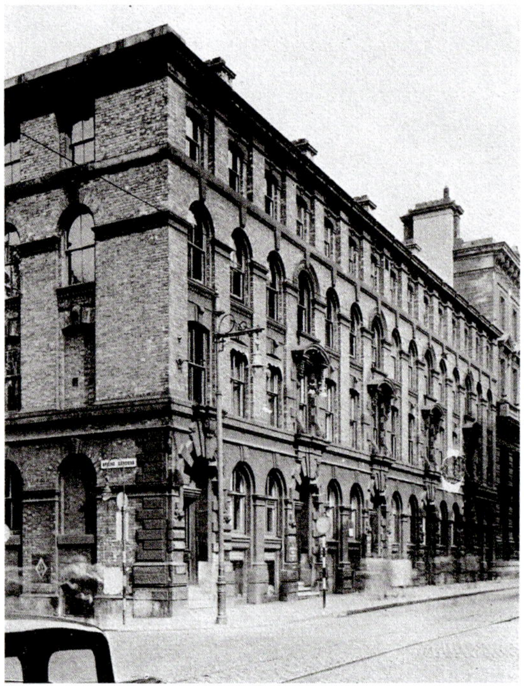

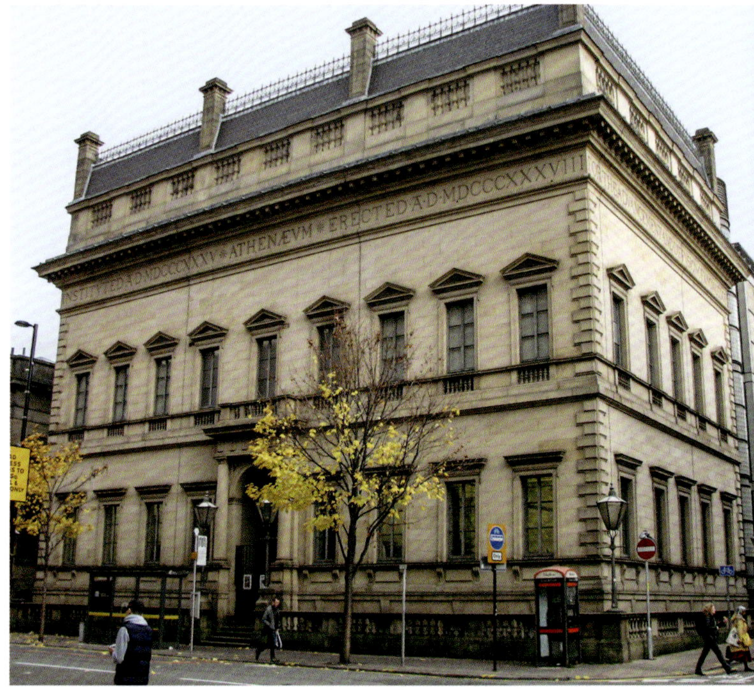

that the cotton industry had recovered from the crisis of 1825 only because of demand from foreign markets (which was to lead to a boom in mill and warehouse building by the mid-1830s).[83] Free Trade found its rationale in a situation that was both localised and bound up with Cobden's personal interests.

Cobden's architectural ambitions achieved their most distinctive expression through his collaboration with Walters. Industrialist and architect met in 1837 when Cobden was in Istanbul to learn about new dyes, while Walters was employed there by the engineer Sir John Rennie to construct a musket factory.[84] Such work was not at all unusual as the British and Ottoman empires exchanged knowledge and technology to mutual benefit; indeed, the Ottoman empire imported more of Manchester's manufactured cotton than all of Europe put together.[85] Only two years later William Fairbairn was employed by the sultan as an engineering consultant to build mills and design portable buildings, as well as make machinery for the Turkish government in his Manchester mills. A little earlier, in 1834, William Henry Barlow had been sent out by the London firm of Maudslay, Sons and Field to design arsenals and help with the manufacture of ordnance.[86]

When Cobden returned to Manchester it was Walters whom he called in to design his own warehouse (known as Harvest House) in 1839 (fig. 39). Taking over from the house on Mosley Street, and not far from the north side of the Infirmary, this has a few palazzo-like appurtenances such as a prominent cornice and stone quoins (unconvincingly repeated to outline the end bays) and possibly the curious stone ornament that links the window trim on the second floor. Elements of an industrial scale seem to have been merely overlaid onto the decorum and scale of a townhouse, which in a sense was exactly what had happened. Cobden's warehouse thus rode the wave of the commercialisation of this street, but it also retained the vestigial appearance of a residence, to the extent of its part-residential purpose on the top floor.[87]

Walters also designed a warehouse on Mosley Street for Cobden's friend Salis Schwabe (1845), a key figure on the Manchester Infirmary board[88] (fig. 40). Here Walters's sketchy mannerism was developed towards a more Roman sense of scale, framing basement and ground-floor windows as well as first- and second-floor windows in two striding attached arcades, bolstering the corner with quoins and carving out rugged details at all levels. The Schwabe warehouse was a powerful if still unresolved presence, like Cobden's warehouse, its industrial–commercial functions all too dominant over its residential allusions.

As Walters's warehouse designs developed over the next few years, so they became more confidently residential in association, and the encouragement for this may have come, if a little belatedly, from Manchester's Athenaeum (1836–7), designed by Sir Charles Barry as a palazzo-style club with Florentine and Roman references,[89] and built on Princess Street just round the corner from Mosley Street (fig. 41). Barry was London based and his building had very different functions from Walters's warehouses, but the institution came out of the same Manchester configuration of civic-minded industrialists, and James Watt was again held up as the exemplary figure for those who were to use the building.[90] There is also a direct link to the palazzo warehouse because Cobden was a prime mover among the industrialists who set up the Athenaeum.[91] What they wanted was a clubhouse for the youth of Manchester's commercial classes, to promote 'a powerful sense of enfranchisement, a legitimate civic and national responsibility'.[92] If Charles Dickens's testimony is a guide, these ambitions convinced some: it was 'neutral ground, where we have no more knowledge of party differences, or public animosities between side and side, or between man and man, than if we were at a public meeting in the commonwealth of Utopia'.[93] But the Athenaeum, far from being a 'cultural island in a sea of shops and warehouses',[94] as some have claimed, was directly linked to – if not the prototype of – the palazzo warehouse tide. On the one hand it extolled the civic-minded virtues and Free Trade rhetoric of Cobden and his kind, while on the other it articulated the architectural possibilities of Italian Renaissance palaces for Victorian cities.

While it has long been thought that Cobden and Walters were behind the invention of the palazzo warehouse,[95] I am suggesting that what they did was bound up in the specifics of urban change, politics and class identity. There has often been a tendency to see Manchester's early nineteenth-century industrial explosion and urban chaos as a product of some generalised 'laissez-faire capitalism' transformed towards mid-century by some apolitical drive for 'civic order'.[96] But it was the industrial bourgeoisie itself that produced the kind of civic order most pointedly expressed in Portland Street and Piccadilly Gardens. It was this class's own counter-culture that aspired to fill the vacuum of urban leadership brought about by the neglect or even active obstruction of change by an older landed class in collaboration with small landowners and the petit bourgeois,[97] 'the Tories and the Residuum' in the language of the day.[98]

The Mechanics' Institute was closely related to the Athenaeum as well as to the emergence of this new bourgeois cityscape[99] (fig. 42). Set up in rented rooms, the institute first acquired purpose-built accommodation in 1827 on Cooper Street, parallel with Mosley Street. The building, described as 'a neat, unpretending structure', was centred on a 1,000-seat lecture theatre, with a library and classrooms in the interstices around it.[100] Fairbairn

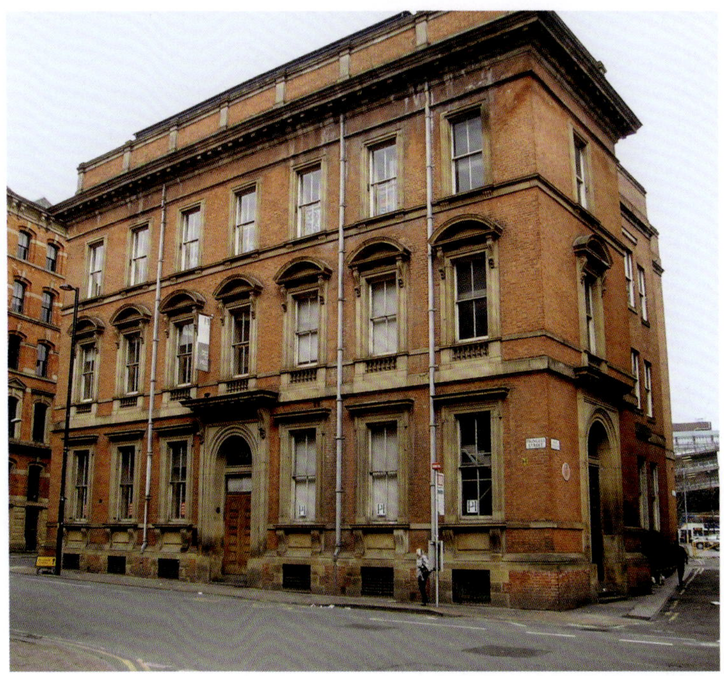

[42] Mechanics' Institute, Princess Street, 1854–5. Architect: J. E. Gregan.

[43] Richard Burnet's 'Spiral of Success' (1826). Engraving from *A Word to the Members of the Mechanics' Institutes* (1826).

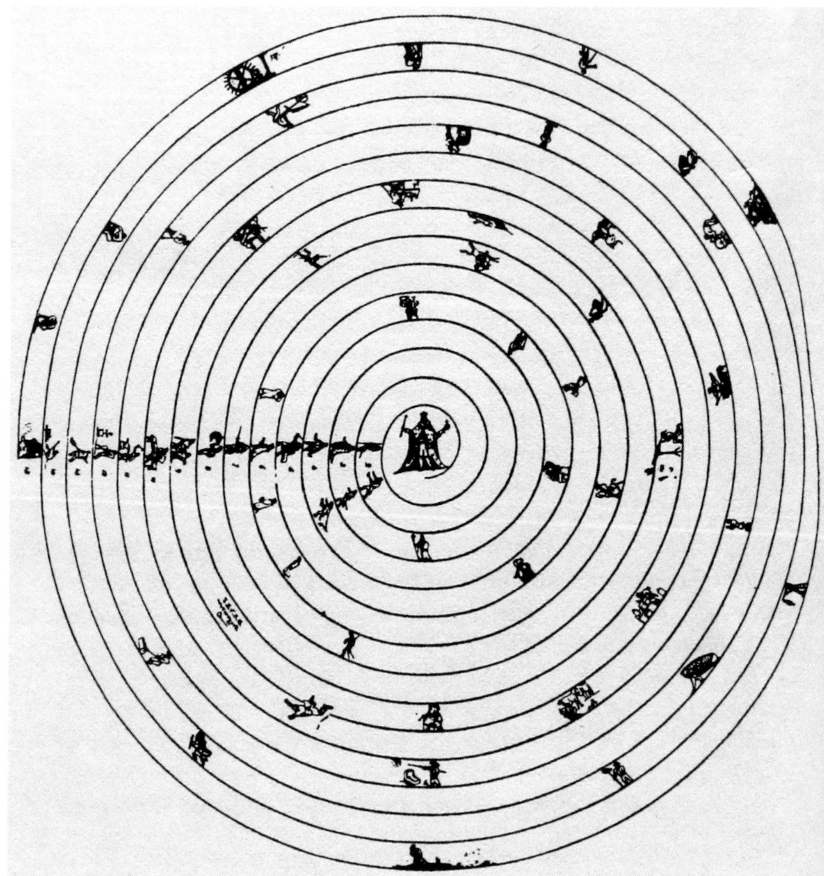

was its first secretary (becoming president in 1840), with the banker Benjamin Heywood as first chairman of the board, and funds were contributed by local manufacturers such as James McConnel.[101] When it was rebuilt in 1854–5 by J. E. Gregan, the architect of Heywood's bank a few years earlier and, with Walters, the most significant of the palazzo warehouse architects, the new Mechanics' Institute was placed a few yards down Princess Street from the Athenaeum, and designed as another Italian Renaissance palace. Again the lecture theatre was the crucial space, slotted at the back in a double-height room behind the three-storeyed Italian frontage and its pedimented *piano nobile* windows. As Maxine Berg has shown, the mechanics' institutes movement was the expression of the allied interests of Free Traders and political economists, bringing representatives of the working class into their vision of the benefits of technology.[102] The 'superior workmen, foremen or overlookers' were the target audience here, with Watt their exemplary figure. A limited scientific education would be the 'means of improvement' by which a disciplined and loyal workforce would be called into being by the philanthropy of their employers, much as workers were also encouraged to attend the institutes' exhibitions.[103] So the institute's building was intended to embody the architecture of enlightened charity, the projection of a common enterprise in which the central idea of benevolent technological change was part of the ideology of a social order based on industry. And we can perhaps imagine Richard Burnet's 'Spiral of Success' (1826) hanging on one of the institute's walls (fig. 43). This was a diagram intended to 'stir up the spirit of emulation', figuring the hierarchical ranking of society as a 'pyrotechnical wheel', a kind of efficient watch-spring, a system of positions and duties. The long spiral route to the centre encouraged the idea that 'the best informed and most industrious' might 'get forward' and push the more ignorant back onto the outer circles, but essentially it is an image of fixed distinctions, a mechanism that moves but keeps its working parts in place.[104] The point about the institute is that architecture drawn into unison is a measure of the industrial classes in unison; the industrial bourgeoisie is represented as belonging to recognisably the same entity – the industrious classes.

There was, then, a charged relationship between palazzo warehouses, the Infirmary as a hub of visible civic leadership for Manchester's industrial class, the development of Portland Street and these new institutions (fig. 44). The dynamic international businesses locating on Portland Street and mediating between local and world markets should be evidence enough, but so too was the seismic political change whereby ways were found to represent the interests of the new industrial elite and their supporters, to devise an architecture of Free Trade that was also instrumental in the new urban configuration of classes, embodying the new divisions of labour.[105] Architects were chosen who understood how to harness street architecture to their clients' ends.

LET US TAKE A CLOSER LOOK AT THE AESTHETICS AND functionality of the palazzo warehouse. Walters's work spread beyond Cobden as other industrialists, driven by emulation and class interest, took up the new architectural aspirations and as Cobden's own commercial interests in the city dried up.[106] The area on and around Portland Street became dotted with Walters's warehouses. Three were built on the old Portland Place frontage in the 1850s, taking on the prestige of that location and offering a concerted and sophisticated version of what Richard Lane had characterised as the flatness and attempt to disguise flatness that were inherent in warehouse architecture[107] (fig. 45). With Brown's warehouse (1851–2), on the corner of Aytoun Street and Portland Place, Walters seems finally to have arrived at the main architectural features and scale of the new palazzo warehouse typology[108] (fig. 46). It might be understood as a cross between the Athenaeum and Schwabe's warehouse, with a rusticated arcade on the ground floor and the owner's offices on the fourth floor, marked with pedimented windows. Deeply carved ornament

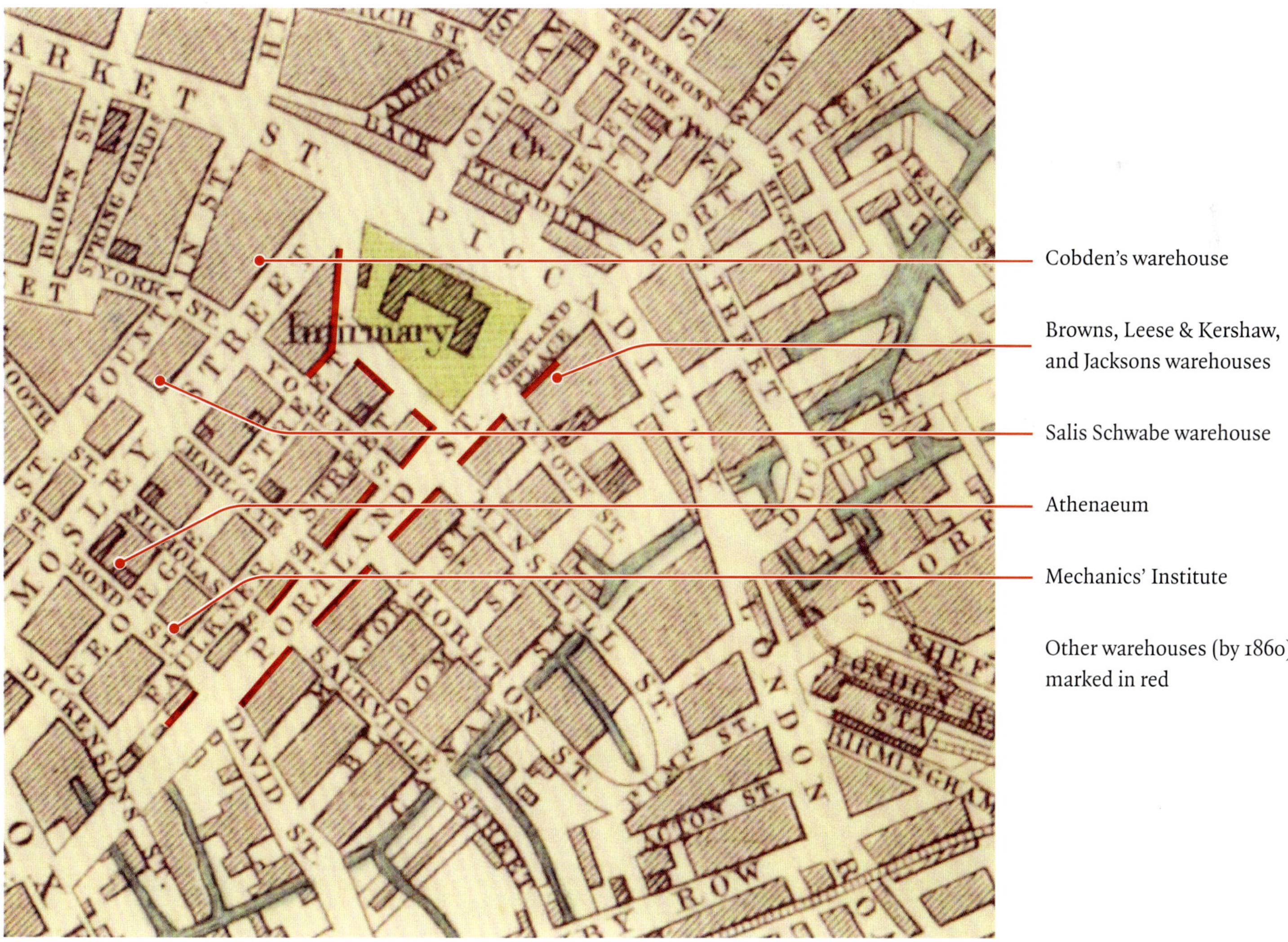

[44] Map of Manchester, 1870: detail showing the extent of the Free Trade cityscape. Published by John Bartholomew & Son.

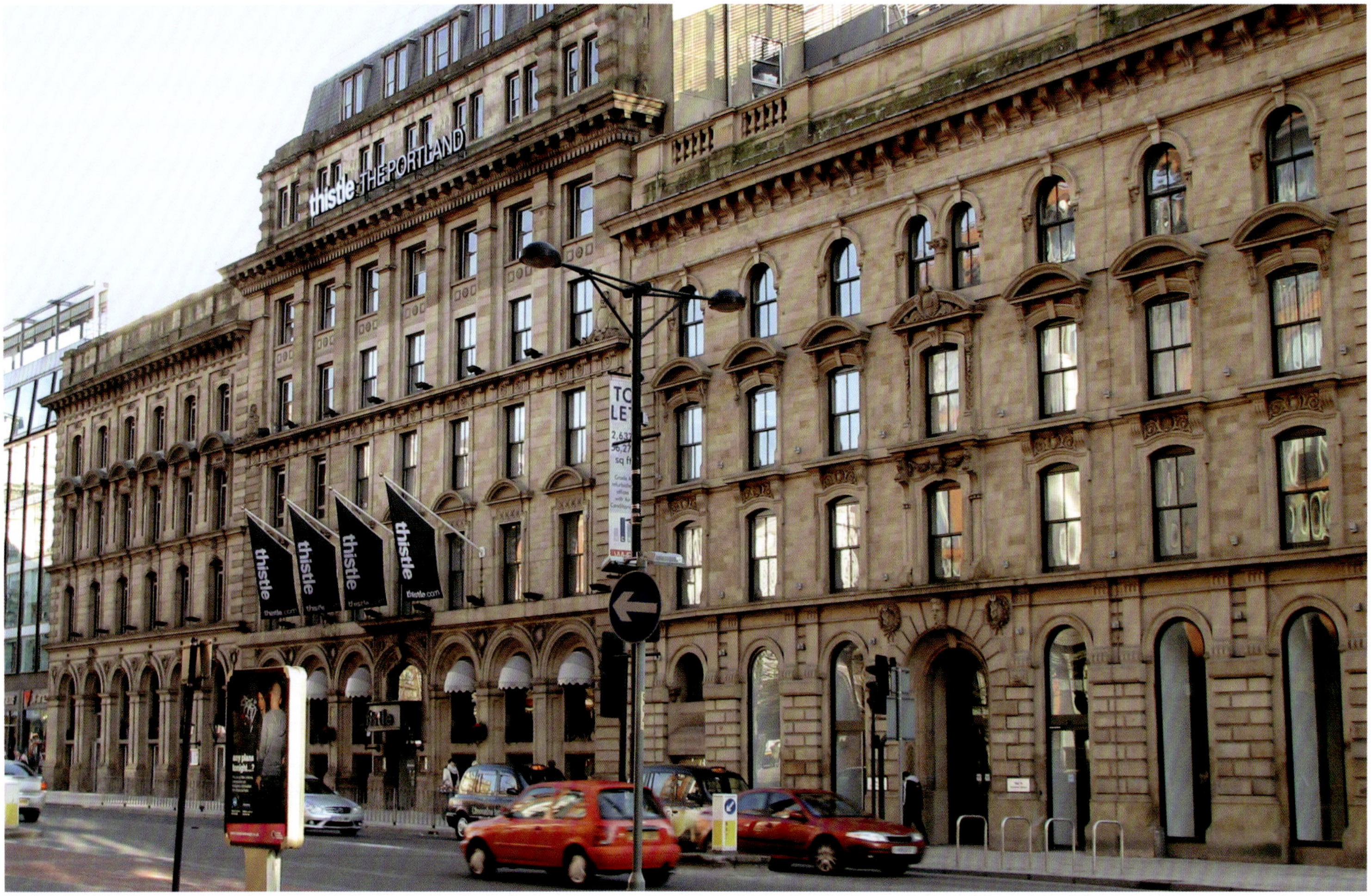

appears across the facades, becoming more lively with its more figurative subjects. On the longer side elevation the pediments occur only over the central six windows, perhaps in an attempt to differentiate the rhythm and create a false centrality to match the main entrance on the short front facing Piccadilly. The attic is hidden by a large balustrade, and the basement is cleverly absorbed into the ground-floor arcade. What might appear to be a four-storey building is actually six storeys. Although each storey is no more than eleven feet high, the exterior effect of vertical scale is created by devices that run one floor into another, for instance, lintels that seem also to act as pediments, and pediments that intrude into the floor above. As with all these warehouses, the palatial elements had to be accommodated within a far more extensively fenestrated facade than in the Renaissance prototypes.

In the warehouse for Kershaw, Leese & Sidebottom (1852), next door to Brown's, the main offices were now on the *piano nobile*, and Walters fitted five storeys into a facade only slightly taller than that of Brown's (fig. 47). Visual continuity with its neighbour was achieved by the same materials and, more subtly, by the minor cornice at third-floor level picking up the line of its neighbour's pedimented windows. E. and J. Jackson warehouse (1858), third in date of these neighbouring warehouses, returns to the scale of Brown's but enhances its vestigial ground-floor arcade (fig. 48). These three warehouses were built for single owners, unlike warehouses for multiple occupation elsewhere, and in each Walters played variations on a collective urban identity for the new class.

Walters had found an architectural subtype that fused his clients' different demands and was echoed in the work of other warehouse architects. A well-mannered street elevation inspired by Renaissance Genoa, Venice or Rome presents private offices on the right and a general office to the left. Passing through the central entrance, one reaches a large top-lit open area with

[45] Three of Edward Walters's warehouses side by side, facing Piccadilly.

[46] Brown's warehouse, Piccadilly, 1851–2. Architect: Edward Walters.

[47] Kershaw, Leese & Sidebottom warehouse, Portland Street, 1852. Architect: Edward Walters. Engraving from *Building News* (12 February 1858).

[48] E. and J. Jackson warehouse, Portland Street, 1858. Architect: Edward Walters.

warerooms on either side. Iron columns, cased in wooden pilasters, support the upper floors, which are divided into sale and pattern rooms for goods. At the back a loading area is sheltered by the projection of the floor above, its hoist presses powered by a steam engine below. Behind the image of the elite urban home, then, was not only a staff of clerks and a large team of warehousemen but also all the relatively small-scale industrial machinery their work demanded. It seems to have been vital, though, not to allow any hint of industry on the main front of the building; this was to be a zone for architectural expression (and was reviewed as such in the architectural press), emblematic of association and aspiration.

Walters's skill was not so much to vaguely 'gentrify' Manchester businessmen[109] as to pointedly reinforce their self-perception as the only properly urban elite. The rise of the palazzo warehouse was essentially about architectural powers of representation. Referencing Italian palazzos (which Walters had seen at first hand in 1837), this class was to emulate Renaissance merchant-princes: the appropriation distinguished their warehouses in both location and architectural quality from the warehouses that dominated Manchester's property market.[110] The public understood this: Brown's warehouse, wrote the *Illustrated London News*, '[befitted] the establishment of a merchant prince', while *Bradshaw's Railway Guide* admired '[these] structures fit for kings and which many a monarch might envy ... The artistic display is all but equal to the noble enterprise which gave them being.'[111] For Cobden the link between his version of Free Trade and early modern Italian architecture was self-evident. The journal he kept while visiting Genoa in 1847, for instance, recorded his meetings with businessmen about Free Trade and, side-by-side, his observations on architecture: 'Walked ... through the city, to view the exteriors of those palaces erected from two to three centuries ago for the merchant-princes of Genoa ... striking specimens of taste and splendour. The Strada Nuova, a narrow street with a pavement of broad flags, is full of these palaces ... Visiting macaroni and vermicelli manufacturers.'[112] Cobden was dissatisfied with his fellow Manchester industrialists because they failed to live up to their historical analogues: if they operated more like Continental manufacturers, they would 'become the De Medicis, and Fuggers, and De Witts of England, instead of glorying in being the toadies of a clodpole aristocracy'.[113] He was also aware from his travels in Italy of the support contemporary Florentines felt for his brand of Free Trade politics, as if a slumbering culture had become newly energised.[114]

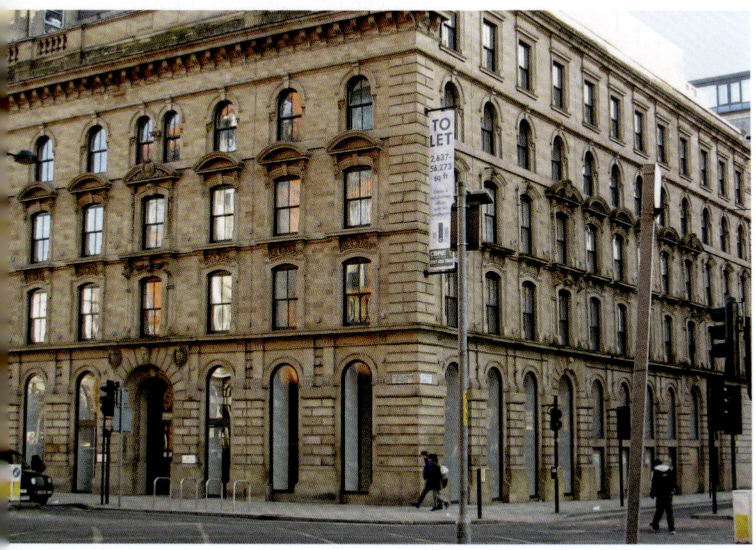

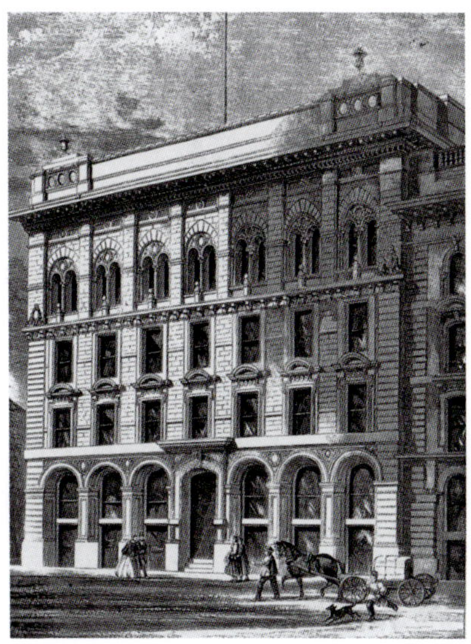

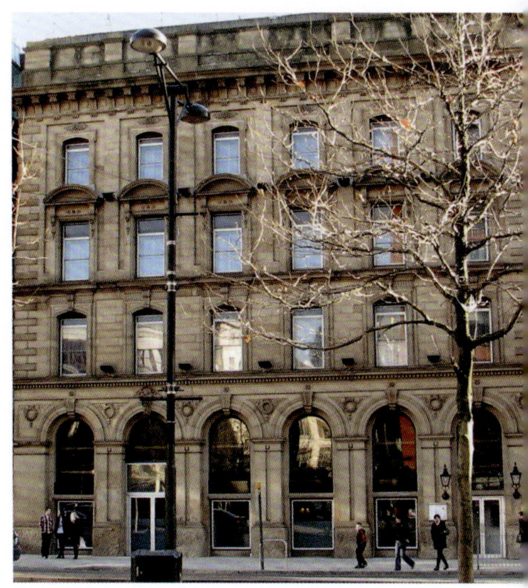

As Cobden would have it, this link between Manchester and Genoa, the Industrial Revolution and the Renaissance, was less about revivalism than figural fulfilment. In Erich Auerbach's explanation, the figural relation occurs when two separate events without temporal or causal connection are joined via a collapsed perspective whereby 'the first signifies not only itself but also the second, while the second involves or fulfils the first ... both occurrences are vertically linked to Divine Providence, which alone is able to devise such a plan of history and supply the key to its understanding'.[115] So the Free Trade of Manchester, whose existence in the city is attested by the palazzo warehouse and the other architecture discussed here, is the fulfilment of a previous historical appearance in the forms of the Renaissance city-state. With Cobden we are clearly dealing with a relationship forged by ideology rather than divine providence, which is carried by aesthetic packages or ideologemes (units of ideology) across the vertical axis, and which is as much a goad as an exemplification.[116]

If the image of grand residence was a matter of historical association, it was also about the locality of these palazzo warehouses on and around Portland Street. When, soon after arriving in Manchester, Cobden himself had essayed the conversion of his house into a warehouse, he was taking up a tradition of merchants who, when they first wanted to display their wares, would convert or expand their own town centre residences to take advantage of the much larger rents from business firms than from private residents.[117] 'Dwelling after dwelling', in the words of one observer in the early years of the century, 'metamorphosed into warehouses.'[118] In Mrs Linnaeus Banks's popular novel *The Manchester Man* (1876), set in the early part of the century, this transition from house-warehouse to warehouse is described in terms of a property on the other side of Piccadilly:

> *Though the house of Mr Ashton was in Mosley Street, the premises extended as far as Back Mosley Street, where was the warehouse door. The workpeople entered at a side door under a gateway which led to the stable, gig-house, and courtyard between house and warehouse ... You may look in vain for house and warehouse now. A magnificent block of stone warehouses, having three-fold frontage, occupies the site.*[119]

The transition is a crucial context for this *Bildungsroman*, which tells the story of the rise of a poor man, Jabez Clegg, to become a member of Manchester's industrial bourgeoisie, a kind of fictional founding myth of the rise of the city itself. All this happens around Mosley Street, where Cobden and Salis Schwabe had their palazzo warehouses.

The architect's synthesis of such ideas was crucial to the palazzo warehouse phenomenon. The warehouses on Portland Place had a strong contextual affiliation with the industrialists' residences that had stood on that spot as well as with the Queen's Hotel right beside them, whose Georgian domestic scale was maintained even as the hotel was extended in 1856.[120] Walters varied the spacing of the multiple windows needed for the palazzo warehouse type but he always kept the type balanced between residential and business associations. Rustication and carved detail were kept bold and entrances were emphasised with carved ornament; the *piano nobile* was made apparent; and the rear was kept for workaday concerns. The palazzo warehouse was, therefore, a kind of lineage-seeking mnemonics of dignified residence, a trace left behind just as the wealthy themselves were removing to the suburbs.[121] And all this was also a way of making the warehouse distinct from the mill, of making it urbane.[122]

Walters's warehouses on the Portland Place end of Portland Street encouraged other textile retailers to relocate their wholesale and storage facilities in the most up to date of warehouses. These were designed by the most aspirational architects in the city and drew upon the details of Renaissance palaces now frequently reproduced in the architectural press.[123] The warehouse that J. E. Gregan designed for the corner of Parker Street and Portland Street used these details more lightly than many, giving its facades a more minimal rhythm of pediments (fig. 49). But the purpose was the same. Inside, on a typical floor, the large sale and sample rooms and 'counting houses' (accounts departments) took over all the outside windows, their interior depths extended and given as much natural light as possible by the use of slender iron columns (fig. 50).

Portland Street was recognised as the crux and apogee of this development, surpassing older warehouse areas like Cannon

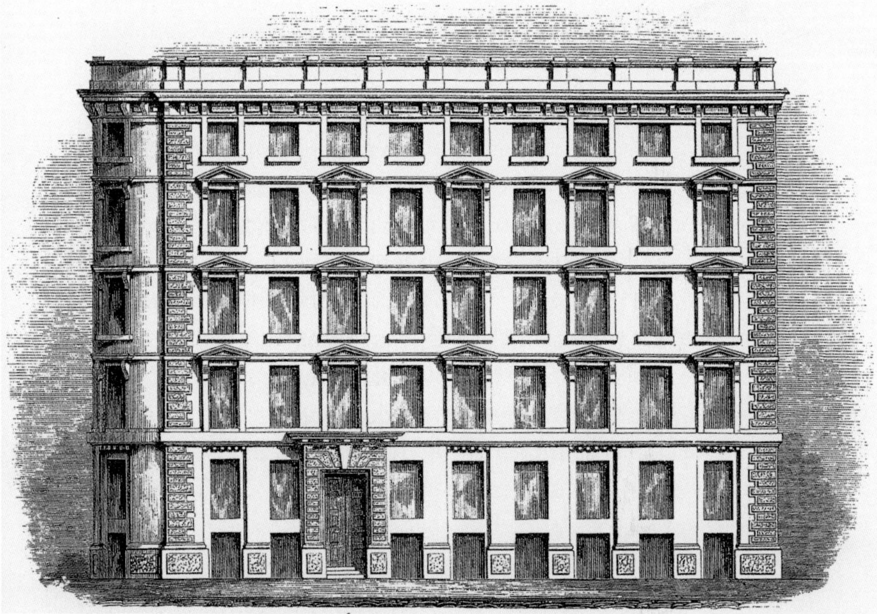

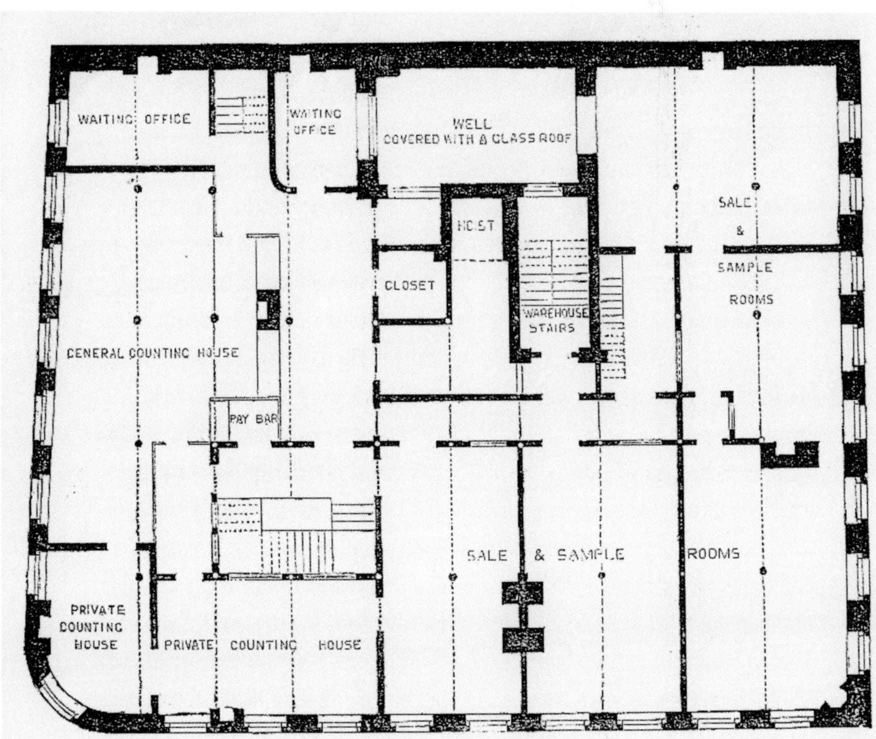

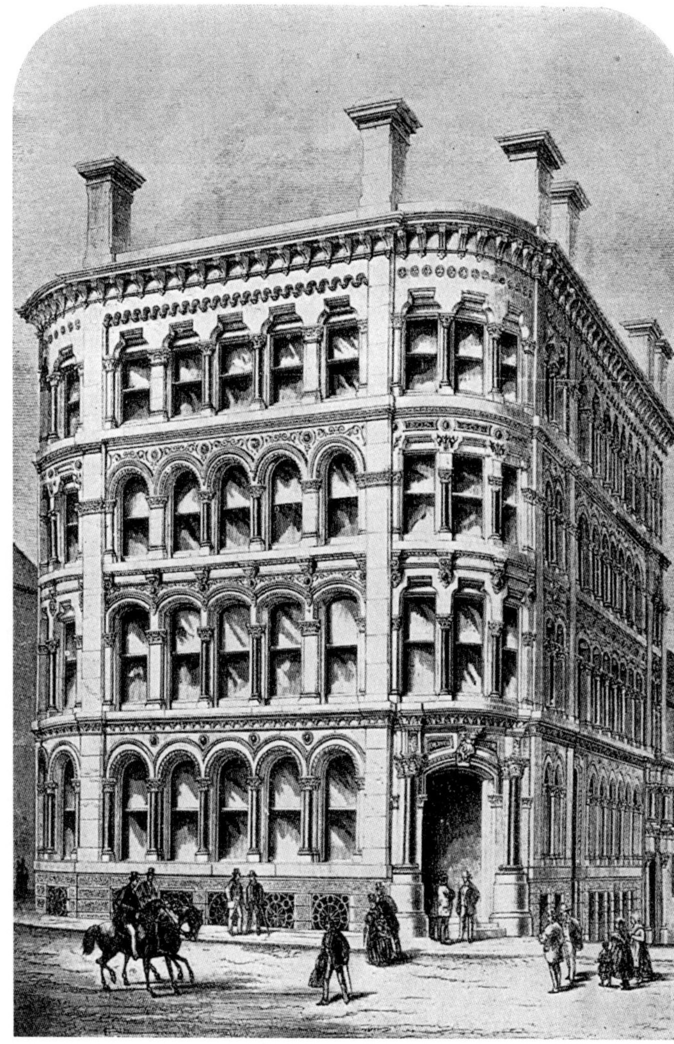

[49] Warehouse on Portland and Parker Streets, 1850: elevation. Architect: J. E. Gregan. From *Builder* (31 August 1850).

[50] Warehouse on Portland and Parker Streets, 1850: plan. Architect: J. E. Gregan. From *Builder* (31 August 1850).

[51] Pickles warehouse, Portland Street and Princess Street, 1870. Architects: Clegg & Knowles. From Cecil Stewart, *The Stones of Manchester* (1956).

Street. 'Portland Street now bristles with scaffold-poles', one contemporary observed in 1858, 'and stone fronts, finely carved, will soon make it one of the best builded streets in England.'[124] In the ensuing three decades almost the entire street was taken over by warehouses for which, remarkably, the Infirmary continued as a formal reference point.[125] Beyond Walters's three warehouses were Hugh Balfour & Co. (Clegg & Knowles, 1858), Louis Behrens & Sons (P. Nunn, 1860), the Circus (Shaw & Webster, 1866), a branch of the multisite Lloyd's Packing Warehouses, Carver's warehouse (Clegg & Knowles, 1869), Pickles warehouse (Clegg & Knowles, 1870) (fig. 51), Lowthian, Williamson & Co. (1877), the Manchester Warehouse Property Company (Royle & Bennett, 1880) and so on.

Who were the companies that commissioned these warehouses and how might they have understood their presence on Portland Street? Some had been established recently but were expanding rapidly. Behrens & Sons, for instance, was founded in 1840, had strong links with New York and manufactured mainly fustians and velvets for the American market.[126] The firm of Lowthian, Williamson & Co. was set up in 1877 and immediately located itself in this already warehouse-themed district. The firm had grown out of Lowthian, Fairlie & Co., established a century earlier, and the relocation and renaming seems to have been an integral part of the firm's desire to see itself and its products as constantly evolving at the high end of the trade.[127] A notable feature of contemporary trade descriptions was an emphasis on the capaciousness, technical advancement and specialised provisions of the Portland warehouses. The Watts brothers moved their business here after trying different locations in Manchester.[128] Other firms, like P. J. Villy, needed a Manchester base for operations that were essentially based elsewhere – in Villy's case in the French market with its centre in Paris.[129] One of the first firms to build a Portland Street warehouse, A. and S. Henry, had spent its early years in Philadelphia.[130]

For a period of about three decades from around 1850 to 1880, Portland Street was therefore the prime location for these thriving businesses and their cutting-edge warehouses. It 'rose in character', Reuben Spencer wrote, looking back from the end of the century, 'almost at a bound, and has become a great centre of the commercial power of our city'.[131] This was a process, of course, with businesses using their street presence to reinforce and reaffirm their mutual upward mobility. Many of these merchants became aldermen, mayors or MPs. The model Manchester man typified by a Schwabe or the fictional Jabez Clegg, the cliché of the absolute bourgeois, was now widely emulated, while the politics of Free Trade was less pointed and more taken for granted, more mainstream. The expertise of these men in urban governance was matched by their patronage of medical and philanthropic charities or by their desire to establish new city institutions. And this collective purpose was, for a time, represented in their architecture.[132] It was as if the inherent fragility of this new hegemony might be bulked up and thus denied by the cohesiveness and unity of expression in their architecture.

As we have seen, palazzo warehouses were drawn to the street line and their much fenestrated elevations enabled by iron structures within. Continuity down the street was established by similar cornice heights and materials, and especially by the rhythms of arcades on the ground or first floors and the embellished floors above, where the owner's offices tended to be located. One important detail for pedestrians was that the basement windows, to gain greater daylight, had holes opened in the pavement and then covered over with iron bars or grilles. Later the windows were often canted away from pedestrians.[133] Another detail was the iron guards fitted to kerbstones to protect them from the wear and tear of the heavy carts that constantly travelled Manchester's streets, from canal to mill to warehouse or to railway station. Such details epitomise the potentially conflicting functions that had to be kept in control if Portland Street were to play its special commercial and civic (or emblematic) role. In a sense, the street was in a constant state of potential breakdown. Just as a new promenade and statues in front of the Infirmary would not stop beggars or gangs of boys congregating there, so a regularised street would not ensure only well-behaved traffic. Both required bolstering, maintaining and policing. A demonstration or modelling of behaviour is also related to this. The merchant Joseph Leese's journeys to and from his home in Ardwick to his warehouse in Portland Place were ostentatious displays of self-discipline and punctiliousness, public

[52] Portland Street, between Princess Street and Nicholas Street. Photograph taken in 2015.

demonstrations of how the self-made Manchester man behaved in the streets he claimed as his own[134] (Leese probably always travelled in a carriage and so was not limited to a walking commute from his place of residence).

But the street was never entirely in the hands of this class. While its north-eastern end was rapidly shaped by the assertion of new political power in the 1840s and 1850s, which extended the development of the Infirmary, most of the rest of the street was developed in a longer cohabitation with petit bourgeois and working-class Manchester. In 1848 there was still a great variety of businesses along Portland Street. There were manufacturers of tinplate, files and copper rollers, of cabinet cases and musical instruments. There were two curriers, eight beer retailers and one spirit maker; a sawmill; makers of watches, shoes and boots; a rag merchant, four bakers, several grocers, two chemists, three butchers, a plumber, a blacksmith, several tobacconists and greengrocers, two tailors, a cooper, a tripe dresser, a hairdresser, an auctioneer, a bookseller, two confectioners, a sadler, a pattern card maker, a whipmaker and an upholsterer. There were land agents and estate agents, taverns, eating houses and lodging houses, small-ware and earthenware dealers, two painters, an engraver, a carver, a music teacher and even a statuary shop. A variety of textile concerns could also be found – two milliners, a sock manufacturer, and several linen drapers and silk manufacturers. All were part of the complex local economy.[135] Architects had played little or no part in this streetscape of small pieces, of buildings, reused, extended or demolished in part or whole and rebuilt. From the 1850s, Portland Street was straightened, widened and

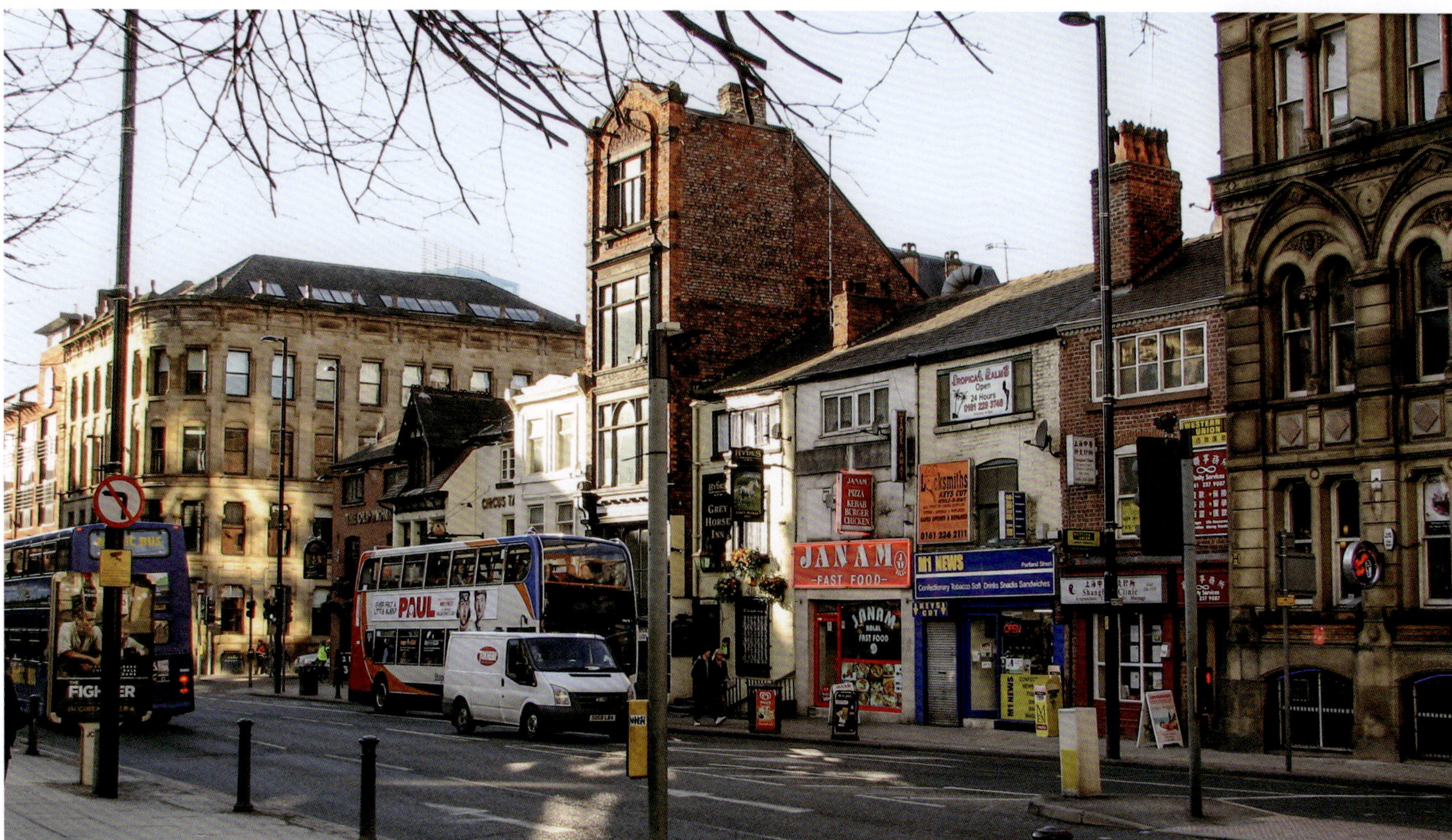

lengthened to accord with its new-found importance. As a result of the 1853 Manchester New Streets Act, it was finally extended to Oxford Street, displacing the older canal-related industrial clutter as the logic of homogeneous commercial development demanded.[136]

Although large warehouses took over parts of the Portland streetscape, they had not attained dominance even by 1868, more than twenty years after Engels's book.[137] From Piccadilly to Chorlton Street warehouses certainly loomed large, but otherwise there was the same mixture of myriad smaller businesses. The juxtaposition was acutely embarrassing to some. Here is the *Manchester Critic* in 1873:

> *it seems odd to see such queer old-fashioned hovels as still exist in Portland Street mixed up with such palatial buildings as the warehouses of Messrs. S. and J. Watts and Co., Mr Sam Mendel's old warehouse, and others. Tripe shops, pork-shops, pie-shops, greengrocer's shanties, and huckster's stalls are to be found cheek-by-jowl with millionaires' establishments rivalling the palaces of the Doges of Venice.*[138]

It was not really until the 1880s that the streetscape was dominated by warehouses. And even in 1891 the *Manchester City News* was complaining that, while old Portland Street had 'consisted principally of a mass of wretched hovels, the last of [these had] scarcely disappeared even yet'.[139] Again, the moral aspect of this is a strong element in the contrasts Victorian writers made with older buildings and smaller businesses. Survivals such as the block between Princess Street and Nicholas Street, a jumble of low-rise Georgian and Victorian structures to this day, was described by one architectural observer: 'it is as if a rabble from some hidden purlieu was invading the street and waiting to be driven back by the police'[140] (fig. 52). The conceit is not entirely fanciful. The hypocritical plan had not worked; the class difference of incomplete development remained architecturally manifest.

This incompletion is almost always the effect of a mutually advantageous yet temporary alliance of interests in urban development. Individual developers may diverge in their aims as time moves on; reluctant or simply negligent landowners may never sell. In Portland Street the incompletion of such an ad hoc project – a coalition of arriviste ambitions, a cityscape of Free Trade – is less remarkable than the fact that it got so far without any formal planning or concerted municipal intent.

THE RELATION BETWEEN ARCHITECTURAL IDENTITY AND civic propriety, and the shifting nature of both, can be highlighted with two exceptional buildings. One was a kind of apotheosis of the role of architecture in the world-view of Free Trade, the work buildings did as 'hieroglyphs of its darkest secret'.[141] The other tested the balance between commerce and civic responsibility, indeed the very idea that there was an identifiable collectivity behind Free Trade, and instead proposed that the market's competitiveness demanded its own expression quite distinct from expressions of collectivity and communal decorum.

The climax of the Cobden–Walters link came with their most overtly political work, the severe yet sumptuous Free Trade Hall (1853–6) (see fig. 26). With this – started only two years after that other apotheosis of Free Trade, the Crystal Palace – the cityscape of Free Trade was extended beyond the Piccadilly–Portland Street nexus and its Athenaeum and Mechanics' Institute outriders. Two temporary buildings had previously housed meetings of the Anti-Corn Law League: a wooden hall with iron pillars and then a brick building, both on land in St Peter's Fields that Cobden had donated in 1840.[142] Politically, the area was highly charged, and the eventual permanent architectural intervention undoubtedly responded to this. The land was part of the 'wide unbuilt space' that had been the site of the Peterloo massacre nearly forty years earlier, in 1819, when a huge peaceful demonstration for political representation was ended by troops and yeomanry being unleashed on unarmed crowds.[143] Cobden had long understood the massacre to have been caused by Manchester's enfeebled status, that it had not been incorporated,[144] and his answer was to sweeten the bitterness with an appeal to 'amalgamate all ranks', meaning 'the artisans and working-class radicals and the so-called "shopocracy"'.[145] He argued for what he called the 'democratic principle' in his writing on incorporation, attempting without success to gain the support of reluctant Radicals.[146] It was an argument that appropriated the mass agitation for suffrage (as

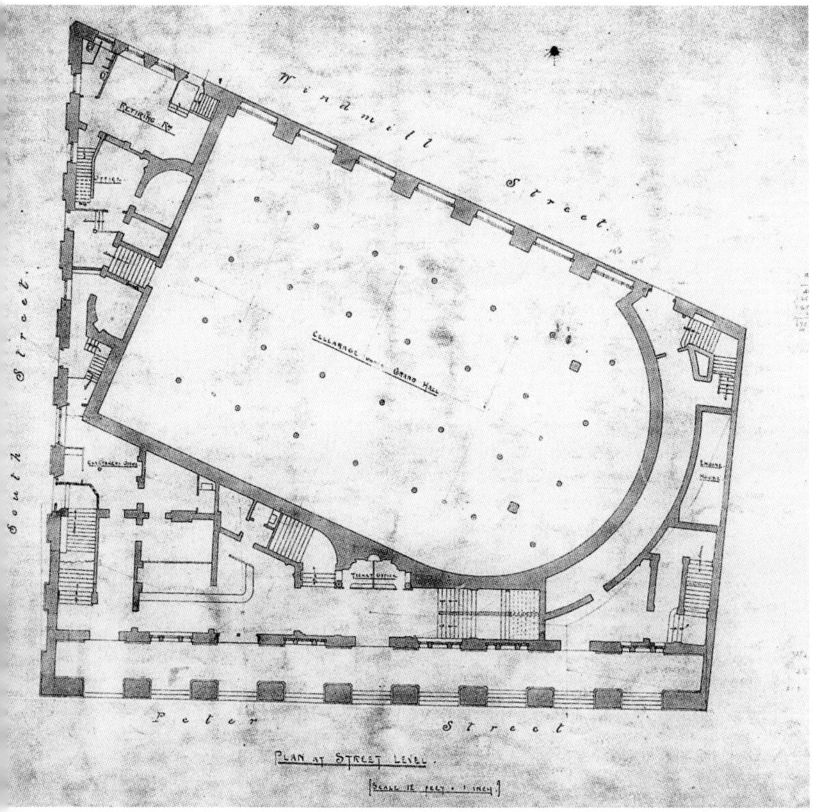

[53] Free Trade Hall, Peter Street, 1853–6: ground-floor plan. Architect: Edward Walters. Manchester Libraries, Information and Archives.

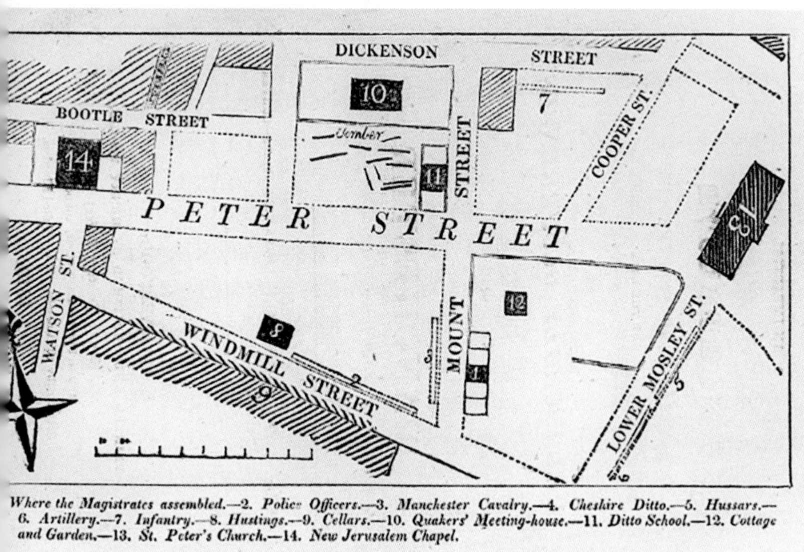

[54] Map of St Peter's Field, 1819. The Free Trade Hall was built on the triangle of land bounded by Peter Street, Windmill Street and Mount Street. Manchester Libraries, Information and Archives.

well as its repression by a reactionary government and its provincial functionaries still obsessed with the spectre of the French Revolution) to the ends of Manchester's developing urban status led by the industrial bourgeoisie.

The site Cobden owned was the very epicentre of the events of 1819 – 'the exact spot where the blood of Peterloo was spilt'.[147] How and why he had taken ownership of the site is not known, but he cannot have been unaware of the site's mnemonic potency. To situate a monument to Free Trade here was another erasure of the memory of Peterloo, the tragic event now appropriated by and aligned with the movement for the repeal of the Corn Laws. Indeed this kind of memory is exactly what the Free Trade Hall was not about: it was not about a history of conflict and its sites but rather, we might say, about 'history' and 'architecture' as abstracted or detached forms of value. Free Trade was to be both nationalised and naturalised – to become economic logic – across party lines.[148] That this was a civic and an urban agenda too is evident from the cityscape of buildings associated with Free Trade a few streets away. Beckoning across to them now was to be the grandest of the city's new palace fronts. Dressed in ultra-confident sixteenth-century garb (Verona's Gran Guardia Vecchia is the most likely source), two tall storeys of arches, of coupled columns and crisply carved swags, were contained within beautifully articulated end bays.[149]

As well as providing meeting spaces, the Free Trade Hall was a way of memorialising success, the diversion of unruly democratic energies into trade and civic order. Inheriting the awkward corner site used for the temporary buildings, Walters's design found space for a large hall by positioning it at the back of the site, following the angle of the street on that side (fig. 53). Given its largely independent structure, this hall was virtually a building within a building. The main Peter Street front exploited the residual space at its corner to accommodate a vestibule and ticket office on the ground floor behind an arcade open to the street, and an assembly room on the first floor. It should be emphasised how closely this site mapped onto crucial elements of the demonstration at St Peter's Fields forty years earlier (fig. 54). Maps of the location of that event showed how the hustings had been placed at the back of this same area – effectively, the speakers' temporary platform was in the middle of what became the audience's seating in the new large hall, while the inn where the magistrates had gathered and from where they had ordered the action of the troops, was across the side road (Mount Street) from the hall.[150] The site for the performance of dissidence and its violent suppression was first roofed over in the temporary halls and then, with Walters's stone edifice, monumentalised as a room for the city's new-found order. The intention had never been for the Peterloo events to be memorialised by the building but rather for it to be built over or buried by it. The radicalism of civil rights had morphed into the liberalism of a socio-economic movement.

Establishing the authority of the changed memory of the site, the facade redirected the viewer towards more conventional forms of historical association. Convention was the key ruse, pointing away from class conflict and towards culture as a way of life; here it meant the settled verities of early modern Italy and the humanist tradition through reasserting and crowning the palazzo tradition in nearby streets. Accordingly, the facade worked both as a screen for the various functions within and as an arcade allowing public access from Peter Street (unlike the temporary buildings which had used the side street for their entrances). Walters had learned, it seems, from the warehouses that succeeded his own along Portland Street (including, possibly, the Watts warehouse then being built), and the new hall provided equivalents for their experiences. Their clever interlocking of spaces can be seen in the suite of rooms grouped along the Free Trade Hall's front; their control of ceiling light was taken up by Walters in the three glazed domes he designed for the main hall; and the way in which warehouses transmuted the acts of viewing and buying into a kind of performance was taken up by the galleried and relatively low-ceilinged space of the hall.

The Free Trade Hall made a claim to own public discourse or discourse about publicness. As Manchester's largest public hall, it continued the tradition established by its temporary predecessors of being used for a variety of political meetings, events and entertainments, and adopted a spirit of political generosity, playing down its moment of triumph – not just the decade-old repeal of the Corn Laws but Chartism's now moribund state – at the building's completion and emphasising its openness to any political and social uses.[151] This continued the Free Trade movement's 'culture of theatre', its use of banquets and balls, lectures and dramatic performances, both for fund-raising and morale-maintaining purposes.[152] Architecturally it became the city's pre-eminent public hall and expressed its commitment to the public realm of the city's streets, its mass articulated by the Palladian rhythms of a confidence previously unseen in the city. The bold ground-floor arcade strode its way across the full length of the long side and wrapped around three bays of the short side of the building, providing, as Walters claimed, 'a most desirable shelter for the public'.[153]

Sculptural decoration declared the benefits of Free Trade. Carved by the sculptor John Thomas and closely based on Walters's drawings, the principal decorations were placed in panels over the upper windows.[154] Free Trade here was associated with female personifications – the principal figures in all the panels are generic. One sitting figure holds a spindle and is flanked by a steam locomotive, a printing press and cogged wheels (fig. 55). In another panel an Indian female figure sits on the back of a lion and holds an ivory tusk, with other fruits of empire behind her. America is represented by a female with a bison, with tubs of molasses around. All of the panels have bales of cotton – the Manchester thread – among their accoutrements. Free Trade, of course, had little tradition, and the city itself had no particularly strong figurative iconography, not even a settled gender for its urban identity (Charity – as discussed in the Introduction – does not seem to have taken off as an embodiment, perhaps for obvious reasons). On the Free Trade Hall, a tradition was invented for Free Trade by association with emblems of the continents and of Agriculture, Commerce, and the Arts and Manufactures. The attributes of the sculpted women – young, healthy, 'pure', 'maidenly' (neither quite sexual nor quite maternal) – are associated with the political movement. In the central panel, the openness of Free Trade was embodied in a female figure with arms outstretched above sheaves of corn and masted ships behind her (fig. 56). Her frontal, four-square mode of address

[55] Free Trade Hall: sculptural panel over upper window. Sculptor: John Thomas.

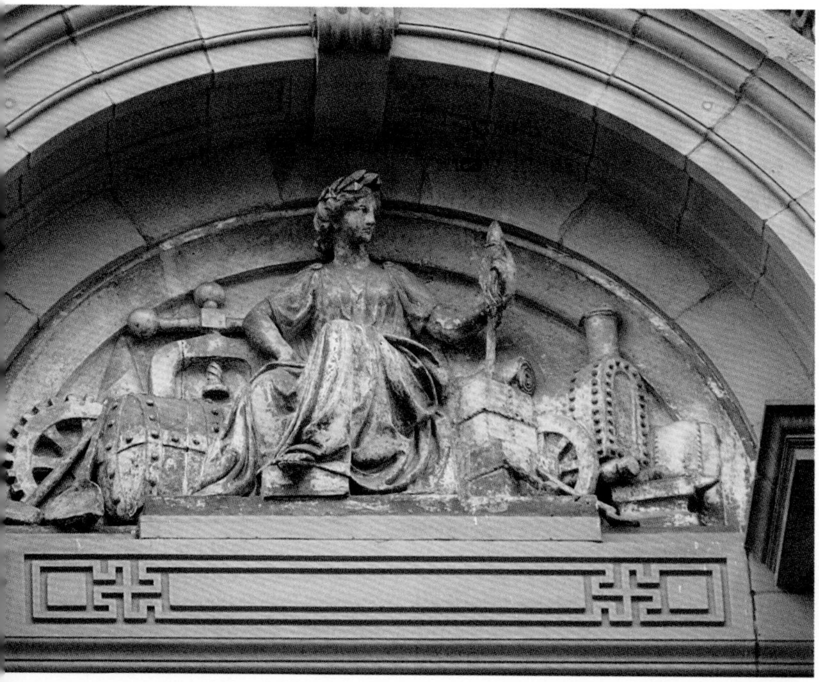

[56] Free Trade Hall: central sculptural panel over upper windows. Sculptor: John Thomas.

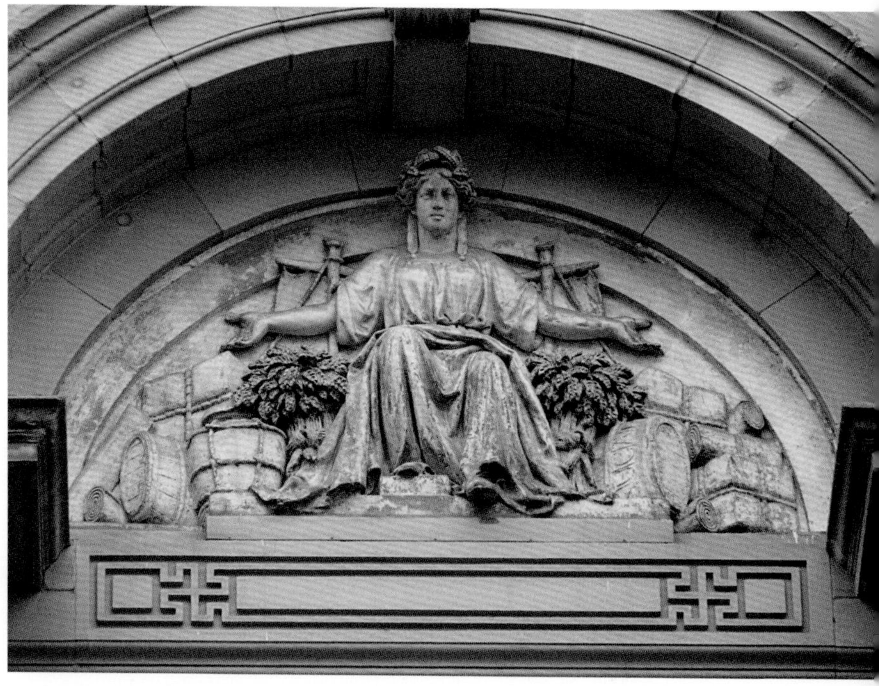

might be understood as the medium through which this bounty and global commerce were to be realised. But this itself was an act of amnesia. On this site radical women, many of whom had formed their own reform societies, had played an unprecedented prominent part in the demonstration that led to Peterloo (as they did when Peterloo was commemorated in Chartist demonstrations in the early 1840s).[155] They wore white, symbolising the purity of their cause, and carried carefully embroidered banners. They bore red caps of liberty made of silk or satin and decorated with gold lace, and presented written addresses to the speakers.[156] They were also disproportionately targeted during the massacre, in which four women died and some 168 were wounded, and their prominence led to cruel and salacious parodies in the press and by printmakers.[157]

The building that finally took over the site of the massacre therefore elides any memory of those groups of organised female protestors from nearly forty years before. It delivers instead a form of sculptural allegorisation that is more conventional and more vaguely inclusive. In their meetings female protestors had often given wider meaning to their personal experiences by drawing on 'biblical, classical and historical references', and notable women from history had provided them with precedents for their campaigns.[158] Indeed, the cap of liberty, while it had associations with the French Revolution, was a Roman symbol denoting liberation from slavery.[159] The symbolic registers of these women, both the sculpted allegories and the real protestors, had some points of overlap, for instance, the rigmarole of purity, the theatrics of display and gesture, and the classical allusions. But the women at Peterloo had carried symbols made with their own skill and labour, products of their work in the textile economy. They challenged the idea that the public sphere was or should be exclusively masculine, and emphasised the links between women's work, including as nurturers, and the demand for a qualified ('universal' but still male) political liberty.[160] The woman of Free Trade, the allegorical figure in stone, is not a labouring figure but a replacement for the labour of others who are not present; she may have a public presence because she is carved on the facade of the building but her role is constrained by a petrified, highly conventionalised form of allegory. One journalist wrote dismissively of the women at Peterloo: 'We met her unblushing front at every turn. Her badges and her banners were everywhere unfurled and she imagined herself triumphant and unconquerable.'[161] She would be made invisible (much as, later in 1819, the cap of liberty had been made illegal), first by violence and then by the desiccated allegorisation of Free Trade.

In all this, publicness – as in the Infirmary and the palazzo warehouses – was associated with the political beliefs of Free Trade. It took over public space, saved it from the memory of state violence and popular outrage but also redefined it, casting it as a liberal private version of public facility. The triumph of the idea of Free Trade was made into stone, its final arrival as political common sense. 'Dedicated – like the United States of America – to a proposition',[162] the Free Trade Hall housed its public functions in the richest outward finery of the Italian Renaissance, a street architecture both expressive and decorous. It also arrived at the watershed of this particular architectural–political alliance. The year after its completion, 1857, was to see defeats for Cobden and Bright in the election and a consequent crisis in the Manchester Free Trade movement.[163] But, with Disraeli's Tories abandoning protection, Free Trade had become economic common sense.

Finished only a year after the Free Trade Hall, the Watts warehouse (designed by Travis & Mangnall) was the most ostentatious warehouse in Manchester (fig. 57). Built for the textile firm of S. and J. Watts, the warehouse was a development of their father's proto-department store, the Manchester Bazaar, housed elsewhere in the city.[164] The Watts family were prominent among Manchester's new industrial bourgeoisie: they were eminent subscribers and donors, keen to see their city made civic. James Watts himself was Manchester's mayor between 1855 and 1857 and was knighted in the latter year. The building of the brothers' warehouse was perceived by their peers, if not by others in a different position in Manchester's stratified society, as an act of civic boosterism at the very moment when the city was at the forefront of the country's attention because of the Art Treasures Exhibition (1857). The Watts warehouse was 'an honour to our country, and speaks well for the future of Manchester ... the most splendid adornment of this city'; 'Watts's is the sight of Manchester'; and, more ambivalently, 'the people of the day were astonished at the temerity of its owners'.[165]

'Temerity' is important here. Portland Street's decorum was certainly tested by the Watts warehouse. Watts disturbed the balance between medical and commercial interests in its location – obviously when the House of Recovery sold some of its land to the Watts brothers in 1851 and then, seeking to benefit from the increased land values, entirely in 1855.[166] As the largest building in the city, this monster warehouse challenged the residential allusions of nearby palazzo warehouses. Its exterior was a display board of architectural styles, while its interior housed a cornucopia of finished textile products. And it disturbed the architectural balance. It was a hundred feet high, took up a whole block and was lit on all sides by arrays of windows; some even claimed that it was a danger to 'public taste' in its appeal to the mere effect of scale.[167] Thus it brought a new kind of architectural rivalry to Portland Street, dwarfing Walters's nearby buildings and creating a new roofscape by breaking up the outline of its upper parts (using a different architectural prototype – the Fondaco dei Turchi in Venice). To one writer its battered base suggested the Egyptians, 'the ground floor is certainly Italian, the first Elizabethan, the second Italian, the third Francois Premier, the fourth a plain story of square columns ... and above ... large French Gothic rose windows'.[168] Despite the continuity of cornice lines and string-courses, the sheer bulk and eclecticism of surface details broke with the Walters subtype. Inside, further natural lighting was provided by five light-wells and a top-lit central staircase, an extraordinary assembly of decorated iron banisters and flights of steps, in a space that scales up suddenly from intimacy to tiered distance, paralleling some of the same devices inside the Free Trade Hall (fig. 58). The grid of iron columns seems to have encouraged a crude and no doubt temporary division of internal space. Exterior and interior were linked by the idea of each floor containing a variety of products (millinery, drapery, ladies' hats,

[57] Watts warehouse, Portland Street, 1857. Architects: Travis & Mangnall. Engraving, *Illustrated London News* (1856).

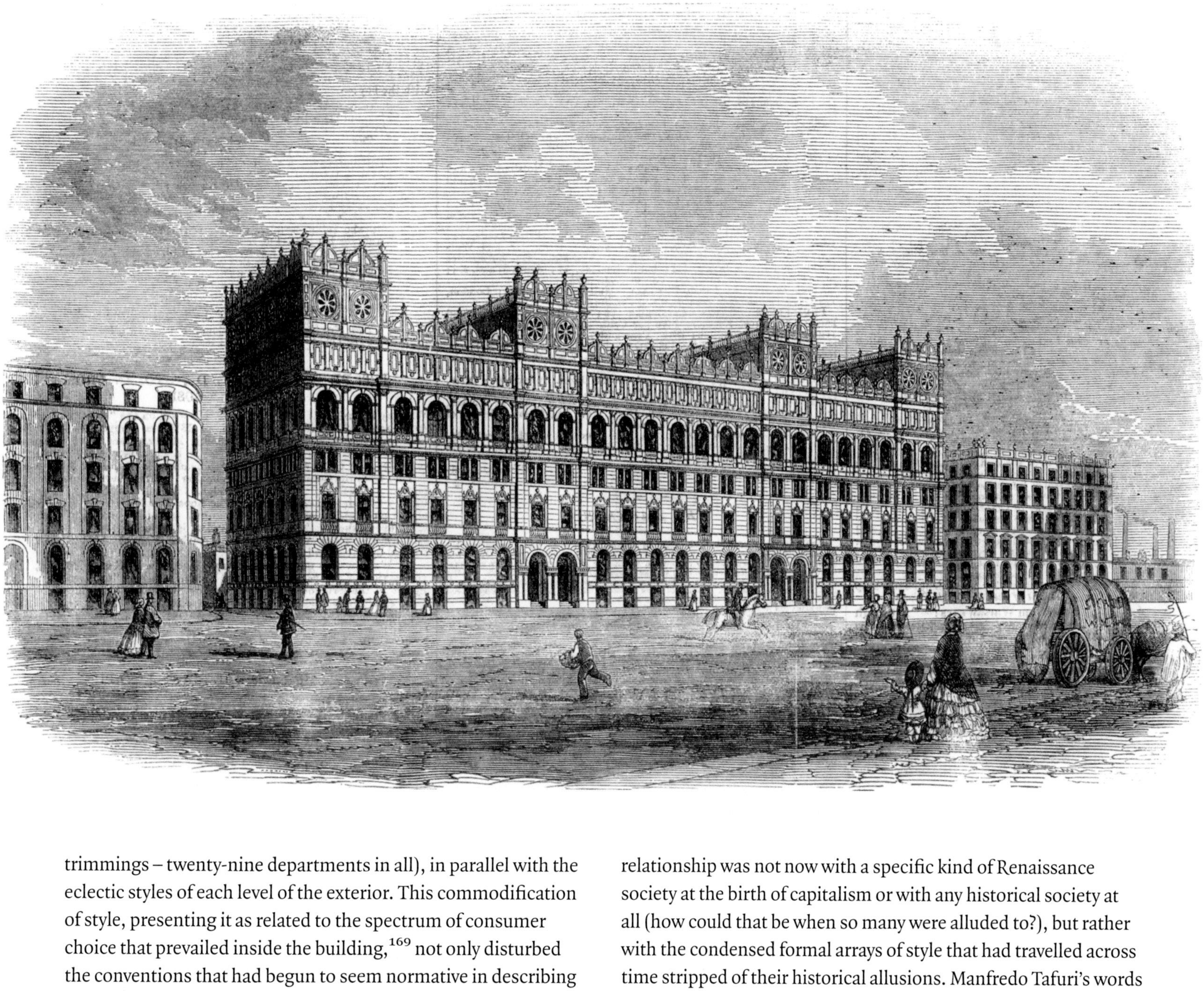

trimmings – twenty-nine departments in all), in parallel with the eclectic styles of each level of the exterior. This commodification of style, presenting it as related to the spectrum of consumer choice that prevailed inside the building,[169] not only disturbed the conventions that had begun to seem normative in describing the street but also established an entirely different relationship with the historical basis for the styles that it appropriated. The relationship was not now with a specific kind of Renaissance society at the birth of capitalism or with any historical society at all (how could that be when so many were alluded to?), but rather with the condensed formal arrays of style that had travelled across time stripped of their historical allusions. Manfredo Tafuri's words on Chicago seem apt as a summing up of the Watts warehouse: 'by projecting its image into the commercial center of the city, [it]

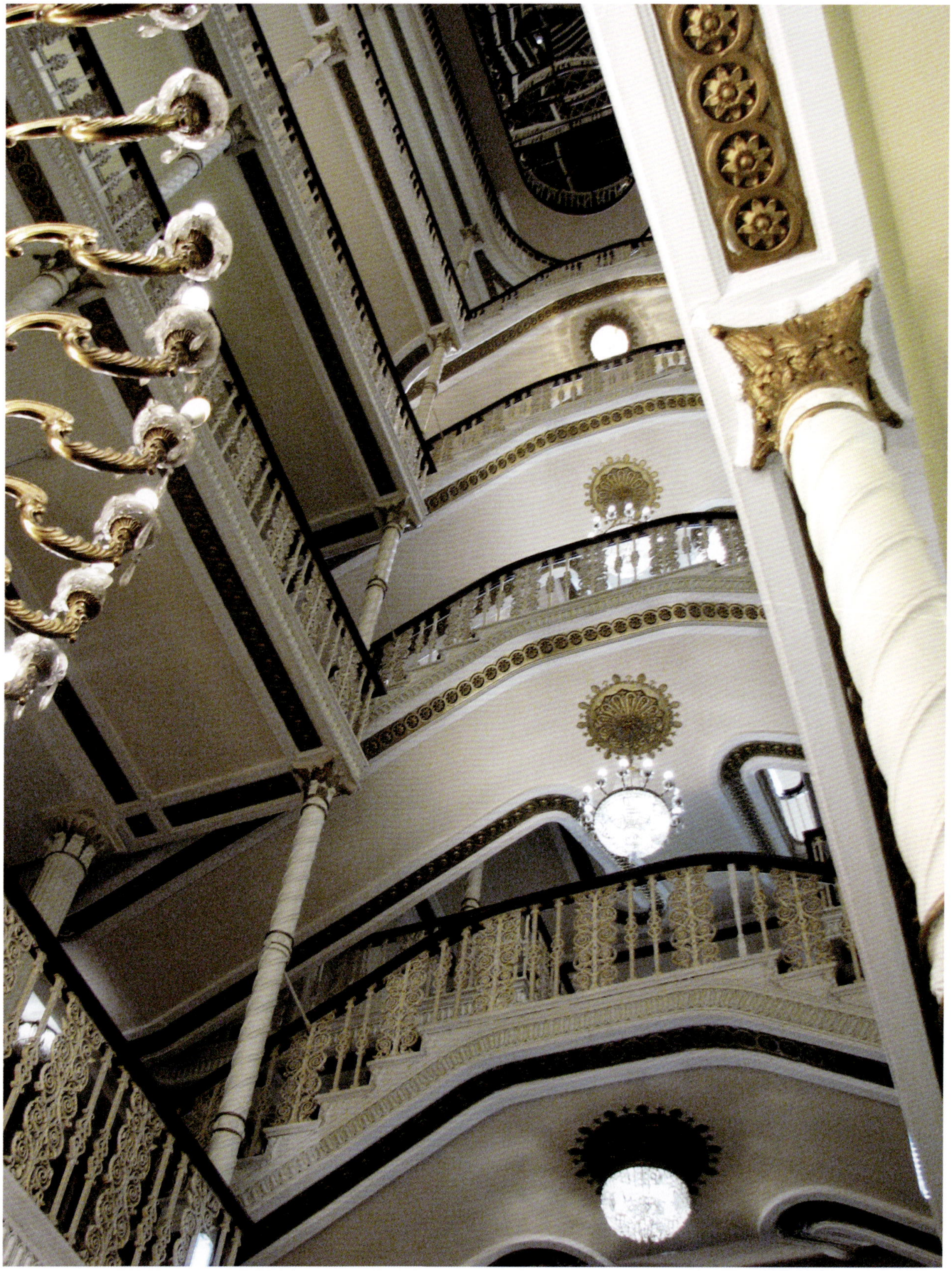

[58] Watts warehouse, Portland Street, 1857: staircase. Architects: Travis & Mangnall.

creates an unstable equilibrium between the independence of the single corporation and the organization of collective capital.'[170] The individualised image within a contest of such images has now become not so much an alternative to the discipline inherent to the collective, but its immanent logic.

And so the Watts warehouse signalled another image of bourgeois identity. Less 'tender concealment', this was now a form of spectacular enchantment: middle-class emporium as imperium. The global complex of trade and the calculating gaze of accumulation were now directed at the sensuous delights of consumption. The palazzo warehouse may have continued elsewhere on the street, but with Watts an architectural imagery that was shared for a brief period was dispersed; the spectacular needs of a consuming public were now prioritised over the collective identity of the industrialists.[171] Part of the Watts warehouse's avowed civilising mission was the necessary demolition of embarrassingly poor housing on this site: housing 'of a moral character that any great city can do without'.[172] These people were displaced elsewhere, probably to the new bye-law housing in grids of streets to the west. With this displacement and demolition, the warehouse became naturalised; the 'irregular' or 'small' were made to seem out of place, ripe for redevelopment. If the working classes were the victims here, it was because they were the collateral casualties of a political and then commercial battle over space, first between the landed classes and industrialists, and then between different sections of the shopocracy.

THE AREA IN AND AROUND PICCADILLY AND DOWN THE length of Portland Street had been produced within a certain view of Manchester's fortunes, in which the old power of landownership had come to be eclipsed by a new logic of capital accumulation. The financial (the necessary surpluses), political (the distinct ideology) and technical (the architect, the manufacturers, the warehousemen) means had been assembled to reshape this area both in the image of the industrial bourgeoisie and in service to its developing ascendancy. As David Harvey has written, 'the preindustrial city had to be disciplined, weaned away as it were from its mercantilist proclivities, its monopolistic practices, and its assertion of the primacy of place over a capitalist organization of space in which relative rather than absolute locations had to dominate'.[173]

Long before Hitler's bombs and post-war replanning, the specifics of this cityscape of Free Trade had already been dismantled. It was a victim of changes in the later Victorian era: the Nightingale ward and a need for a bigger hospital site; the final flight to the residential suburbs; a different understanding of architecture's relation to morality; and a new sense that competitive commercialism could be an architectural matter. Even more telling than the loss of some of these buildings was the loss of an understanding of their concerted significance in representing the ideas of the industrial bourgeoisie. Cobden was no architectural theorist and, as his architectural right-hand man, Walters was virtually mute. But where an idea takes on the belief that it is obvious – and this is what happened to Free Trade – it loses its urgency, the sense that it needs renewal, and becomes the way of the world.

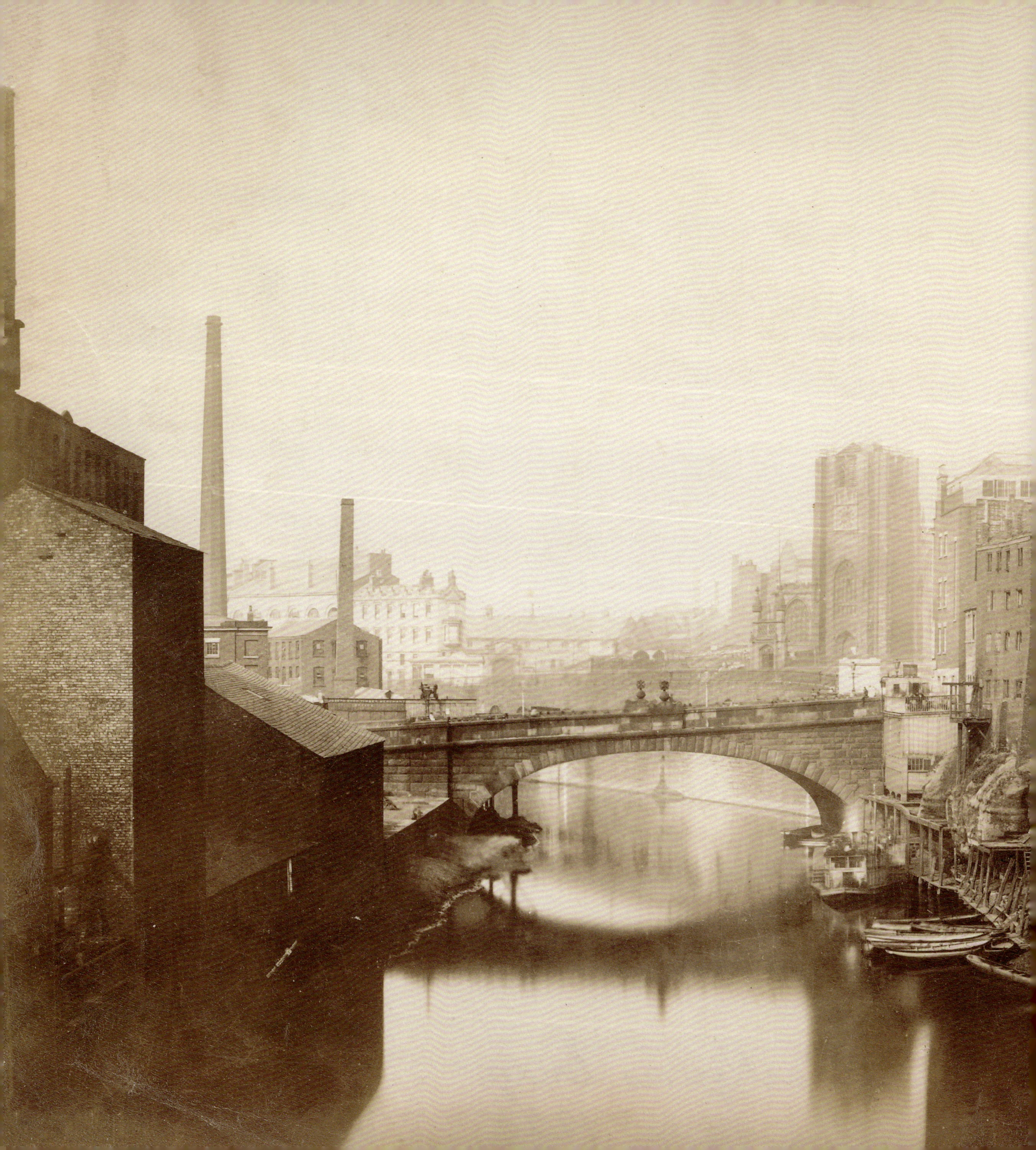

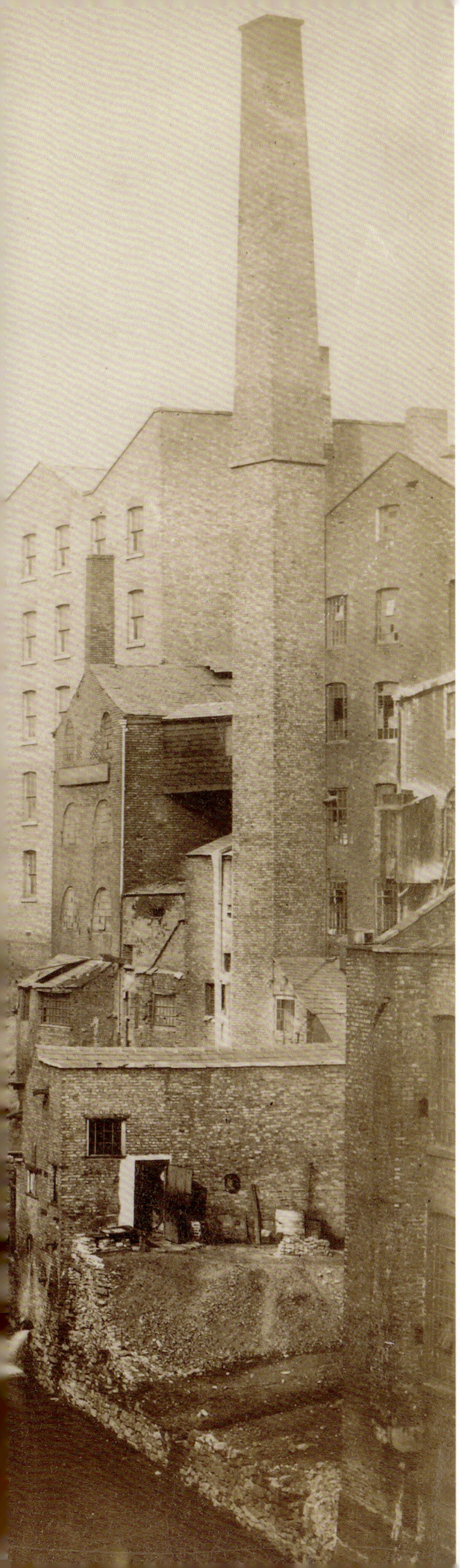

[59] James Mudd, 'The River Irwell from Blackfriars Bridge', 1859. Albumen silver print. Canadian Centre for Architecture, Montreal.

3 Ancient and Modern

Photography Imagining an Epoch

THE IMAGE SEEMS EMBLEMATIC, OVER AND ABOVE WHAT is represented (fig. 59). The photograph is solidly, even reassuringly, balanced, as if there were nothing arbitrary about the scene. The lack of any apparent movement adds to the sense of gravity and quietness. The city appears as an epitome of itself.

When the photographer James Mudd chose this view, 'The River Irwell from Blackfriars Bridge' (1859), from midway across a bridge and looking along a river which fills the foreground before the next bridge, he organised the scene around an imagined equivalence between two positions. There is the place from which the photograph is taken and there is another place or position in the picture's depth, somewhere on that far bridge. Yet, where that other equivalence should be, there are two stone orbs marking the midpoint of the bridge's parapets, a mirror image reminding us of the parapet beside which our own lens must be located. It is as if a vanishing point, denied by the sudden bend of the river leftward just beyond the bridge, has been bracketed for future reference. Below this midpoint is a flattened oval created by the arch of the bridge and its reflection in the stilled water (no doubt a result of slow shutter speed). That oval, in turn, is like a frame that contains a summary of the image as a whole: darker and more solid geometries on the left give way to diffuse reflections and misty forms that fill the rest of the shape. It even has its own cross-hair where the waterline cuts the vertical drain shadow. Thus, beneath our equivalent position on the far bridge, there is a metaphoric mirroring of the camera eye on our bridge.[1]

Another group of equivalences traverses the river from bank to bank, crossing the scene from either side, joined or reconciled by the bridge that spans the river. But again these equivalences are contained by a set of mirror images, the repeated verticals of chimneys on either bank of the river that seem to diminish towards the middle area of the image. The thick tapering vertical of a chimney on each side reinforces the side edges of the image, fencing in the scene. The other equivalences across the image are starker and less assimilable, establishing it as contained and symmetrical. To the left of the river the brick walls and slate roofs of industrial buildings are simplified and flattened out, producing broad planes of dark tone sharply defined by straight edges and angled geometries in high contrast with the speckled effect of individual bricks in a plane of wall or the lines of slate on a simple angle of roof. These buildings are aligned towards the river but present no face onto it. To the right, however, a busier amalgam of riverside clutter and the apparently contingent proximities of buildings seem to indicate both a complex shifting of uses and the deteriorating and impermanent aspect of the whole. On this side, formal distinctions are made by localised characteristics and differences of material; the scale of incident seems smaller, keyed to the patterns of fenestration, the angles of boats and the irregular rhythms of wooden pillars. On this side of the photograph, then, an extraordinary density and simplicity of form edits out incident and information. On the other side, however, the bank of the river presents an extraordinary density of information. One side seems to offer the city as made anew, resulting in part from its own new abruptness of form and in part from a newly abrupt editing of surface and tone, plane and space. The other side offers the city constantly decaying and renewing in local, ad hoc and incomplete ways: the city as palimpsest, as a tracing of its various irreducible pasts.

Mudd himself wrote about photographic composition, if not in ways that relate directly to this image. He emphasised a difference between the photograph as document and the photograph as work of art, dismissing 'early photography' (before the 1860s) for its concern with detail:

> *The ardent experimenter of that period looked with pride and wonder at the picture of a stack of grim chimneys, taken perhaps, from his little laboratory window, or his surprising view of a dead brick wall and water tubs. He could count every brick: that was the marvel. But the novelty of this soon wore off, and something more was desired – namely beauty in the object itself. So the photographer went to nature, and the hills, and fields, and streams became fitting subjects for his art.*[2]

It may be possible to understand the Irwell view as combining these approaches: both the 'marvel' of 'every brick' and the kind of broader treatment that Mudd called 'certain agreeable outlines and combinations of forms'.[3] And yet the abrupt changes of tone and plane on the left, their sheer abstract density, seem to point to a position, an aesthetic, quite distinct from the oppositions that he conjured up in his writing.

The bricks and slates and flat planes, of course, belonged to real buildings which housed real work. The *Manchester Directory* tells us that in 1859, when this photograph was taken, the buildings on both sides of the river contained a great diversity of trades. To inventorise the various buildings and their occupants in the image is to gain a picture – perhaps oblique to the one presented in Mudd's image – of the tangled functions and juxtaposed building uses of this area of Manchester and Salford. On the Salford bank to the left, there was Sharp & Galloway's sugar-refining business, Clegg's Court Printing Company and a variety of businesses: timber merchants, fish curers and egg importers, a chimney-top maker and a packing-case maker, a number of spinners and cotton manufacturers in Bridge Mills (beside the river), manufacturers of iron safes and patent springs, as well as various other iron merchants, small-ware manufacturers and makers of engineers' tools. On the Manchester side there was Franklin's Furnace and Machine Company and the Northampton Patent Enamelled Leather Cloth Company, as well as gunmakers, a silk merchant and a toy manufacturer, a brass founder and coppersmiths, a cork manufacturer, a beer retailer, a cotton-waste dealer and traders in oil and tallow.[4] Such are the multifarious enterprises that feed off the larger industries of the city, that cluster in the rented spaces or 'flats' of its mills or in small workshops, that share sources of power and that use the same dump for their effluent. Not so much a less developed phase of industry, they coexist and are more flexible, at least compared to the monolithic character of the city's central warehouse districts or of its larger mills elsewhere.

Beyond the banks of the river, a great variety of buildings and their functions are shown in Mudd's photograph. The building to the right of the stumpy cathedral tower is Ben Lang's Music Hall, and above this is the chimney of a copper-works. Those distant chimneys to the left of the cathedral are part of School Mills on the River Irk, while the buildings immediately above Victoria Bridge and to its left are the centuries-old Chetham's College and the much more recent Palatine Buildings and Hotel.[5] Victoria Bridge was itself a relatively new addition to the river, replacing the medieval Old Salford Bridge in 1838. Formal equivalences in the photograph are therefore made out of seemingly somewhat incompatible material: sites of learning and sites of manual labour; places of worship and places of manufacture; the medieval and the ultra-modern; classical embellishment in stone and sheer surfaces of brick.

The idea of a memory crisis in the nineteenth century is a theme common to many modern writers who have identified it with the effects, including the traumas, of urban upheaval.[6] In Charles Baudelaire's poem 'Le Cygne', the camp of shacks in the Place du Carrousel suggests (or throws up) the *Aeneid*; the loss of the old Paris has shattered landmarks and separated the modern from its continuity with the past. Antiquity, to put it rather differently, seemed at this historical moment to be the necessary consequence of modernity.[7] To pick up my argument in the Introduction, however, the issue of memory and change, of a city in the convulsions of sudden transformation, had its earlier and specifically industrial manifestation in Manchester. Here the shock was equivalent to a natural disaster; its actors and their interests were much less recognisable, its urban pleasures much less obvious. If Manchester was not just a new city quantifiably but a new quality of urban experience and a new kind of city whose form was changing with a jarring rapidity, how might we expect a new medium of visual representation to manifest these phenomena, to relate the old and the modern in meaningful ways? One of the questions that therefore lurks behind an image like 'The River Irwell from Blackfriars Bridge' is whether this photograph, or perhaps any photograph at that time, could depict the new kinds of urban spaces that many saw epitomised by Manchester. In particular, could photography's particular relation to time (its anterior future tense) be used to fix the disappearing past and the fast-developing present, to capture potent images of the relation between old and new? It is a question that, I shall argue, finds several different answers in Mudd's work, especially through its mutating reproductions.

While 'The River Irwell from Blackfriars Bridge' is one of the most emblematic images of the industrial city, it has also, perhaps because of that status, become one of the most enigmatic, its layers of meaning and its history of multiple uses accompanying different texts unrecognised and unexplored. This chapter discusses how the idea of epochal change achieves its significance through representation. I take the view that the medium – photography in this case – has a power peculiar to itself rather than an entirely dependent or functional relation with power (even *power* in the Foucauldian sense).[8] Photography can signify without having to be absorbed by language; it can conjure up what Roland Barthes called the *studium* – the regulatory or ideological aspects of vision – without being determined by it.[9] This encapsulates, for instance, a broader argument that rejects both the essentialising impetus in modernist accounts of photography (where photographic meaning is folded in upon itself) and the contextualising tendencies of post-modernism (where meaning is entirely the function of some other cause).[10] The chapter will take this 'historical and ontological complexity' of photography as fundamental to understanding why a certain image of a city becomes representative across different sites of its viewing, as well as in understanding what is excluded from that image by these discursive functions. To help focus the discussion, the sites to which I shall refer – this photograph as well as others by Mudd – are identified under three thematic groupings: the city as iconic of industrialism; the city as topoi (or the places of the pre-industrial city); and the city as a theatre of memories.

MUDD'S PHOTOGRAPH HAS BECOME PERHAPS THE SINGLE most reproduced image of nineteenth-century Manchester. Whether this has anything to do with Mudd's range of interests

[60] William Wyld, *Manchester from Kersal Moor, with Rustic Figures and Goats*, 1852. Watercolour. Royal Collection.

as a practitioner, or indeed his proximity to influential groups, is unclear, though both the ambiguities and the inclusiveness of the image may be linked to these conditions. He was the most important of Manchester's early photographers, equally concerned with the experimental, evidentiary and aesthetic sides of his métier even if, as his writing shows, he was capable of polemicising against one or other of them at times. His career flourished within the circles of Manchester's industrial bourgeoisie, and as a member of the Manchester Literary and Philosophical Society he received many commissions from fellow members (the most notable was his work for Charles Beyer from 1856, where he portrayed Beyer, Peacock and Company's new locomotives in silent perfection before they left their Manchester yard; see fig. 2).[11] Mudd benefited from the 'vigorous polytechnic culture' of that society, where industrial entrepreneurialism, professional and scientific knowledge, and antiquarianism all interacted, mutually legitimating themselves in what has been described as 'a constant synergistic ferment'.[12]

He had actually started out in a different class from many of his associates, as a pattern designer for a calico printer, a position that was much closer to the aspirational artisan so mythologised by Victorian biographers like Samuel Smiles (James Watt being the prime example). Mudd was also exactly the kind of artisan that the Mechanics' Institute, established in 1824 and supported by Manchester's industrial and scientific leaders, was intended to help (see Chapter 2).[13] Textile work continued for a time alongside his photography, the two with clear points of complementarity in their printing and chemical processes (he collaborated with Joseph Sidebotham, who was also involved in both fields). Mudd brought what Steve Edwards has identified as a petit bourgeois subjectivity into productive contact with the industrial bourgeoisie he encountered in the Literary and Philosophical Society.[14] Later, he became eminent in the Manchester Photographic Society (formed in 1855), which was supported by many of Manchester's most prominent scientists and industrialists, including William Fairbairn, J. P. Joule and James Nasmyth (all vice presidents of the society).[15] Mudd's images of the city are therefore likely to have had at least points of correspondence with the industrial bourgeoisie's attitudes to Manchester, though it is not straightforward to establish what those were.

Part of the problem is how long these images' emblematic qualities have remained unexamined. In the twentieth century Mudd's Irwell photograph was almost invariably associated with, and seen to illustrate, the 'first industrial city' or 'shock city' of the Industrial Revolution, and this somewhat schematic connection has persisted. No other image of Manchester has the ubiquity of this photograph, not even William Wyld's two paintings (and subsequent engravings) of Manchester from Kersal Moor (1835 and 1852)[16] (fig. 60). The image has had a far longer life than any, now lost, moment of public display, and part of the reason might be that, with every new reproduction that the photographic medium made possible, the image was visually adjusted to its new context. Cut and mounted in a portrait format so that most of the right-hand or Manchester bank was seen but none of the Salford bank, the photograph was sold by the Petschler firm as a *carte de visite* in the 1860s.[17] Restored to most of its extent, it was reproduced in two books of reminiscences at the turn of the twentieth century: Louis Hayes's *Reminiscences of Manchester and Some of its Local Surroundings from the Year 1840* (1905) and Joseph Corbett's *The River Irwell* (1907), which will be discussed later. At the other end of the twentieth century the photograph, cropped at the bottom and on either side, was used in H. J. Dyos and Michael Wolff's *The Victorian City: Images and Realities* (1973)[18] and reproduced as the cover image of Robert Kargon's *Science in Victorian Manchester: Enterprise and Expertise* (1977), while Gary Messinger published a detail of the right bank in his *Manchester in the Victorian Age* (1985), where it faces a long quotation from Friedrich Engels about one of the most appalling views in Manchester. The Engels connection was reinforced by the image being used on the cover of the 1987 Penguin edition of *The Condition of the Working Class in England*, where it was cropped so that only its right bank was visible. Finally, Mudd's photograph was reproduced in Alan Kidd's general history of the city, *Manchester* (1993).[19]

If the image has a remarkable ubiquity, equally remarkable is the lack of commentary on it, let alone analysis of it. It simply stands for Manchester, and for the Industrial Revolution and the

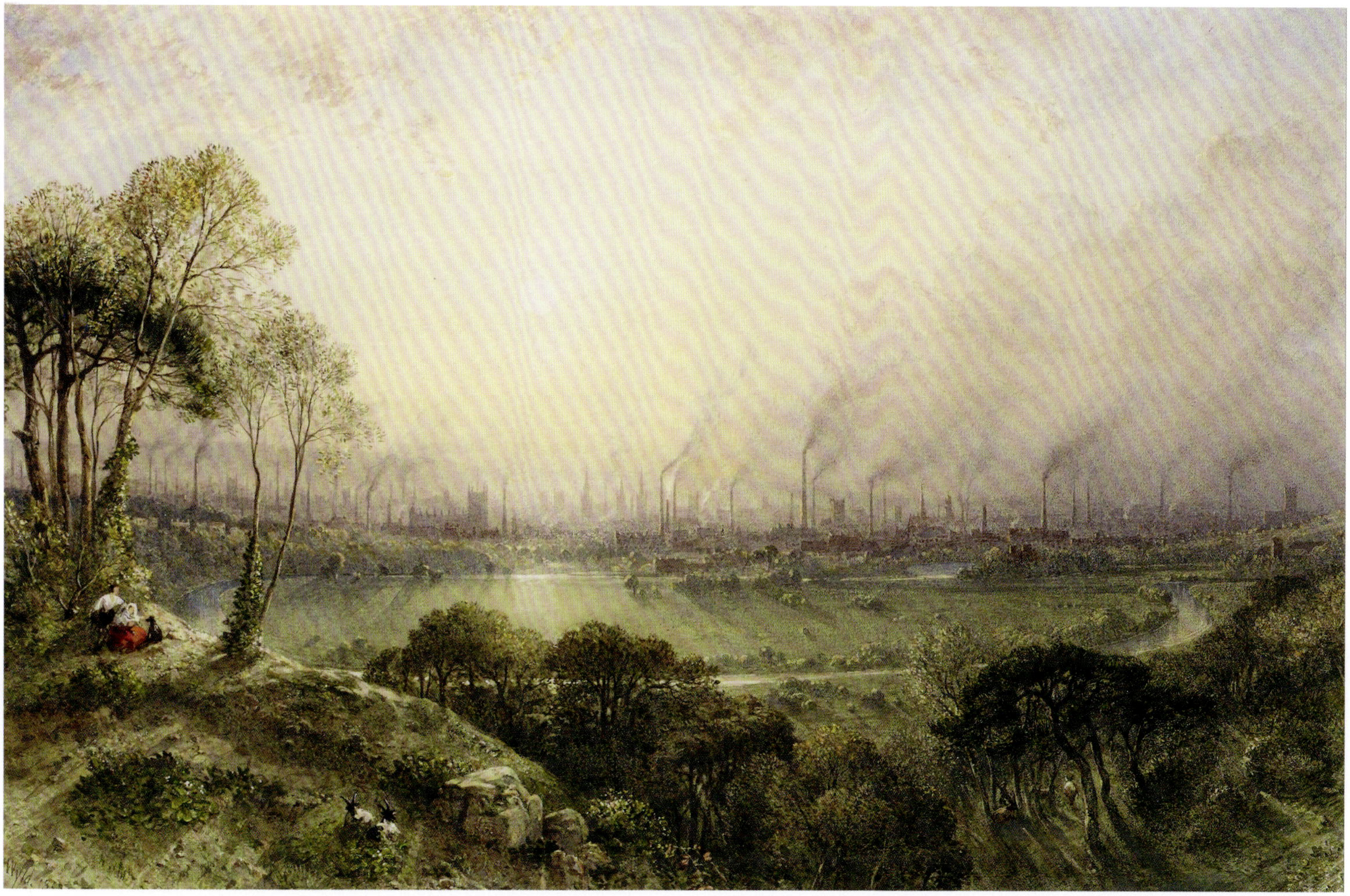

industrial city more generally. It has become iconic not just of the city but – because of Manchester's paradigmatic status – of the impact of industrialism on cities per se. The shock city is what is read into those chimneys, those planes of wall and their dwarfing and hemming in of the cathedral tower. And all this regardless – I want to suggest – of any contradictory readings, not least the contradictory qualities within the image itself. Associating it with Engels is particularly inapposite, not simply because Engels does not describe the specific aspects of Manchester brought out by the image but because the image does not appear to have been made with any revelatory or critical purpose, as will become apparent later in this chapter. The image is dominated by a river and a cathedral tower, on the face of it quite conventional elements in city views before the Industrial Revolution. Yet the river is a feature that for 200 years since the Industrial Revolution has not been especially eminent or even easily visible in central Manchester, though it forms the boundary between the twin cities of Manchester and Salford. During that time, it has usually been treated as an open sewer or ignored in a city that is rarely remembered for its natural topographic features – and yet the image has been the occasion for some remarkable acts of river remembering that have, as we shall see, an anti- or pre-industrial aspect to them.[20] The cathedral, equally, has never been regarded as one of Manchester's most impressive buildings. And so the contradictions may be seen to reside partly in the river and in the cathedral's specific combination of oldness and newness. The cathedral had been upgraded from a medieval collegiate church only because of the city's tumultuous expansion and was therefore nominally expressive of the new city status; the river had been made into an industrial sewer by the same process. One made up, promoted, the other brought low, both from the same causes. However, this is to jump too quickly to conclusions.

The photograph's ubiquity can be explored further through its association with Engels's book. Published fourteen years before Mudd took his photograph, *The Condition of the Working Class in England* was not translated into English until 1886 (in New York; first published in the UK in 1892). The photograph's subsequent association with the book was clearly intended to evoke Engels's description of 'Ducie Bridge über d. Irk', as the map to the original German edition called it, and so Mudd's bridge and Engels's bridge come into ahistoric juxtaposition, as if to reinforce the arguments made about each other (fig. 61). Ducie Bridge was actually several hundred yards to the east of Blackfriars Bridge, following the Irk up-river after its junction with the Irwell, but Engels's text points the reader back in the direction of the cathedral. Engels's account of Manchester employs the device of a viewing point, a set-piece prospect of the cityscape. While it is often referred to, it needs quoting at length:

> *The river from this bridge, mercifully concealed from mortals of small stature by a parapet as high as a man, is characteristic of this whole district. At the bottom flows, or rather stagnates, the Irk, a narrow, coal-black, foul-smelling stream, full of debris and refuse, which it deposits on the lower right bank. In dry weather, a long string of the most disgusting blackish-green slime pools are left standing on this bank, from the depths of which bubbles of miasmatic gas constantly rise and give forth a stench unendurable even on the bridge forty or fifty feet above the surface of the stream. But besides this, the stream itself is checked every few paces by high weirs, behind which slime and refuse accumulate and rot in thick masses. Above the bridge are tanneries, bonemills, and gasworks, from which all drains and refuse find their way into the Irk, which receives further the contents of all the neighbouring sewers and privies. It may easily be imagined, therefore, what sort of residue the stream deposits. Below the bridge you look upon the piles of debris, the refuse, filth, and offal from the courts on the steep left bank; here each house is packed close behind its neighbour and a bit of each is visible, all black, smoky, crumbling, ancient, with broken panes and window-frames. The background is furnished by old barrack-like factory buildings. On the lower right bank stands a long row of houses and mills, the second row being a ruin without a roof, piled with debris; the third stands so low that the lowest floor is uninhabitable, and therefore without windows or doors. Here the background embraces the pauper burial-ground, the station of Liverpool and Leeds railway, and, in the rear of this, the Workhouse, the 'Poor-Law Bastille' of Manchester, which, like a citadel, looks threateningly down from behind its high walls and parapets on the hilltop, upon the working peoples' quarter below.*[21]

As he tells us straightaway, Engels's 'view' is hardly a view at all and the prospect he describes is an anti-prospect, one intended to repel the senses, debase the imagination and provoke a moral and political reaction in the reader.[22] There is no outside here; significant difference has been abolished. The bridge itself is not a form that connects, that gathers the elements into unity – as it might be described as doing in Mudd's image – but a partially obstructed outlook onto a scene of dislocation and chaos. Similarly, the customary picturesque modality of broken forms and irregularity was usually intended to engineer a continuity between nature and art, a continuity that 'blithely cauterized' the details of blight, poverty and decay, remaking or mediating them so that disgust could be contained within the represented scene.[23] In Engels's description, however, this modality is implied but at the same time made gross, pushed beyond the niceties of containment; there is no bridging synthesis that can transcend it. The scene is revealed to be inhabited by nothing but piles of debris and refuse, below the bridge and on the left bank as much as on the right, the products of a violent dichotomy between humanity and nature. The very words 'slime', 'debris' and 'refuse' are used two, three and four times respectively in the description, as if to convey the banal repetition of the obscene in what is glimpsed beyond the parapet.[24]

At the level of this description the organising devices of the prospect and the picturesque provide a parallel between Ducie Bridge and the way in which Engels organises his account of Manchester as a whole. Engels also reiterates his trope of Manchester as a place that insulates its misery from the eyes of the 'money aristocracy': by the shops that line the main thoroughfares, by the immense hotels and warehouses, and even by the large gardens and villas of the bourgeoisie.[25] The 'mercifully concealed' (*zartfühlenderweise ... verhüllt*) view from Ducie Bridge

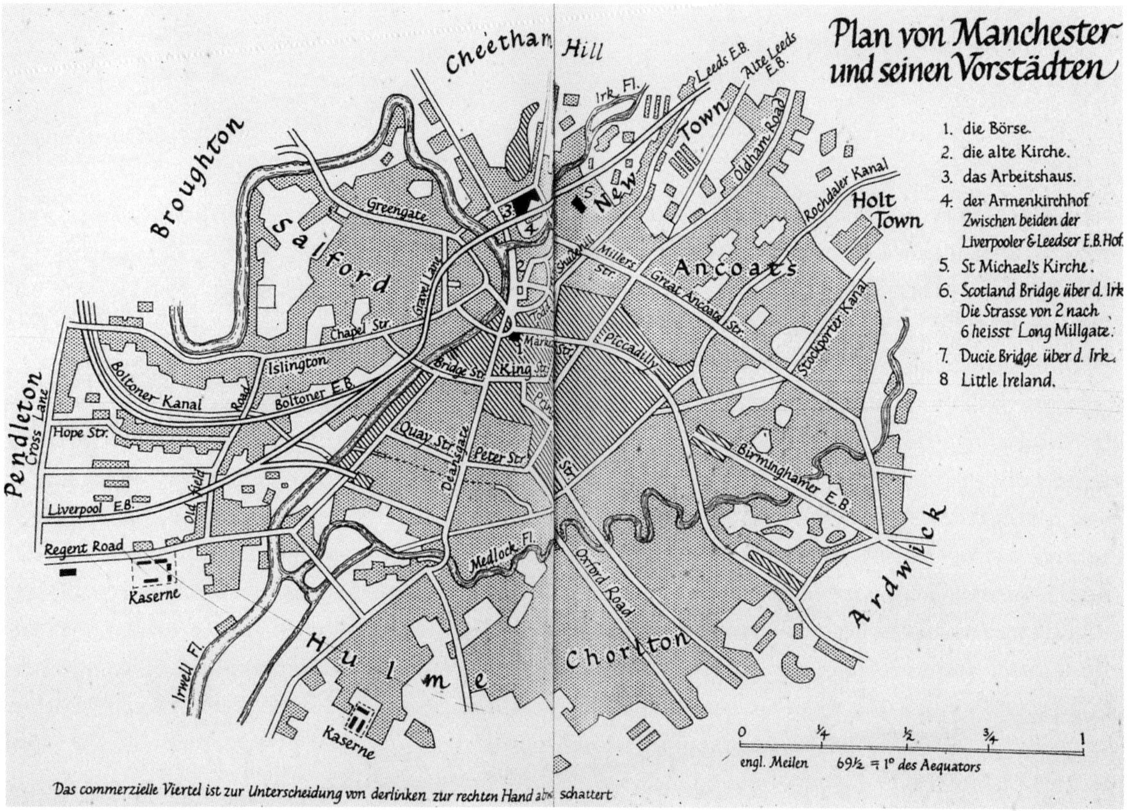

[61] Friedrich Engels's map of Manchester, from *Die Lage der arbeitenden Klasse in England* (1845).

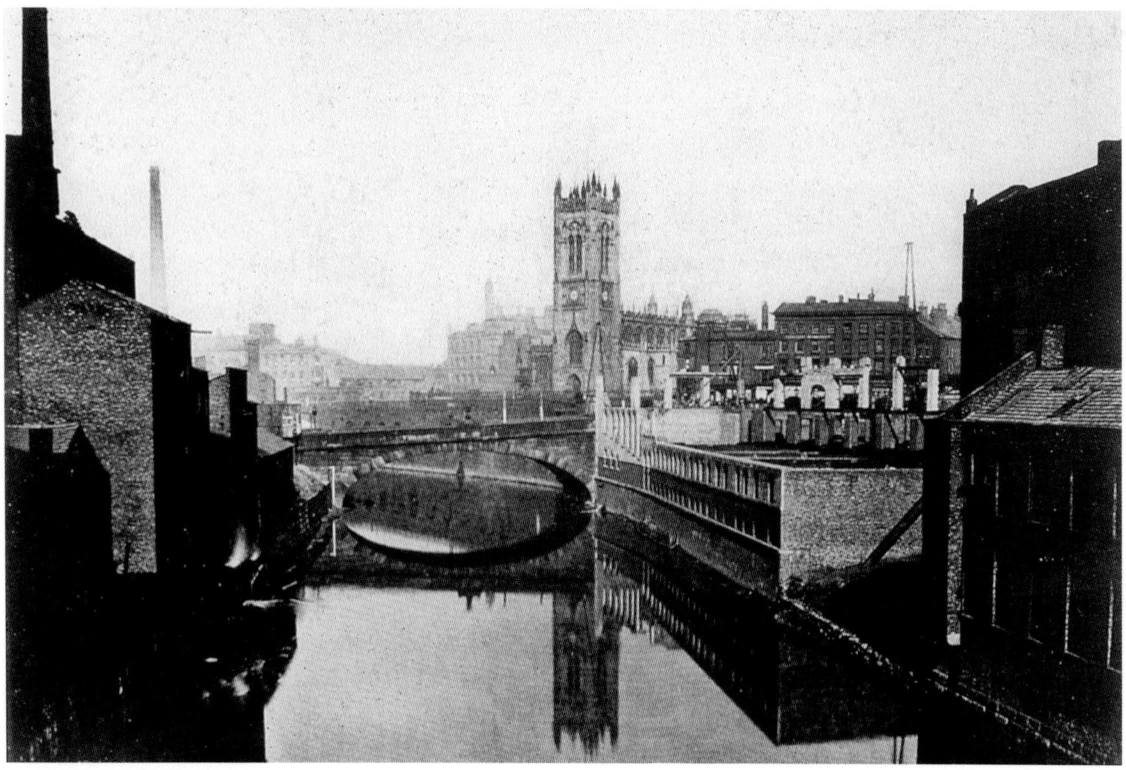

[62] Alfred Brothers, 'Victoria Bridge'. Photograph from Brothers, *Manchester As It Is* (1878).

therefore epitomises the larger ways in which Manchester's 'hypocritical plan' (*heuchlerische Bauart*) as a whole works systematically towards 'so tender a concealment' (*so zartfühlende Verhüllung*) of its underside.[26] As Engels's map shows, the result is a kind of dystopian diagram where the workhouse, the pauper's graveyard, the cathedral and the Exchange are suddenly in close axial proximity. The city is a work of design and intent, not the result of change or natural occurrences.[27] Chaos – shock – is seen to signify. Going behind these facades or, in the case of Ducie Bridge, looking over this high parapet reveals the obscene: the hidden squalor that issues from naked relations of power. Henri Lefebvre's definition of the obscene is useful here, precisely because he brings it back to its roots in architecture and space. For Lefebvre the obscene is understood as a general category of social practice that is banished or excluded from the scene by a process of 'repressing those gestures which are not prescribed by monumental space'.[28] This was also the crucial point for Engels. The disorder and disintegration of Manchester, the obscene, is a necessary part of causes and effects, the logic of capitalist development that has grown up there; it is only the other side of the scene.[29]

Mudd's view of the River Irwell clearly seemed to historians and their publishers to offer a visual parallel to Engels's description of the Ducie Bridge prospect. It looks towards the same area of the city, if from a different location. It could be seen to encompass a similar range of industrial and residential buildings, and it had some of the same background features. In the strangely limpid atmosphere and still waters of the Irwell could be imagined the same pollution as in the Irk and the same, seasons-negating inversion of the qualities of landscape. And on the right bank of the Irwell, especially, could be seen the same close-packed and propped-up buildings, which seem to subside into the river, 'smoky, crumbling, ancient'. It is apparent why Mudd's view was the chosen parallel rather than, say, Alfred Brothers's photograph taken from the same spot nearly twenty years later in 1878 (fig. 62). Brothers's view was published in his book of that year, *Manchester As It Is*, a companion volume to his *Old Manchester*, published in 1875. While the left-hand bank is almost identical to Mudd's and, judging by the pattern of shadows, may even have been taken at the same time of day, the right-hand bank has undergone a total transformation in the two intervening decades. From Victoria Bridge to the right edge of the view, the old buildings and the debris of the bank have been swept away, replaced by new buildings rising sheer from the river's edge and extending in an almost unbroken line from the bridge. Centrally positioned in the image, rebuilt so that its tower could regain its significance from the factory buildings, and even with its reflection clear and complete in the river below, the cathedral has been given a new visual authority. It is now irrefutably the main motif of the picture. Manchester as it is, Brothers's picture seems to say, might still be an industrial city but it has become much more a city of monuments and moral order; the tender concealment has extended its effect along the banks of the Irwell. Brothers himself proclaimed the transformation with some pride:

> *There is probably no place in the United Kingdom where, in so short a period, commercial progress has wrought such wondrous changes in the external aspects as it has in Manchester ... everything appears modernised or new, testifying to the fact of this extraordinary development, and conveying to the mind the idea that the place is only the creation of yesterday.*[30]

Where Brothers's photograph represents the modernisation of the cities of Manchester and Salford as something achieved, the concrete epitome of a new era, Mudd's photograph – once it is juxtaposed with Engels's text – is seen to present a transitional or unresolved moment.

It has long been argued that the processes of deep-rooted and traumatic change in early nineteenth-century British cities also entailed similar changes in the ways they were understood and represented. The paradigm that became dominant was the product of a new group of professional administrators and reformers who, as James Donald has described it, 'devised new technologies of social observation and political calculation to tackle the perceived problems created by urbanisation'.[31] It was this paradigm, epitomised in Manchester by the researches of James Phillips Kay (later Sir James Kay-Shuttleworth), that Engels had set out to challenge. Kay aimed to identify and tabulate the signs of disease within the urban organism, to remake them as data so as to bring them within the regulative functions of modern government. Engels wanted to give a different kind of legibility to the city: he saw it as a problem of interpretation rather than of mere tabulation, an interpretation that would indicate and indict the underlying economic and social relations. Although Kay and Engels stood for two newly emergent models of urban representation, it is difficult to align Mudd's photography with either of them. If photography was to play a role in recording and disseminating images of the social ills of the industrial city, for technical and administrative reasons it would not be able perform this function for several more decades.[32] According to the available evidence, Mudd's image made no contribution to policing the city – at least not in any sense that might be equated with the work of social investigators and their disciplines – and it has not been deployed retrospectively to point to the city as a systematic manifestation of social relations. Yet it does seem to have been involved in a coming to terms with something new, and that coming to terms involved a testing and sorting of visual formulae, embodying some sense of epochal change as it acknowledged and captured the cohabitation of different spatial and representational regimes within the city. If it attempted to equalise these, to balance them with the compositional formulae of picture making, this in itself might be considered in relation to other indications of loss and compensation. But, again, this is to reach conclusions too soon.

ONE OF THE EARLIEST APPEARANCES OF MUDD'S PHOTOGRAPH was in a portfolio of loose mounted prints titled *Views of Old Manchester and Salford*, including some twenty-seven photographs taken between 1858 and 1877.[33] The portfolio must be considered as one among many destinations for Mudd's print rather than its point of origin. There is no printed text, except for titles, in relation to which what has been called photography's 'code of legibility' might be constructed.[34] Instead, as we shall see, the images – through their selection as a group in the portfolio and the interconnections within the group – act as a kind of dynamic device for mapping place in relation to epochal change. They map the difference between now and then, between a past that was decisively different from the photographic present. The range of the dates when the prints were taken demonstrates that their grouping under this rubric of epochal change is more likely to have been retrospective than intended at the time the first images were taken, or perhaps it was developed at some time during the creation of the portfolio.[35] The obvious rationale behind the collection is signalled by their identification as 'views'; its images make a claim to be topography, with all that implies about a descriptive recording that apparently stops at the surface of its subjects. There are bridges, houses, churches, pubs, warehouses, marketplaces and various public buildings. None of the buildings presented as the central motif of these photographs dates from much later than the mid-eighteenth century (there are many more marginal buildings that are nineteenth century), and most date from before then. Some of these buildings, such as Ordsall Hall in Salford, were threatened by general neglect, some by the demand for commercial space in the heart of the city, some by new road-building and road-widening schemes brought in by the Improvement Acts of the new municipality, and others by the erection of larger and more modern and monumental edifices, particularly warehouses and public buildings.

A case in point is the cathedral that appears in 'The River Irwell from Blackfriars Bridge'. There is a curious feeling of redundancy about it. Its tower is marginal to those sets of equivalences that were identified at the beginning of this chapter as structuring the photograph, both those that traverse the image and those that cross it in depth. Dwarfed by the other verticals and without a balancing element, the cathedral seems inadequate in both size and symbolism for the city around it. Perhaps the stumpy medieval tower is the crux here, the gesture that enables some kind of coherent meaning for the image. If anywhere, this is where 'old Manchester' might be found in the image, in the Gothic forms and the old Anglican authority of the cathedral, a monument that owes nothing to the Industrial Revolution. If we somehow see the cathedral as its focus, the image could be understood as structured not by formal equivalences but by a set of oppositions as in the contrasted towns of A. W. N. Pugin's *Contrasts* (the image

[63] 'A Catholic Town in 1440' and 'The Same Town in 1840': contrasted towns from A. W. N. Pugin, *Contrasts*, 2nd edn (1841).

[64] James Mudd, 'Manchester Cathedral', *c.*1864. Albumen silver print. Canadian Centre for Architecture, Montreal.

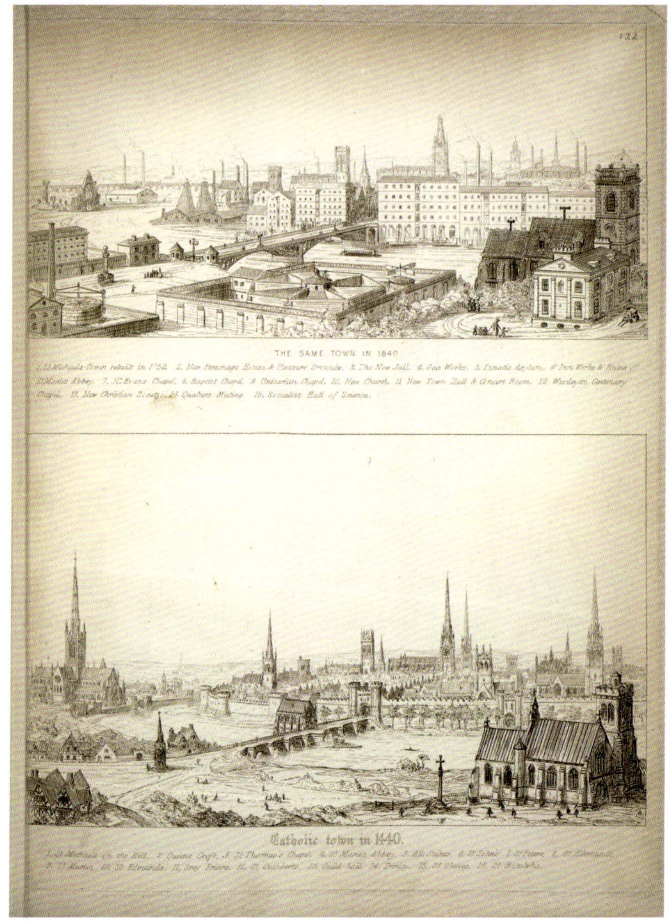

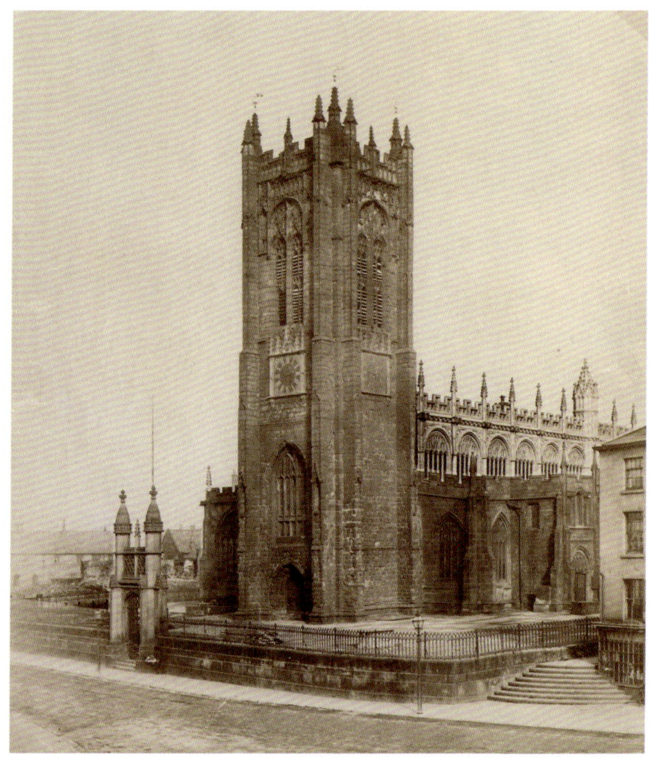

was added to the 1841 edition): religion and industry, traditional and modern, old and new, but with only the faith in a utopia of the past to outface the dystopian present (fig. 63).[36]

When Mudd's River Irwell photograph was taken, the cathedral had existed in name for only twelve years, the existing collegiate church having been converted into a cathedral in 1847. The hasty upgrading was all too apparent, certainly in Mudd's image. By 1859 it was clear that the cathedral would have to be substantially remade. The tower had recently suffered the truncation of its upper section and the blunting of its pinnacles, and the pitched slate roof that covered it had a decaying flagstaff passing through its centre. A square wooden balustrade had just been completed ('it reminded you of the framework of a scaffold', wrote one contemporary[37]). It is this dilapidated and even threatening appearance of the cathedral, epitomised by the stump of the tower, that is captured in the photograph, at a time when it was well known that its upper sections were to be pulled down and the tower to be remade from the foundations up.[38]

In two other images in the portfolio we see what then happened. The viewer is drawn nearer by stages to the cathedral. First, the building is approached close enough to isolate it from the city, centralising the tower and allowing study of the building's various volumes in detail (fig. 64). Then, as we come closer still, its main west door fills the pictorial space (fig. 65). The sequence is a little baffling, but it demonstrates Mudd's concern with temporality. The first image shows the restored upper part, but in drawing nearer we focus on the as yet unrestored stonework in the arch around the west doorway.[39] It is as if we were moving backwards in time between the two images, whereas they were actually probably taken on the same day.

If the cathedral tower, as a motif, is seen as the motivation for Mudd's 'The River Irwell from Blackfriars Bridge', the photograph can be understood as a piece of antiquarianism, an attempt at preserving memory in the face of rapid change. If, on the other hand, the equivalences are seen as a more significant structural element in the image, it takes on a rather differently determined relationship to the city's development; it could be evidence of what the incorporation of the city had brought about. Both positions

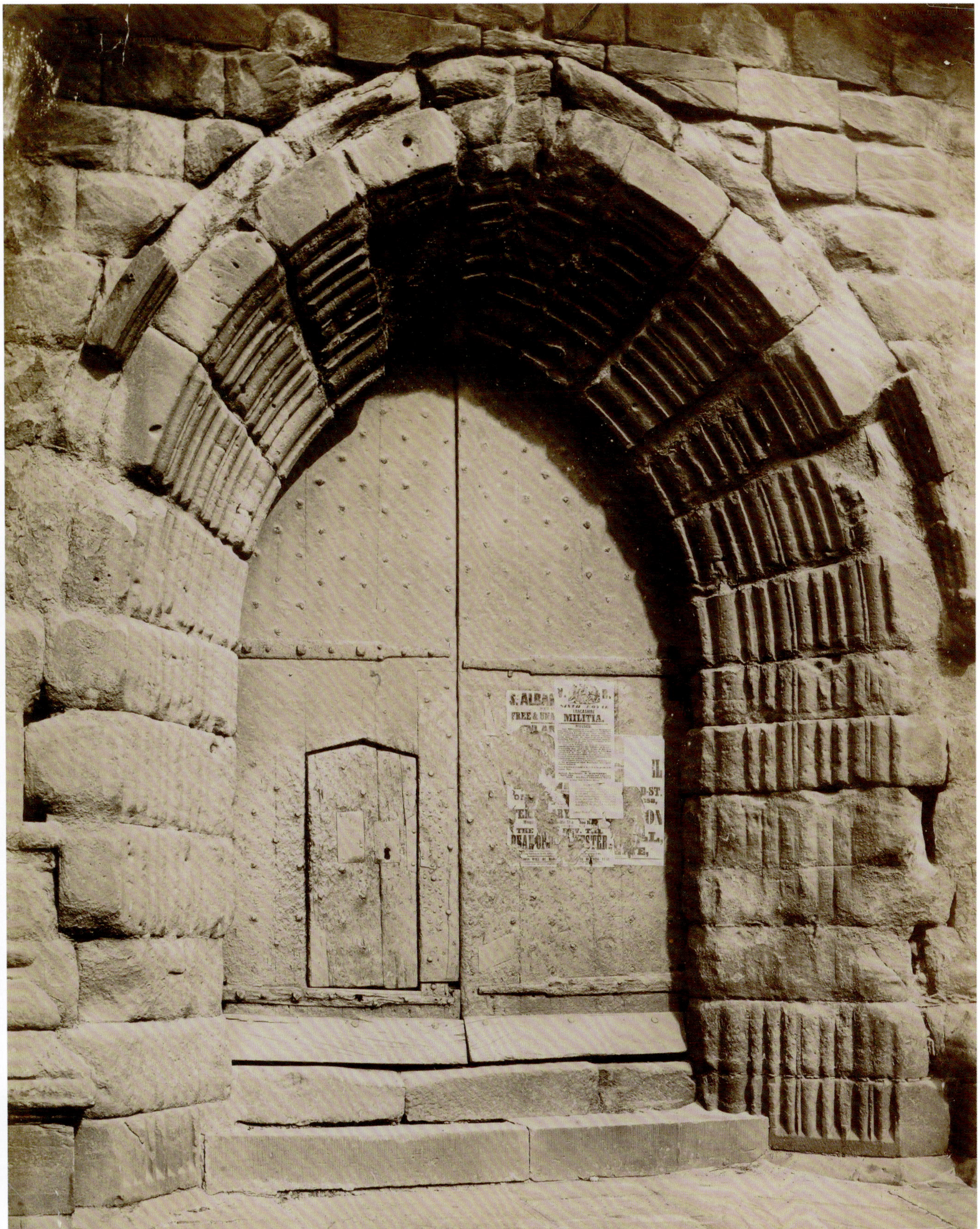

[65] James Mudd, 'The Old West Doorway', c.1864. Gelatin silver print. Canadian Centre for Architecture, Montreal.

cannot be held simultaneously, it seems, yet both are licensed by the River Irwell photograph. To put this differently, meaning can be found both in the institutional spaces within which the photograph is inscribed *and* in its capacity to allow an interrogation of its ontology.

If we understand it as an antiquarian and topographical enterprise, the portfolio *Views of Old Manchester and Salford* was not exceptional in mid- and late nineteenth-century Manchester. James Mudd's brother Richard Mudd wrote several articles on the early history of Manchester for the *Strines Journal*. In 'Ancient Edifices in Manchester' he included woodcuts, taken from newspapers of the 1820s, illustrating many of the buildings that also appeared in *Views of Old Manchester and Salford*. The text's argument that these 'ancient edifices' were under threat is balanced by a pride in the new monumental city, and – in common with other antiquarian texts of the period – in the machinery that powered the Industrial Revolution.[40] (This conjunction of the medieval and the industrial will be taken up more fully in Chapter 4.) Particularly important as records of Manchester's pre-industrial edifices were *James's Views*, a set of lithographic prints published in 1825, and a group of drawings by John Ralston from 1822 (published as lithographs in 1823–5). Both sets of views were republished in Alfred Brothers's *Old Manchester* (1875) and provided some of the historical evidence for the 'Old Manchester and Salford' display at the Royal Jubilee Exhibition in 1887.[41] Ralston and James's views were important because they recorded some of the older buildings that were demolished when Market Street was widened in the 1820s and when Victoria Street was built by the improvement commissioners in the later 1830s. Another important source for pre-industrial Manchester was Russel Casson and John Berry's 'Plan and Prospect of Manchester and Salford in 1751', reproduced in a photolithograph by Alfred Brothers and published in Richard Wright Procter's *Memorials of Bygone Manchester, with Glimpses of the Environs*. Casson and Berry's plan was particularly valuable for the images of major and notable buildings that were used in a frame around the map. Procter's book, as with similar works within the genre, catered for what it claimed was a 'newly awakened' interest in Manchester's history.[42]

What can be identified here, then, is a context for antiquarian views of Manchester, where a recuperative project to preserve records of the old town, and thereby to create what might be termed a pre-industrial imaginary, seems to go hand in hand with the celebration of new municipal pride. A related dynamic can be found in the popular 1876 novel *The Manchester Man* by Mrs Linnaeus Bank (Isabella Varley). As mentioned in Chapter 2, the story develops along the lines of a kind of foundation myth in which all the clichés of the pre-industrial city – green fields, clear water, family-like working relations and the various details of antiquarian knowledge – are put into suspension by the rise of the 'Manchester Man', Jabez Clegg, who is found at the beginning of the novel like Moses floating in a cot on flood waters and becomes one of the new city's industrial leaders. As mentioned earlier, in this and the antiquarian accounts, antiquity is not only the complement of modernity but also its necessary consequence. In this setting a record like Mudd's photograph of the 1857 Art Treasures Exhibition is as much a marker of new urban pride as, say, the new consciousness of Manchester's city status from the late 1830s, the establishment of public parks and public libraries in the 1840s and 1850s, or the building of new streets and various street improvements throughout these decades.[43] This remaking of the monumental image of the city culminated in the building of the new Town Hall and the rebuilding of the Exchange in the 1870s, and Mudd's portfolio collects together views taken from across this period.[44]

Since 1838, when Manchester was incorporated as a municipal borough, a new architectural image for the city had been promoted by the city's middle classes (as discussed in Chapter 2 and also in Chapter 4), an image that was driven forward by the new borough administration and enabled by a newly installed group of architects in the city, whose aspirations were promoted by the Manchester Architectural Society, established in 1837.[45] But the city presented in *Views of Old Manchester and Salford* is one that is determinedly focused on the pre-industrial: its spaces and buildings thus represent, among other things, the remnants of a time before the emergence of the shock city. And this pre-industrial architecture is presented as fragments, increasingly isolated

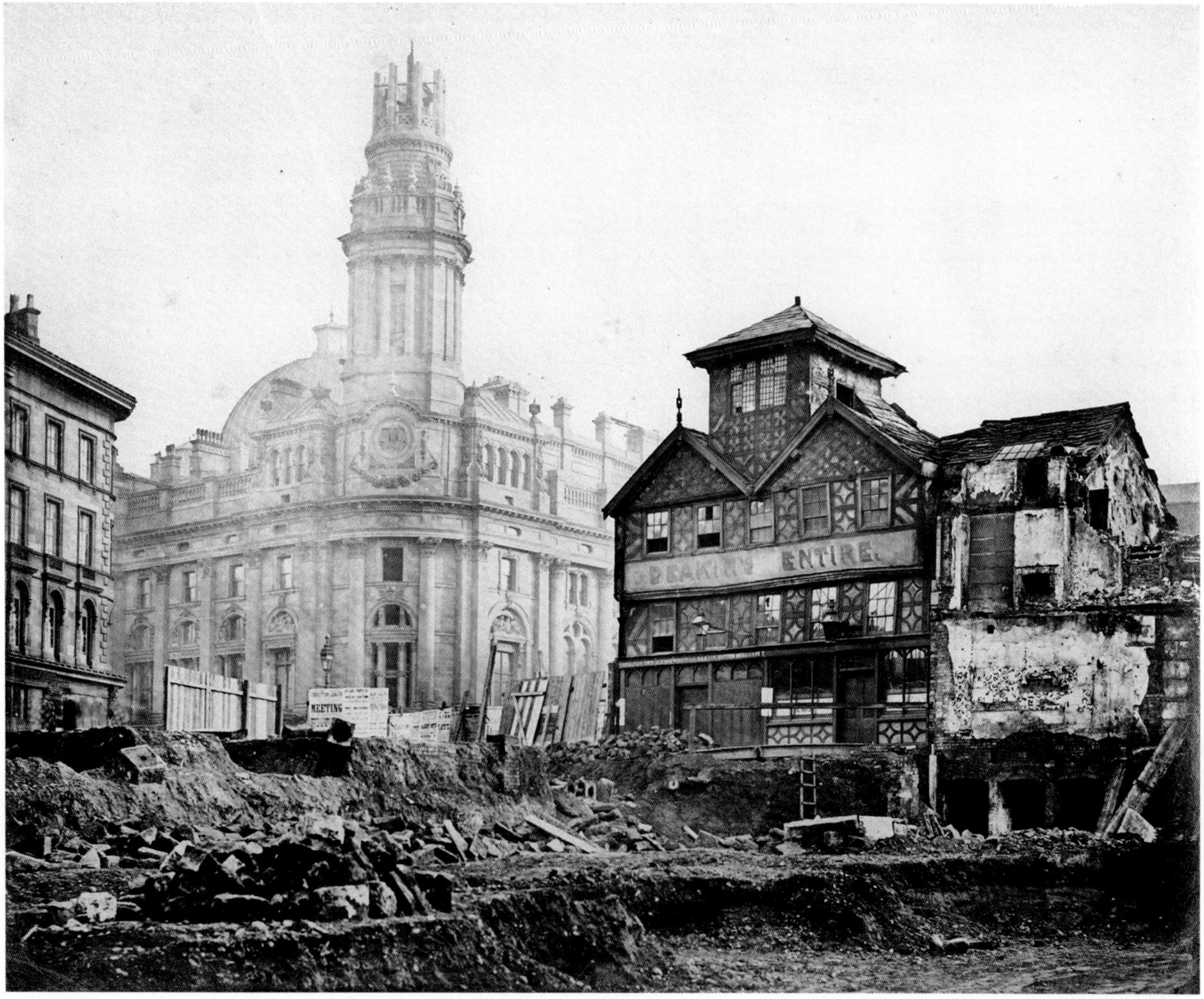

[66] James Mudd, 'Ancient and Modern Manchester', 1875. Albumen silver print. Manchester Libraries, Information and Archives.

and often depicted at a moment before impending demolition or improvement. If the artefacts in the photographs seem too threatened by change to suggest an urban museum of the pre-industrial, then at least – the project seems to suggest – the images themselves might constitute some form of photographic mausoleum of the pre-industrial. It is as if it were possible to imagine the pre-industrial only after the industrial, and its associated urban and architectural forms, has passed into the civic reformation of the city. In this conceptual ordering, in Mudd's attempt to identify differently epochal times, his work seems distinct from what has been called the 'metropolitan picturesque' or the 'picturesque of demolition' in images of nineteenth-century London and Paris.[46] Though he deals with similar subjects, Mudd does not focus on the fragment that must be aged or chaos that must be conventionally framed, or aestheticised, to make it art; instead, his photographs make oppositions, juxtapose with purpose (as we shall see).

To call a building 'pre-industrial', it follows, is to beg a number of questions about what constitutes or represents the industrial in the built environment. Is it, for instance, to do with a new set of functions, typologies or building technologies, or does it simply encompass any building in a certain period (and if so perhaps 'proto-industrial', a modern term favoured by many historians, might be better)?[47] But 'pre-industrial' is neither a misreading of the history of the Industrial Revolution nor a concept imposed on the *Views of Old Manchester and Salford* portfolio, because it seems itself to be commented on and thus to acquire a visual formulation in several prints, which is summed up in the title of one of them – 'Ancient and Modern Manchester' (fig. 66). This image, dated 1875, presents an explicit contrast between the pre-industrial

[67] Friedrich Engels's map of Long Millgate, from *Die Lage der arbeitenden Klasse in England* (1845).

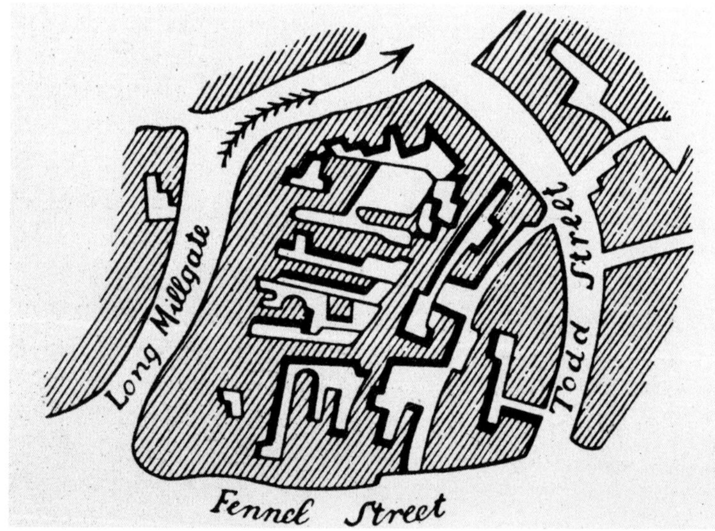

structure of a pub, the Vintner's Arms, on the right, and to its left one of the modern city's new monumental buildings, the Royal Exchange, one of whose many incarnations was just then being completed (see Chapter 6).[48] Mudd gives them parity in terms of the space they occupy in his image so that a series of comparisons can be drawn in the somewhat stark contrast between the two buildings. Where the slender tower of one is still awaiting its stone copula, the squatter tower of the other is obviously dilapidated; where one seems to rise miraculously from the ground because its base is hidden, the other has its foundations violently exposed by the neighbouring demolition site; and, finally and most tellingly, where one despite its heavy neo-baroque masonry appears softened and almost ethereal in its limited range of grey tones, the other is all sharp tonal contrast in the pattern of black beams against white plaster, the gridded panes of leaded windows across its front, and even the angular wooden paling to the left. There seems no point of reconciliation between the two architectural modalities. 'Deakin's Entire', the advertisement on the upper part of the older building, can only seem ironic in this setting. The Vintner's Arms' skinned and toothless neighbour to the right – made anonymous by its half-demolition – is only one stage along from the dismemberment that faces the pub. Other images in the portfolio fixed the Old Shambles, the area around the Vintner's Arms, at various stages in its transformation: some, from ten years earlier, showed it surrounded by shops and other pre-nineteenth-century pubs; others from a later moment showed it as an isolated medieval monument surrounded by a wilderness of demolition.

Another group of photographs was taken around Long Millgate, nearer the cathedral, and several of these use a similar trope to the 'ancient and modern Manchester' view. For Friedrich Engels writing in 1845, Long Millgate had been another typification of Manchester's 'hypocritical plan', where shops and beer-houses fronting the road presented a relatively acceptable face but behind them, in the courts and lanes, dwellings were crammed and tangled in such a way that it was 'impossible to convey an idea'[49] (fig. 67). In 'Long Millgate and Grammar School' (1875) Mudd presents this outer, public face with a view down the empty street (presumably a result of the image's long exposure time) and with the newly erected Manchester Grammar School, grey and muted, filling the end of the street (fig. 68). In another photograph, 'Bakehouse Court, Long Millgate' (1875), the half-demolished older buildings, with their outer walls ripped off and their interiors indecorously exposed, seem almost propped up by the more rigid, if again greyer, forms of the grammar school behind them (fig. 69). And yet in these photographs the contrast of new and old is considerably inflected by making the old appear more photographically substantial – more crisply detailed, more declaratively black and white – than the new.

All these images – 'Ancient and Modern Manchester', 'Long Millgate and Grammar School' and 'Bakehouse Court, Long Millgate' – devise a form of legibility for the city. They bring out the other – the 'modern' – aspects of the project into explicit juxtaposition with the records of 'ancient' scenes that are the avowed aim of *Views of Old Manchester and Salford*. By comparison with early nineteenth-century English watercolourists, whose urban scenes also often screened or contrasted a notable architectural feature with more humdrum buildings or activities in front of it,[50] Mudd's photographs force a reading of the city as a place of epochal contrasts where the new epoch threatens (or perhaps promises) to strip away the old entirely; for one to come about, the other must

[68] James Mudd, 'Long Millgate and Grammar School', 1875. Albumen silver print. Manchester Libraries, Information and Archives.

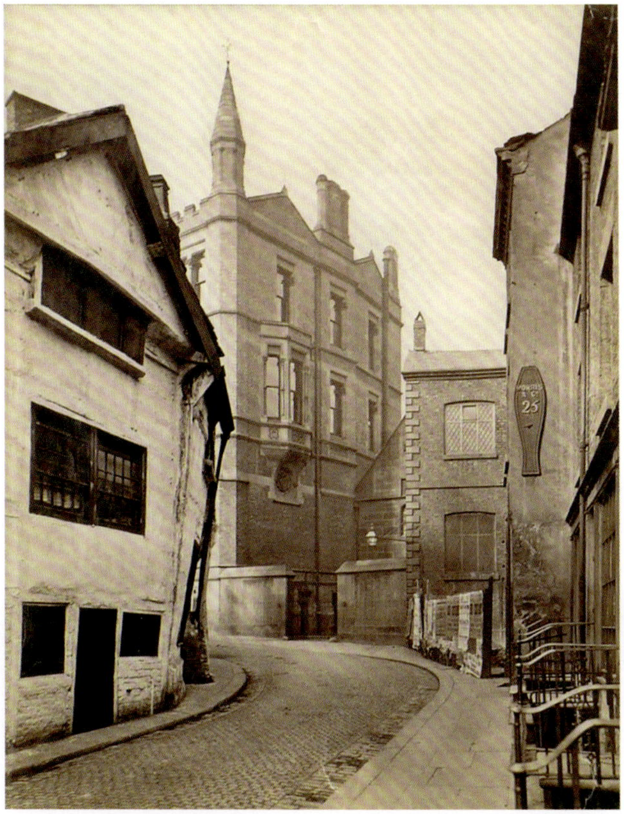

[69] James Mudd, 'Bakehouse Court, Long Millgate', 1875. Albumen silver print. Manchester Libraries, Information and Archives.

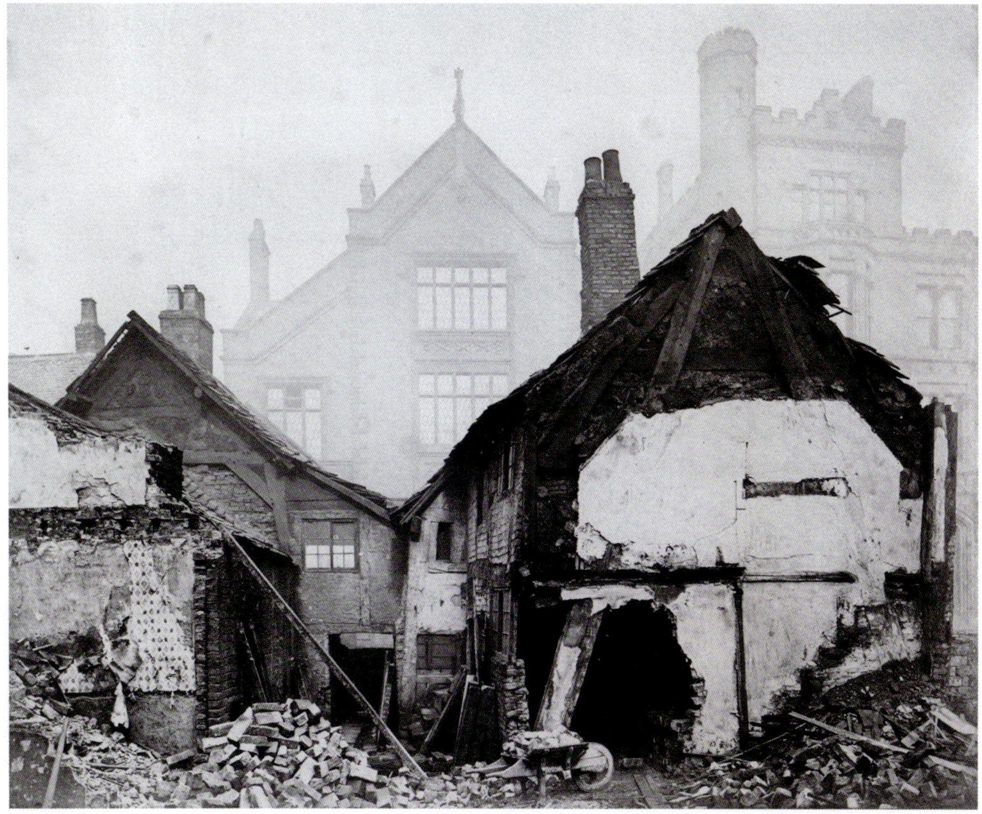

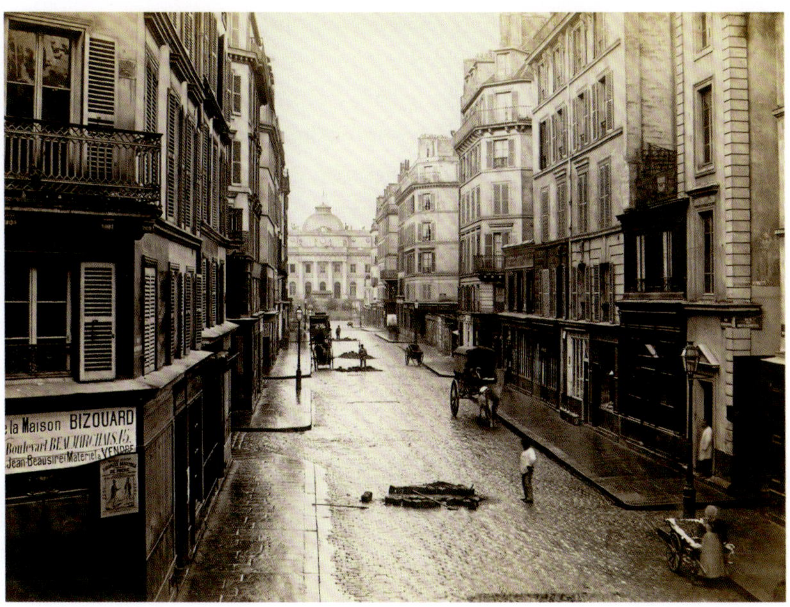

go. It is a temporal pairing that is fundamentally unstable: ancient and modern are seen as distinct categories but also as bound together by an inherent antagonism because one can seemingly come into existence only as a result of the demise of the other.[51]

Pertinent photographic comparison with Mudd's images can be found in Charles Marville's contemporary work in Paris.[52] Marville was commissioned in 1858 to produce before-and-after pictures of the redevelopment of Paris under Baron Haussmann (fig. 70). The official function of these photographs was to visualise this change as a necessary and progressive eradication of the irrational and the derelict. However, as Shelley Rice has argued, while Marville's work functioned within this new administrative concept of urban space, his photography can also be understood as an inadvertent

[70] Charles Marville, 'Rue de Constantine, Paris', c.1865. Albumen silver print.

[71] James Mudd, 'The River Irwell from Blackfriars Bridge', 1859: detail. Albumen silver print. Canadian Centre for Architecture, Montreal.

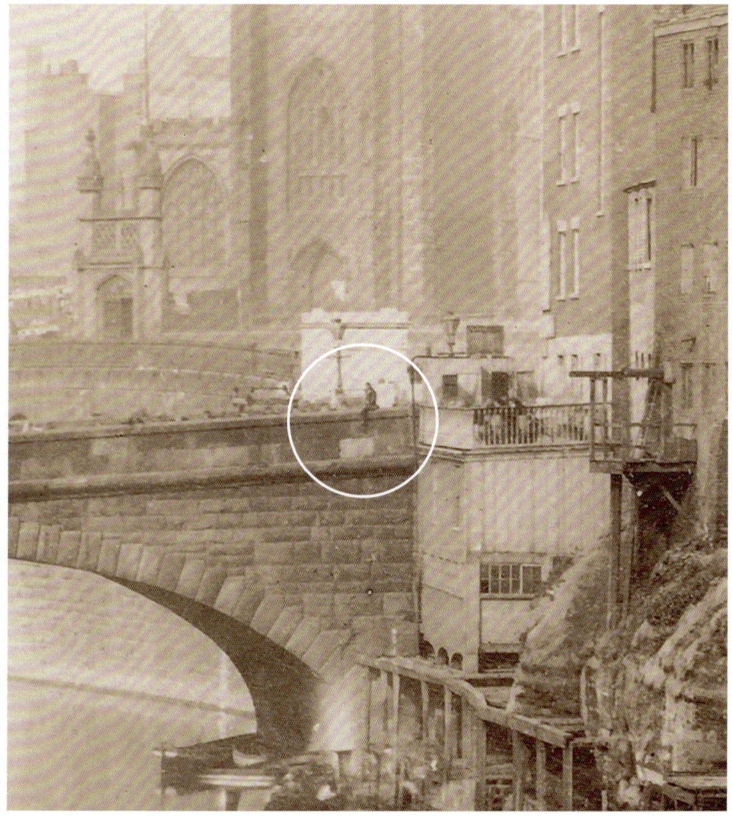

form of resistance to modernisation. The pictures' long exposures edit out the transient, and their consequent stillness emphasises narrative time and linear history between the contrasting prints; they record stages in a measurable process rather than a constantly mutating interaction of different elements. Marville used them to search for classical balance and for clearly separated moments of experience, avoiding the new patterns of mobility and the newly modern forms of randomness and synchronicity otherwise associated with modernisation.[53]

Mudd's photographs attempt a non-synchronic representation of temporality; they seem to want to hold space and time in suspension through the device of the old/new, or ancient/modern, dichotomy. Like Marville's images in this respect, they evince an essentially conservative refusal of simultaneity. The dynamism of social relations, the actions and motivations of actual people – that shaping of space to which Engels's writings constantly draws attention – are all seemingly edited out of the photographs or are not available within their means.[54] In 'Ancient and Modern Manchester' two buildings of different historical moments are contrasted as different stages in an advancing historical process. This is not simultaneity, that uneven time that is so often the subject of Marxist thought, since, although the buildings can be seen to occupy the same city, the rhetoric of their presentation is that one building eclipses the other, causes the other's demise: this will follow that. Something is clearly *happening* in these images but the processes of change can be rendered only at the level of the detail (the wheelbarrow, the builder's ladder, the ramshackle hoardings) or of the momentous contrast.[55]

If this seems to be all that photography at this time can do with this theme, then 'The River Irwell from Blackfriars Bridge' itself offers something else. The image's stillness seems to be a way of figuring stasis in the face of change; it is less a symptom of a before-and-after rendition of historical time than an attempt to place before and after in coincident time, to find that there are equivalences rather than outright oppositions between the different forms that they take. Human presence, its absence or diminution, is relevant here. The only people still enough to appear in the photograph are minute figures sitting on the parapet of Victoria Bridge. One of these, on the Manchester end of the bridge, has swung a leg over the parapet in a punctuating moment of masculine swagger (fig. 71). He is certainly not 'the "right man" in the "right place"', as Mudd's own strictures on photographic composition had proposed, but he is nevertheless a usefully symptomatic figure.[56] He and the other figures are too distant securely to register their social identities, but despite his dapperness his swung leg certainly breaches the decorum expected of the middle classes in public, and in this sense he may evoke a correspondence as much as the stone orbs near him. But he is exceptional.[57] In general, the few people who feature in Mudd's portfolio do not have any particular class identity, and the buildings manifest no fixed class either. This does not mean that depicted buildings were not associated with particular groups and classes. Bakehouse Court, as part of Long Millgate, was certainly a working-class slum, but then it had also been a set of shopkeepers' houses and premises. Both of these previous lives belong to the past, before the photograph's moment of demolition: the photograph thus captures coincident time. Ben Lang's Music Hall was a well-known place of working-class entertainment, with a beer-house beside it, and was notably diverse in its facilities – 'at once a vault, a refreshment-room, a boathouse, and a singing gallery'.[58] But, in general, Mudd's images are premised on a spatiality of segregation that respects the facades and the itineraries of the respectable city of class interest – so the music hall is only one part of a complex space of different interests and activities. In other words, the images represent a city whose public spaces enable the freedom of movement of the roving and recording bourgeoisie while the working classes are only implied in the abject, obscene spaces beyond the facades, or at most as blurred figures in doorways or, possibly, distant figures on a bridge.

New and old in these photographs are to be read as alternatives, utterly different styles of architecture, modes of looking and perhaps even forms of life. A 'pre-industrial' imaginary is contrasted with an 'industrial' civic urbanism, establishing a sealed circuit of mutually confirming and consoling opposites and transcending the diffuseness and the conflicts of the present. The specific ideological nature of this binary structure is evident by comparison with Engels. While Engels was also interested in the relation of old and new, their cheek-by-jowl relationship has no currency of preferences, let alone one of betterment. For Engels it is the very nature of capitalist development to uncouple attachments in time as well as space, to misuse and contravene the forms of an older epoch as much as to draw the peripheral into the metropolitan. What we are looking at is a problem created by the present, not inherited from the past:

> *True, this is the Old Town, and the people of Manchester emphasise the fact whenever anyone mentions to them the frightful conditions of this hell upon earth; but what does that prove? Everything which here arouses horror and indignation is of recent origin, belongs to the industrial epoch. The couple of hundred houses which belong to Old Manchester have been long since abandoned by their original inhabitants: the industrial epoch alone has crammed into them the swarms of workers whom they now shelter; the industrial epoch alone has built up every spot between these old houses to make a covering for the masses whom it has conjured hither from the agricultural districts and from Ireland.*[59]

As well as being a product of the modern, this 'old town' is essential to a certain imaginary: 'However, it is the Old Town, and with this reflection the bourgeoisie is comforted.'[60]

WHILE MUDD'S 'RIVER IRWELL FROM BLACKFRIARS Bridge' seemed in the later nineteenth century to provide a way of epitomising the contrast between the pre-industrial and the industrial cities, or in more recent decades to offer a near-canonic, if unexamined, visualisation of the industrial city, other alternatives in understanding the image have also been available. When the photograph was reproduced at the turn of the nineteenth century, whether re-photographed or printed from the original negatives, it was associated both with the memory of a different kind of city and with the use of the city for rather different purposes than industrial production. Louis Hayes's *Reminiscences of Manchester and Some of its Local Surroundings from the Year 1840* was driven by the desire to record what its author called 'green' memory – the 'bright and the happy incidents of our lives ... [in] dear old Manchester'.[61] He reproduced Mudd's view as a half-tone cropped at the sides and top, which made the cathedral tower more prominent and the central areas more composed than the truncated and split chimneys to the sides (fig. 72). The photograph is used as a parallel to Hayes's childhood memories of the grimy cathedral and especially of Ben Lang's Music Hall, with its 'strong flavour of corduroy and tobacco', its tripe stalls and hot potato sellers outside, and its ditties 'wafted along to you on the breeze'. From the music hall, Hayes tells us, wooden steps led down to the steamer which would take revellers to the Pomona Gardens.[62] And there, as Hayes expects us to, we see a waiting steamer in Mudd's photograph as if it were our own memory prompt, its steam whitening the bridge behind. A curious and complicated movement in time is taking place here: not just the 'escalator', as Raymond Williams called it, that always seems to

[72] James Mudd 'The River Irwell from Blackfriars Bridge', 1859, as used in Louis Hayes, *Reminiscences of Manchester and Some of its Local Surroundings from the Year 1840* (1905).

[73] James Mudd 'The River Irwell from Blackfriars Bridge', 1859, as used in Joseph Corbett, *The River Irwell* (1907).

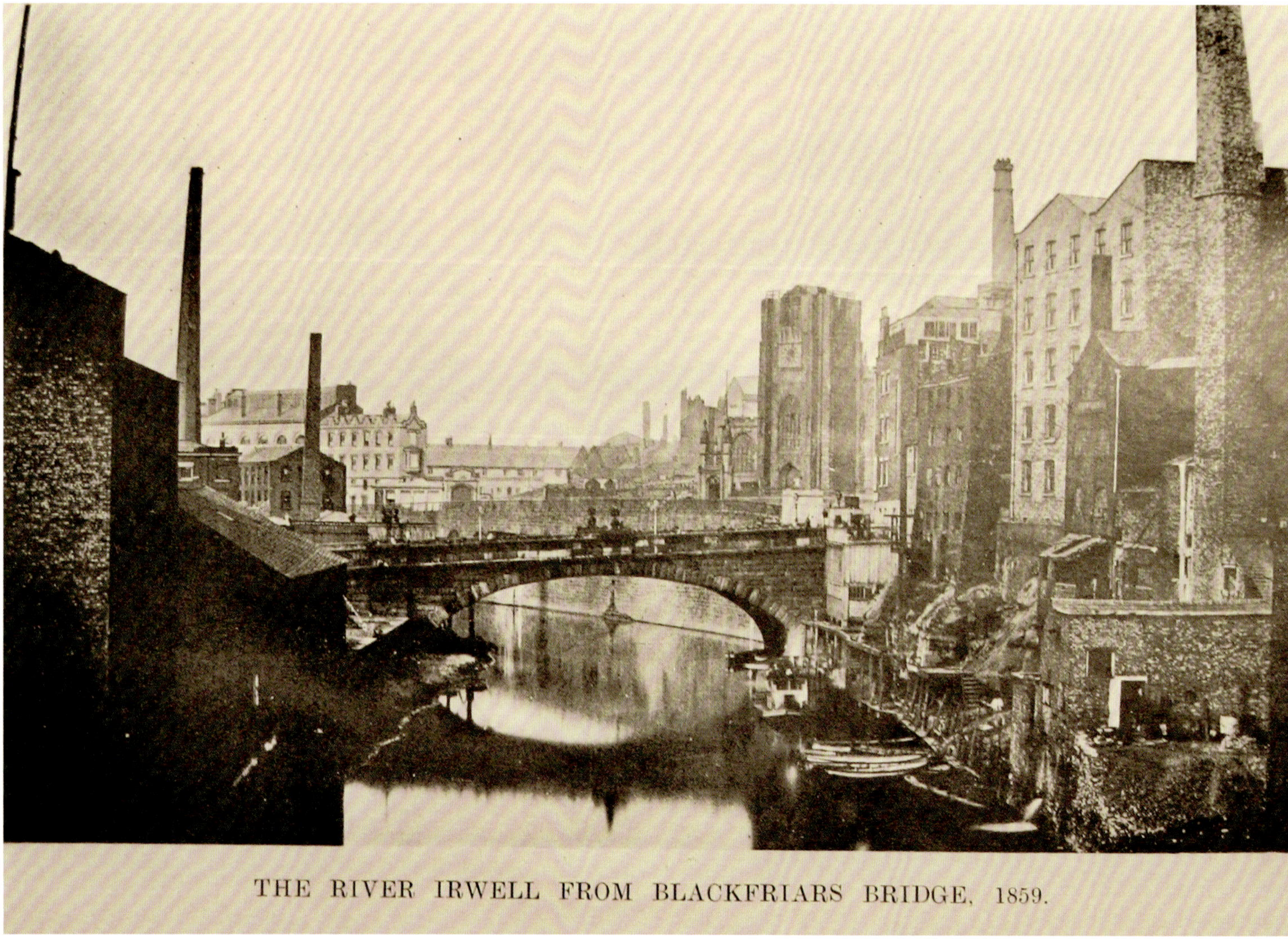

move back to another childhood or pastoral moment, but also the play of different values, different qualities of experience, different attitudes and positions towards the present.[63] And it's the present, the way it will reassert itself, that disturbs attempts to fix the past as an 'enamelled world':[64] its alternative smells and sounds, its visible sewage outlets, always remain just as latent within the image. The Fall of Industrial Man is, after all, the other of Memories of Childhood Fishing.

The relation between photograph and text in Hayes's book also raises a broader question of hierarchies of meaning in relation to modes of reading and modes of looking (between text and image), which gains a particular gloss with photography's indexical relation to its object. Does Hayes's text help us to read Mudd's image better, or is Mudd's photograph confirmation of or independent testimony to the truth of Hayes's account – that is, does it illustrate it? There seems no reason to doubt that Hayes wanted the

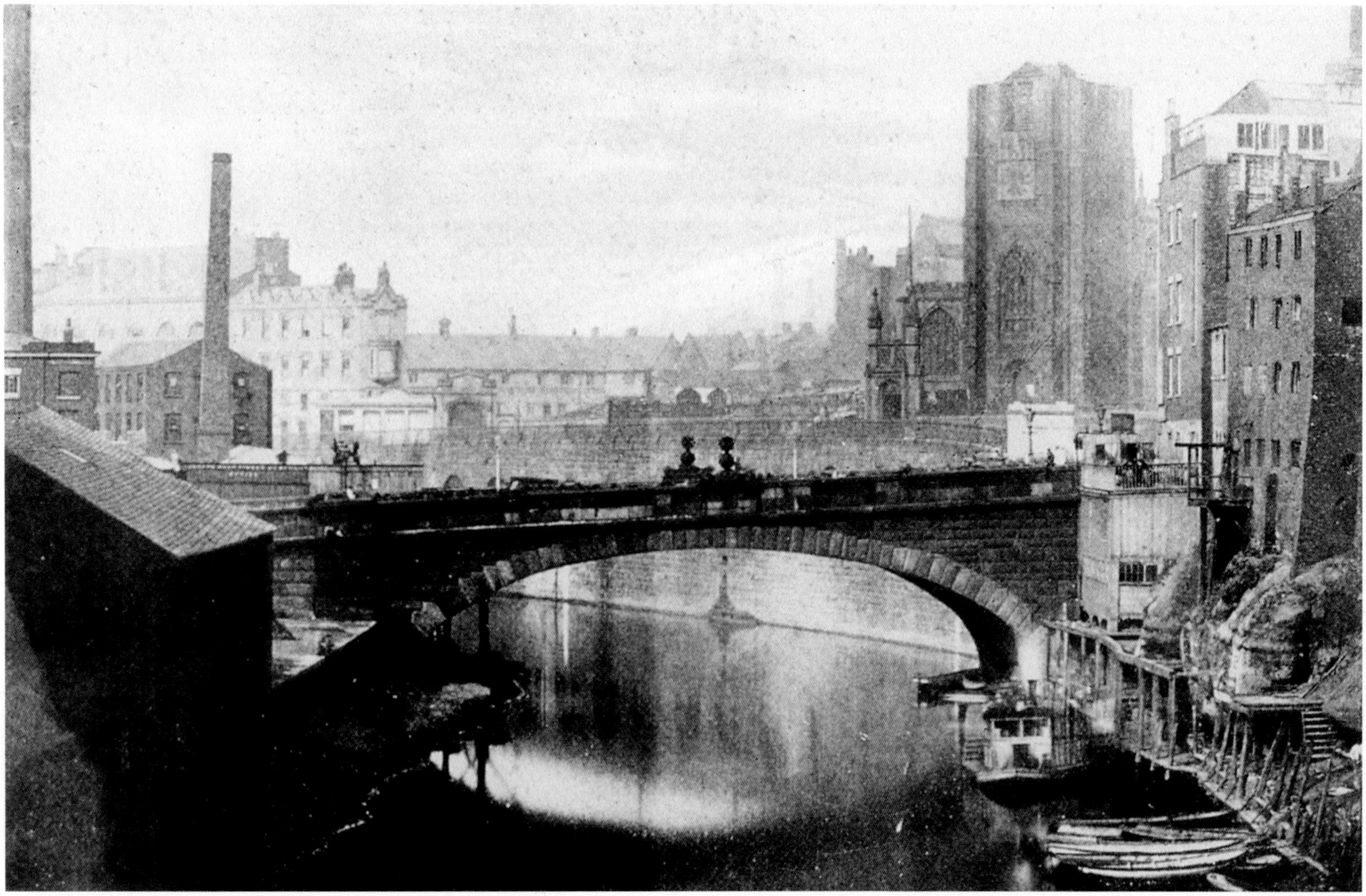

photograph to perform what Carol Armstrong has called its 'proof function': it acts 'as a stand-in for and trace of actual experience, [it] has the power to demonstrate or refute imaginative and textual hypotheses'.[65] In her book *Scenes in a Library*, Armstrong wants to see the mid-nineteenth-century photograph as fundamentally intransigent, as resisting or transcending its assimilation to printed texts or at least as differentially related to them.[66] Armstrong believes that photography is neither the servant of some larger discursive construction nor reducible to some singular photographic character perceived in the isolated photographic object. Hayes's *Reminiscences* belongs to a later period, in which Armstrong asserts that the photographic image was understood to be wholly assimilated to the text, when it was regarded as 'the prime possessive tool and mnemonic device of [a] positive mode of subjectivity'.[67] But, if the relation between the photograph and text in this later period cannot convincingly be described as one where the photograph refuses such assimilation, it is often unclear which has assumed priority, and while the photograph has a 'proof function' this is not its only role (and even that role is shared with the text). Hayes's book, for example, establishes a relationship between at least three moments: the 'Year 1840' of the title and of the 'strong flavour of corduroy and tobacco'; the year 1859 of Mudd's photograph with its waiting steamer; and the year 1905, with which the two previous moments are triangulated to make 'dear old Manchester'. The text is not parasitical on the image because the dyadic relationship of looking and reading is superseded by a triadic relationship of moments, none of which is wholly located in image or text but all of which work together through a naturalised self-reflexivity. This is important beyond debates within photographic theory, of course, because it shows the formal mechanisms and the psychic forms required if the industrial city is somehow to be remade as a subject for memory.

Joseph Corbett, the author of *The River Irwell* (1907), was not only borough engineer of Salford but also chairman of the Agecroft Rowing Club, and this second interest plays a prominent role in his book. Corbett views the Irwell with the eye of a man who uses the river for leisure and closely observes its river-borne traffic. Mudd's photograph serves to illustrate a strategic stop along a tour of the river from the cathedral to Runcorn and back, and then up-river to Prestolee (fig. 73). The view is more drastically edited down than in Hayes's version, so that, while the entire span of the bridge and the cathedral tower are preserved, the image is cut just above the tower and the river banks extend only to just above the waterspout. Effectively, Corbett has erased as much as he can of the obviously industrial elements in the photograph, and the tonalities of the image are more subtle than in Hayes's version, making the bridge stand out more from the embankment beyond it, softening the edges of the picture and shaping volumes so that they appear more solid and the depth more vertiginous. In conventional terms, it is a more picturesque image, with the cathedral tower given bulk and shifted further off-centre so that it can more effectively anchor the composition. Corbett's caption to the picture points particularly to the elements of riverside leisure within the scene:

> *On the right of the picture are several rowing boats and a small Paddle Steamer moored to rough wooden stages against the rocky bank of the river. The Cathedral Tower is in process of pulling down and rebuilding. To the right of it is the end of 'Ben Lang's Music Hall' with a view platform on its roof.*[68]

Elsewhere in *The River Irwell*, antiquarian details continue to provide the setting for the text's focus on the river as a place of leisure. Just above Victoria Bridge on the Salford side had stood a woollen cloth hall, Corbett tells us, and on the sloping riverbank in front of it were a 'number of rowing boats for hire in "Mary Ann's Boathouse"'.[69] Below the bridge on the Manchester side 'there was a very busy landing stage, connected in later years with "Ben Lang's Music Hall", where many rowing boats were on hire, and where small steamers started for pleasure trips down the river to Pomona Gardens and other holiday resorts'.[70] And, while the music hall itself is described, this is only a prelude to the information that 'Mr Lang owned the paddle steamers "Punch", "Judy" and two others which plied on the river ... Cargo barges were frequently pooled up the river ... In 1841 two vessels, the "Lingard" and the "Mary" ... were towed to Victoria Bridge by the steamer "Jack Sharp".'[71] It is only a short step from here to the memory – now Corbett's father's – of a pre-industrial Irwell with shoals of fish and eels in the water, and swallows and house martins flying above.[72]

The role of Mudd's picture within Corbett's narrative is to trigger a set of observations whose antiquarian nature is assembled from anecdote and various chronological and statistical data. As with Hayes, the past in Corbett's book seems to be constructed by another triangulation of three moments that are seen to have an inevitable relationship: the moment of writing (1907), the moment of looking (1859) and the moment being imagined (the more distant past, the pre-industrial). Where Hayes's distant past was an urban one suggested by vivid sensory memories, Corbett's is a pastoral one made up of different rhythms and forms of movement: a heterochronic (even hetero-motive) time of mooring, rowing, towing, paddling, poling and plying.[73] As with Hayes, Mudd's picture attests to the truth of what Corbett claims: it is the apex of the triangulation. There, he can say, observe that the river is used for many purposes, and acknowledge it as a site for industrial traffic and industrial waste, but prefer another memory of it as a locus of pleasure and a conduit between the city and the countryside (if not the hundreds of watermills of the Irwell basin, 'the most hard-worked and overtasked stream in the universe').[74] Since this distant remembered past, the Irwell has been tamed and industrialised, but the pre-industrial remains as much a kind of idyll in the language itself and the prompts that it offers as in the selective use of the image. As Richard Procter, who also remembered childhood scenes there, wrote:

> *No such wild pranks are permitted to the Irwell now: its margins are higher and less easily surmounted; utilitarians have confined it with stones, and embanked it with earth ... houses have displaced the verdure in all directions, and the pellucid character of the river has been destroyed by chemical refuse.*[75]

BOTH CORBETT'S AND HAYES'S USE OF 'THE IRWELL FROM Blackfriars Bridge' make claims for a different understanding of the photograph from that of the shock-city icon or the contrast of epochs, and these are claims that seem to be almost entirely repressed by those other narratives of the city. In their books, Mudd's image is deployed as part of a pre-industrial imaginary, a structure of feeling that reduces temporality to an idealised pastoral landscape (that is, one without the disjunctive recognition of its place in industrial capitalism, one that can always be pushed back in time). By these means society can be represented without industry (while exploiting the now fully industrialised medium of the photographically illustrated book). Here memory is construed as something located beyond a generation, something whose material presence now consists of fragmentary remains, a world of anecdotes attached without consistency to visual details.

In this pursuit of a genealogy for the photograph we have now passed from what seems to be a mid- and late twentieth-century preoccupation with industrial imaginary back to a mid- to late nineteenth-century concern with the relations between the pre-industrial, the industrial and the civil, and then to another phase, which seems to be located in the late nineteenth and early twentieth centuries, in the city as a site for memory, particularly of a memory associated with a pre-industrial imaginary. The argument, then, is not that this image of a nineteenth-century city is dependent for its meaning on its institutional uses and contexts, nor that we can reach back to some originating scene where photograph and city were equally transparent. To argue that photographs like 'The River Irwell from Blackfriars Bridge' have no unity of signification, or that their meanings are not confined to the agency of makers and functions (if they could only be reconstructed), does not have to entail that their meaning is determined by context. Instead of seeing the photograph as part of an archive, we can understand it, as we can understand the city it represents and the moment of its exposure in that city, as an archive in itself. This is not to say that it means in an entirely associational way, that we find in it what we bring to it; clearly there is purpose of some kind in it, there is a domain of things, a range of possible content. The new is there as much as the old.

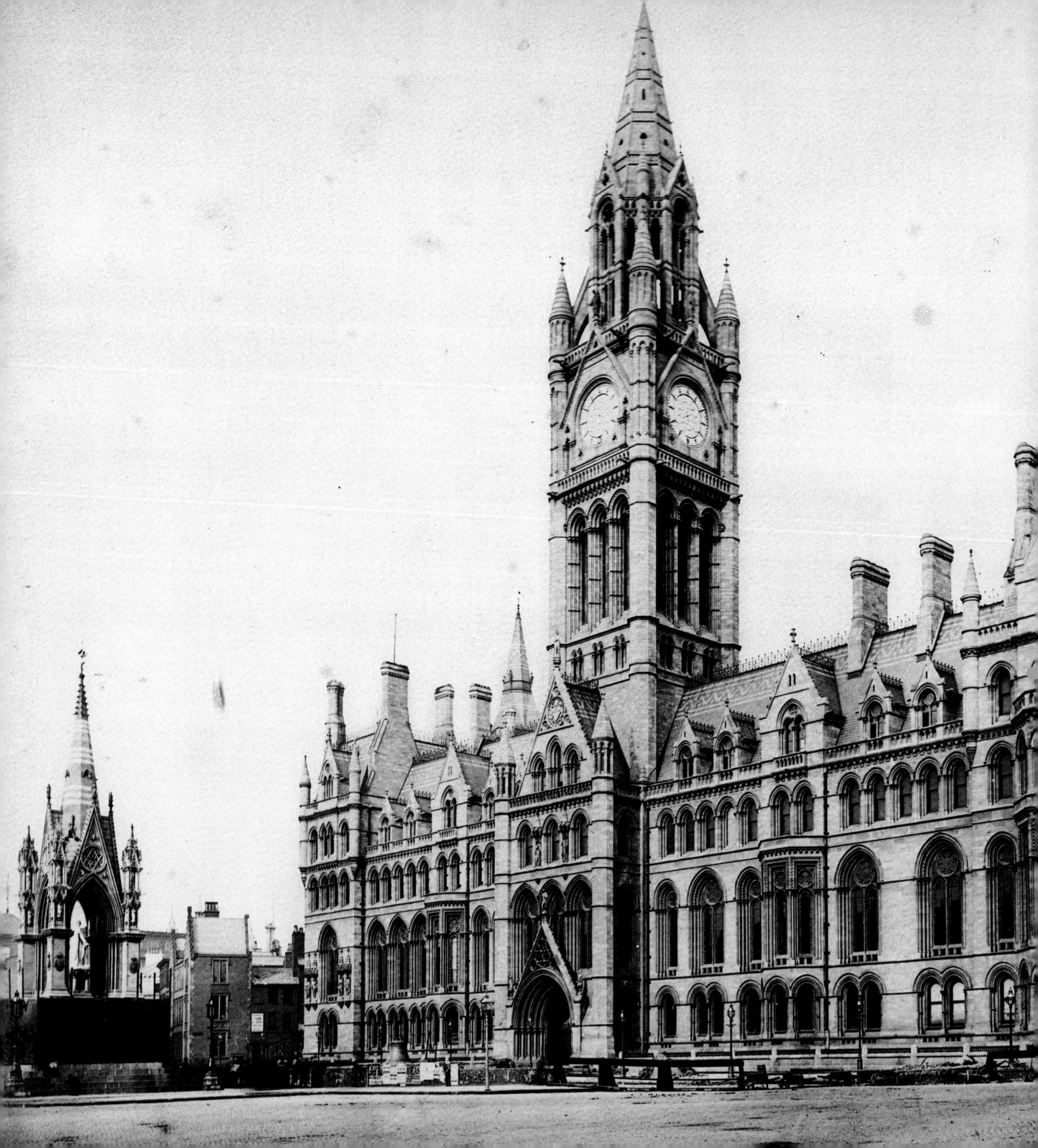

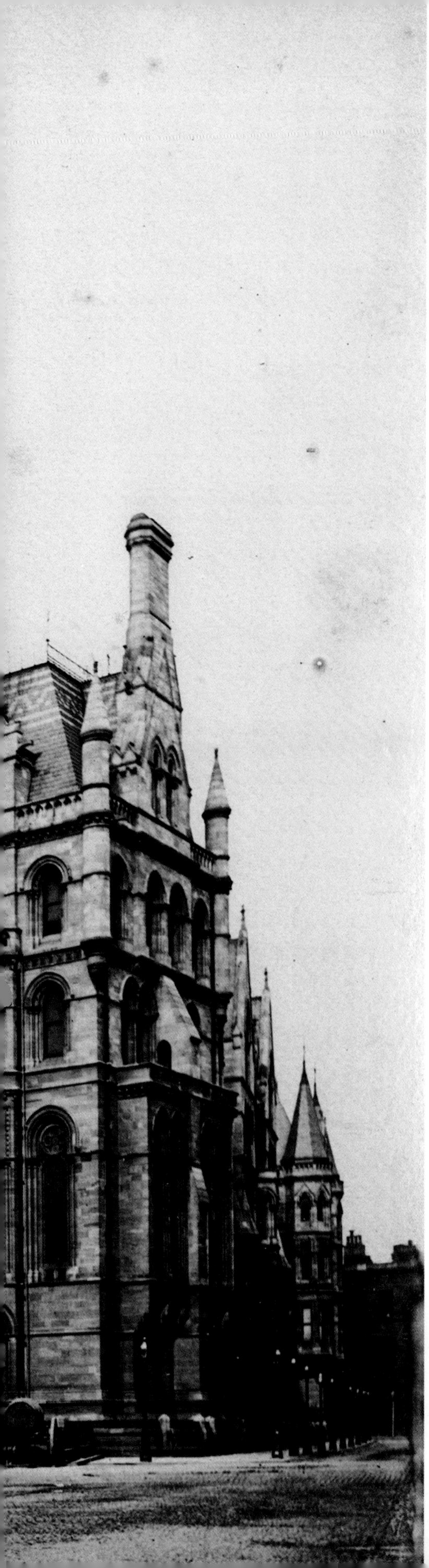

[74] Manchester Town Hall, 1867 77.
Architect: Alfred Waterhouse. Photograph: James Mudd, *c.*1877.
Manchester Libraries, Information and Archives.

4 Industrial Greatness

The Town Hall as a Gothic Machine

AN UNEXPECTED IMAGE APPEARED IN THE FIRST OFFICIAL publication about the new Manchester Town Hall, soon after its completion in 1876 (fig. 75). The engraving by T. Raffles Davison is unusual in this kind of architectural publicity – not because of how this detail of the building is depicted but in its staffage. This is partly because the boy shown is evidently poor and partly because of the ideas the boy's presence brings together so compactly. At near centre is a carved roundel under an oriel window. The carving, we are told, represents 'a girl in the dress of the last century spinning in the primitive way then in vogue'.[1] To either side, the wall's alternating courses of masonry are drawn out across the full breadth of the print, like a net stretched taut just behind the picture plane. What we are being shown appears to be something about the newly assertive town council: its rule is everywhere, and especially in the management of 'gas', written twice on the glass and energising the handsome street lamp, representing its main municipal use as well as symbolising cleanliness and illumination. The boy is a contemporary street type, an urchin or 'street arab', usually associated with 'rowdyism'.[2] The only remaining brace holding up his trousers is angled in a structural improvisation not unlike the buttresses and groins depicted in neighbouring images of the publication. Of course, this 'Gothic' urchin is poor; his pathetic cuteness is coherently arranged and detailed. He evokes neither pity nor distress. And he is surely intended as a potential beneficiary, in some way, of the dynamic municipal urbanism that has produced what is in front of him (even if municipal control does not ensure progressive employment policies).[3] Although he perches on his toes as if to peer

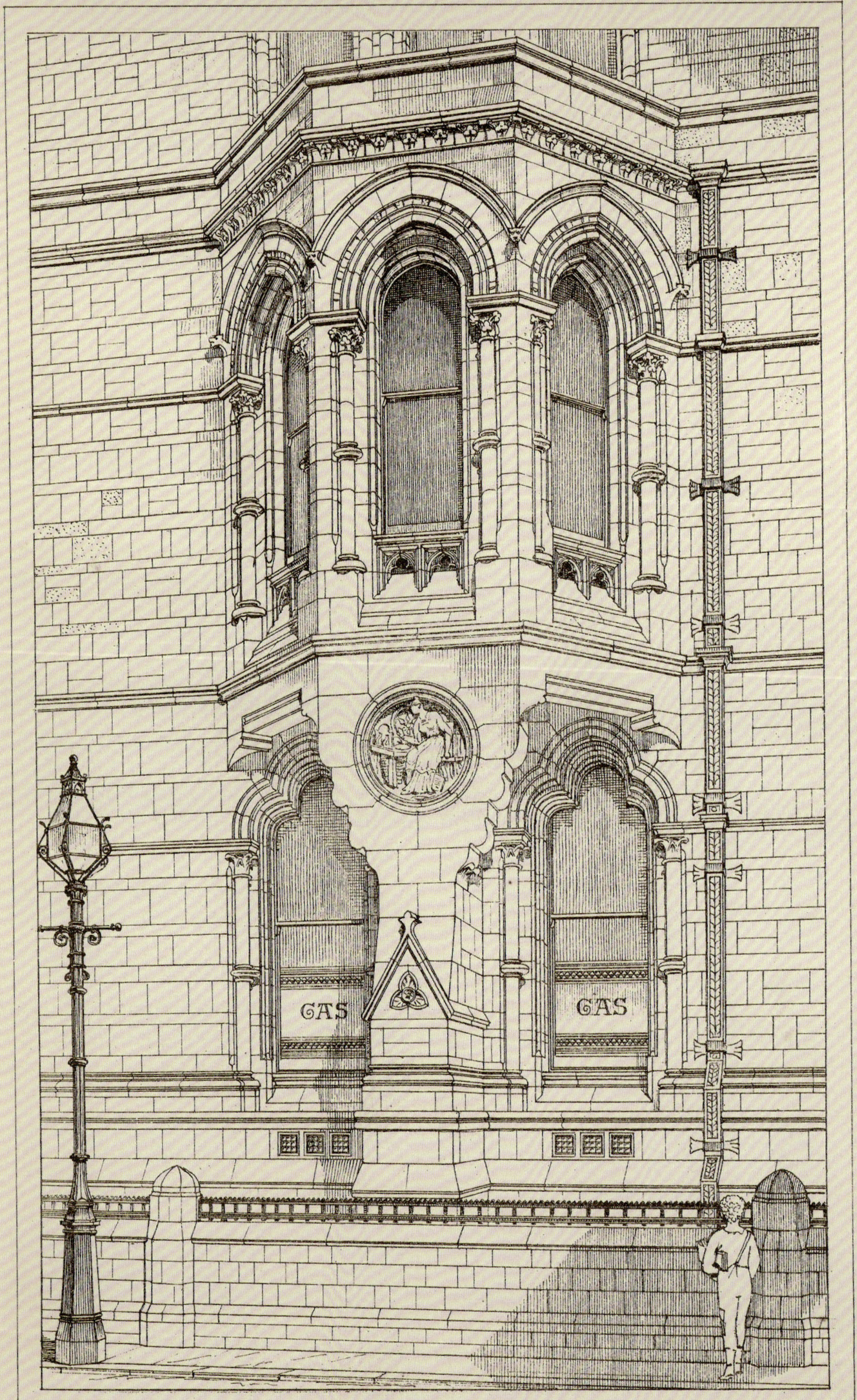

BAY IN LLOYD STREET.

[75] 'Bay in Lloyd Street', 1878. Engraving by T. Raffles Davison, from William Axon (ed.), *An Architectural and General Description of the Town Hall, Manchester* (1878).

over the wall, he doesn't engage convincingly with the building except as a measure for the height and subdivision of the wall or perhaps as a moral anti-equivalent to the anthropomorphic street lamp. Furthermore, he's not so much anomalous as almost too purposefully made marginal: he's in the shadow yet not darkened by it, very clearly on our side of the wall. He may be an antitype of the idealised worker (more adolescent, more decorous) with her simple machine sculpted above. More subliminally, he is also an antitype to that abstract equivalent (and likely product) of machine power, the sliced silhouette of mouldings that is the oriel's buttress. More overtly, through him we are alerted to the content of the building, not just what it contains but what we are led to believe it stands for, that is, not only gas but cotton, its manufacture and its various machines, the temporality of ancient and modern, and a whole way of justifying, of 'spinning', Manchester's new urban order. The bringing of light, the city made safe, the 'street arab' made picturesque.

If the image tells us something about a detail of the building and introduces the theme of how cotton and its machines can be understood as relating to it, the building's ancientness – or shall we say its overtly old newness? – must also be addressed, for it is evidently there as much in the pointed arches as in that 'primitive way' of spinning. Here is another way of putting it, from a decade earlier and at the start of the campaign to build the Town Hall: 'It is to be intimated that, without any absolute limitations to any particular style, the preference of the Council is in favour of Gothic'[4] (fig. 74). These are the strangely tentative words with which the civic leaders of the shock city, the grimy cradle of urban industrial culture, announced the decision that its most signal public building would look medieval. And that is what the pointed arches in the engraving are doing – looking medieval. But why should that be so? Why should Manchester's leaders in 1866 want or need a municipal palace in a Gothic style?[5] While it is already clear that cotton would play a part in the building's iconography, how, if at all, would the modern machines and their industrial environments that were the business of the men who dominated the administration of the municipality, find a place in this medieval-style new Town Hall?

Such questions have tended to be sidestepped by architectural historians and others rather than answered directly or at any length.[6] The reasons of an earlier Victorian generation are alluded to, particularly Gothic as the sign of a revived medieval life-world that embodied religious virtue (whether in its closely related ecclesiological or its Puginian Catholic forms) as a 'backlash' against industrialism and as a form of nostalgia.[7] Marginal, though influential, cultural critics (like Ruskin) are seen to have their views magically carried into an industrial culture for which they had little or no sympathy.[8] In terms of architectural theory, Gothic is seen to have finally merged its rationalist and antiquarian traditions and become inevitable.[9] Relatedly, as this is like a medieval cloth hall and Manchester is Cottonopolis, 'modern gothic' or Gothic 'adapted to the requirements of the nineteenth century' is fitting; its choice is a celebration of 'collective glory' or a 'particular capacity to express the local'.[10] Perhaps Victorians simply lacked a 'vision of modernity'.[11] Perhaps the conjunction of industry and Gothic is inexplicable, a contradiction or even an irony.[12] Or perhaps it can be explained if Gothic is understood as a veil, a disavowal of industry and its technologies.[13] More so, the turn to Gothic is perhaps proleptic of decline or irrelevance, of a culture that doesn't know how to be industrial, that 'escapes' into a medieval dreamland; and so, having pushed aside the enfeebled aristocrat, the once dynamic industrialist in turn gets complacent and can only erect 'historical screens' around himself.[14]

None of these shrugged-off explanations are necessarily wrong, they are either applied too broadly or don't take us very far. Part of the problem may be the term 'Gothic Revival' itself, which, provided with its founding history in Charles Eastlake's *A History of the Gothic Revival* (1872), invested the manifold phenomenon with a backward, history-seeking impetus: it was definably always about a 'self-conscious use of antique forms' and the '[mastering of] the grammar of an ancient art', even as some of its architects attempted to 'accommodate … the common requirements of social life'.[15] (It was also, of course, cast as retrospective in its search for a tribal, even racial, founding moment – not just revival but 'Gothic' revival.)

[76] Manchester Town Hall, 1867–77. Architect: Alfred Waterhouse. Coloured lithograph, from William Axon (ed.), *An Architectural and General Description of the Town Hall, Manchester* (1878).

One of the key figures in building the Town Hall, Abel Heywood, called it a 'worthy monument of the industrial greatness of Manchester', and I propose to take this seriously in what follows – that it was indeed a specifically *industrial* greatness that was monumentalised.[16] Suppose, then, that a significant part of the Gothic Revival *is* industrial culture, that it is, in metaphoric and appropriately problematic ways, both nature and machine, both ancient and modern. That is what is central to this chapter.

TO SEE THE CITY ANEW IS PERHAPS WHAT THE VIEW OVER Manchester with which this book opened was really about: to see its emerging order, to see some sense in its pattern of building, to see from a new height and angle (see fig. 1). Its perversity in ignoring the very building whose completion it had been commissioned to commemorate may be explained by this sense of the new urban prospects – imagining become realisation – that were now provided. As well as a cityscape dramatically shaped by the industrial bourgeoisie in the preceding decades, it also shows how the Town Hall relates to this city; how, as it were, it looks at Manchester; and how it joins the order that has already emerged there. If this is so, we might well ask: how does the city look at the Town Hall, or at least how was that reciprocal look imagined by the new building's creators?

Sanctioned by the architect Alfred Waterhouse's drawings and reiterated in print and photograph, the most common view of the Town Hall was from the north and back towards the position of the 1876 engraving (fig. 76). Of course, there are many views that align with the principal entrance and show the main front facing Albert Square, but frontal views were quite awkward because of the limited depth of the square and were difficult to manipulate if something of its setting was to be included in the view (the building always ends up seeming stark and isolated). Understandably, then, the angled view, centred on the north-east corner and looking obliquely down the main front, was the most common way of representing the building, and it certainly accords with the picturesque effects associated with Gothic Revival buildings. It shows the Town Hall as a complex object, an informal yet imposing pile-up clustering around a projecting pavilion on the corner. It is a kind of city analogue or city compressed, declaring that the dynamic between formal and informal, functional order and digressive expression, is an overt part of its makers' conception of the Town Hall's urban presence. Elsewhere, and similarly, the Town Hall's main towers, at the base and peak of the triangle of land it occupies – over the main Albert Square entrance and the minor Cooper Street entrance – while central to their facades, do not face down major streets but create their own, more proximate relationships (with the Albert Memorial, for instance). Waterhouse believed Gothic to be particularly well suited to the 'atmosphere' of Manchester, and that it engaged in a form of dialogue with a set of Gothic Revival buildings nearby.[17]

If we look at the plan, this observation can be extended further to show how the Town Hall articulated with other important hubs within the city (fig. 77). There were four main public entrances into the building, one on each of its frontages. The 'principal entrance' on the frontage facing Albert Square was only nominally the main entrance; its architecture and positioning relative to the building's internal functions marked it out as mainly ceremonial, and its relation to the external city was largely with the symbolic public space of the square (though the city's legal district lay beyond the square). Two distinct urban spheres were addressed by the Lloyd Street entrance (to the right of the plan), which serviced municipal politics, health and sanitation, and the Cooper Street entrance (on the upper or south-west side of the plan), which serviced commerce and the offices in charge of the city's gas and water utilities. The fourth entrance, marked by the great picturesque assemblage on the north-east, might thus just as well be called the financial corner of the building (though it also gives access to the mayor's apartments). We might understand this entrance and its corner as both hailing and making itself permeable to the Royal Exchange further across the city to the north-east, and the flow of cotton brokers bringing their business from there to the Town Hall's treasury department through a dedicated entrance at this corner of the building.[18]

More than a political space, then, the building was conceived as a dynamic and multifunctional administrative centre in the city's economic life, taking in revenues and servicing businesses, often

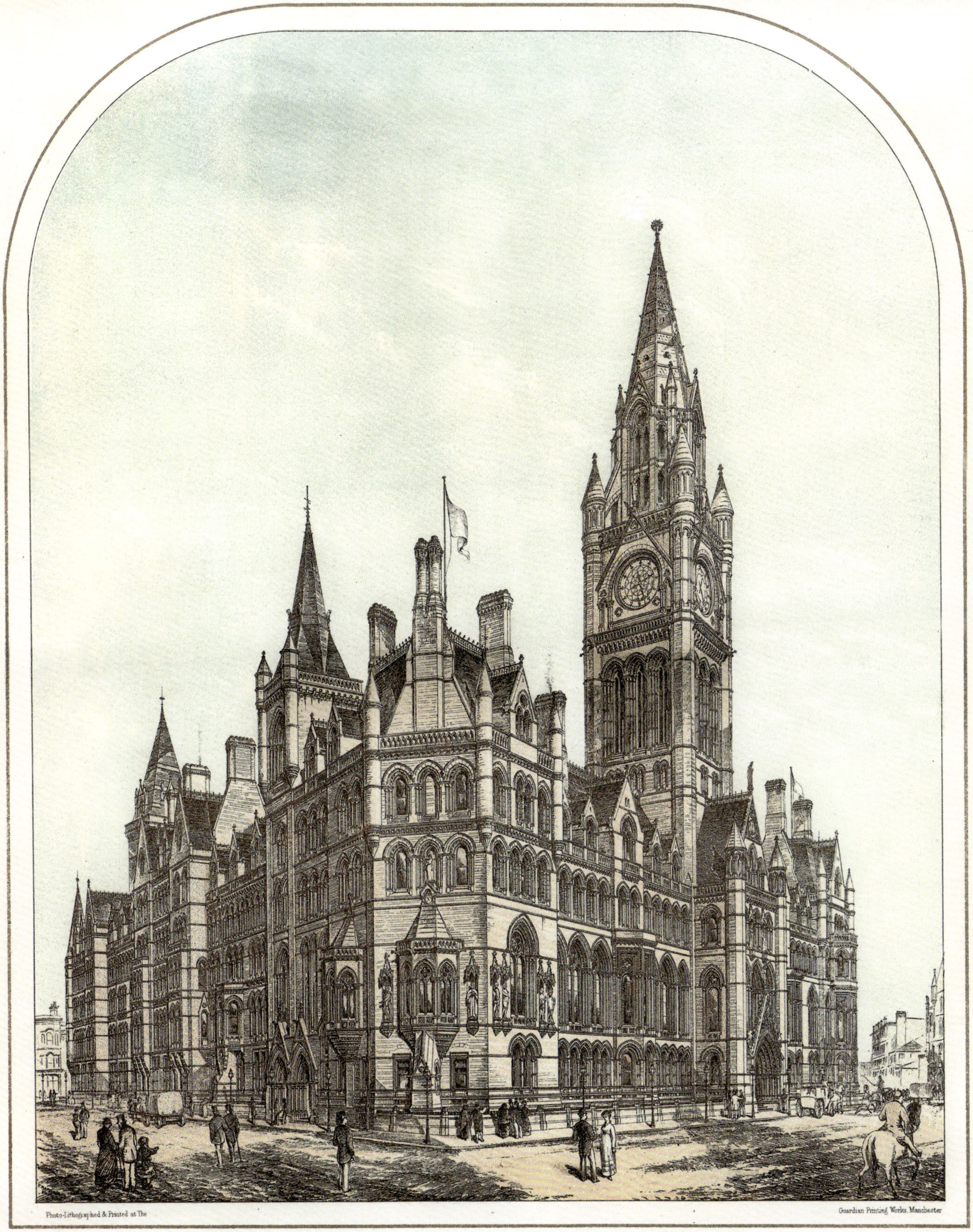

Photo-Lithographed & Printed at The Guardian Printing Works, Manchester

THE NEW TOWN HALL, MANCHESTER.

ALFRED WATERHOUSE, F.R.I.B.A., ARCHITECT.

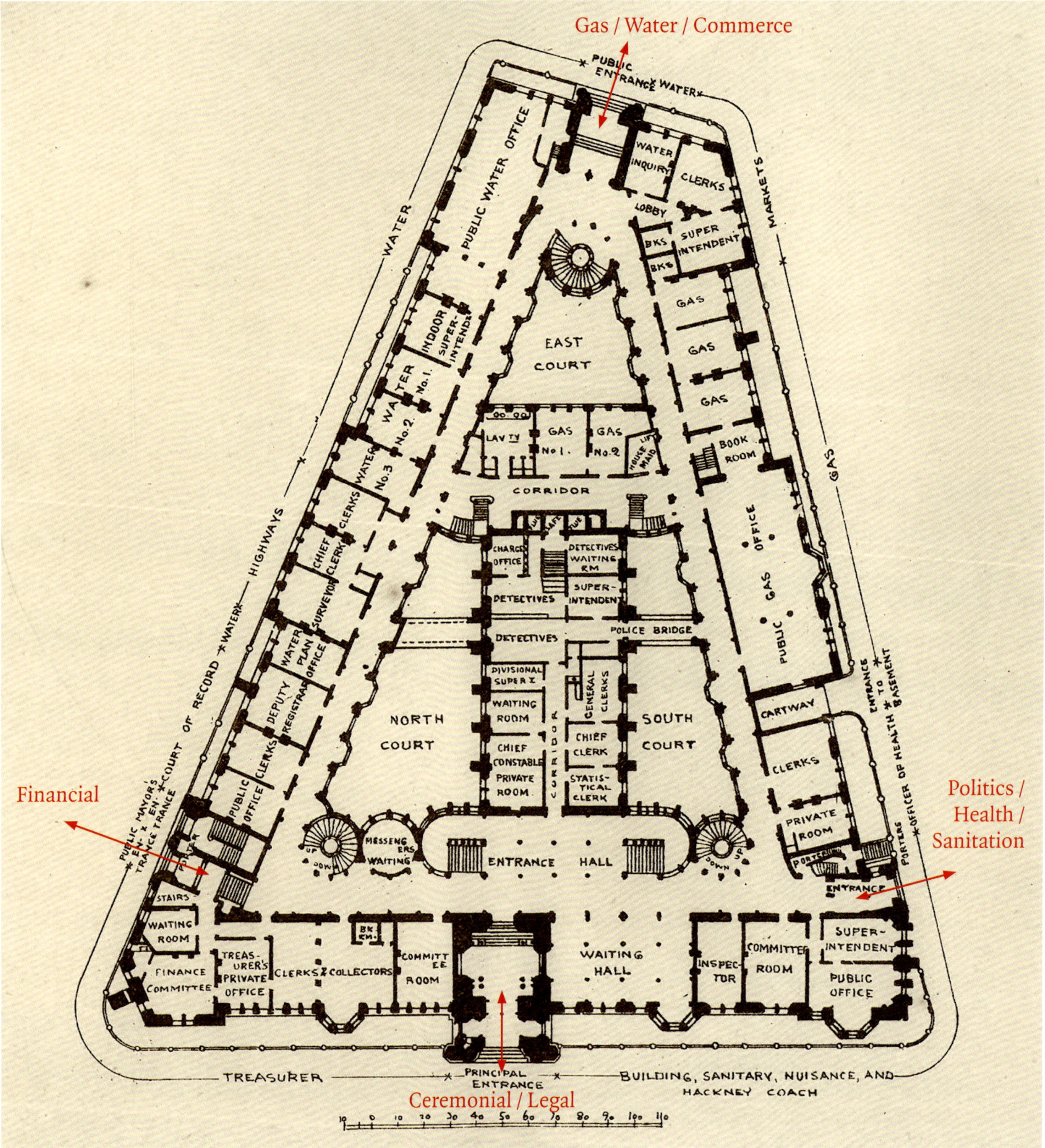

Gas / Water / Commerce
PUBLIC ENTRANCE
WATER
WATER INQUIRY
CLERKS
LOBBY
BKS
SUPER INTENDENT
MARKETS
PUBLIC WATER OFFICE
INDOOR SUPER-INTENDS
WATER No. 1.
WATER No. 2.
WATER No. 3
CLERKS
CHIEF CLERK
SURVEYOR
WATER PLAN OFFICE
DEPUTY REGISTRAR
CLERKS
PUBLIC OFFICE
EAST COURT
GAS
GAS
GAS
LAV'TY
GAS No 1.
GAS No 2
HOUSE MAID
LIFT
BOOK ROOM
CORRIDOR
CHARGE OFFICE
DETECTIVES WAITING RM
DETECTIVES
SUPER-INTENDENT
DETECTIVES
POLICE BRIDGE
PUBLIC GAS OFFICE
GAS
HIGHWAYS
COURT OF RECORD
PUBLIC MAYOR'S EN- & EN-TRANCE TRANCE
DIVISIONAL SUPER T
WAITING ROOM
CHIEF CONSTABLE PRIVATE ROOM
CORRIDOR
GENERAL CLERKS
CHIEF CLERK
STATIS-TICAL CLERK
NORTH COURT
SOUTH COURT
CARTWAY
CLERKS
PRIVATE ROOM
ENTRANCE TO BASEMENT
OFFICER OF HEALTH
PORTERS
Financial
Politics / Health / Sanitation
STAIRS
WAITING ROOM
MESSENGERS WAITING
ENTRANCE HALL
UP
DOWN
ENTRANCE
FINANCE COMMITTEE
TREAS-URER'S PRIVATE OFFICE
CLERKS & COLLECTORS
BK. RM.
COMMITTEE ROOM
WAITING HALL
INSPEC-TOR
COMMITTEE ROOM
SUPER-INTENDENT
PUBLIC OFFICE
TREASURER
PRINCIPAL ENTRANCE
BUILDING, SANITARY, NUISANCE, AND HACKNEY COACH
Ceremonial / Legal
10 0 10 20 30 40 50 60 70 80 90 100 110

[77] Manchester Town Hall: ground-floor plan showing main entrances and functional orientations. From William Axon (ed.), *An Architectural and General Description of the Town Hall, Manchester* (1878).

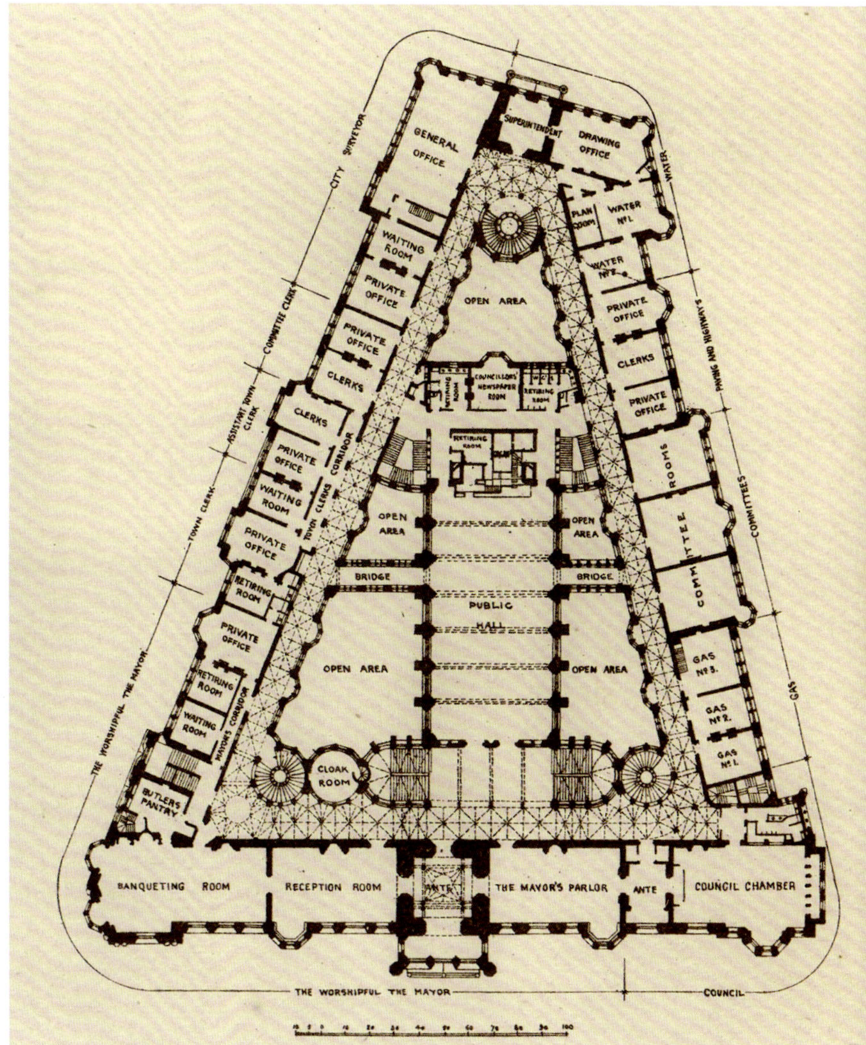

[78] Manchester Town Hall: first-floor plan. From William Axon (ed.), *An Architectural and General Description of the Town Hall, Manchester* (1878).

with little difference between municipal and private interests.[19] This explains why the council chamber, as the main political space of debate and discussion, was made marginal within the Town Hall's plan, placed on the north-west corner of the first floor at the end of a group of reception spaces (even Waterhouse downgraded it, referring to it as part of a 'suite of entertaining rooms'), with banked seats for the public located on a gallery above the councillors in the chamber (fig. 78).[20] In the centre of the building, instead, was the Great Hall, a place for meetings and ceremony, for the representation of the city's history (however equivocal that might be, as we shall see), rather than for the work of politics, and best accessed from the 'principal entrance'. The relative marginalisation of representative politics was itself, of course, a political act. (As T. C. Horsfall recognised, 'I know nothing more disheartening than the contrast between the vast building in which the Council meets and the smallness of the policy which proceeds from it.'[21]) The industrial bourgeoisie were investing in town halls across the north-west, defining themselves as integral to the new civic realm and the administration of public utilities, and so the new political dispositions (whether Tory or Liberal) of local government were to be tied to the interests and fortunes of this class – as with the Free Trade Hall, capital was symbolised as public spirit and public spirit as capital.[22] The highly profitable administration of gas and water utilities was one of the main reasons: this was 'municipal capitalism' at full flow, with each of the corporation's utility departments working effectively as an 'autonomous business'.[23] Industrialists had invested heavily in gas and water early in the century, and these utilities had become hugely profitable by the time the Town Hall was first mooted. They required 'huge trading department[s]' and therefore occupied large areas of the Town Hall's ground and first floors.[24] Another suspension of the everyday political world can be detected in the entrance sequence, where the ceremonial functions of the building were centred. The entrance was on a kind of pseudo-axis. Leading to the Great Hall at the heart of the building but not on an axis with it, it was not continued through the Town Hall and was not even strictly central to the facade. Sculpture around the entrance engaged the Town Hall with the great and distant figures of the area's past (its conqueror the Emperor Agricola, as well as Henry III and Elizabeth I, who gave privileges to the city) and a higher symbolism (St George) – but, again, not with the realm of institutionalised politics.

In the entrances and their relation to the plan, therefore, we see how the Town Hall embodied the disposition of Manchester's now dominant class. Spaces for political debate by the minimal representative democracy that existed were marginal and minor, spaces for commercial functions (especially the local monopoly of gas) and the management of the city's economy were dominant

[79] Manchester Town Hall: ground-floor staircase.

[80] Manchester Town Hall: ground-floor plan showing the flow of functions within and beyond the Town Hall. From William Axon (ed.), *An Architectural and General Description of the Town Hall, Manchester* (1878).

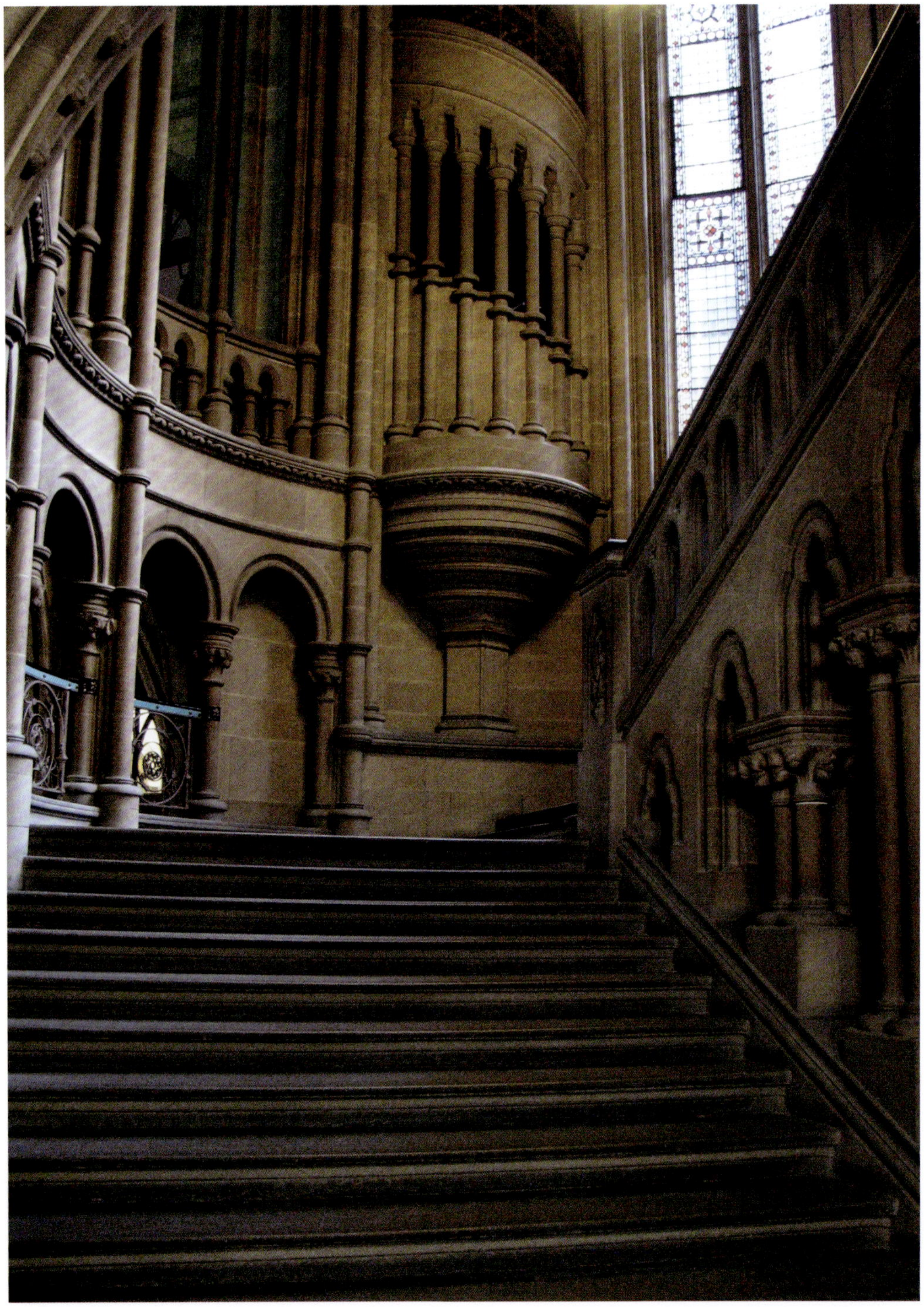

and clustered around most of the entrances, while spaces for civic ceremony were, as expected, central to the building – as were, as we shall see, pomp and glamour – but they were also curtailed and made appendix-like. Spaces for policing, it should be added, were also important to the plan; indeed, the chief constable's office and his police department were located below the Great Hall; they are central in the ground-floor plan, but for more everyday functions they were accessed by a bridge above and a cartway below leading straight into the courtyard and the cells in the basement.[25] (This caused an interesting planning problem for Waterhouse – a corridor giving public access to the police department is on axis with the entrance hall, yet this could not be allowed to seem like the culmination of the entrance sequence. The twin grand staircases on either side do more than enough through their sheer architectural éclat to direct attention elsewhere (fig. 79).)

This kind of functionality, whereby the building points to and embraces different constituencies beyond it in the surrounding city, complemented another aspect of the Town Hall – the idea of the building as a smoothly organised circulation system, one that justified the term 'machine-like' in the relation between its component parts, major and minor. The spatial system conducted a flow of functions through and around it in discretely provided routes (ceremonial, functional and public, as well as for the police, the mayor and employees) (fig. 80). All this was an explicit part of the Town Hall's purpose.

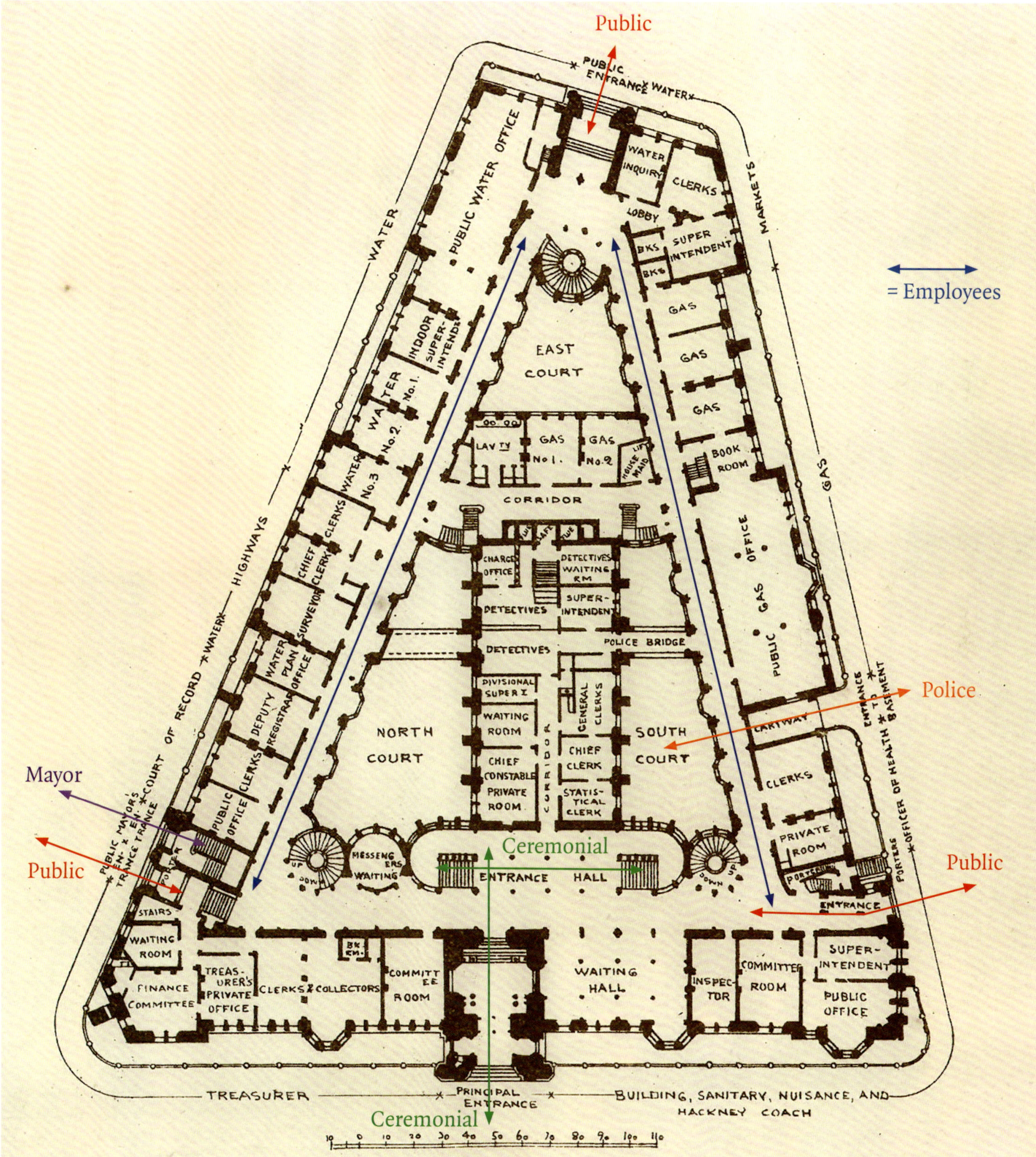

Public
PUBLIC ENTRANCE
WATER
WATER INQUIRY
CLERKS
LOBBY
SUPER INTENDENT
BKS
PUBLIC WATER OFFICE
MARKETS
= Employees
EAST COURT
INDOOR SUPER-INTENDS
WATER No. 1.
WATER No. 2
WATER No. 3
GAS
GAS
GAS
LAV TY
GAS No. 1.
GAS No. 2
HOUSE MAID
LIFT
BOOK ROOM
CORRIDOR
CLERKS
CHIEF CLERKS
SURVEYOR
HIGHWAYS
GAS
CHARGE OFFICE
DETECTIVES WAITING RM
DETECTIVES
SUPER-INTENDENT
PUBLIC GAS OFFICE
DETECTIVES
POLICE BRIDGE
WATER PLAN OFFICE
DEPUTY REGISTRAR
COURT OF RECORD
DIVISIONAL SUPER T
WAITING ROOM
CHIEF CONSTABLE PRIVATE ROOM
CORRIDOR
GENERAL CLERKS
CHIEF CLERK
STATISTICAL CLERK
NORTH COURT
SOUTH COURT
Police
CARTWAY
ENTRANCE TO BASEMENT
OFFICER OF HEALTH
CLERKS
PRIVATE ROOM
Mayor
PUBLIC MAYOR'S EN-TRANCE
PUBLIC OFFICE
CLERKS
Public
PORTER
Ceremonial
MESSENGERS WAITING
ENTRANCE HALL
UP
DOWN
PORTERS
Public
ENTRANCE
STAIRS
WAITING ROOM
FINANCE COMMITTEE
TREASURER'S PRIVATE OFFICE
CLERKS & COLLECTORS
BK RM.
COMMITTEE ROOM
WAITING HALL
INSPECTOR
COMMITTEE ROOM
SUPER-INTENDENT
PUBLIC OFFICE
TREASURER
PRINCIPAL ENTRANCE
BUILDING, SANITARY, NUISANCE, AND HACKNEY COACH
Ceremonial
10 0 10 20 30 40 50 60 70 80 90 100 110

[81] The old Town Hall, Manchester, 1819–34. Architect: Francis Goodwin. Photograph: James Mudd, c.1870. Manchester Libraries, Information and Archives.

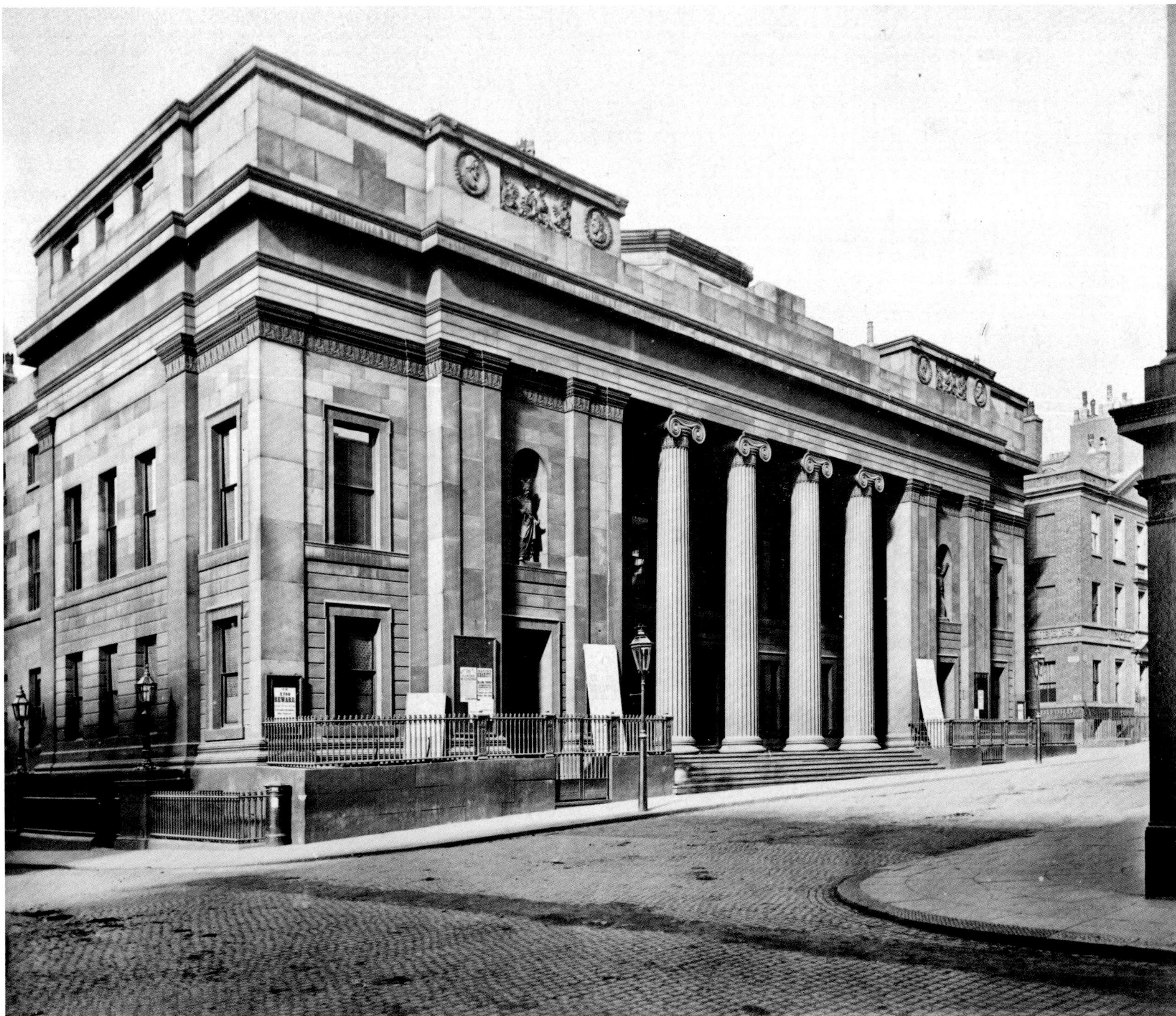

And this purposiveness had a demonstrative element to it. The new building was conceived as an expansive replacement for the confined and overburdened spaces of the old Town Hall on King Street, built when the town was a third the size of the city in the 1870s[26] (fig. 81). Designed in 1819 by Francis Goodwin (and completed by Richard Lane in the 1834), the original Town Hall was in the then fashionable Greek Revival style, with a frontage inspired by the Erechtheion. It was intended mainly as a building for meetings and assemblies rather than for administrative toil. Nor was it a centre of political power when it was first built, before the Municipal Corporations Act of 1835, because that lay in the hands of the police commissioners and the Court Leet (though their officers were given space in the Town Hall). The latter used to meet in a house on Brown Street, a 'murky chamber', in the words of Richard Cobden:

> *Ascending by a flight of steps in Brown Street, leading up to several other apartments, and to a dancing master's academy amongst the rest. I reached the door of the manor court room, which is large, and altogether destitute of furniture, whose row of tall old-fashioned windows would, but for the crust of smoke and dirt that covered them, have afforded a cheerful light. The atmosphere of the room was heavy and stale; it had probably been confined ever since the last public meeting of the teetotallers was held there, a month before. To the left of the door lay a heap of sawdust ... The jurors were now penned within a small enclosure at the furthest extremity of the room; the representative of the Lord of the Manor took his seat in a small desk springing from the wall; his legal agent sat below.*

After the jury retired they were conducted 'into a closet under the stairs in which were deposited the bonnets, shawls, cloaks and clogs of the nymphs who were threading the mazes of the quadrille and waltz in the dancing academy above'.[27] Whether the indolent nature of proceedings is a true picture is less interesting than the casual dilapidation that is its complement – this is the trope that is linked to a pre-industrial or 'ancient' Manchester whose depictions are discussed elsewhere in this book, and in Cobden's view was more evidence for incorporation.[28] The contrast could not have been greater between the discreet if unfocused elegance of Goodwin's building and the Court Leet, with its 'impanneled' jury, in its last years.[29] And yet Goodwin's Town Hall was equally unsuited to the administration of the rapidly growing city. Crucially, it made little provision for the council's new responsibility (from 1819) for supplying gas, even though the building's funding was based on promised revenues from that source. The gas directors shared space with the borough reeve's officers and the police commissioners. In addition to other scandals, the old Town Hall came to represent for many the follies of administration in the pre-incorporation town.[30] Its decorations, for instance, were conceived entirely without reference to Manchester's industrial make-over, and instead focused on the recent wars with France, which were fast becoming history. Frescoes on its ceiling represented 'the figures of Britannia, crowned by the genius of Immortality, and commanding Peace to descend on Europe ... then comes a figure bearing the fasces, descriptive of Constitutional Law, who overthrows Hypocrisy and Tyranny'.[31] And so on.

If the new Town Hall marked a purposive new era – the victory and eminence of the industrial bourgeoisie – it also celebrated their fortunate escape in terms of the global cotton trade. When the proposal for a new building was first seriously discussed in 1863, it came out of the work that the council was doing to relieve the effects of the cotton famine due to the American Civil War.[32] While this meant that more municipal office space was needed, it also had deeper implications for the city's status as Cottonopolis. The war was profoundly challenging for industrialists, '[severing] in one stroke the relationships that had underpinned the worldwide web of cotton production and global capitalism since the 1780s'.[33] The ensuing economic scramble was largely about finding new suppliers of raw cotton as mills reduced their shifts or shut down completely. The consequent global reconstruction of the supply and trading of cotton was thus also a moment marking both survival and renewal (even the prospect of peace in 1865 had caused global panic). 'The misery that appeared to be hanging over us', as Edward Potter of the Manchester Chamber of Commerce put it, had been dispelled.[34] This, it might be proposed, remained as a kind of embedded memorial function of the

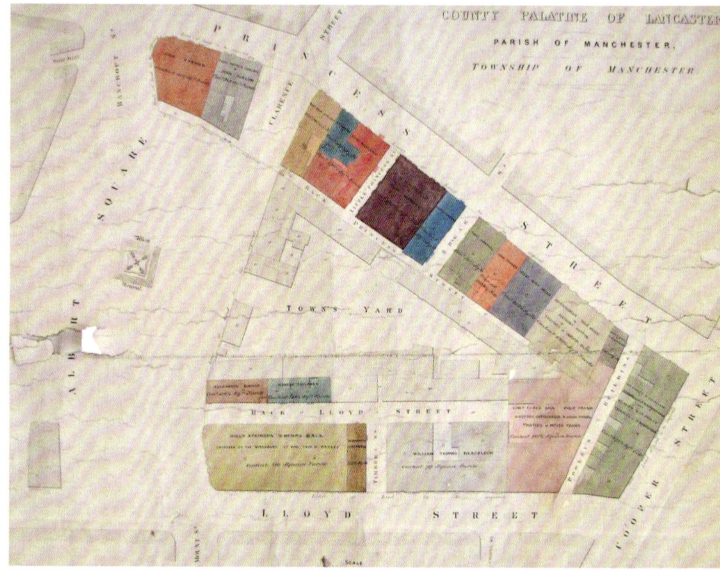

[82] The 'Town's Yard': site plan, c.1860. Manchester Libraries, Information and Archives.

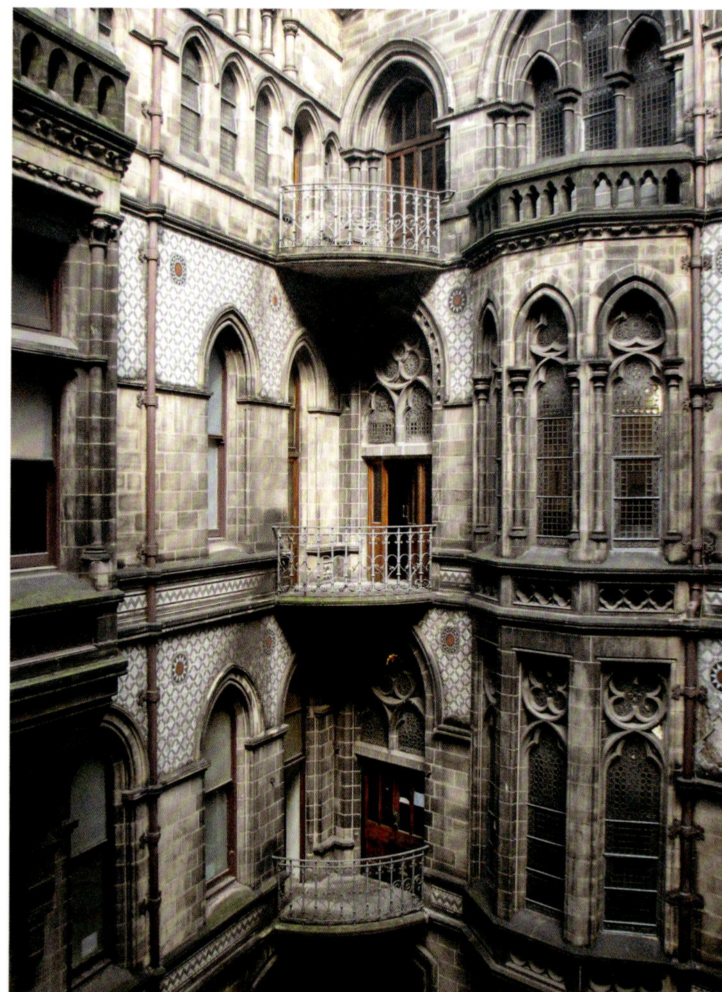

[83] Manchester Town Hall: courtyard. Architect: Alfred Waterhouse.

eventual building, its imagination of civic collectivity a celebration of the industrial bourgeoisie as the leadership and new paternalist class of the city. The subjects of the crisis caused by war, and the organisation of relief for the indigent, may not have found figurative form in the Town Hall but they were both there in its initiation; they had brought to a head the inadequacies of the old building.

Whatever its use of historical styles, the new Town Hall certainly embodied a radically new conception of municipal space. This stemmed in part from the way Waterhouse rethought a muddled collection of municipal facilities, including waste disposal, on the old 'Town's Yard' site (fig. 82). Changes to this site, bounded by Albert Square, Princess Street and Lloyd Street, were integral to street improvements in this part of the city, fluidly collating distinct functions and extending the building's glamour and authority beyond it.[35] The recognition of the resulting smooth circulation can be seen in the kind of praise given to Waterhouse's design, then and more recently.[36] It won the competition held in 1867 largely because of its plan, particularly how the interior corridors running along all three sides of its triangular plan brought clarity to the challenging plot shape.[37] Most impressive, as we have seen, was its organisation of entrances, corridors, stairs and rooms to give lucid form to a new city within a city. And this again was not only an internal matter; it also had implications for the larger city around it. The relentless length of the building's corridors was relieved by views onto the miniature 'cityscape' of the inner courtyards (fig. 83). This also allowed all the offices and meeting rooms to be placed on the outer side, to make municipality oversee the city as much as to be part of its reform (as we saw in Raffles Davison's image – see fig. 75 – at the outset of this chapter). In these street facades the smoothness of the internal organisation was complemented by notably complex elevations.

On the two long sides of this triangular site the building has always been faced directly by other buildings as part of a street corridor. Although there are broad symmetrical elements here high up on the facade, the pedestrian's experience is more likely to be of asymmetrical features such as the tower and the broached spire over the mayor's apartments, and the unexpected diversity of corbels and oriels, as well as of acute raking views and physically

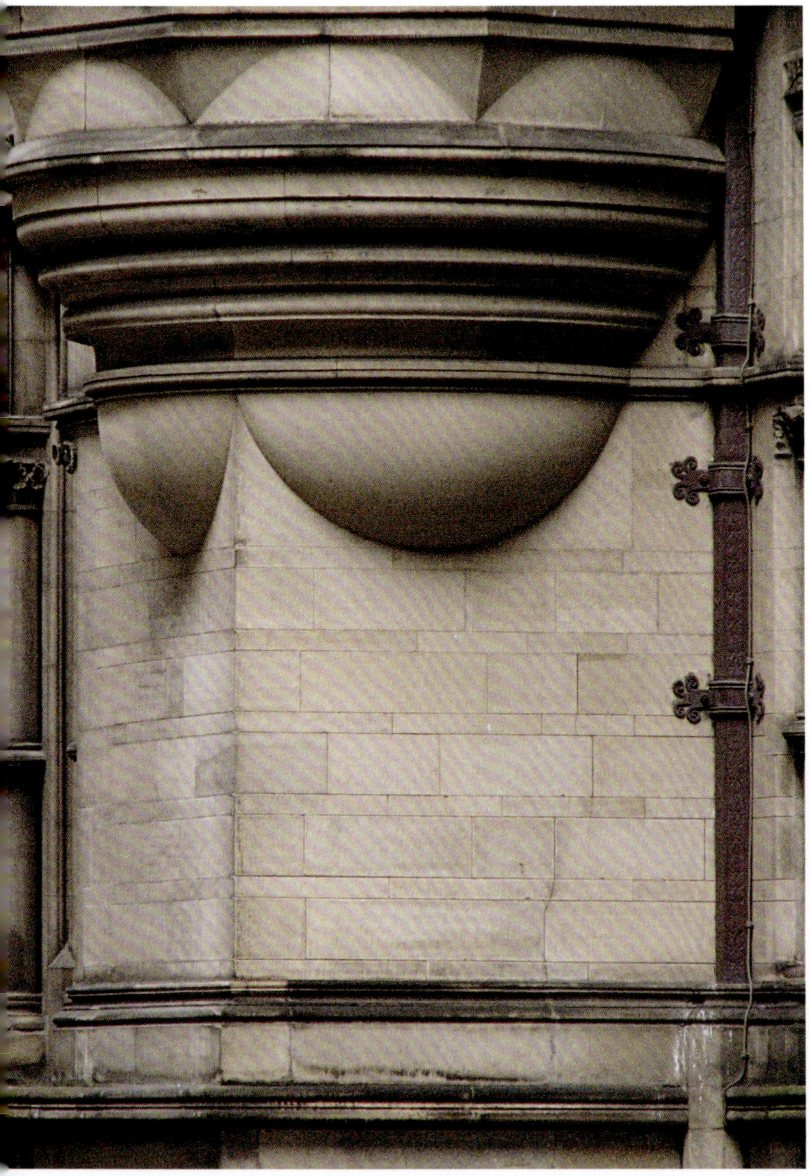

[84] Manchester Town Hall: detail of the Princess Street side.

close masses of stone, the building's constantly surprising detail (fig. 84). The design here plays with the building line: a boundary wall occasionally emerges from the building mass and is marked by domed posts; buttresses and flying buttresses abut this line or are set back within it; the wall planes advance and recede. It is as if the city's diversity beyond were reflected in these facades: to walk along the building's flanks was to see a gamut of apparent improvisations and abbreviations.

Here it's relevant to recall what could be termed the crisis of the street earlier in the century. Already discussed in Chapter 1 on Ancoats, this can also be identified in the writing of social reformers like James Kay, in the condition-of-England novels of the 1840s, and in Friedrich Engels's descriptions of the industrial city.[38] In these accounts of social alienation the street is barely knowable or 'civilised'. Hardly a street at all, it is sketched in as chaotic or deserted or half-made, a fraught zone of 'brutal indifference' or antagonism between men and women, masters and workers – a 'dissolution', Engels wrote, 'into monads'.[39] Its identity is in flux as much as the class and sexual identities of those who use it. The street crisis became, in the 1860s and later, a desire to reassure Manchester that the street was manageable, was civilised: there is a trope of 'street architecture',[40] for instance, and a subgenre of literature on 'Manchester streets and Manchester men'.[41] And there was also an architectural response to the same concerns, a carving out of ideal streets and streets that represented and negotiated urban complexity, both of which, I suggest, can be found in the Town Hall. The crisis had been 'solved', or at least sublimated, into these two forms of the imaginary street: a street placed firmly within the realm of civic governance, and a complementary street suggested by making various virtuous gestures to the old-fashioned compromises of the city outside the Town Hall.

AS A BEAUTIFUL MECHANISM, THE TOWN HALL MUST have been particularly attractive to the industrialists of Manchester who had agitated for the Municipal Corporations Act (1835) and had dominated the city's council ever since its subsequent incorporation in 1838.[42] Many of Manchester's mayors, including the first two after incorporation, were industrialists. They saw the town council as a local parliament dominated by their own class but expressive of the needs of the propertied classes of the city as a whole: as one wrote, 'a town council … is opposed to that principle of centralization which is the bane of continental governments. It fosters a love of freedom. It teaches the people to rely upon their own exertions, to think and act for themselves: and that is the characteristic of a free people.'[43]

The key men behind the building of the new Town Hall were Abel Heywood, who was mayor when the project was inaugurated and who was associated with it throughout its building, and Joseph Thompson, a local industrialist. Heywood's life itself might

[85] Manchester Town Hall: ceiling mosaic in the entrance hall.

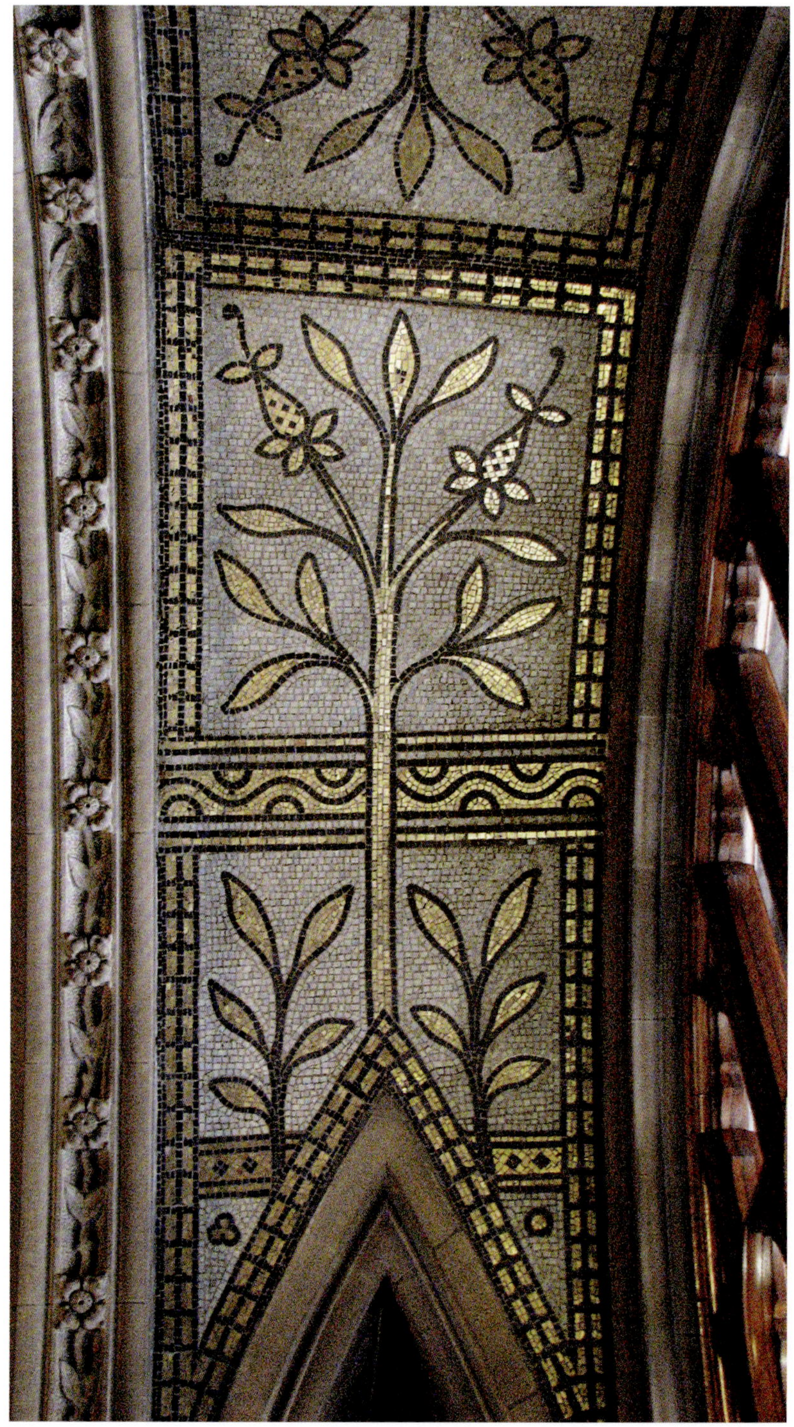

be understood as a long process of political incorporation. From a humble background, he was educated at the Mechanics' Institute and became a bookseller, printer and wallpaper manufacturer. Once an avid Chartist, he became a Cobdenite Free Trader and one of the main campaigners in securing Manchester's municipal status in 1838.[44] Thompson, who owned mills in Ardwick just outside the city centre, was a founder and long-term member of the Manchester Reform Club and had worked with John Bright. He sat as a councillor on the key building committee driving the project forward, and was already a supporter and friend of its architect, Alfred Waterhouse, from his involvement with previous buildings in the city.[45] Both Heywood and Thompson were members of the bourgeoisie, Liberal in their political affiliations (even if Heywood had held Radical beliefs earlier), who were making the town over into their image and for whom Free Trade was the reigning theology in the contest for global markets and local eminence.

Cotton and cotton machines were crucial to this industrialist conception of the building and of its relation to the city's 'industrial greatness'. As Raffles Davison's engraving indicated, one level of controlled connection between the Town Hall and the mills and warehouses that had made industrial Manchester was cotton's appearance as image and decorative motif. This occurs most obviously in the building's ceremonial entrance spaces. Moving through the main portal, we stand immediately beneath a groined ceiling, a dark space in which tesserae impart Byzantine glitter in a mosaic of cotton plants (fig. 85). As we step further into the building, the floor mosaic is scattered with cotton flowers. Upstairs, on the landing outside the Great Hall the flowers are replaced by bees – the workers devoted to their naturally ordained pollination (knowing nothing of the struggle between labour and capital) – around which runs a border of cotton ropes in a cable pattern (fig. 86). Inside the Great Hall there are crossed cotton shuttles on the ceiling, as well as more bees and cotton plants, and of course the cotton subjects in Ford Madox Brown's great series of paintings (1879–93) on either side of the hall. The subjects seem to have been decided by Thompson and Waterhouse consistent with their understanding of the symbolic programme of the building,

[86] Manchester Town Hall: landing outside the Great Hall.

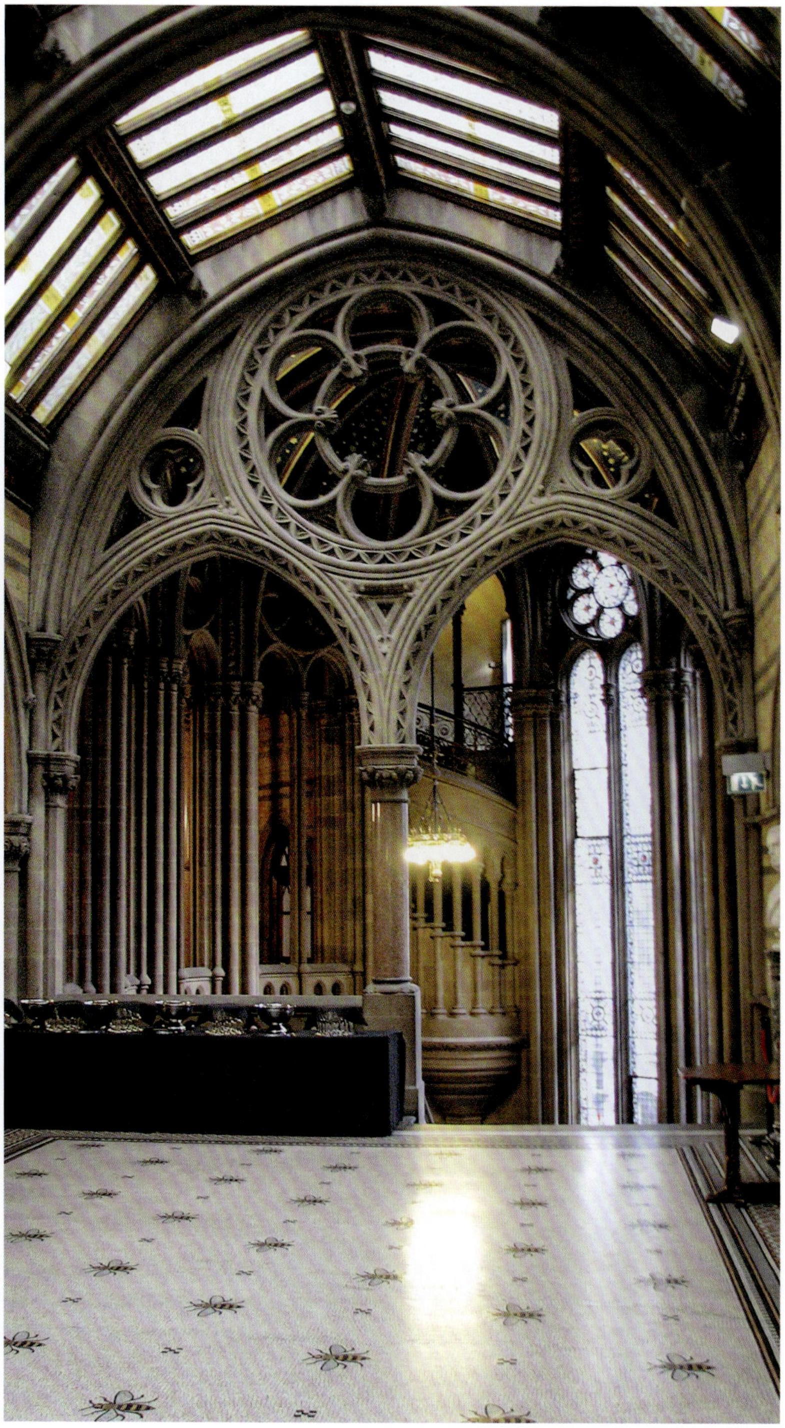

and they included 'John Kay Inventor of the Fly Shuttle' and 'The Establishment of the Flemish Weavers in Manchester' (more about both of these at the end of this chapter). Brown's works (spaces for panels were provided in Waterhouse's design of the Great Hall) were commissioned only after the Town Hall was finished, but clearly it was hoped that they would synchronise their subjects' pan-historical vision of the place of cotton, industry and scientific knowledge in Manchester's past with the same vision in the architecture of the Town Hall.

The many allusions to 'cotton and all its works', so many in fact that they sometimes threatened to swamp any other allusion,[46] were clearly part of a larger set of references and embodiments of Manchester and its past. But what is to stop us moving from the overt cotton reference in Brown's iconography to, say, an implicit reference to millwork (the shafts, gears, pulleys, straps and belts that transfer motive power within a mill) or to the chimneys and iron columns of steam power in the clustered and ringed shafts that divide the wall and frame each of Brown's paintings? (fig. 87). Or, indeed, to think outwards from the more literal ways in which the Town Hall parallels how millwork animates a mill, such as the Town Hall's three basement boilers whose smoke-producing furnaces passed their smoke through a system of tubes and shafts; or the hot water pipes from the boilers that conducted water around the main rooms and corridors via channels below the floors.[47] A looser parallel world – the transubstantiation of the process of manufacture – I suggest, haunts or, perhaps better, echoes through the building in many other ways, concealed, suggestive and sometimes also uncontrolled. And certainly the idea of the building, particularly the mill, as a collection of machines organised within a building that was itself like a machine – 'a mechanical monster whose body fills whole factories', in Marx's words – was shared by the industrialist and his critic.[48]

The links between Town Hall and mill thus take several different forms. One example is the spiral stairs at the corners of the inner courtyard (fig. 88). The architectural-historical way, then and now, of giving these stairs resonance through precedence is to refer to the 'courtyard stair by François I at Blois'.[49] Like all Gothic Revivalists, Waterhouse was heavily steeped in such historical

[87] Manchester Town Hall: Great Hall, showing the architectural surround for one of Ford Madox Brown's murals.

[88] Manchester Town Hall: spiral stair in the corner of the courtyard.

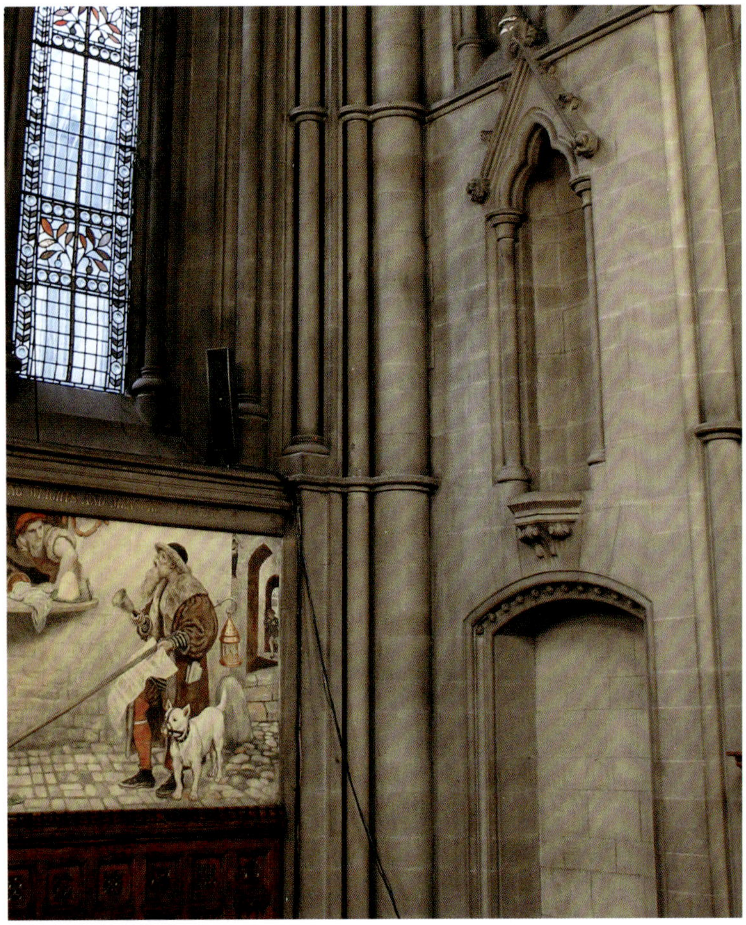

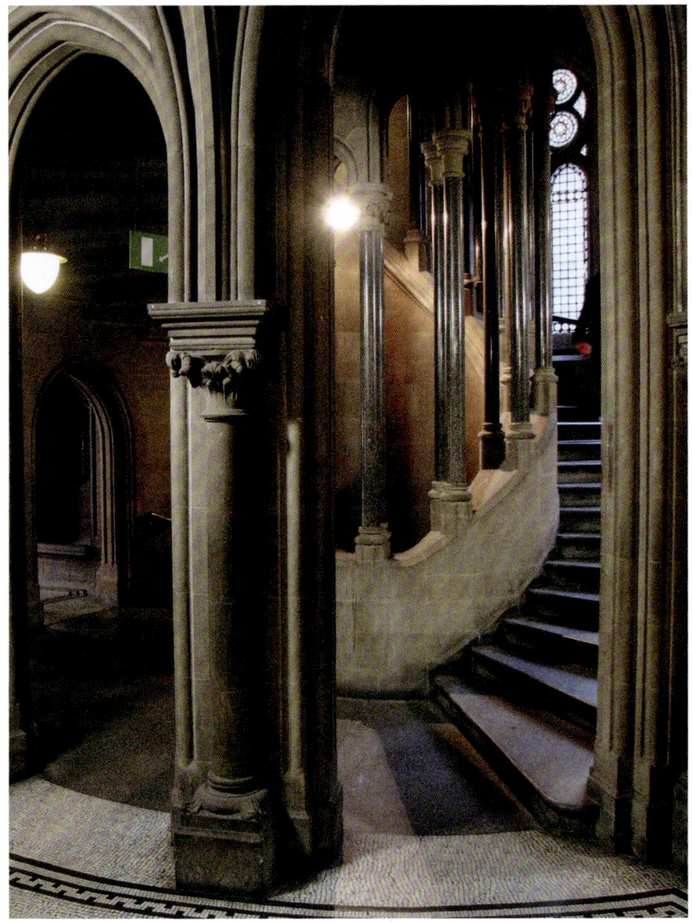

precedents, and he made the link himself, no doubt preferring references from the canon of high architecture.[50] But, whether or not one can see visual similarities with Blois, there are also the flues set within these same stairs at the Town Hall. We could say with more conviction that the spiral stairs are like the chimneys in an Ancoats millyard because the device derives more directly from a peculiar Manchester innovation – the combined chimney and stair tower, which appeared in the first two decades of the century, without any architectural pretentions, as a means of using the stone steps to give structural support to the newly tall chimney stacks of the time.[51] Not unlike a chimney, the open flue in the Town Hall's spiral stairs is a source of heat, for it conducts warm air from heating coils at the bottom of each stair to every level of the building. It is, of course, also dressed up as an elegant Gothic structure, all sprung dynamism in its stretched columns and winding stair, with panelling underneath. So, if it has any relation to these Ancoats mills it is as a kind of allegorisation of the shock to civic city story, a development and refinement to harness the industrial form to a civic purpose.

This is to think in terms of precedent or appropriation. Alternatively, we might consider a shared line of techno-scientific and architectural thinking that linked the medieval and the industrial. Some Victorian polymaths especially privileged parallels between the Industrial Revolution and the medieval period, appropriating and shaping the latter to explain or justify ways of understanding industrial objects and technological change. Particularly influential was the work of two prominent scientists at Cambridge University, who also distinguished themselves as architectural historians and are often regarded as founding figures in the discipline: William Whewell, professor of mineralogy, and Robert Willis, Jacksonian Professor of Natural and Experimental Philosophy. Both were opposed to romantic ideas of the medieval past and sought to dispel their gloom and religiosity. In their architectural histories, Whewell was interested in the origins and development of Gothic architecture, while Willis focused on Gothic cathedrals in England and the relation between Gothic and classical in Italian medieval buildings. They were concerned with expanding architectural nomenclature as a means to scientific and historical precision, with Whewell likening this to the classification system of botany.[52] They were also intrigued by the promise of systematic analysis that their friend Thomas Rickman had brought to the study of the Gothic, and presented their work as interrelated with his.[53] Rickman had created a classificatory framework for a historical succession of English Gothic styles, underpinned by a method that separated Gothic architecture into individual building parts: a teleology built on a taxonomy.

What I shall argue here is not that Willis's and Whewell's turn to Gothic was motivated by the Enlightenment rationality they espoused and in whose terms their work has often been appraised,[54] but that their understanding of Gothic was closely associated with the values and interests of the industrial bourgeoisie, who saw history in an industrial perspective. This was the same ideology that informed the Gothic Revival Town Hall in Manchester. My argument is not that all Gothic Revival architecture should be perceived in this way, nor that there is a particular variant of this based on appearance or structure. Instead I believe that this understanding of Gothic was based in a particular time and place and deployed by a particular class formation. It was deployed not in a theoretical way, or at least one that made articulate sense of the conjunction (that is not how ideology works), but instead as an assertive form of materiality, a construct in matter and idea, an 'existence as an ensemble of apparatuses, intellectuals, rituals and forms of practice', as Jan Rehmann has defined ideology.[55] Just as this was a class that struggled with other classes, it also erased the traces of contest, displacing them or denying that any such struggle was happening (the Gothic Revival's anachronistic recourse to historical scenarios of chivalry or religion are common examples of this). Willis's and Whewell's work, with its direct links to the Manchester cottonocracy (Whewell had also been born in Lancashire[56]), gives us some insight into this, some sense of the frameworks, terms and practices by which medieval buildings might be made to correspond to an industrial world of invention and manufacture, to justify a certain view of that world and to help accommodate science and history to the interests of the industrial bourgeoisie. More specifically, the effect of their work was to make a particular version of industrial change seem to require the alienation of other social classes from their participation in technical and craft-based forms of knowledge.[57] A key to all this is to see the connections in Willis's and Whewell's work between the technology of the Industrial Revolution and the architecture of the Middle Ages, and how these were understood as analogous cultural products.[58]

The medieval and the industrial both developed through what Whewell, indebted to Francis Bacon's empiricism, called the 'philosophy of discovery'.[59] Changes in Gothic, for instance, worked through 'reformation, selection of the good, rejection of the mere customary'.[60] If engineering and machinery were crucial to discovery in the Industrial Revolution, architecture was the key to the same model of discovery earlier. And the principal discovery was the pointed arch, which was developed, so Whewell claimed, from the mechanical need for vaulting.[61] Medieval buildings thus exemplified the dispelling of the 'indistinctness of ideas' of late antiquity: 'notions of support and stability once again became conspicuous ... a new decorative construction was matured, not thwarting and controlling, but assisting and harmonizing with the mechanical construction.'[62] Every part or member of the building, and almost every moulding, became devoted to the sustaining of weight, and so 'Architecture prepared the way for Mechanics'.[63] Architecture was an intricate mechanism, the relation of its parts a matter of calculation and synchronisation. It was clearly a model for the way Victorians themselves should conceive of building.

Both thinkers brought a mathematical and analytical precision to their writing. Willis's descriptions are detailed accounts of what can be seen in annotated drawings. Here he is, for instance, on pier arches: 'Thus at Geneva, Pl. III. Fig. 23, *mpn* is the section of the pier arch, which differs from *ab*, Fig. 22. only in having edge-beads *mn* applied to the first order, and chamfers to the second p'[64] (fig. 89). And here again, on banded archways: 'the section of the upright is the same as the section of the arch, so that the shaft appears to pierce and pass through its capital and to be carried over the arch, while the impost mouldings and foliation of the capital appear like a band fastened round the mouldings of a continuous archway.'[65] Shafted arches are divided into new subclassifications: vaulting shafts, bearing shafts, subshafts, face shafts, edge shafts and nook shafts.[66] In these descriptions, which form the main content of Willis's *Remarks on the Architecture of the Middle Ages*, Gothic buildings are divided up into parts and understood to have the precision and purposiveness of the parts of an industrial machine; they are diagrams of petrified kinematics whose 'connection and distribution of the parts' can be separately analysed and taxonomised.[67] This was the case with vaults, imposts, piers, arches, capitals, windows and doorways. Of clustered columns Willis writes:

> *the clustering of a pier is not merely a kind of enriched fluting, for every shaft and moulding which compose it bears a definite relation to the parts which lie above it, every one of which receives, in the decorative sense, an independent support from some member of the cluster.*[68]

Much as with cotton machines, these parts had not necessarily developed simultaneously, and Willis separates them for purposes of analysis.

The same precision is found in Willis's descriptions of machine parts as Gothic parts. Here he is on epicyclic trains from his book *Principles of Mechanism* (1841; fig. 90):

> *A train of mechanism the axes of which are carried by an arm or frame which revolves round a centre, as in figs. 211, 212, 213, is termed in this work an* Epicyclic train ... *Thus in fig. 211,* CB *is the frame or*

[89] Details of Gothic pier arches, and other details from medieval buildings, from Robert Willis, *Remarks on the Architecture of the Middle Ages* (1835).

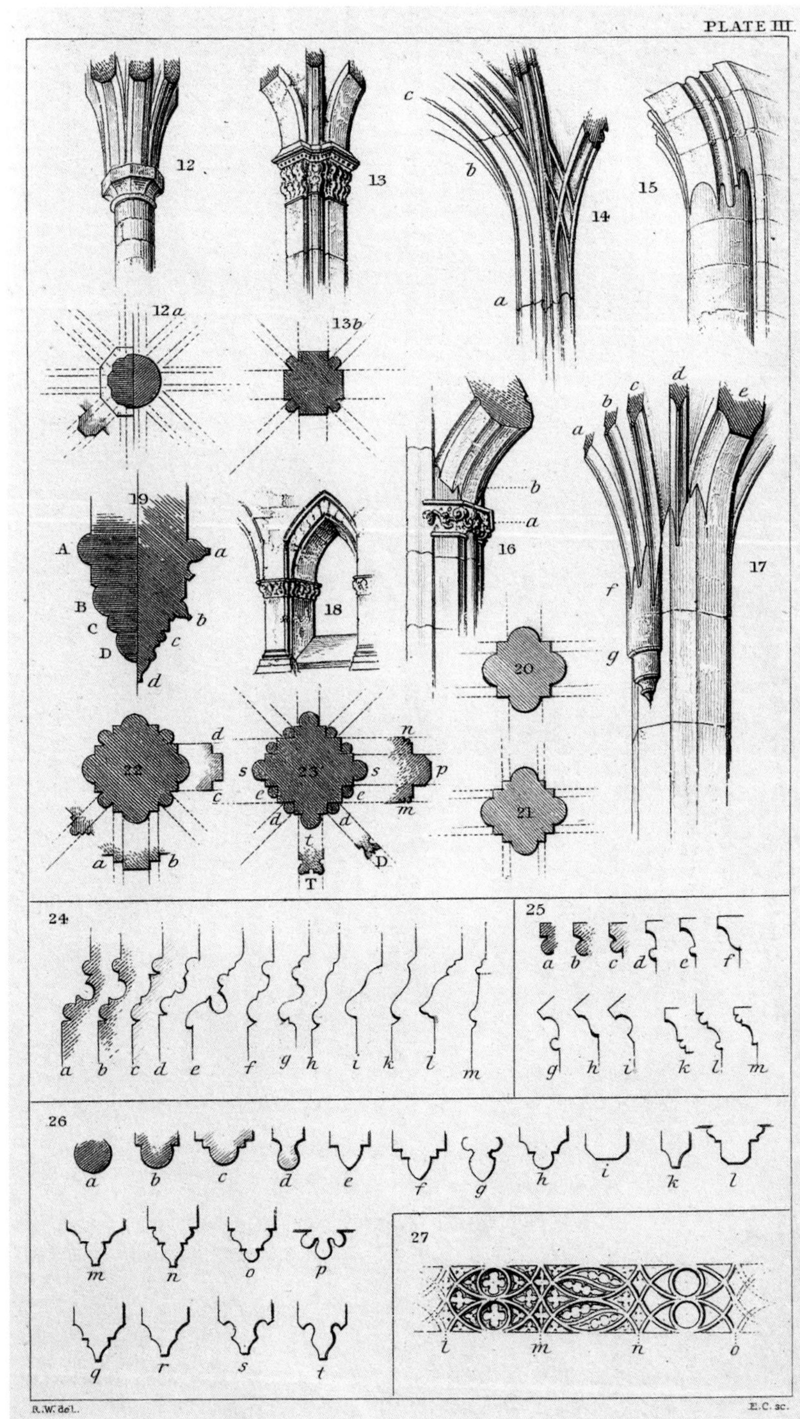

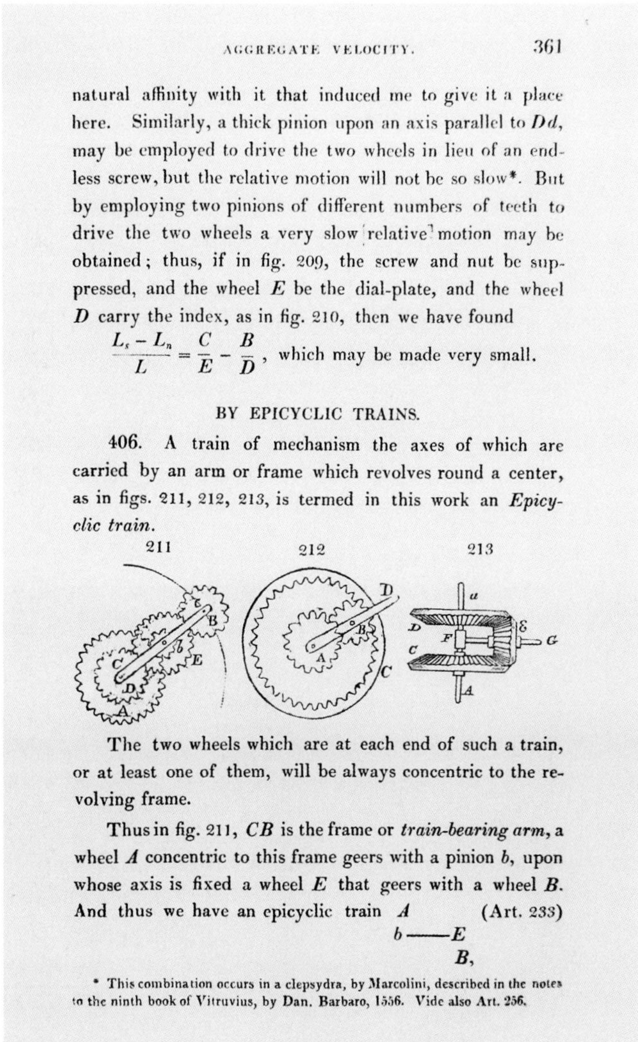
AGGREGATE VELOCITY. 361

natural affinity with it that induced me to give it a place here. Similarly, a thick pinion upon an axis parallel to *Dd*, may be employed to drive the two wheels in lieu of an endless screw, but the relative motion will not be so slow*. But by employing two pinions of different numbers of teeth to drive the two wheels a very slow relative motion may be obtained; thus, if in fig. 209, the screw and nut be suppressed, and the wheel *E* be the dial-plate, and the wheel *D* carry the index, as in fig. 210, then we have found

$$\frac{L_s - L_n}{L} = \frac{C}{E} - \frac{B}{D},$$ which may be made very small.

BY EPICYCLIC TRAINS.

406. A train of mechanism the axes of which are carried by an arm or frame which revolves round a center, as in figs. 211, 212, 213, is termed in this work an *Epicyclic train.*

211 212 213

The two wheels which are at each end of such a train, or at least one of them, will be always concentric to the revolving frame.

Thus in fig. 211, *CB* is the frame or *train-bearing arm*, a wheel *A* concentric to this frame geers with a pinion *b*, upon whose axis is fixed a wheel *E* that geers with a wheel *B*. And thus we have an epicyclic train *A* (Art. 233)

b —— *E*

B,

* This combination occurs in a clepsydra, by Marcolini, described in the notes to the ninth book of Vitruvius, by Dan. Barbaro, 1556. Vide also Art. 256.

[90] Epicyclic trains, from Robert Willis, *Principles of Mechanism* (1841).

train-bearing arm, *a wheel* A *concentric to this frame geers with a pinion* b, *upon whose axis is fixed a wheel* E *that geers with a wheel* B.[69]

Analytic description, developed through Willis's research in architectural terminology, is a lesson in naming, in combining language and diagram, in discerning difference between parts and in denoting the articulations essential to the whole.[70] It works for stone or metal, for old churches as much as new machines. Whewell applied the term 'consilience' to the convergence or putting together of inductive knowledge from different sources, and Willis's diagrammed buildings and machines belong to the same approach.

Like Whewell, Willis was less interested in development as staged progress, and more in a process of change through invention (what he called 'imitation' and 'transitions') and functional decline (or obsolescence).[71] For Willis the logic of Gothic was in its constructional system, its fitting of parts together. While architectural historians have tended to refer this back to French rationalist theory in architecture, it seems more likely that the theory subtended an approach that Willis had actually learned through his scientific work, his interest in comparative anatomy and particularly his visits to machine makers and cotton mills in industrial England, including those of William Fairbairn, Henry Maudslay and Joseph Whitworth.[72] All of these men were committed to developing tools for the more accurate production of geometric forms in machinery: Maudslay's slide rest, for example, bypassed the guidance of the workman's hand in cutting machine parts. (As we shall see, this form of industrial prosthesis also interested Willis.)

Therefore Whewell and Willis had not just a common approach to Gothic architecture and to the products of industrialism, but also a way of seeing and thinking of the two in the same terms. To use Willis's tripartite scheme, this worked from the level of the elements (or pieces of the machine), up to the forces that moved it (its 'train of mechanism') and finally to the whole mechanism ('actual and complete machines').[73] Joints or meeting points were particularly important in this scheme, whether in the anatomy of an animal, the bay of a Gothic church or the relation of machine parts. A crab's claw, for instance, was illustrated by Willis in his *Principles of Mechanism* to show 'Hooke's joint and the universal joint of flexure', both of which had application for machinery.[74]

This comparative and cross-disciplinary approach is particularly noteworthy in the case of cogwheels, a telling feature of the machine allusions in the Town Hall. Just visible in Raffles Davison's engraving (see fig. 75) are the defensive 'teeth' on the metal railings that run on low walls around much of the outside of the building to deter potential intruders (fig. 91 a). There is more than an allusion to cogged edges in these railings, and they are repeated prominently and even more overtly on various handrails in the entrance spaces where the lines of teeth are located either adjacent to curved metal decoration or as integral to the curving handrails themselves (figs 91 b and 91 c). This is not a motif like

[91 A–C] Manchester Town Hall: cogged exterior and interior handrails.

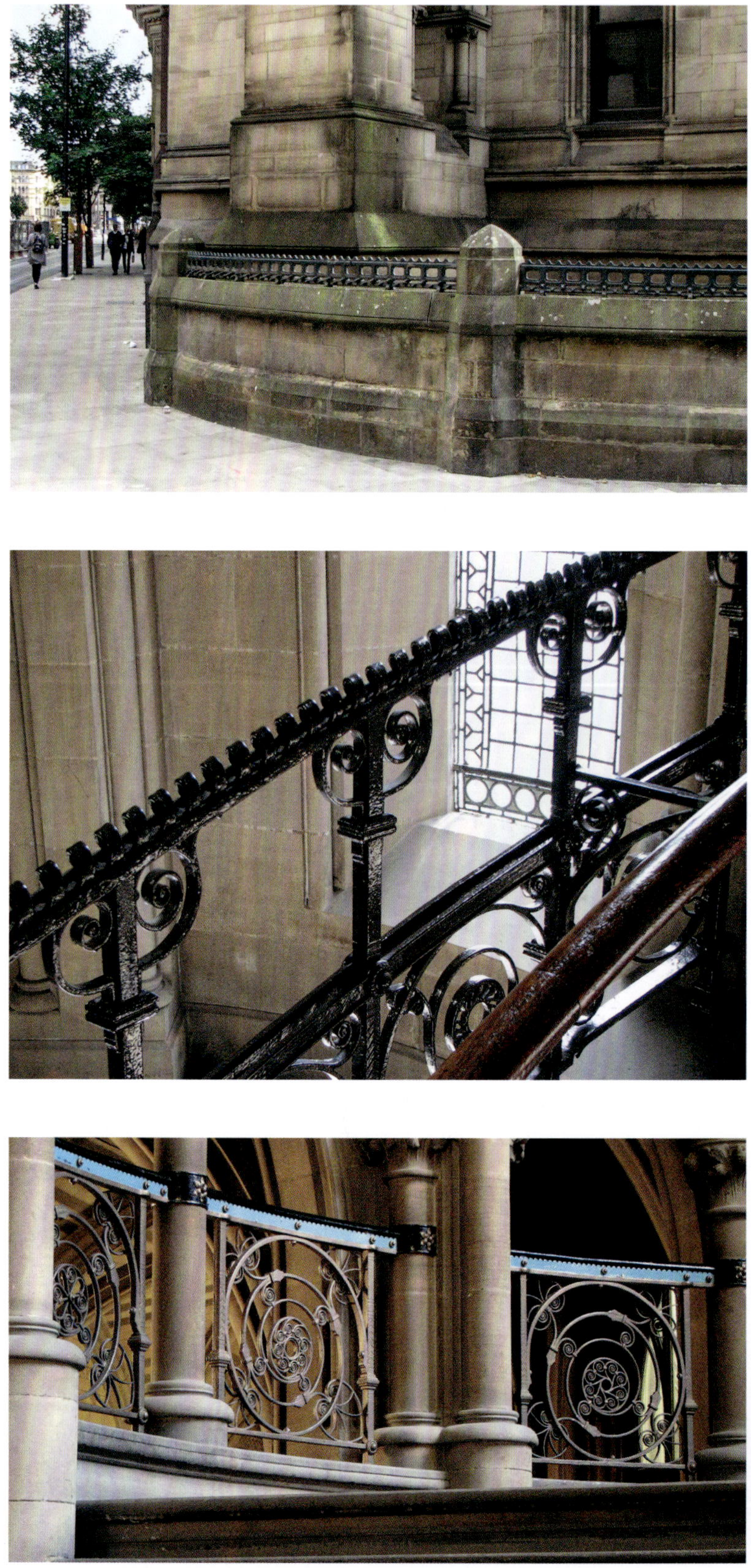

any other in this context; it has been designed into the building's more functional elements rather than its symbolic programme.

The cogwheel, William Blake's 'wheel without wheel', was the key component of industrial machines.[75] Cogwheels also had great figurative value (one whose political valences have largely been lost in the use of the analogy today) in epitomising the nature of class struggle: Louis Auguste Blanqui, the French socialist, wrote of 'the cogs of this machine, assembled with an astonishing art, [that] touch the poor man at every instance of the day'.[76] It is that 'astonishing art' that I am concerned with here, and what it meant to its creators. Central to any theory of machinery, the cogwheel was a subject of vital importance to industrialists and of great interest to anyone writing about cotton machines in which cogwheels had replaced the levers and belts of spinning wheels.[77] One engineer, speaking to the Manchester Literary and Philosophical Society in 1819, argued that the city had an 'eminently distinguished' interest in the subject.[78] And the interest was considerably augmented by a fortuitous link, because south Lancashire's thriving watch industry was crucial to the technology of the cotton machines, with many clockmakers moving into important roles in the rapidly developing cotton industry.[79] (Although their craft skills would soon be superseded by gear-cutting machines, the memory of their craft was sometimes marked by mill workshops being called clockmakers' shops.[80]) Cogwheels were of particular interest to William Fairbairn, the great Manchester-based engineer, who carefully described their varied contributions to the transmission of motion[81] (fig. 92). And the cogwheel was equally, if more theoretically, important to Robert Willis, whose descriptions in his 1841 book *Principles of Mechanism* show how the teeth of wheelwork similar to the Town Hall's railings were designed to combine grip, smoothness of motion and lack of friction so that they communicated motion efficiently[82] (fig. 93). This was the applied science of 'kinematics', and it was developed further by Whewell, with Willis's support, in his *Mechanics of Engineering* (also 1841). Willis had also published several papers on gear teeth in the late 1830s and invented an instrument to be made of card or metal – the odontagraph – to help workmen in the making of such teeth (this could be seen

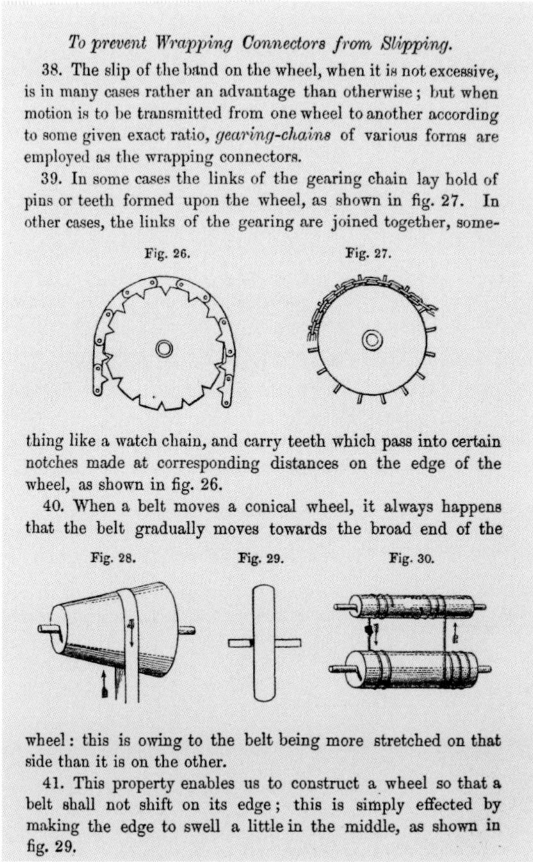

To prevent Wrapping Connectors from Slipping.

38. The slip of the band on the wheel, when it is not excessive, is in many cases rather an advantage than otherwise; but when motion is to be transmitted from one wheel to another according to some given exact ratio, *gearing-chains* of various forms are employed as the wrapping connectors.

39. In some cases the links of the gearing chain lay hold of pins or teeth formed upon the wheel, as shown in fig. 27. In other cases, the links of the gearing are joined together, something like a watch chain, and carry teeth which pass into certain notches made at corresponding distances on the edge of the wheel, as shown in fig. 26.

40. When a belt moves a conical wheel, it always happens that the belt gradually moves towards the broad end of the wheel: this is owing to the belt being more stretched on that side than it is on the other.

41. This property enables us to construct a wheel so that a belt shall not shift on its edge; this is simply effected by making the edge to swell a little in the middle, as shown in fig. 29.

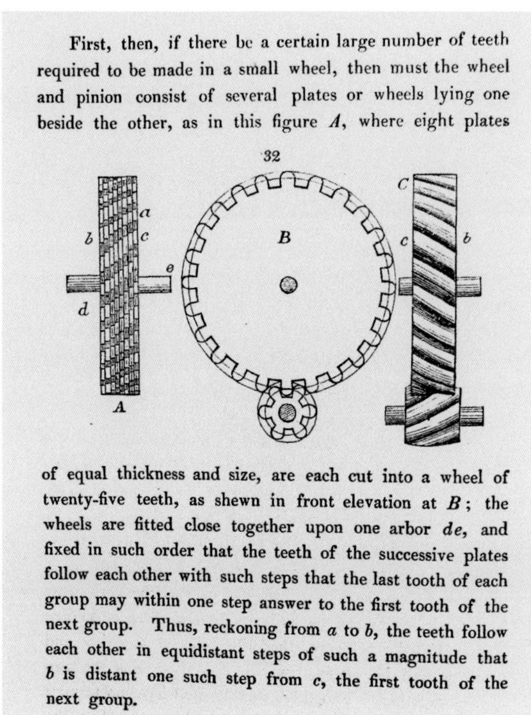

First, then, if there be a certain large number of teeth required to be made in a small wheel, then must the wheel and pinion consist of several plates or wheels lying one beside the other, as in this figure *A*, where eight plates of equal thickness and size, are each cut into a wheel of twenty-five teeth, as shewn in front elevation at *B*; the wheels are fitted close together upon one arbor *de*, and fixed in such order that the teeth of the successive plates follow each other with such steps that the last tooth of each group may within one step answer to the first tooth of the next group. Thus, reckoning from *a* to *b*, the teeth follow each other in equidistant steps of such a magnitude that *b* is distant one such step from *c*, the first tooth of the next group.

[92] 'To Prevent Wrapping Connectors from Slipping', from William Fairbairn, *Treatise on Mills and Millwork* (1861).

[93] Combining cogwheels, from Robert Willis, *Principles of Mechanism* (1841).

as an equivalent to Maudslay's slide rest, a mechanical contraption that allowed for greater precision in the making of a key machine part, though it was more a device to measure than to manufacture)[83] (fig. 94). Complementarily, Willis also invented what he called the cymagraph for copying architectural mouldings[84] (fig. 95). In their making and measuring, and by inserting a prosthetic mechanism between them and the hand of the worker or the measurer (like Maudslay's slide rest), the iron edges of the wheel and the stone edges of the moulding achieve an equivalence. Such prostheses were sized up from the hand but not for handcraft; they were part of an industrial culture that valued 'technical dexterity' instead of craft skills.[85] They were the intended instruments of deskilling, of controlling a workforce,[86] as much through the making of machine parts by iron and brass turners as through the recording of medieval structures by draughtsmen. But at the same time these tools not only made a worker into a prosthesis of the machine, as we saw in the Ancoats factories. They also had a different direction of effect, which enabled a scholar like Willis to enter into the abstracted forms of work (or calculation) necessary to render his conception of the medieval building as petrified machine.

Willis thus went well equipped to mine his medieval material. With his patented cymagraph, together with the more familiar pantograph (an instrument that enabled a plan to be drawn at a different scale) and a camera lucida, to help him measure and represent medieval cathedrals, he was in a sense placing reproducible 'precision' above judgement, skill and interpretation.[87] In analysing Canterbury Cathedral, for instance, Willis produced a version of the material history of the past whose ideological implications were bound up with the tools and effects of recording. Canterbury may have been a medieval building but Willis's way of understanding it might better be termed 'industrial Gothic'; in other words, it was an approach imbued with the world-view and protocols of the industrialist and his engineers, even using similar tools. And so at Canterbury Willis was concerned with attributing forms, like patented inventions, to different builders; he described architecture as made of abstracted machine-like parts or members (a 'membrology'), each with its

To accompany Profr. Willis' paper on the Teeth of Wheels.

Fig. 3.

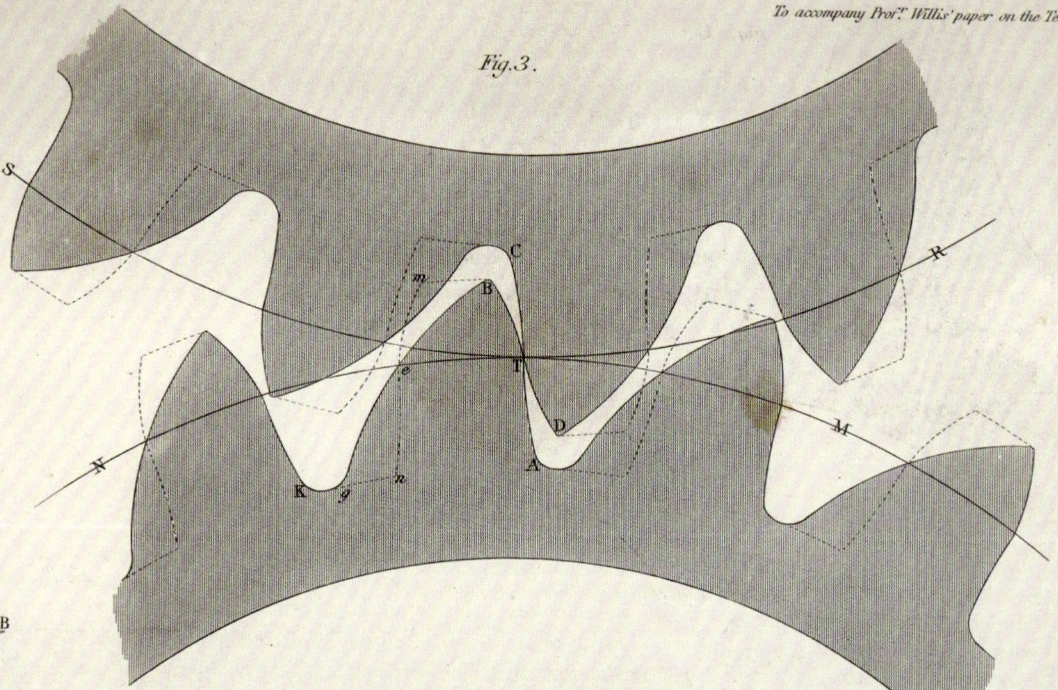

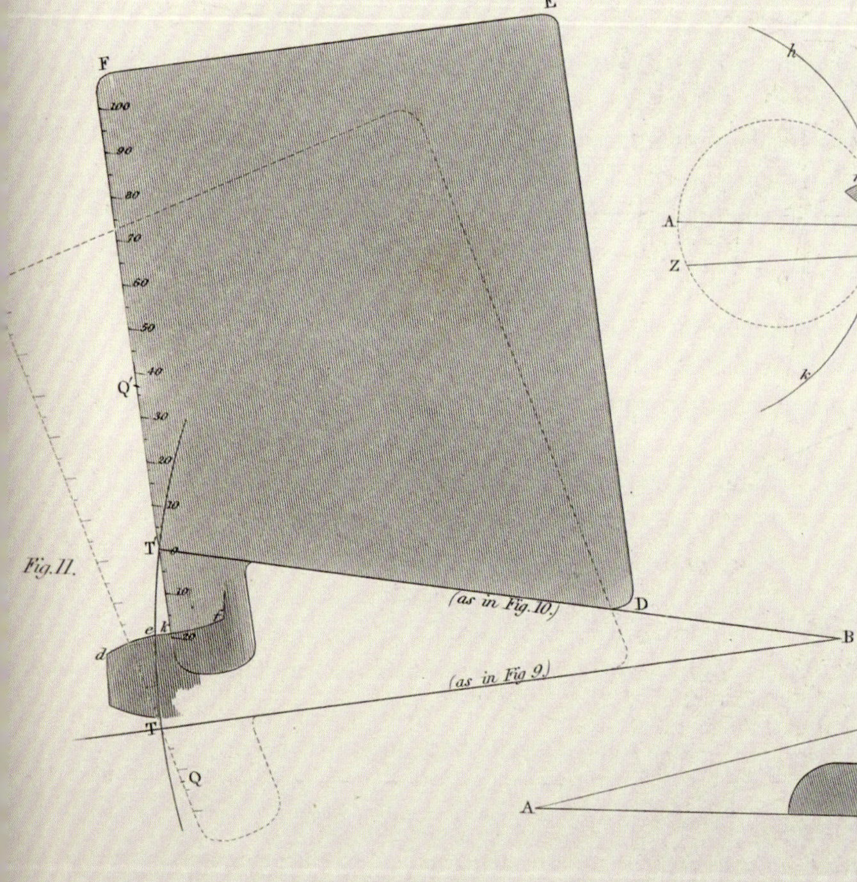

Fig. 11.

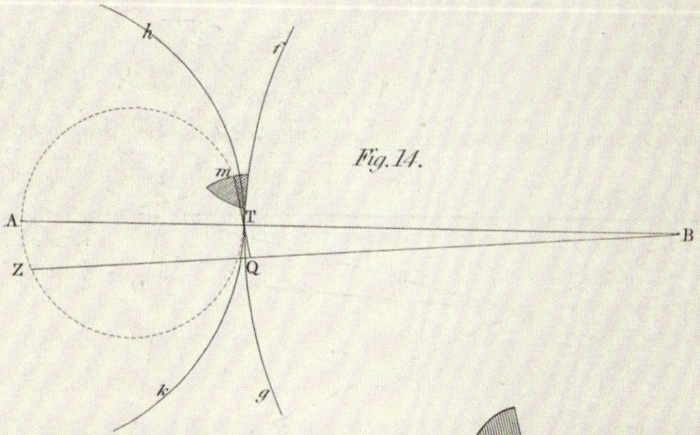

Fig. 14.

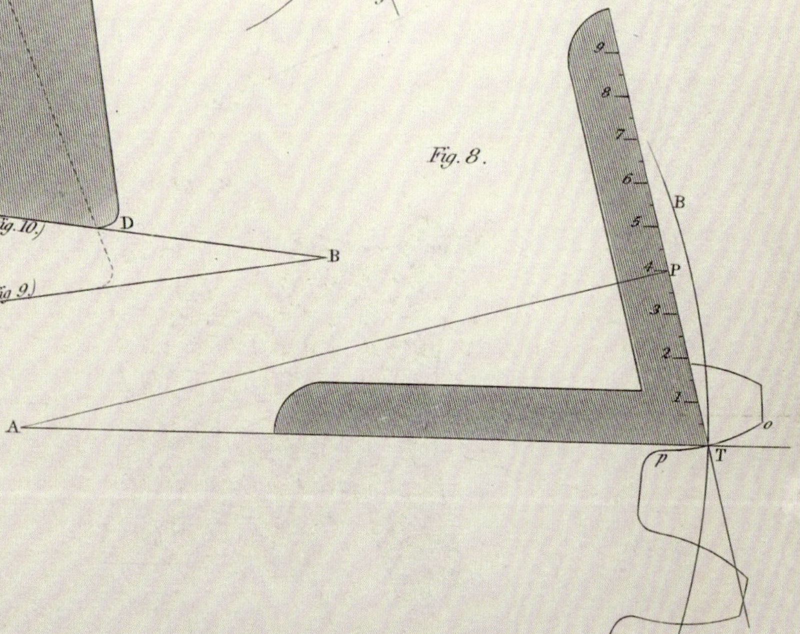

Fig. 8.

, 59, High Holborn.

J.W. Lowry sc.

[94] Robert Willis's odontagraph. Engraving from 'On the Teeth of Wheels', *Transactions of the Institution of Civil Engineers* (1838).

[95] Robert Willis's cymagraph. Engraving from 'Description of the Cymagraph for Copying Mouldings', *Civil Engineer and Architect's Journal* (1842).

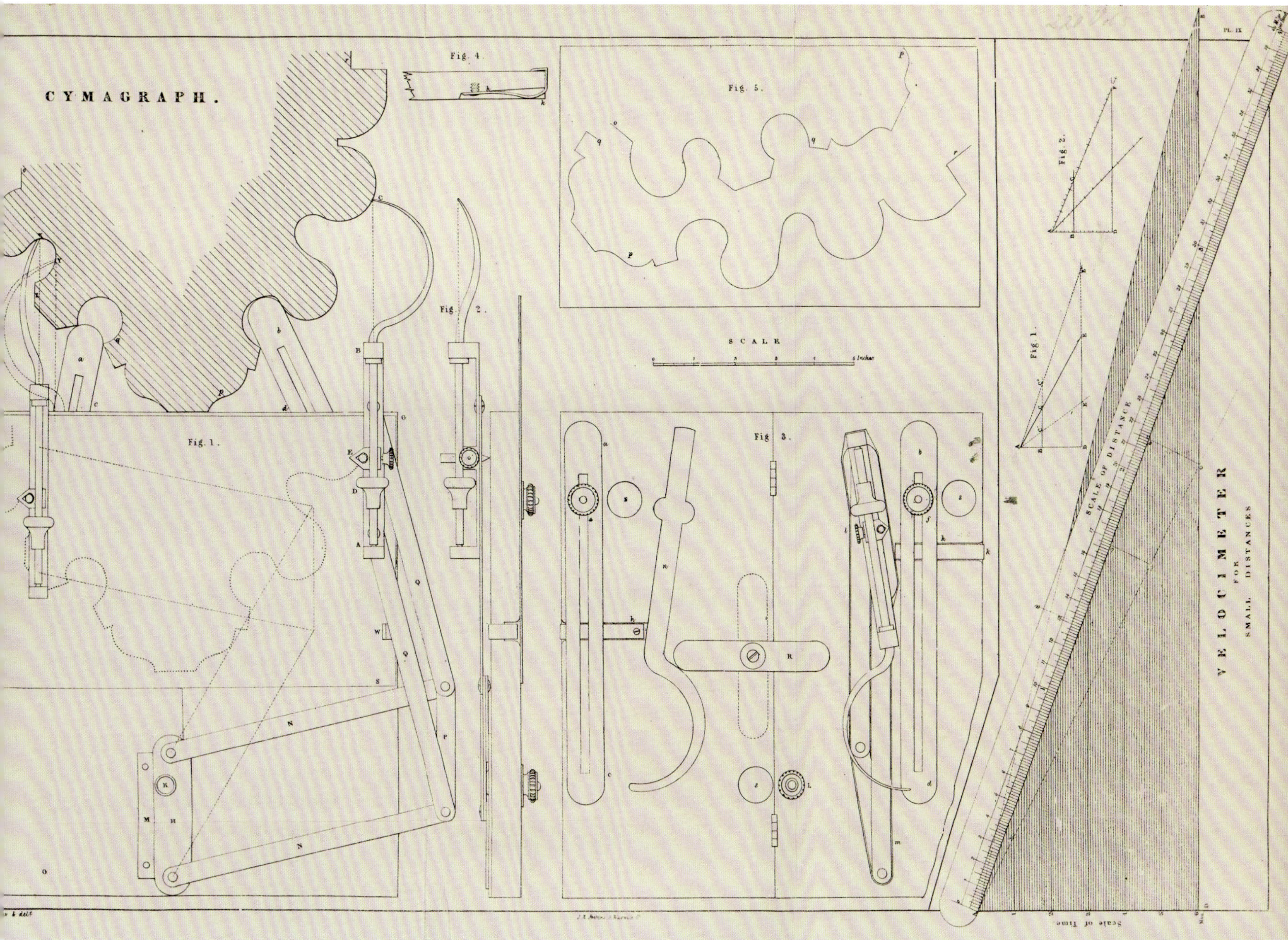

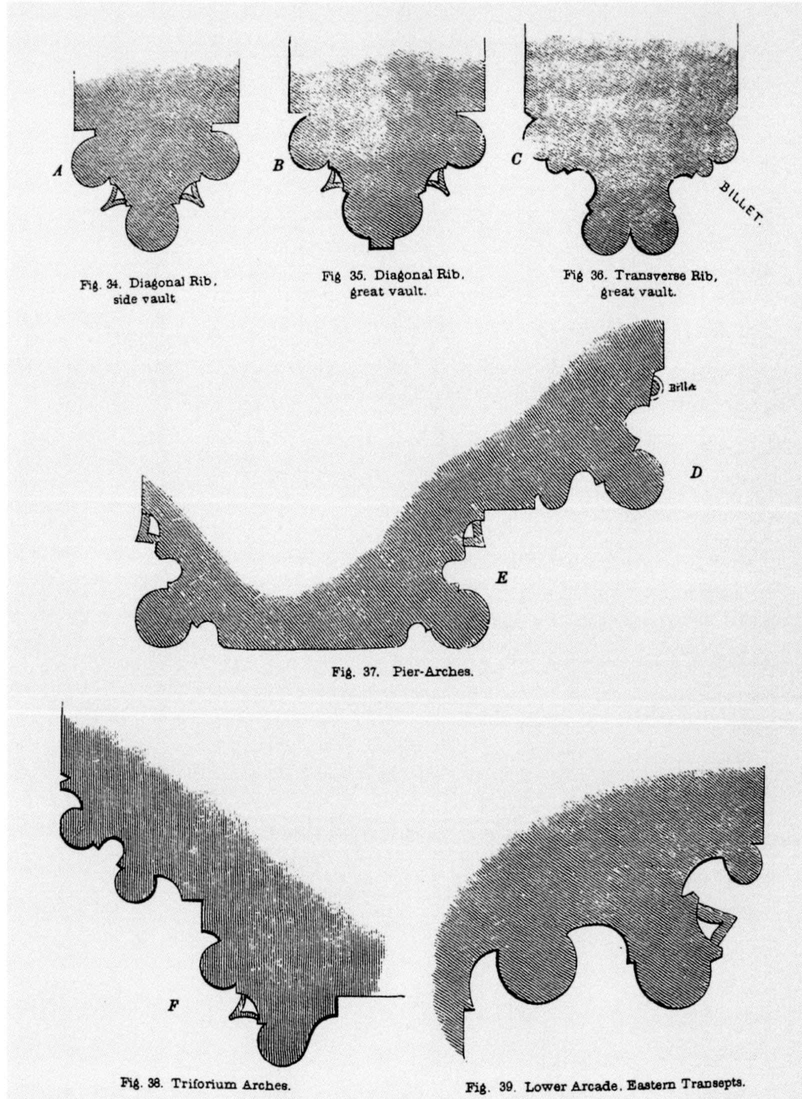

[96] Sections of mouldings from rib-vaults at Canterbury Cathedral, from Robert Willis, *The Architectural History of Canterbury Cathedral* (1845).

unique name and a serial interchangeability with other similar parts (fig. 96). The medieval past could thus become part of the new cultural economy, just as clockmaking had contributed to industrial machine making. What Jonathan Crary has called the 'uprooting of vision' in the early nineteenth century is also found here. The new means for recording medieval architecture gave it 'unprecedented mobility and exchangeability'; it was rendered through the 'industrialization of image-making' and thus also the industrialism of seeing and knowing.[88]

As a consequence, Willis also saw objects without the imprint of the hands that had made them, and with the implicit understanding – an extension of his own methods – that those hands were docile prostheses of the architect. By his extraordinary, impossible, picturing of objects through their sectional profiles (and even more impossible grouping of them), he took them out of direct experience and made them reproducible. Maintainable and replaceable, they became functional parts rather than meaningful objects.[89] The profiles became paragons of lucid and efficient objects, like the paragons of machinery produced by technical drawing.[90] As Ben Marsden has written, 'the "science of pure mechanism" as a universal and permanent intellectual apparatus [trumped] the local, the individualistic and the transitory, the intuitive and insufficiently communicable knowledge of the artisan inventor'.[91] This architecture as mechanism – or industrial Gothic – was the product, in other words, of a form of displaced class war in which whatever knowledge or autonomy was left to the artisan was finally stripped away. Following from this, the cogged railings at the Town Hall show neither the acclaimed adaptability of Gothic to the industrial nor the reverse, the adaptation of the industrial to the Gothic, but instead a mutual adaptation, a consilience between the two.[92] Both the cymagraph and the odontagraph would be useful tools if we were to record the membrology of the Town Hall; they are essential to recording its ideology.

VICTORIAN HISTORIES OF TECHNOLOGICAL INVENTION have certain reiterated themes. The arrival of the steam engine is regarded as pivotal in the development of the Industrial Revolution, and John Kay's flying shuttle as the trigger for the revolutionary development of cotton machines.[93] (India's pre-eminent global status for cotton manufacture at the time of Kay and Arkwright is never mentioned.) Similarly, stone vaulting or the pointed arch were regarded as the key to Gothic architecture: revolution cast in terms of invention '[dispenses] with any consideration of the human factors of classes and of the social organization of production'.[94] Cotton brokers, merchants and manufacturers, like clients of Gothic Revival buildings (they were often one and the same), were frequently reminded of the basis in nature of the material they worked with, and this is where another genre, the history of the cotton industry, comes in. The iconography of the

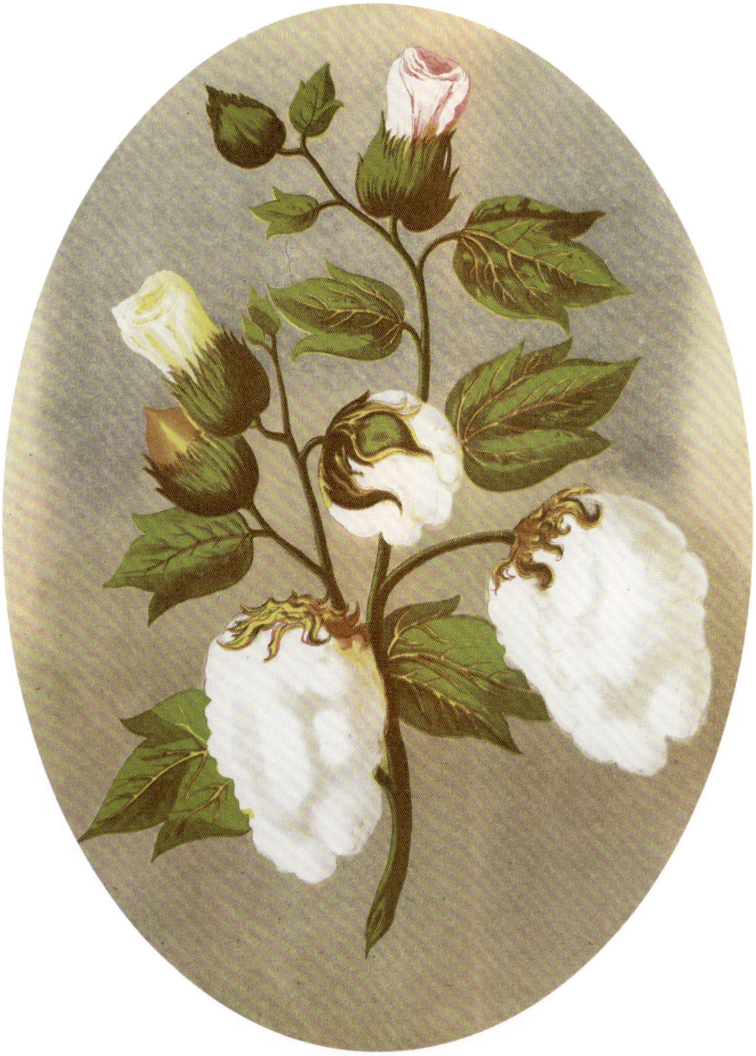

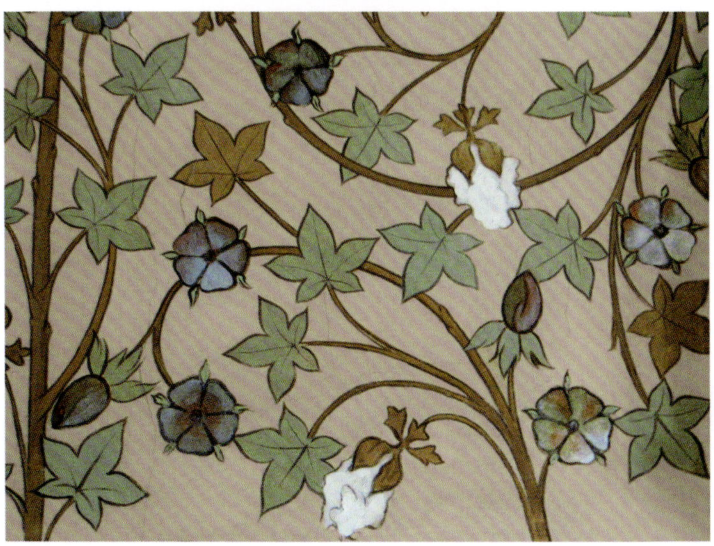

[97] Frontispiece showing cotton bolls, from Evan Leigh, *The Science of Modern Cotton Spinning* (1873).

[98] Manchester Town Hall: painted ceiling.

Town Hall reiterates much of this history.[95] The textile product was constantly traced back through its distribution, manufacture, picking and cultivation to the living plant; in much the same way as Gothic architecture was often traced back to what were thought to be its original vegetal forms. These shared accounts are indicated as much in the tendrils and bursting bolls in the decoration of the Town Hall as in contemporary histories of cotton manufacture (figs 97 and 98). The origin myths of both cotton making and Gothic making are about certain primitive things that grow out of nature – the loom as a kind of architecture, the primitive Gothic church as a kind of, well, loom. The utopia of 'beautiful' machines (as the historian of cotton manufacture, Edward Baines, saw it) was the end-point of this past and the source of analogical power.[96] What was not retained was workers' knowledge and skill as a source of metaphorical amplification, nor their sharp decline in income with the growth of industrial production.[97] Just as with the sculpted roundel on the walls of the Town Hall, the spinning girl is vaguely yet firmly historical, an ideal type of the past, while the urchin boy is an empty cipher for contemporary fecklessness and wasted labour (see fig. 75).

A similar utopia is suggested by the many wheeled devices in the metalwork and stone and in the wooden furniture of the Town Hall (fig. 99). We know that Waterhouse was explicit in disagreeing with Ruskin over the use of 'cast and machine-made ornaments of any kind', and in some parts of the Town Hall this is taken much further, so that the ornament clearly evokes the machine and its parts (as has been shown, with the teeth of wheels).[98] The balustrade of the circular stair contains round and curving springs of wrought iron, as organic as they are machine-like. When the stair lands on the first floor this balustrade becomes a parapet whose ornament is spring-like and wheel-like, coiled and revolving. In the stonework and its tracery are further wheels and circular motifs, the largest of which are in the screens over the main, ceremonial staircases; they are linear articulations of circles held suspended within other circles (see fig. 86). How many times are similar shapes to be observed in cotton machines? I am referring not so much to the Gothic decoration of a cotton machine – although there are examples of this[99] – but to a range of

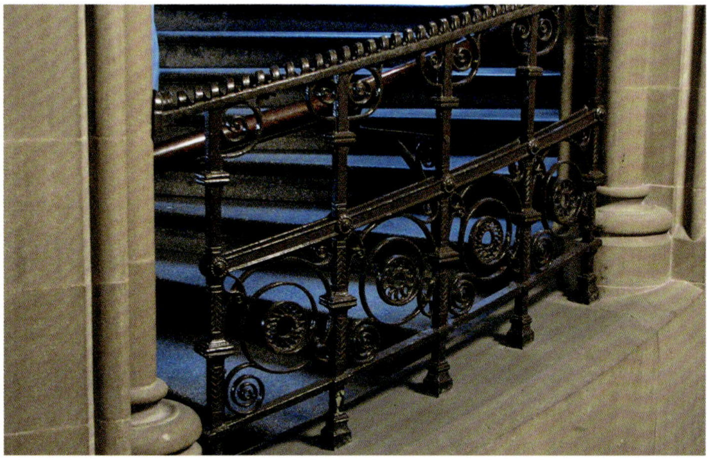

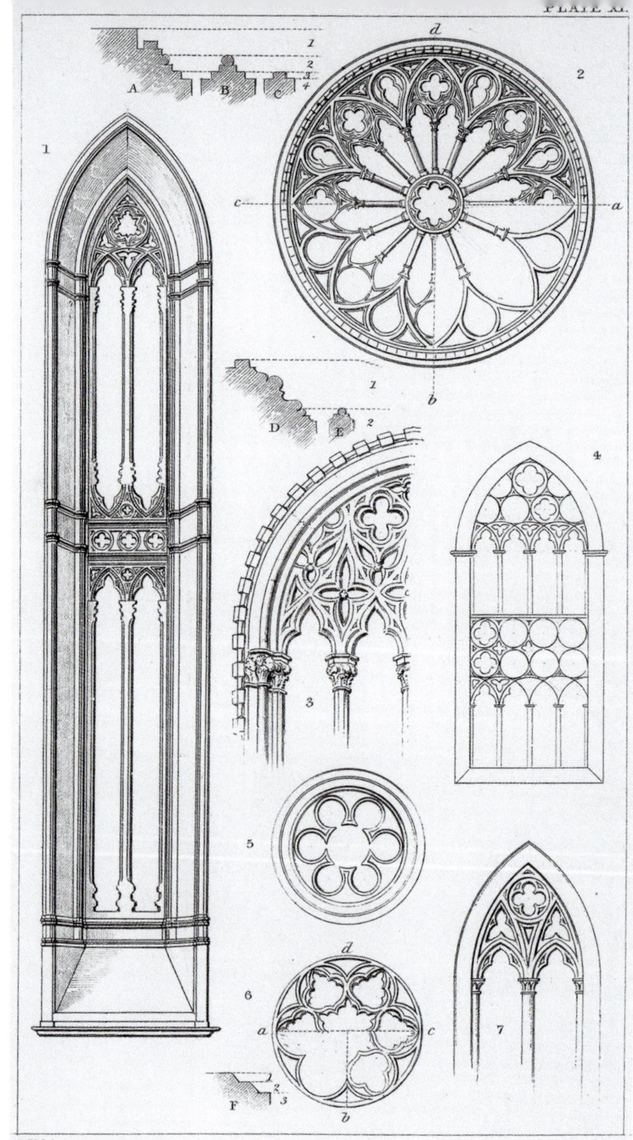

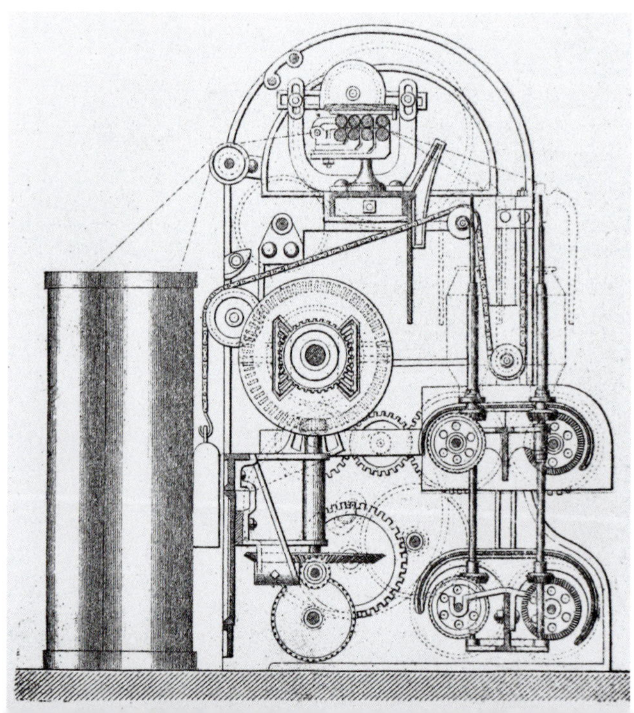

[99] Manchester Town Hall: wheeled devices in a balustrade.

[100] Foliated window (figure 5) in Modena Cathedral, from Robert Willis, *Remarks on the Architecture of the Middle Ages* (1835).

[101] Slubbing frame, from Evan Leigh, *The Science of Modern Cotton Spinning* (1873).

rhyming forms: Gothic roundels, formed out of circular apertures surrounding an intersecting central one, are like round punctured machine parts (figs 100 and 101); arcaded or foliated circular windows are like yarn rollers on dressing machines and warping frames (figs 102 and 103); and clustered shafts of vaulting piers are like the gears and pillars of millwork. Even flamboyant tracery is like wheels with ogee-shaped radii in cotton machines (figs 104 and 105). And those piers, through which we pass in the entrances and which frame the machine-like organ in the Great Hall, which are attached and unattached, clustered and single – could we think of them as passing through levels of the building, as in millwork, as some stilled form of motive power (see fig. 79)? Is the grand staircase a petrified machine? The question is part of the association. Gothic seems to allow this kind of allusiveness: its roundels, flutings, caps, shafts and shaft rings suggest equivalence at least or, to use Whewell's term, consilience. To see the Florentine church of Orsanmichele drawn by Willis as 'a system of mouldings' is to see machinery;[100] to see a cotton machine is to see a Gothic screen; to see the Town Hall's interiors is to see both Florentine Gothic tracery and Victorian machines.

Going further, can the plan of the Town Hall be understood in this way too? If so, humans become equivalents for the threads of cotton, and the building's beautifully lucid and efficient layout, and the movement of people through it, the equivalent for the

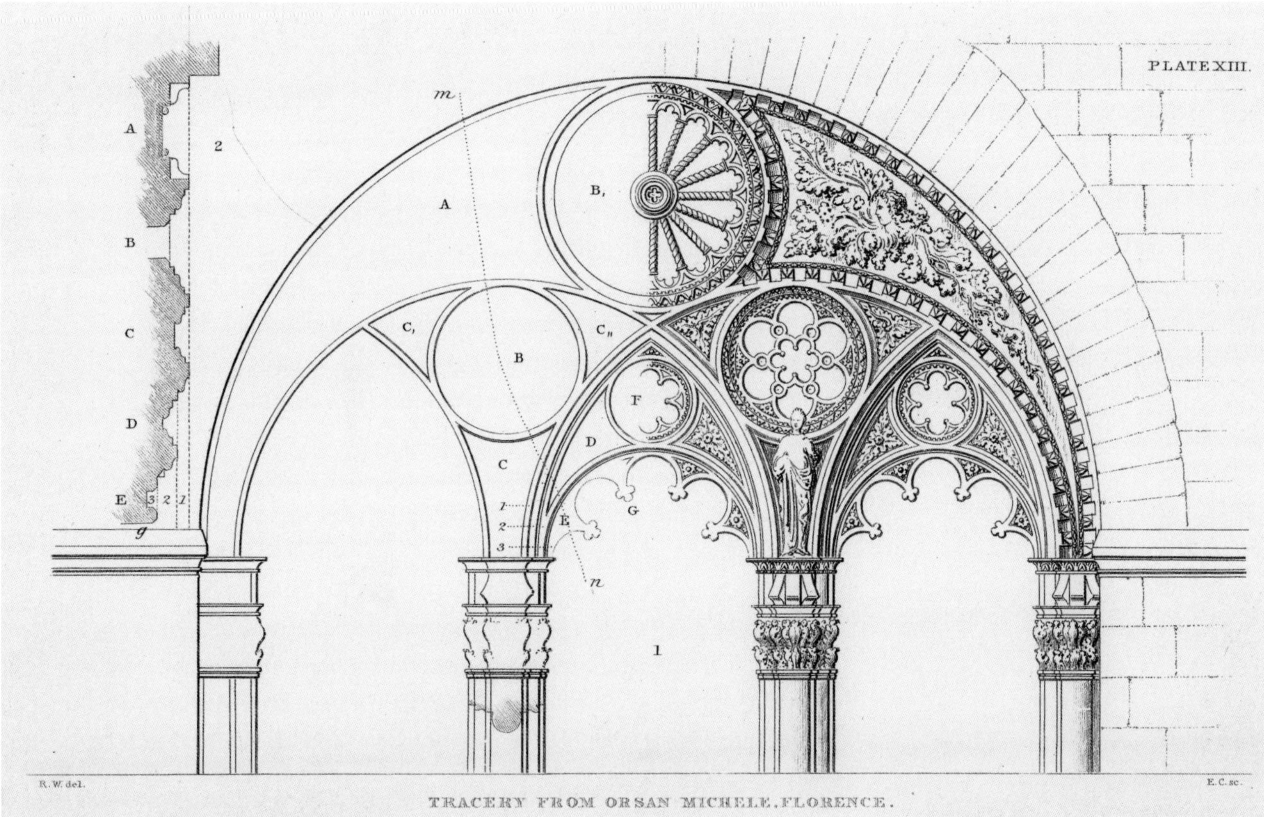

[102] Tracery from Orsanmichele, Florence, from Robert Willis, *Remarks on the Architecture of the Middle Ages* (1835).

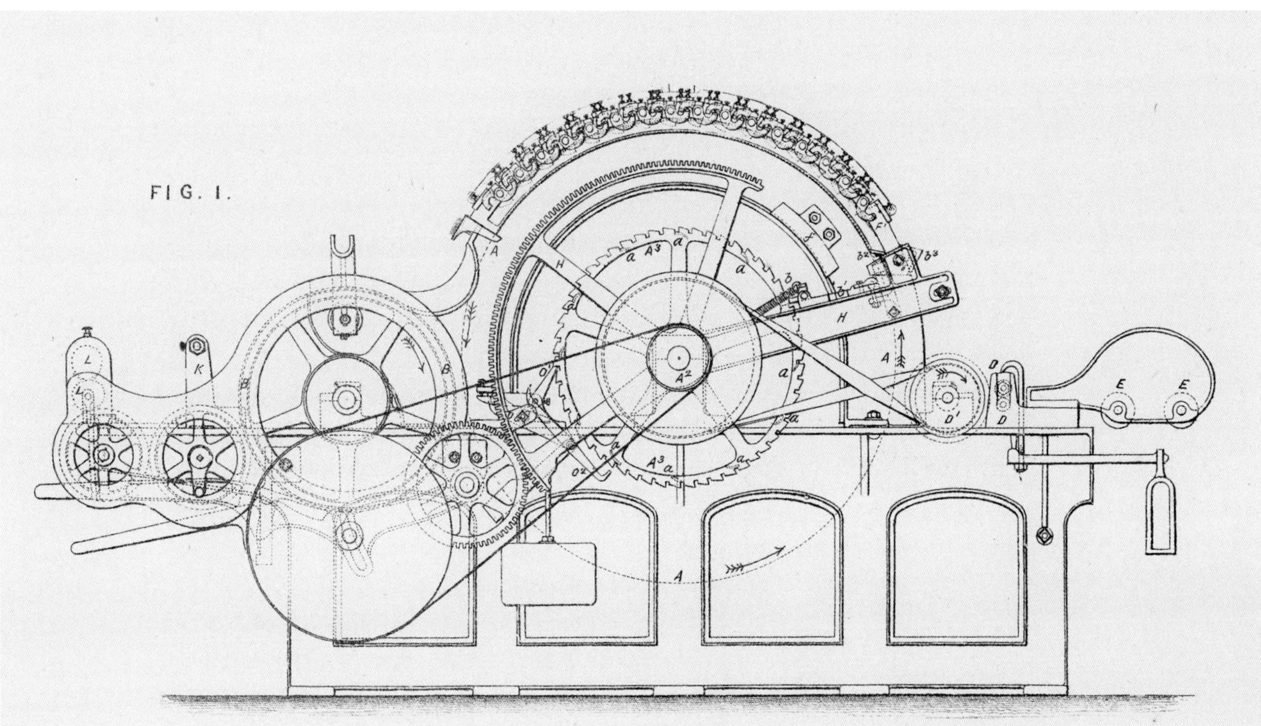

[103] Self stripping carding engine, detail from Evan Leigh, *The Science of Modern Cotton Spinning* (1873).

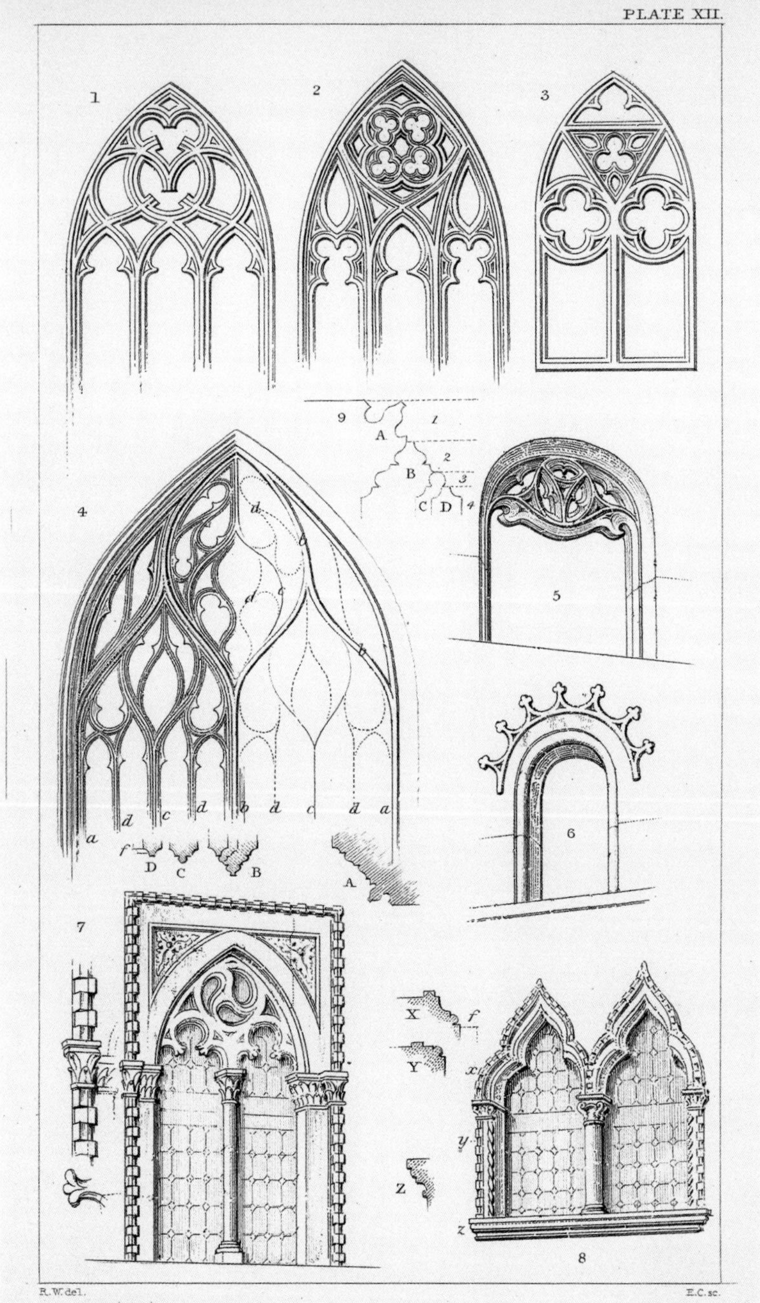

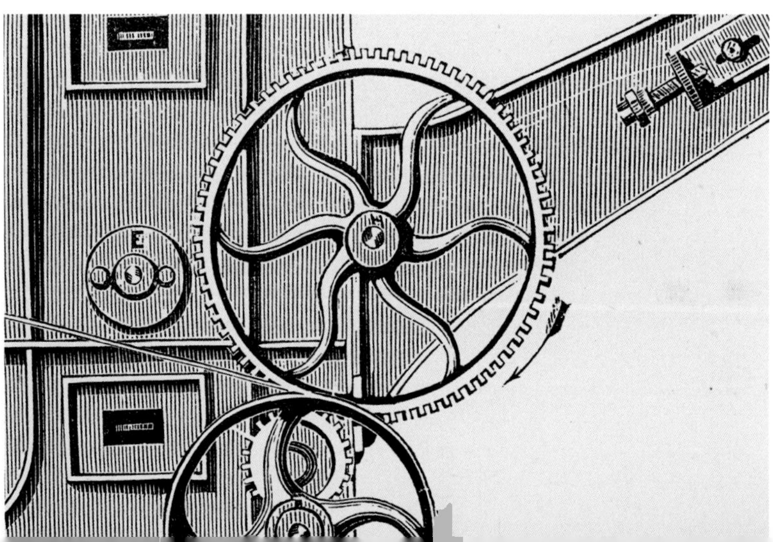

[104] Flamboyant tracery, from Robert Willis, *Remarks on the Architecture of the Middle Ages* (1835).

[105] The saw gin, detail from Evan Leigh, *The Science of Modern Cotton Spinning* (1873).

flow of cotton through the machine[101] (fig. 106). At least as represented in technical illustrations, machines were pictured as narrative images, with an account of sequential processes, much as the Town Hall's plan is a narrative account of sequences and movement through the different parts of the building.[102] The machine's moving parts would therefore be equivalent to the spiral stairs at the three corners of the plan, neighboured by the round cloakroom on the main front and then the entrance hall with its rounded end walls. A subsidiary wheel in the machine is an equivalent to the small spiral staircase that links the cloakroom to the storey above and that appears corbelled out over the main staircase (fig. 107; see fig. 79). The spiral stair was quite deliberately paired by Waterhouse with a pedestal supporting a statue to John Bright on the other side of the main staircase:[103] twinned with Free Trade, then, but might we also think of this spiral stair as a supplementary machine part, or indeed – to look at it in elevation – can we think of its run of columns, each doubly shaft-ringed, as millwork?

But cogs and wheels seem mere allusions when we have the most blatant products of machinery before us – polished shafts of granite (fig. 108). Appearing all over the major floors of the building, in the entrance spaces and around the stairs, and framing the ceremonial route, these shafts had come from quarries using steam-powered equipment and been polished by steam-powered lathes.[104] Their presence in the waiting hall is particularly unavoidable where they are human sized and crowd the space (fig. 109). In this hall they hold up a ceiling made with the very latest method of fireproof construction, the so-called Dennett system with its 'groined vaults formed in concrete and filled to the floor level'.[105] (This was a concrete whose most important constituent, gypsum, was ground by machine-powered millstones.) But the shafts are the more immediate product of machines, and the granite trade was itself admired in Manchester as exemplary for its 'unskilled labour, machinery, and that spirit of progress'.[106] Grouped and separate, gorgeous in their mixture of greys and reds, the columns are a kind of 'spectacle of dispossession',[107] of the mechanisation of production, of skilled control over labour. Moreover, they divide the space into three aisles, their

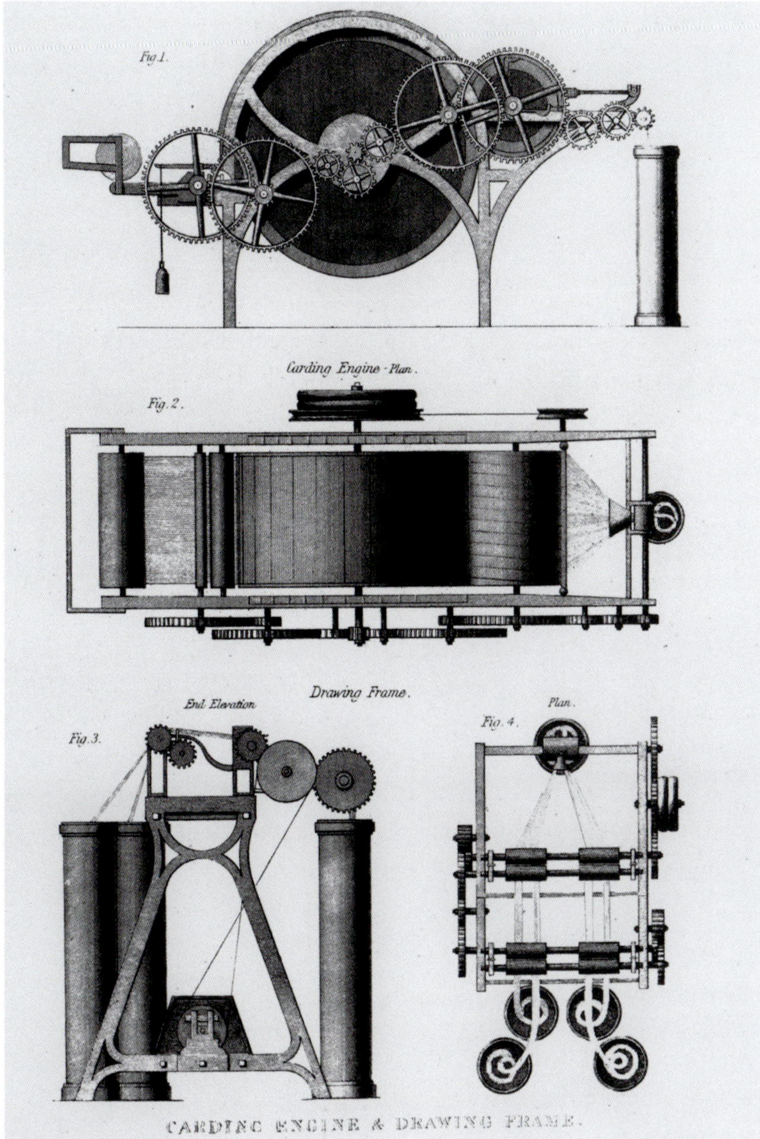

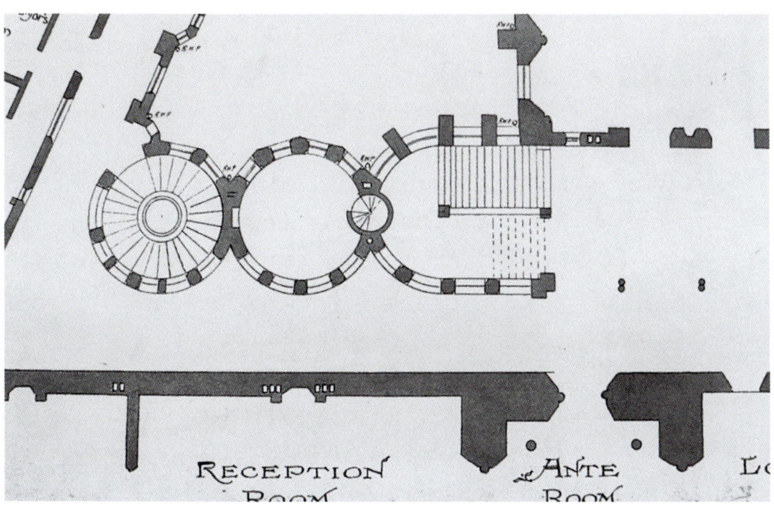

[106] Carding engines and drawing frames, from Edward Baines, *History of the County Palatinate and Duchy of Lancaster* (1836).

[107] Manchester Town Hall: plan of main and spiral staircases. Manchester Libraries, Information and Archives.

[108] Manchester Town Hall: polished granite shafts by a staircase.

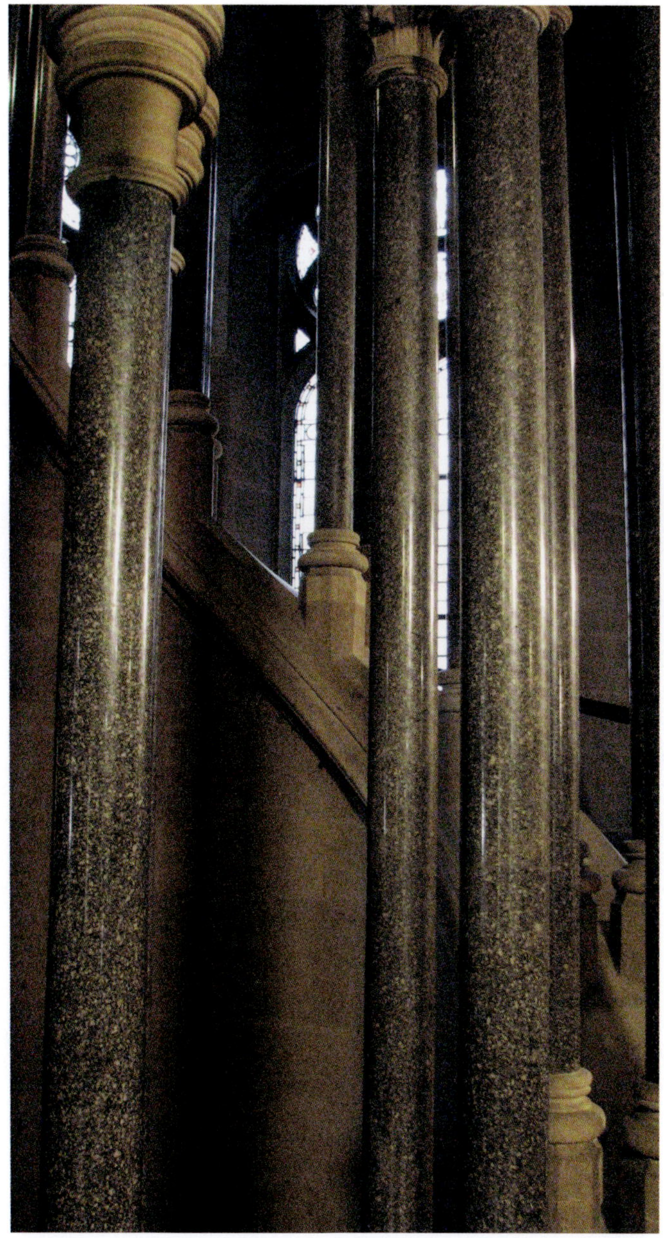

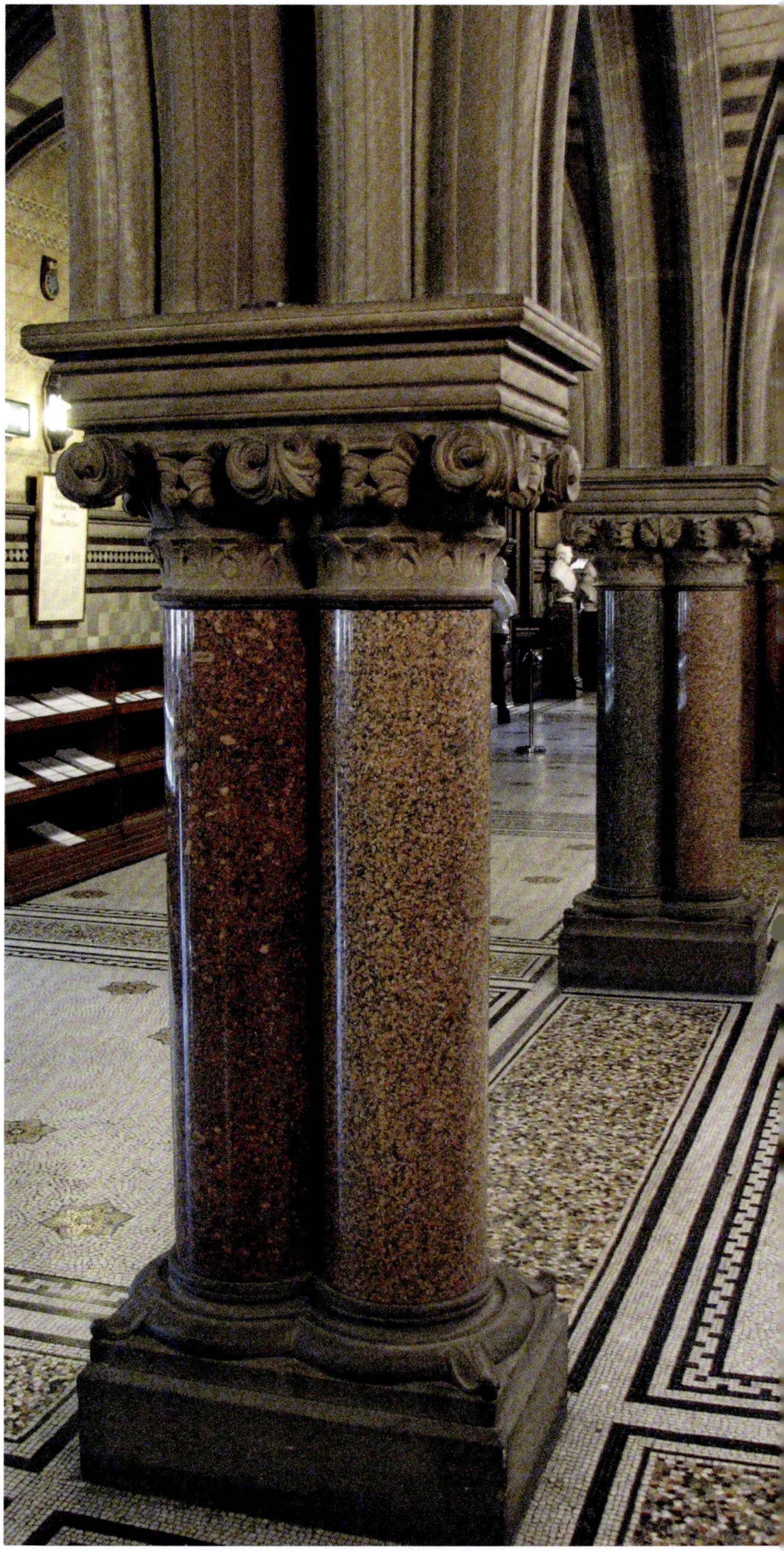

[109] Manchester Town Hall: polished granite shafts in the waiting hall.

short glinting shafts, perfectly round in girth and rigidly straight through their length, are always proximate to the sculpted bodies of the industrial bourgeoisie that decorate these spaces, as well as to the bodies of visitors as they tread the mosaic of cotton flowers. They are proximate too to Ure's philosophy, in which (describing millwork) 'polished shafts ... were at rest or in motion, so truly and silently did they revolve'.[108] They are medieval and industrial.

THE TOWN HALL IS NOT A MILL. IT DOES NOT LOOK OR function like one, at least not in any literal sense. Those aspects of it that could be called a historical dream world are much more obviously medieval: not just its sculpted spinners but also its minstrels' galleries, the costume drama of elegant knights and avuncular lords sketched in Waterhouse's drawings, and the battery of armorial shields ornamenting its objects and surfaces (including the anachronistic shields of Fairbairn, Whitworth, and Owens in the chimney-piece of the Mayor's Parlour). But by 1866, thirty years after Manchester's Court Leet was abolished, feudal privilege was declared history, mere armour fetish. So these affiliations are expressive of a particular inner logic in the life of the industrial middle class, its ability to 'functionalise different temporalities'.[109] Having eclipsed the old Tory landed gentry, the agrarian-capitalist order, the ascendant class now ran the city's municipality, shaped its new urban spaces and was increasingly its representatives in Parliament.[110] This was the peak of its world-historical moment. And this is how it took over its class enemies' turf; how it placated them and sometimes even trotted them out for ceremonial purposes and more marginal decoration;[111] how it moderated pressure from below or enlisted it for its own purposes;[112] how it differentiated itself from the mere worker or the one-time noble; how it justified its new social eminence; how it appeared to ride out crises in its market or its workforce (including two recent ones – the cotton famine of the early 1860s and the glut in the world market of 1866[113]); how it projected its ownership of municipal state power; and how it self-mystified. But, far more than just mobilising already existing things for legitimacy,[114] this steamocracy was bent on 'improvement', on technological development, style, the naturalising of history: all these were its means and all are integral to the Town Hall. Gothic is more historical, more developed and more industrial now; it justifies, because it is made to mirror the constant revolutions in the technological basis of industry. And it also has representational purposes. We learn Manchester's worthiness through these spaces: that business is based on the harnessing of nature's bounty and natural labour (not, say, slavery, colonial exploitation or child labour);[115] that nature becomes 'purely a matter of utility' through technological progress and scientific analysis (Dalton and Joule have statues in the first entrance space);[116] and that political acumen is best allied to liberalism (hence Prince Albert's statue in the square, while busts of Richard Cobden, John Bright and Charles Pelham Villiers in the sculpture hall make it a Valhalla of Free Trade and its associated technologists[117]).

In more general terms, the workings of government had recently come to be analogised with machinery.[118] By 1861 J. S. Mill had elevated this into the very image of good government. As opposed to the conservative notion of government as 'a sort of spontaneous product ... a branch (so to speak) of natural history', government-as-machinery was made and worked by men, 'even by ordinary men' and so represented society proportionately.[119] Mill knew Whewell's work well, so this analogy had strong descriptive power, repeated again and again in the opening pages of his *Considerations on Representative Government*. It is through machines that power gets distributed, but the well-functioning machinery of government is only one side of this. Society too has its elements and 'aggregate interests', which must be classified and brought into 'definite groups' if the whole is to be properly – mechanically – organised by the synecdochal representations of government.[120] To act on the minds of men and on public business, as Mill put it, is a good way also to understand the beautiful mechanisms of the Gothic Town Hall.

A vulgar modernist of mid-twentieth-century vintage looking at the Town Hall might say that Waterhouse and his clients simply could not or would not follow through on the logic of the machine–Gothic scenario; that the mill and its machines reach no tangible, visual synthesis with the Gothic in the Town Hall; and that no machine aesthetic is achieved is down to a failure of logic, of imagination, of nerve. Thus the success of heroic 1920s modernism. A certain kind of Victorianist of later vintage would mirror this in wanting to see machines and mills literalised in the building programme for this chapter's interpretation to be acceptable. But perhaps a different kind of synthesis is possible.

The argument here is not for a weak 'modern Gothic' but for something better described as a 'steam-powered industrial culture' articulated with the politics of Free Trade.[121] Whether this is a form of what the art historian Michael Baxandall called the 'period eye' is a tantalising question. 'Living in a culture, growing up and learning to survive in it,' Baxandall asserts, 'involves us in a special perceptive training.'[122] What that meant for Baxandall's fifteenth-century merchants was a specific relation to materials based on their ability to measure – or 'gauge' – commodities visually, which was then translated into a painter's invocation in his work of 'his public's general disposition to gauge ... a habit of analysis ... very close to the painter's analysis of appearances'.[123] Add to this similar dispositions towards dancing and sermons and you have a 'cognitive style', a way of seeing shared across painting and daily life. Perhaps this was something like industrial Gothic and the industrial bourgeoisie, and what Heywood meant by 'industrial greatness'. Perhaps. But Baxandall's period eye works curiously like that of the 'class of over-cultivated person' he evokes in his own time, a group of people who need 'specialised categories' if they are to understand paintings.[124] Cognitive style is, then, something highly cultivated, based on collective everyday rewards – the reassurances of money, holiness and physical pleasure. This is fundamentally a static world, captured in painting as a 'deposit of a social relationship' (another telling analogy is of paintings as 'fossils of economic life').[125] There is little here of the 'imperious sense of change' that Marc Bloch, of the 1930s Annales school of historians, demanded of history writing.[126]

There is not some fundamental difference between building and machine; indeed, what has been described is a spectrum of different forms of resemblance between the Gothic and the industrial. They range from specific machine products like columns to machine representations like cogwheels, to possible allusions to machines and an industrial way of looking at medieval architecture. This is a distinct machine aesthetic, an industrial Gothic, as appropriate for the riot gates of the police station in the basement as for the pinnacles on the roof. And what is to be observed in all of the Town Hall's industrial allusions and echoes are the satisfactions of this medieval modern: 'the beautiful labour of the machine'.[127] The Town Hall is a demonstration of various forms of expertise over architecture's history as much as over the city's, and it equates this knowledge with that of other experts – businessmen, industrialists, engineers, scientists – from the industrial middle class. The Town Hall is the home and central hub for what Disraeli called a 'Venetian oligarchy';[128] it is their political and bureaucratic machine, the product of dispossession.

Understanding Andrew Ure's work in relation to a still rapidly evolving factory system, Marx argued that it was precisely because of Ure's 'undisguised cynicism' that he 'blurts out the thoughtless contradictions of the capitalist brain ... [producing] the classical expression of the spirit of the factory'.[129] In parallel with the more mature factory system three decades later,[130] there was another cynicism. Gothic revival, mills, millwork and cotton machines were made to work together to carry ideas about the perfecting of the machine that was society, but also to give human form to the machine in terms of the borrowed language of a previous culture, a medieval culture understood as oriented around religion, the body and nature but also assimilated to a certain idea of consilience in industrial culture. This is what Walter Benjamin called a 'narcotic historicism', though both the 'cult of machinery' and the historical form could be the narcotic.[131] If, in its main architectural statements, the Town Hall stops short of literalising the Gothic–machine connection, that too is part of the collective dream. Gothic is there to convince us that we are not alienated from work or nature after all, and in that sense Ruskin is relevant, even if the consequences are not what he desired.[132] The abolition of craft skills in the cotton factory has its compensation in the invocation of skill's effects in Gothic, much as for Ure and Fairbairn it was compensated for in millwork. Gothic is no longer the genre that works through fear of the machine but instead through its naturalisation, its reverse engineering into nature. That is why the machine need not – must not – be fully visible.

PERHAPS THIS SHOULD NOT BE THE FINAL WORD. AS A coda, we might consider an image enshrined in the Town Hall after its completion. Earlier I suggested that the murals Ford Madox Brown painted for the Great Hall were intended to establish a sense of Manchester's history and of the relations between its past and its industrial present. It is worth examining one of Brown's works to see how far this synchrony really went and what tensions might be evident. The painting *John Kay: Inventor of the Fly Shuttle, AD 1753* (1888–90) is the only one of Brown's subjects that is squarely part of the Industrial Revolution[133] (fig. 110). The nineteenth-century subject of *Dalton Collecting Marsh-Fire Gas* is closer to Brown in time, but it is a contemplative pastoral scene and, while Dalton's experiments on the properties of gases certainly had industrial applications, the scene itself gives no indication of them. Similarly, *The Opening of the Bridgewater Canal, AD 1761* may celebrate the first of the major canals that would serve Manchester's industrial expansion, but the labour of building the canal and its effects are either played down (as with the coal barge treated as part of the ceremony) or entirely absent, elided by anecdote and historical detail.

What is immediately different in the painting of John Kay is that it shows a crisis, which is played out around a machine in an interior. A mob is breaking through the windows and the inventor is in the act of being swaddled in a woollen sheet by his wife and two workers: he has to become fabric so that he can be smuggled out of the house unobserved.[134] This wrapping is done in a frenzy, all odd limbs, bent backs, a surplus of garments twisted and knotted and with Kay's head oddly grey and white emerging to kiss his wife like a maniac half-constrained by a straitjacket.[135] The grasping hands around Kay are, as it were, those displaced from the invention 'without hands' to the left.[136] This panic implies that other and much bigger turmoil outside, mostly hidden beyond the windows and for which we are not invited to feel any particular sympathy. And the cause of all this, the object of the mob's ire, is the flying shuttle, two of which are on the floor while a third is in mid-air, knocked off the machine, it seems, by the inventor's sprawling son.

The flying shuttle was a remarkably simple invention, yet it was the first innovation to really open up the potential of mass

[110] Ford Madox Brown, *John Kay: Inventor of the Fly Shuttle*, AD 1753, 1888–90. Oil on canvas. Manchester Town Hall.

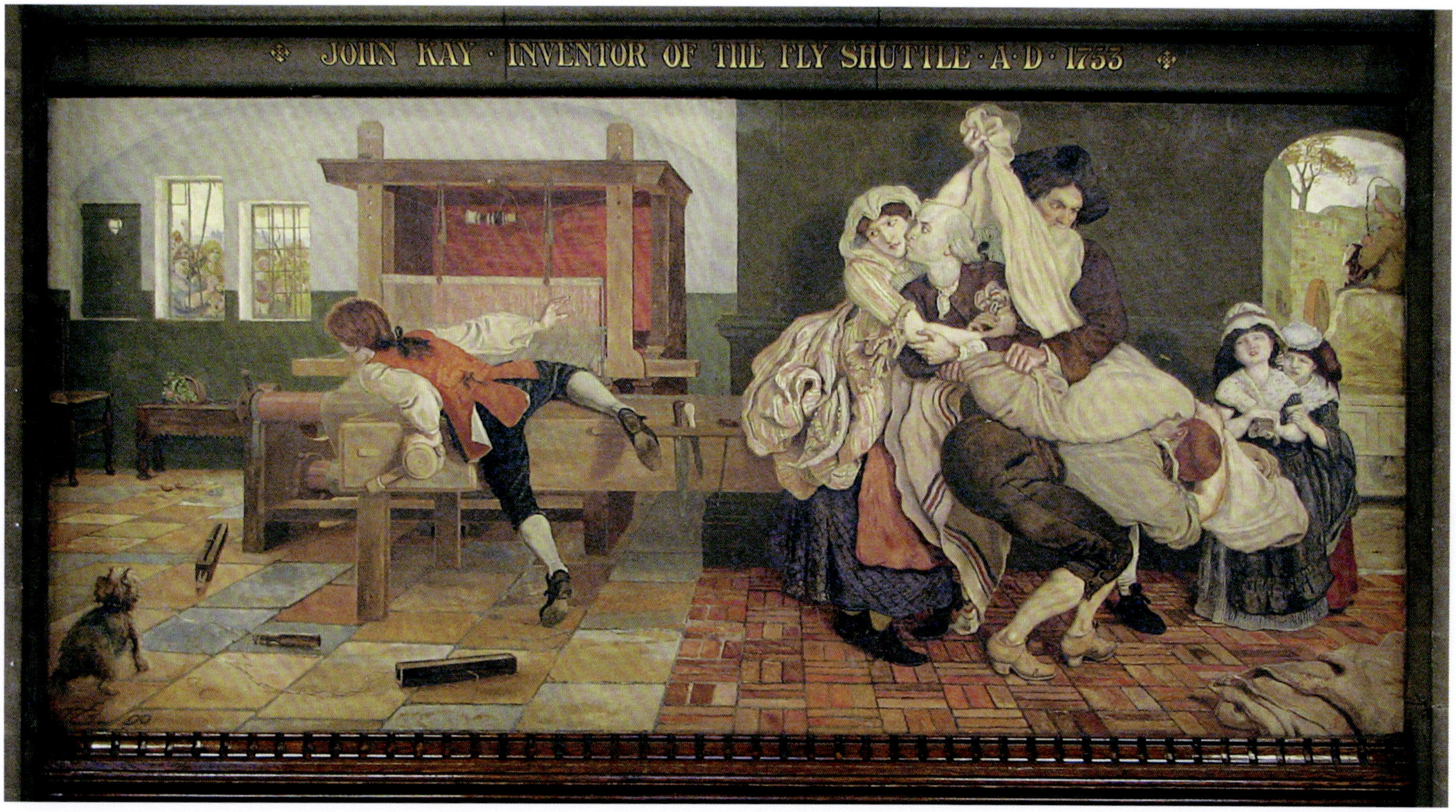

manufacture in the textile industry. The wheeled shuttle itself is like a wooden model of a hollowed-out boat, sometimes pointed at both ends or sometimes – as with the early examples in the painting – blunt ended. In the hollow is placed a spool for the thread, which passes out of both ends of the shuttle so that it can feed the loom. By the jerk of a cord, the shuttle is shot through the loom, carrying the weft threads along a track from end to end of the warp threads. This was the first automation in the textile industry and it meant that weavers' productivity was doubled at a stroke, but it also had the knock-on consequence of requiring more spinners to supply them with yarn. So the shuttle did not so much change the way wool was manufactured as increase weavers' productivity, cut the costs of labour and cause a ripple effect of increased demand across the textile-manufacturing sector. Brown emphasises the simplicity of the invention by placing the heavy carpenter's bench in the foreground with the tools for making the shuttle – vice, chisel and other implements – prominently displayed. In a portent of their destruction, the flying shuttles have come loose from their threads on the loom. They have, in effect, been dis-automated and seemingly resituated at a historical moment when they might as well be the lure of a gimmick rather than a technological transformation.[137]

All this has become the target of destruction because another group of people, the weavers, have been made vulnerable by it, and may be eliminated by its labour-saving effects. The point is made not just by the mob at the windows but also by the near-typological relation between two of the paintings in the mural scheme.[138] Six works previously in the Great Hall sequence of paintings Brown had celebrated *The Establishment of the Flemish Weavers in Manchester*, AD 1363 (fig. 111). Those weavers not showing

[111] Ford Madox Brown, *The Establishment of the Flemish Weavers in Manchester*, AD 1363, 1881–2. Mural painting by the Gambier Parry process. Manchester Town Hall.

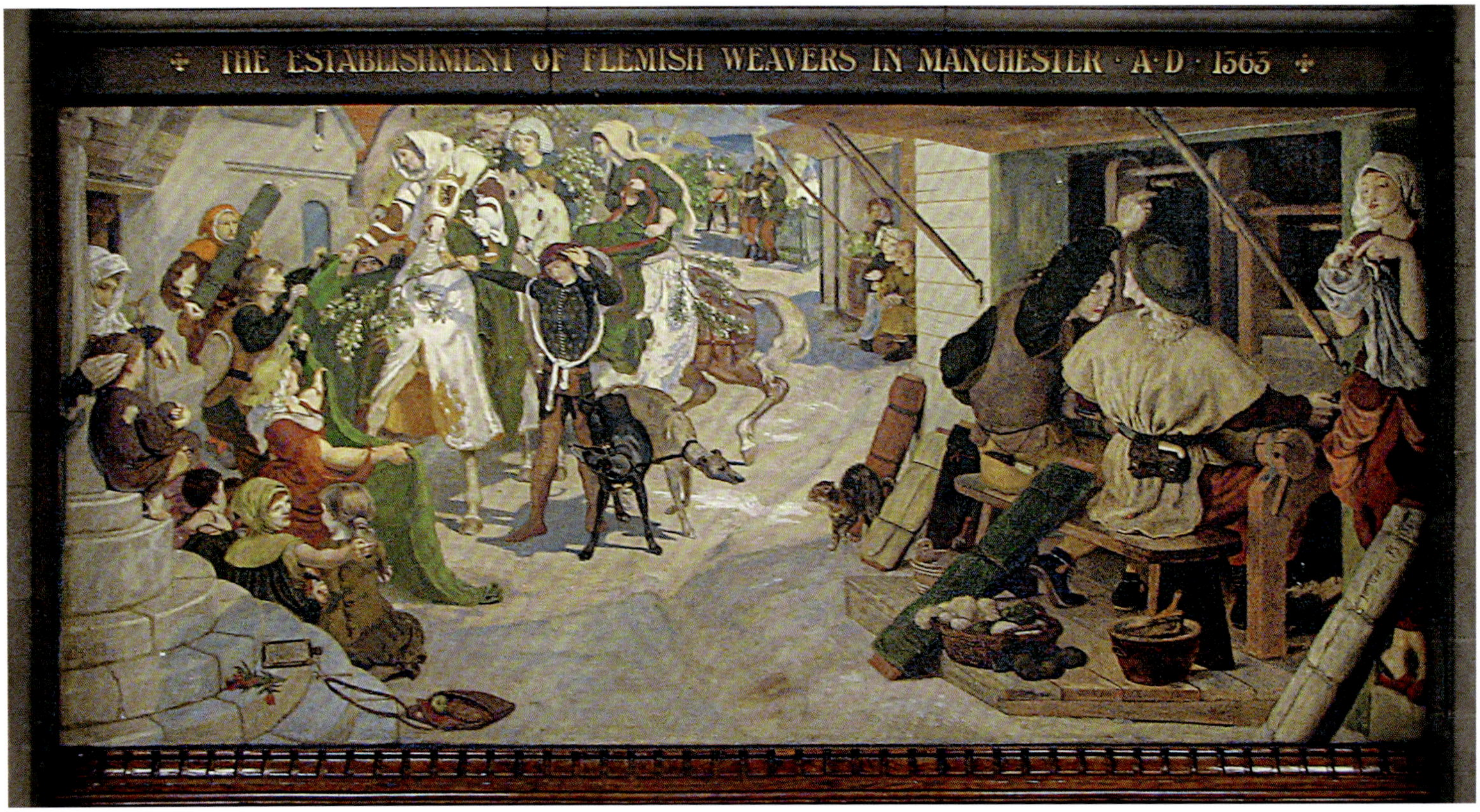

their wares to the queen work under a canopy in the open air, at looms not unlike the one standing in Kay's workshop. Four centuries later those weavers' descendants are the mob breaking the windows: this is their dis-establishment. We do not see much of them but there is a prominent pitchfork and a stretch of countryside. By contrast, Kay's escape will be through a door at the far right, where a cart and a high brick wall await him in a kind of millyard.

But what is most relevant to the concerns of this chapter is the room in which the event takes place. The Flemish weavers are shown integrated in a great sweep of shadow that loops across the foreground of the painting and then coils into the shapes of the road and the queen's entourage. As part of this curve that expresses both community and hierarchy, the Flemish weavers work in something that is part dwelling and part shop, happily integral to the street scene. Kay's room – the founding scene of technological innovation – is contrasted in almost every aspect. Kay's father ran a woollen manufacturing business in Bury, just outside Manchester, and it may be that Brown was imagining this space as a kind of store-room in a mill or warehouse – hence the readily available woollen garments and the waiting cart. It is an obviously improvised space, a room made of two spaces without any obvious join, simply and abruptly pushed together (and, in its blunt bareness, unlike any of the other spaces in the murals). To the left the floor is paved with clay tiles; to the right, these change suddenly to brick. To the left the ceiling is shallowly vaulted and painted an airy blue; to the right, without explication, this becomes a darkly painted wall with equally dark panelling below. And to the left stands the loom, untended save for the son's body perched in front of it (his hand against the threads and his posture may even remind us of the children underneath the looms in the mill images discussed in Chapter 1: see figs 22 and 23). The loom, wooden, squarish and solid as a four-poster bed, occupies an area of relative calmness between the two frenzied activities, but there is a latency to it, an expansive potential suggested by its continuity with the workbench, and perhaps also a sense that its multiplication through industrial production will break the constraints of the room. As a sundered, even schizophrenic, space, this seems inevitable.[139] All this, then – the disjointed room and the potent loom, and perhaps even the sick frenzy – makes a kind of proto-factory. It is not Gothic, certainly not Gothic Revival, but rather something improvised, in the process of both coming together and bursting its bounds.

Brown's painting is equivocal about technological change and its effects, a strange mix of comic and tragic registers.[140] When the murals had been commissioned, this subject was regarded by the decorations subcommittee, which decided on the murals (and on which sat Joseph Thompson), as one that was part of their own industrial genealogy: after the title of Kay's subject they wrote, 'Machinery in great part the cause of Manchester's prosperity'.[141] Brown's Kay is far from heroic, and his invention breaks the harmonies portrayed elsewhere in the murals, but there is no sympathy either for those breaking with 'most sinister intentions' into the workshop.[142] What is clear is that Brown had lodged at the heart of the Town Hall – a depicted room within the room of the Great Hall – an image that in many ways is quite discrepant with the Gothic machine. Far from espousing the synchrony of industrial and medieval forms that, I have argued, run through the Town Hall, this is an image that is deeply ambivalent about progress or at least its means and its spaces. At best this is about the abruptness of change, the in-betweenness of its spaces – neither medieval nor yet modern.

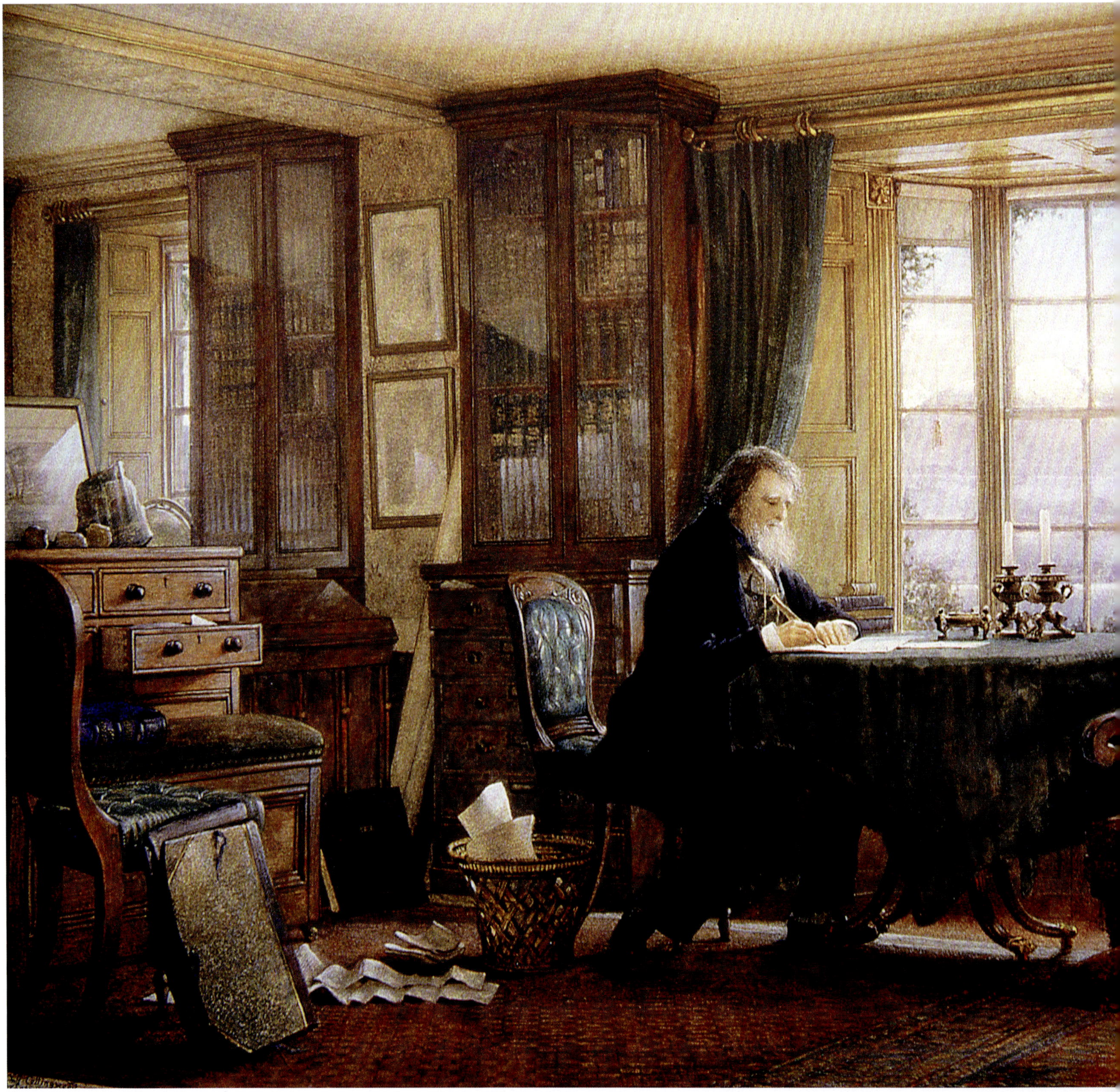

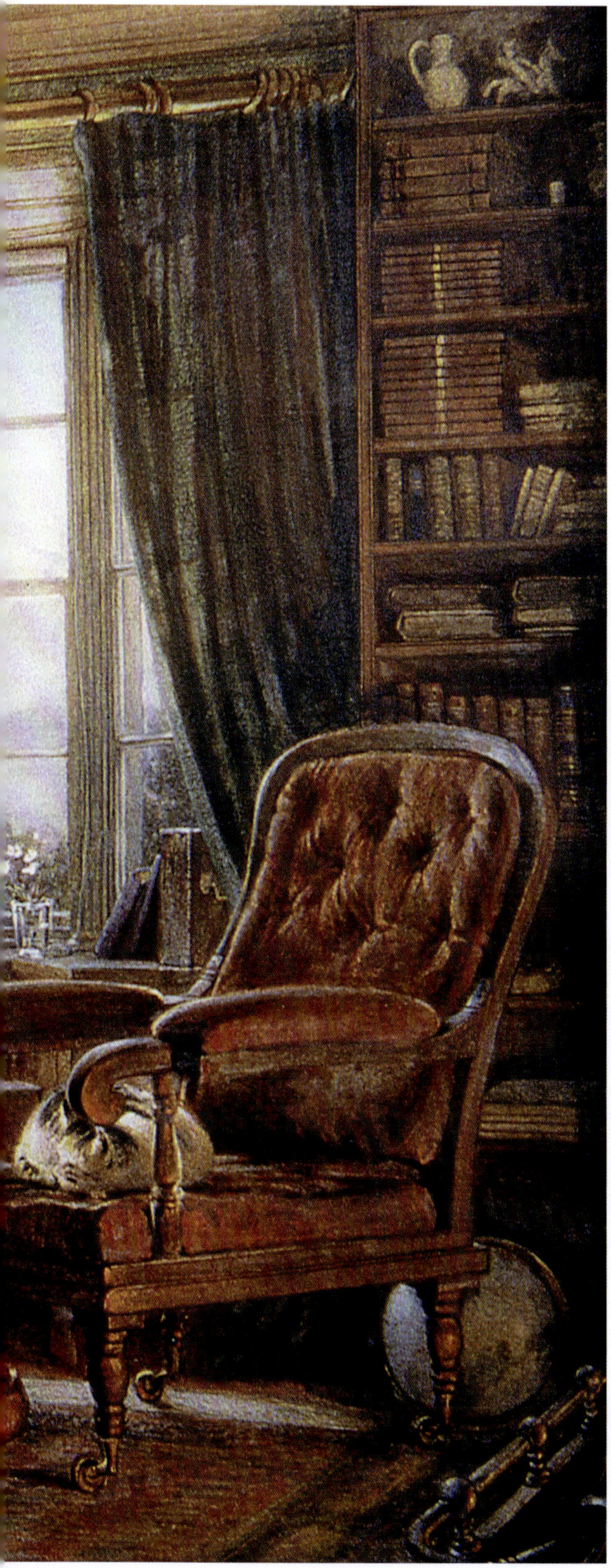

[112] W. G. Collingwood, *John Ruskin in his Study at Brantwood*, 1882. Watercolour. Ruskin Museum, Coniston.

5 Devil's Darkness

Industrial Pollution and Culture as Philanthropy

IN HIS 1882 PORTRAIT, W. G. COLLINGWOOD, RUSKIN'S dutiful assistant, captures little of the famously driven, painstaking intelligence of his employer (fig. 112). To the contrary, for at the centre of the picture Ruskin is a psychological void, little more than a cipher for the industrious scholar, as if the painting had inadvertently captured the sitter's final years of guttering lucidity. But the products of Ruskin's intellectual labour, even its waste, are everywhere evident. 'Slips of proof and sheets of paged revise', Collingwood explained, 'are laying on the floor, and the spent copy is in the waste-paper basket.'[1] And through these means, by concentrating on the room's minutiae and its assembled objects as an image of a lifetime's passions, the painter does achieve something suitably reverent. This is the art critic as St Jerome, seated in his study at Brantwood in the Lake District, portfolio at the ready, books to hand, tabby asleep, globe at bay and, on the chest of drawers, a row of mineral specimens and a Turner watercolour of Florence from Fiesole. Below these, 'on the velvet cushioned top of the case for framed Dürers', Collingwood tells us, 'is a favourite MS bible of the fourteenth century which he used to read as a beginning to his day's work'.[2] The early morning sun, which enters the orderly, well-dusted room, also lights the slopes of the mountain (known as the Old Man of Coniston) beyond.[3] A fender in the corner assures us of the warmth of a coal fire in the grate, while the arm of the trusty 'Ruskin shovel', made to the sage's design by a local blacksmith, is just visible. And yet, as Ruskin himself felt, all this comfort, this harmony with nature, this steady glow of the mind long projected onto its surroundings, could suddenly be put at risk by its inferred opposite: soot, smoke poisoning, darkness.

[113] John Ruskin, *Ice Clouds over Coniston Old Man*, c.1880. Watercolour. The Ruskin – Library, Museum and Research Centre, University of Lancaster.

Geological time cut across by the newly catastrophic time of industry.

The threat was persistent, and its source was clear. This is Ruskin writing in his diary as he looked out from the same study window six years earlier, on 22 May 1876 – 'dark on the Old Man. Since morning however the clouds have been natural in their old white wreaths – now it is getting Manchestery'.[4] And, again on 7 August 1877, 'Terribly hot, dark, moist, thunderous cloud, ending in mere Manchester blackness'.[5] Or this nightmarishly industrial and Gothick scene noted on 13 August 1879:

> *The most terrific and horrible thunderstorm ... rolling incessantly, like railway luggage trains – quite ghastly in its mockery of them – the air one loathsome mass of sultry and foul fog like smoke – scarcely raining at all, – increasing to heavier rolling with flashes quivering vaguely through all the air, and at last terrific double streams of reddish-violet fire, not forked or zigzag, but rippled rivulets ... with grand artillery-peals following; not rattling crashes, or irregular cracklings, but delivered volleys ... and now half past seven seems settling down into Manchester devil's darkness.*[6]

Finally, an entry from 8 January 1880: 'Deadly fog-rain these three days, without a gleam – today – Manchester smoke – with the usual deviltry of cloud moving fast in rags, with no wind'[7] (fig. 113). With every precise observation, and every shudder of panicky fear – as if a fatal future were gathering in the very sky above – the notes in the diary, which had started by simply separating clouds from smoky pollution, so often end by identifying the whole infernal scene with Manchester. Much of this observation was carried over into one of Ruskin's last books, *The Storm Cloud of the Nineteenth Century* (1884), where the 'plague-cloud', a 'sulking', lowering presence, was named again as 'Manchester devil's darkness'.[8] What Ruskin saw out of the study window was not just the scree on the sunny slopes of the Old Man of Coniston, in harmony with the mineral specimens and painted landscapes around him, but also the smoky pall of the archetypal industrial city nearly seventy miles to the south and west. An ethical way of seeing, based on the ekphrastic lessons of nature, was judderingly disturbed by an insurgent aesthetic, modern and industrial.[9] Another mineral was the cause; mined and burned, rapidly increasing in use,[10] and threatening the world Ruskin himself had created even as he enjoyed its blessings in the form of his own coal fire.

WHAT HAS BEEN CALLED THE 'FOSSIL ECONOMY' – OUR over-reliance on fossil fuels for the last two centuries and the gap this has opened up in the human relation to nature (which Marx understood as a 'metabolic rift') – has deep and continuing relevance to culture.[11] But, while histories of the fossil economy have an urgency today as we scramble to understand and to hold back the mounting climatic changes whose terrifying effects were unleashed by the Industrial Revolution, the cultural logic of this economy – its moral sustenance, its hero worship, its finagling, its necessary justifications and disavowals, its profession of good works – requires equal attention. This chapter is concerned with following this cultural logic to understand how it worked across the industrial city and its satellites through a set of connections that linked different kinds of space, energy systems and human labour with the cultural forms of architecture, broadly conceived. This logic is not deeply hidden, yet it needs a different perspective on it if we are not to take it at its own estimation, a perspective that provides the means of recognising and re-establishing its linkages. The denial and disavowal of the drives behind, and the effects of, the fossil economy were largely, of course, a product of its long historical moment and the way in which the interests of capital were placed above those of the worker and the earth itself; but they were also a product of the disciplinary separations and professional territorialisation that arose out of this moment and that continue, despite our self-acclaimed interdisciplinary moment, to obscure accounts of Victorian culture and its relation to industrial change. Niklas Luhmann's idea of a dynamic of differentiation is useful here, that making sense of reality in the modern period has been a matter of devising 'distinct semi-autonomous levels which we come to think of as multiple and coexisting realities with their own specific intelligibilities'.[12] By contrast, the idea of totality is the hypothesis and even the desire for connection, a 'law of mutually interacting "coincidences" rather than one of truly rational organisation'.[13] The idea or category of totality itself motivates attempts to connect separate

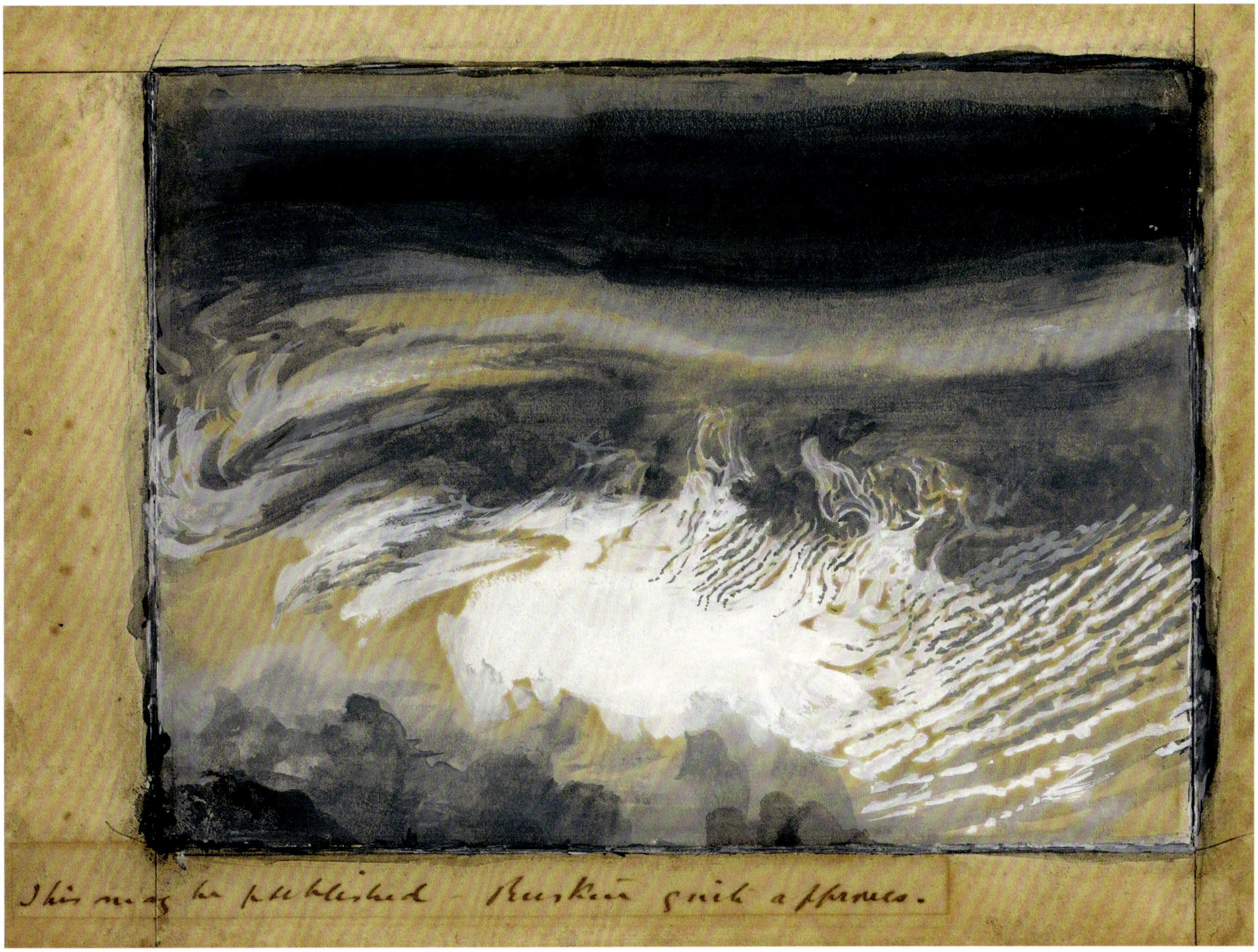

disciplines and imagine collective processes. Even if such totality is occluded – it is, in Fredric Jameson's words, 'what organizes history but is unrepresentable within it ... necessarily always absent ... [yet] always perceptually present' – it can at the same time be substituted for and allegorised.[14] As so often with the perception and representation of industry, Manchester presents the best test case. The very speed of the making of vast fortunes based on the gathering of new technologies and new forms of work and workforces, and the will and means to shape the city to these interests, also entailed a twofold action: of profound imbrication and of profound separation as these processes and their effects operated within the work of culture, whether through religion, philanthropy, the making of architecture or, as we shall see, the collecting and reading of books.

What follows in this chapter is a kind of rudimentary pursuit of Ruskin's smoke from one of its sources outside Manchester into the city and its effects, material and symbolic. But first, a few things must be said about this pursuit or tracking, the artifice required and method as a kind of structure. It is in one sense simply a smutty tale of small flakes of soot, and like all smutty tales it has to have a moral. In this tale, environmental history, architectural history and history of technology all play a part; they must all play a part as each individually presents a fragmentary or partial account. The necessary transdisciplinary or adisciplinary nature of this, however, is less important than its attempt to make sense of architecture's position in relation to a chain of production and waste, not just from a mine to a pithead along rail tracks and to a mill and its consumption of coal, but further into the very buildings that were paid for by the textile industry's profits and that found ways to minimise the effects of its by-products. As a method, this is less a system than a persistence, insisting on the pathway of links made by fossil fuel consumption. My intention is to put stone carved into ornament back into some meaningful cultural relationship with coal carved into fuel.

The approach thus has something in common with the so-called it-narrative, or novel of circulation, a literary subgenre common in the eighteenth and nineteenth centuries. In such works, many of which were stories of money (a golden guinea, a rupee, a shilling, a banknote) – for instance, *The Secret History of an Old Shoe* and *The History and Adventures of an Atom* – an object is followed (it often narrates its own story) as if it were a character passing through layers of society high and low and physical locations, often far-flung. These objects are therefore curious spy-avatars whose mobility but apparent lack of agency is used to cut through propriety, hierarchy and convention, often mimicking the values of circulation and exchange and seeming to explain them by putting them under different lights. Recently, it-narratives have received attention from literary critics, for whom the portability of these objects – often animistic and satiric – and their allegorisation of a range of anxieties about an emerging world of consumerism, are seen to resonate with recent critical trends for thing theory, affect and the non-human as actant.[15] But I am not interested in an exercise in this 'new materialism' here, and do not imagine smoke as having agency.[16] Instead my pursuit of smoke across spaces reveals the human complexities of the desire to exploit, as well as the exculpation of this desire in the realm of culture.

This chapter does not mimic an it-narrative; it cannot quite provide the life and adventures of a smut. And, anyway, it's clear that the authors of it-narratives chose simple artefacts – wares and other objects that represent exchange value – rather than waste products like smoke (even if, like Tobias Smollett's atom, they may pass through various waste processes). But the literary form does parallel and has something to say about Ruskin's fear that what he traced back to Manchester was something that would destroy what he most valued, that his St Jerome's study beside the lake and the mountain would be infested by the personified substance, 'devil's darkness', of industrial capitalism. This helps us to develop another way of connecting industry and culture through the practices of Rylands & Sons and the library created in the heart of Manchester by Enriqueta Rylands.

Smoke travels in ways that are threatening; its unruly character puts at risk any notion of proper place. It was often used by Victorian writers as a substance that represented as much the depravity of working-class environments as the precarity of middle-class circumstance, both metonym and medium. There is a chapter in Elizabeth Gaskell's *North and South* (1854–5) when, having been expelled from the pure air of her father's idyllic country parsonage and newly ensconced in a rented house in the industrial city of Milton (a fictionalised Manchester), Margaret Hale's attempts to impose order – repapering the rooms, unpacking and arranging – are undermined: 'a thick fog crept up to the very windows, and was driven in to every open door in choking white wreaths of unwholesome mist ... the heavy smoky air [even] hung about her bedroom'. This is 'as thick a fog of circumstance', Gaskell suggests, as of pollution. The invasive substance breaches the house's skin as much as it breaches the weaker distinctions; it is irrepressible evidence of the lowering of class status (or the ever-present threat of it), but it also pervades and obscures, undermining the signs and codes of social stability.[17] The 'barrier to hope' is a trap that does not allow the 'intercourse' between classes that was Gaskell's great concern: 'intercourse is the very breath of life', she writes in *North and South*.[18] There is also Gaskell's complementary use of smoke in *Mary Barton* (1848), where it stands for the constraints of class as conveyed by the determinations of environment. Mary Barton herself is 'bound to Manchester' and cannot 'quit the old smokejack'; when she attempts to she finds herself '[looking] towards the factory-chimneys, and the cloud of smoke which hovers over Manchester, with a feeling akin to the "Heimweh"'.[19] Although it was not always as negatively construed as we may now assume, smoke is represented in such novels as one of the most insidious elements of the trap that is environmental determinism; it is familiar and even linked to homeliness, but because it is noxious and never quite comes to rest, it can drift and destabilise both place and substance. Less often depicted, however, is the fact that smoke's release in the form of effluent from more solid material forms also means that it evades possession (or, as lawyers found, is very hard to attribute to one owner), and this is where the it-narrative form, more than the Victorian novels it prepared the way for (with Gaskell's smoke or Dickens's dust in *Our Mutual Friend* or fog in *Bleak House*), is useful.

Although they are fictional stories, it-narratives describe mobile forms of sociability or connectedness between things, people and places, different cuts or sections through the norms and forms of social and economic structure. Their objects make unfamiliar what they pass through or make familiar what is exotic, rendering the world differently legible.[20] Similarly, the spaces and architecture of things in constant motion – especially a substance like smoke which permeates what it is contained by, floating into and out of it – causes spaces to be drawn together by new or newly revealing connections, 'changing the cartography of the sensible and thinkable',[21] bypassing the antitheses essential to the maintenance of the very idea of the city (town and country, near and far, traditional and modern, high and low, centre and suburb).[22] This drawing together offers something of an alternative also to the delimitations of disciplinary, professional or sociological notions of architectural and urban space, a 'partitioning of times and spaces, sites and functions'.[23]

To track the spaces traversed by smoke is to engage in what Fredric Jameson has called a 'cognitive mapping'.[24] Turning back to the engraving of Manchester discussed in the Introduction (see fig. 1). one response to that view is to see it as a collection of buildings – a collection of streets, warehouses and mills, cultural buildings, buildings for local government and for leisure – all built at different times and for different purposes and clients. Whether we study them individually or in groups, by typology or morphology, as civic boosterism or urban dystopia, we end up with a collection, the *musée imaginaire* of our own projection – something with too partial a grasp of the historical forces actually at work. And yet the image also makes unavoidable a different connective tissue, the environmental conditions of smoke pollution – smoke as both medium and effluent. Properly understood, this offers a different angle or narrative. We map a different set of connections, which make a different sense; an architectural history comes into view that includes the coal mine and the smoke-stack and the cotton plantation, as well as the philanthropically endowed library made possible by exploitation. Fossil capitalism is what binds all these together, connecting different kinds of space, energy systems and human labour with the cultural forms of architecture. To follow smoke is to follow that rationale. It is also not to take the logic of fossil capitalism on its own terms. The denial and disavowal of the drives behind the fossil economy were largely a product of its long historical moment and the way the interests of capital were placed above those of the worker and the earth itself; but they were also a product of the disciplinary separations and professional territorialisation that arose out of this moment and that continue to obscure accounts of Victorian culture and its relation to industrial change.

By cognitive mapping Jameson wanted to indicate the necessary work of revealing and plotting the links, relationships, co-productions and routes of the complexity that is capitalism; to put it differently, to provide a guide to knowing it other than on its own sublime and mystificatory terms.[25] Ruskin's *Storm Cloud* itself has some of these mapping elements – drawing together subjective experience, precise climatic observation and vast global changes – but it is far from offering a navigational aid. Linking it-narratives and cognitive mapping, as Toscano and Kinkle have recently done, is to allow for orientations or tracks that intersect with the circularity of the commodity chains of production and consumption, but also to acknowledge or intercut what those chains disassociate or differentiate (in this case that would obviously be high art as much as waste).[26] Of course, it-narratives also have highly conventionalised sentimental elements – a moral or apotheosis – but again these are of use here, for one thing because their imaginative and satirical aspects question the conventions of mimeticism associated with historical analysis. Although it does have a more general period temporality about it, the route traced

[114] Pillar and stall system in a coal mine, from Matthias Dunn, *A Treatise on the Winning and Working of Collieries* (1848).

[115] Dip level and rise level in a coal mine, from Matthias Dunn, *A Treatise on the Winning and Working of Collieries* (1848).

[116] 'A section of Bradley Mine near Bilston', *c.*1805. Engraving.

[117] Coal hauliers, from *First Report of the Commissioners (Mines) of the Children's Employment Commission* (1842).

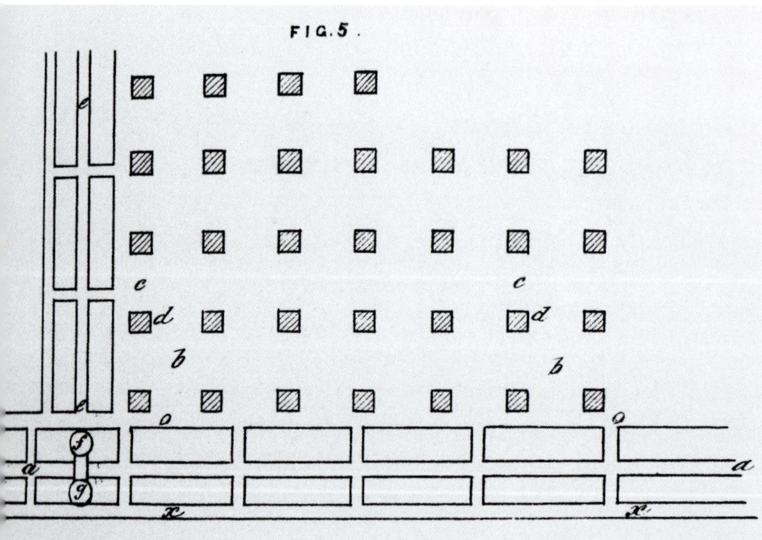

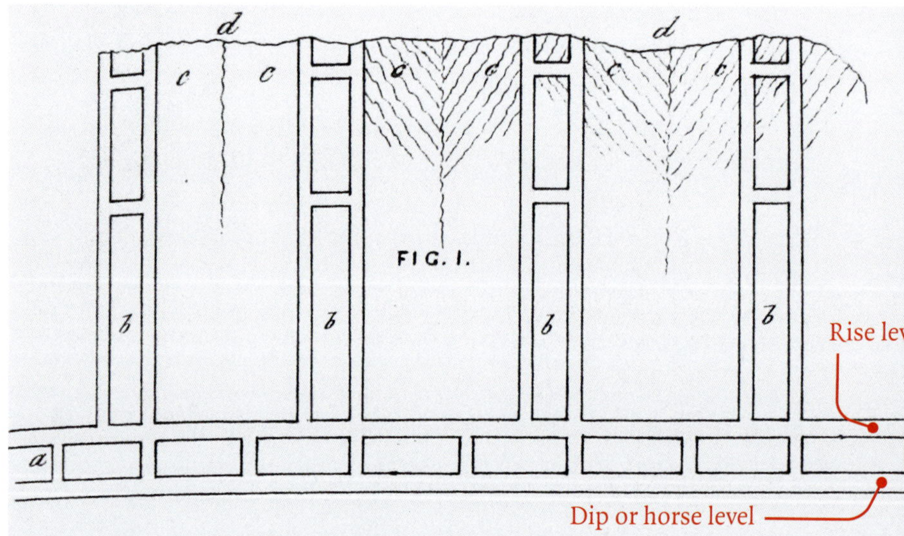

across a world of spaces is not temporally specific – this is not an actual smut traversing spaces at a particular moment; instead, the smut narrative necessitates a breaking with the idea of fixed coordinates in the abstract space and time of capitalism.[27] While it has a connecting logic in terms of production and its effluent – the carbon trail that links the making of energy and its waste – in what follows I also attempt to register the 'phenomenological richness' of a tracking that involves a spatio-temporal drifting and merging with other objects and other routes.[28] The map thus created is an itinerary, both literal and metaphorical, from a mine to a library, a cotton mill to a book, a boiler to a bookcase. The new simplifications, and the unexpected forms they take, are inherent to the model – as in the fabular forms of the it-narrative or indeed in the diagrams that the urban theorist Kevin Lynch (from whom Jameson took the term 'cognitive mapping') encouraged his subjects to draw in order to represent their memory (or mental maps) of moving across familiar places in what Lynch understood as otherwise a city largely alienated from them because its logic was obscure.[29] But the simplicity also brings out coordinates and significances that are not registered and that are not mappable in more formalised or institutionalised models of space and its geographies.

THE LIKELY ULTIMATE SOURCE OF RUSKIN'S DEVIL'S darkness was the south Lancashire coalfield and its seams.[30] The 'architecture' of these subterranean workings is where our story starts, at the beginning of the carbon trail. The mines around Wigan were worked by leaving pillars of coal to hold up the roof, with stalls or compartments between them; this was known as the pillar and stall system, as opposed to the long-wall system which brought in stone walls or wooden supports[31] (fig. 114). This first architecture of coal was tunnelled into the ground and, after underground service roads had been dug, its apparently ordered spaces were made by productive extraction from the coal seams, the 'stores of past photosynthesis'.[32] The size of the pillars was a matter of controversy: the larger were generally the more safe, the smaller generally the more productive.[33] Their extractive removal was a matter of experience and luck. The troglodytic passages (usually called roads or galleries) were planned as a grid iron or, in a variation often found in Lancashire mines (and known as the 'Lancashire system'), in the form of paired passages differentiated between a 'dip level' (or a lower horse road) and a 'rise' (or higher level), each enabling haulage and the ventilation of the complex[34] (fig. 115). From the rise level the tunnels for the working places were driven, again in the form of paired passages.

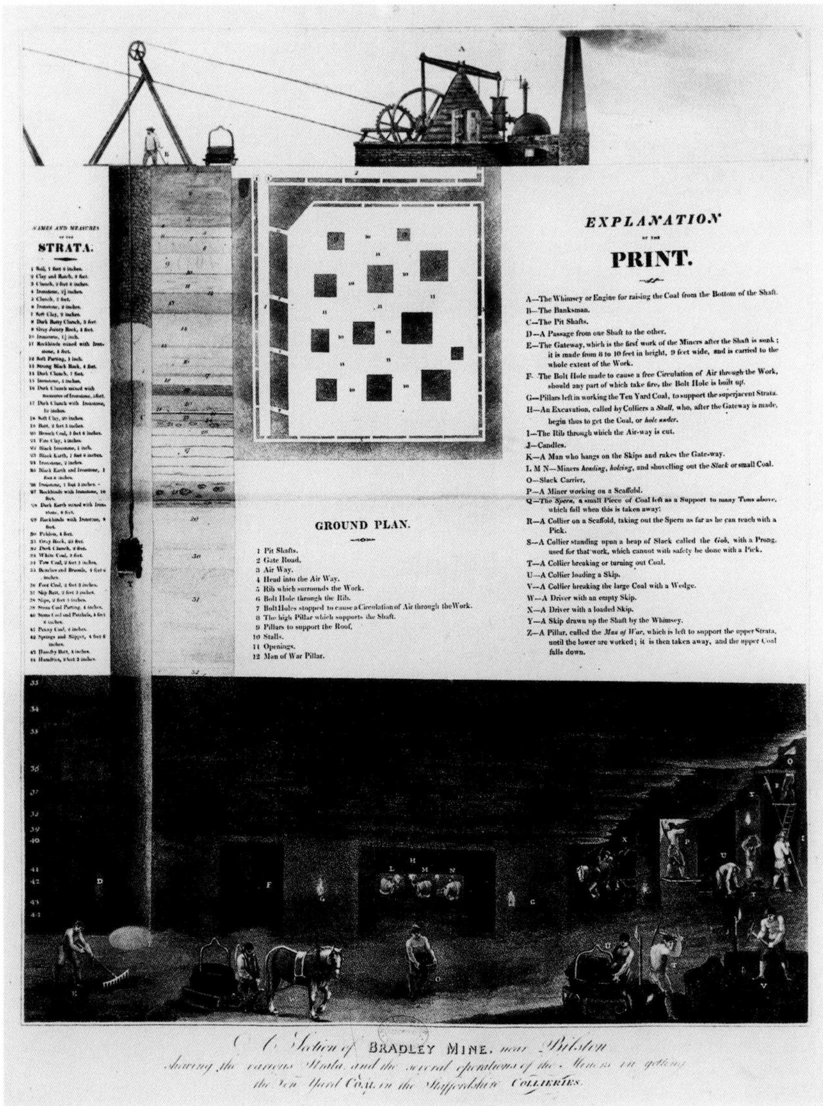

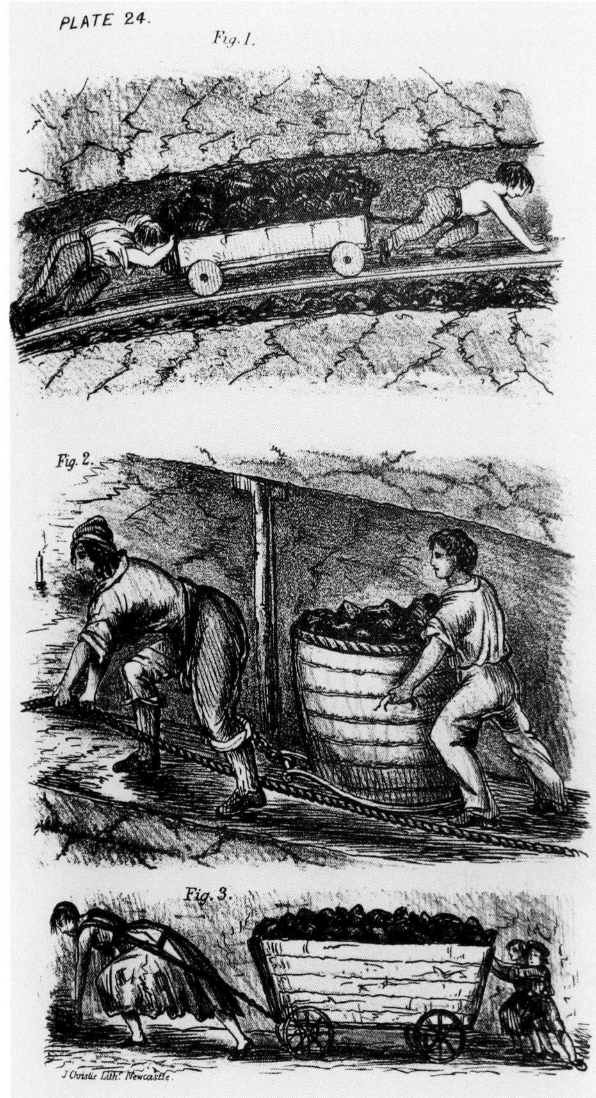

The mine may be 'a master site of capitalism', but representation is clearly a problem when it comes to underground workings, and this is manifest in more ways than a simple scarcity of images.[35] The less vernacular vocabulary used to describe mines – of galleries, chambers, roads, pillars, passages and circulation – indicates the struggle to reconcile the danger of the precarious conditions with the reassurance of familiar forms of stability and order. And, likewise, in the few images available we see ideal layouts, spatialised systems of extraction and movement that take as little account of local variations and modifications as they do of the conditions of work within these mines. More like marketing brochures than blueprints – and owing much to the sections through mines in Diderot's *Encyclopédie*[36] – mine layout diagrams imagine mole's-eye views of subterranean cities without dwellings or sunlight, through whose schematic spaces pass the substances of coal, bodies and air (fig. 116). Such diagrams are certainly distinct in terms of their intended viewers and the relative skill of their artists, from the better-known subterranean imagery of narrow passages and barely clad figures, often women and children, produced for the 1842 Parliamentary Report[37] (fig. 117). Made for the purposes of the Parliamentary Commission, these provide occasional glimpses of how mine layouts might have been experienced. (For instance, Betty Harris, a thirty-seven-year-old drawer in a pit in Little Bolton, could perceive little beyond the 'very steep' road and the occasional rope to help guide her up it.[38]) Although these images must have been the work of non-professional artists, they are not quite as direct and objective (by a hand that 'might as well be a lens'[39]) as some have claimed. Their architectural aspect demonstrates they are effectively sectional drawings; they imagine miners moving through passages as if the passage sides were, somehow, magically transparent.

The diagrammatic mode of mining engineers often pointed to the causes of disaster, if more for economic purposes than out of human empathy. The Lancashire coalfield was notorious for its gassy seams that caused frequent explosions. The pillars of mine passages were also likely (as the top and middle figures of fig. 118 show) either to disjoint (to be 'deranged by creep', as one mining expert put it) and the floor to fill up and be joined by crumbling coal from the roof, or the pillars to collapse because they were too weak (a phenomenon known as 'thurst'). One inspector calculated the death rate in Lancashire and Cheshire mines for the years 1851 to 1853 as 215 lives per annum out of a total mining workforce of 38,000.[40]

Despite the reassurances of the grid and its thick crossing points or doubled passages, a ruinous instability – the environmental danger to labouring bodies subordinated to the primacy of the movement of coal – marked smut's life from its beginning.[41] To prevent thurst and creep destroying the whole mine, a further architectural form was devised, the barrier made of coal, often twenty or thirty yards thick.[42] Drifts (c–c) and levels (a–a) (in fig. 119) were defended by these barriers, leaving the working spaces (b) undefended but allowing the principal communication routes to be unaffected by any collapse. The specification of passages was key to the operation of the whole: circulation (of air) was designed into the system, interconnecting with the larger operation of collecting and transporting coal (fig. 120). Mine ventilation plans take this to a further level of abstraction, with the downcast shaft (A) now the centre of flow (fig. 121). Levels of abstraction, then, but also 'creep' and 'thurst'. This was the collier's world – its architecture, its space – and, despite mining's technological advances in the previous century and unlike textile manufacture, little of it changed across the nineteenth century: it was hardly a

[118] Disjointed or collapsed pillars in coal mines, from Matthias Dunn, *A Treatise on the Winning and Working of Collieries* (1848).

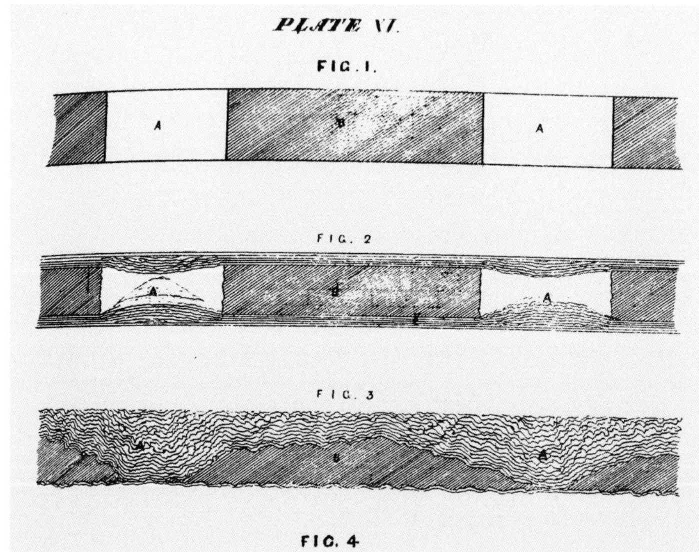

[119] Mine layout showing barriers, drifts and levels, from Matthias Dunn, *A Treatise on the Winning and Working of Collieries* (1848).

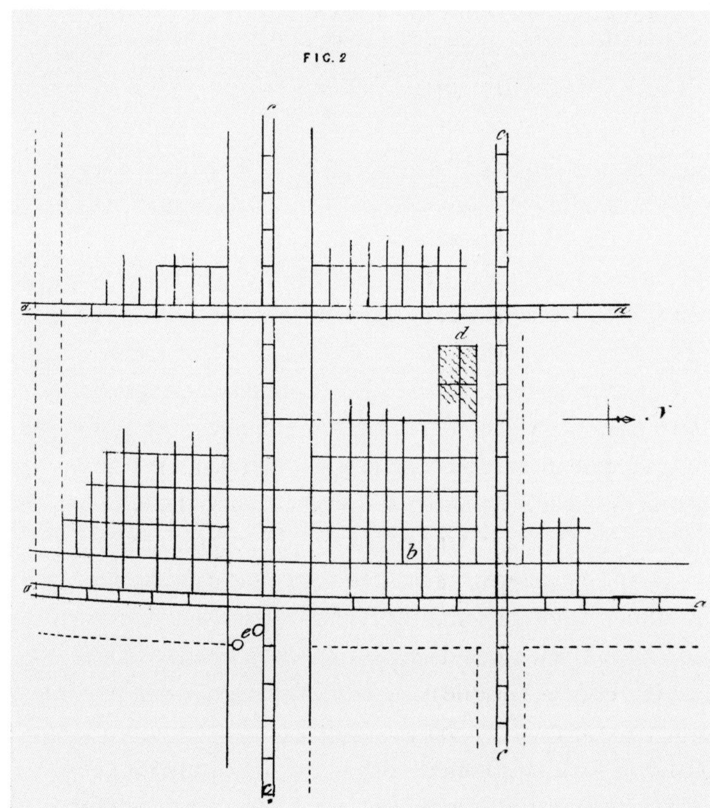

[120] Mine layouts showing ventilation doors (E), from Matthias Dunn, *A Treatise on the Winning and Working of Collieries* (1848).

[121] Mine ventilation plan, from Matthias Dunn, *A Treatise on the Winning and Working of Collieries* (1848).

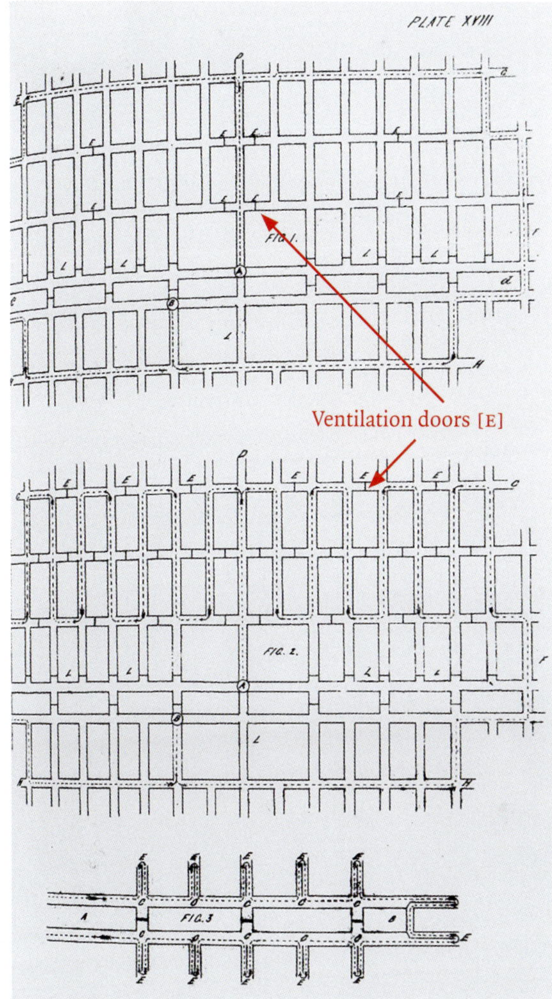

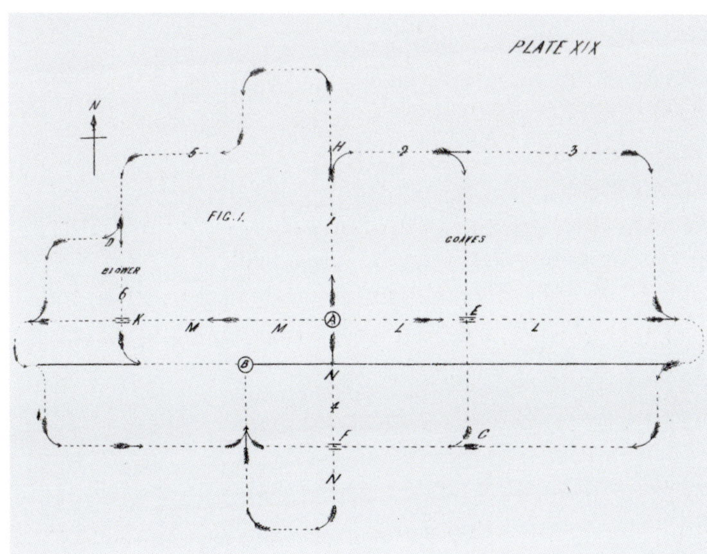

site of technological innovation.[43] Steam-driven pumps and fans may well have been present by the mid-nineteenth century, but the miners still hacked at the coalface with picks and shovels, working at the head of the smaller passages in the layout diagrams.[44]

If the mine was a kind of grid found and tunnelled out of the earth, whose extractive productivity depended on an eating away not just at its edges but also at its own nodes and passages, it was also a colonial city exploiting subterranean resources, part of larger industrial and commercial empires. Comparisons with towns were common: as one mining manual put it,

> *[the mine workings] might remind one of a town having long streets reaching from boundary to boundary in one direction, and these crossed by other streets at right angles to them. In this case the streets and back streets would be in reality the parallel and cross roads, and the blocks of buildings the pillars of solid coal.*[45]

In other words, and taking into account that this is another form of reassurance (now of governance by design), the subterranean mine mirrored the form of the company towns or the by-law streets of the industrial towns above ground.[46]

One such town was Wigan, in the heart of the Lancashire coalfield and increasingly important as one of the ring of satellite towns around Manchester. Since the 1830s the three Gidlow pits, just north of Wigan, had been owned by the textile company Rylands & Sons to provide coal for its Gidlow mill[47] (fig. 122). They belonged to one of the most successful Victorian commercial enterprises, from 1860 onwards the single largest textile firm in the world, whose founder, John Rylands, was Manchester's first multimillionaire, the 'Wellington of commerce'.[48] The key to Rylands & Sons' success was not managerial style or any particular technological innovation but its marketing skills, its accounting systems, its portfolio built up through constant acquisitions and prudent diversification while grounding itself in the domestic market, and its 'vertical integration' of the disparate elements of cotton textile manufacture and its ancillaries in a company system.[49] Indubitably large in its combined capacity, Rylands & Sons' commercial empire was also remarkably differentiated in its operations even within one industry. Securing

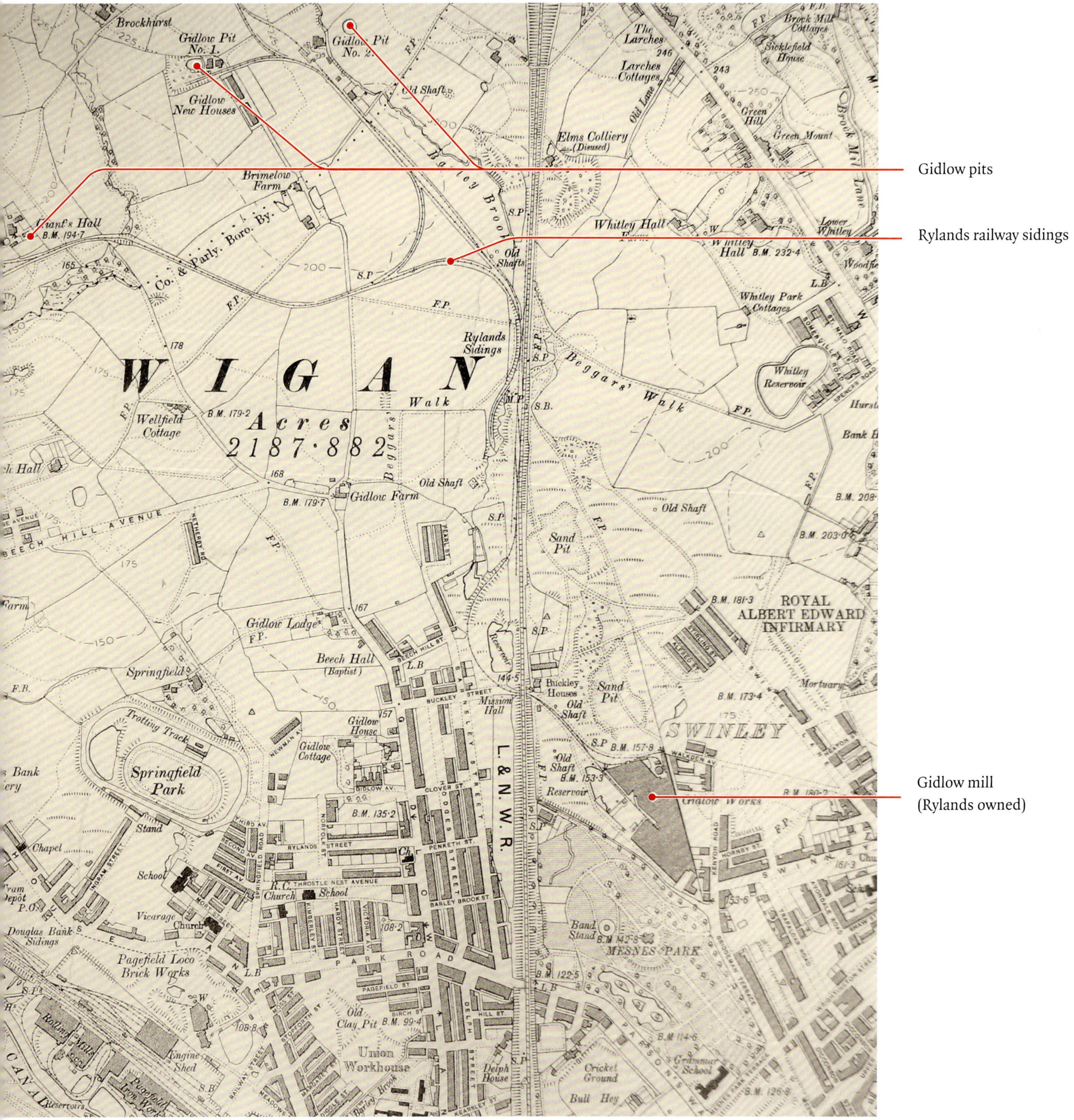
Gidlow pits
Rylands railway sidings
Gidlow mill
(Rylands owned)
Gidlow Pit No. 1.
Gidlow Pit No. 2.
Gidlow New Houses
Brockhurst
Brimelow Farm
Elms Colliery (Disused)
Larches Cottages
Whitley Hall
Rylands Sidings
WIGAN
Acres 2187·882
Beggars' Walk
Gidlow Farm
Gidlow Lodge
Beech Hall (Baptist)
Springfield Park
Trotting Track
ROYAL ALBERT EDWARD INFIRMARY
SWINLEY
Gidlow Works
L. & N. W. R.
MESNES PARK
Union Workhouse
Pagefield Loco Brick Works
Grammar School
Cricket Ground
Whitley Reservoir

[122] Ordnance Survey map of Wigan, 1909, showing the Gidlow mines and mill.

[123] Gidlow mill, Wigan, 1865: perspective. Architect: George Woodhouse. From Evan Leigh, *The Science of Modern Cotton Spinning* (1873).

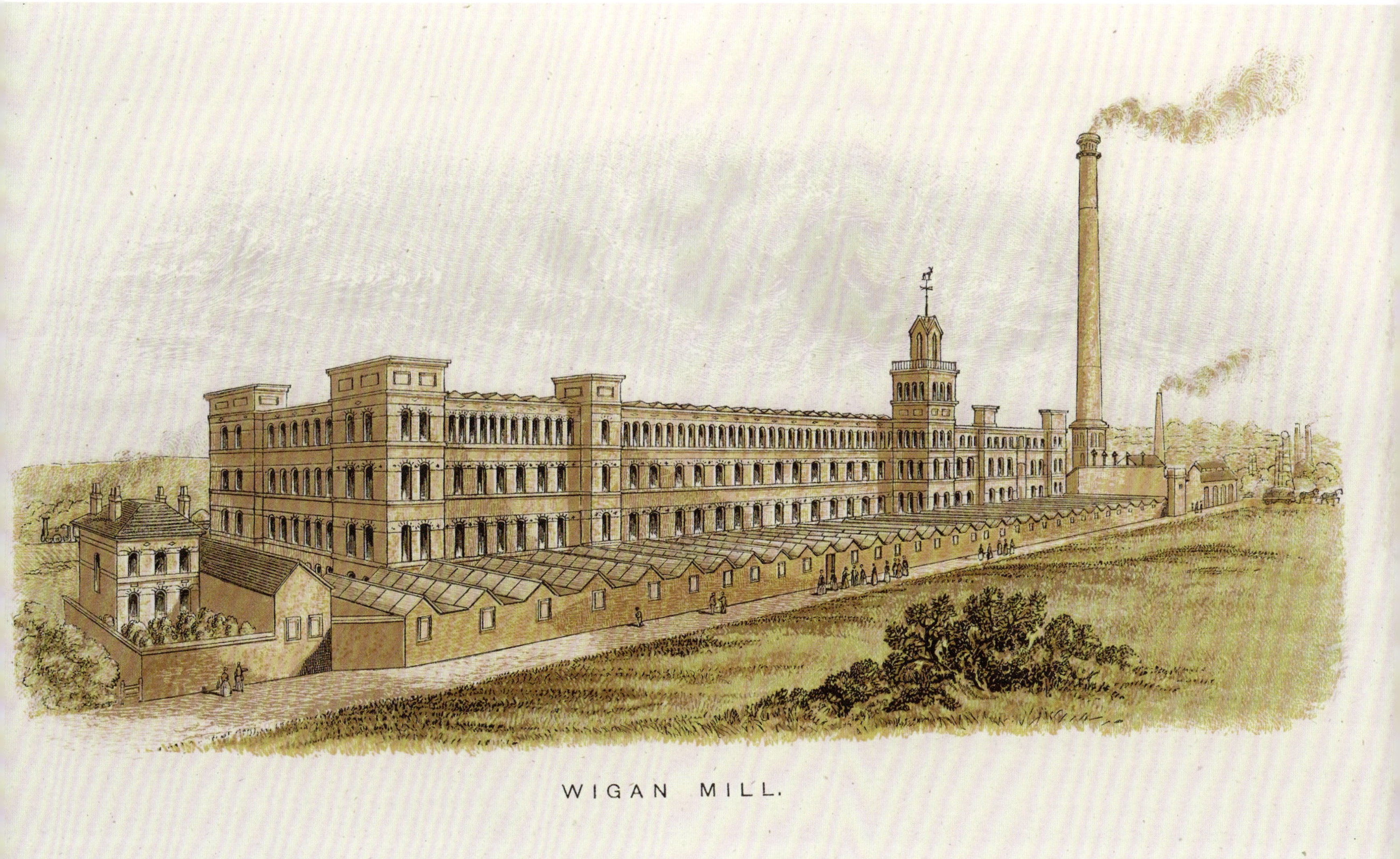

the supply of cheap local fuel by the owning of mines in Wigan, as well as their railway spurs and their onward connections to the main line, was typical.[50] But the Gidlow collieries were as subject to the dangers of subterranean construction as any, to which Rylands's prudence did not extend. In 1859 an older lower level of working collapsed under the weight of those above, flattening the buildings on the surface. The collapse was blamed on a misjudgement of the size of the pillars.[51] (Architecture, it might therefore be observed, had both an ideal and a precarious existence at the start of this narrative.)

Coal was essential to cotton's steam-powered manufacture and, likewise, the Gidlow pits would not have existed without cotton. We return, then, to our story of smoke and its previous life as coal travelling through, indeed actually forming, these different spaces. After it was hewn and brought to the surface, the coal was loaded onto wagons and pulled by steam engines from the mine

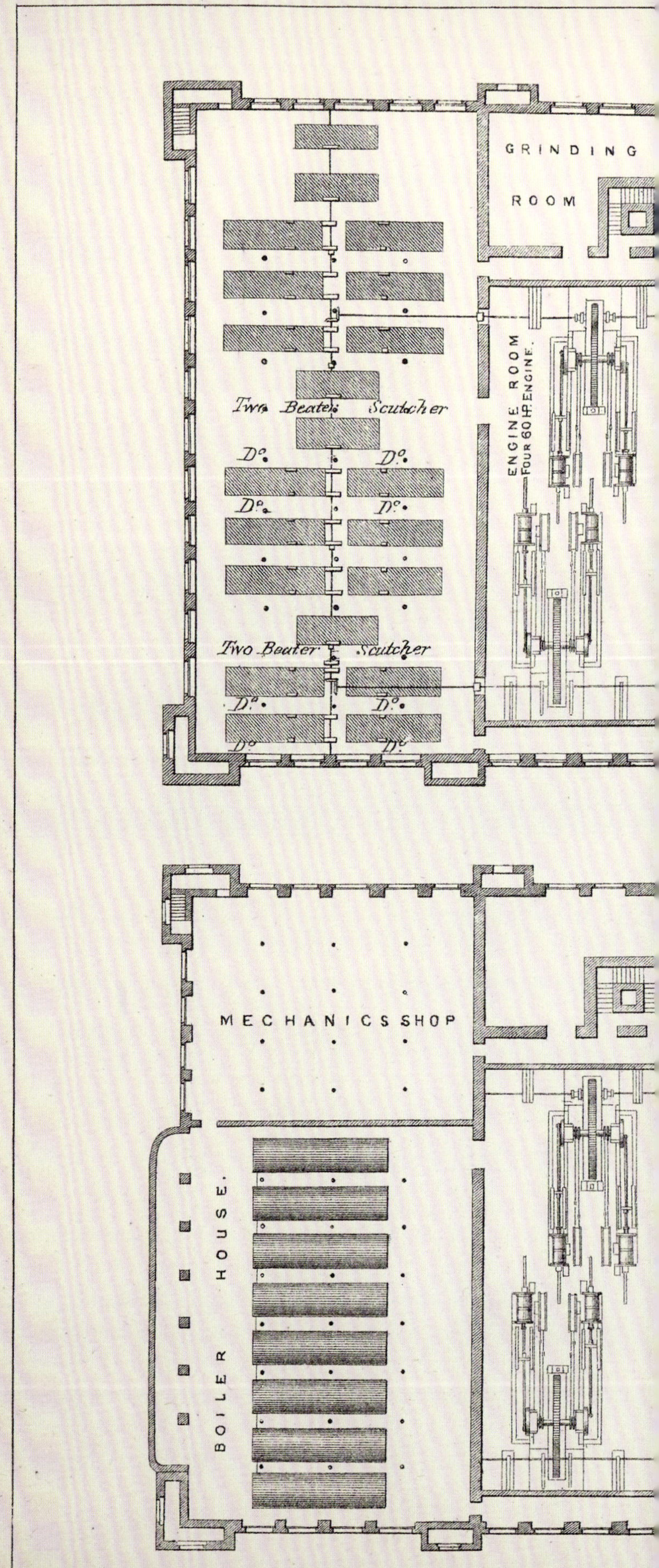

[124] Gidlow mill, Wigan, 1865: plans. Architect: George Woodhouse. From Evan Leigh, *The Science of Modern Cotton Spinning* (1873).

to the Gidlow mill nearby (fig. 124). This mill, designed by the specialist mill architect George Woodhouse and much celebrated in manufacturing circles when it was finished in 1865, replaced the mill that Rylands had bought with the land; it was unusual for the company in that it was its only purpose-built mill (the company's sixteen other mills were acquired second hand).[52] It was remarkable partly for its size, partly for its state-of-the-art machinery and partly for its fireproofing throughout, but mainly for the single-storeyed sheds, learned from recent Indian mills designed by William Fairbairn, which gave the structure a very different profile from those of McConnel & Kennedy's earlier in the century[53] (fig. 123). As mentioned in Chapter 4, the curtailing of cotton imports from the slave plantations of the American South as a result of the American Civil War had led to Britain's sudden reliance on greater cotton production in India. What we see in the Gidlow sheds is direct evidence of the back-and-forth movement between Britain and India of the technologies and architectural forms rapidly developed to service these new arrangements.[54] Ironically, it was in these sheds, and their 1,500 looms, that Rylands & Sons' famous 'Dacca' calico was woven. The perspective view of fig. 123, drawn for a history of cotton manufacture rather than for the clients, was only propositional: only a little over half of what is shown was actually built. And it is opaque and provisional in another, critical, sense for, like Bertolt Brecht's famous lament about photographs of the Krupp factory, it tells us next to nothing about the social realities it shaped and presided over.

Coal, while essential, was used in the marginal spaces of the mill. The objective was to get it into the building as quickly as possible, combust it and then convey its waste out rapidly. Its route in was the railway track; its exit in the form of carbonaceous smoke was via the lofty but primly Italianate chimney that dominated the area. Gidlow's coal fed eight boilers, and it was in the boiler room, marked on the mill's exterior by a tower, that the vital energy transfer occurred. Together with steam engines, the boilers formed what Marx called the 'motor mechanism' of the industrial system.[55] The process is described in a diagram of a rectangular steam boiler, plate 2 of Thomas Tredgold's then

PLATE XXXIII

GIDLOW MILL, WIGAN.

GENERAL PLANS.

SCALE 40 FEET TO 1 INCH

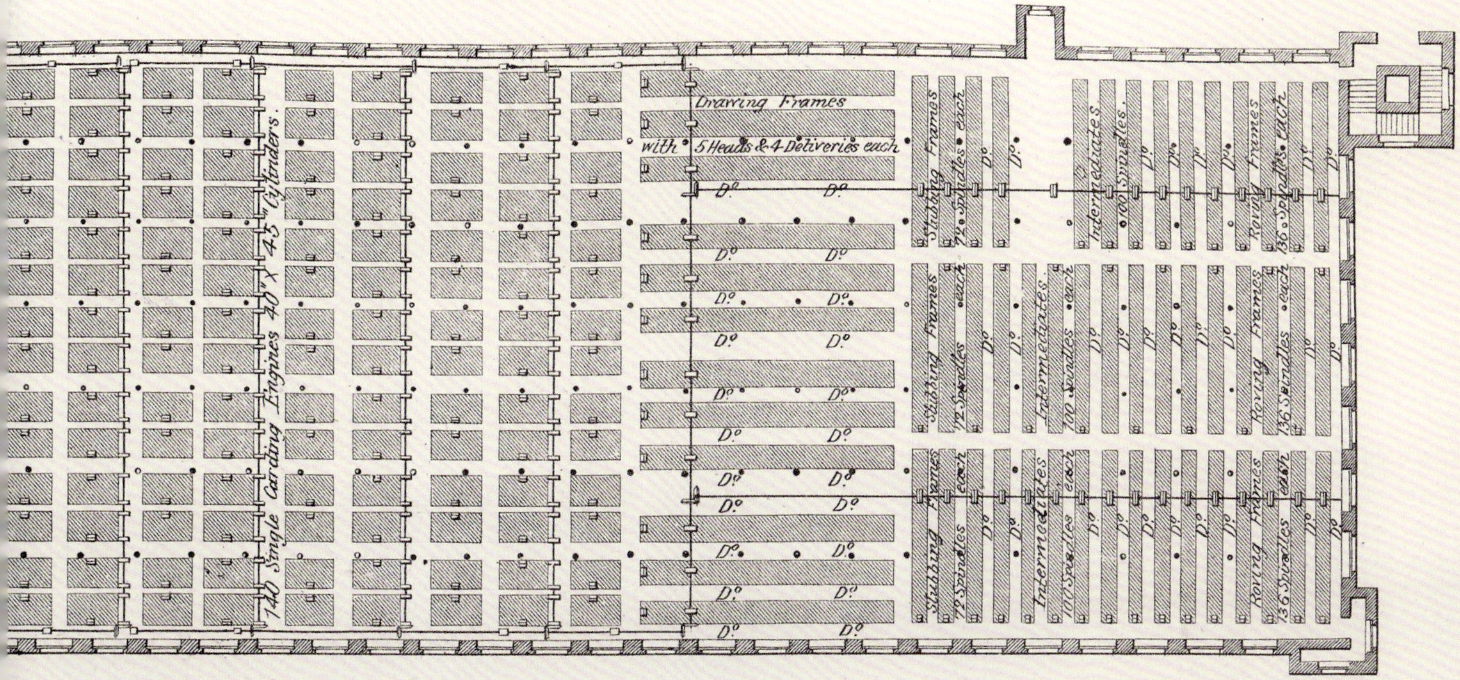

PLAN OF CARD ROOM.

PLAN OF THROSTLE ROOM

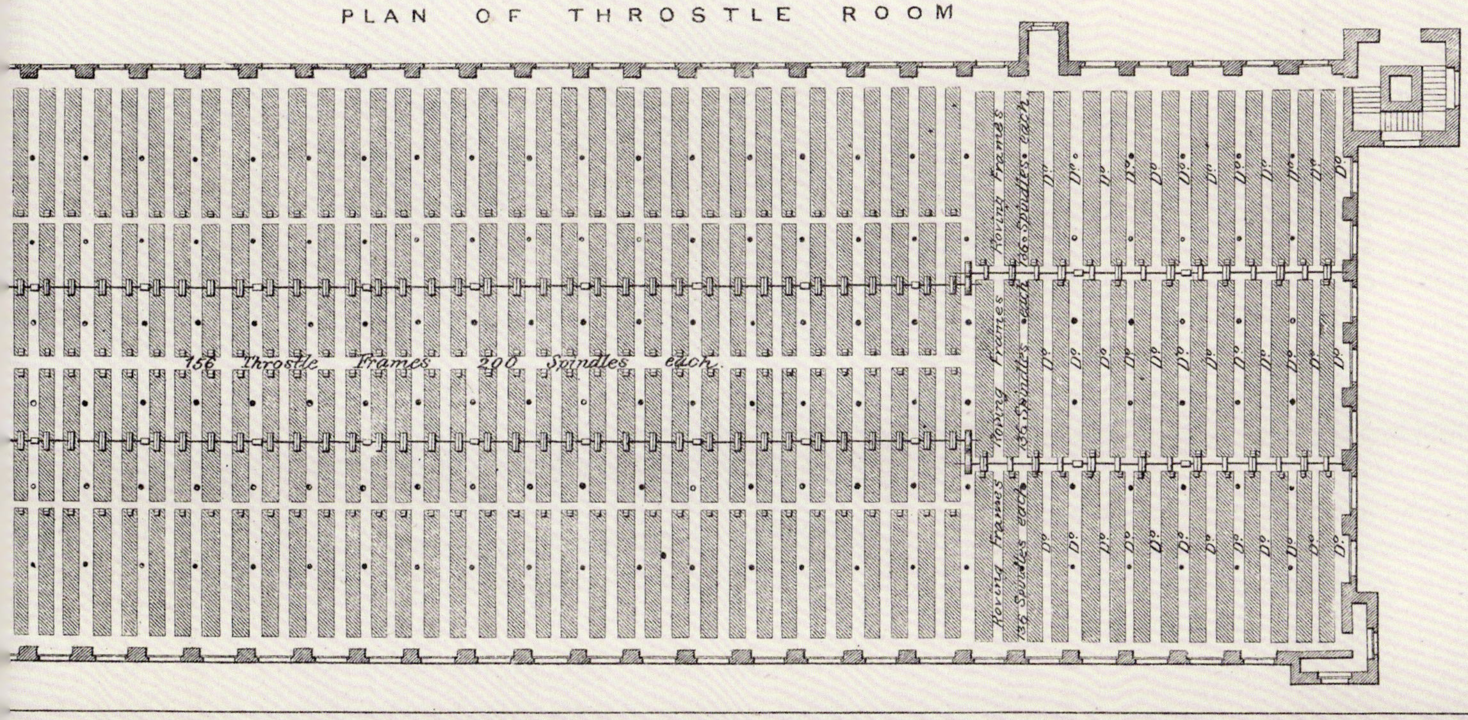

J. GALLOWAY, LITH: MANCHESTER.

[125] Rectangular steam boiler, from Thomas Tredgold, *The Steam Engine*, 2nd edn (1838).

[126] Details of alternative designs for chimneys, from Thomas Tredgold, *The Steam Engine*, 2nd edn (1838).

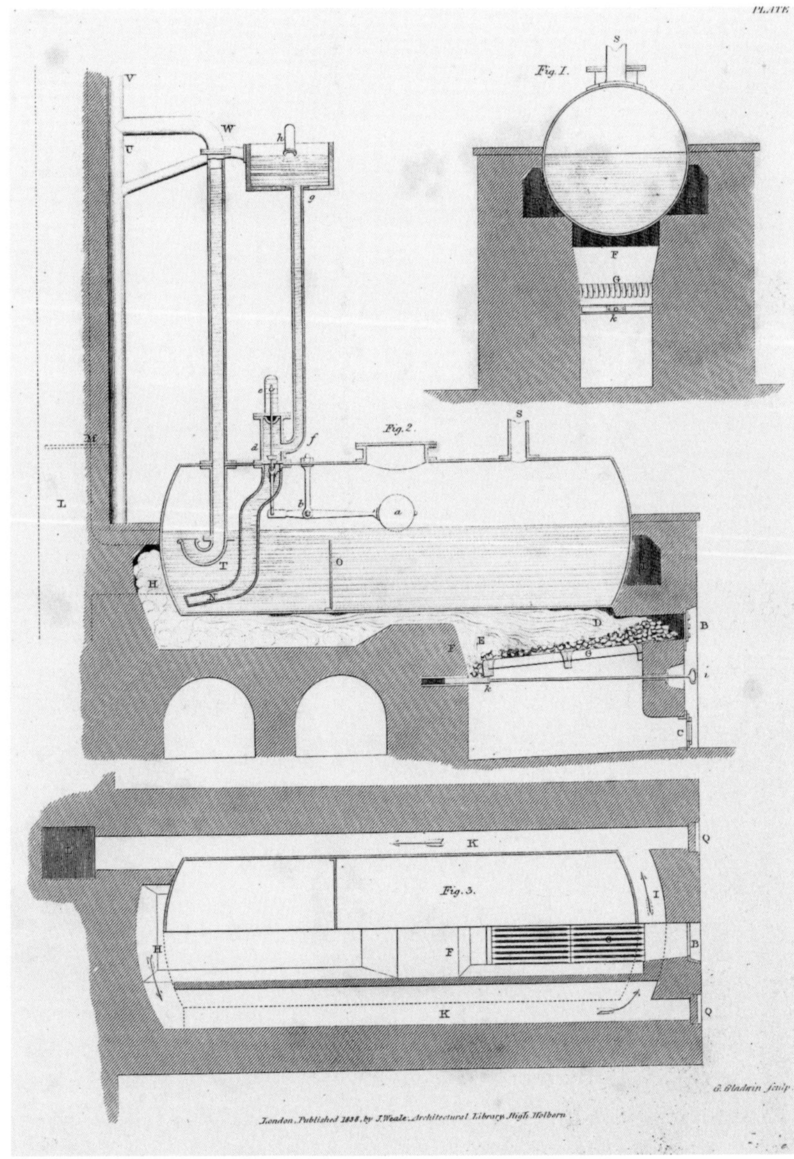

still standard *The Steam Engine: Its Invention and Progressive Development* (1827)[56] (fig. 125). Tredgold's plate shows movements across bodies and through passages. Coal is shovelled through a fire door (B) onto a grate above an ash pit, and set ablaze. The inflamed coal's current of fumes passes around the boiler, heating its water before passing up a chimney (L). (Gidlow's boilers may well have used 'economisers', clusters of pipes located in the flue which made the heating more efficient.) Water has entered the boiler itself by pipes (M and N) and steam – the product of this part of the process – leaves the boiler via a pipe (S) which takes it to the steam engines. That is the end of the coal: it has created steam that will impel the engines as the prime movers of industrial process; it has been transformed into ashes and smoke and, its thermal energy exhausted, its waste is now expelled from the mill in one architectural flourish and returned, apparently, to nature.

One inference here, at this point in the narrative of smoke, is that engineering, even the mechanical engineering of steam boilers, is never far from architecture (though it may be from architects).[57] So if smoke is given an honorific exit here through a part of the mill's exterior defined as architectural, its production and movement might already be described as spatial, especially via the flues that made it circulate under and around the suspended body of the boiler. (Perhaps architecture could even be defined here as the barrier around, and sometimes within, which air and gas circulates.) Coal and smoke were thus done with as far as Rylands & Sons were concerned: the power they released coursed through the mill, energising what Marx called that 'vast automaton'.[58] And this elaborates further the point about boilers, that to make distinctions between architecture and machine, or architecture and engineering, in the mill (as we have seen in previous chapters) is almost entirely spurious – as is the idea that circulation is something only humans do in human-sized spaces. Coal, steam, labouring bodies and mechanical power all circulate, are all geared or attuned to the same end in the mill. At least that is the theory, or 'philosophy of manufactures' as Andrew Ure conceived it, with the 'benignant power of steam' at the centre and the 'collocation of its members' summoning 'myriads of willing menials ... [assigning] the regulated task'.[59] Having left the complex architectural organism that gave it birth, the waste, barely regulated, continues on its way.

The unusually high chimney at Gidlow, of 204 feet, separated from the main building, released smoke far away from possible local litigants and simultaneously made a point about the company's sense of social obligation (see fig. 123). Such

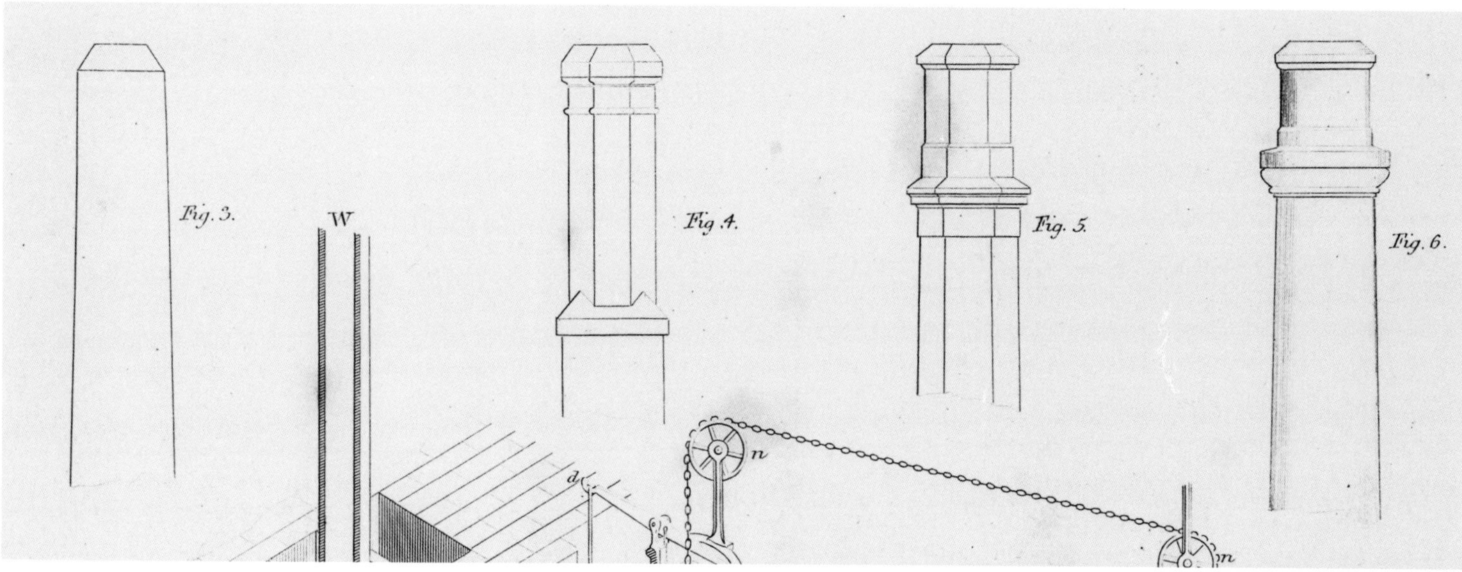

architectural grandiosity, with its elements of base and capital and its pronounced lip just below its summit, was not uncommon by this time. Tredgold's first plate gives us some tops for similar chimneys: an obelisk form, an octagon top for a square shaft, an octagon chimney in both shaft and top and a columnar chimney (fig. 126). In 1858 the engineer Robert Rawlinson had devoted a whole book to various designs for free-standing chimneys, ventilating shafts and water towers, openly espousing the lessons of minarets and campaniles in promoting towers as distinctive markers in their landscapes. As he termed it, this was 'the "infusion of design" into the utilitarian'.[60] The adoption of such designs might make a point about the mill's and thus the mill owner's civic-mindedness and modernity, his projection of an understanding that what the mill was doing was not just a matter of profit but also of culture even at the moment of the expelling of waste. But tall chimneys had another purpose, more technical and thus less often remarked: they increased the draught to the boilers, so improving the intensity of combustion and making the whole operation more efficient.[61]

UP TO THIS POINT IN THIS SMUTTY TALE, COAL AND smoke have been extracted, refined and transformed within a sequence of tight, shaped passages, vessels and vehicles. But, on leaving Gidlow's chimney, smoke was released to the prevailing winds, wafting eastwards and northwards, mingling with the smoke from the many domestic fires of Wigan and Manchester and settling in the city's saucer-like topography. In the words of one Ruskinian witness, 'air currents meet the gaseous products of combustion, mixed with minute material particles, and are hindered or directed in their course thereby, and move forward, dirty, irregular, and scattered'.[62] Industrial chimneys in Manchester alone numbered well over 500 by 1843, and would double by 1890, while domestic consumption of coal was more than double that of London per capita.[63] The subject of smoke was almost obsessive for speakers at the Manchester Literary and Philosophical Society and at the Statistical Society. As smoke left Gidlow and other mills, its particles and sulphur dioxide gas dropped and draped and encrusted in a kind of industrial melanism, blackening trees, acidifying soil and destroying plants. (Famously, it even made moths adapt their camouflage.[64]) This was the 'deep, lead-coloured cloud' that Elizabeth Gaskell's character Margaret Hale saw from far off, fed by the 'unparliamentary smoke' that avoided regulation.[65] Yet, if we are to believe Reuben Spencer, chairman of Rylands & Sons, the same smoke was the 'incense of industry'; his fictional counterpart, Dickens's Josiah Bounderby, described smoke as 'the healthiest thing in the world in all respects, and particularly for the lungs'.[66] Later in the century the Ruskinian T. C. Horsfall remarked that, although legislation existed in the 1840s to limit smoke pollution, it was circumvented by 'magistrates who believed that the emission of black smoke was the inevitable and innocuous accompaniment of the meritorious act of manufacturing'.[67]

There was certainly no dominantly negative view of smoke.[68] In many of the images that viewed Manchester from outside the

[127] Photographic evidence of damage from smoke pollution, from *Regina* v. *Spence*, 1857–9. Photograph: James Mudd. Salford Art Gallery and Museum.

[128] Manchester Assize Courts, 1859–64: main entrance. Architect: Alfred Waterhouse. Engraving from Charles Eastlake, *History of the Gothic Revival* (1872).

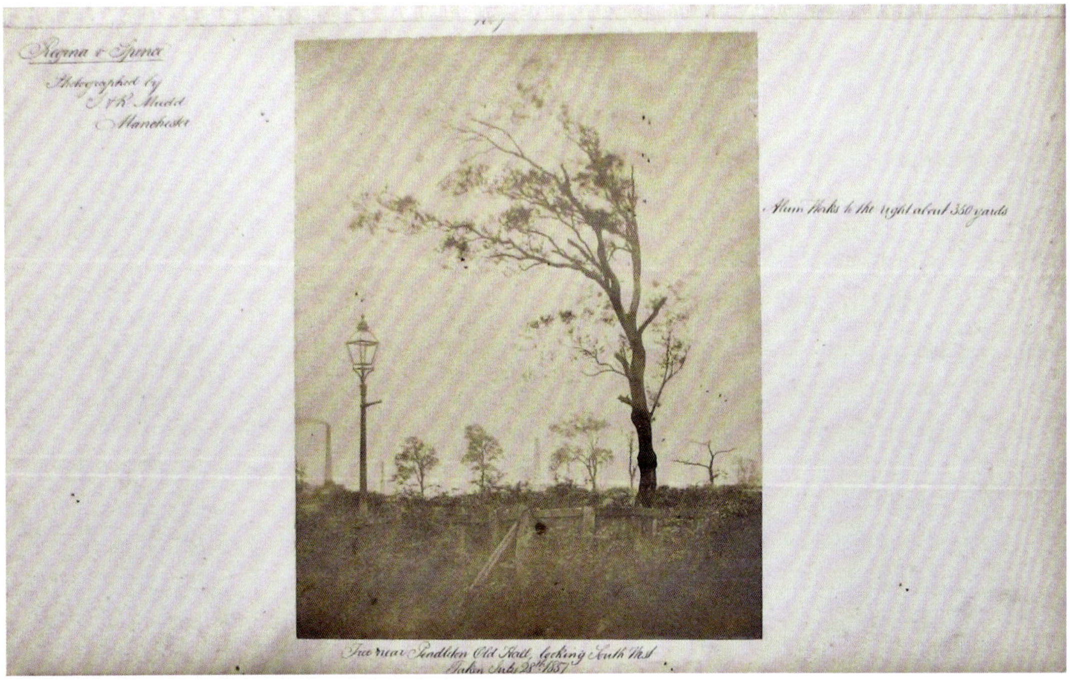

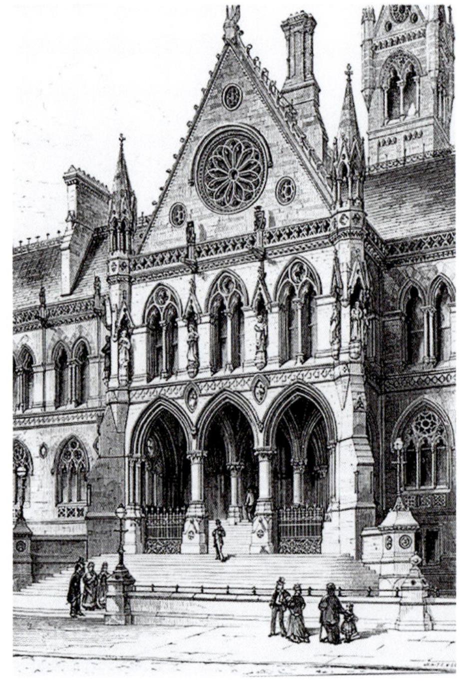

city, the range of smoking chimneys is a trope not of a degraded godless modernity, nor even of pollution but of productivity, a city at work. And, in the case of one of the most canonical of Manchester images, William Wyld's *Manchester from Kersal Moor* (1852), smoky chimneys are part of an almost divinely ordained scene, with its golden light, easeful river and figures resting as if in flight from Egypt (see fig. 60). Here, unlike Ruskin's later *Storm Cloud*, the observation of natural atmospheric conditions is brought into a desired compatibility (harmony would be a step too far) with the observation of the man-made atmosphere. Industry is put in its place, contained by a world-view that has not abolished differences or recognised capital's all-encompassing nature.[69]

Some imagined the ideal mill owner not only as living in Gothic harmony with nature but, as with Disraeli's Mr Millbank, '[consuming] his own smoke'.[70] Others thought smoke could work to the good as a 'deodoriser' of sewage,[71] and devised schemes to draw smoke into sewers through fans and to make it run in flues interconnected with sewers.[72] One such scheme was by the industrialist Peter Spence, whose chemical works in Pendleton had given rise to one of the rare occasions of a successful legal prosecution for pollution (fig. 127). As if in compensation, Spence envisaged a system of sewers conveying both gases and effluent, each negating the worst effects of the other, with the combined product made into manure. There would no longer be a forest of chimneys; instead, one vast chimney, 600 feet high, would discharge the cleansed leftover gases into the atmosphere, literalising the description of Manchester as the 'chimney of the world'.[73]

Nevertheless, the by-product would inevitably descend onto the city. Carbon was deposited, pervading the streets, blackening what had been polychrome, falling upon brick and stone, and infiltrating ornament. Within three years of its completion, the polychrome Assize Courts (architect: Alfred Waterhouse, 1859–64) was said to have lost 'all traces of colour on the outside of the building'[74] (fig. 128). Such evidence, it might be said, was among

[129] Rear of a mid-nineteenth-century warehouse in Jackson's Row, Manchester.

[130] Manchester Town Hall: window and spandrel in the courtyard.

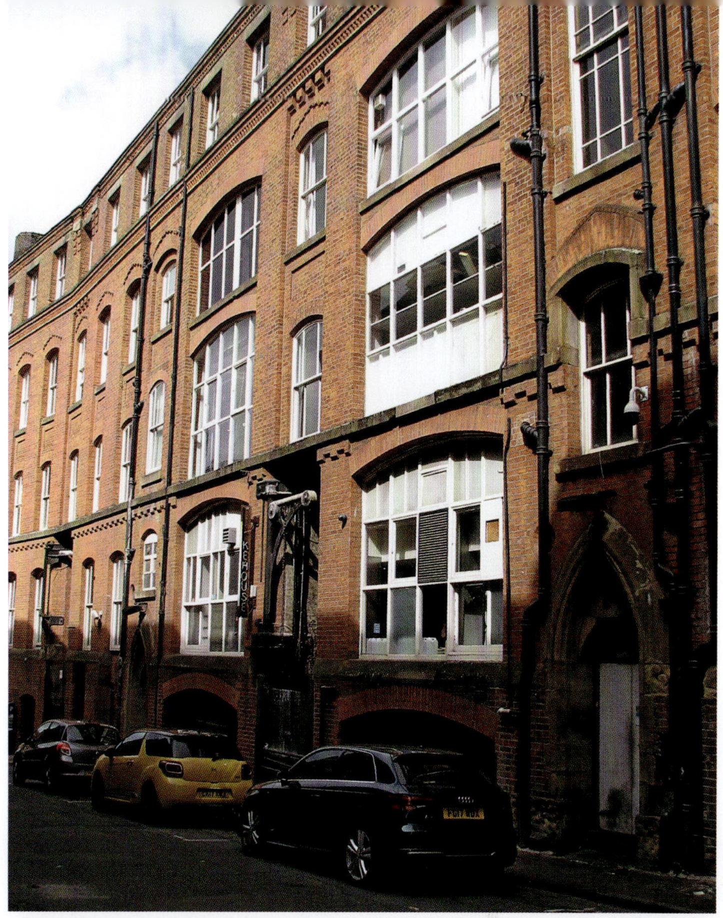

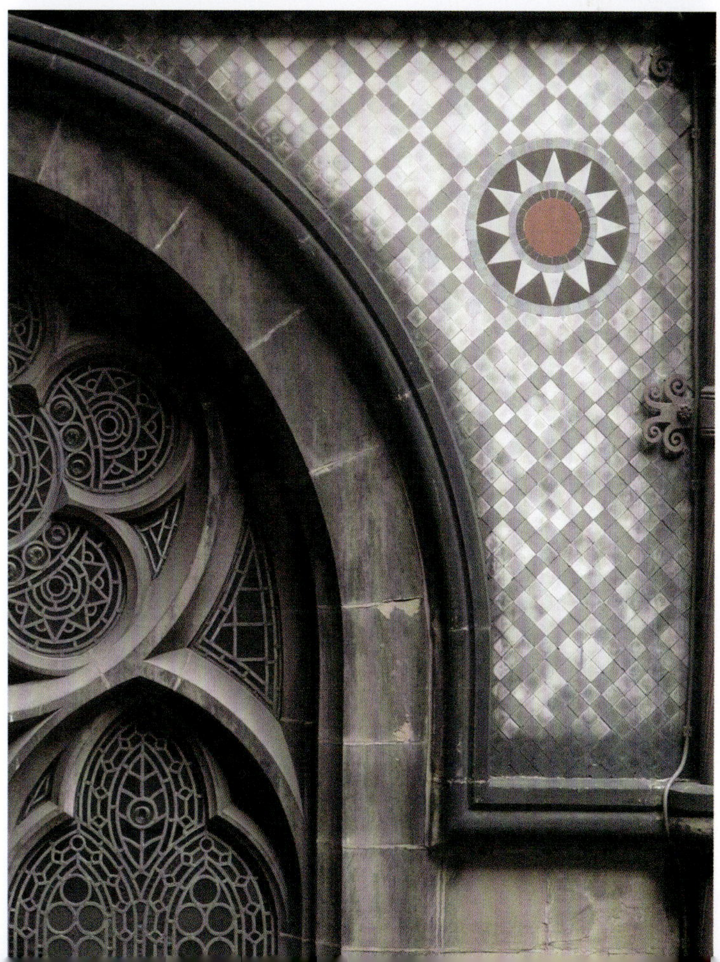

the many inklings of a new epoch of environmental pollution for architecture, which we now understand started with the gradually accelerating adoption of steam power as industrialists sought to secure their sources of energy both from competitors and from the collective actions of their workforces.[75] Indeed, if steam power and its human proprietors were the central dynamic in the rapid agglomeration of buildings and facilities that constituted the industrial city, they were also the cause of its grimy coating and vitiated air.

Manchester's architects, in common with many of its scientists, were highly aware of smoke's negative effects and searched for ways to mitigate them.[76] As stone and brick were seen to crumble, and mortar to swell and become porous, they realised that alternatives had to be found.[77] Walls were opened up with larger expanses of glass so that more light might enter; architectural colour was taken away from exteriors; deeply stained glass was avoided; terracotta and tile were more often used as facing materials, and self-cleansing materials such as glazed bricks, mosaic and enamelled iron were advocated[78] (figs 129 and 130). As Caen stone, Bath stone and limestones were all vulnerable, alternative stones were examined for their ability to resist smoke's effects, with granite, porphyries and most sandstones preferred.[79] Ornament was rendered more broadly so it could still be read from afar when clogged with soot, and there was an awareness that the more sheltered parts of an exterior were more affected by decay.[80] Nevertheless, even the most smoke aware of buildings – such as the Town Hall or, as we shall see, the John Rylands Library – proved unable to withstand 'the evil influence of the peculiar climate of Manchester'.[81] If coal (taking over from water power) and its combustion had made this world, the resistance to or mitigation of its effects was also a continual undercurrent, one might say a problematic, of Victorian architecture.

THE DESIGN OF ONE MANCHESTER BUILDING, IN PARticular, was marked by a high level of obsession with the exclusion of smoke. It is, in several ways, complementary to the mill and mines at Gidlow, and not just because they were built by the same family (fig. 131). This was the library endowed by John Rylands's

[131] John Rylands Library, Deansgate, 1890–9. Architect: Basil Champneys.

[132] Map of Manchester, 1890, showing the John Rylands Library and Town Hall. Published by W. H. Smith.

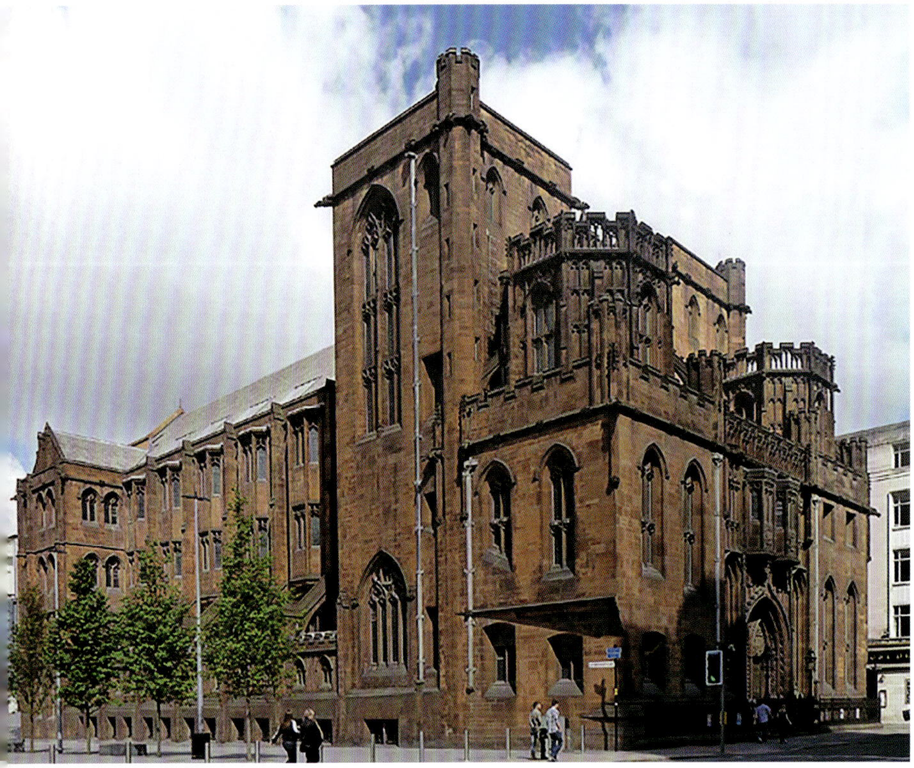

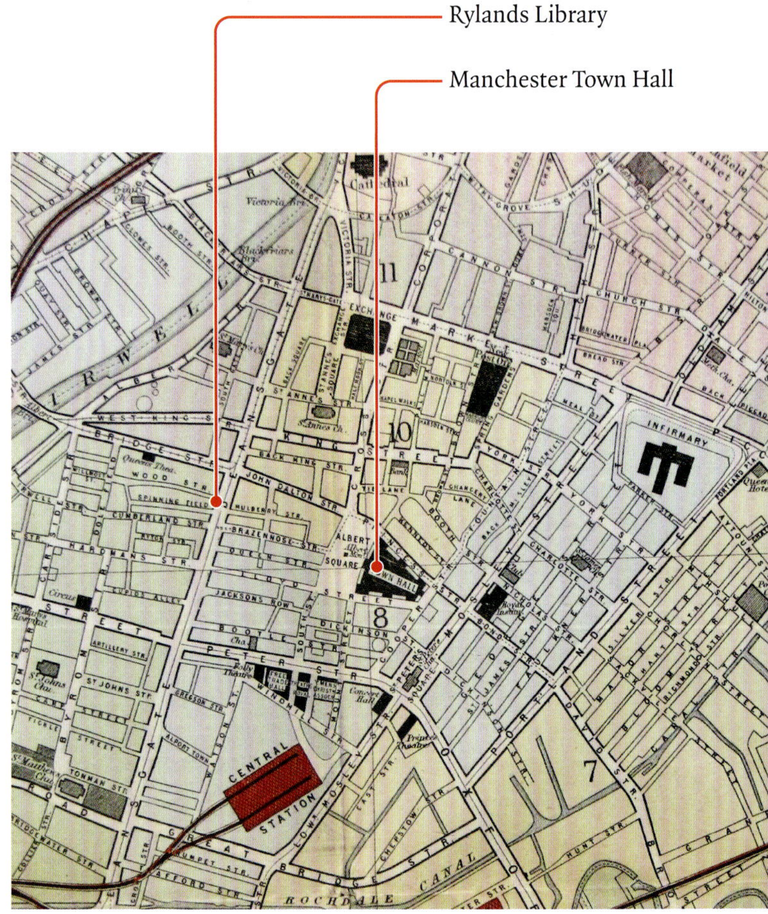

widow, Enriqueta Rylands, as a memorial to her husband, who died in 1888; it was filled with the precious books and manuscripts that she added to her husband's largely theological collections.[82] Just west of Deansgate, its site was in a slum-ridden and semi-industrial area often described as one of the most insalubrious in Manchester; its 'narrow and loathsome streets, and close courts defiled with refuse' were little changed from what Engels and James Kay had seen forty years before.[83] The area was often infused with the 'murky mass [of smoke hanging] like a shroud' over the city.[84] In 1890 life expectancy for men in Deansgate was estimated at 28.78 years.[85] Despite at least thirty years of concern and various municipal improvements,[86] Deansgate was still a survival of shock city and Charity still the middle-class means of engaging with it. The Wood Street mission, a private charity for the poor and indigenous (of which John Rylands was a trustee), was close by the library's site.[87]

Locating the Rylands library here was an act understood as philanthropic in at least two ways. First, it was a cleansing and purging of dirt and poverty from the immediate environs and, second, it was the arrival of a gift that, if paid for from the world of polluting industry, would nevertheless be redolent of a different world altogether – quiet and clean, pre-industrial, religious, scholastic.[88] The area was being cleaned up, supported by government legislation and municipal endeavour.[89] A potential axial link to the nearby Manchester Town Hall must also have been important to the choice of site, offering the possibility for remaking a slice of the central city, spatially linking Rylands's civilised philanthropic largesse to the seat of the city's government by its industrialist class (fig. 132).

Ventilation was central to the design of the library, just as it had been to the Gidlow mines and even the Gidlow mill's boilers and chimney. And we might even think of the library as a kind of

[133] John Rylands Library: bookcases.

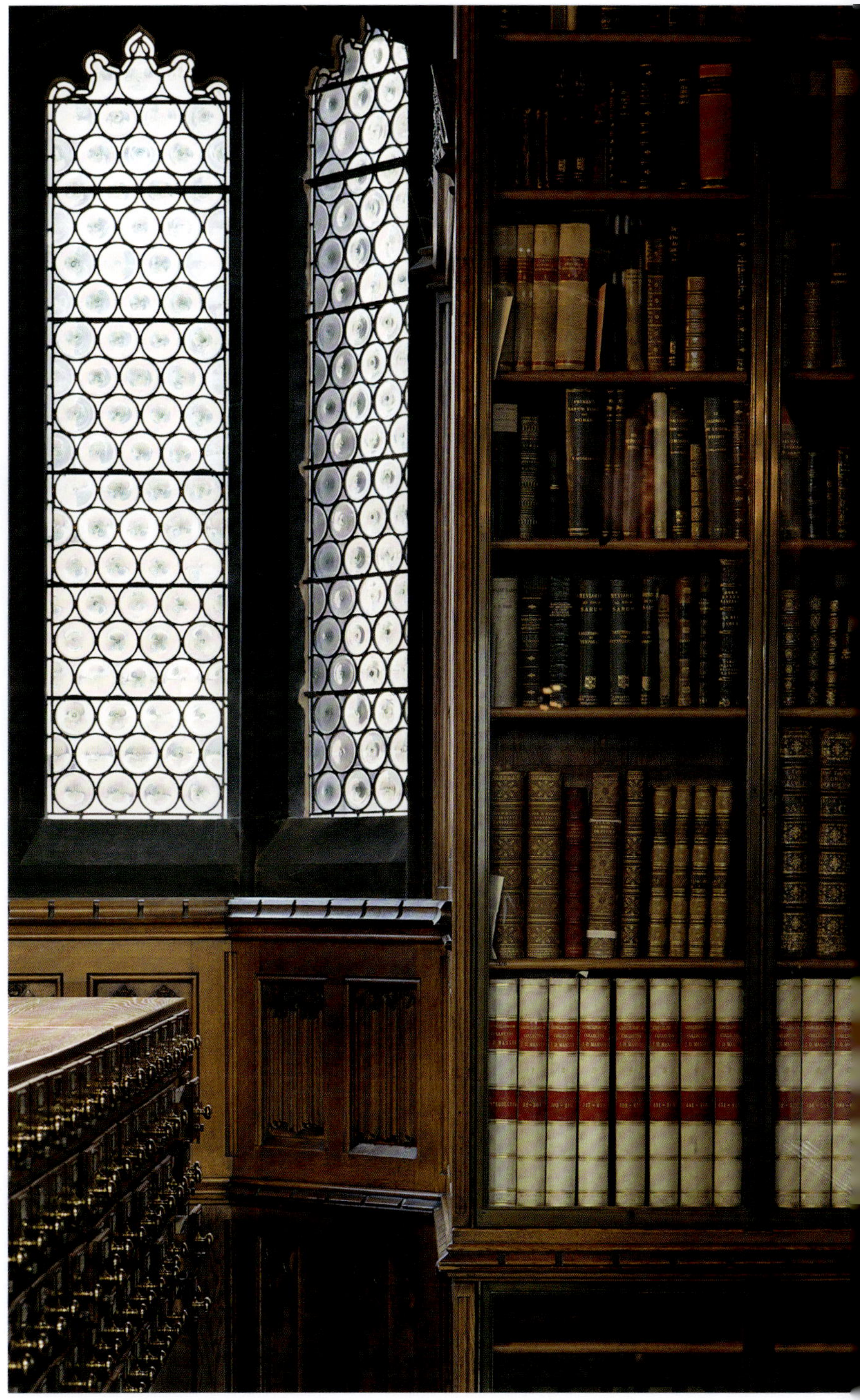

inversion or antithesis of a mine. Its rock face to be picked at were the bookcases, added to the walls (rather than extracted to form walls) or free-standing within rooms like the pillars of coal and stalls or compartments between them.[90] The deposit of past mental labour accumulated here, we might say, in this site of addition, while physical labour was expended or consumed in that other site of extraction. To juxtapose the ground-floor plan of the Rylands library with a diagram of a coalfield with paired passages and a pillar and stall grid would be absurd to a certain kind of architectural history, a pseudo-isomorphism at best. But, if anything about this coming together is forced, that is only the product of a certain interest, a need to keep them separate (the promiscuity of such relationships can certainly be found in Victorian periodicals).[91] Library and mine are both products, after all, of the same industrial complex, the beginning and the end of it. (Indeed, Francis Bacon had linked the speculative aspects of natural philosophy metaphorically with the work of mining.[92]) Together, they stand for the birth and after-life – or, really, half-life – of our smut: its entering into productive life as coal, its transmutation into waste and its exclusion, or attempted exclusion, from another kind of life dependent upon it which disowns, even disavows, it. There will be closer connections and analogies to discuss in the library, but smoke remains the unavoidable medium, tying the by-product of library to the production of cotton. 'The entire proposal', Rylands's architect Basil Champneys wrote, 'has originated in the desire to preserve the valuable works from injury.'[93] This 'injury' was the threat from the very smoke that had helped create the wealth expended on the library's books.

Smoke thus had to be kept out of the library, and Champneys and his various consultants wrestled with this practical problem on a number of levels, while also using the idea of the pollution-free building to charge the library's remarkable spatial drama. It was the library's ventilation that took most time to resolve in the design, and the solution was eventually a belt-and-braces combination of measures arrived at over several years. Air would be drawn in by electric fans low down in the building and sprayed with water, passed over hot water pipes and then be drawn

[134] John Rylands Library: ground-floor plan. University of Manchester.

[135] John Rylands Library: library or main-floor plan. University of Manchester.

[136] John Rylands Library: gallery floor plan. University of Manchester.

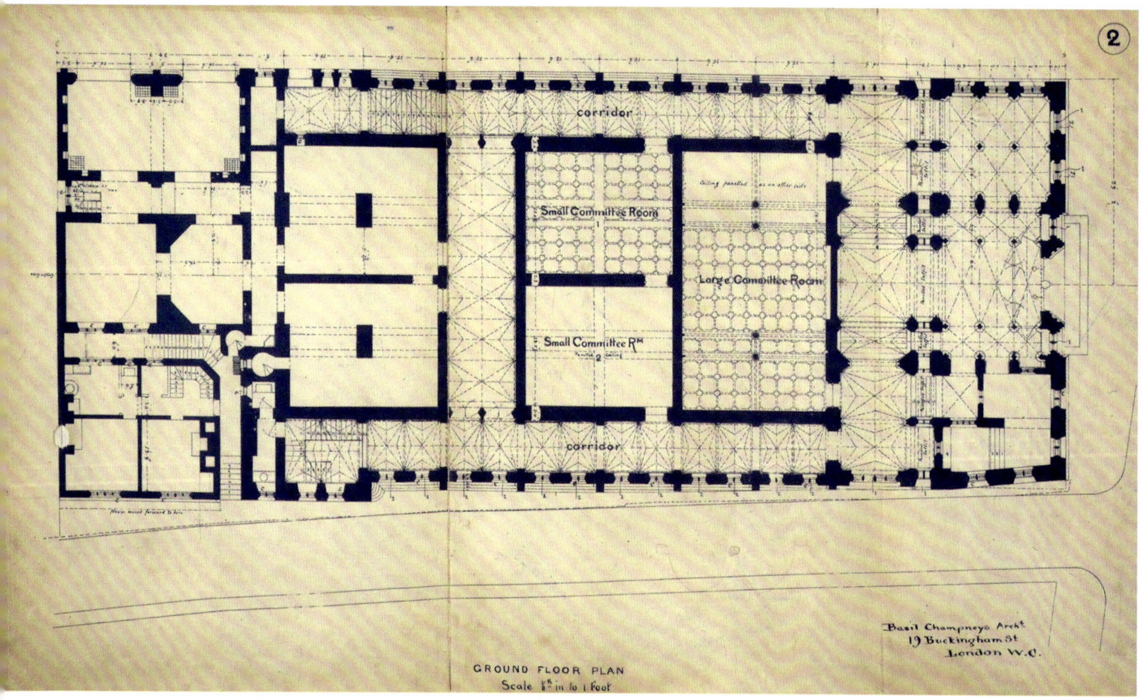

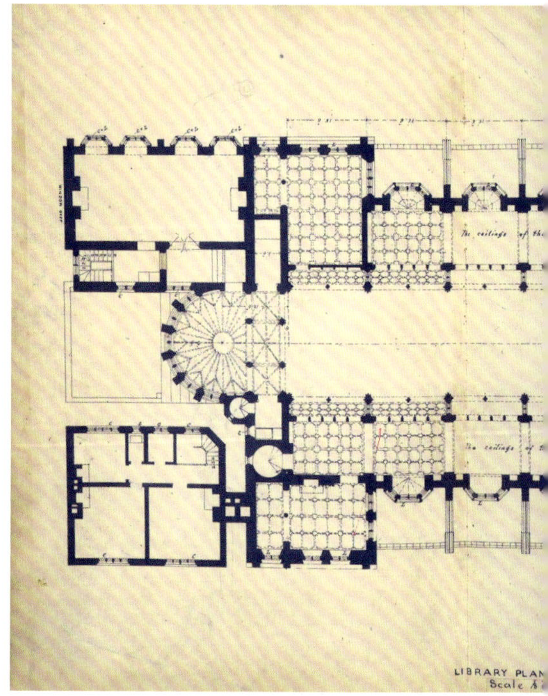

through jute or hessian screens, while foul, or 'vitiated', air was taken out via extract flues connected with two exhaust chambers in the roof. Air circulation was vital if mildew and mould were not to damage the books.[94] Inevitably, the weakness was that the building could never be kept sealed even if windows were airtight (delivery entrances, for instance, were only partially protected by screen doors), and this may be one reason for the elaborate spatial sequences between the main entrance and the reading room itself. The ineffectiveness of even these methods was all too quickly demonstrated when, as early as 1907, barely eight years after completion, the beautiful stone vaulting over the reading room was reported to have blackened.[95] The precious books themselves, however, were provided with some of the most hermetically sealed containers in the history of bookcase design, precision-made glass caskets with seals between doors and frames made airtight by rolls of velvet packed with wool[96] (fig. 133). If the building science was arcane, the use of electric lighting to avoid the fumes of gas certainly was not.[97]

But this attempt to exclude smoke was about more than convenience and conservation. It could be suggested that the nuisance of smoke, which was actually the politics of smoke, was remade into the poetics of smoke through the ornament and the sequence of spaces that make the library's entrance route so extraordinary (figs 134–6). The route starts with the placement of the entrance right on the street, where it is guarded by two short towers stepping back from the street line. The library thus sits implacable within a hostile world, castellated and intricate, defensive and precious (fig. 137). The progress of visitors, on entering, is directed through a sequence of spatial experiences, whereby the smutty city is symbolically discarded before entering the purified library precinct. Visitors pass through the relatively narrow doors into an entrance space, a kind of decompression or detoxifying chamber that expands upwards suddenly like a lofty forest (fig. 138), with the forest ceiling held high by tall slender columns compressed into small vaulting bays (fig. 139). A set of reception spaces follow, through which visitors are compelled to turn and turn about,

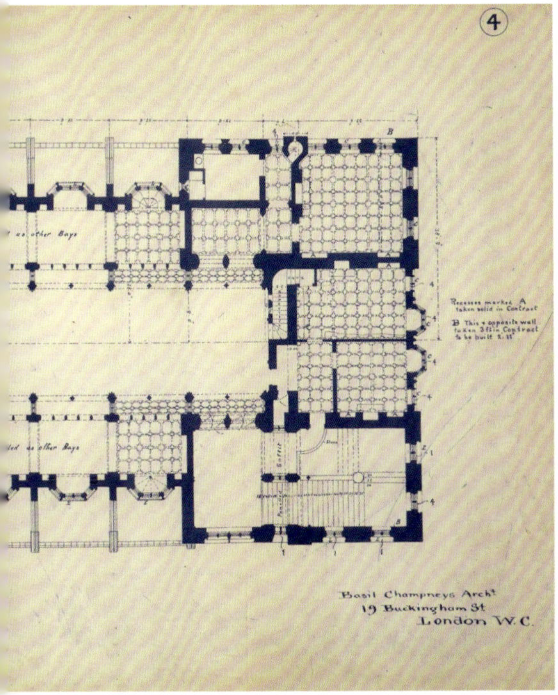

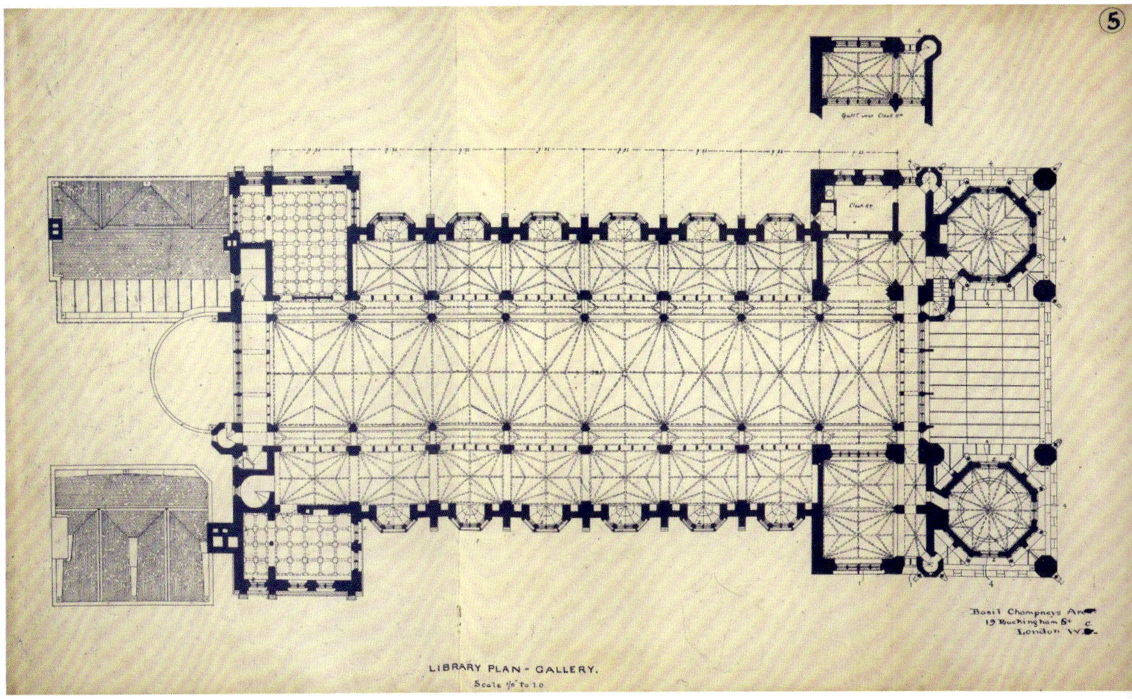

seeing and passing various screens, trellises and traceries. These create an ambience – more symbolic than functional – of being screened and even filtered, the sense of levels of admittance (fig. 141). The visitor turns left and left again, moves up stairs and under stone canopies, with fan vaults and an otherworldly stone lantern high above (fig. 140). The movement spirals upwards and then turns into the sudden tall volume of the south tower, with the Manchester street a world now long abandoned. Finally the visitor arrives in the reading-room nave of the library, a space suspended above street level and held within a containing cocoon or layered casket of corridors on all sides[98] (fig. 142).

The religiosity of many elements of the library is not so much my concern here, though the fact that this terminal space is so like a nave and that books are so nearly invisible within it, needs some comment. Some of the correspondence between Champneys and Enriqueta Rylands was much exercised with where the line might be drawn between the religious and the secular, or rather between the High Church and the Nonconformist. Enriqueta tended towards the second term in these pairings ('[I want to] avoid anything that gives an ecclesiastical appearance'), though she only seems to have realised the problem late in the design, by which time only minor modifications could be made.[99] She was concerned that, despite her husband's considerable collection of theological texts, the library should not be seen narrowly as an evangelical foundation or even a kind of missionary establishment (in contrast to its surroundings), but instead that it should stand for the cultural in Matthew Arnold's sense of 'sweetness and light' (and thus also deny Arnold's charge of philistinism thrown at the industrial bourgeoisie). Her choice of figurative sculpture came from the literary tradition, the heritage of the classics, the idea of history as a canon of figures of authority, and a more abstract or generalised realm of the spiritual, even if it had more than a hint of Protestant Nonconformity about it.[100] That the library might be a transition from the industrial to the cultural so that the cultural transcends the realm of the commodity, the factory, the working day, the office and its ledgers, the 'faith in machinery',[101] the mine

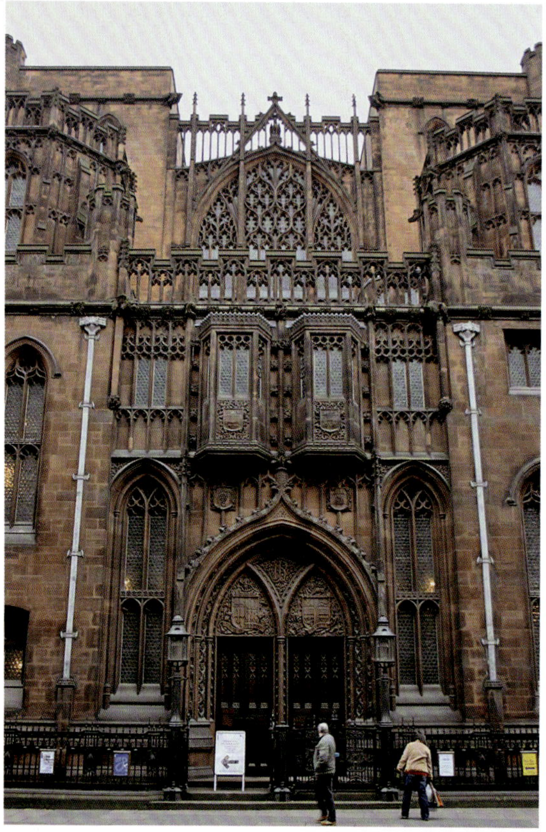
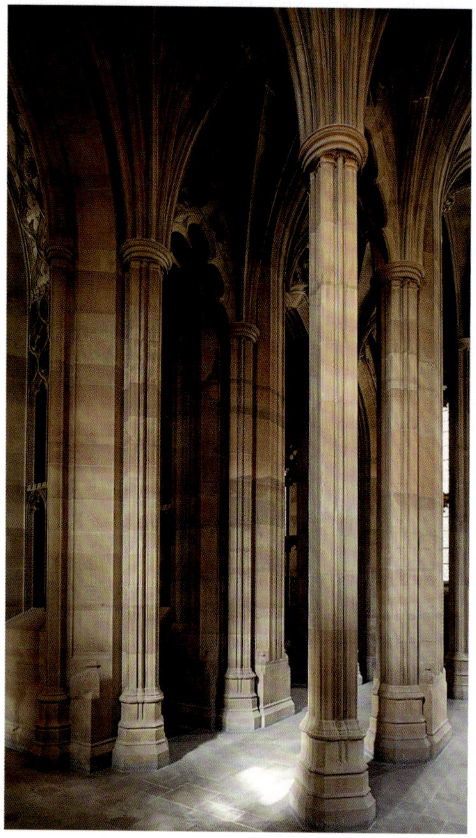
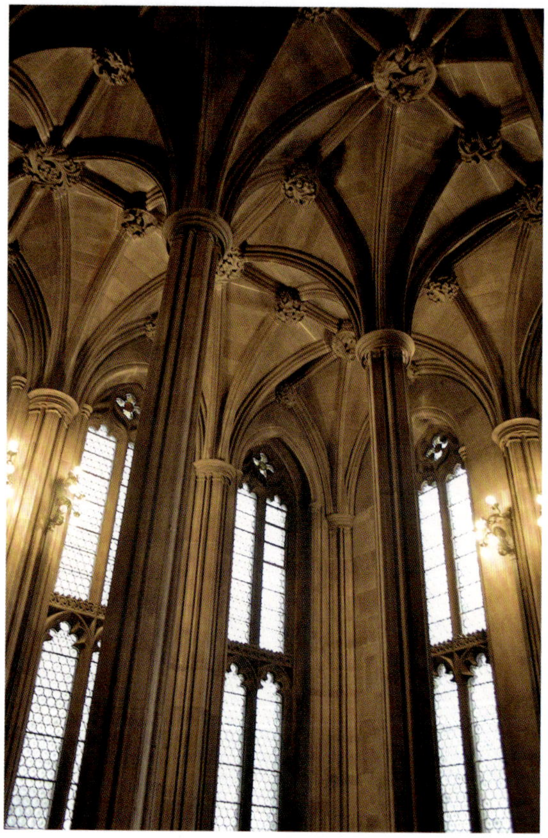

clockwise

[137] John Rylands Library, Deansgate, 1890–9. Architect: Basil Champneys.

[138] John Rylands Library: entrance interior.

[139] John Rylands Library: vaulting above entrance space.

[140] John Rylands Library: view up to the oculus.

opposite

[141] John Rylands Library: staircase from the ground floor.

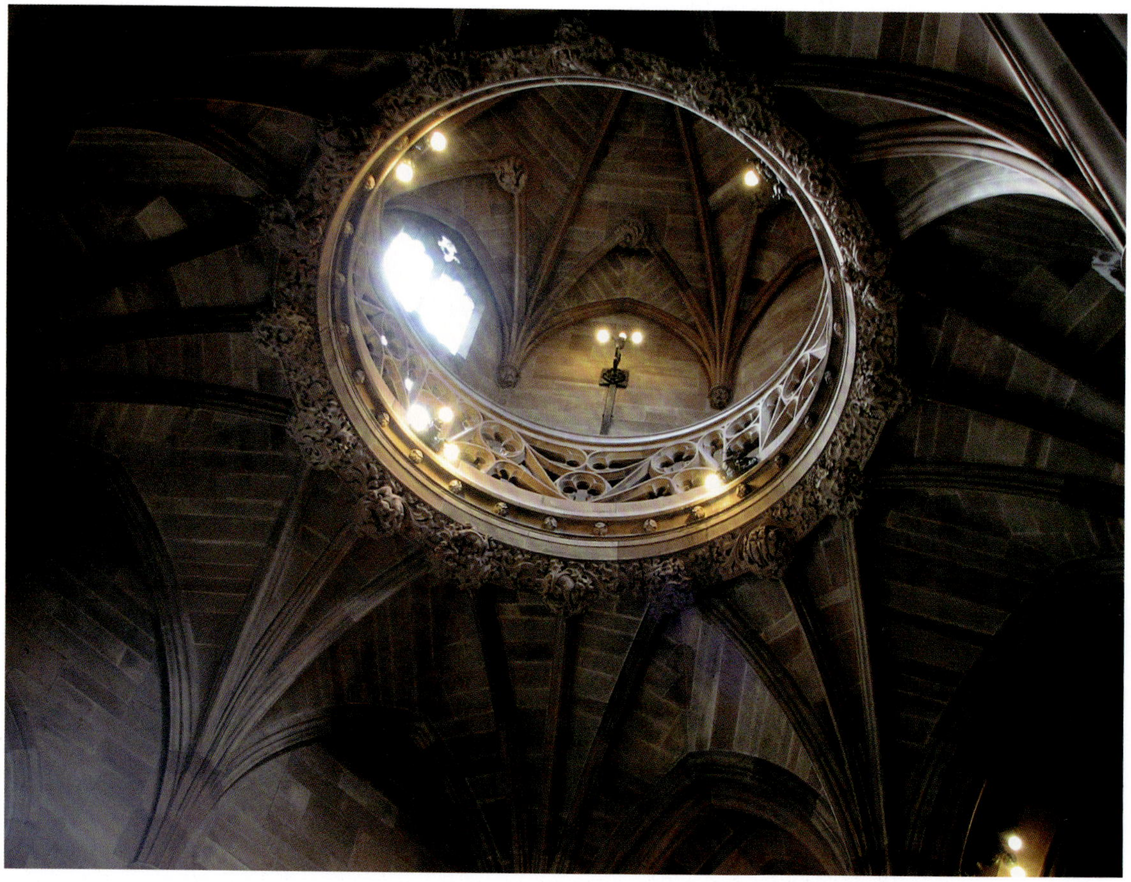

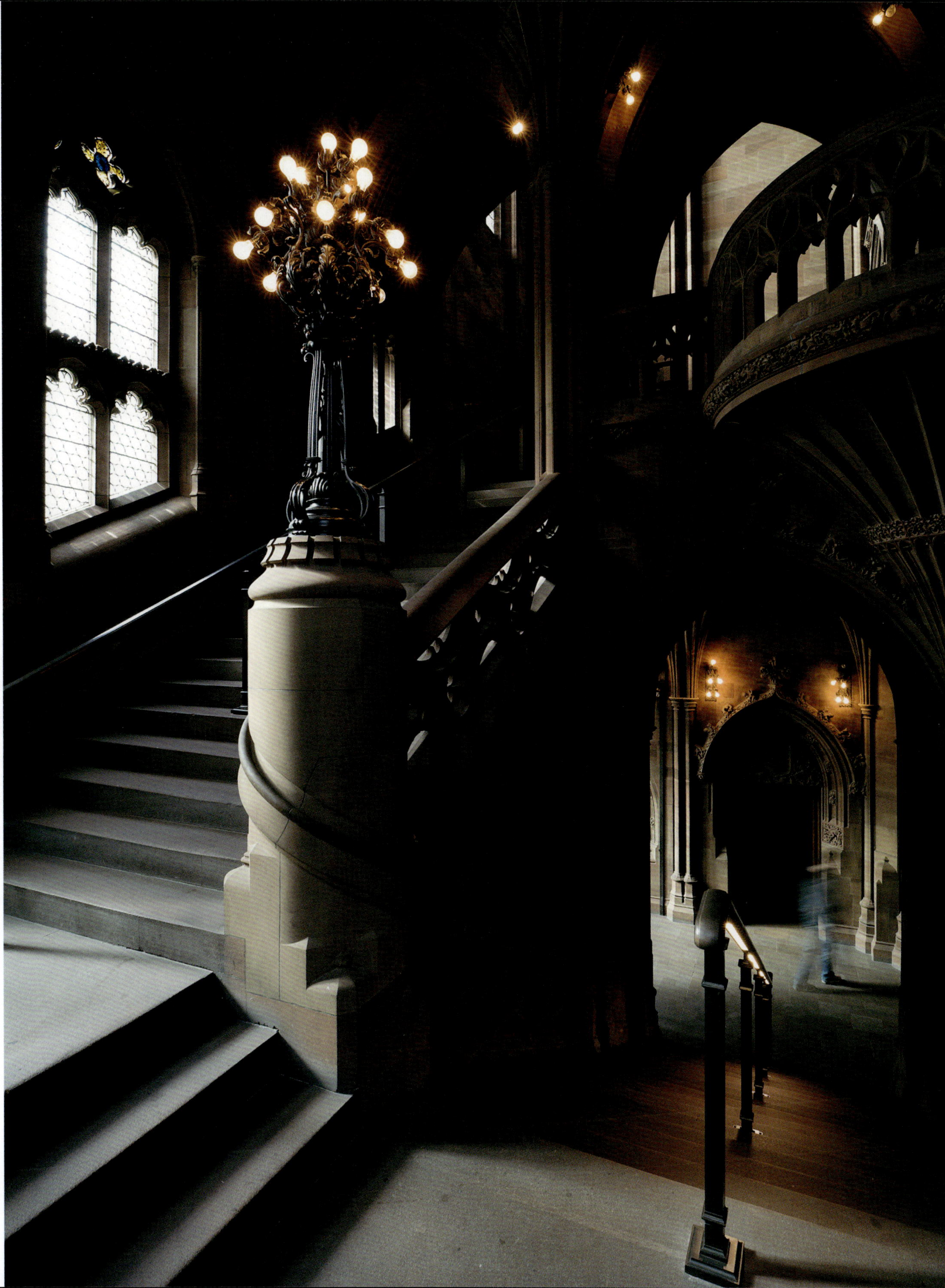

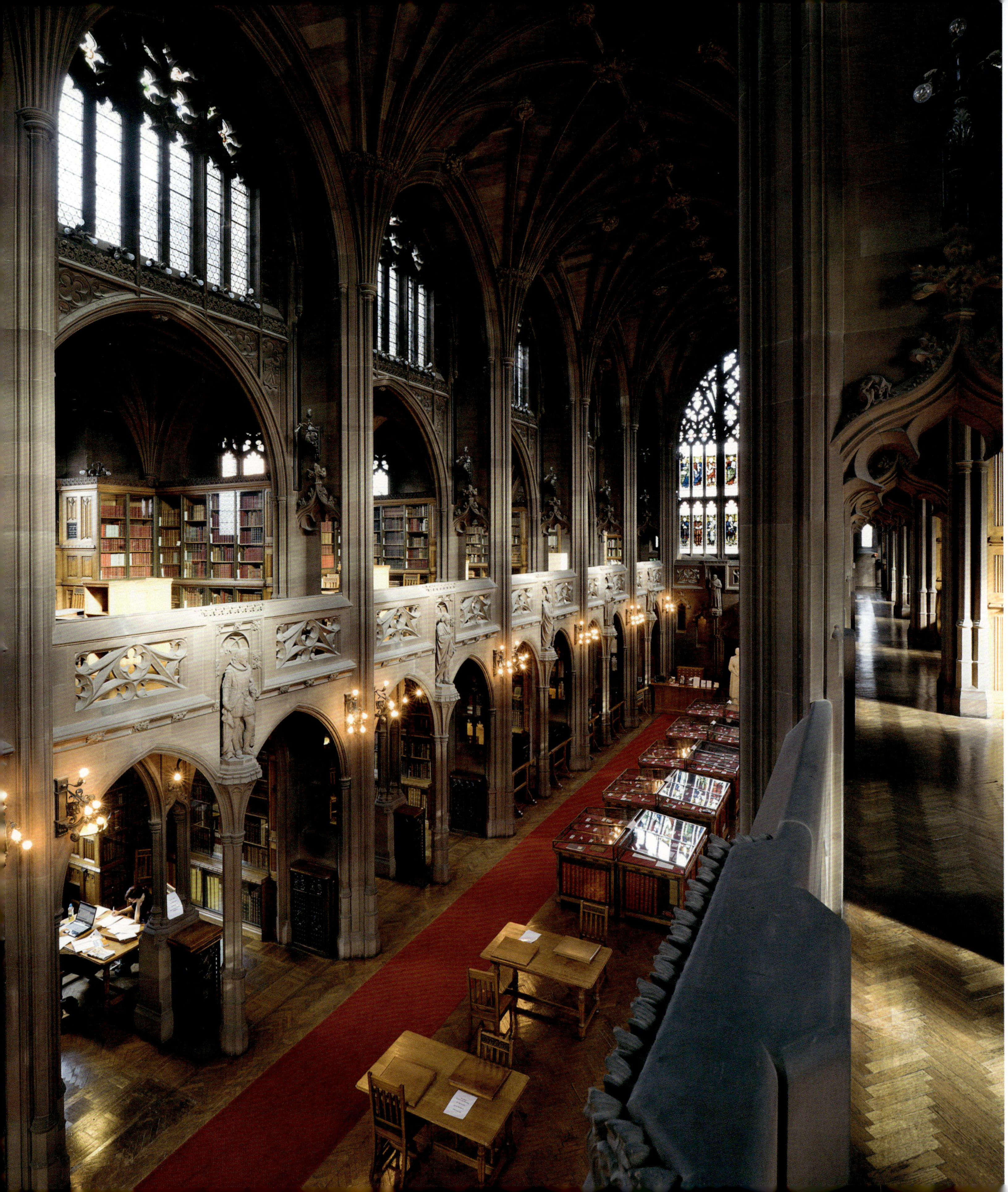

[142] John Rylands Library: the reading room.

and the mill, and their various surpluses and wastes – in short everything that Rylands & Sons had created and mastered – is, of necessity, at a different level from the overt iconography with which Enriqueta was concerned, such as her insistence on the stained glass having secular subjects or the niches for her historical figures having semi-domes rather than Gothic tabernacles. This – reaching yet another level – is exactly why the library's architecture as a way of rendering the experience of the transition into the cultural is so important; it is both more spectacular and more subliminal.

Along the way to the reading room, extensive sandstone surfaces flaunt their exposure to air. This sandstone, known as shawk, had been quarried near Dalston in Cumbria, and was paler than the dark red Barbary sandstone, quarried in Penrith, that was used for the exterior and that Enriqueta Rylands believed to be sufficiently durable to stand up to the city's pollution.[102] A repeated motif carved into this interior stone is of organic forms rustled by the wind, a motif that is as wave-like as it is leaf-like (fig. 143). Plants were often taken as the measure of smoke's bad effects, their stunted, 'blanched and sickly' forms used as an analogy with the blighted physiques, life expectancy and 'deterioration of race' of urban slum dwellers.[103] In Collingwood's painting of Ruskin, it is interesting to observe a tumbler of water holding Grass of Parnassus, a wild flower, placed on the window sill as another emblem of purity (see fig. 112). 'Lovely architecture', Ruskin had written in 1865, was possible only in 'cloudless air', by contrast with the 'black air' that 'renders all ornament invisible in distance, and then chokes its interstices with soot'.[104] The very existence of ornament – its legibility, its articulation of the free or 'savage' expression of the craftsman, in Ruskin's terms – was testament to a continuing anti-modernity, to a resistance against all that industrial modernity stood for and produced. The library's leaf ornaments, furthermore, also thematise air as free and 'purified', circulating the building with the ascending visitor. (This, it

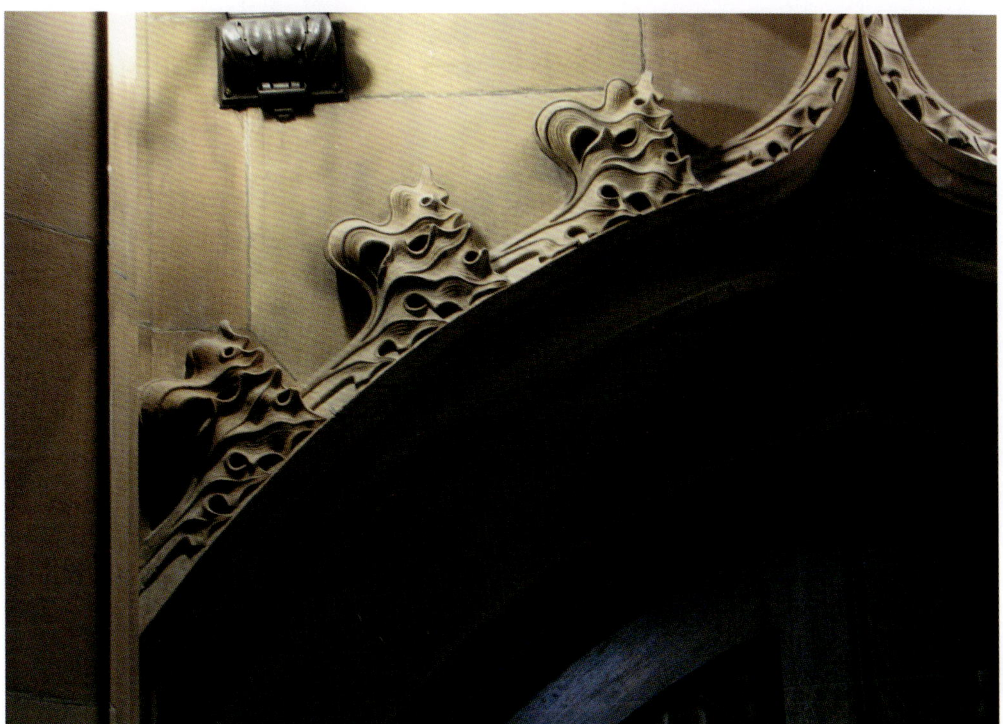

[143] John Rylands Library: decorative carving.

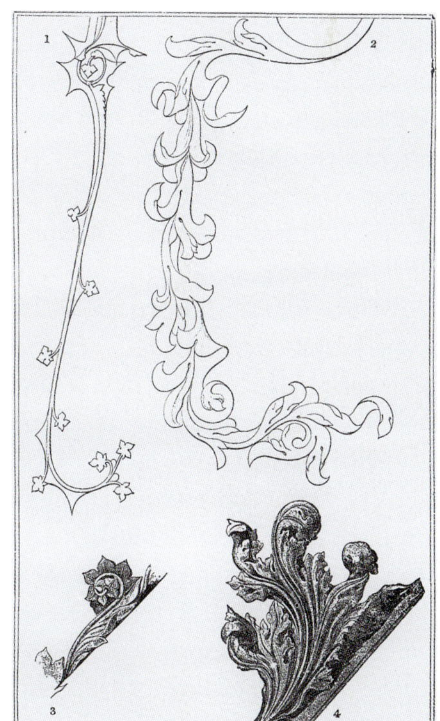

[144] 'Temperance and Intemperance in Curvature' (Figure 4 is a carved crocket from St Mark's, Venice): plate from John Ruskin, *Stones of Venice*, vol. 3 (1853).

needs saying, is neither a programmatic figuring of the symbolic attributes of smoke and purification, nor a jump into the purified spaces of a health-obsessed modernism.) Gothic Revivalists were always concerned with sourcing such motifs, and Champneys no doubt meant his readers to be reminded of the crockets on the gables of St Mark's Basilica in Venice – the city that was a type for Britain's imperial state, of course, but also the Venice that was medievally distant from the disturbing newness of industrial forms (fig. 144). But that was only a temporal distance. In Ruskin's words, those Venetian crockets had a pre-industrial vitality about them: '[they] appear to consider themselves at greater liberty even than the finials, and fling themselves, hither and thither, in the wildest contortions'.[105] They were part of those crests of arches on the upper part of St Mark's that, in one of his most famous lines, Ruskin had described as crests that 'break into marble foam, and toss themselves far into the blue sky in flashes and wreaths of sculptured spray'.[106]

We are far from the Gidlow pits and mill here, or so Champneys and Enriqueta Rylands would have it and as the Ruskinian motifs would appear to testify. (As such, this is part of a series of disavowals in Enriqueta's life that might reward a more directly socio-psychological study.)[107] If Ruskin himself regarded St Mark's crockets as a little too 'intemperate', perhaps even morbidly excited ('the fatal weakness of decay ... the infallible indication of decline'),[108] a Ruskinian like Champneys was not to be dissuaded from them – they would have had the generic Ruskinian stamp, regardless of Ruskin's own quibbles. But perhaps the craftedness of the Rylands ornament, its breezy organicism, might better be understood as bearing a false testimony – that, despite the deskilling of industry and the replacement of human energy with fossil fuel energy, the product of craft would still survive: those who caused its demise were also those who would preserve it. The ornament also reminds us of the Victorian idea that culture, symbolised by the library itself, was a 'stream of fresh and free thought', a 'pursuit of perfection', a place and an activity that were completely apart from the world of coal and cotton and machinery that belonged, so Matthew Arnold had said, to the non-cultural zone of the 'vast residuum'.[109] (If Arnold's arguments – very much a product of the 1860s and his attempts to move beyond the condition-of-England debate – seem renewed, or rather reincarnated, in the John Rylands Library, this had much to do with the formation of a new set of interests at the *fin de siècle*.[110]) Smoke has been banished from this other world of the library, where a purer air flutters its stone plants, much as industry has been confined to the world of the utilitarian, the quotidian, the unfeeling and unthinking. Meanwhile, of course, beyond the library, smoke continued on its prevailing drift northwards to the Lake District and Ruskin's house at Coniston.

FOR RUSKIN, LECTURING IN 1865, MANCHESTER WAS THE site of a transformation of people into things (or, we might say, the ingredients of it-narratives):

> *[a city which is] mere crowded masses of store, and warehouse, and counter ... all chief magnitude of edifice is to enclose machinery; [a city] in which the streets are not the avenues for the passing and procession of a happy people, but the drains for the discharge of a tormented mob, in which the only object in reaching any spot is to be transferred to another; in which existence becomes mere transition, and every creature is only one atom in a drift of human dust, and current of interchanging particles, circulating here by tunnels underground, and there by tubes in the air; for a city, or cities, such as this no architecture is possible.*[111]

Smoke was a product of 'mental vileness ... loathsome insanity'; it manifested 'total carelessness' of the beauty of nature.[112] In fact the 'happy people' of Ruskin's desire have themselves become like smoke, drifting and transiting and circulating to no purpose, with no value, a 'current of interchanging particles'. 'The Empire of England,' as Ruskin declared at the close of his first *Storm Cloud* lecture, 'on which formerly the sun never set, has become one on which he never rises.' 'Blanched Sun, – blighted grass, – blinded man' – what is the meaning of these things? he asks. Is the poisonous smoke actually 'dead men's souls', the traces of industrial culture's victims[113] – the remains, perhaps, of the crushed or asphyxiated Gidlow miners?

The ironies of the John Rylands Library are barely implicit; the hypocrisies of this attempt at redemption through the accumulation of cultural capital are in plain sight. Enriqueta Rylands was certainly a Ruskinian. Although she did not meet Ruskin himself, she was a close friend of the prominent Ruskinian Canon Rawnsley, a co-initiator of the National Trust, whose founding motivation was to preserve the Lake District from the despoliations of industrialism.[114] Enriqueta also collected Ruskiniana, including Ruskin's letters (some on vellum) and special editions of his writings.[115] And she owned several sets of Cook and Wedderburn's collected *Works of John Ruskin*. To open one of her copies of volume 34, which contains *The Storm Cloud*, is to find pages of handmade linen rag paper in a state of beautifully soft, virginal whiteness. This and the other volumes and sets were kept in one of Champneys's hermetically sealed bookcases where they were airlessly preserved from the effects of smoke, a precious treasure within a casket set within the larger casket of the building. There are few better examples of Walter Benjamin's famous dictum that 'there is no document of civilization which is not at the same time a document of barbarism'.[116] Whatever the moral here, to trace this smutty story – the cognitive map by which smoke crosses and contaminates the city but also the library that seeks to deny it – is to reconnect the psychic to the social and the economic. There is not some separable typological convenience we could call the 'architecture of smoke (or coal)' nor a simple correspondence. The architecture is, instead, as much the subterranean grid as the carved crocket, as much the bookcase sealed with velvet and wool as the belching chimney or the damp coalface. Isn't there more than an analogical relation between the boiler suspended in flues being heated by currents of smoke and the library sealed from the industrial pollution that also sustains it? This is, of course, not only to reveal the marks of labour, of conflict and violence, within the library, but to show something of the library as a complex of disavowal.

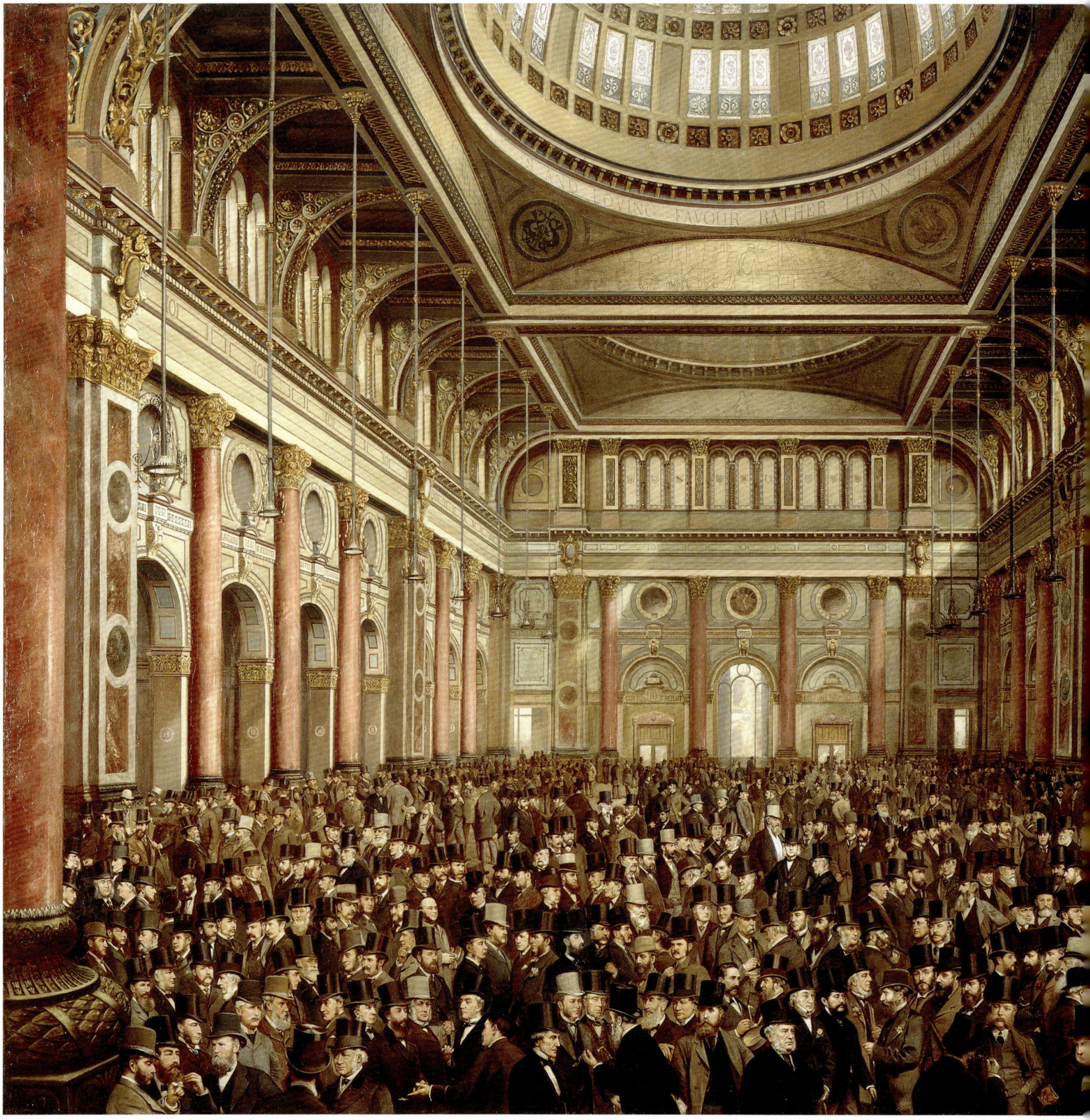
AND LOVING FAVOUR RATHER THAN SILVER

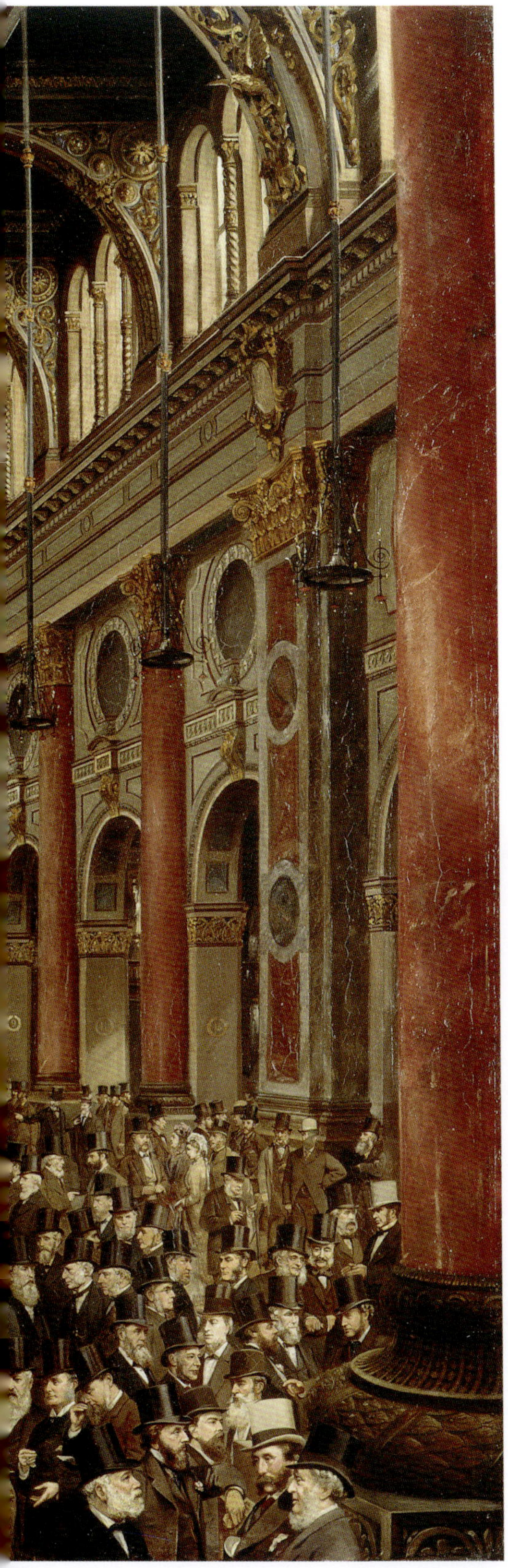

[145] Frederick Sargent and H. L. Saunders, *Interior of the Manchester Royal Exchange*, 1877. Oil on canvas. Manchester Art Gallery.

6 The Largest Room

Making a Deal with the Architecture of the Exchange

THE IMAGE SHOWN IN FIGURE 145 IS BOTH IMPOSING and diminishing. Imposing because of the boxed-in scale of what it depicts, its rhetoric all about size and the relationships of size, about the measure of men and of their architecture. Diminishing not so much because of where we as viewers are placed, and not because the figures depicted are fitted into less than a third of its overall space, but because we must be either part of it or not part of it, not part of its address and therefore of its measure. We are shown a huge space, vaulted and domed, ringed on its three visible sides by arches and red stone columns. At the front, like the proscenium of a stage, two of these columns, perhaps free-standing, seem to frame or guard the space beyond them. The top hats of several men come up close to the column bases and their coats brush or rest against them. They are only the outer breakers of a sea of such men, besuited in greys, browns and black, a crest of faces in earnest conversation or poised and meditative, some looking out towards us.[1] The painting places the viewer in the Strangers' Gallery, somewhere opposite the central round window on the far wall, so that they can range over this tightly packed, zoological yet homogeneous array of individuals.[2] The light that comes from above and that slants across the surfaces of the building seems not to affect these men. Individually portrayed yet filling the floor of this room from side to side and from end to end, the transcribed physiologies must hold their own; their over-proximate sociability is essential to what is portrayed. This is *Interior of the Manchester Royal Exchange*, as painted in 1877 by Frederick Sargent and H. L. Saunders.

While this painting is densely peopled, it might be better to think of its subject not as a crowd but as a coordinated and even harmonious congestion, a kind of ideal theatre for one class's performance – or even the reverse: a virtual scenario of our own audition to be accepted by those before us. The individuality of the men is the discrete module of a collective sense of distinction and purposefulness. An accompanying 'Key to the Interior of the Royal Exchange' names everyone portrayed, acting as a kind of register of the represented.[3] They are members (who pay an annual subscription) and what they belong to is the great club of gentlemanly commerce, a nirvana of middlemen and their dealing, of buying and selling, of knowledge of the market and the glamour of global trading.[4] They fit to some extent with Alois Riegl's characterisation of corporate portraiture: '[a group of] completely autonomous individuals who associated themselves with a corporation solely for a specific, shared, practical, and public-spirited purpose'.[5] The public spirit might be less relevant here, or at best an accretion from other associations, but the combination of the individual and the corporate is exactly right; it is one of the things that separates this collective from, say, the street-betting gatherings of the working classes that were a notable if semi-legal feature of Manchester's street life.[6] And, following Riegl, this individualised collective is the product of massed physiologies that address and open up to the viewer, that depend on the viewer if membership is to be understood as confraternity, if indeed speculation is to be seen not as red in tooth and claw but as gentlemanly, discreet, attentive and working according to collective codes.[7] In an exchange with Walter Benjamin, Adorno wrote of how Balzac 'assesses [people] in terms of their purchase price', and he does this by stripping them of their 'bourgeois standardization', both of which procedures have a 'speculative impulse'. In other words, as with financial speculation, there is a risk involved in physiological description (Adorno emphasises the proximity of the analogy): to portray individual difference is a 'speculative adventure' that risks 'intoxicating gain or a fraudulent trap'.[8] All the more so, it might be added, with the mass of speculators in this painting, where – almost as a result of the artist's compositional challenges – the patchwork artifice of individuality is made plain. Yet there is also an imposing quality about the flatness of distinctions; there seems to be something more than a corporate body, for that would surely imply boundedness and hierarchy within the group. But boundedness, we might say, is only a limit condition of the architecture. There is, in an important sense, a pressure enacted by these bodies on the walls that contain them, and this is a condition of the success of the institution – that it grows, that it expands.

Membership is also crucial to another image, this time a graph drawn in 1908 for an engineer advising the Manchester City Council[9] (fig. 146). The shape described by the graph's pink wash is like the section of a mountain. The foothills, to the left, represent the early years of the nineteenth century, then there are steep rises from the 1830s to the late 1860s, smaller and uneven peaks over the next decade or so and then the return of steep rises from the 1880s until the section comes to an end at its highest point in 1908. The pink mountainside stands for the increasing membership numbers of the Manchester Royal Exchange. But against it the graph posits an unevenly stepped line, from the first level, the number 452 on the left, jumping briefly to the second level at 799, rearing up to 1,634 from the 1850s to the 1870s, and then rising exponentially to 4,413 in the mid-1870s and staying there to the graph's end-point. The stepped line is the floor space of the Exchange building in square yards, the amount of the pink mass (the number of members) that can actually be accommodated. Its steps up represent new or expanded buildings. The building had been extended three times in a hundred years; the first two proved entirely inadequate to the challenge of the pink wash, while the third held its own for nearly thirty years. The narcotic of trading has overcome its feudal past; in Walter Benjamin's terms, the phantasmagoria of ever-expanding space is joined to a phantasmagoria of time.[10] In the last few years up to the present of the graph the pink wash has caught up and once more exceeds the floor space line. Even though the details of capacity – how many members should fit into, say, a hundred square yards, and what does the space need to accommodate beyond the besuited body and top hat, what kind of movement and what social distance? – are unclear, the graph clearly reveals a mismatch. The Exchange simply cannot keep pace; the growing membership

[146] Graph showing the membership of the Royal Exchange in relation to its space, from T. de Courcy Meade, 'Paper Submitted to Improvement and Paving Committees of Manchester City Council' (1908).

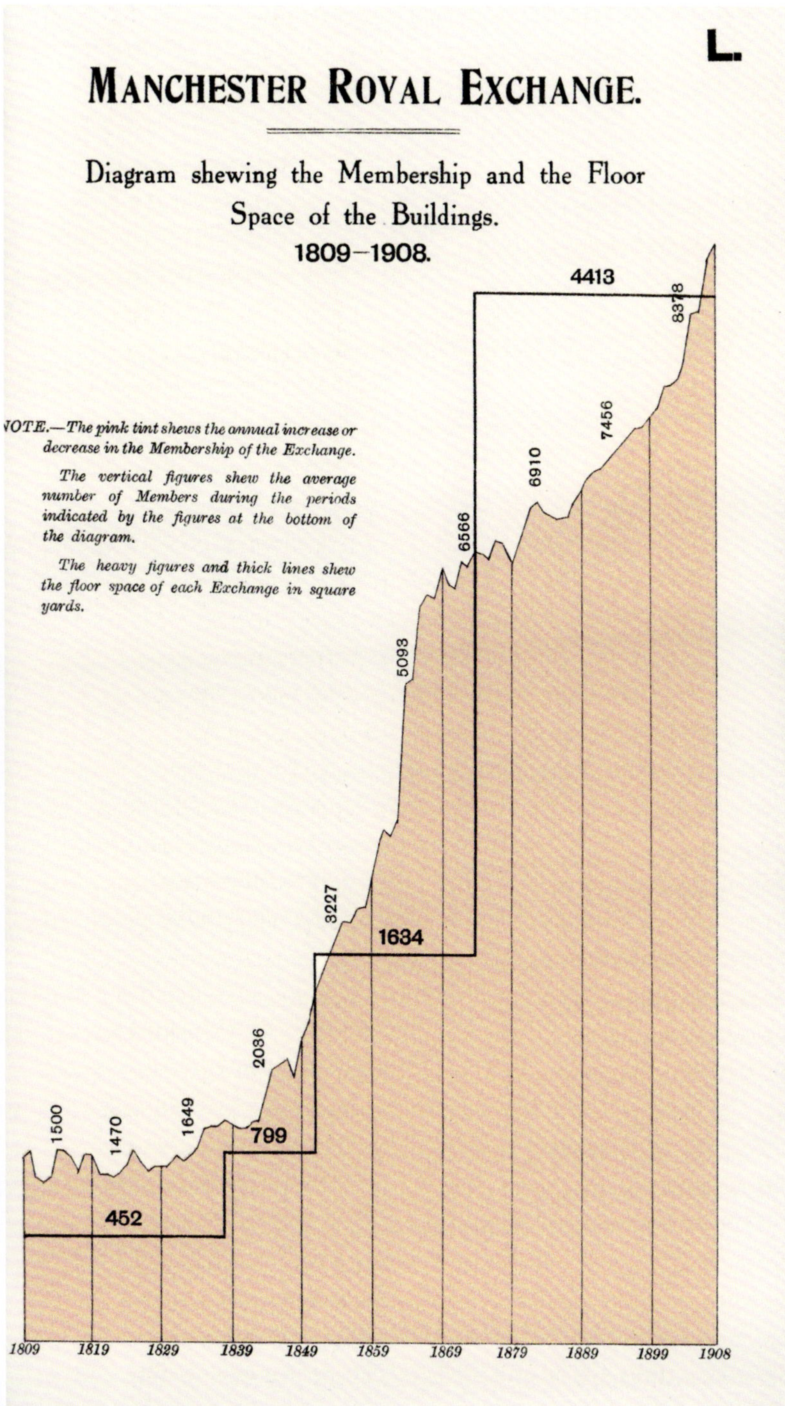

constantly outpaces or quickly outgrows the expanding floor space. Despite its crowd, Sargent and Saunders's painting actually represents the only period in the Exchange's graphic history when, for three decades, the building's floor space was comfortably in excess of membership. But it's clear that busyness in the form of intense sociability, of being seen together, was what must still be conveyed.

These are two glimpses of a building that is curiously difficult to define in terms of its functions. If we say it was about a capacious emptiness and the filling of the space for short, intense periods with a multitude of men, we would have an oblique definition of it, and one that should not be dismissed. It was about money too, of course, passing into and out of goods, animating their passage, and that abstraction, the very commodification of these goods, is what happened in the Exchange. Yet the goods never entered the Exchange, never entered this room as more than the occasional sample, nor did the money. Men did. And there they performed the curious, immensely important rituals and activities of their class: acquiring and moving capital, engaging with the mysterious actions of the market, observing the spectral circulations of objects and signs. The building we see in the painting is only one of several iterations of what the Exchange was in architectural terms, but it memorably captures what this chapter considers as fundamental to it.

From the early eighteenth century until its final (and current) form in the 1920s, the Exchange was expanded or rebuilt many times (the stepped line of the graph only records the major changes). In the nineteenth century it became key to Manchester's position dominating the global cotton trade. The world was, in some measure, directed from here. Manchester's maps often used an orientation device centred on the Exchange, which was more about symbolic order than about actual orientation in the city. Concentric rings marking hundred-yard distances rippled out from the Exchange to the edges of the map, superimposing a kind of geometry on the city that could never be brought about in its streets. By implication they also calibrated distances to Manchester's satellite towns and to its extraterritorial cotton empire beyond. Other maps made the compass points intersect

[147] Map of central Manchester, 1836, showing the compass points crossing on the Exchange. Published by James Pigot. From J. T. Slugg, *Reminiscences of Manchester Fifty Years Ago* (1881).

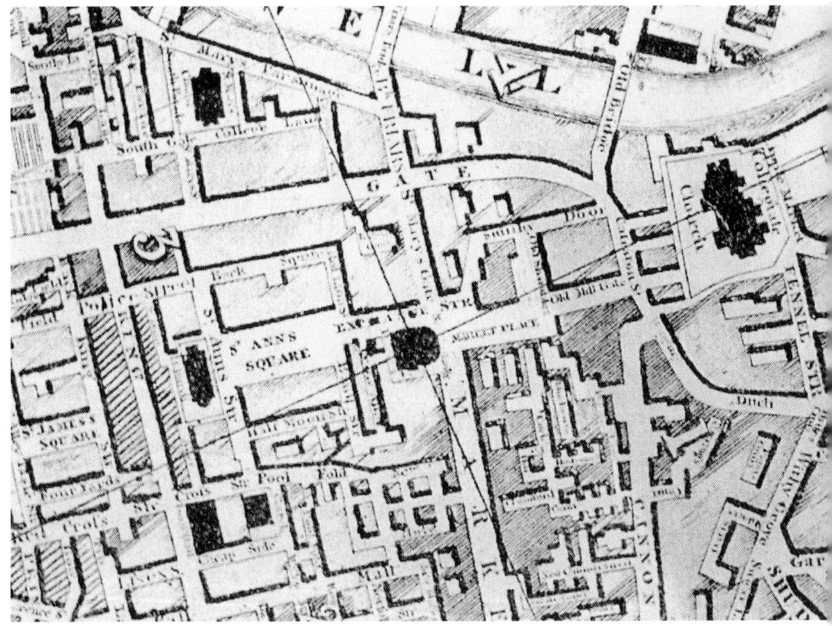

on the building itself, so that every other street or building on the map was seen in relation to the Exchange; every other place in the world was presumably oriented to it, worlded by it[11] (fig. 147). Both superimpositions implied that orientation was possible by overlaying geometry onto an object that was both worldly and abstract. Dealing with the Exchange's history as part of Manchester always implies the world beyond it, but at the same time an architecture- and image-based account has the advantage of cutting through to the material history of the Exchange, a history of human beings in actual spaces.[12] Capacity and membership are key to this, as is the building's tension with the city around it, the bursting of its frame as its overcapacity forces onto its locality (its urban grain, its local municipal encumbrances and constraints, its building envelope) the inevitable periodic recognition of its more than local significance.

MANCHESTER'S FIRST EXCHANGE IS EVIDENCE OF AN architectural ambition not usually associated with the early eighteenth-century town (fig. 148). Built right in the middle of Market Place in 1729 by the then Sir Oswald Mosley, it was central to the town's commercial world and also about halfway between St Ann's and the collegiate church (then known as Christ Church), the twin edifices that mark religious presence in the town centre. It was free-standing but positioned so that its length followed the east–west flow of Market Street Lane (later to become Market Street) through Market Place, while its pedimented front faced southwards (fig. 149). From the images that survive it seems somewhat dumpy: a temple front imposed on an edifice only one bay wider to either side of its three arched entrances. But the images are deceptive. This was the only properly temple-fronted institutional building in the town at that time and the only mainly stone-faced one (other buildings were wood, brick and stucco). One visitor described it as 'an hansome building, but crouded up in a low situation'.[13] It was the basic arrangement seen here of central space and classical frontage – if later bloated, extended, lifted up and elaborated in a multitude of ways – that remained the Exchange's essence over the next 150 years. But what was increasingly lost with the various later iterations was any sense that the Exchange was spatially integrated with, or even containable by, its environing town.

The architecture might have been upgraded from its surroundings, but it continued to house the same set of functions. Its two storeys created the necessary space within the market square without the need to acquire and demolish properties around it, and in this additional space not only could part of the market be covered but there was also the kind of meeting space for merchants with which the town was poorly supplied, a space capacious enough to be adaptable for balls, plays, lectures and scientific demonstrations, as well as meetings of the Court Leet.[14] In the image that appeared on the margins of Casson and Berry's *c.*1746 map we can see that the three entrances not only led into an open ground-floor space but were matched by three similarly open entrances on the other side, establishing a permeability that would also be a marked feature of some of the Exchange's later versions. The ground floor seems to have sheltered some of the market around it, being regularly occupied by butchers' stalls.[15] The intended association was clearly with the free-standing market halls of country towns rather than the

[148] Map of Manchester, c.1746: detail showing the first Exchange in Market Place (just left of centre). Published by Casson and Berry. Chetham's Library, Manchester.

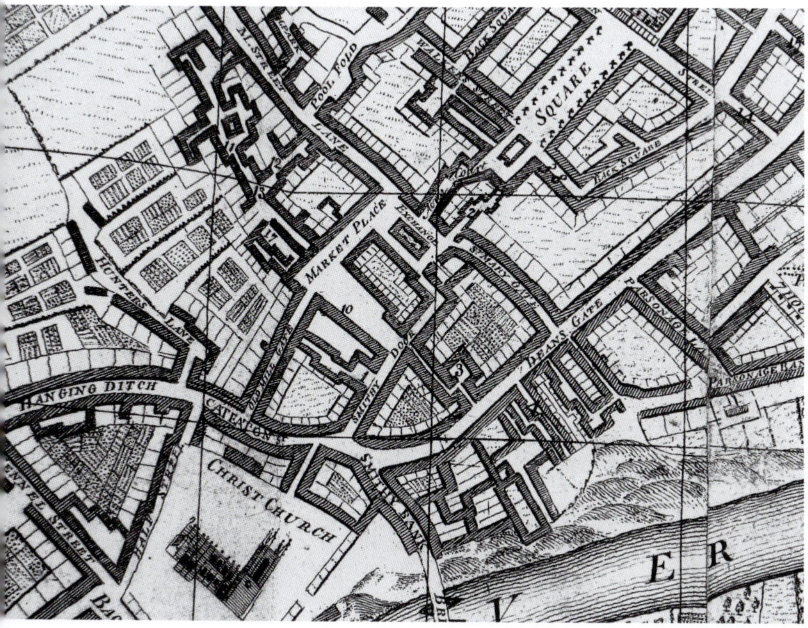

[149] The first Exchange, as represented in the border of map of Manchester, c.1746. Published by Casson and Berry. Chetham's Library, Manchester.

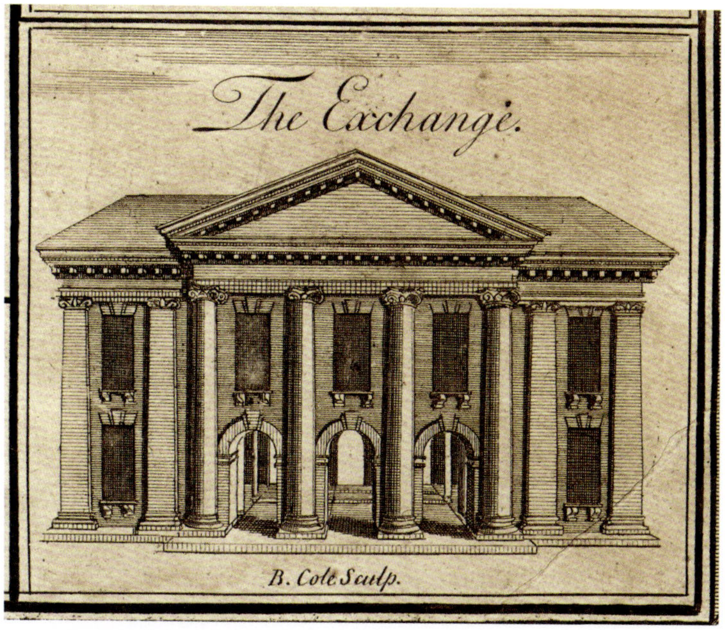

disdained 'Box'd ... Compass' of Daniel Defoe's 'Exchange-Alley' in London.[16]

The Mosley link and the presence of the Court Leet show that the Exchange was to some extent merely a new container for old medieval and landed institutions; it brought a focus to the town's market activities and kept them within its established forms of oversight.[17] Partly because of this, it was much despised by later commentators, its name regarded as a misnomer and its physical state a sure sign of the decrepit institutions it housed: '[the Exchange] had seldom been used for the purpose its name seems to designate, but was a harbour for vagrants and dirt'.[18] The immediate area was clearly in need of regular cleaning because of the market, and from an early date the Exchange was allotted its own scavengers.[19] According to Joseph Aston, merchants did not even gather in the Exchange during the building's last year, such was its inconvenience and squalor, but preferred to meet in the open space around it, gathering in a 'corner' (a term that would extend as much to a commodity – 'cornering a market' – as to a particular space); some had long met in an 'unofficial Exchange' a little distance away on King Street.[20] The use of the open space continued on the site of the building when it was demolished in 1792.[21] For a time after demolition, Manchester's merchants made do with nearby venues – coffee shops, taverns, rented rooms and even an open flagged passage. But clearly the situation was unsustainable.

THE INTERREGNUM WAS CRUCIAL. BY THE TIME A NEW Exchange building was completed in 1809 Manchester's relation to the cotton trade had moved on definitively. In 1770 cotton goods had accounted for 2.6 per cent of Britain's economy; by 1801 that figure had grown to 17 per cent; and thirty years later it had grown to 22.4 per cent.[22] What Sven Beckert has called 'war capitalism' was one reason, tying the development of the economy directly to the acquisition and redevelopment of territory during the long wars against the French, the appropriation of slave labour and the opening up of new markets.[23] (And this is a crucial example, in accelerated form, of the tying together of primary accumulation and capital accumulation in what Marxists have called 'uneven and combined development'.)[24] The two final decades of the eighteenth century saw an explosion in exports of cotton by a factor of

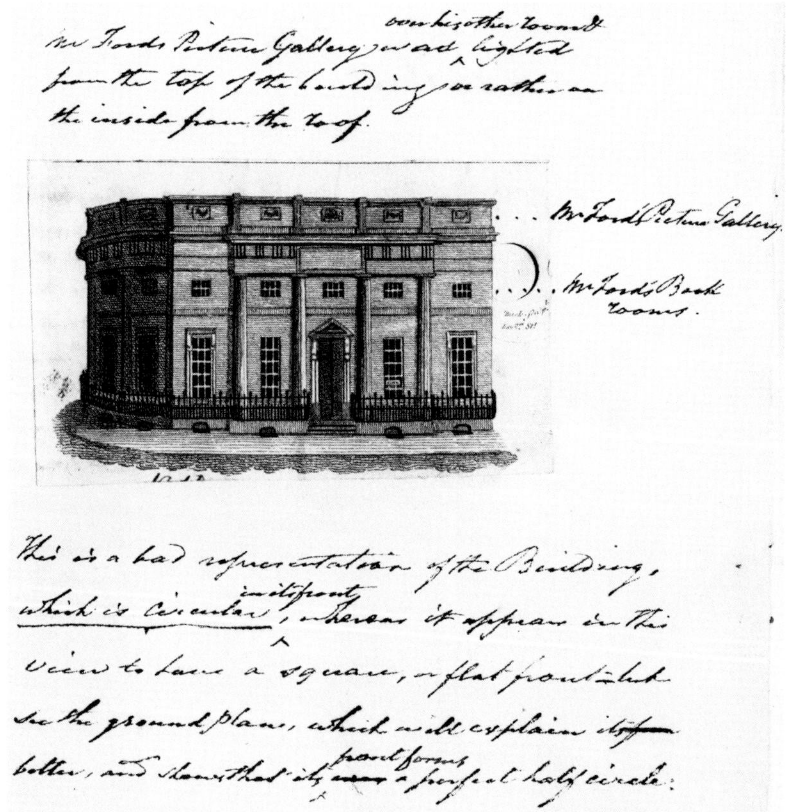

[150] The new Exchange, 1809. Architect: Thomas Harrison of Chester. From 'Description of the Manchester Exchange by Joseph Aston with notes by WF', undated MS (probably c.1812). Chetham's Library, Manchester.

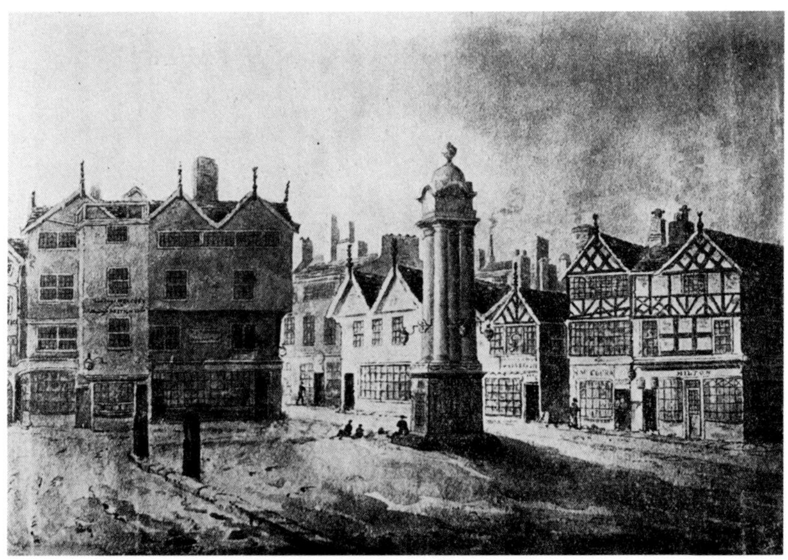

[151] The site of the old Exchange in 1790, now marked with a pillar. Watercolour. From W. H. Thomson, *History of Manchester to 1852* (1967).

more than sixteen. With the surpassing of or elimination of non-European rivals, global trade was opened up to British speculation, becoming what has rightly been called its 'financescape', its spreading transnational territory for the movement of capital.[25] Linked to all this were the extraordinary technological changes in cotton manufacture and in the factories that housed them (as seen in Chapter 1).

The Exchange is bound up with war capitalism: it was both at the heart of what helped to generate war capitalism and a product of it, and was active in the transition to industrial capitalism proper. We see the first tensions in its position in the new years of the century as the institution was caught between the rapidly growing and vast extent of the markets and commodities that it was now serving, and the contingencies, provisions and extemporisations of its material existence in a specific locality. Environmentally, the situation was grim. In 1808, as the new Exchange was nearing completion, one visitor described Manchester as the epitome of shock city: 'abominably filthy, the Steam Engine is pestiferous, the Dyehouses noisome and offensive, and the water of the river as black as ink or the Stygian lake'.[26] Nevertheless, Manchester had assembled all the components required to become the centre for the global cotton trade: its manufacturers and importers; its factories, technologies and workforce; and its financial and other services. The era of the modern exchange had arrived. Manchester's fortunes were linked to Liverpool's, like 'coupled nucleii', but, where the Liverpool Cotton Exchange was primarily a raw cotton market, the Manchester Exchange was more diversified and its move to a membership system fundamentally different.[27]

In 1804 it was decided at last to erect 'a handsome building ... for the purposes of a commercial coffee room and tavern ... [which] would afford great accommodation to the merchants and manufacturers of this town and neighbourhood'.[28] This barely indicates the great shift in understanding that took place, for the new building would be almost entirely separate from the market in actual goods, which would now be wholesale and occupy a spectral or virtual space in its dealings. And dealing would now be brought entirely inside, institutionalised, made part of a newly

[152] The Exchange (Thomas Harrison's design, with modifications by Alexander Mills) in its immediate context: detail from Ordnance Survey map of Manchester, 1851.

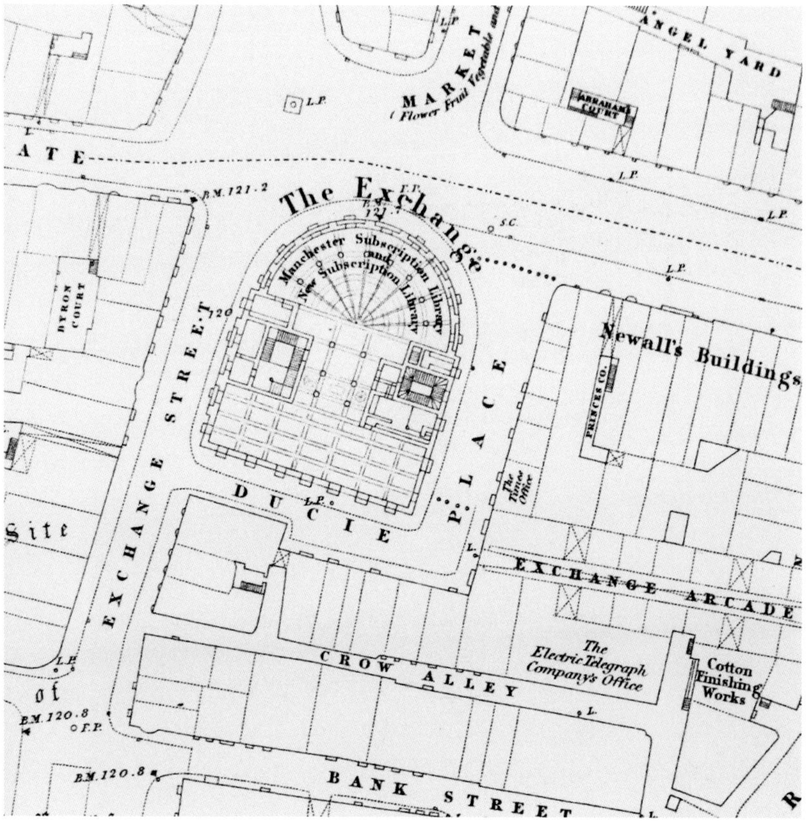

regularised space (street dealing outside increasingly became para-legal, the activity of another class). Closely assembled bodies, operating individually and collectively, would take their place in the Exchange and commodities (predominantly cotton), not goods, would be their trade. And those bodies would now be 'members', who paid an annual subscription rate to a club, a private institution, with which they were now formally identified (membership subscriptions had, within a year, far exceeded expectations).[29] It is as if the courtyard spaces of the exchanges of London and Amsterdam and of the eighteenth-century piece halls were now roofed over and emptied of their non-human traffic. And, just as corn exchanges and coal exchanges emerged as specialised places of dealing, so the cotton exchange would emerge out of the incubator of Manchester. What is remarkable is how closely the architecture kept pace with all this; it might be claimed that the new building showed a better understanding of these new expectations – how they could be accommodated and enabled, what they implied for the locality – than any other cultural expression of the time, even if it was found wanting periodically.

A competition was announced and Thomas Harrison of Chester, one of the most distinctive architects of the Greek Revival, was appointed to design the new building (fig. 150). Opened in 1809, the building had a new site, to one side of where its predecessor had stood and taking over property offered to the town by Lord Ducie. A subscription was raised, 'Lord Ducie contributing without charge, 592 yards, which were given to the public streets, and the subscribers paying rent for 1200 square yards'.[30] This shifting of the Exchange's site was an important aspect of the new building. While the now vacated old site became an open public space, marked by a pillar and often the subject of artists' views (fig. 151), the new site to its south involved the demolition of existing buildings, initiating the long process by which the Exchange became engaged in a kind of struggle over space with the town around it (within five weeks of completion the architect was being asked for designs to extend the building).[31] The Exchange was not now positioned to emphasise the flow of Market Street Lane but as an object in its own carved-out area, a kind of whirlpool drawing energies towards itself in a new vortex of urban space (fig. 152). The town of small family-based businesses for which the first Exchange had catered had been broken and expanded by a more urgent force, of which the new Exchange was the cutting edge.[32] The older, limited policy of 'street improvements', such as the widening of streets to make them more 'convenient' (specifically, in 1776, for the merchants of the Exchange in its immediate streets[33]), was now taken over by a different dynamic, whereby the interior capacity of the Exchange, with its ever-increasing need for more room, was the prime cause of urban change in the vicinity of the building.

If Vittore Zanetti's print of 1810 is to be believed, the Exchange may have been no higher than the shops adjacent to it, but its scale was distinctly different (fig. 153). It also offered a gamut of modern conveniences directed at the town immediately around it. From the globe-shaped lamps fixed to its columns to the tall, regular

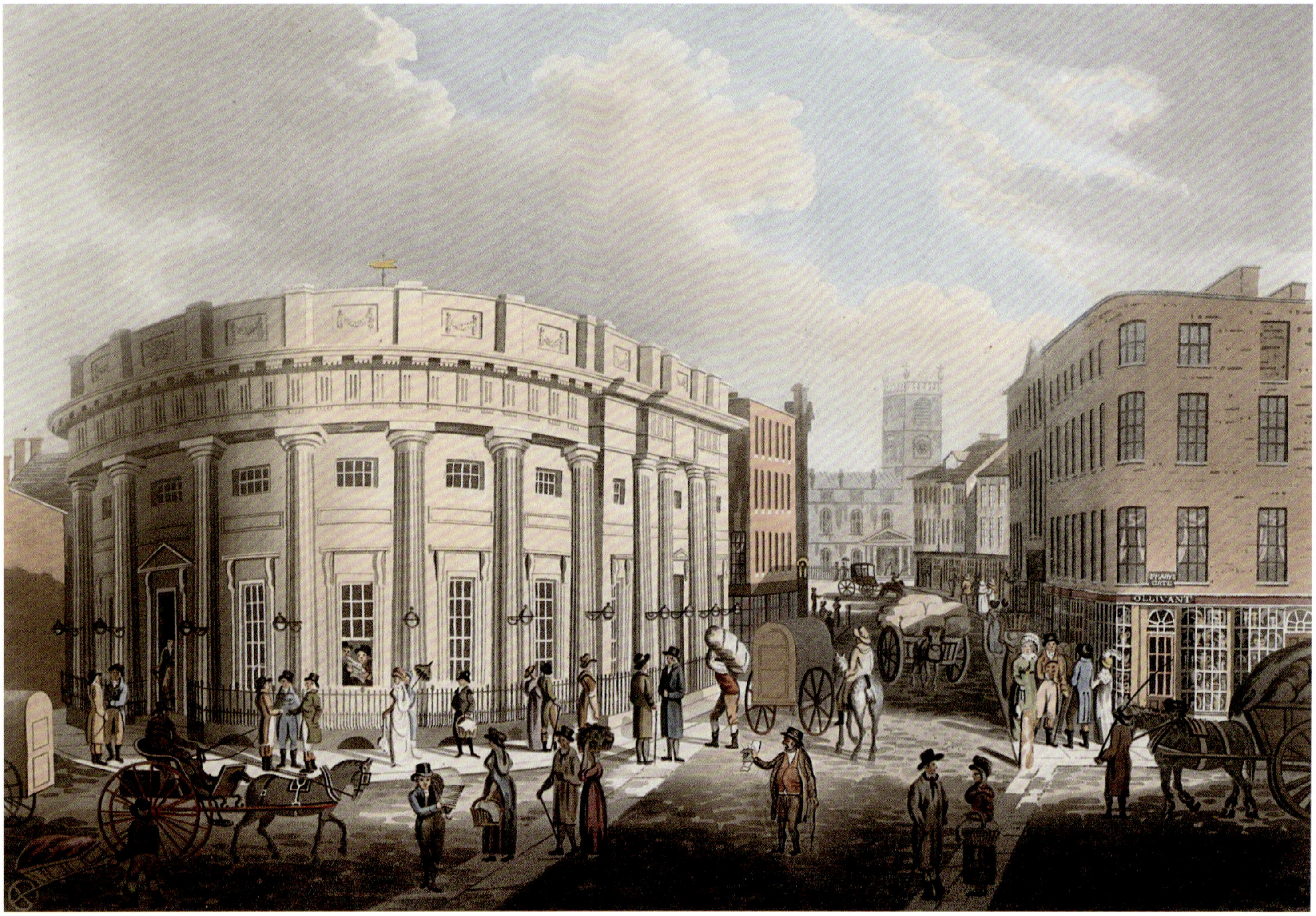

Georgian windows reaching low to the ground, their sashes enabling the creation of large openings (well demonstrated by one figure who sits at an open window, his newspaper half outside the frame), and to the door reached only a step or two from the street (again demonstrated by a man who stands half-in, half-out), the building is depicted as having a more human scale and a more open and immediate relation to its surroundings. Joseph Aston, writing in 1816, claimed something similar:

> *The utility and elegance at once broke down the barriers of custom, and the ancient site of colloquial commerce was abandoned for ever; and such was the popularity of the Exchange, founded, certainly, on the advantages it possesses for the purposes intended, that it can now boast of nearly sixteen hundred annual subscribers.*[34]

We need not be party to Zanetti or Aston's concern with civic boosterism to understand the declarative nature of this. The architecture's pitch is to do with asserting something new about civic sociability; its gathering or assembly function is also a part of identifying difference with, as well as breaking down, the 'barriers of custom' from a time now pushed firmly into the past, and of moving 'colloquial' practices of commerce into new, purposeful and para-public forms, forms fit to be paraded as part of an image of a town that was both more differentiated in its behaviours and more geared to the urgency of its changes.

Something of great novelty was happening here. We might find it particularly focused on that door unusually placed on the central and furthest outer point of the curving facade. This appears both to invoke and to go against a whole tradition of

[153] Vittore Zanetti, 'Manchester Exchange', 1810. Coloured aquatint and etching. British Library.

[154] The Market Place in 1823. Engraving of 1874, based on drawing by John Ralston, from Richard Wright Procter, *Memorials of Manchester Streets* (1874).

[155] Plan of the Exchange (Thomas Harrison's design of 1809), from Joseph Aston, *A Picture of Manchester* (1816).

[156] Portrait of Colonel Thomas Stanley, c.1805–20, by Thomas Lawrence (or a follower). Oil on canvas. Manchester Art Gallery.

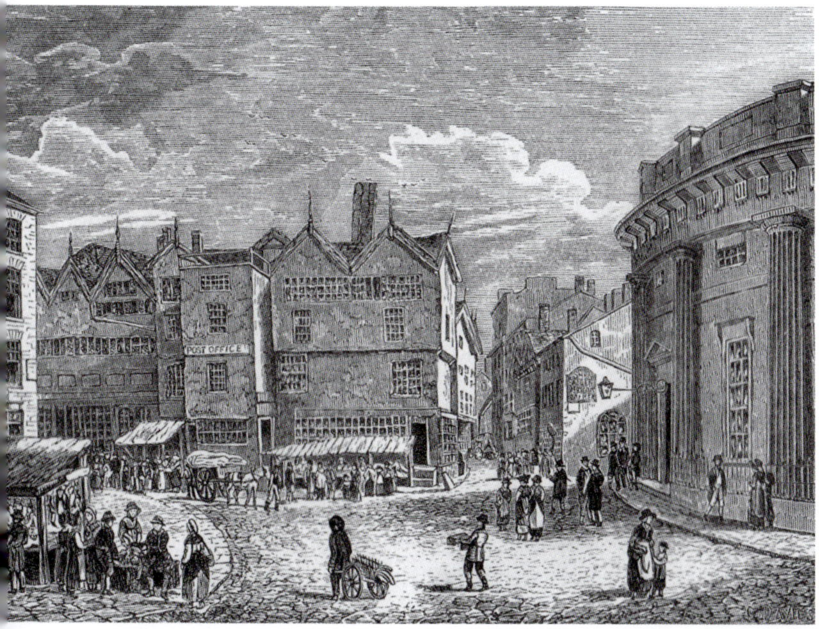

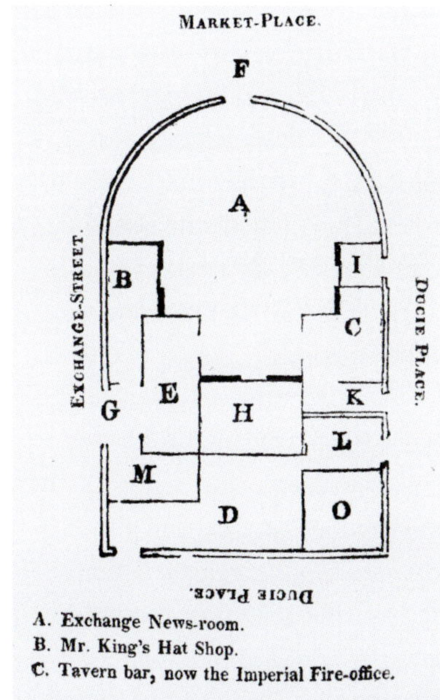

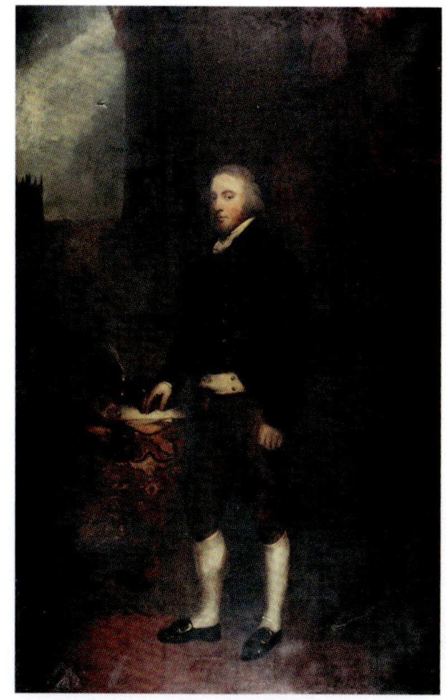

basilical and ecclesiastical structures and their derivatives, where the main entrance was at the other end of the building and the apsidal end represented the holy of holies, which was not to be encountered abruptly from direct entrance. But Aston and Zanetti make no bones that this is the main entrance, that it leads straight into the exchange room and that the side entrance is subsidiary (a small entrance at the south end of the building is not even mentioned by Aston and is rarely depicted in views).[35] The apse is the front. This door, leading straight in, positioned close to the level of the street, opening without a portico onto the open area of Market Place and the commotion of traffic and market stalls there, retains some relation to the permeability of market buildings and of the first Exchange building, but it also marks another way in which the Exchange has shifted in relation to the town around it (fig. 154). As a song written to mark the opening expressed it, 'You've seen the Exchange's outside / By exchanging you see it within' – it is as easy as that.[36] One could say that, while the marks of distinction and difference are announced in the architectural dress of the Greek Revival, the reorientation of the building's phenomenological relation to the town is at least as profound.

Cotton, which was now the dominant trade in the Exchange, was achieving a focused cultural expression in the architecture of that building just as its discursive ideological forms were to be developed with the establishment, first, of a 'commercial society' from 1794 – tellingly, after the loss of the American colonies and amidst the upheavals in France – and then in 1820 when it re-emerged as the Manchester Chamber of Commerce.[37] Here, many of the same traders could vocalise and harmonise their practices in relation to imperial government, newly energised by war capitalism.[38]

Central to all this was the exchange room itself, over 4,000 square feet in size. This might be reached directly from that door midway at the apsidal end or, less directly, from a door at the side on Exchange Street (visible to the right in Zanetti's view). Either way, the entrance sequence was curiously informal (fig. 155). From the west entrance, past a hat shop to the left and a drapery shop to the right, visitors entered the vestibule proper before encountering the exchange room (often known as the 'exchange newsroom' because of its informational function). The equivalent spaces on the other side from the entrance housed a tavern (which later became the Imperial Fire Office) and staircase. It was in the exchange room that the town's businessmen would meet to negotiate deals. Newspapers were provided on tables and over a central fireplace hung a portrait of the local MP Thomas Stanley, painted by Thomas Lawrence (or a follower)[39] (fig. 156). Stanley's career as a Whig MP started in 1780 and spanned more than three decades, the period during which the city's expansion made the inadequacy of its parliamentary representation increasingly blatant. The portrait, now in poor condition, seems to position Stanley in the Exchange itself. With the cathedral visible through its tall window, a kind of triangulation of powers – political, religious, financial – is suggested, which accords with the building's other gestures towards its surroundings. As well as its tall windows, the exchange room was lit from a semicircular panelled and glazed dome. A master's office adjoined it, and a gallery ran around the curved side of the space supported by Ionic columns. From the gallery, members could turn one way to use the library, and the other to look down upon their fellows at business below (one of the functions of the Exchange was to enable this very business of presenting itself as spectacle).[40] A picture gallery occupied part of the attic storey, no doubt included for its association with luxury goods.[41] There was also a room let out to the Post Office, following discussion with Manchester's postmaster, and this was a crucial facility for the communicational aspects of the Exchange, if one that marked an uncertain alliance between the private company or club and the public facility.[42] The flat-fronted end of the building, with its own minor entrance and its lettable rooms, was clearly treated as secondary. Above this end was a dining room that could cater for 300 people. Importantly, Harrison understood the necessarily mutable nature of his building; there was some inbuilt potential for expanding the main room into the master's office and the warehousing space.[43]

Already by the 1820s this inner remodelling, with its consequent clarification of the space, had occurred (see fig. 152). The old master's office and the warehousing space were entirely swept away in these revisions, making room for an opening out of the main exchange room right to the southern end of the building. This must have more than doubled its size, and certainly made the remaining shops peripheral (income from their lettings would also have been less important). The plan now met the expectations of its outer form: a great narthex space was provided by the lateral vaults on its southern end and a shortened nave was newly suggested in the middle of the building, while the curved north end was more apse-like.

As this implies, the idea of the exchange as a building form or typology had been quite loose in the early modern period, encompassing a range of commercial and meeting functions, and the first and second versions of the Manchester Exchange had inherited this.[44] Exchanges essentially housed merchants, which meant that they often also accommodated shops, taverns and eating places around a hall or courtyard, and often attracted more informal transactions in their vicinity (it was said in the 1840s that some 500 prostitutes would use the surroundings in the evenings for their own marketplace).[45]

Communication and commercial information were ramified through the Exchange, creating and extending networks – Hermes was the presiding deity.[46] This is what the large room was all about but also the sociable spaces off and around it, which sometimes extended into the nearby town and its taverns and coffee houses. Establishing creditworthiness on the basis of reputation, character and trust might well depend on both direct personal knowledge and the kind of information circulating informally by word of mouth as much as in print.[47] Also, members needed knowledge of prices and price movements, exchange rates, taxes, emerging markets, new commodities and threats to production. Hence the newsroom (Manchester boasted nine local newspapers by 1825), which was 'opened to subscribers resident in Manchester and its environs, to the distance of six miles, at two guineas each per annum; and to other persons who reside at a greater distance than six miles, but who have a warehouse open occasionally in town, one guinea per annum'.[48] Joseph Aston (the source here) noted also that the newsroom was a good incentive for merchants to end their habit of meeting outside, and the building itself now encouraged the idea that it was indeed possible to 'assemble in comfort'. Where exchanges housed a range of trades, as in London or Amsterdam, the individual trades had found their own spaces, leading to the trope of the 'microcosm', or the 'Babel of Tongues', being attached to exchanges and, relatedly, the desire to see the building as an epitome of its world-girdling trade.[49] Of course the emergence of its global significance became apparent in Manchester only in the late eighteenth century and it was then that the Exchange was rapidly transformed from gathering point in an essentially regional market to a vital node of a global network of trade and information.

What actually happened in the Exchange? We have impressionistic accounts from some contemporaries. Here is a visitor in 1841, who is worth quoting at length:

> *Were I asked how a stranger could best form a notion of the character of Manchester manufacturers, I should recommend him to visit the Exchange of Manchester at the period of 'high change'; that is, about noon on a Tuesday. It is the parliament of the lords of cotton – their legislative assembly – which enacts laws as immutable as those of the Medes and Persians, but, unlike every other parliament in the world, very much is done and very little is said ... Transactions of immense extent are conducted by nods, winks, shrugs, or brief phrases, compared to which the laconisms of the ancient Spartans were specimens of tediousness and verbosity. There is a kind of vague tradition, or rather remote recollection, that a man was once seen to gossip on the Exchange ... It has been my fortune to visit this place in a season of great commercial prosperity and activity, and more recently at this period of stagnation and depression. On the first occasion, a stranger would imagine that he had got into one of those communities of dancing dervishes whose rule inculcates silence and perpetual motion. It seems as if each man was incapable of remaining in the same spot for three continuous seconds ... The aspect of the Exchange at this period of commercial distress is perfectly appalling, there is a settled gloom on every countenance, accompanied with a restlessness of eye quite out of keeping with the contracted brow and the compressed lip. Eagerness is changed into obstinacy ... Whether trade be active or dull, 'high change' lasts little more than an hour: after the clock strikes two the meeting gradually but noiselessly melts away, without your being very well able to account for the disappearance of the several forms: before three the building is as empty and deserted as the catacombs of Egypt.*[50]

The passage is fascinating as much for its description of behaviour in the Exchange as for the way it steers wide of the specificities of the kinds of transactions taking place. Behaviour, we might say, stands in for trade. Exchange is embodied almost solely by gesture. All those laconic 'nods, winks, shrugs, or brief phrases' are how the bourgeoisie negotiates: sociability is a financial transaction. This may be a hall, an open space, but there must be no loud noises in it, no collective address.[51] An aggrandising reference is made to the ancient world. As for where this happens, and how it happens in relation to a specific space, all is vague again. What we know is that there must be intensity (the 'high change' of the middle of the day when most members would be present), proximity and movement. The Exchange must be a club but also a kind of transactional ballroom, a choreography of bodies, reputations and protocols of homosociality.

Thirty years after its completion, Harrison's Exchange was enlarged and entirely refronted by Alexander Mills between 1846 and 1849[52] (fig. 157). This was on top of an extension in 1841 – the brief jump to 799 square yards on the pink mountain graph we saw at the start of this chapter (see fig. 146). After Mills's additions

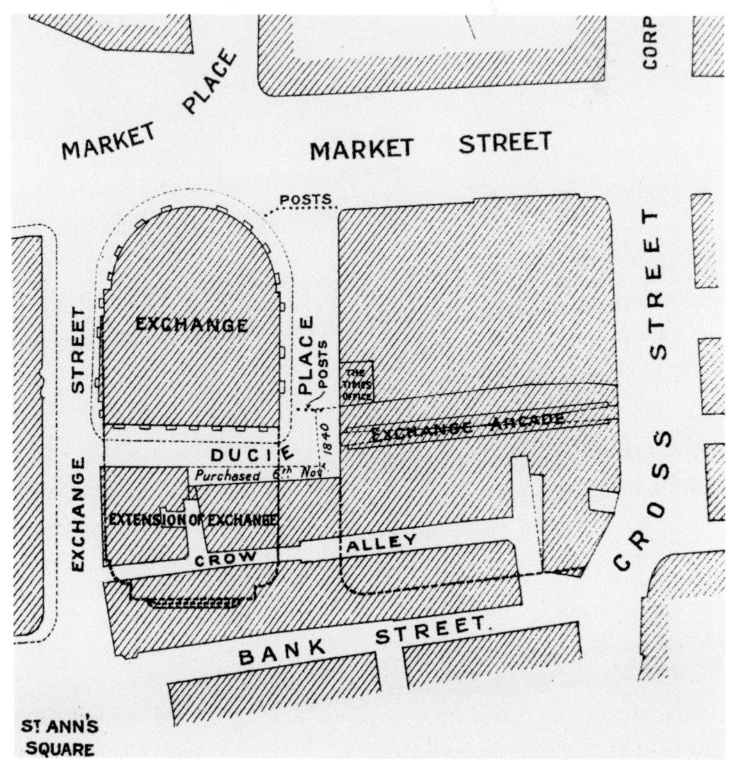

[157] Site plan showing the Exchange in relation to its surroundings following Alexander Mills's redesign of 1846–9, from T. de Courcy Meade, 'Paper Submitted to Improvement and Paving Committees of Manchester City Council' (1908).

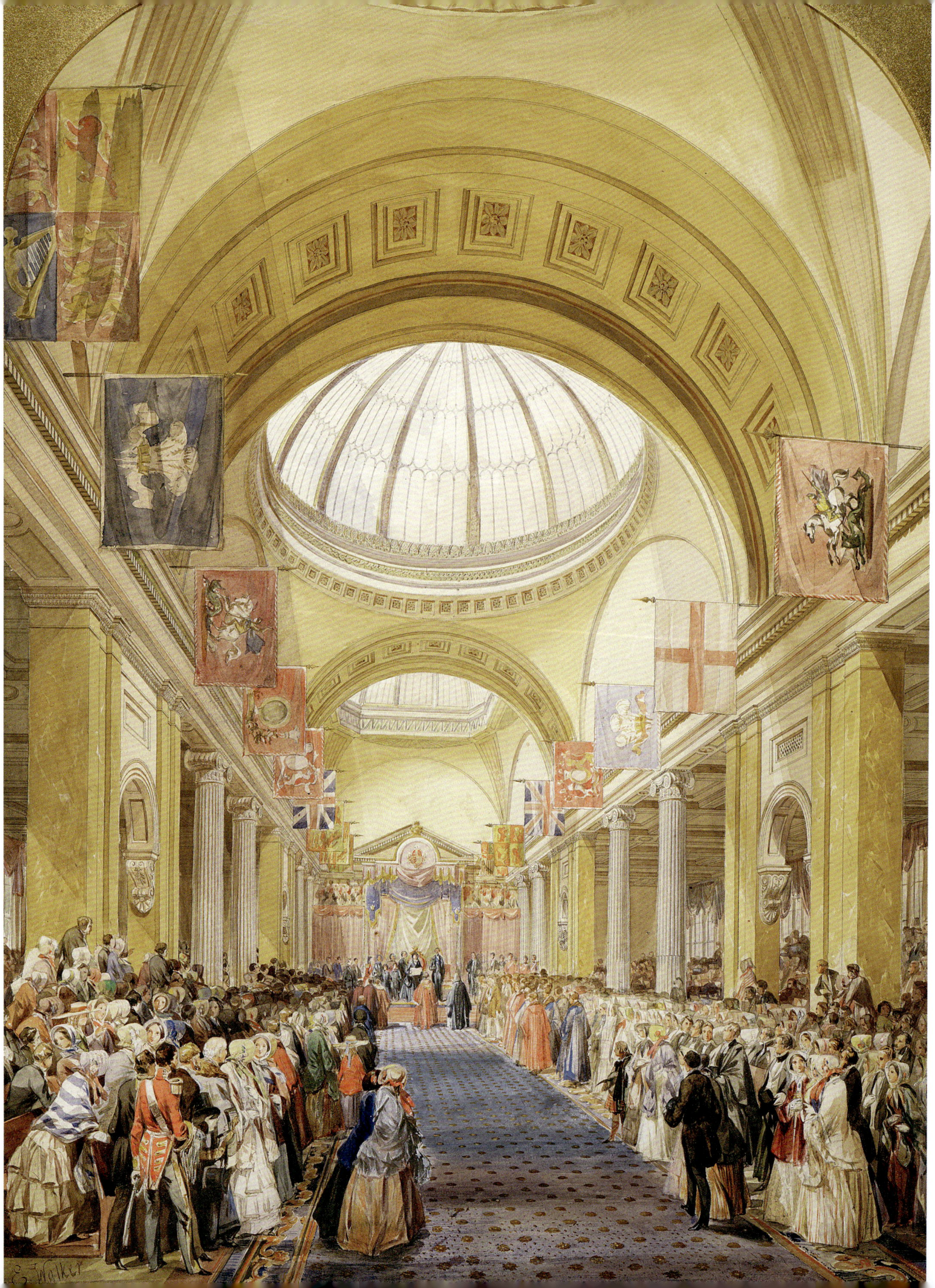
E. Walker

[158] Edmund Walker, *Visit of Queen Victoria to the Royal Exchange, Manchester in 1851*. Watercolour. Manchester Art Gallery.

[159] The Royal Exchange in its urban context, as adapted by Alexander Mills, 1846–9, following Thomas Harrison's design, c.1868. From H. J. Dyos and Michael Wolff, *The Victorian City: Images and Realities*, vol. 2 (1973).

[160] The Exchange after enlargement and refronting by Alexander Mills, 1848, from Edwin Simpson, *A Sketch of the History of the Manchester Royal Exchange* (1875).

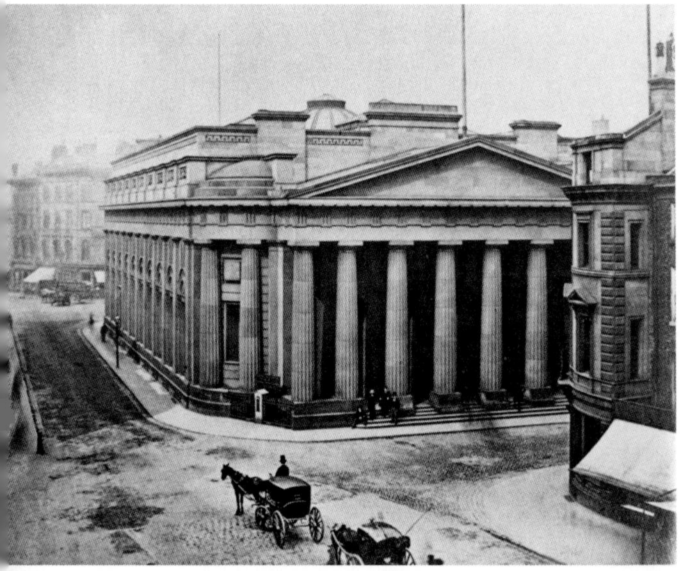

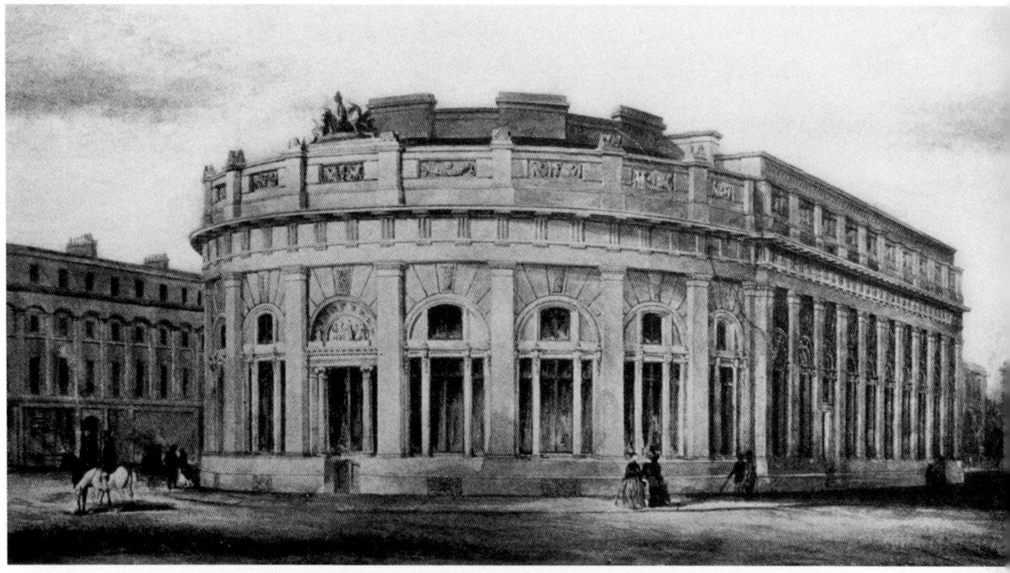

capacity more than doubled to 1,634 square yards. In conventional architectural terms, this combination of Harrison's and Mills's conceptions was probably the most distinguished of all iterations of the Exchange. Mills updated the building stylistically (by taking it back in time) and giving it a more forthright unity, but he also reversed its primary orientation, expanding the building and extending it southwards, which ate up more of the shops and businesses on this side of it. The interior could be understood as both a room and a hall for ceremonial events such as the queen's visit in 1851 (pillars that blocked the view down the length of the building were removed for this visit to create a space more like a throne room than an exchange[53]) (fig. 158). A succession of vaults and domes carried the eye down the length of the building towards what was now a definitive apsidal climax, complete with coffered semi-dome. To either side, pairs of columns screened almost aisle-like spaces into which trading floor activities might expand.

Not so much floating in the stream (as with the first Exchange), the building was now a blockage – a sizeable lump in the urban mass (fig. 159). A wide low pediment was positioned over the south front, signalling its new function as the main entrance (though this had to be temporarily reversed with the queen's visit, when one of the windows on the north side was reconverted into a door, the south entrance being too congested for royal dignity).[54] The Doric columns that supported the pediment and then also followed the building round its corners, the continuous cornice wrapping the building and the low dome over the main space all made the building strongly compact, emphasising a newly militant visual and physical autonomy from its surroundings – and one imagines, stressing the idea of the Exchange as a place of solidly implanted practices, of trust and of gentlemanly behaviour. These features also associate it with the numerous other institutional buildings, including banks and mints, that had by then been built in this Greek Revival style. The curved corners on the south side also presaged the great semicircular side of the building, the Doric columns – now attached as half-columns – continuing the stiff striding rhythm established at the front. Harrison's idiosyncratic doors on the north and west fronts have been erased by a sequence of grand arched windows occupying much of the height of the ground storey from just above the ground almost up to the cornice (fig. 160). Mills's refacing seems to have emphasised the openness or transparency of the building at this end while establishing a more conventional sense of decorum as regards its entrances: at one end it looks like a building for entertainment, perhaps a coffee house or even a theatre, while at the other it looks like a mint. Or, to put it differently and to return to the earlier analogy of Harrison's building drawing urban energies towards itself like a whirlpool and then radiating them outwards, Mills's building sealed itself up in an obdurate carapace and channelled those energies towards the new front, while it established the other end of the building as an image of transparency, an aquarium of traders. And yet the new rigid harmony and consistency of Mills's design hid its much greater impact on the city around it.

AS THE PINK MOUNTAIN GRAPH (SEE FIG. 146) SHOWED, the newly erected building of the late 1860s, which replaced Mills's, could be regarded as the first definitive Exchange in that it staked out a capacity consonant with the industrial and global scale of the business within. It so increased the floor space that, for nearly four decades, its capacity was more than equal to its membership. A second look at the graph, however, shows that the rise in membership had already slowed before the new building was designed, though Mills's work, despite being twice the size of its predecessor, had since shortly after its completion been inadequate to the number of members it ostensibly housed. Which was the greater period of the Exchange then? The middle decades of the nineteenth century, when it was flush with members and constantly bursting as a building, or the later decades, when its rise in membership stuttered and slowed down but its building had achieved a grandeur and scale beyond requirement?

Certainly grandeur, if of a stuffily distinguished kind, would appear to have been the projected character of the new building (fig. 161). This redevelopment had been kick-started in 1864, barely eighteen years after Mills's refurbishment job, when a new building, which would have an exchange room with nearly three times the capacity of the existing one (from 1,634 square yards to 4,405 square yards), was first planned. The site was again extended with land acquired, absorbing Ducie Place and Crow Alley (including, tellingly, the old headquarters of the Anti-Corn Law League). A competition was launched in 1867 while the old building was demolished. The local firm Mills & Murgatroyd (the same Alexander Mills) emerged as the winner.[55]

The exterior is a piece of neoclassical urban theatrics. A pedimented entrance portico facing eastwards to Cross Street is now raised by flights of steps above the road level, and the facades are articulated by double-height pilasters. Above a rusticated basement containing shops, the pilasters run from front to rear. In one corner of the site, at the junction of Market Street and Exchange Street, a tower with a dome and lantern provides a signal function – it was little more than that – on the city's skyline, anticipating the picturesque effects of the town hall then about to be built (see Chapter 4). Above a strong cornice, which ties the building together, the roofline was provided with a range of eye-catching devices – squat Italianate corner towers and attic storeys surmounted by miniaturised temples, lamps, and various sculptural accretions. It is as if the compact Greek Doric of Mills's resurfaced building had been reimagined for a different era, where the overriding consideration was much less about the relation to the street and much more about the generalities of institutional form. This could be a museum or a government building. Its decoration can be understood as an attempt to dress the facade so as to draw attention away from the building's now huge size. The road, the market and the surrounds are now neither to be opened up to (as with Harrison) nor to be defended from (as with Mills) but to be looked down upon, as the Exchange's bulk raises it disdainfully above street level. The new character of the building – both institutionally aspirational and nostalgic for a vision of authority – coincides with what Sven Beckert has characterised as the emergence of a new, state-led, conception of cotton trading.[56] Cotton in all its varieties was now standardised, with contracts specifying lot sizes of certain qualities. This was another move in the globalisation of the cotton trade through the internationalisation of its prices, agreed terms for its classification and rules for the arbitration of disputes. And the power of defining these now lay with the state. But the development also coincided with the immediate aftermath of the American Civil War and (as we saw in Chapter 4) this moment of great relief for the cotton industry was

[161] The Royal Exchange as redesigned by Mills & Murgatroyd, 1867–74. Photograph: James Mudd, *c.*1875. Manchester Libraries, Information and Archives.

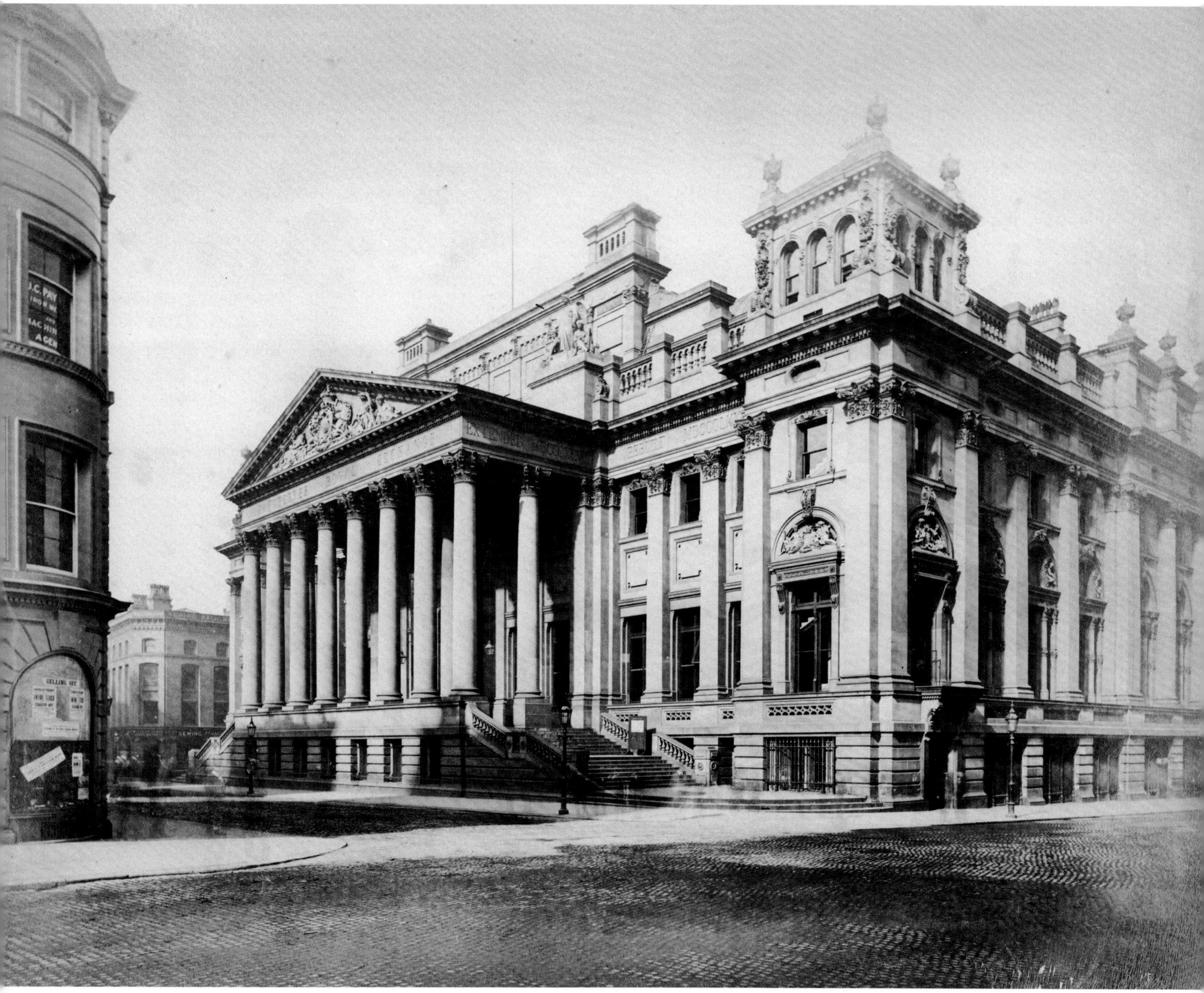

[162] The Royal Exchange: site plan showing the size of the Mills & Murgatroyd redesign compared with the extent of the existing building, from T. de Courcy Meade, 'Paper Submitted to Improvement and Paving Committees of Manchester City Council' (1908).

[163] The Royal Exchange: plan, from *Directory and Guide to the Manchester Royal Exchange* (1905).

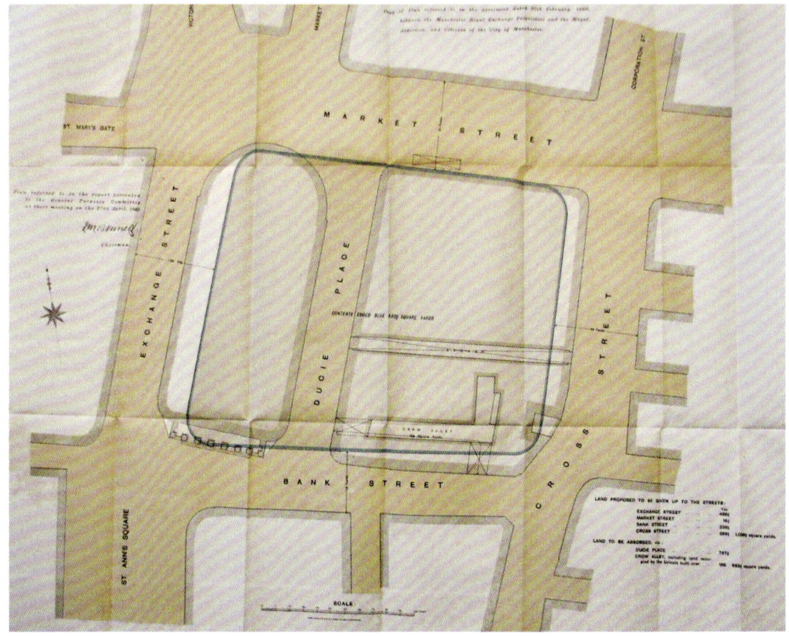

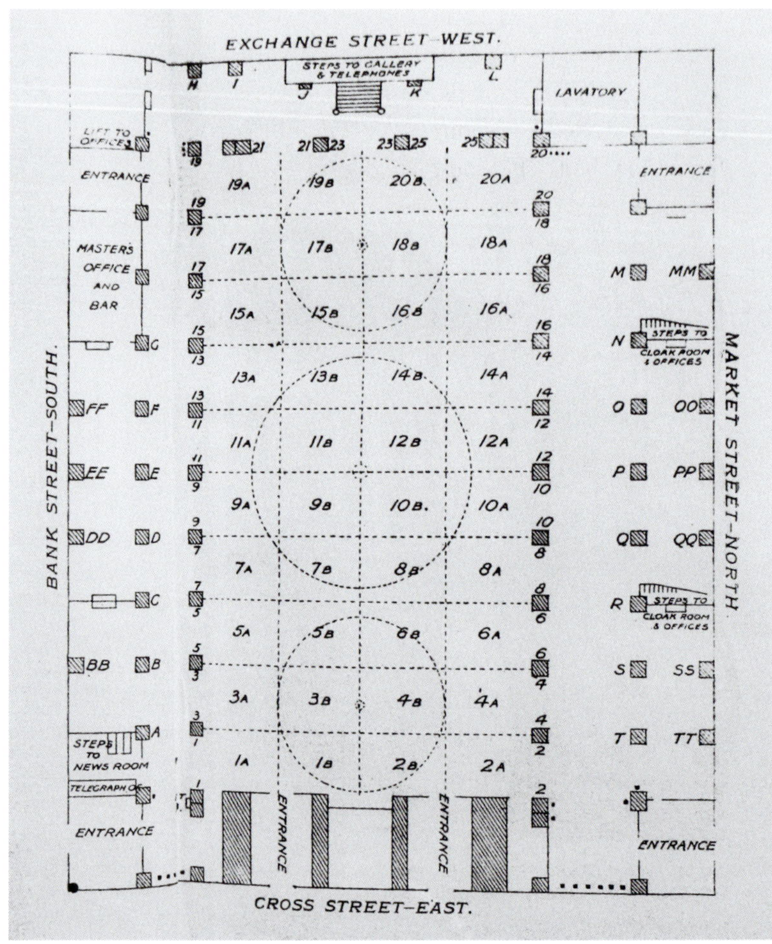

expressed in civic and institutional renewal. This institutionalisation, this new alignment with the organs of governance, took architectural form with the new Exchange of the late 1860s.

Within the building, constructed in two parts, was created the 'largest room in the world for commercial purposes'.[57] The Royal Exchange, whose honorific had been bestowed during the queen's visit in 1851, extended from Cross Street to Exchange Street, some 206 feet in length and 192 feet in width. Within a century and a half the size of the room in the first Exchange had been increased tenfold (fig. 162).

How would anyone orient themselves within such a large space? This chapter started with a painting of Mills & Murgatroyd's interior a few years after its completion, showing a sea of businessmen filling the room from side to side (see fig. 145). There is no sense of disorder in the painting, despite the multitude; while the businessmen are distributed evenly, they are not rigid or regimented. That, of course, might be a compositional device: Sargent and Saunders might simply have organised their portraits to ensure that the image bore some relation to business at 'high change' (the depicted individuals – 231 were identified in an accompanying key – had probably paid for their portraits, the cost determined by their size and visibility). But, in this huge space, how were businessmen to know where to find their partners, where to make a deal and where to direct their communication of those 'nods, winks, shrugs, or brief phrases'? The *Directory and Guide to the Manchester Royal Exchange* was the required manual. It was small enough to fit into an overcoat pocket and so stuffed with information that it seemed to provide all the data necessary for the businesses it promoted. Members were told the by-laws and their privileges and given the complete list of newspapers, periodicals and directories subscribed to by the Exchange. There was a list of firms, each with its telephone number, in the copy I consulted dating from 1905 (the tenth edition). Most relevantly, with regard to the use of the exchange room, there was another list of the principals and representatives of firms. Here most entries were given 'the letters, or number, in the Pillar or Square column [which] indicates the Member's usual position while on the Exchange'.[58] The plan of the Exchange, to which this list refers, was the single most important orientation device in the *Directory* (fig. 163).

The plan's purpose was to locate members of the Exchange. A new member would note the letter or number (or both) listed beside his entry and find it on the plan. The plan's central area combined both letters and numbers; around the pillars there were two numbers; and further to the sides, in the 'aisles' of the room, there were letters only. Walking into the room, a new member might look up and position himself under one of the three domes (the centre points marked on the plan would not have been of much use here), if he were in one of the more central locations, and compare it to the plan which projected the domes onto the floor space. Relating a dome overhead to the pillars along the side of the space – perhaps by counting off the number of pillars down the sides of the room or by seeing the numbers or letters marked on them – he would find his allotted location. Once he had found that location two or three times, he would probably use the plan only to locate members with whom he might want to conduct business.

The plan has only superficial similarities with the conventions of architects' plans. The user or member is clearly not the builder, client or fellow architect. The plan is distinctly cursory about all the outside walls of the Exchange, generalising its overall shape into one rectangle, and any relation to the city beyond is barely mediated by the names of the streets immediately around it. But entries are emphasised from these streets, endowing the Exchange with a sense of thin membranes and a permeability that reminds us of both the first Exchange and the Harrison-designed Exchange. Inside the building, the plan barely distinguishes between the footprint of different columns – all are crudely generalised into either a square or a double square. Necessary ancillary rooms are indicated – master's office and bar, telegraph room, steps to the newsroom and lavatories. It is the projected domes and the imagined grid of squares across the central area that are the real spatial rationale for the plan, a grid that is entirely invisible within the building itself.[59] If this is abstract rationality, it is of a kind that remains closed to outsiders; its space has not become part of the public domain and is only partially accessible to the public gaze.

A different kind of sense is made out of Sargent and Saunders's painting (see fig. 145) by the *Directory* plan. Studying the painting again, we seem to be facing towards the east or Cross Street side of the building, and to be looking between the two pillars marked 21/23 and 23/25 on the plan. And with some licence too, because the span we look between is either considerably widened (given the perspectival recession of the walls on either side) or, by implication, the pillars 21/23 and 23/25 have been edited out and we look at two others. With the *Directory* plan in mind, we can now understand that the distribution of members is even – if not regimented – across the floor of the Exchange, and made even in such a way that they can be related to the gridded squares on the plan. The immediate foreground, with the licence of the fictionally widened span, is taken up either by half of the square 19b and half of the square 20b, or (if the pillars have been edited out) by the squares 19a, 19b, 20b and 20a. The painters' image is not intended to guide the new member as much as to impress him with the corporate order.

We might say that two salient conceptions of architecture are simultaneously expressed by the exchange room. The first is more familiar: the saturation of surfaces with the re-creation of architectural forms from history (the columns, the domes, the gold-painted capitals, the ornamental panels and so on). The accumulation of reference here, its overproduction, exists in relationship to the commodities being traded, and there is a shared kind of emptiness to these figures (of architecture, of accumulation). This conception of architecture is also linked to the other institutions (and architecture) of bourgeois life – the kind of public formed by joining clubs and societies, attending concerts, gaining distinction through committees, trusteeships and executive positions. And we remember that the accompanying key to the painting made clear the painting's role as an exhibition of membership. The second conception of architecture, the trading logic of space, is linked to the first as a stage and enabler for networking and insider knowledge of codes of behaviour, but

[164] The Royal Exchange, as redesigned by Bradshaw Gass & Hope, 1914–21.

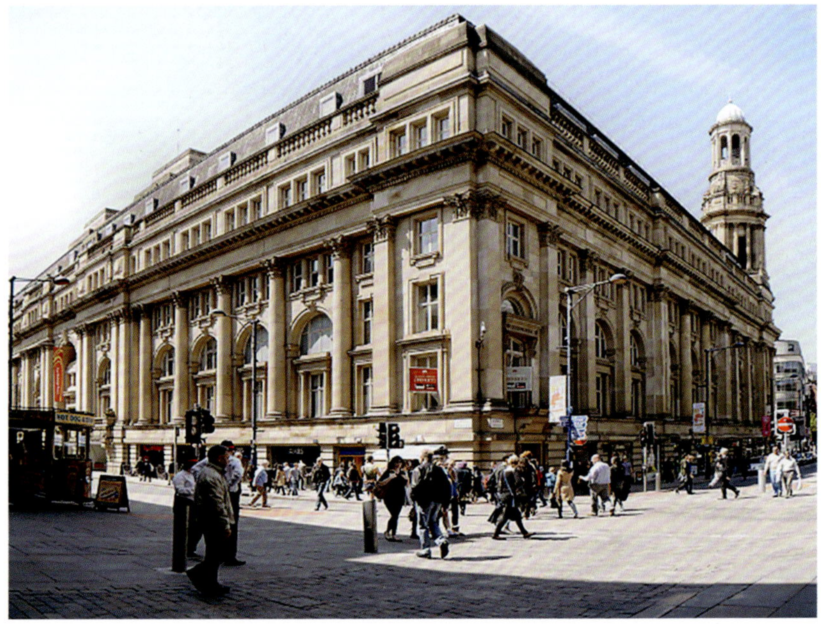

its 'invisible' aspects effectively organise its productive capacities, empowering the bourgeoisie to operate both collectively and in competition with each other. The porous, gridded, dome-encircled and grid-projected space is the instrument for this. This is the equivalent of the factory floor, if quieter (more of a 'hum and buzz of hundreds of conversations'), without commodities and machine-less.[60] In a famous insight Karl Marx suggested that the factory, which creates an exploited and atomised workforce, also inadvertently teaches collectivity and solidarity within the division of labour, thus forming the proletariat.[61] Similarly, it might be conjectured that the exchange room offers a parallel lesson. As the city of Free Trade architecture (Chapter 2) had given the class its urban identity, the exchange room teaches the bourgeoisie that, while as a class it might be competitive and might be portrayable as individuals, it is also socialised by its common space and commonality of activity (the two are inextricable here). This is in part what all the coffee houses, restaurants and taverns, and even the library, around the Exchange, and what membership itself, were about – the solidarity of collective socioeconomic life. But collective class identity is brought into its most intense expression – just as the factory floor was with its attendance on the machine – with the gathering, organising and activating functions impelled by the architecture of the exchange room. 'All that is solid becomes more so.'[62]

MEMBERSHIP OF THE ROYAL EXCHANGE FINALLY PEAKED at 11,539 in 1920. Thereafter, Britain's centrality to the cotton industry declined, and by 1939 subscription had slipped to 5,062.[63] A newly expanded, and in certain key aspects rebuilt, structure bridged the 1920s peak to the Exchange's tumultuous fall, the short post-war boom already retreating by the time of its completion in 1921. The Exchange is still there (now partly occupied by a theatre that was designed in the 1970s to stand autonomously within its large room). The commission to rebuild it had been won in the inauspicious year 1914 by the Bolton-based architects Bradshaw Gass & Hope, and was finally completed seven years later[64] (fig. 164). The architects now accepted the reality that the Exchange could no longer be considered as just another free-standing building. Their design was neither especially open to the city (as Harrison's building had been) nor a compact object in its flows (as Mills's design had suggested) nor even the aloof institution of Mills & Murgatroyd's confection, but instead accepted its logic as a monster block (seemingly denied by the previous incarnation). Another room of the same scale was added to the exchange room, the entrance was replaced (and established on the other side of the complex), the exterior was reclad and its height and capacity extended with an attic storey and a mansard roof. Finally, an arcade for shops was drilled through the block from east to west.

The Exchange was now a huge mega-structural thing, an architected city block containing ten floors of offices, shops at ground level, restaurants and once again a post office. From the exterior, most of the older signs of the Exchange had been reduced to the angle tower still on its north-west corner – like the surviving leg of an upturned table – with the entrances now placed east and west. The rest was a collocation of different architectural forms – corner dome, dormered roof, three-storeyed arched entrance, attic storey, attached columns and pilasters arranged according

[165] Interior of the Royal Exchange (with the Royal Exchange Theatre, 1976) in 2014.

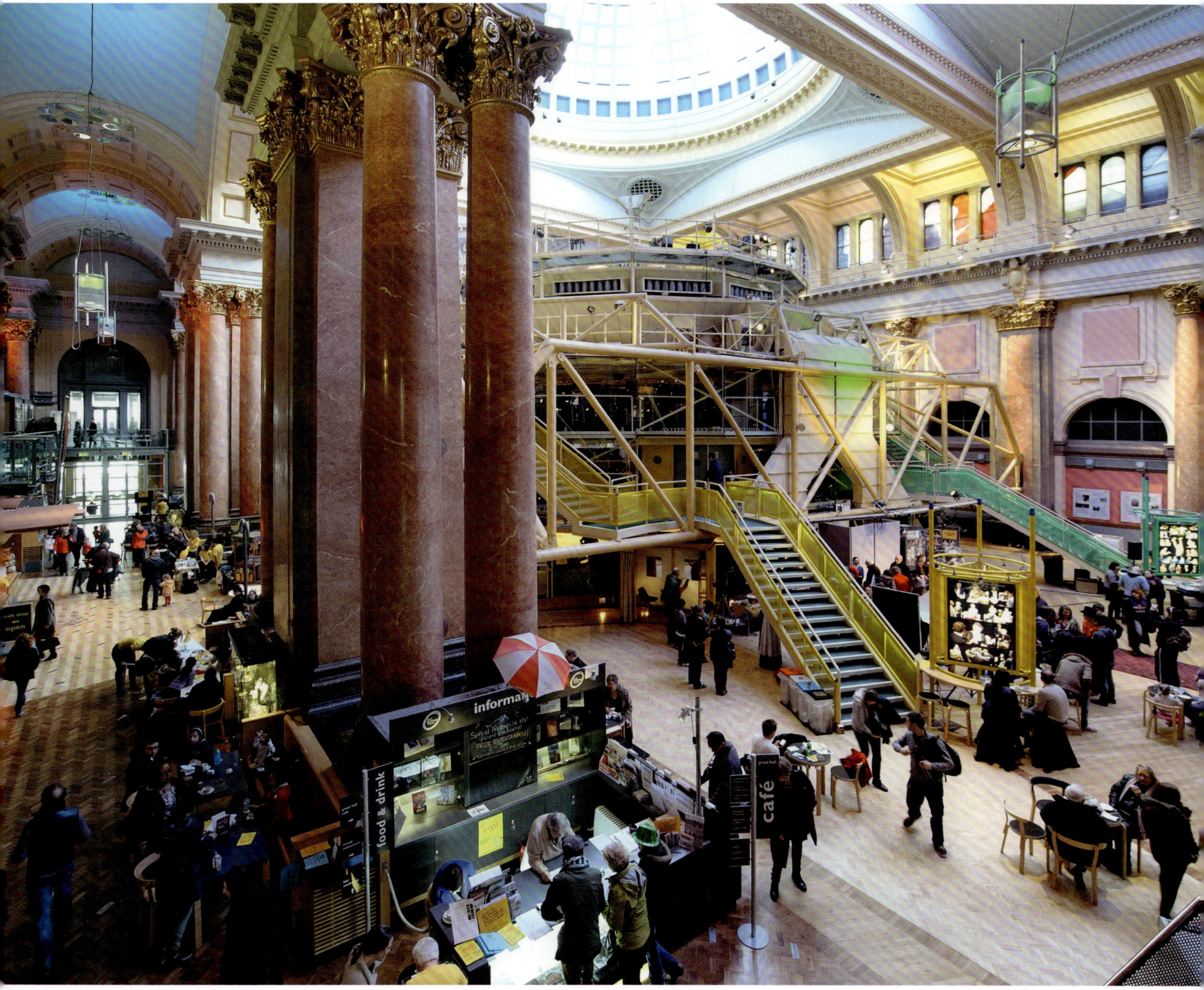

to different rhythms – all barely held together visually by a cornice and a band above the basement level. It would be easy to mistake this as a kind of department store, except that it outscaled anything yet conceived. It was impossible to step back from this mass and scan its various parts. The point about this new iteration was that architecture was not to express the unity of a whole building, to project certain ruling ideas of an institution (as with Mills & Murgatroyd's design), nor even the innovative ideas of Harrison's conception about what an Exchange should be. The passer-by, the pedestrian, would perceive not so much a unity as a congeries of different relations to the streets and the surrounding city.

As with every iteration of the building, the entrances are particularly telling. The first Exchange had been open on two sides to the surrounding market. Harrison's building had expressed its porosity in a subtler and more guarded way. In Mills's reworking the entrance was shifted away decisively from the market and to the southern side, where it was framed by a Doric temple front. Mills & Murgatroyd's redesign relocated the entrance on the east side within a raised portico. The sequence is extraordinary – turning and turning about the ingress function, addressing it to the city in very different ways. And in its final iteration, the function received its most modest form, with entrances one bay wide and barely announced on the building's east and west sides, narrow funnels as if the city outside meant little to the multiply-domed spaces inside.[65]

At the heart of all this, cocooned as it were in the surrounding layers, was an exchange room twice its previous size (fig. 165). The hugely increased capacity of the room was manifest in its triplet of domes above, with three more beyond. In photographs after its completion, the same sea of hats, many now bowlers, can be seen at 'high change' but there was a new communicational element. Huge boards on the walls recorded the transactions in raw cotton taking place in New York and Liverpool, the prices of cotton around the world and the movement of ships on the Manchester Ship Canal, while 'smaller boards [announced] the telephone numbers of those members for whom there are telephone calls'.[66] 'Attendance on the boards', as it was known, was now a crucial addition to the currency of information and interaction. And above the boards, around the rim of the centremost dome, was written the hopeful admonition, 'Who seek to find eternal treasure must use no guile in weight or measure'.

All this – the domes, the space, the human network, the global information – might be understood as creating a 'vision of totality', an even more overwhelming one than had been seen in any of the iterations of the Exchange.[67] This is not to say that it was transparent or explicable. The levels of abstraction, the opacity or incomprehensibility of operations on exchanges, are famous. How could a 'unifying viewpoint' be found for the complexities of production, distribution and consumption, and the vast multitude of commodities, that an institution like an exchange enabled to be brought together?[68] So what relation do these seemingly incompatible statements have with each other – the 'vision of totality', architecturally established or enabled, and something that has no 'unifying viewpoint'? Is there a way of, as it were, parsing from the 'nods, winks, shrugs, or brief phrases' down below, through the invisible gridding of the floor, the boards and their information, all the way to the domical pretensions above? Or is it a vision that is riven by contradiction between the decipherable and the indecipherable, the palpable and the spectral – the telephone numbers, the cotton prices, the redolent place names on the boards, the obscure codes and manners, and the quasi-theological domes above (with their 'frozen cosmology'[69]) as if the denizens and doings of such a place have some relation to the gods and the heavens? The kind of cognitive mapping essayed with smoke in Chapter 5 is relevant to what is going on in the Exchange: the movements of cotton can be traced through architectural spaces and seen as excluded by their abstraction from this destination. The difference is that we have here a set of components that play with the belief that they represent totality, through various representational codes, but at the same time do not add up to a cognitive whole: they map at the same time as they refuse mapping.

WE MIGHT PERHAPS LOOK OUTSIDE THE EXCHANGE TO find an indirect but highly specific materialisation of cotton's global logic. A new kind of acceptance of the Exchange's expansive space can be found in the report commissioned from the city's

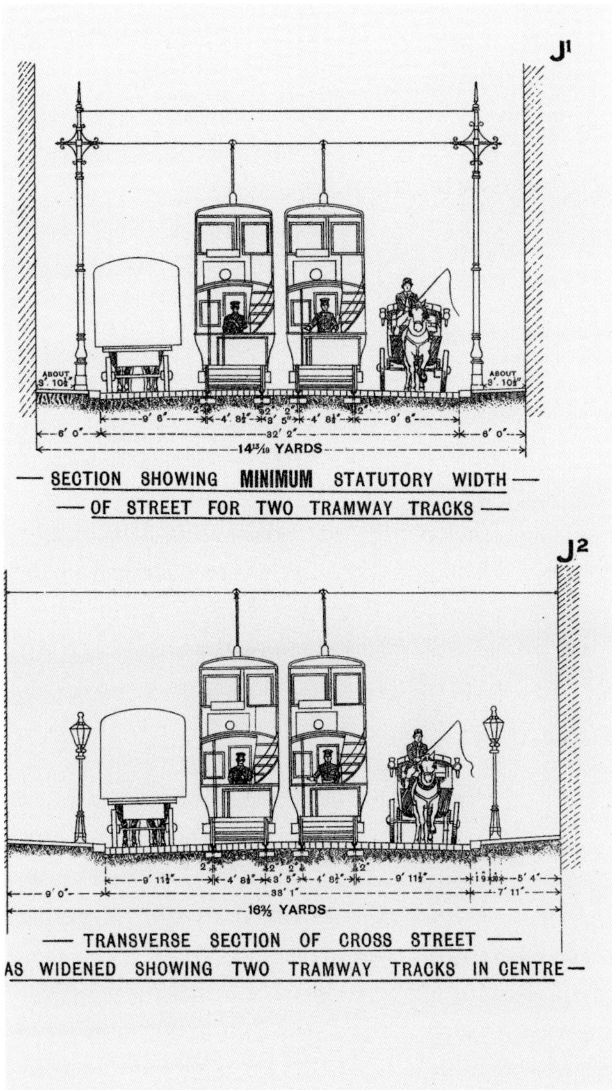

[166] Transverse sections of Cross Street, showing the effect of the Exchange's expansion on pavements and roads, from T. de Courcy Meade, 'Paper Submitted to Improvement and Paving Committees of Manchester City Council' (1908).

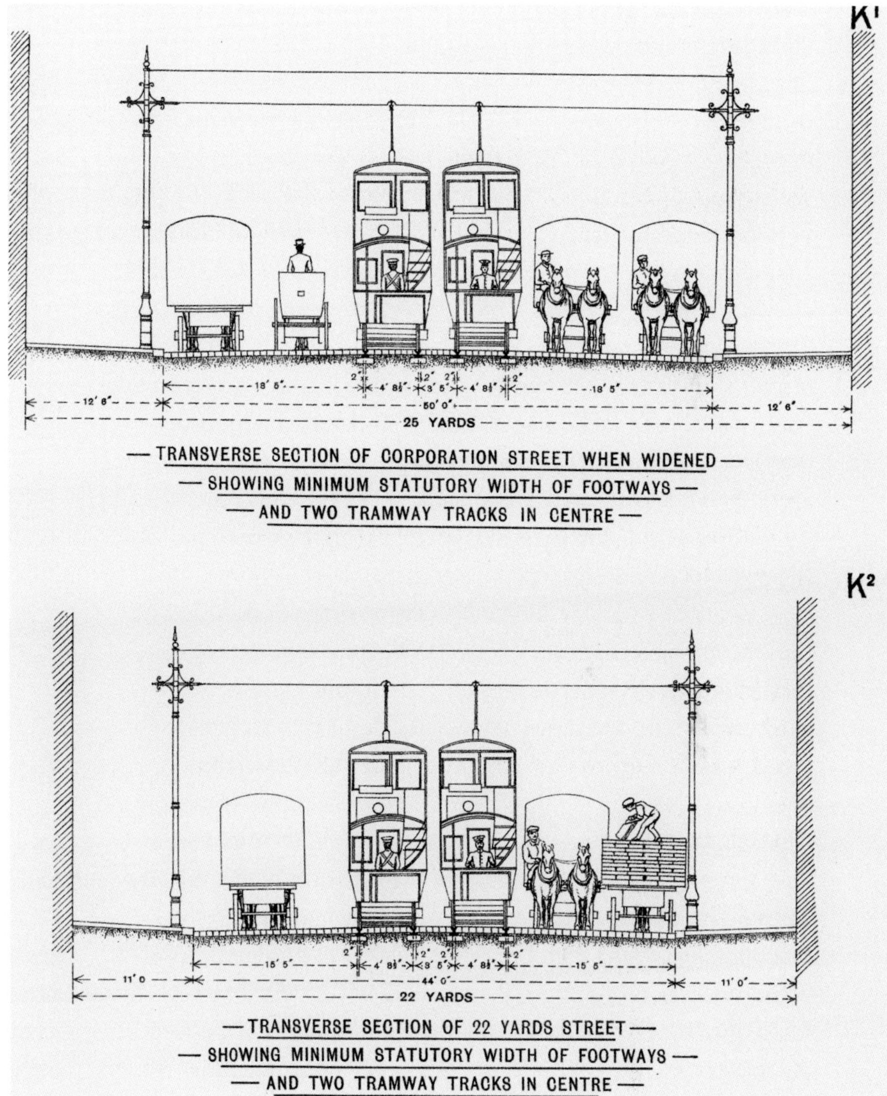

[167] Transverse sections of Corporation Street, showing the effect of the Exchange's expansion on pavements and roads, from T. de Courcy Meade, 'Paper Submitted to Improvement and Paving Committees of Manchester City Council' (1908).

surveyor, one Thomas de Courcy Meade, by a parliamentary subcommittee in 1908 (the same arguments were also used when a parliamentary bill was brought forward five years later[70]). Meade reasoned that the building could never be conceived of as a private trading concern because it was always tied to the city's commercial interests, and its increasing scale overtook any notion of give and take between it and its surroundings. Meade traced this history forwards from the first street-widening Act in 1776, showing how the Exchange was progressively inflated, pushing at the city and bursting its bounds. Expansion and overcrowding inside had led periodically to widening, improvement, lengthening and adjustment in the streets outside. Meade's understanding of the 1866 Mills & Murgatroyd scheme is telling. That building had taken over streets but had also 'given up to the streets areas on

[168] Site plan showing proposed extensions in 1913, with figures showing the growth in membership and the size of the Royal Exchange, from *Proposed Extension of the Manchester Royal Exchange* (1913).

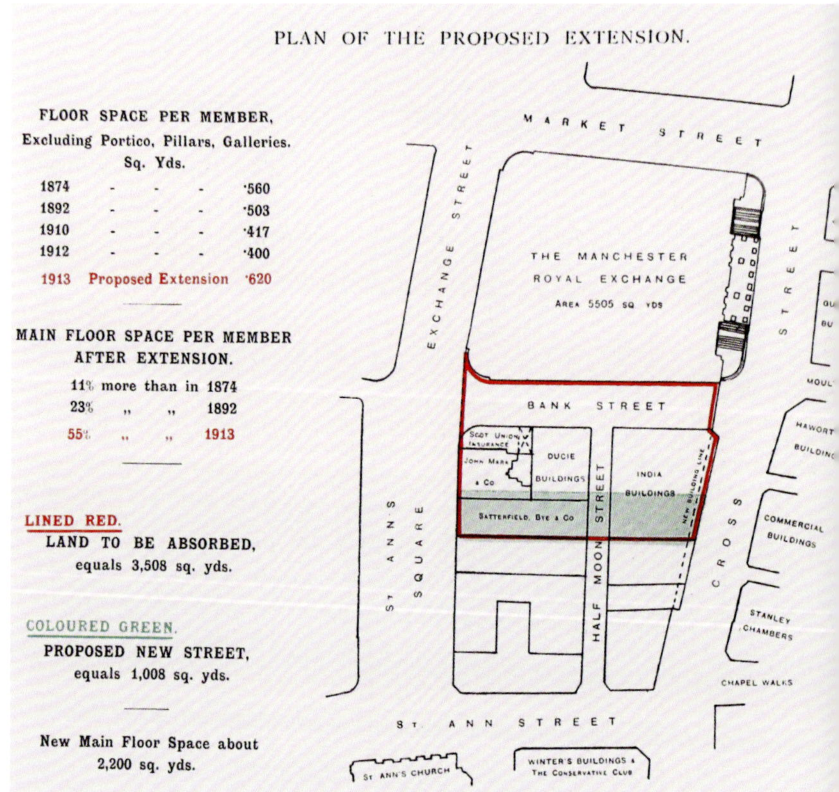

Cross Street, Bank Street, and Exchange Street'.[71] For Meade the surveyor public space could be gained, despite the Exchange's own impetus: the swallowing up of streets and lesser buildings could produce a civic benefit in what the Exchange had 'given up', in other words wider and more regularised streets would result. And so, in his plan, 'Proposed Site for the New Royal Exchange', a great blue-bordered squarish mass (it includes pavements and their rounded corners) sits astride the city's existing streets (in yellow), showing how the Mills & Murgatroyd scheme extinguished Mills's portico and expanded well beyond it (see fig. 162). But Meade's arrows show gains – the twenty-yard-wide Exchange Street and the twenty-yard wide Cross Street. The expanded Exchange, taking over Ducie Place and the neighbouring block of buildings to the east, has actually released more land for the flow of streets on three sides of it. 'Land to be absorbed' is complemented by 'land to be given up to the streets'.

Meade's historical reflections had a bearing, of course, on his present. In 1908, examining the various proposals and counter-proposals, he was most interested in their implications for the surrounding city. He showed the squarish mass as an established fact but more recently another local factor had entered the equation – trams arrived in the city, first horse-drawn in 1877 and then electrified in 1901. One line runs directly down Cross Street, right beside the east side of the Exchange. There was now a problem with the extensions that the proprietors wanted on this boundary of the building. Meade shows two diagrams: one with two sections for Cross Street and the other with two sections for Corporation Street. Each of these has variations of existing and widened widths, with trams on tracks, traffic on either side and pavements on either side beyond (the electric cables in one diagram are attached to the neighbouring buildings) (figs 166 and 167). The Tramways Act in 1870 for horse-drawn trams had laid down minimum widths between the tracks and the pavement, though this was modified by the Manchester Corporation Tramways Act of 1900 to allow the reduction of pavements to a minimum of six feet on roads with tramways.[72] 'Improvement' and 'street widening' – always a matter of a few feet to the good here and a few feet to the worse there, depending on your relation to it – now clearly measure the relation between globalisation and locality. What followed – though now in the Exchange's immediate environs – was a return to the issue of bodies in space, of capacity as a calculus of the number of persons to size of space (pushed to its extreme, as we have seen, at those moments in the middle of the day before and after 'high change').[73] The diagrams therefore show an equivalent to Sargent and Saunders's painting, measuring congestion where traffic is now the unit of density as much as human bodies (in the roadway itself, human bodies were strictly contained within the volumes of their vehicles). On Cross Street, Meade counts some 42,000 pedestrians passing every working day within an aggregate width of pavement of just over twenty-three feet. On each of these days over a thousand vehicles pass on each of four lines of traffic, over 4,000 daily within a road width of 36 feet. This congestion, Meade argued, was directly in relation to the successive enlargements of the floor space of the Exchange as its membership increased, which for the past twenty years had been at a rate of 1.53 per cent per annum. There was 'no reason to suppose that the rate of increase ... is likely to be less in the future'.[74] The scale and expansiveness of the world-circling business of cotton, the pressure of members' bodies on the bounds of the Exchange (as well as the new suburban expansions allowed by the tram), are here distilled to a matter of negotiating a few feet on a pavement – this was one of its measures. The measure was succinctly pictured when a bill came to Parliament a few years later (fig. 168).

On one level, what was at stake here was traffic management: the increasing traffic of the early twentieth-century city was one pressure on urban space, but added to it, on a more fundamental level, was the pressure of the continually space-eating Exchange. The Exchange's architectural history records no simple movement from obscurity to rationality, from pre-industrial mercantilism to the attainment of the civic city of free circulation. If the Exchange was a kind of thermometer, to use Engels's analogy, of the dynamic technological, geographical and social changes as a result of the Industrial Revolution, the temperature neither rises evenly nor settles into predictable patterns.[75] And, if it is a thermometer, it is part of the phenomenon whose changes it registers. As this chapter has shown, architecture and urbanism made the global financing of the cotton trade visible but they also made it happen. In the Exchange's triadic space – interior, locality, world – the two outer spaces of interior and world seem most obviously to be speaking to each other (however abstracted that dialogue might be), while the middle space seems to go missing, a mere consequence of the dialogue beyond it. But the street is both a border and a river: a border that registers the material impact of the Exchange's expansive, globally defined logic on its immediate Manchester environs; and a river that conducts the city's flows around its great constructions.

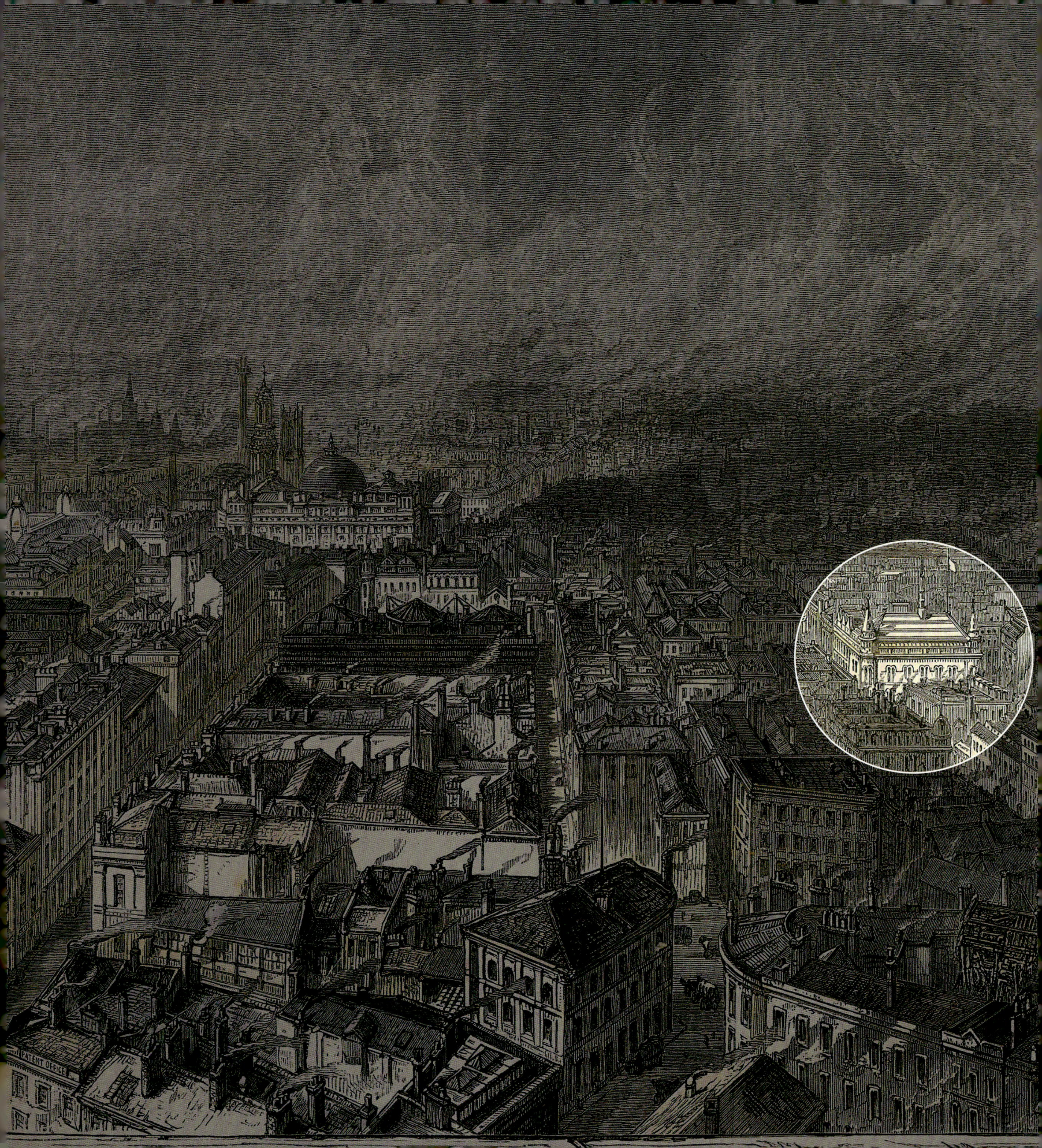
PATENT OFFICE

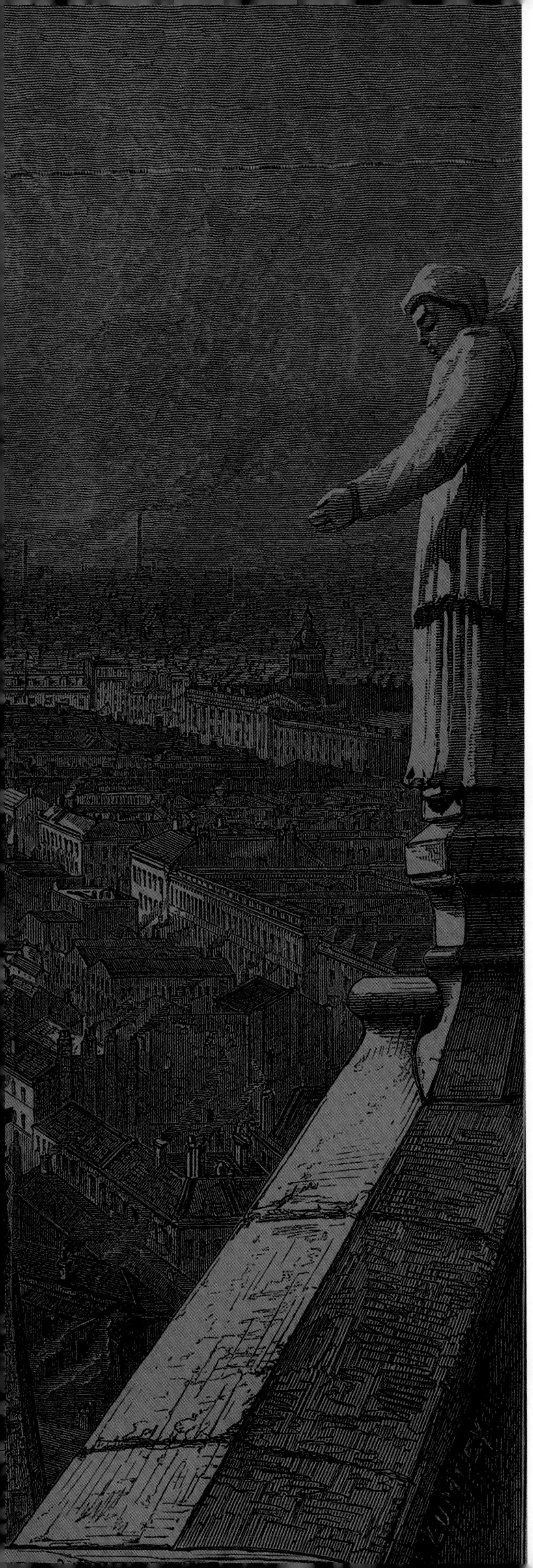

[169] 'Bird's-Eye View of the City from the New Town Hall Tower'. Engraving published in *The Graphic*, 14 October 1876.

Coda

CHARITY'S GESTURE IN THE IMAGE WITH WHICH THIS book started could be taken as pointing directly towards one of the best-lit buildings in the engraving (fig. 169). Never, though, was a building or its users less in need of charity. What we see is a steep roof with bands of coloured tiles. There is a jauntiness about its *flèche* and projecting corner turrets (even a white flag that seems attached to the roof). Below all this is a more orderly facade – an ornate attic storey above a range of coupled Gothic windows. Not visible in this view are the sculpted panels on those turrets, representing allegories of the arts and the sciences, a reprise of the sculptures on the Free Trade Hall.[1] This building is the Reform Club, and it was one of a number of neo-Gothic buildings erected in the streets around the Town Hall in the 1860s and 1870s. The height of the view gives prominence to the coupled and pointed second-floor windows; behind them is a billiard room that runs the whole length of this storey. Below it, not visible on the engraving, are the club's double-height dining room and meeting room. The whole building is devoted to the principle of the bourgeoisie's right to leisure; the new Venetian oligarchy at play, conveniently located near its political and bureaucratic machine – the Town Hall.

Fifty years later the American photographer Alvin Langdon Coburn, then living in north Wales, was commissioned to produce five photogravures for a commemorative volume, *The Manchester Reform Club, 1871–1921* (1922).[2] Coburn was – in any conventional understanding of the term – a modernist, fully credentialised by his Cubist-inspired vortographs of 1917. But what his Manchester clients wanted from him was more akin to his Symbolist-tinged pictorialist work of the early years of the twentieth century.

Coburn himself related this work, with its urban subjects, to James McNeill Whistler's notions of a city's essential nature: the artist, so the Whistlerian credo went, should evoke the time

> *when the evening mist clothes the riverside with poetry, as with a veil, and the poor buildings lose themselves in the dim sky, and the tall chimneys become campanili, and the warehouses are palaces in the night, and the whole city hangs in the heavens, and the fairy-land is before us.*[3]

This was strictly for those with the time to dream about such conditions; the dissolution of the city's harsher materialities is a kind of Midas-like transmutation into poetic veils and loose historical associations. It also depended upon another illusion. For workers, apparently mired in their humdrum existence, there was only – as the poet Arthur Symons, one of Coburn's collaborators, wrote – 'a listlessness, a hard unconcern, a failure to be interested'.[4]

Coburn's images trace an ascent through the Reform Club's interiors. We pass with them up the main staircase, into the dining room on the *piano nobile*, to the library and finally to the billiard room (accorded two images, one of a 'well-known corner' and the other looking across the unused tables). The most striking aspect of these photographs is their solemnity, their portentous sense of absence; although everything is ready to use or move through, no club members are to be seen. The staircase seems tight and constricted, a zone of tense transit (fig. 170). Above a barred landing rail the stairs reach up to a trapped marble bust – John Bright, senior statesman of the Liberal Party and one of the sainted founders of Free Trade – and what we can see of three framed portraits. Black, four-square newel posts guard the route like outer bastions of some angular castle wall. In the dining room, decanters and plates are laid out on fresh tablecloths and empty chairs wait to be pulled out, while the pearly light – surely not smog – reaches in through long vertical windows and settles blurredly on the polished wood and light fittings (fig. 171). The library is a tight masculine space, one corner of which is firmly centred on in the photograph with a triangle of patterned carpet closed off by shelves of glowing book spines (fig. 172). Members might be 'almost lost in [the] depths' of this obscure corner, the haunt of 'the ghosts of bygone members'.[5] A low, wide, leather seat, 'the most comfortable and seductive of armchairs',[6] signifies the active body's place of retreat. It seems both to hail us as its desired occupant and to mark some absent person, suggesting an equivalence between both. The light itself, whether scattered across most of the image by the book spines, more softly spread by the carpet or picked up in measured highlights by the armchair and side table, offers a compensating animation for the absence at the photograph's centre.

In photographs of the billiard room, named in the book as the club's most important room for its encouragement of interaction among coteries of members, male sociability is signalled in one image by casually placed Thonet chairs in the 'well-known corner'. But this is strangely counteracted in another image by the billiard tables themselves (fig. 173). Here the repeated tabletops and the clustered light shades overhead are evocative of some workspace where labour is to be intensely lit but saved from degrading repetition by the refinements (skill, improvisation, strategy) of the game. Labour at the billiard table – leaning down and attending to the cue, the work of potting balls – is, it is picturesquely inferred, a summoning up of the factory floor. (Members of the Royal Exchange also had a plentiful supply of billiards tables.) Coburn's photographs cannot but direct us to these kinds of ideas. Their ostensible subject might be the different rooms and services provided by the Reform Club, but they also induce in us a vicarious identification with the club's values and pleasures. They may intimate the industrial world this all derives from, but their main job is to conjure up the benefits of a gentlemanly public life, the fraternal influence endowed by association and the ghostly auras of the worthies who have gone before.

The language of Coburn's book itself parallels the images. It intimates insubstantial but redolent matters like 'exudations of grey cloth', the 'abode of the spirit', 'seams of genuine history', a 'lingering tradition' and a 'dynastic character'.[7] It includes an elegiac essay by Arthur Symons in which he wrote of how he could recall previous members as he 'saw and spoke to them in the hall, on the stairs, in the dining room, at committee meetings … They are all gone, and there are very few of their contemporaries and comrades left.'[8] Any hint of decline has been made over into

[170] 'The Staircase from the Second Landing', 1922. Photogravure. Photograph by Alvin Langdon Coburn for *The Manchester Reform Club, 1871–1921* (1922).

[171] 'The Dining Room', 1922. Photogravure. Photograph by Alvin Langdon Coburn for *The Manchester Reform Club, 1871–1921* (1922).

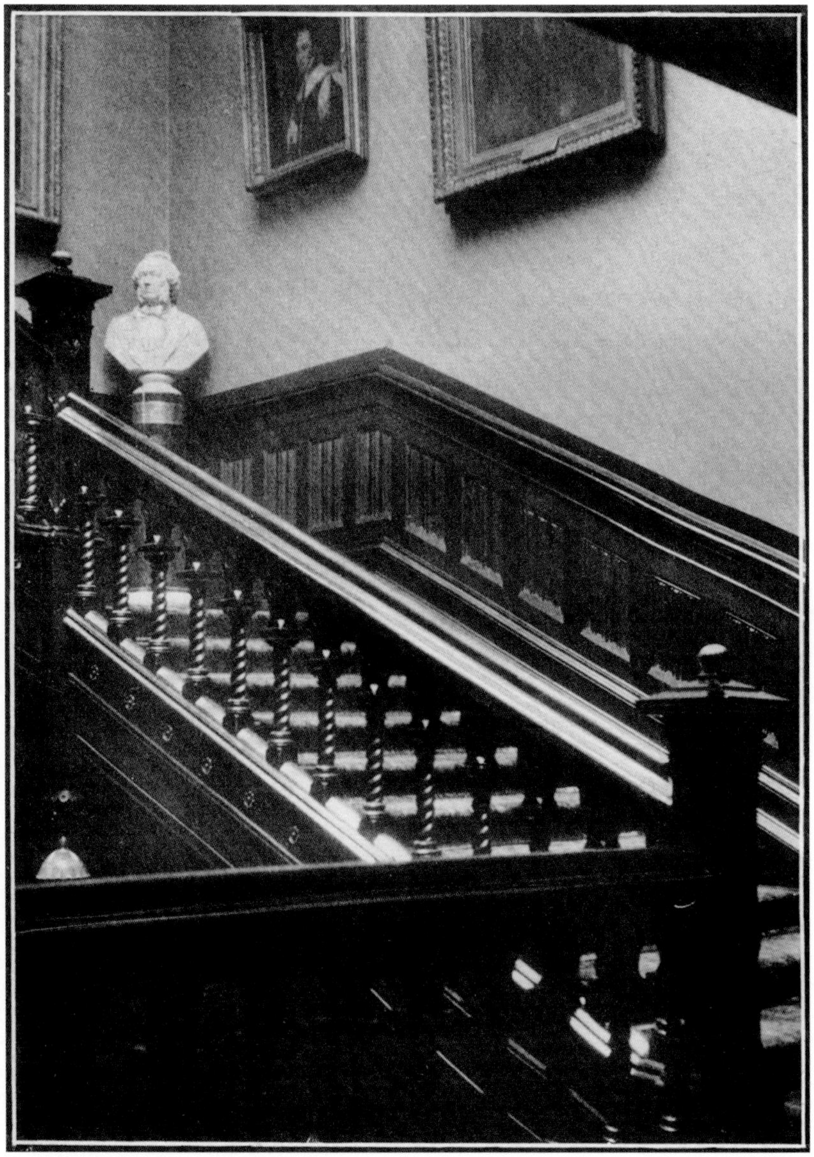

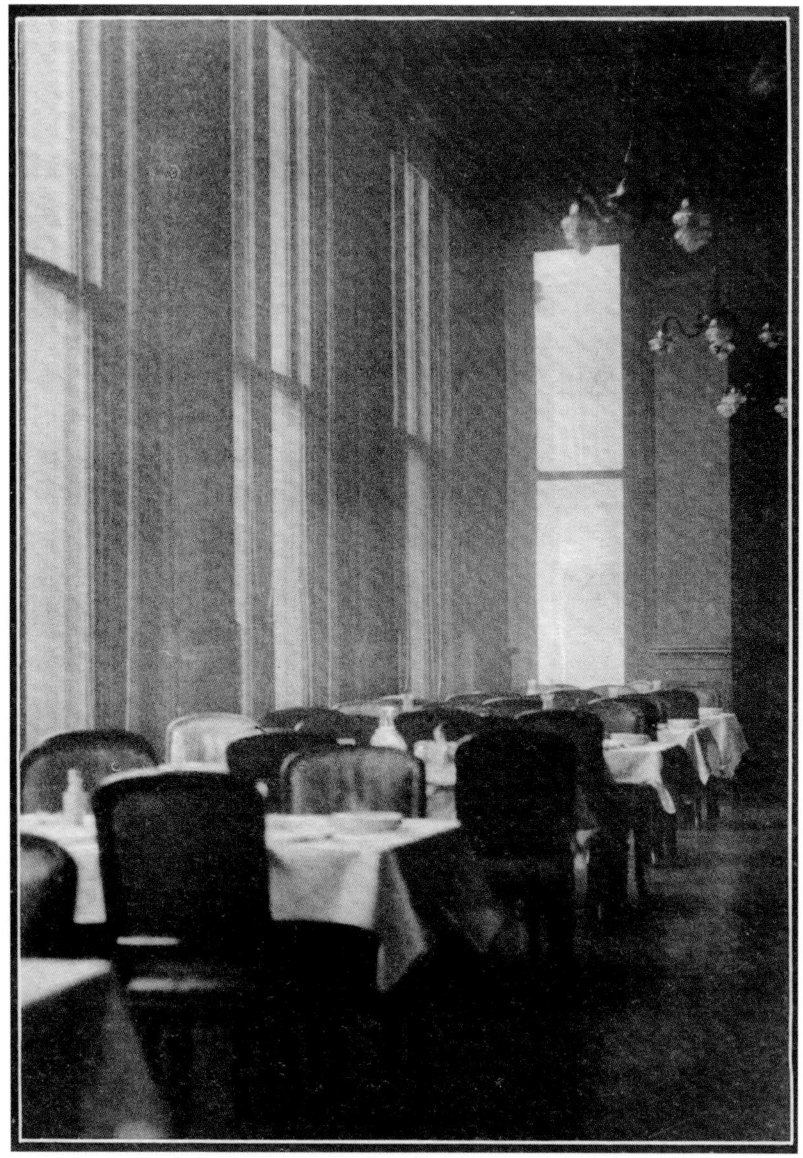

[172] ‘A Corner of the Library’, 1922. Photogravure. Photograph by Alvin Langdon Coburn for *The Manchester Reform Club, 1871–1921* (1922).

[173] ‘The Billiard Room’, 1922. Photogravure. Photograph by Alvin Langdon Coburn for *The Manchester Reform Club, 1871–1921* (1922).

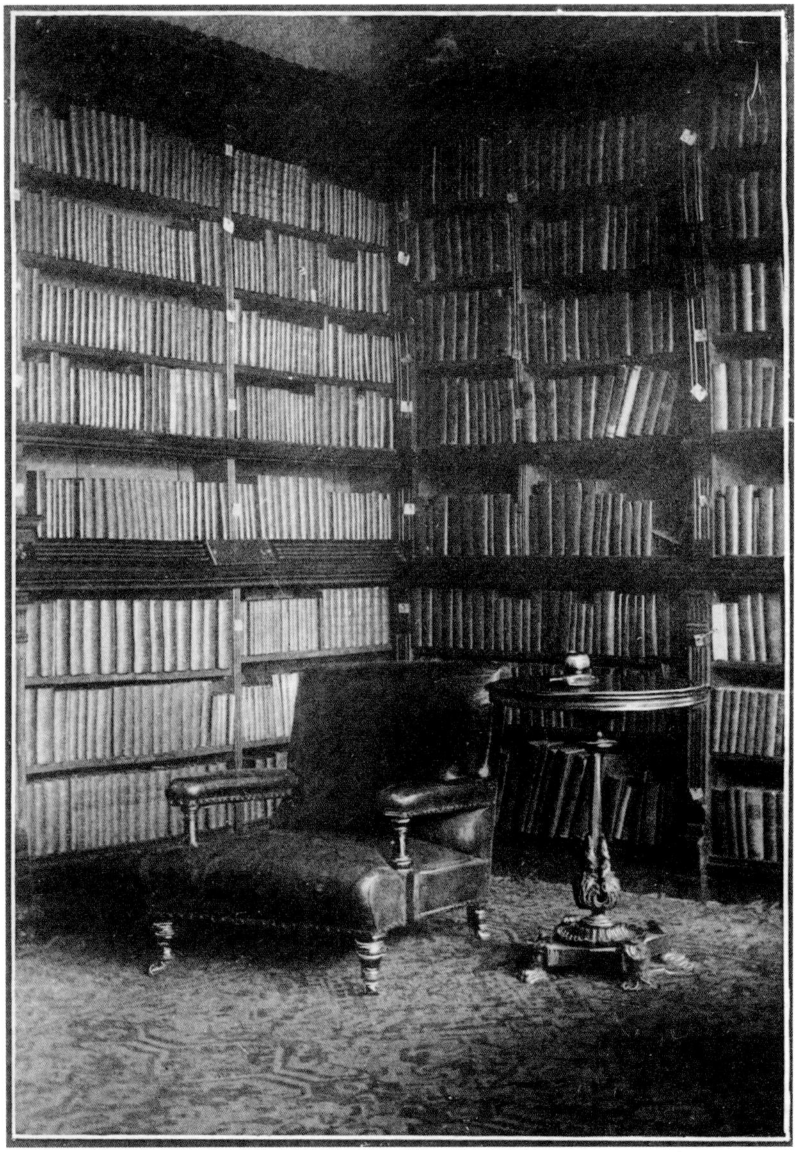

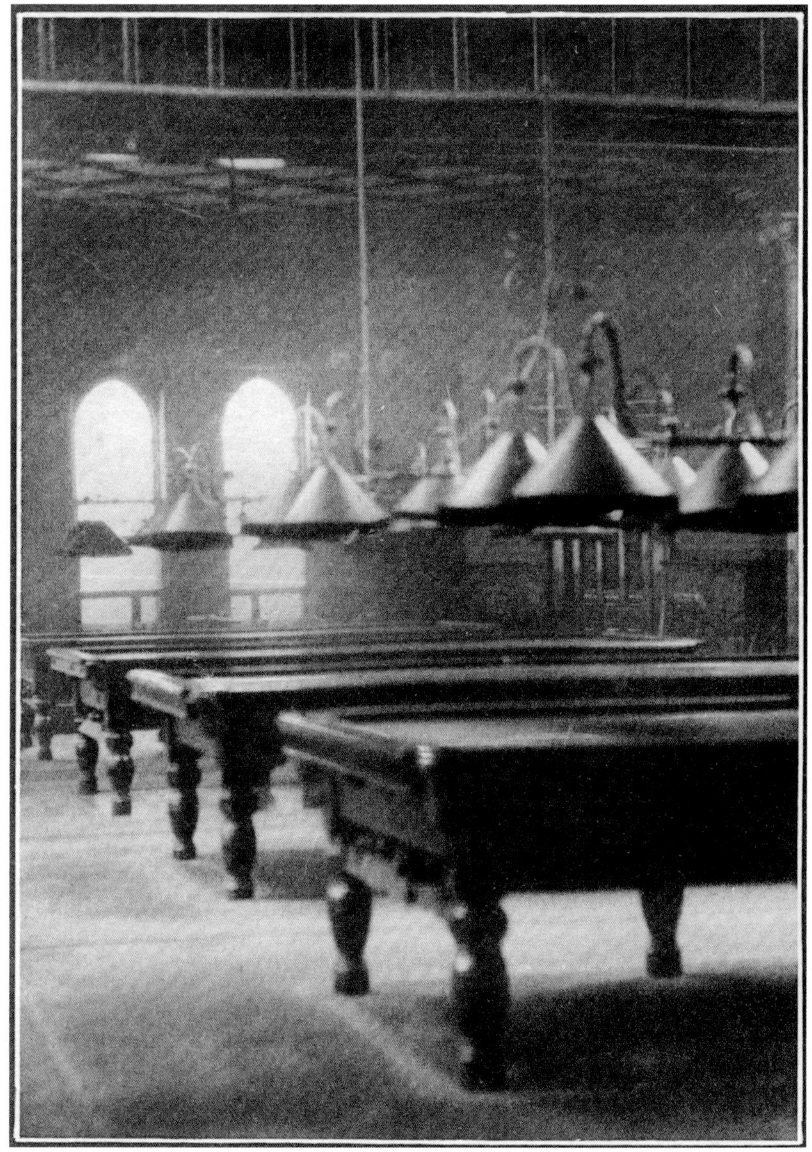

'commemoration' – a temporal mode that can just as well suggest generational handover as duty and sacrifice. In other parts of the book the years of the recent Great War are seen as a barrier to a period that was now 'distant and dim'.[9] The club, so its historian tells us, has a 'curious look of vicissitude': it is a 'monument' in its 'power to awaken memories and to change the current of thought'.[10] And memory – its losses mitigated by this steady contemplation, with its mournful yet enjoyable melancholy – is what Coburn's images seem palpably confident in addressing.[11]

The light that plays along surfaces and objects is one of the pleasures of Coburn's images, and it helps relate a particular set of notions about time and the world. The Reform Club is yet another space, like the Royal Exchange, where the collectivity of class attempted to hold the world in its scope. It is yet another Valhalla for the industrial bourgeoisie – like the Town Hall, Piccadilly Gardens, the Free Trade Hall, the John Rylands Library, and many of the city's other institutions that had sprung up in the mid and late nineteenth century. It has some echoes of the way the Town Hall, the central building of the civic-minded industrialist's world, had transmogrified the machinofacture of the steam-driven mill. Little of this Manchester modernity relates to Baudelaire's idea of the juxtaposition of a deep antiquity with the transitoriness of modern life,[12] or of the charms and dislocations caused by the commodity that Benjamin found expressed everywhere in Baudelaire. Instead, these are places where different settlements had been reached with the convulsions of industrial capitalism and its threats of a non-architecture and a non-city, through which we look at a disjointed past, as if over a chasm of our own making: we reorient ourselves around epochal change. This is what throws up the machine building, the forest of chimneys, the cathedral beside the mill and the infirmary beside the warehouse, the ever-expanding Exchange and the Free Trade townscape. And this is what makes Manchester a distinct kind of capital of the nineteenth century.

Yet what Coburn makes of Manchester's industrial Gothic is rather different. He seems to have replaced the great defining feature of Manchester's modernity – accommodation with shock – with another threshold, the more recent, relatively displaced, effect of the Great War. This is the city in slack water, the moment of stillness before the tidal stream turns and bridles.

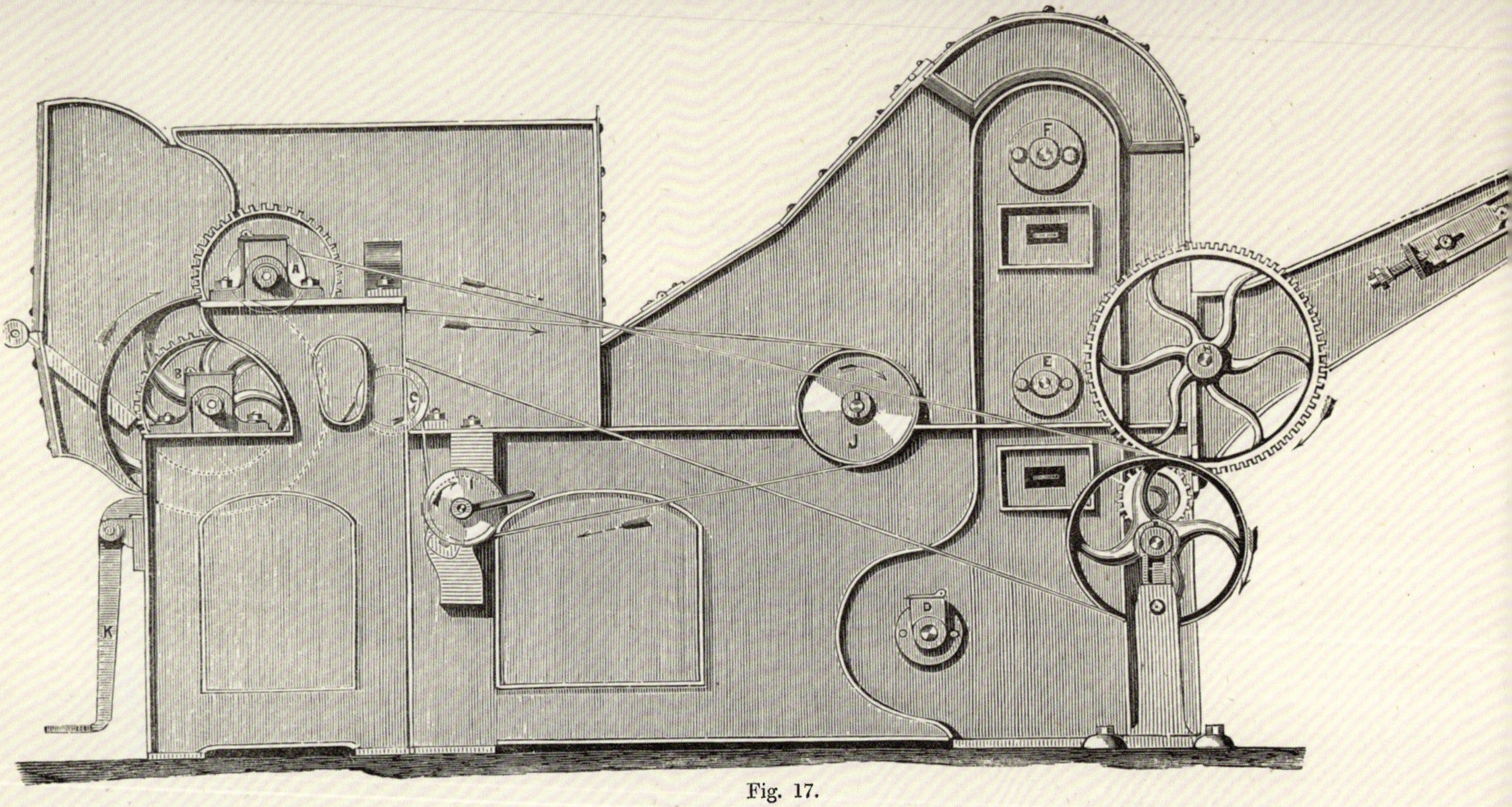

Fig. 17.

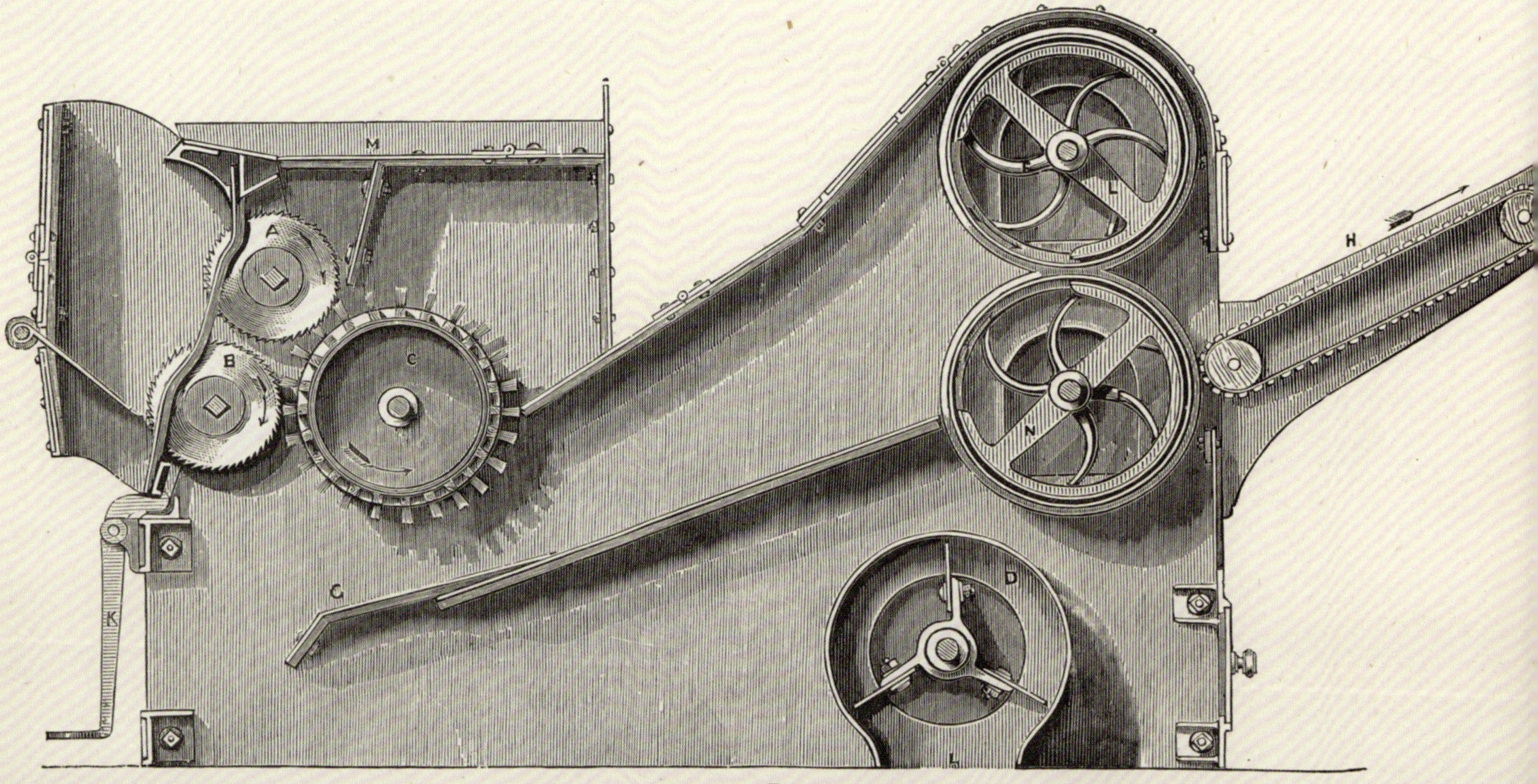

Fig. 18.

The saw gin, from Evan Leigh, *The Science of Modern Cotton Spinning* (1873).

Notes and References

Introduction: Shock, Smoke and Charity *pages 1–17*

1 It appeared as part of a long article assessing the city's recent developments in *The Graphic*, 14 October 1876, pp. 369–84. Generally, this is boosterish, comparing the city positively with London, but it characterises Manchester as a 'city of anomalies' and there is at least one other image in the article that is equivocal about the city's modernity, 'The View from Blackfriars Bridge', in which the river and the cathedral are framed by sewage outlets and smoking chimneys. For more on this kind of view see Chapter 3.

2 Or perhaps even Hugo's own famous description of Paris from the roof of the cathedral: *Notre-Dame de Paris, 1482* (1831), book 3, chapter 2.

3 This was certainly the assessment of a contemporary article in a Manchester-based journal, in which a similar set of buildings were 'difficult to surpass ... yet [there is] high death rate and "primitive" sanitary arrangements': *British Architect* 3 (8 January 1875), p. 19.

4 Friedrich Engels, *The Condition of the Working Class in England* (1845), London: Penguin, 1987, pp. 276–7.

5 Engels, *Condition*, p. 85.

6 A Manchester journalist wrote in 1870, 'The town is encircled by a huge cordon of beastliness and filth, enough to strike fear into the heart of every civilised inhabitant': as quoted in Simon Gunn, *The Public Culture of the Victorian Middle Class: Ritual and Authority in the English Industrial City, 1840–1914*, Manchester: Manchester University Press, 2000, p. 62.

7 Asa Briggs, *Victorian Cities* (1963), Harmondsworth: Pelican, 1968, p. 96.

8 Andrew Lees, *Cities Perceived: Urban Society in European and American Thought, 1820–1940*, Manchester: Manchester University Press, 1985, pp. 61–6; W. O. Henderson, *Industrial Britain under the Regency: The Diaries of Escher, Bodmer, May and de Gallois*, London: Routledge, 2013.

9 Joseph Aston, *A Picture of Manchester*, Manchester: Aston, 1816, p. 31; Alexis de Tocqueville, *Journeys to England and Ireland* (1835), trans. George Lawrence and K. P. Mayer, Garden City, NY: Doubleday, 1968, p. 105; Roger Lloyd-Jones and M. J. Lewis, *Manchester and the Age of the Factory: The Business Structure of Cottonopolis in the Industrial Revolution*, London: Croom Helm, 1988, pp. 32–7; Roger Scola, *Feeding the Victorian City: Food Supply of Manchester*, Manchester: Manchester University Press, 1992, pp. 158–9; François Vigier, *Change and Apathy: Liverpool and Manchester during the Industrial Revolution*, Cambridge, MA: MIT Press, 1970, p. 98.

10 The industrial novel of this period often takes up both forms of shock response – the graphic and appalling detail of one, and the palliative or campaigning motivations of the other: Catherine Gallagher, *The Industrial Reformation of English Fiction, 1832–1867*, Chicago: University of Chicago Press, 1985.

11 Mary Poovey, *Making a Social Body: British Cultural Formation, 1830–1864*, Chicago: University of Chicago Press, 1995; Stathis Kouvelakis, *Philosophy and Revolution: From Kant to Marx*, London: Verso, 2003, pp. 207–19.

12 Léon Faucher, *Manchester in 1844: Its Present Condition and Future Prospects*, Manchester: Heywood, 1844, pp. 16–25.

13 Edwin Chadwick, 'Report on the Sanitary Condition of the Labouring Population', *Parliamentary Papers*, 1842, extracted in Alasdair Clayre (ed.), *Nature and Industrialization*, Oxford: Oxford University Press, 1977, pp. 132–6.

14 Briggs, *Victorian Cities*, p. 89.

15 The usage is common: see, for instance, Peter Hall, 'The First Industrial City – Manchester 1760–1830', ch. 10 in *Cities in Civilization*, New York: Pantheon, 1998. For a challenge to this status see Michael Fores, 'The Myth of a British Industrial Revolution', *History* 66 (1981), p. 183.

16 Engels, *Condition*, pp. 61–2.

17 The literature on class is unfathomably vast but, specifically on the industrial bourgeoisie and the working classes in Manchester, see Gunn, *Public Culture of the Victorian Middle Class*; Boyd Hilton, *A Mad, Bad, and Dangerous People? England 1783–1846*, Oxford: Oxford University Press, 2006, pp. 125–33, 156–61; François

Crouzet, *The First Industrialists: The Problem of Origins*, Cambridge: Cambridge University Press, 1985; Anthony Howe, *The Cotton Masters, 1830–1860*, Oxford: Clarendon Press, 1984; Michael J. Turner, *Reform and Respectability: The Making of a Middle-Class Liberalism in Early Nineteenth-Century Manchester*, Manchester: Chetham Society, 1995; Patrick Joyce, *Work, Society and Politics* (1980), Brighton: EER, 2017. See also Michael Andrew Zmolek, *Rethinking the Industrial Revolution: Five Centuries of Transition from Agrarian to Industrial Capitalism in England*, Chicago: Haymarket, 2014, pp. 609–75; and Dror Wahrman, *Imagining the Middle Class: The Political Representation of Class in Britain, c.1780–1840*, Cambridge: Cambridge University Press, 1995.

18 Fredric Jameson, *The Political Unconscious: Narrative as a Socially Symbolic Act*, London: Methuen, 1981, p. 20; Fredric Jameson, *Signatures of the Visible*, London: Routledge, 1992, p. 47. 'Displaced class struggle' is David Harvey's term: *The Urban Experience*, Baltimore: Johns Hopkins University Press, 1989, p. 85. 'Social war' is Engels's term: *Condition*, p. 69.

19 Andreas Malm, *Fossil Capital: The Rise of Steam Power and the Roots of Global Warming*, London: Verso, 2016, p. 18. As Malm points out, the semantic confluence of meanings in the word 'power' (as in 'steam power') is crucial (pp. 11–13). The exertion of power comes from the control of power, one sociopolitical, the other thermodynamic.

20 For Manchester's regional significance in the early eighteenth century see Michael Nevell (ed.), 'From Farmer to Factory Owner: Models, Methodology and Industrialization', special issue, *Archaeology North West* 6, no. 16 (2001–3), pp. 33–5.

21 Eric Hobsbawm, *The Age of Revolution, 1789–1848* (1962), London: Abacus, 1996, p. 53.

22 One contemporary wrote that 'the entire country is ruined in outward appearances ... Lancashire ... must have been a very beautiful country. What it now is all men know': George Saintsbury, *Manchester*, London: Longmans, 1887, p. 101.

23 For the interdependence of Manchester and Salford, and the consequent frictions, see John Garrard, *Leadership and Power in Victorian Industrial Towns, 1830–80*, Manchester: Manchester University Press, 1983, pp. 86–90.

24 Giorgio Riello, *Cotton: The Fabric that Made the World*, Cambridge: Cambridge University Press, 2013, pp. 151–2.

25 Briggs, *Victorian Cities*, p. 94.

26 Briggs, *Victorian Cities*, pp. 112, 88. See also Terry Wyke, 'Rise and Decline of Cottonopolis', in Alan Kidd and Terry Wyke (eds.), *Manchester: The Making of the Modern City*, Liverpool: Liverpool University Press, 2016, pp. 68–118.

27 See, for instance, the chapter 'The Emergence of the City, 1844–60' in Arthur Redford, *The History of Local Government in Manchester*, London: Longmans, 1939. For commentary on this kind of triumphalist narrative see Patrick Joyce, *Democratic Subjects: The Self and the Social in Nineteenth-Century England*, Cambridge: Cambridge University Press, 1994, pp. 165–71; and specifically on the queen's visit see Gunn, *Public Culture of the Victorian Middle Class*, pp. 165–6. Another reason for the sense that an era had ended was the legislation settling the long campaigns for restrictions on the factory working day: Robert Gray, *The Factory Question and Industrial England, 1830–1860*, Cambridge: Cambridge University Press, 1996, pp. 210–11. One economic historian has recently argued that the 1850s – specifically the Great Exhibition – mark the completion of the Industrial Revolution: E. A. Wrigley, *The Path to Sustained Growth: England's Transition from an Organic Economy to an Industrial Revolution*, Cambridge: Cambridge University Press, 2016, p. 198.

28 Harold L. Platt, *Shock Cities: The Environmental Transformation and Reform of Manchester and Chicago*, Chicago: University of Chicago Press, 2005; Howard Spodek, *Ahmedabad: Shock City of Twentieth-Century India*, Bloomington: Indiana University Press, 2011; Agata Zysiak, Kamil Smiechowski, Kamil Piskata, Wiktor Marzec, Kaja Kazmierska and Jacek Burski, *From Cotton and Smoke: Lodz – Industrial City and Discourses of Asynchronous Modernity, 1897–1994*, Lodz: Lodz University Press, 2018; Tom Hulme, *After the Shock City: Urban Culture and the Making of Modern Citizenship*, Woodbridge: Boydell, 2019.

29 Jürgen Osterhammel, *The Transformation of the World: A Global History of the Nineteenth Century*, Princeton: Princeton University Press, 2014, pp. 272–5.

30 Briggs, *Victorian Cities*, p. 96.

31 The point here isn't so much to question Paris's status as to expose the grounds for it. For more on this status see André Dombrowski and Hollis Clayson (eds.), *Is Paris Still the Capital of the Nineteenth Century?*, Oxford: Routledge/Ashgate, 2016.

32 Walter Benjamin, 'Exchange with Theodor W. Adorno on the Essay "Paris, the Capital of the Nineteenth Century"', in *Walter Benjamin: Selected Writings*, vol. 3, 1935–1938, trans. Edmund Jephcott, Howard Eiland and others, ed. Howard Eiland and Michael W. Jennings, Cambridge, MA: Belknap Press, 2002, p. 52. It was Adorno who suggested the title be changed from 'Paris, the Capital of the Nineteenth Century' to the less emphatic and more allusive 'Paris, Capital of the Nineteenth Century' (p. 58). This was done in the 1939 version.

33 Benjamin, 'Paris, the Capital of the Nineteenth Century', in *Walter Benjamin: Selected Writings*, vol. 3, pp. 32–4.

34 There are reasons, however, to doubt the connection between Fourier and the arcades: David Harvey, *Paris, Capital of Modernity*, New York: Routledge, 2003, p. 82.

35 Benjamin, 'Paris, the Capital of the Nineteenth Century', pp. 37–8.

36 Benjamin, 'Exchange with Theodor W. Adorno', p. 54.

37 Benjamin, 'Paris, the Capital of the Nineteenth Century', pp. 34–6.

38 Theodor Adorno, *Prisms* (1967), trans. Samuel Weber and Shierry Weber, Cambridge, MA: MIT Press, 1981, p. 237.

39 Benjamin, 'Paris, the Capital of the Nineteenth Century', p. 43. For more on the 'dialectical image' see Fredric Jameson, *The Benjamin Files*, London: Verso, 2020, pp. 223–8.

40 'Ventriloqual precision' is from T. J. Clark, *The Painting of Modern Life: Paris in the Art of Manet and his Followers*, London: Thames & Hudson, 1985, p. 69.

41 On how the Paris material has been used in the last two decades to refocus Benjamin's work away from cultural critique and on consumption, see Esther Leslie, 'On Making-Up and Breaking-Up: *Woman* and *Ware*, *Craving* and *Corpse* in Walter Benjamin's *Arcades Project*', *Historical Materialism* 1, no. 1 (1997), pp. 66–90.

42 Adorno is referring to an earlier draft of Benjamin's text, where the words 'underworld' and 'hell' play a part, indicating a suppressed or 'dark' mythic side to modernity. Adorno's understanding of Hell is clearly much closer to the industrial shock city than Benjamin's more mythological thinking. See Walter Benjamin, 'The Arcades of Paris' (1928–9), in Walter Benjamin, *The Arcades Project*, trans. Howard Eiland and Kevin McLaughlin, ed. Rolf Tiedemann, Cambridge, MA: Belknap Press, 1999, pp. 873–84, especially p. 875. Adorno also thought that the later draft cut out this dimension 'because the determination of the nineteenth century as hell became untenable with the rise of the Third Reich': Adorno, *Prisms*, p. 238.

43 Benjamin, 'Exchange with Theodor W. Adorno', pp. 54–5. See also Graeme Gilloch, *Myth and Metropolis: Walter Benjamin and the City*, Cambridge: Polity Press, 1996, p. 106.

44 It is clear that for Benjamin – and this is better represented in the *Konvoluts* for the arcades project than in the prospectus that Adorno read – Hell is actually the commodity form and its commercial spaces, especially in the figure of the prostitute and in the idea of fashion (and the mannequin) as 'the parody of the motley cadaver ... [coupling] the living body to the inorganic world': Benjamin, *The Arcades Project*, pp. 62–3, 66, 79.

45 Benjamin, 'Exchange with Theodor W. Adorno', p. 55. Benjamin may well have intended more on what he refers to (in the introduction to the 1939 version of the 'Paris' essay, as well as later in it) in Louis Auguste Blanqui's work as 'the terrifying features of this phantasmagoria. Humanity figures there as damned ... a vision of hell'. However, this seems more an image of monotonous routine repeating itself than of any more specific form of industrial life. See Benjamin, 'Paris, Capital of the Nineteenth Century', in *The Arcades Project*, pp. 15, 25. For Benjamin on women as factory workers – though his reference is vague and not specific to Paris – see Leslie, 'On Making-Up', pp. 75, 81–2.

46 Benjamin, *The Arcades Project*, p. 391.

47 Benjamin, 'Exchange with Theodor W. Adorno', p. 58.

48 Benjamin, *The Arcades Project*, p. 391. Giedion's quote is also here.

49 This is T. J. Clark on how L. S. Lowry related crowd and city: T. J. Clark, 'Lowry's Other England', in T. J. Clark and Anne M. Wagner, *Lowry and the Painting of Modern Life*, London: Tate, 2013, p. 69.

50 Benjamin, 'Paris, the Capital of the Nineteenth Century', p. 43.

51 The distinction between two different forms of experience is found in Walter Benjamin, 'Some Motifs in Baudelaire' (1939), in Walter Benjamin, *Charles Baudelaire: A Lyric Poet in the Era of High Capitalism*, London: Verso, 1983, pp. 109–54; and in Walter Benjamin, 'The Return of the *Flâneur*', in *Walter Benjamin: Selected Writings*, vol. 2, 1927–1934, trans. Edmund Jephcott, Howard Eiland and others, ed. Howard Eiland and Michael W. Jennings, Cambridge, MA: Belknap Press, 1999, pp. 262–7.

52 Benjamin, 'Some Motifs in Baudelaire', p. 111.

53 This is Benjamin quoting Baudelaire, in *Walter Benjamin: Selected Writings*, vol. 4, 1938–1940, trans. Edmund Jephcott, Howard Eiland and others, ed. Howard Eiland and Michael W. Jennings, Cambridge, MA: Belknap Press, 2002, p. 48.

54 Walter Benjamin, 'The Paris of the Second Empire in Baudelaire' (1938), in Benjamin, *Charles Baudelaire*, pp. 36, 53.

55 This relates to Engels's thoughts on the relation between the monadic, individuating, effects of the modern city and its crowds: Engels, *Condition*, pp. 68–9. It should also be said that the *flâneur* is a residual figure for Benjamin, whose fate is determined by the commodified transactions of industrial modernity.

56 Benjamin, 'Some Motifs in Baudelaire', p. 132.

57 Mark Traugott, *Armies of the Poor: Determinants of Working-Class Participation in the Parisian Insurrection of June 1848*, Princeton: Princeton University Press, 1985, chapter 1; Harvey, *Paris, Capital of Modernity*, pp. 155–9. See also the accounts of carpenters, locksmiths, tailors, shoemakers and typographers in Jacques Rancière, *Proletarian Nights: The Worker's Dream in Nineteenth-Century France* (1981), trans. John Drury, London: Verso, 2012.

58 As quoted in Benjamin, 'Some Motifs in Baudelaire', pp. 132–3.

59 Benjamin, 'Some Motifs in Baudelaire', p. 134. Also, 'the reflecting mechanism which the machine sets off in the workman can be studied closely, as in a mirror, in the idler' (p. 134). Benjamin seems to be writing about nineteenth-century Paris while having 1920s modernism always in mind. Hence also, for instance, the link he makes between the assembly line and the film strip 'in the process of consumption' (*Selected Writings*, vol. 3, p. 94). A similar case is Manfredo Tafuri who, while suggesting that relationships of production are 'immanent' in Benjamin's crowd behaviour, also avoids (perhaps because of his similar desire to tie in the avant-garde of the 1920s) the issue of how they could become deep-seated or inherent if factory production was still marginal to mid-nineteenth-century Paris: Manfredo Tafuri, *Architecture and Utopia: Design and Capitalist Development* (1973), trans. Barbara Luigia La Penta, Cambridge, MA: MIT Press, 1976, p. 80.

60 Charles Dickens, *Hard Times* (1854), Harmondsworth: Penguin, 1969, p. 65.

61 This is Fredric Jameson's own translation from Adorno's *Aesthetic Theory*, in his *Late Marxism: Adorno, or, The Persistence of the Dialectic*, London: Verso, 1990, p. 190. See also Theodor Adorno, *Aesthetic Theory* (1970), trans. Robert Hullot-Kerner, London: Bloomsbury, 1997, p. 46.

62 David Harvey's *Paris, Capital of Modernity* is more explicitly an account of the emergence of a distinct kind of city, *sui generis*. His case for Paris reasserts the economic sense of 'capital', placing class struggle around the uses and identity of the city as central. Modernity is understood as being produced out of the catastrophic failure of the working classes in the 1848 revolutions

and by the newly powerful middle classes supporting Louis-Napoléon. The circulation of capital and a new middle-class confidence in its own representation – especially in urban and architectural scale – are key, but so too is the problem of rendering the city as a totality. We should also mention Richard Sennett's *The Fall of Public Man* (New York: Alfred A. Knopf, 1977) and Marshall Berman's *All that Is Solid Melts into Air: The Experience of Modernity* (New York: Simon & Schuster, 1982), in both of which Paris again plays a crucial role in how modernity can be understood.

63 Clark, *Painting of Modern Life*, p. 36. The source for this, Guy Debord, wrote of '*capital* accumulated to the point where it becomes an image' (italics in original): Guy Debord, *The Society of the Spectacle*, New York: Zone Books, 1994, p. 4. My thanks to Steve Edwards for this reference.

64 Clark, *Painting of Modern Life*, pp. 9–10.

65 For another Paris, the 'third city' or city of 'nonbourgeois low modernity', which is closer to what I will argue about some aspects of Manchester, see Molly Nesbit, *Atget's Seven Albums*, New Haven: Yale University Press, 1992, pp. 132–51.

66 Clark, *Painting of Modern Life*, p. 29.

67 C. Redding (ed.), *The Pictorial History of the County of Lancaster*, London: Routledge, 1844, p. 11.

68 And yet the idea that consumption is somehow other, and equal, to production is a curiosity of postmodernism. The overemphasis on consumption in postmodernist approaches finds its more recent echo in an overemphasis on Manchester as commercial rather than industrial – or at least the artificial separation of the two in the case of many warehouses. (The industrial, it seems, remains an uncomfortable subject in thinking about modernity.) See, for example, Patrick Joyce, *The Rule of Freedom: Liberalism and the Modern City*, London: Verso, 2003, p. 9. The narrowing can be because of a focus on the city centre, where warehouses certainly were more important in the economy: Lloyd-Jones and Lewis, *Manchester and the Age of the Factory*, p. 37; Alan Kidd, *Manchester*, Keele: Keele University Press, 1993, pp. 23–30. It also leaves out the fact that Manchester's leading cotton manufacturers owned premises outside the city in its satellite towns as well as within it.

69 T. J. Clark and Anne M. Wagner, 'Preface', in Clark and Wagner, *Lowry*, p. 19.

70 For a very different argument for Manchester as capital of the nineteenth century, one centred on the 1857 Manchester Art Treasures Exhibition, see Janet Wolff, 'Manchester, Capital of the Nineteenth Century', *Journal of Classical Sociology* 13, no. 1 (February 2013), pp. 69–86.

71 London – a consumer, political and financial fulcrum; a bureaucratic capital; a locus of rentier residence, of docks and light industries, but arguably neither the site nor the engine of industrial change – was in many ways marginal to the Industrial Revolution. Of course, the case for 'capital of the nineteenth century' might be made on these bases, certainly that for global dominance: Osterhammel, *Transformation of the World*, pp. 263–4, 270.

72 Engels's argument, right at the end of his book, was that industrial England (with Manchester at its cutting edge) would replace Paris as the place of revolution: Engels, *Condition*, pp. 290–2.

73 David Harvey, *Urban Experience*, p. 33.

74 Which would also indicate, perhaps surprisingly, that we could think of Manchester's position as sharing something with the ideas about alternative modernity developed to explain colonial or non-Western forms of the modern: see Gwendolyn Wright, 'Building Global Modernism', *Grey Room* 7 (2002), pp. 130, 134 n. 24; Swati Chattopadhyay, *Representing Calcutta: Modernity, Nationalism, and the Colonial Uncanny*, London: Routledge, 2006, pp. 4–5; Jyotri Hosagrahar, *Indigenous Modernities: Negotiating Architecture and Urbanism*, London: Routledge, 2005, pp. 4–5. 'Bastard birth' is from Perry Anderson, quoted by Alexander Anievas and Kerem Nisancioglu, *How the West Came to Rule: The Geopolitical Origins of Capitalism*, London: Pluto, 2015, p. 55.

75 Benjamin, 'Some Motifs in Baudelaire', p. 122.

76 Henri Lefebvre, *Marxist Thought and the City* (1972), trans. Robert Bonnono, Minneapolis: University of Minnesota Press, 2016, p. 10.

77 Benjamin, 'Paris, the Capital of the Nineteenth Century', p. 34.

78 Hilton, *A Mad, Bad, and Dangerous People?*, p. 125; Harvey, *Urban Experience*, p. 26. There were also alliances, though these tended to be later: Martin Daunton, '"Gentlemanly Capitalism" and British Industry, 1820–1914', *Past & Present* 122 (1989), pp. 119–58. 'Bourgeois' does have a somewhat alien sound to it in a later British nineteenth-century context, but early on it was just as (in)frequently used as 'middle class', and its refusal to be a neutral description seems appropriate here: Franco Moretti, *The Bourgeois: Between History and Literature*, London: Verso, 2013, pp. 6–12.

79 On 'industrial enlightenment' see Joel Mokyr, *The Gifts of Athena: Historical Origins of the Knowledge Economy*, Princeton: Princeton University Press, 2002; Joel Mokyr, *The Enlightened Economy: Britain and the Industrial Revolution, 1700–1850*, London: Penguin, 2009.

80 This, in opposition to what one Foucauldian admits is an approach that 'makes resistance sometimes difficult to identify': Joyce, *Rule of Freedom*, p. 188. Neither industrialists nor their operatives would have thought this, but perhaps this is to be dismissed as a 'somewhat romantic dualism of high power and low resistance': Joyce, *Rule of Freedom*, p. 209.

81 Sven Beckert, *Empire of Cotton: A New History of Global Capitalism*, London: Allen Lane, 2014; Riello, *Cotton*.

82 Harvey, *Urban Experience*, pp. 33–4. The classic text on slavery and the Industrial Revolution is Eric E. Williams, *Capitalism and Slavery* (Chapel Hill: University of North Carolina Press, 1944), though its limitation of slavery to mercantilist economies has long been superseded. For more recent discussion of industry and slavery after 1833 see Beckert, *Empire of Cotton*; William Darity Jr., 'British Industry and the West Indies Plantations', in Joseph E. Inikori and Stanley L. Engerman (eds.), *The Atlantic Slave Trade: Effects on Economics, Societies, and Peoples in Africa, the Americas and Europe*, Durham, NC: Duke University Press,

1992, pp. 247–82; and Mark Harvey, 'Slavery, Indenture and the Development of British Industrial Capitalism', *History Workshop Journal* 88 (Autumn 2019), pp. 66–88. 'Cheap natures' is from Jason Moore, 'The Rise of Cheap Nature', in Jason Moore (ed.), *Anthropocene or Capitalocene? Nature, History and the Crisis of Capitalism*, Oakland, CA: PM Press, 2016, pp. 78–115.

83 The literature here is vast, and more of it is drawn on elsewhere in this book, but for a taste see Crouzet, *First Industrialists*; Peter Maw, *Transport and the Industrial City: Manchester and the Canal Age, 1750–1850*, Manchester: Manchester University Press, 2013; N. F. R. Crafts and C. K. Harley, 'Output Growth in the Industrial Revolution: A Restatement of the Crafts–Harley View', *Economic History Review* 45 (1994), pp. 703–30; Maxine Berg and Pat Hudson, 'Rehabilitating the Industrial Revolution', *Economic History Review* 25 (1992), pp. 24–50; and E. A. Wrigley, *The Path to Sustained Growth: England's Transition from an Organic Economy to an Industrial Revolution*, Cambridge: Cambridge University Press, 2016. I can't enter here into the debates about the problems of the term 'Industrial Revolution' (or perhaps better '*capitalist revolution*'), though it is still unavoidable in indicating the huge shift of productive forces in play. On understanding the change in global terms see Kenneth Pomerantz, *The Great Divergence: China, Europe, and the Making of the Modern World Economy*, Princeton: Princeton University Press, 2000. For a summary of the debates in a global context see Osterhammel, *Transformation of the World*, pp. 637–72; and Anievas and Nisancioglu, *How the West Came to Rule*. For discussions of debates in the English context see Gray, *The Factory Question*, pp. 1–20; and more recently Zmolek, *Rethinking the Industrial Revolution*.

84 See particularly Joyce, *Rule of Freedom*; Poovey, *Making a Social Body*; Chris Otter, *Victorian Eye: A Political History of Light and Vision in Britain, 1800–1910*, Chicago: University of Chicago Press, 2008. Otter and Joyce also link Foucault's ideas with those of Bruno Latour and 'new materialism'.

85 On the exclusion of form and labour from Foucault see Sianne Ngai, *Theory of the Gimmick: Aesthetic Judgement and Capitalist Form*, Cambridge, MA: Belknap Press, 2020, pp. 34–9.

86 Otter, *Victorian Eye*, pp. 12, 258.

87 On this see also Jacques Bidet, *Foucault with Marx*, trans. Steven Corcoran, London: Zed Books, 2016, pp. 87–8.

88 For a related argument about what he calls 'neoliberal self-description', see Jan Rehmann, 'The Unfulfilled Promise of the Late Foucault and Foucauldian "Governmentality" Studies', in Daniel Zamora and Michael C. Behrent (eds.), *Foucault and Neoliberalism*, Cambridge: Polity Press, 2016, pp. 134–58.

89 Martin Hewitt's critique of work on Manchester is particularly useful here: Martin Hewitt, *Making Social Knowledge in the Victorian City: The Visiting Mode in Manchester, 1832–1914*, London: Routledge, 2020, pp. 1–9.

90 Still the best guide to Foucault's ocularcentrism and its relation to French philosophy is Martin Jay, *Downcast Eyes: The Denigration of Vision in Twentieth-Century French Thought*, Berkeley: University of California Press, 1993, pp. 381–416.

91 T. J. Clark, 'Lowry's Other England', in Clark and Wagner, *Lowry*, p. 21.

92 Faucher, *Manchester in 1844*, p. 21.

93 Quoted in Briggs, *Victorian Cities*, p. 135.

94 T. J. Clark, *Image of the People: Gustave Courbet and the 1848 Revolution*, London: Thames & Hudson, 1973, p. 33. On Manchester's emerging art world see John Seed, '"Commerce and the Liberal Arts": The Political Economy of Art in Manchester, 1775–1860', in John Seed and Janet Wolff (eds.), *The Culture of Capital: Art, Power, and the Nineteenth-Century Middle Class*, Manchester: Manchester University Press, 1988, pp. 45–82.

95 What visitors might be guided towards is well represented in Joseph Perrin, *The Manchester Hand-Book, an Authentic Account of the Place and its People*, Manchester: Hale and Roworth, 1857. On the exhibition see Tristram Hunt and Victoria Whitfield, *Art Treasures in Manchester: 150 Years On*, Manchester: Manchester Art Gallery / Philip Wilson, 2007; and Helen Rees-Leahy (ed.), 'Art, City, Spectacle: The 1857 Art-Treasures Exhibition Revisited', special issue, *Bulletin of the John Rylands Library*, 87 (2005). Tourists seeking industrial sites continued throughout the century: Paul Readman, 'Manchester: Shock Landscape?', chapter 5 in *Storied Ground: Landscape and the Shaping of English National Identity*, Cambridge: Cambridge University Press, 2018.

96 Maw, *Transport and the Industrial City*, pp. 210–11.

97 These cavalry barracks, also known as the Hulme Barracks, were notorious as the home of the 15th King's Hussars who charged protestors in 1819. There were many other barracks and prisons, too small to be named on this map.

98 Engels, *Condition*, p. 90; Nesbit, *Atget's Seven Albums*, p. 141.

99 For more on these issues see the now classic analysis in Harvey, *Paris, Capital of Modernity*, pp. 107–40; and for another English industrial city see R. J. Morris, *Men, Women and Property in England, 1780–1870: A Social and Economic History of Family Strategies amongst the Leeds Middle Classes*, Cambridge: Cambridge University Press, 2005.

100 The term is a Chartist one: Malm, *Fossil Capital*, p. 239.

1 · Ancoats, 1826: The Shock of the Factory
pages 19–45

1 The notebook is now in the Staatliche Museen Preussischer Kulturbesitz, Berlin. A complete facsimile is published in Reinhard Wegner (ed.), *Die Reise nach Frankreich und England im Jahre 1826*, Munich: Deutscher Kunstverlag, 1990. A translation has appeared in David Bindman and Gottfried Riemann (eds.), *Karl Friedrich Schinkel, 'The English Journey': Journal of a Visit to France and Britain in 1826*, trans. F. Gayna Walls, New Haven: Yale University Press for Paul Mellon Centre Studies in British Art, 1993.

2 *Manchester Guardian*, 22 July 1826.

3 Schinkel was accurate in the number of windows in his nearer block but, if we are to believe a watercolour view of 1820 (fig. 16) less so with the second block. This may be accounted for by remodelling work in the six-year interim period between the two views.

4 On Stimmung see Kurt W. Forster, *Schinkel: A Meander through his Life and Work*, Basel: Birkhäuser, 2018, pp. 26–7.

5 Bindman and Riemann (eds.), *Karl Friedrich Schinkel*, p. 175.

6 Angelika Wesenberg, 'Art and Industry', in Michael Snodin (ed.), *Karl Friedrich Schinkel: A Universal Man*, New Haven: Yale University Press, 1991, pp. 57–63.

7 Bindman and Riemann (eds.), *Karl Friedrich Schinkel*, p. 4. One possible reason for Schinkel's short stay may be that Beuth had already stayed there in his 1823 journey. Even in his itinerary Schinkel had noted under Manchester only 'Kirche alt / Dampfmaschinen, Sägemaschinen [Old church / steam engines, sawing machines]': Bindman and Riemann (eds.), *Karl Friedrich Schinkel*, p. 212.

8 Bindman and Riemann (eds.), *Karl Friedrich Schinkel*, p. 180. It is not that Schinkel was against the manifestation of industrial modernity, rather that this kind of modernity had to be rendered into an orderly relation with the verities of architecture: Forster, *Schinkel*, pp. 60, 130.

9 Bindman and Riemann (eds.), *Karl Friedrich Schinkel*, p. 180.

10 On the images produced by industrial spies and for industrial tourists see Celina Fox, *The Arts of Industry in the Age of Enlightenment*, New Haven: Yale University Press for Paul Mellon Centre for Studies in British Art, 2009, pp. 378–406.

11 Compare, for instance, Olivier Bernier, *The World in 1800*, New York: Wiley, 2000; Jonathan Schneer, *London 1900: The Imperial Metropolis*, London: Yale University Press, 1999.

12 Maxine Berg, *The Age of Manufactures*, London: Fontana, 1985, p. 30.

13 S. D. Chapman, 'Fixed Capital Formation in the British Cotton Manufacturing Industry', in J. P. P. Higgins and Sidney Pollard (eds.), *Aspects of Capital Investment in Great Britain*, London: Methuen, 1971, p. 59.

14 Andreas Malm, *Fossil Capital: The Rise of Steam Power and the Roots of Global Warming*, London: Verso, 2016, p. 156 and especially pp. 121–64. Malm's argument is supported by very different kinds of historians: Joel Mokyr, *The Enlightened Economy: Britain and the Industrial Revolution, 1700–1850*, London: Penguin, 2009, pp. 101–2, 125; E. A. Wrigley, *The Path to Sustained Growth: England's Transition from an Organic Economy to an Industrial Revolution*, Cambridge: Cambridge University Press, 2016, p. 206. For a useful summary of historians' debates on the rise of the factory system see Joshua B. Freeman, *Behemoth: A History of the Factory and the Making of the Modern World*, New York: Norton, 2019, pp. 12–13. The classic description of this 'labour of superintendence' is Marx's: Karl Marx, *Capital: A Critique of Political Economy*, trans. Ben Fowkes, Harmondsworth: Penguin, 1976, vol. 1, pp. 548–50.

15 John Kennedy, 'Observations on the Rise and Progress of the Cotton Trade in Great Britain', *Memoirs of the Literary and Philosophical Society of Manchester*, 2nd series 3 (1819), p. 128. This immigration accounted for much of the city's fivefold increase of population between 1801 and 1851: Arthur Redford, *Labour Migration in England, 1800–50*, Manchester: Manchester University Press, 1964; Colin Pooley and Jean Turnbull, *Migration and Mobility in Britain since the Eighteenth Century*, London: Routledge, 1998.

16 Edward Baines, *History of the Cotton Manufacture*, London: H. Fisher, 1835, p. 226.

17 P. Deane and W. A. Cole, *British Economic Growth, 1688–1959*, Cambridge: Cambridge University Press, 1962, p. 52.

18 Land had been offered for sale along both undug canals as early as 1794: Peter Maw, *Transport and the Industrial City: Manchester and the Canal Age, 1750–1850*, Manchester: Manchester University Press, 2013, p. 10.

19 The juxtaposition of houses and industrial structures may well have been deliberate: Jacqueline Roberts, '"A Densely Populated and Unlovely Tract": The Residential Development of Ancoats', *Manchester Region History Review* 7 (1993), p. 16. For middle-class surveillance see Martin Hewitt, *Making Social Knowledge in the Victorian City: The Visiting Mode in Manchester, 1832–1914*, London: Routledge, 2020, pp. 17, 33. Hewitt mentions that even architects were involved in what he calls this 'visiting mode' (p. 19).

20 C. H. Lee, *A Cotton Enterprise, 1795–1840: A History of McConnel & Kennedy Fine Cotton Spinners*, Manchester: Manchester University Press, 1972.

21 Quoted in John W. McConnel, *A Century of Fine Cotton Spinning*, Manchester: Faulkner, 1913, p. 9.

22 McConnel, *A Century of Fine Cotton Spinning*, p. 10.

23 V. A. C. Gatrell, 'Labour, Power, and the Size of Firms in Lancashire Cotton in the Second Quarter of the Nineteenth Century', *Economic History Review* 30, no. 1 (February 1977), p. 100. Gatrell's article drew attention away from large-scale firms such as McConnel & Kennedy, which he viewed as exceptional. See also Roger Lloyd-Jones and A. A. Le Roux, 'The Size of Firms in the Cotton Industry', *Economic History Review* 33, no. 1 (February 1980), pp. 72–82. For qualified refutation of the idea that large-scale industry dominates because of efficiencies of scale, see David Harvey, *Paris, Capital of Modernity*, New York: Routledge, 2003, pp. 167–9.

24 Robert C. Allen, *The British Industrial Revolution in Global Perspective*, Cambridge: Cambridge University Press, 2009, pp. 136, 148–9. On the new use of 'innovation' as a term of praise in this period see Peter Gay, *The Enlightenment, vol. 2, The Science of Freedom*, New York: Norton, 1969, p. 3.

25 James Wheeler, *Manchester, its Political, Social and Commercial History, Ancient and Modern*, London and Manchester, 1836, p. 153. For Kennedy's adaptations of the mule see Kennedy, 'A Brief Memoir of Samuel Crompton', *Memoirs of the Manchester Literary and Philosophical Society*, 2nd series 5 (1831), pp. 340–4; William Fairbairn, *A Brief Memory of the Late John Kennedy*, Manchester, 1861, p. 4.

26 Michael Huberman, *Escape from the Market: Negotiating Work in Lancashire*, Cambridge: Cambridge University Press, 1996, p. 17.

27 Gatrell, 'Labour', p. 109.

28 Mike Williams and D. A. Farnie, *Cotton Mills in Greater Manchester*, Preston: Carnegie, 1992, p. 98. Richard Tattersall was one of the earliest mill architects in Manchester. He worked with William Fairbairn on the Shaddon mill in Carlisle in 1836 before, seemingly, developing his own mill expertise: Ron Fitzgerald, 'The

Development of the Cast Iron Frame in Textile Mills to 1850', *Industrial Archaeology Review* 10, no. 2 (Spring 1988), pp. 141–2.

29 Lee, *Cotton Enterprise*, p. 101.

30 Lee, *Cotton Enterprise*, pp. 20–1, 90–100. For the dependence of the cotton industry on slave labour see Sven Beckert, *Empire of Cotton: A New History of Global Capitalism*, London: Allen Lane, 2014, especially chapter 4, and on the new American plantations chapter 5.

31 Lee, *Cotton Enterprise*, p. 105.

32 The 1833 Factory Commission gives a figure of 1,551 spinners working in the company's mills, the highest in the city. The next largest was Birley & Kirke at 1,402 (spinners and weavers), followed by A. & G. Murray at 805 (all spinners): Roland Smith, 'Manchester as a Centre for the Manufacture and Merchanting of Cotton Goods, 1820–30', *University of Birmingham Historical Journal* 4, no. 1 (1953), p. 50. Of McConnel & Kennedy's employees by this date, 1,079 were women and 340 children (employed as piecers and scavengers). Twelve hours was the normal weekday shift, and nine hours on Saturdays: Smith, 'Manchester as a Centre', pp. 56–7.

33 On this see David Harvey, *The Urban Experience*, Baltimore: Johns Hopkins University Press, 1985, pp. 64–5.

34 McConnel, *A Century*, plate between pp. 10 and 11.

35 John Rylands Library Special Collections, McConnel and Kennedy Papers, MCK/4/4. The plan was made for insurance purposes.

36 James Montgomery, *The Theory and Practice of Cotton Spinning*, 2nd edn, Glasgow: Niven, 1833, p. 15.

37 Lee, Cotton Enterprise, p. 102; McConnel, *A Century*, p. 11. The firm was riding a wave of adoption here rather than leading the way. Philips and Lee had adopted gas lighting in 1805 in their cotton-spinning mill in Salford: W. O. Henderson, *J. C. Fischer and his Diary of Industrial England, 1814–51*, London: Frank Cass, 1966, p. 57. On how 'modern gas lighting began as industrial lighting' see Wolfgang Schivelbusch, *Disenchanted Night: The Industrialization of Light in the Nineteenth Century*, Berkeley: University of California Press, 1995, pp. 14–20.

38 Michael Huberman, 'Industrial Relations and the Industrial Revolution', *Business History Review* 65, no. 2 (Summer 1991), p. 361.

39 McConnel & Kennedy were supplied with coal from the Clayton Colliery in Bradford, on the eastern edge of Manchester: John Rylands Library Special Collections, McConnel and Kennedy Papers, Ledgers for 1817–1827 and 1827–1831.

40 Beckert, *Empire of Cotton*, p. 150.

41 Montgomery mentions 'a wall to surround the whole premises, if deemed necessary': Montgomery, *Theory and Practice*, p. 16.

42 I. Miller and C. Wild (eds.), *A and G Murray and the Cotton Mills of Ancoats*, Lancaster: Oxford Archaeology North, 2007, pp. 61–140.

43 Chapman, 'Fixed Capital', pp. 75–6.

44 Marx, *Capital*, pp. 497, 499, 503. Scale drew Marx's attention because it also helps typify the ecological deprivations of capitalist industry: Marx, *Capital*, pp. 637–8. Scale is also repeated as a key factor in many later accounts: Chapman, 'Fixed Capital'.

45 Roger Lloyd-Jones and Merv Lewis, 'Housing Factory Workers: Ancoats in the Early Nineteenth Century', *Manchester Region History Review* 7 (1993), p. 35; Miller and Wild (eds.), *A and G Murray*, p. 74.

46 Maxine Berg, 'Small Producer Capitalism in Eighteenth-Century England', *Business History* 35, no. 1 (1993), p. 18. Also on the deceptions of scale see Mokyr, *The Enlightened Economy*, pp. 339, 347. For debates on whether large-scale manufacture has been exaggerated in accounts of the Industrial Revolution, see N. F. R. Crafts, *British Economic Growth during the Industrial Revolution*, Oxford: Clarendon Press, 1985; N. F. R. Crafts, S. J. Leybourne and T. C. Mills, 'Trends and Cycles in British Industrial Production', *Journal of the Royal Statistical Society: Series A (Statistics in Society)* 152, no. 1 (January 1989), pp. 43–60.

47 John Kenneth Galbraith, 'Was Ford a Fraud?', in *The Liberal Hour*, Harmondsworth: Penguin, 1963, p. 132, as quoted in Owen Hatherley, *The Chaplin Machine: Slapstick, Fordism and the Communist Avant-Garde*, London: Pluto, 2016, p. 24.

48 Maw, *Transport and the Industrial City*, pp. 42–7, 211–12. Road transport, however, remained important for McConnel & Kennedy: Michael Freeman, 'Transporting Methods in the British Cotton Industry during the Industrial Revolution', *Journal of Transport History*, new series 1 (1980), pp. 59–74.

49 John Hassell, *Tour of the Grand Junction Illustrated with a Series of Engravings*, London: Hassell, 1819, p. 1. The Grand Junction Canal passed through the southern Home Counties and so, when Hassell illustrated waterside mills, he showed them against the hills and trees of their landscape settings. See also John Aikin, *A Description of the Country from thirty to forty miles around Manchester*, London: J. Stockdale, 1795, pp. 112, 114.

50 The buildings were already in existence, at least by 1805, when they are shown marked on the Rochdale Canal Company section maps: Greater Manchester Records Office.

51 See the map of 1819 reproduced in Michael E. Rose, with Keith Falconer and Julian Holder, *Ancoats: Cradle of Industrialisation*, Swindon: English Heritage, 2011, p. 12. The watercolour may have been commissioned by the firm itself – it was included in their later history of the firm: McConnel, *A Century*. It is in the collections of the Manchester Central Library.

52 Alexis de Tocqueville, *Journeys to England and Ireland* (1835), trans. George Lawrence and K. P. Mayer, Garden City, NY: Doubleday, 1968, p. 94.

53 Montgomery recognised that engine houses 'ranged in a line with other buildings ... gives the whole a more neat and uniform appearance': Montgomery, *Theory and Practice*, p. 16.

54 Charles Dickens, *Pickwick Papers* (1836–7), London: Penguin, 1994, p. 763. Dickens was describing factories in Birmingham.

55 *Lancashire Illustrated, from original drawings by S. Austin, J. Harwood, G. and C. Pyne, etc., with historical and topographical descriptions*, London: Fisher & Jackson, 1832, p. 42.

56 Peter Maw, *Transport and the Industrial City*, p. 211. The limit was 20 yards.

57 A similar pattern of development had occurred along the banks of the Mississippi, where the distinctive fan shape of cotton plantations was a result of having their short ends on the waterfront: Daniel Brownstein, 'Mapping the Cancer Corridor along Louisiana's Gulf Coast', *Musings on Maps*, 4 December 2013, https://dabrownstein.com/2013/12/04/mapping-the-cancer-corridor-along-louisianas-gulf-coast (accessed 26 March 2020).

58 On factory entrances see Richard Biernacki, *The Fabrication of Labour: Germany and Britain, 1640–1914*, Berkeley: University of California Press, 1995, pp. 122–8. Biernacki's examples come from a later period, the mid-nineteenth to the early twentieth centuries.

59 Jonathan Crary, *24/7: Late Capitalism and the Ends of Sleep*, London: Verso, 2014, p. 63.

60 De Tocqueville, *Journeys to England and Ireland*, pp. 95–6; Robert Owen, *The Life of Robert Owen Written by Himself*, London: Effingham Wilson, 1857, vol. 1, p. 26; Benjamin Disraeli, *Coningsby, or, The New Generation* (1844), Harmondsworth: Penguin, 1983, pp. 178–9.

61 Bindman and Riemann (eds.), *Karl Friedrich Schinkel*, p. 175.

62 For the mill as heterotopia see Kevin Hetherington, *The Badlands of Modernity: Heterotopia and Social Ordering*, London: Routledge, 1997, pp. 109–38.

63 Mikhail Bakhtin, 'Forms of Time and Chronotope in the Novel', in *The Dialogic Imagination: Four Essays*, trans. Caryl Emerson and Michael Holquist, Austin: University of Texas, 1981. For re-alerting me to the chronotope, if to very different ends, I am indebted to Gail Day and Steve Edwards, 'Differential Time and Aesthetic Form: Uneven and Combined Capitalism in the Work of Allan Sekula', in James Christie and Nesrin Degirmencioglu (eds.), *Cultures of Uneven and Combined Development*, Leiden: Brill, 2019, pp. 253–88.

64 'Palace of infamy' is from the account of a factory in G. W. M. Reynolds's serialised novel *The Slaves of England*, no. 1, *The Seamstress* (1850), as quoted in Catherine Gallagher, *The Industrial Reformation of English Fiction, 1832–1867*, Chicago: University of Chicago Press, 1985, p. 135. There are also ways of seeing the palace as an epitome of the modern: Hetherington, *The Badlands of Modernity*, pp. 1–19. On the country house as utopia see Lewis Mumford, *The Story of Utopias*, New York: Peter Smith, 1941, pp. 193–234.

65 Frances Trollope, *The Life and Adventures of Michael Armstrong the Factory Boy* (1840), Stroud: Nonsuch, 2007, pp. 26–8.

66 Trollope, *Michael Armstrong*, pp. 118–20.

67 Thomas Markus, entry on 'Factories, to 1850', in Patrick Goode (ed.), *The Oxford Companion to Architecture*, Oxford: Oxford University Press, 2009, p. 303.

68 Markus, 'Factories', p. 304; Gillian Darley, *Factory*, London: Reaktion, 2003, pp. 21–6; Fox, *The Arts of Industry*, pp. 416–17.

69 John Jones, *The Cotton Mill, A Poem*, Manchester: Aston, 1821, p. 10.

70 John Jones, *Poems by John Jones*, Manchester: T. Smith, 1856. The collection ends with the poem 'A Tribute in Memory of John Kennedy, Esq.' For working-class poetry critical of the factory system see Paul A. Pickering, *Chartism and the Chartists in Manchester and Salford*, Basingstoke: Macmillan, 1995, pp. 16–17.

71 McConnel & Kennedy's wages have been described as average for the cotton industry in Manchester at this time, but also as 'comparatively high' in relation to those paid in other working-class jobs at the time: Frances Collier, *The Family Economy of the Working Classes in the Cotton Industry, 1784–1833*, Manchester: Manchester University Press, 1964, pp. 16–18. Cotton spinning also enabled families to earn more because of its employment of women and children. But wages would fluctuate according to conditions of trade.

72 Berg, *The Age of Manufactures*, pp. 12–15.

73 Lee, *Cotton Enterprise*, pp. 124, 126–7; Beckert, *Empire of Cotton*, p. 188. Jones's contemporary, the Murray's mill operative John Doherty, campaigned extensively against these conditions: R. G. Kirby and A. E. Musson, *The Voice of the People: John Doherty, 1798–1854, Trade Unionist, Radical and Factory Reformer*, Manchester: Manchester University Press, 1975.

74 See the (admittedly later) Chartist poetry collected in Brian Maidment, *The Poorhouse Fugitives: Self-Taught Poets and Poetry in Victorian Britain*, Manchester: Carcanet, 1987, pp. 39–59. Jones's work fits within none of the traditions that Maidment identifies.

75 David McConnel, *Facts and Traditions Collected for a Family Record*, Edinburgh: Ballantyne, 1861, pp. 61, 144–5. The Polygon was later home to William Fairbairn, John Rylands and Alexander Henry.

76 Aikin, *A Description of the Country*, p. 205.

77 Karl Marx, *The Eighteenth Brumaire of Louis Napoleon* (1852), London: Lawrence & Wishart, 1934, p. 10.

78 A suitable arms was created, though apparently never registered: McConnel, *Facts and Traditions*, pp. 1–3.

79 John Kennedy, 'A Brief Memoir', pp. 318–45. See also Christine MacLeod, *Heroes of Invention: Technology, Liberalism and British Identity, 1750–1914*, Cambridge: Cambridge University Press, 2007.

80 Rose, *Ancoats*, p. 5. Murray bought it from William Rawlinson, a Manchester merchant.

81 Clare Hartwell, *Manchester*, London: Penguin, 2001, p. 273.

82 Harold L. Platt, *Shock Cities: The Environmental Transformation and Reform of Manchester and Chicago*, Chicago: University of Chicago Press, 2005, p. 52.

83 Friedrich Engels, *The Condition of the Working Class in England* (1845), Harmondsworth: Penguin, 1987, pp. 94–5.

84 C. W. Chalklin, *The Provincial Towns of Georgian England*, London: Edward Arnold, 1974, p. 205; Rose, *Ancoats*, pp. 40–2; Roberts, '"A Densely Populated and Unlovely Tract"', pp. 15–26; Engels, *Condition*, pp. 95–7. Marx quoted Sir John Simon's report on such housing: Karl Marx, *Capital: A Critique of Political Economy*, trans. Ben Fowkes, Harmondsworth: Penguin, 1976, p. 811.

85 Lloyd-Jones and Lewis, 'Housing Factory Workers', p. 33.

86 John Rylands Library Special Collections, McConnel & Kennedy Papers, Ledgers for 1817–1827 and 1827–1831; Rose, *Ancoats*, p. 37. Both firms' ownership of houses rose in the next few decades, though they never provided for more than a 'small proportion of the workforce': Mike Williams, 'The Mills of Ancoats',

Manchester Region History Review 7 (1993), pp. 29, 30. It would be good to know more about the houses owned in 1826: Were they built by the companies? Had they been acquired with a view to possible future expansion of the mill buildings?

87 De Tocqueville, *Journeys to England and Ireland*, p. 94.

88 The area had been designated Police District 1 in 1792, one of fourteen such districts. The Police Commissioners were meant to oversee the provision of sewers, drains and paving, and the improvement and widening of streets but in general, especially in areas like Ancoats, they were overwhelmed by the sheer volume of new building and new streets These districts became linked to the supply of gas for street lighting, with any profits from gas provision ploughed back into town improvements: Roberts, '"A Densely Populated and Unlovely Tract"', p. 21.

89 James Phillips Kay, *The Moral and Physical Condition of the Working Classes*, London: James Ridgway, 1832, p. 11.

90 Angus Bethune Reach, *Manchester and the Textile Districts in 1849* (1849), Helmshore: Helmshore Local History Society, 1972, pp. 6–7.

91 De Tocqueville, *Journeys to England and Ireland*, p. 95.

92 Engels made this point in his *Anti-Dühring* (1878), Peking: Foreign Languages Press, 1976, p. 335.

93 Robert Owen, 'Report to the County of Lanark' (1820), in Robert Owen, *A New View of Society and Other Writings*, ed. Gregory Claeys, London: Penguin, 1991, p. 283. Such conditions also haunted the visions of other utopians reacting to the Industrial Revolution: see James Silk Buckingham, *National Evils and Practical Remedies, with a Plan of a Model Town*, London: Peter Jackson, 1849.

94 W. H. Chaloner, 'Robert Owen, Peter Drinkwater and the Early Factory System in Manchester', *Bulletin of the John Rylands Library* 37, no. 1 (September 1954), pp. 78–102.

95 Vidler points out how the title page of the Owenite newspaper *The Crisis* pitted a scene of an unpaved street in a town with various social ills against a scene of tranquillity in one of the villages: Anthony Vidler, *The Scenes of the Street and Other Essays*, New York: Monacelli, 2011, p. 61.

96 Mumford, *The Story of Utopias*, p. 111.

97 On Owen see Richard Price, *Labour in British Society: An Interpretive History*, London: Croom Helm, 1986. See also Thomas Markus, *Buildings and Power: Freedom and Control in the Origin of Modern Building Types*, London: Routledge, 1993, pp. 286–93; Michael J. Lewis, *City of Refuge: Separatists and Utopian Town Planning*, Princeton: Princeton University Press, 2016, pp. 169–78.

98 Robert Owen, 'A Sketch of Some of the Errors and Evils Arising from the Past and Present State of Society' (1817), in *A New View of Society and Other Writings*, p. 167.

99 John Bellamy Foster, *Marx's Ecology: Materialism and Nature*, New York: Monthly Review Press, 2000, pp. 141–77.

100 Friedrich Engels, *The Housing Question* (1872), ed. C. P. Dutt, London: Lawrence & Wishart, 1942, p. 54.

101 Owen, 'Report to the County of Lanark', p. 229. I also wonder about the exemplary presence of Fairfield, just outside Manchester, only two miles east of Ancoats, a startlingly serene expression of the Moravian tradition, with its church, square and terraces designed in 1785 by Benjamin Latrobe.

102 Maxine Berg, *The Machinery Question and the Making of Political Economy, 1815–1848*, Cambridge: Cambridge University Press, 1980.

103 Kennedy, 'Observations on the Rise and Progress', pp. 119, 121, 124, 125.

104 John Kennedy, 'Observations on the Influence of Machinery upon the Working Classes of the Community', *Memoirs of the Literary and Philosophical Society of Manchester*, 2nd series 5 (1831), pp. 26–9.

105 Kennedy, 'Observations on the Influence', p. 31.

106 Kennedy, 'Observations on the Rise and Progress', pp. 129–30.

107 '[The division of labour] changes the status of the human body (the human status of the body): it creates *men-bodies* whose bodies are body-machines; they are fragmented and dominated, utilized for an isolable function or a movement; their integrity is destroyed, but they are simultaneously fetishized; their useful organs are subject to both atrophy and hypertrophy': Étienne Balibar and Immanuel Wallerstein, *Race, Nation, Class*, trans. Chris Turner, London: Verso, 1991, p. 282.

108 Richard Byrom, *William Fairbairn: The Experimental Engineer*, Market Drayton: Railway & Canal Historical Society, 2017, pp. 63–4. This was an important stage in Fairbairn's own development of his 'factory-architect business [which] offered a complete package deal to the manufacturer': Berg, *Machinery Question*, pp. 200–1. It has also been pointed out that other consultant engineers for mills 'spent little of their time on mill carcases': Andrew Saint, *Architect and Engineer: A Study in Sibling Rivalry*, New Haven: Yale University Press, 2007, p. 75.

109 Miller and Wild (eds.), *A and G Murray*, pp. 52–3.

110 Markus, *Buildings and Power*, pp. 280–1; Byrom, *William Fairbairn*, p. 64.

111 Huberman, *Escape from the Market*, p. 34.

112 Williams and Farnie, *Cotton Mills*, p. 20; Lee, *A Cotton Enterprise*, p. 104.

113 Markus, *Buildings and Power*, p. 265.

114 Jennifer Tann, *The Development of the Factory*, London: Cornmarket, 1970, p. 19. Tann gives the source here as portfolio 303 in the Boulton & Watt archive, Birmingham. (Due to restrictions during the COVID-19 pandemic in the latter part of my research I was unable to see the original drawings.) The drawings – a plan and a section – are dated July 1809, clearly after the building had been finished. They were supplied to Boulton & Watt, as accompanying notations show, for the supply and fitting of gas retorts. Gas fitting had become another of Boulton & Watt's specialisms: Schivelbusch, *Disenchanted Night*, pp. 18–19.

115 Treating the subject strictly in terms of technological problems and solutions, architectural historians have long established a succession of stages for various aspects of fireproof and wide-span mill construction. The canonic buildings are, successively, William Strutt's six-storey Calico Mill (1792–3) in Derby (though this had wooden beams); Benyon, Marshall and Bage's five-storey flax

mill in Shrewsbury (1796–7), which had iron beams and columns; and Philips, Wood and Lee's seven-storey Cotton Twist Mill at Salford (1799–1801): Turpin Bannister, 'The First Iron-Framed Buildings', *Architectural Review* 107 (April 1950), pp. 236, 241–2. See also A. W. Skempton and H. R. Johnson, 'The First Iron Frames', *Architectural Review* 131 (March 1962), pp. 175–86. These are two of several articles in the mid-twentieth century attempting to establish the history of iron-framed constructions, ultimately as precursors to modern skeleton frames. The spur for these articles was probably Sigfried Giedion's *Space, Time and Architecture*, Cambridge, MA: Harvard University Press, 1941, pp. 124–5. See also Markus, *Buildings and Power*, pp. 270–2.

116 I am echoing here part of Adorno's critique of Benjamin: Walter Benjamin, 'Exchange with Theodor W. Adorno on the Essay "Paris, the Capital of the Nineteenth Century"', in *Walter Benjamin: Selected Writings*, vol. 3, 1935–1938, trans. Edmund Jephcott, Howard Eiland and others, ed. Howard Eiland and Michael W. Jennings, Cambridge, MA: Belknap Press, 2002, p. 58.

117 Marx, *Capital*, p. 519.

118 Mark Harvey, 'Slavery, Indenture and the Development of British Industrial Capitalism', *History Workshop Journal* 88 (Autumn 2019), pp. 66–88.

119 Eric Hobsbawm, *The Age of Revolution, 1789–1848*, London: Abacus, 1992, p. 50.

120 Edward Baines, *History of the Cotton Manufacture in Great Britain*, London: Fisher, Fisher, and Jackson, 1835, p. 5.

121 Montgomery, *Theory and Practice*, pp. 169–70. The similarity of these descriptions to those in guidebooks is not surprising given the rising interest in visiting factories as part of a tour of the city: Robert Gray, *The Factory Question and Industrial England, 1830–1860*, Cambridge: Cambridge University Press, 1996, pp. 136–7.

122 Marx, *Capital*, p. 519.

123 Baines, *History*, p. 208.

124 Huberman, 'Industrial Relations and the Industrial Revolution', p. 354; Michael Andrew Žmolek, *Rethinking the Industrial Revolution*, Chicago: Haymarket, 2014, p. 453.

125 Beckert, *Empire of Cotton*, p. 191.

126 Gray, *The Factory Question*, pp. 80–1.

127 A. E. Musson and Eric Robinson, *Science and Technology in the Industrial Revolution*, Manchester: Manchester University Press, 1969, p. 182.

128 The image represents the Orrell, or Travis Brook, mill in Stockport, which had been finished only the previous year and was therefore unlikely to be filled with a full stock of machines yet: Fitzgerald, 'The Development of the Cast Iron Frame', pp. 139–41.

129 Andrew Ure, *The Philosophy of Manufactures, or, An Exposition of the Scientific, Moral, and Commercial Economy of the Factory System*, London: Charles Knight, 1835, p. 13.

130 It recalls Jean-Paul Sartre's words about 'the [automatic] machine that dreamed through them [i.e. female workers] about erotic experience'. The machine requires the human semi-automaton to complete itself, the body functions mechanically as hand(maiden): Jean-Paul Sartre, *Critique de la raison dialectique*, vol. 1, Paris: Gallimard, 1960, pp. 290–1, as quoted in Fredric Jameson, *Marxism and Form*, Princeton: Princeton University Press, p. 291.

131 The dangers of wearing flowing garments around machinery was to be a particular concern of the 1840 Select Committee on the Act for the Regulation of Mills and Factories: see Gray, *The Factory Question*, p. 95.

132 Ure, *The Philosophy of Manufactures*, p. 21. On the factory–ballroom link see Gray, *The Factory Question*, p. 85.

133 Jules Michelet, *Le Peuple* (1842), as translated in Schivelbusch, *Disenchanted Night*, p. 134.

134 Steve Edwards, 'Factory and Fantasy in Andrew Ure', *Journal of Design History* 14, no. 1 (2001), p. 19.

135 Ure, *The Philosophy of Manufactures*, p. 44.

136 Robert Willis, *Principles of Mechanism*, London: John W. Parker, 1841, p. iv.

137 Karl Marx, *The Poverty of Philosophy* (1847), New York: International Publishers, 1963, p. 141.

138 Fredric Jameson, *Representing Capital: A Reading of Volume One*, London: Verso, 2014, p. 102.

139 Tijana Vujosevic, *Modernism and the Making of the Soviet New Man*, Manchester: Manchester University Press, 2017, pp. 37–64; Hatherley, *The Chaplin Machine*, chapter 2.

140 Jameson, *Representing Capital*, p. 102.

141 See Gray, *The Factory Question*.

142 Lee, *A Cotton Enterprise*, p. 114; Joel Mokyr, *The Lever of Riches: Technological Creativity and Economic Progress*, New York: Oxford University Press, 1992, pp. 98, 166. On steam and the labour force see Malm, *Fossil Capital*, pp. 121–64.

143 There was a direct link between the development of self-acting mules and the events of 1825–6: Kirby and Musson, *Voice of the People*, p. 32.

144 Boyd Hilton, *Corn, Cash, Commerce: The Economic Policies of the Tory Governments, 1815–1830*, Oxford: Oxford University Press, 1977, pp. 202–31; Žmolek, *Rethinking the Industrial Revolution*, pp. 670–3.

145 Boyd Hilton, *A Mad, Bad, and Dangerous People? England 1783–1846*, Oxford: Oxford University Press, 2006, pp. 398–9.

146 See the account in Archibald Prentice, *Historical Sketches and Personal Recollections of Manchester*, London: Gilpin, 1851, pp. 275–80.

147 Wheeler, *Manchester*, pp. 123–4; J. L. Hammond and Barbara Hammond, *The Skilled Labourer, 1760–1832*, London: Longmans, 1927, p. 127.

148 Wheeler, *Manchester*, pp. 127–8. On 8 May the firm reported to a correspondent in Glasgow that 'the disposition to tumult seems to be mainly subsided here': John Rylands Library Special Collections, McConnel & Kennedy Papers, Letterbook September 1825–July 1826.

149 *Manchester Gazette*, 15 July 1826; *Manchester Guardian*, 22 July 1826; David Walsh, 'The Lancashire "Rising" of 1826', *Albion* 26, no. 4 (Winter 1994), pp. 623–44.

150 *Manchester Gazette*, 22 July 1826.

151 On the description of riots see Erich Auerbach, *Mimesis: The Representation of Reality in Western Literature*, Princeton: Princeton University Press, 1953, pp. 50–76.

152 For more on this see Beckert, *Empire of Cotton*, pp. 150, 182. Between 1792 and 1815, 155 military barracks were constructed in industrial areas: E. P. Thompson, *The Making of the English*

Working Class, Harmondsworth: Penguin, 1968, p. 663.

153 Prentice, *Historical Sketches*, p. 280. Problematic industrial relations at McConnel & Kennedy were not exceptional for the time, even though the firm's size, innovativeness and reinvestment were. There was agitation for higher pay in 1810, a four-month dispute in 1811 and further strikes in 1813 and 1818, and over the whole period the increasing employment of female and child workers to reduce labour costs: Huberman, 'Industrial Relations', p. 371; Huberman, *Escape from the Market*, pp. 25–6. Attempts to cut pay recurred in 1823, 1825 and 1826, and later and more determinedly in 1829, while on the workers' side there was agitation to reduce output: Huberman, *Escape from the Market*, pp. 40–2. A particularly long dispute broke out in 1829 about a cut in piece rates: Huberman, *Escape from the Market*, p. 82.

154 *Manchester Guardian*, 22 July 1826. Although McConnel & Kennedy were relatively unaffected, their correspondence for this year makes several references to the bankruptcies and other economic difficulties of smaller firms: John Rylands Library Special Collections, McConnel & Kennedy Papers, Letterbook September 1825–July 1826. The firm's size and Continental trade may have protected it from the worst effects of the recession.

155 Bindman and Riemann (eds.), *Karl Friedrich Schinkel*, pp. 175, 179. It has proved impossible to find out more about the 6,000 deported Irish workers, though their expendable treatment is typical of this time. For more on Irish workers in England see Thompson, *Making of the English Working Class*, pp. 469–85; Mervyn Busteed, *The Irish in Manchester c.1750–1921: Resistance, Adaptation and Identity*, Manchester: Manchester University Press, 2016.

156 Kirby and Musson, *Voice of the People*, p. 42.

157 See the extract from *Critique of the Power of Judgement* (1790) in Robert R. Clewis (ed.), *The Sublime Reader*, London: Bloomsbury, 2019, pp. 123–37.

158 Jacques Rancière, 'Lyotard and the Aesthetics of the Sublime: A Counter-Reading of Kant', in *Aesthetics and its Discontents*, trans. Steven Corcoran, Malden, MA: Polity Press, 2009, p. 92.

159 Schinkel's reactions to the sublime experiences of nature – the abrupt, the dread inducing, the bodily threatening – were also often shadowed by, or paired with, the sense of precarious or turbulent social existence: Forster, *Schinkel*, p. 91.

160 Kay, *The Moral and Physical Condition*, p. 10.

161 Berg, *The Machinery Question*, pp. 164–5.

162 Benjamin Heywood in 1834, as quoted in Berg, *The Machinery Question*, p. 160.

163 Quoted in Barry Bergdol, *Karl Friedrich Schinkel: An Architecture for Prussia*, New York: Rizzoli, 1994, p. 9.

2 · City of Free Trade: The Urbanism of the Industrial Bourgeoisie *pages 47–77*

1 This would also be to ignore protectionist policies preventing British dominance and, even in Britain itself, the repeated tendency to protect businesses and the economy when their dominance is threatened: Sven Beckert, *Empire of Cotton: A New History of Global Capitalism*, London: Allen Lane, 2014, p. 158. On Free Trade see Joel Mokyr, *The Enlightened Economy: Britain and the Industrial Revolution, 1700–1850*, London: Penguin, 2009, pp. 63–78.

2 T. J. Clark, *The Painting of Modern Life: Paris in the Art of Manet and his Followers*, London: Thames & Hudson, 1985, p. 36.

3 George Saintsbury, *Manchester*, London: Longmans, 1887, p. 136.

4 Karl Marx, 'The Chartists', *New York Daily Tribune*, 28 August 1852, as republished in Christopher Harvie, Graham Martin and Aaron Scharf (eds.), *Industrialisation and Culture, 1830–1914*, London: Macmillan / Open University, 1970, p. 163. On Free Traders' attempts to convince Chartists of their 'unity of interest' see Dorothy Thompson, *The Dignity of Chartism*, London: Verso, 2015, pp. 28–37.

5 John Seed, 'Unitarianism, Political Economy and the Antinomies of Liberal Culture in Manchester, 1830–1850', *Social History* 7, no. 1 (1982), pp. 1–25; A. C. Gatrell, 'Incorporation and the Pursuit of Liberal Hegemony in Manchester, 1790–1839', in Derek Fraser (ed.), *Municipal Reform and the Industrial City*, Leicester: Leicester University Press, 1982, pp. 23–8; Mary Poovey, *Making a Social Body: British Cultural Formation, 1830–1864*, Chicago: University of Chicago Press, 1995.

6 The concepts are Foucault's, particularly from his posthumously published lectures at the Collège de France: Michel Foucault, *Security, Territory, Population: Lectures at the Collège de France, 1977–1978*, trans. Graham Burchell, Basingstoke: Palgrave Macmillan, 2007. For use of them in the case of Manchester see Patrick Joyce, *The Rule of Freedom: Liberalism and the Modern City*, London: Verso, 2003.

7 Joyce, *Rule of Freedom*, p. 98.

8 Marx, 'The Chartists', p. 161.

9 Friedrich Engels, *The Condition of the Working Class in England* (1845), Harmondsworth: Penguin, 1987, p. 86.

10 Engels, *Condition*, pp. 89, 87.

11 Clark, *The Painting of Modern Life*.

12 John J. Parkinson-Bailey, *Manchester: An Architectural History*, Manchester: Manchester University Press, 2000.

13 Engels, *Condition*, pp. 85, 87.

14 The year given in one source for the first appearance of the name 'Portland Place' is 1776: T. Swindells, *Manchester Streets and Manchester Men*, Manchester: J. E. Cornish, 1907, p. 7. It is not known if 'Portland' had any local significance, but its use may well have been an attempt to link it to contemporary London developments. The *Manchester Guardian* published several letters about the origins of these names in the mid-1870s: see *Manchester Guardian*, 14 December 1874, 16 December 1874, 18 December 1874, 29 December 1874, 15 January 1875.

15 C. W. Chalklin, *The Provincial Towns of Georgian England*, London: Edward Arnold, 1974, pp. 92, 95.

16 See Lewis's *Map of Manchester*, 1788; Laurent's *Topographic Plan of Manchester and Salford*, 1793; and Green's *Map of Manchester and Salford*, 1794.

17 Swindells, *Manchester Streets*, p. 15.

18 W. A. Shaw, *Manchester Old and New*, London: Cassell, 1894, p. 39; Charles Reilly, *Some Manchester Streets*, Liverpool: University Press of Liverpool / London: Hodder & Stoughton, 1924, p. 69.

19 Where the River Tib crossed the 'high road below the Infirmary' was described in 1783 as 'the old boundary of the town': James Ogden, *A Description of Manchester by a Native of the Town* (1783), Manchester: Heywood, 1887, p. 11.

20 John Pickstone, 'Ferriar's Fever to Kay's Cholera: Disease and Social Structure in Cottonopolis', *History of Science* 22, no. 4 (December 1984), p. 403.

21 John Pickstone, *Medicine and Industrial Society: A History of Hospital Development in Manchester and its Region, 1752–1946*, Manchester: Manchester University Press, 1985, p. 11.

22 Pickstone, *Medicine and Industrial Society*, pp. 11–12.

23 T. R. Williamson, 'On the Origin and History of the Manchester Statistical Society', *Transactions of the Manchester Statistical Society*, 1875–6, pp. 9–24.

24 See William Brockbank, *Portrait of a Hospital, 1752–1948*, London: Heinemann, 1952; F. Renaud, *A Short History of the Rise and Progress of the Manchester Royal Infirmary from the Year 1752 to 1877*, Manchester: J. E. Cornish, 1898, pp. 7–8, 79–80.

25 Joseph Aston, *A Picture of Manchester*, Manchester: Aston, 1816, pp. 116–25.

26 Gary A. Boyd, *Dublin, 1745–1922: Hospitals, Spectacle, and Vice*, Dublin: Four Courts Press, 2006, p. 77. There are also similarities in the role St George's Hospital, London, played in the development of the area around Hyde Park Corner: see Dana Arnold, *The Spaces of the Hospital: Spatiality and Urban Change in London, 1680–1820*, Abingdon: Routledge, 2013, pp. 106–10.

27 Pickstone, *Medicine and Industrial Society*, pp. 18–20.

28 Pickstone, *Medicine and Industrial Society*, p. 19.

29 Renaud, *Short History*, pp. 25, 53. Here, as elsewhere, I am modifying the revisionist idea that 'competition between a pre-industrial aristocracy and a new industrial elite played no significant part in the social or political dynamics of class formation in early or mid-nineteenth century Manchester': Martin Hewitt, *The Emergence of Stability in the Industrial City: Manchester, 1832–67*, Aldershot: Scolar Press, 1996, p. 36. Hewitt can't help but contradict this statement when dealing with conflicts over local government and the exclusion of Liberals and Unitarians from it in the early nineteenth century, or with the campaign for incorporation (pp. 68, 70–3). See also Gatrell, 'Incorporation', pp. 16–60.

30 Renaud, *Short History*, p. 46; Pickstone, *Medicine and Industrial Society*, p. 30.

31 Swindells, *Manchester Streets*, pp. 7–15. There were landed connections among these industrialists, Houldsworth most notably: Simon Gunn, 'The "Failure" of the Victorian Middle Class', in Janet Wolff and John Seed (eds.), *The Culture of Capital: Art, Power and the Nineteenth Century Middle Class*, Manchester: Manchester University Press, 1988, p. 22.

32 Despite his revisionist arguments, Hewitt writes that 'In Manchester no middle-class pockets were created and fortified against the spread of the industrial city ... [by the 1840s] the city was bereft of a resident haute bourgeoisie': Hewitt, *Emergence of Stability*, pp. 54–8. For the persistence of elite residences in another northern industrial city centre at this time, see R. J. Morris, *Men, Women and Property in England, 1780–1870: A Social and Economic History of Family Strategies amongst the Leeds Middle Classes*, Cambridge: Cambridge University Press, 2005, pp. 181–2.

33 Richard Wright Procter, *Memorials of Manchester Streets*, Manchester: Thomas Sutcliffe, 1874, p. 83.

34 *Manchester Mercury*, 5 March 1816.

35 Discussion had started in 1824 and been revived in 1836, the centenary of Watts's birth: Christine MacLeod, *Heroes of Invention: Technology, Liberalism and British Identity, 1750–1914*, Cambridge: Cambridge University Press, 2007, pp. 116–17.

36 William Fairbairn, *Observations on Improvements of the Town of Manchester Particularly as Regards the Importance of Blending in those Improvements, the Chaste and the Beautiful, with the Ornamental and Useful*, Manchester: Robinson, 1836, p. 16.

37 Fairbairn, *Observations*, p. 22.

38 Fairbairn, *Observations*, pp. ix–x, 32.

39 Manchester's population increased from 233,000 in 1831 to 388,000 in 1851, a rise of 67 per cent in a mere twenty years.

40 Swindells, *Manchester Streets*, pp. 81–3.

41 Pickstone, *Medicine and Industrial Society*, pp. 100, 102, 105–6. It was moved out to a new building designed by Richard Lane in Cheadle.

42 Renaud, *Short History*, pp. 110–11.

43 Richard Lane, report to Building Committee, 16 June 1846, Central Manchester University Hospital NHS Foundation Trust Archive. The architect's desire to use stone facings to link the complex and create 'one uniform imposing building' can be followed in the correspondence with the Building Committee: Richard Lane to Building Committee, 16 April 1846, and Report, 16 June 1846, Building Committee Minutes 1845–49, Central Manchester University Hospital NHS Foundation Trust Archive.

44 Pickstone, *Medicine and Industrial Society*, p. 102.

45 Pickstone, *Medicine and Industrial Society*, p. 104.

46 Pickstone, *Medicine and Industrial Society*, pp. 103–4. The alliance between industrialists and medics was also evident in the latter's opposition to the Ten Hours Bill, which limited factory working hours: Robert Gray, *The Factory Question and Industrial England, 1830–1860*, Cambridge: Cambridge University Press, 1996, pp. 77–9.

47 Richard Lane to Building Committee, 24 April 1846, Building Committee Minutes 1845–49, Central Manchester University Hospital NHS Foundation Trust Archive. These developments are also detailed in the papers of the Manchester Medical Collection, John Rylands Library, MMC/9/6/2/21–44.

48 Richard Lane, report to Building Committee, 24 August 1849, Building Committee Minutes 1845–49, Central Manchester University Hospital NHS Foundation Trust Archive.

49 The Portland Street entrance was, however, little used: Brockbank, *Portrait of a Hospital*, pp. 79, 146.

50 Mrs G. Linnaeus Banks (Isabella Varley), *The Manchester Man* (1876), Manchester: E. J. Morten, 1973, pp. 175–6; Manchester Medical Collection, John Rylands Library, MMC/9/6/2/21–44. Legislation in the late 1840s required factories in a locality to take their time from a designated public clock: Gray, *The Factory Question*, p. 217.

51 See also the accounts in guidebooks that usually described a mutually enhancing ensemble of buildings: George Catt, *Pictorial History of Manchester*, London: Pictorial Times Office, 1845, p. 10.

52 Indeed, there was no serious attempt to remove the hospital until 1875, and then it was because of the value of the land and the cramped site – and no success until the early twentieth century: Brockbank, *Portrait of a Hospital*, pp. 119–28; Pickstone, *Medicine and Industrial Society*, pp. 185–90.

53 The manufacturer Salis Schwabe was treasurer of the Lunatic Hospital and deputy treasurer of the Infirmary as well as a member of the Peel Memorial Committee: Terry Wyke, *Public Sculpture of Greater Manchester*, Liverpool: Liverpool University Press, 2004, p. 113; Renaud, *Short History*, pp. 125, 131.

54 On the creation of the Watt mythology see Ben Marsden, *Watt's Perfect Engine: Steam and the Age of Invention*, Cambridge: Icon Books, 2002, pp. 183–201; MacLeod, *Heroes of Invention*; and Andreas Malm, *Fossil Capital: The Rise of Steam Power and the Roots of Global Warming*, London: Verso, 2016, pp. 204–5.

55 MacLeod, *Heroes of Invention*, pp. 1, 117–18; Patrick Joyce, *Democratic Subjects: The Self and the Social in Nineteenth-Century England*, Cambridge: Cambridge University Press, 1994, pp. 168–9; Adrian Rifkin, 'Success Disavowed: The Schools of Design in Mid-Nineteenth-Century Britain (An Allegory)' (1988), in Steven Edwards (ed.), *Communards and Other Cultural Histories: Essays by Adrian Rifkin*, Chicago: Haymarket, 2018, p. 289.

56 Wyke, *Public Sculpture*, p. 112.

57 Wyke, *Public Sculpture*. See also Benedict Read, *Victorian Sculpture*, New Haven: Yale University Press, 1982, p. 149. A little later, in 1862, Thomas Worthington's memorial to Prince Albert was proposed for a location in front of the Infirmary, where it would join the other heroes of Free Trade. However, in a twist that shows how the aesthetics of Free Trade had already lost any unity, the memorial's Gothic Revival was deemed inappropriate to the Infirmary's Ionic portico. The story is told in Terry Wyke, 'The Albert Memorial and the Making of Civic Manchester', in Clare Hartwell and Terry Wyke (eds.), *Making Manchester: Aspects of the History of Architecture in the City and Region since 1900*, Manchester: Lancashire and Cheshire Antiquarian Society, 2007, pp. 90–115.

58 There were, however, attempts to build a central railway station between Portland, Hunt, David and Oxford streets in the 1860s: John R. Kellett, *The Impact of the Railways on Victorian Cities*, London: Routledge & Kegan Paul, 1969, pp. 167–9. Kellett emphasises how much urban land was owned by railway companies in British cities, as well as how much surrounding land was also indirectly affected by them (p. 290).

59 Pickstone, *Medicine and Industrial Society*, p. 14.

60 Christine Stevenson, *Medicine and Magnificence: British Hospital and Asylum Architecture, 1660–1815*, New Haven: Yale University Press for Paul Mellon Centre for Studies in British Art, 2000, pp. 205–12, 254 n. 55. Others have assumed that asylums were 'designed to keep [problem populations] apart from the rest of society', most usually in countryside locations: Andrew Scull, 'A Convenient Place to Get Rid of Inconvenient People: The Victorian Lunatic Asylum', in Anthony D. King (ed.), *Buildings and Society: Essays on the Social Development of the Built Environment*, London: Routledge & Kegan Paul, 1980, pp. 38, 48. At least one contemporary regarded the existence of the Lunatic Asylum in the heart of the city as symptomatic of the disordered spaces of industrial modernity. The title page of Robert Owen's newspaper *The Crisis* contrasted a scene containing a public house, gallows, dogs fighting and a lunatic asylum with a scene of tranquillity in one of Owen's parallelograms: Anthony Vidler, *The Scenes of the Street and Other Essays*, New York: Monacelli, 2011, p. 61.

61 *Manchester Evening News*, 3 February 1872; *Freelance*, 19 September 1873, both as quoted in Simon Gunn, *The Public Culture of the Victorian Middle Class: Ritual and Authority and the English Industrial City*, Manchester: Manchester University Press, 2000, p. 42.

62 *Builder* 26 (17 October 1868), pp. 760–1.

63 Manchester's Medical Officer of Health expressed the view in 1876 that commerce had done more to sweep away insanitary districts than any sanitary legislation: Gunn, *Public Culture*, p. 47.

64 Roger Lloyd-Jones and M. J. Lewis, *Manchester and the Age of the Factory: The Business Structure of Cottonopolis in the Industrial Revolution*, London: Croom Helm, 1988, pp. 67, 75–80; Gray, *The Factory Question*, pp. 88–90.

65 This argument has some relationship with work on governmentality and liberalism: see Joyce, *Rule of Freedom*, pp. 144–5. However, I want to retain the specific historical context of class-based struggles within the emerging civic city; architecture, to my mind, is a good, if complex and often indirect, expression of these.

66 Gunn, *Public Culture*, p. 18. Gunn's figures are based on propertied or non-manual workers, and on those earning over £100 p.a. See also Gary Messinger, *Manchester in the Victorian Age*, Manchester: Manchester University Press, 1985, chapter 7.

67 Gunn, *Public Culture*, pp. 29–30.

68 Beckert, *Empire of Cotton*, p. 150.

69 Lloyd-Jones and Lewis, *Manchester*, pp. 85–6.

70 Lloyd-Jones and Lewis, *Manchester*, pp. 44–62.

71 See A. V. Cooper, 'The Manchester Commercial Textile Warehouse, 1780–1914: A Study of its Typology and Practical Development', PhD thesis, Manchester Polytechnic, 1991, pp. 55–6, 71.

72 Nikolaus Pevsner, *A History of Building Types*, London: Thames & Hudson, 1976, p. 213.

73 Lloyd-Jones and Lewis, *Manchester*, p. 17.

74 Neither historians nor industrial archaeologists seem to recognise its distinctive representational function. This is why the subtype has received little recognition outside architectural

history: see, for example, Lloyd-Jones and Lewis, *Manchester*.

75 Paul Readman, *Storied Ground: Landscape and the Shaping of English National Identity*, Cambridge: Cambridge University Press, 2018, pp. 221–3.

76 *Builder*, 17 October 1868, p. 759.

77 Boyd Hilton, *A Mad, Bad, and Dangerous People? England 1783–1846*, Oxford: Oxford University Press, 2006, p. 157. Although many industrialists were members of the Court Leet, this did not alter or contradict its essentially medieval, pre-urban mode of operation: Lloyd-Jones and Lewis, *Manchester*, p. 137.

78 Richard Cobden, 'Incorporate your Borough' (1837), in E. A. Axon, *Cobden as a Citizen*, London: T. Fisher Unwin, 1907. On this alliance across industrial bourgeoisie, shopocracy and artisanate see Gatrell, 'Incorporation', pp. 16–60. This still seems to me better described as an ideology, with its specific political forms, rather than as something to do with 'governmentality': for the latter see Joyce, *Rule of Freedom*, p. 101.

79 Lloyd-Jones and Lewis, *Manchester*, p. 32.

80 Richard Cobden to Frederick Cobden, 12 April 1832, Cobden Papers, M87/2/1, Manchester Central Library Archives.

81 Samuel Bamford, *Passages in the Life of a Radical*, vol. 1, Manchester: Heywood, 1844, p. 204.

82 Richard Cobden to Frederick Cobden, September 1832, as quoted in John Morley, *The Life of Richard Cobden*, London: T. Fisher Unwin, 1903, p. 22 (emphasis in original). He was tempted into speculation which cost him hugely in land rents: Morley, *Richard Cobden*, pp. 159–60. Mosley Street's development is possibly the model for 'New Street', where the industrialist Thornton has his mill, in Elizabeth Gaskell's *North and South* (1854–5).

83 Malm, *Fossil Capital*, p. 60.

84 Morley, *Richard Cobden*, pp. 48–88. Cobden noted in his journal for 18 February 1837, 'In the morning breakfasted with Mr Perkins and Mr Walters – spoke to the latter about going to establish himself in Manchester as an architect': British Library Add. MS 43672A. The factory was in Uskudar, across the Bosphorus from Istanbul, and from the journal it seems likely that Cobden first met Walters there.

85 W. H. Chaloner, 'The Birth of Modern Manchester', in C. F. Carter (ed.), *Manchester and its Region*, Manchester: Manchester University Press, 1962, p. 138.

86 William Pole, *The Life of Sir William Fairbairn*, London: Longmans, 1878, pp. 75–82; Mark Crinson, *Empire Building: Orientalism and Victorian Architecture*, London: Routledge, 1996, pp. 126, 251 n. 4; Sibel Zandi-Sayek, 'The Unsung of the Canon: Does a Global Architectural History Need New Landmarks?', ABE *Journal* 6 (2014), https://journals.openedition.org/abe/1271#ftn13 (accessed 5 November 2021).

87 Cooper, 'Manchester Commercial Textile Warehouse', p. 59.

88 A biography of Cobden was written by Schwabe's wife: Mrs Salis Schwabe, *Reminiscences of Richard Cobden*, London: T. Fisher Unwin, 1895.

89 The Palazzo Pandolfini in Florence and the Cancelleria in Rome: see Marcus Whiffen, 'The Architecture of Sir Charles Barry in Manchester and its Neighbourhood', in John H. G. Archer (ed.), *Art and Architecture in Victorian Manchester*, Manchester: Manchester University Press, 1985, pp. 58–61.

90 Joyce, *Democratic Subjects*, pp. 168–9.

91 Swindells, *Manchester Streets*, pp. 32–8.

92 Howard M. Wach, 'Culture and the Middle Classes: Popular Knowledge in Industrial Manchester', *Journal of British Studies* 27, no. 4 (October 1988), p. 387. See also Joyce, *Democratic Subjects*, pp. 166–7.

93 Speech given at the Athenaeum, 5 October 1843, quoted without source in Asa Briggs, *Victorian Cities* (1963), Harmondsworth: Pelican, 1968, p. 95.

94 Wach, 'Culture and the Middle Classes', p. 382.

95 See, for instance, Henry-Russell Hitchcock, *Early Victorian Architecture in Britain*, New Haven: Yale University Press, 1954, vol. 1, p. 387. This part of Hitchcock's book first appeared as 'Victorian Monuments of Commerce' in *Architectural Review*, February 1949, pp. 61–74. Hitchcock's agenda was partly to find British precedents for the work of Louis Sullivan and H. H. Richardson.

96 See, for instance, Michael Hebbert, 'The Art of Street Architecture: The Case of Manchester', in Charles C. Bohl and Jean-François Lejeune (eds.), *Sitte, Hegemann and the Metropolis*, London: Routledge, 2009, p. 239. The use of public institutions to manifest the industrialists' civic identity has often been recognised but only very loosely in terms of architecture: see, for instance, Alan Kidd, *Manchester*, Keele: Keele University Press, 1993, p. 75.

97 John Seed, '"Commerce and the Liberal Arts": The Political Economy of Art in Manchester, 1775–1860', in Wolff and Seed (eds.), *The Culture of Capital*, p. 72.

98 Morley, *Richard Cobden*, p. 123; see pp. 121–5 for Cobden's views on the medieval forms of Manchester's pre-incorporation local government.

99 The Royal Manchester Institution (later Manchester Art Gallery), designed by Charles Barry and built in 1824–35 in a Greek Revival style, should also be mentioned. Its image and governance largely predated the rise of the industrial bourgeoisie but were increasingly infiltrated by them; by the late 1830s nearly 50 per cent of its members were industrialists: Seed, '"Commerce and the Liberal Arts"', pp. 66, 80 n. 102.

100 James Wheeler, *Manchester, its Political, Social and Commercial History, Ancient and Modern*, London and Manchester, 1836, p. 414; Thomas Markus, *Building and Power: Freedom and Control in the Origin of Modern Building Types*, London: Routledge, 1993, pp. 241–2.

101 I. Miller and C. Wild (eds.), *A and G Murray and the Cotton Mills of Ancoats*, Lancaster: Oxford Archaeology North, 2007, p. 160.

102 Maxine Berg, *The Machinery Question and the Making of Political Economy, 1815–1848*, Cambridge: Cambridge University Press, 1980, pp. 145–78.

103 The words are those of Benjamin Heywood, speaking about the Manchester Mechanics' Institute: Berg, *The Machinery Question*, pp. 147, 155. On the exhibitions see Seed, '"Commerce and the Liberal Arts"', pp. 69–70.

104 Richard Burnet, *A Word to the Members of the Mechanics' Institutes*, Devonport, 1826, pp. 16–19. See also Berg, *The Machinery Question*, pp. 156–8.

105 On the classes held in the Mechanics' Institute and their relation to the industrial economy of Manchester see Rifkin, 'Success Disavowed', pp. 282–3.

106 Most of Cobden's commercial interests in Manchester ended in 1847 as a result of neglect (as he pursued political interests in London) and the slump in the Lancashire textile trade that year: Wendy Hinde, *Richard Cobden: A Victorian Outsider*, New Haven: Yale University Press, 1987, p. 187.

107 Richard Lane to Building Committee, 24 April 1846, Building Committee Minutes 1845–49, Central Manchester University Hospital NHS Foundation Trust Archive.

108 *Manchester Critic*, 16 December 1871, as quoted in Parkinson-Bailey, *Manchester*, p. 73.

109 Parkinson-Bailey, *Manchester*, p. 73.

110 In 1815 warehouses constituted 48 per cent of Manchester's total property assets, compared to cotton mills which provided only 6 per cent: Lloyd-Jones and Lewis, *Manchester*, pp. 30–1.

111 *Illustrated London News*, 14 May 1853, p. 372; *Bradshaw's Railway Guide*, London: W. J. Adams, 1848, as quoted in Anthony J. Pass, *Thomas Worthington: Victorian Architecture and Social Purpose*, Manchester: Manchester Literary and Philosophical Publications, 1988.

112 British Library Add. MS 43,674B, entries for 9 January 1847 and 11 January 1847.

113 Morley, *Richard Cobden*, p. 134. Engels was surely making a sly dig at Cobden and the Free Traders with their dreams of Renaissance Italy when he described Salford as 'built in courts or narrow lanes, so narrow that they remind me of the narrowest that I have ever seen, the little lanes of Genoa': Engels, *Condition*, p. 99.

114 Schwabe, *Reminiscences*, pp. 62–5; British Library Add. MS 50751, Richard Cobden to Frederick Cobden, 9 May 1847.

115 Erich Auerbach, *Mimesis: The Representation of Reality in Western Literature*, Princeton: Princeton University Press, 1953, pp. 73–4; see also pp. 195–8.

116 On ideologemes see Fredric Jameson, *The Political Unconscious: Narrative as a Socially Symbolic Act*, London: Methuen, 1981, pp. 87–8.

117 Hinde, *Richard Cobden*, pp. 13–14; Robina McNeil and A. D. George (eds.), *Warehouse Album*, Manchester: University of Manchester Field Archaeology Centre, 1997, p. 9; Roland Smith, 'Manchester as a Centre for the Manufacture and Merchanting of Cotton Goods, 1820–30', *University of Birmingham Historical Journal* 4, no. 1 (1953), p. 64 n. 58.

118 Joseph Ashton, *The Manchester Guide: A Brief Historical Description of the Towns of Manchester and Salford*, Manchester: Joseph Ashton, 1804, p. 272.

119 Banks, *The Manchester Man*, p. 104. The novelist was part of the Free Trade movement and a member of the Ladies' Committee of the Anti-Corn Law League.

120 *Manchester of Today*, Manchester: Historical Publishing Company, 1888, p. 148.

121 London writers recognised it as a particular type, quite distinct from the more utilitarian warehouses that prevailed elsewhere; even when ornamented, these were more mono-functional warehouses than the new Manchester type.

122 On the 'struggle' between factory and warehouse in the early years of the century see Lloyd-Jones and Lewis, *Manchester*, pp. 2–4.

123 See, for instance, *Builder*, 10 March 1849 and 14 April 1849.

124 *Building News* 4 (12 February 1858), p. 158.

125 Although warehouses became less ornate as they reached the other end of the street, they continued to bind the street together. The Behrens warehouse, for instance, used red brick on the upper storeys and attempted to animate its longer frontage with a two-storey 'arcade' above the ground floor rather than with Walters's articulations. Tellingly, it was built for multiple occupation where the earlier palatial warehouses at the other end of the street had been built for single owners. On the Infirmary as reference point see Reuben Spencer, *A Survey of the History, Commerce and Manufactures of Lancashire*, London: Biographical Publishing Company, 1897, p. 94.

126 *Manchester of Today*, p. 87.

127 *Manchester of Today*, p. 106.

128 Shaw, *Manchester Old and New*, pp. 38–9.

129 *Manchester of Today*, p. 109.

130 Swindells, *Manchester Streets*, p. 18.

131 Spencer, *Survey*, p. 87.

132 On the collective interests of this class, against the usual supposition of individualism, see Joyce, *Democratic Subjects*, pp. 86–7.

133 Alyson Cooper, 'Natural and Artificial Lighting in the Manchester Textile Warehouse', in Hartwell and Wyke (eds.), *Making Manchester*, p. 59.

134 Gunn, *Public Culture*, p. 73.

135 Isaac Slater, *A Directory of Manchester and Salford*, Manchester: I. Slater, 1848. Many parts of this economy were, of course, reliant on warehouse activity. Public houses, for instance, were commonly used as meeting places by merchants and industrialists: Lloyd-Jones and Lewis, *Manchester*, p. 36.

136 That the development was for commercial and not industrial ends is clear from the minutes of the Improvement Committee: Manchester Council Proceedings, 21 January 1857, p. 95. Manchester Central Library.

137 Isaac Slater, *A Directory of Manchester and Salford*, Manchester: I. Slater, 1869.

138 *Manchester Critic*, 15 November 1873, p. 561.

139 *Manchester City News*, 31 December 1891.

140 Reilly, *Some Manchester Streets*, pp. 74–5.

141 Theodor Adorno, *Prisms* (1967), trans. Samuel Weber and Shierry Weber, Cambridge, MA: MIT Press, 1981, p. 235.

142 *Manchester Free Trade Hall*, Manchester: Municipal Information Bureau, 1851, p. 1; Terry Wyke, *A Hall for All Seasons: A History of the Free Trade Hall*, Manchester: Charles Hallé Foundation, 1996, pp. 9–15. Cobden was not allowed to raise money, given that his own interests were compromised, but found a way to contribute to the building fund through an intermediary: Richard Cobden to George Wilson, 5 July 1843 and 22 June 1853, Cobden Papers, M20/Index/653 and M20/Index/757, Manchester Central Library Archives. Cobden's active prompting from a distance continued through the development of the building: for

instance, Cobden to Wilson, 11 April 1853 and 20 May 1853, Cobden Papers, M20/Index/755 and M20/Index/756, Manchester Central Library Archives. Little is known about why Cobden wanted to own the Peter Street site apart from as part of a portfolio of property speculation: Saintsbury, *Manchester*, p. 144.

143 Bamford, *Passages*, vol. 1, p. 204.

144 Cobden, 'Incorporate your Borough', pp. 2, 5–6.

145 Cobden, 'Incorporate your Borough', p. 2; Derek Fraser, *Urban Politics in Victorian England*, Leicester: Leicester University Press, 1976, p. 119.

146 Paul A. Pickering, *Chartism and the Chartists in Manchester and Salford*, Basingstoke: Macmillan, 1995, pp. 75, 88–9.

147 Saintsbury, *Manchester*, p. 194.

148 Anthony Howe, *Free Trade and Liberal England, 1846–1946*, Oxford: Oxford University Press, 1997; Frank Trentmann, 'Civil Society, Commerce, and the "Citizen-Consumer": Popular Meanings of Free Trade in Modern Britain', in Frank Trentmann (ed.), *Paradoxes of Civil Society: New Perspectives in Modern German and British History*, New York: Berghahn Books, 2000, pp. 306–31.

149 This cityscape also had outriders in new theatres such as the Theatre Royal (1845) on nearby Peter Street: Viv Gardner, 'The Image of a Well-Ordered City: Nineteenth-Century Manchester Theatre Architecture and the Urban Spectator', in Janet Wolff and Mike Savage (eds.), *Culture in Manchester: Institutions and Urban Change since 1850*, Manchester: Manchester University Press, 2013, pp. 95–122.

150 See C. Wheeler, *A Plan of St Peter's Field* (1823), as reproduced in Jacqueline Riding, *Peterloo: The Story of the Manchester Massacre*, London: Head of Zeus, 2018, pp. 226–7.

151 Wyke, *A Hall*, pp. 16–17, 33. Cobden was concerned to exercise some control over these uses of the hall lest they cause 'embarrassment': Cobden to Wilson, 8 July 1853, Cobden Papers, M20/Index/758, Manchester Central Library Archives.

152 Paul A. Pickering and Alex Tyrell, *The People's Bread: A History of the Anti-Corn Law League*, London: Leicester University Press 2000, pp. 191–216.

153 Quoted without source in Wyke, *A Hall*, p. 29.

154 A detail drawing of the facade survives, showing the female embodiment of Free Trade, signed and dated 9 March 1853 by Walters: Cobden Papers, M497, Manchester Central Library Archives.

155 Anna Clark, *The Struggle for the Breeches: Gender and the Making of the British Working Classes*, London: Rivers Oram Press, 1995, p. 241. For women's reform societies and their presence at Peterloo see M. L. Bush, 'The Women at Peterloo: The Impact of Female Reform on the Manchester Meeting of 16 August 1819', *History* 89, no. 2 (April 2004), pp. 209–32; and Riding, *Peterloo*, pp. 169–85. On Chartists memorialising Peterloo see Pickering, *Chartism and the Chartists*, pp. 35, 160; and James Epstein, *Radical Expression: Political Language, Ritual, and Symbol in England, 1790–1850*, London: Breviary Stuff, 2014, pp. 177–99.

156 Riding, *Peterloo*, pp. 172, 298.

157 Clark, *Struggle for the Breeches*, p. 163; Riding, *Peterloo*, 265; Bush, 'Women at Peterloo', p. 224.

158 Riding, *Peterloo*, p. 175.

159 That, at least, was Henry Hunt's argument in his trial, where his prosecutors regarded it as symbolic of the French Revolution. Interestingly, Hunt in his defence also pointed to an architectural decoration as precedent – 'the representation of the cap of liberty on the front of the town hall at York as evidence of the Englishness of the symbol': Epstein, *Radical Expression*, p. 92.

160 Katrina Navickas, *Protest and the Politics of Space and Place, 1789–1848*, Manchester: Manchester University Press, 2016, pp. 78–9; Epstein, *Radical Expression*, p. 105.

161 *Manchester Comet*, October 1822, as quoted in Bush, 'Women at Peterloo', p. 209.

162 A. J. P. Taylor, 'Manchester', *Encounter* 8, no. 3 (1957), p. 9.

163 Fraser, *Urban Politics*, pp. 206–7.

164 Alison Adburgham, *Shops and Shopping, 1800–1914*, London: Barrie & Jenkins, 1989, p. 19.

165 *Bradshaw's Railway Guide*, p. 18; Shaw, *Manchester Old and New*, p. 38; Swindells, *Manchester Streets*, p. 18.

166 Pickstone, *Medicine and Industrial Society*, pp. 105–6. Pickstone sees this as the beginning of the end for the Infirmary's central site as, although it became financially stable, it also became badly overcrowded as it took over the House of Recovery's functions. The building was briefly used as a hotel – the Art Treasures Hotel – during the Art Treasures Exhibition of 1857.

167 *Builder* 16 (13 February 1858), p. 98.

168 Reilly, *Some Manchester Streets*, pp. 77–8.

169 See, for instance, *Manchester of Today*, p. 161.

170 Manfredo Tafuri, 'The Disenchanted Mountain: The Skyscraper and the City', in Giorgio Ciucci (ed.), *The American City: From the Civil War to the New Deal*, Cambridge, MA: MIT Press, 1979, p. 390.

171 Its completion coincided with the economic upswing, with cotton manufacturing accounting for 40 per cent of British exports and Manchester sitting at the centre of imperial trade in the commodity: D. A. Farnie, *The English Cotton Industry and the World Market, 1815–1896*, Oxford: Clarendon Press, 1979.

172 Quoted without source in Clare Hartwell and Terry Wyke, 'Bibliographical Note', in Hartwell and Wyke (eds.), *Making Manchester*, p. 233.

173 David Harvey, *The Urban Experience*, Baltimore: Johns Hopkins University Press, 1989, p. 28.

3 · Ancient and Modern: Photography Imagining an Epoch

pages 79–98

1 Mudd came close to breaking his own strictures on composition here (and elsewhere); in 1866 he wrote: 'do not let the distant opening be exactly in the centre of the picture': James Mudd, *The Collodio-Albumen Process, Hints on Composition, and Other Papers*, London: Thomas Piper, 1866, p. 47.

2 Mudd, *The Collodio-Albumen Process*, p. 42. There is more than a touch of irony here – and Mudd may well have been playing on it – for, nine years before his book was published, he had been involved in a lawsuit against the industrialist Peter Spence, and had taken photographs of damaged trees to demonstrate the airborne pollution caused by Spence: see the album titled 'Regina v Spence: Plates' in the archives of the Salford Public Library.

3 Mudd, *The Collodio-Albumen Process*, p. 42.

4 *A New Alphabetical Directory of Manchester and Salford*, Manchester: Whellan, 1859.

5 Joseph Corbett, *The River Irwell*, Manchester: Abel Heywood, 1907.

6 It can be found in the writings of Baudelaire, Freud, Benjamin and Proust: see Richard Terdiman, *Present Past: Modernity and Memory Crisis*, Ithaca, NY: Cornell University Press, 1993.

7 Benedict Anderson, *Imagined Communities*, London: Verso, 1991, p. xiv. See also Michel de Certeau, 'The Theater of the *Quidproquo*', in *Heterologies: Discourse on the Other*, trans. Brian Massumi, Minneapolis: University of Minnesota Press, 1986, pp. 150–5.

8 For a now classic Foucauldian approach to photography see John Tagg, *The Burden of Representation: Essays on Photography and Histories*, London: Macmillan, 1988.

9 Roland Barthes, *Camera Lucida*, trans. Richard Howard, London: Vintage, 1993. See also W. J. T. Mitchell, *Picture Theory*, Chicago: University of Chicago Press, 1994.

10 Geoffrey Batchen, *Burning with Desire: The Conception of Photography*, Cambridge, MA: MIT Press, 1997, p. 177.

11 Harry Milligan, 'James Mudd: A 19th Century Industrial Photographer', *Photographic Journal* 114, no. 11 (November 1974), pp. 544–7. Mudd read a paper on 'A Photographer's Dream' to the society in 1865, later published in the *Photographic News*: Steve Edwards, *The Making of English Photography: Allegories*, University Park: Pennsylvania State University Press, 2006, p. 125. Mudd was drawn into the prosecution of a fellow member of the Literary and Philosophical Society, Peter Spence (see n. 2) and his Pendleton Alum Works: Peter Reed, *Acid Rain and the Rise of the Environmental Chemist in Nineteenth-Century Britain*, Aldershot: Ashgate, 2014, p. 86.

12 Peter Hall, *Cities in Civilisation*, London: Weidenfeld & Nicolson, 1998, pp. 314–15; A. Thackrey, 'Natural Knowledge in a Cultural Context: The Manchester Model', *American Historical Review* 69 (1974), pp. 672–709; Robert Kargon, *Science in Victorian Manchester: Enterprise and Expertise*, Manchester: Manchester University Press, 1977, pp. 1–33.

13 Mabel Tylecote, *The Mechanics' Institutes of Lancashire and Yorkshire before 1851*, Manchester: Manchester University Press, 1957, pp. 129–89; Kargon, *Science in Victorian Manchester*, pp. 20–4.

14 Edwards, *The Making of English Photography*, pp. 131–2 and, more generally, pp. 101–3. Edwards's is an eloquent and persuasive argument about Mudd's utopian conception of photography as art and how this relates to Mudd as petit bourgeois, but for my purposes its concentration on the differences between the mechanical, the machine and the landscape as art leaves out the industrial city and the question of whether images of it were 'mechanical documents', 'pictures' or something else entirely (p. 134).

15 Edwards, *The Making of English Photography*, pp. 108, 125–6, 322 n. 147.

16 See Caroline Arscott and Griselda Pollock, with Janet Wolff, 'The Partial View: The Visual Representation of the Early Nineteenth-Century City', in John Seed and Janet Wolff (eds.), *The Culture of Capital: Art, Power, and the Nineteenth-Century Middle Class*, Manchester: Manchester University Press, 1988; Marcia Pointon, *Bonington, Francia and Wyld*, London: Batsford, 1985, pp. 75–7.

17 'Photographs of 19th Century Worthies and Places', Collection of John Harland, Manchester Central Library.

18 H. J. Dyos and Michael Wolff (eds.), *The Victorian City: Images and Realities*, vol. 1, London: Henley / Boston: Routledge & Kegan Paul, 1973. All the other titles mentioned here are cited elsewhere in this book.

19 An earlier engraving, showing the same view as Mudd's photograph, was used on the cover of the 1968 Pelican Books edition of Asa Briggs's seminal *Victorian Cities*. The photograph also appears on the first page of the chapter 'Manchester and the Industrial Revolution' in *Manchester: 50 Years of Change*, London: HMSO, 1995. This is by no means an exhaustive survey of the use of Mudd's image and does not include anything since the turn of this century.

20 Central Manchester actually has four rivers – the Irwell, the Medlock, the Tib and the Irk (some might add Shooter's Brook before it was taken over by the Ashton Canal) – but for much of their urban extent they are either culverted or hemmed in by buildings, and the Tib and the Irk are barely more than streams. This anti-waterways sentiment reached its height in 1945 when the city surveyor planned that this stretch of the Irwell should be covered over to provide an inner ring road: Rowland Nicholas, *City of Manchester Plan*, Norwich: Jarrold, 1945, pp. 114, 188.

21 Friedrich Engels, *The Condition of the Working Class in England* (1845; first translation published in the UK in 1892), Harmondsworth: Penguin, 1987, p. 89.

22 It is one of the few areas of Manchester where Engels didn't employ his racialised matrix for poverty: see Stathis Kouvelakis, *Philosophy and Revolution: From Kant to Marx*, London: Verso, 2003, pp. 207–19.

23 The phrase is Molly Nesbitt's: see her *Atget's Seven Albums*, New Haven: Yale University Press, 1992, p. 71. See also John Macarthur, *The Picturesque: Architecture, Disgust and Other Irregularities*, London: Routledge, 2007, pp. 57–109. Engels certainly understood the conventions of landscape description: see his use of contrasted landscape prospects in Greece, Germany and England in his 1840 article 'Landscapes', in Karl Marx and Friedrich Engels, *Collected Works*, New York: International Publishers, 1975, vol. 2, pp. 95–101.

24 In the original German the words are *Schlamm* (twice), *Abfall* (three times) and *Schutt* (twice), but the point still applies.

25 There was a vast increase in the number of shops in Manchester in this period, by some accounts a 645 per cent increase between 1822 and 1848: David Alexander, *Retailing in England during the Industrial Revolution*, London: Athlone Press, 1970, p. 92.

26 Friedrich Engels, *Die Lage der arbeitenden Klasse in England* (1845), Berlin: Dietz, 1974, pp. 116, 113, as translated in Engels, *Condition*, pp. 89, 87.

27 On Engels's map see Kouvelakis, *Philosophy and Revolution*, pp. 203–5. I go along with Kouvelakis's idea of Engels's map as a 'dystopian figure', but he literalises too much and, in imagining that it enabled 'a "guided tour" of the city' which allows us to 'roam freely', misses the dialectical intent in Engels's play with aesthetic and guidebook codes (p. 396 n. 141). Far from roaming freely, the reader is usually baulked, lost or confused in what Engels calls a 'labyrinth' (a term that recognises that there is an insider knowledge necessary to traverse it and that there is a group that knows and a group that doesn't).

28 Henri Lefebvre, *The Production of Space*, trans. Donald Nicholson-Smith, Oxford: Blackwell, 1991, p. 226. Compare Steven Marcus's Freudian reading of Engels's 'tender concealment': '[the streets represent] a collective effort of isolation, distancing and denial, and work socially to the same ends as the same unconscious defensive processes work toward in individual persons': Steven Marcus, *Engels, Manchester and the Working Class*, London: Weidenfeld & Nicolson, 1974, p. 174.

29 See also Henri Lefebvre, *Marxist Thought and the City* (1972), trans. Robert Bonnono, Minneapolis: University of Minnesota Press, 2016, pp. 3–18.

30 Alfred Brothers, *Manchester As It Is*, Manchester: J. E. Cornish, 1878, p. 1. For Brothers's dual career as photographer and publisher see Steven F. Joseph, 'Alfred Brothers (1826–1912) and his Role in Photographic Publishing', *History of Photography* 11, no. 1 (January–March 1987), pp. 62–76.

31 James Donald, *Imagining the Modern City*, London: Athlone Press, 1999, p. 29.

32 That it is difficult to align any mid-nineteenth-century photography with these models is inadvertently indicated in James Donald's book, where a Jacob Riis photograph of a New York rookery from 1890 is placed opposite an analysis of Engels's text. Similarly, in his now classic account of nineteenth-century photography, John Tagg uses a set of photographs of the Quarry Hill area of Leeds from the 1890s for his case study of the relationship between photography and urban regulation: Tagg, *The Burden of Representation*.

33 The portfolio has the subheading 'Photographed by George Wardley', but it is perhaps more accurate to say that the earlier photographs were the work of James Mudd's studio, where Wardley worked as a studio assistant until 1866: see Priscilla M. Gray, 'James Mudd, Early Manchester Photographer', MA thesis, University of California at Riverside, 1982, pp. 44–52. Wardley and Mudd were both listed on the council of the Manchester Photographic Society in 1861: *British Journal of Photography Almanac*, 1861, p. 1. After 1906 the business was known as George Grundy & Sons. There were two copies of the portfolio in Manchester Central Library, with varying images in them (the variation does not affect the prints discussed here), and a set of loose prints in addition. Most of the photographs were albumen silver prints. I studied the portfolio in 2001, but when I returned to view it again in 2016 the librarians were unable to locate either copy. The portfolio may have been broken up and the prints consigned to what was called 'deep storage', available only as digital images. However, another set of Mudd's images, a Victorian album with photos pasted in and similar in its range of images to the portfolio, had entered the collection since my initial visit: Manchester Central Library, MISC/1222–2014/13. It is from this and the collection at the Canadian Centre for Architecture in Montreal that I have taken the Mudd images used in this chapter.

34 Carol Armstrong, *Scenes in a Library: Reading the Photograph in the Book, 1843–1875*, Cambridge, MA: MIT Press, 1998, p. 2.

35 The collection was given to the Manchester Central Library in 1959 as a portfolio, together with antiquarian views of Manchester and Salford by H. G. James, T. Barritt and F. Wroc. It is unclear whether the portfolio was put together by a collector as a selection of antiquarian views by Mudd/Wardley or whether Mudd/Wardley put the collection together. The Canadian Centre for Architecture in Montreal has thirty-nine views of Manchester by James Mudd, many of which are the same as those at the Manchester Central Library; there is no mention of George Wardley on any of them.

36 This plate, with its contrasted towns, was added to the second edition of Pugin's book: Augustus Welby Northmore Pugin, *Contrasts; or, A Parallel between the Noble Edifices of the Middle Ages, and Corresponding Buildings of the Present Day*, 2nd edn, London: Charles Dolman, 1841. Pugin may well have had Manchester in mind for the upper half of the plate 'The Same Town in 1840', with its gasworks, lunatic asylum and townscape of churches and chimneys, all on the banks of a river.

37 Louis Hayes, *Reminiscences of Manchester and Some of its Local Surroundings from the Year 1840*, London: Sherratt & Hughes, 1905, p. 114. For a description of the tower just before this enforced demolition of its upper parts see Thomas Bullock, *Bradshaw's Illustrated Guide to Manchester*, Manchester: Bradshaw & Blacklock, 1857, pp. 66–7.

38 Thomas Worthington, *An Historical Account and Illustrated Description of the Cathedral Church of Manchester*, Manchester: J. E. Cornish, 1884, p. 43.

39 The restoration campaign is dated 1862 to 1868. The view from the bridge and the close-up of the west door were exhibited together at the Manchester Photographic Society in 1860: Gray, 'James Mudd', p. 72.

40 *Strines Journal* 4 (1855), pp. 97–103. The same volume includes photographs of 'The Nasmyth Gun' and 'The Steam Hammer', possibly by James Mudd. This kind of juxtaposition, or rather cohabitation, can also be found, for instance, in *Views of Old Manchester*. The latter's set of views of the pre-industrial city is, on the page facing the title page, introduced by a 'Hand loom used for weaving previous to the introduction of power looms' and on the inside back cover the views are book-ended by an image of a 'Modern power loom': *Views of Old Manchester*, Manchester: Mancunian Velveteen, 1885.

41 See Alfred Darbyshire, *A Book of Olde Manchester and Salford*, Manchester: John Heywood, 1887.

42 Richard Wright Procter, *Memorials of Bygone Manchester, with Glimpses of the Environs*, Manchester: Palmer & Howe, 1880, p. vii. On the various editions of this plan see W. H. Thomson, *History of Manchester in 1852*, Altrincham: John Sherratt, 1967, pp. 168–70.

43 Arthur Redford and Ina Russell, *The History of Local Government in Manchester*, London: Longmans, 1939–40, vol. 2, pp. 89–91, 205, 210–220.

44 Both are represented in several Mudd photographs not in the *Old Manchester and Salford* portfolio: see the set of loose prints in Manchester Central Library in 2001, and the collection of Mudd photographs in the Canadian Centre for Architecture.

45 Cecil Stewart, 'MSA: A Brief History', in Dennis Sharp (ed.), 'Manchester Buildings', special issue of *Architecture North West* 19 (October–November 1966).

46 Lynda Nead, *Victorian Babylon: People, Streets and Images in Victorian London*, New Haven: Yale University Press, 2000, pp. 31–3; T. J. Clark, *The Painting of Modern Life: Paris in the Art of Manet and his Followers*, London: Thames & Hudson, 1985, pp. 37–8; Alex Potts, 'Picturing the Modern Metropolis: Images of London in the Nineteenth Century', *History Workshop Journal* 26, no. 1 (Autumn 1988), pp. 28–56.

47 John K. Walton, 'Proto-industrialisation and the First Industrial Revolution: The Case of Lancashire', in Pat Hudson (ed.), *Regions and Industries: A Perspective on the Industrial Revolution in Britain*, Cambridge: Cambridge University Press, 1989, pp. 41–68; Maxine Berg, *The Age of Manufactures, 1700–1820*, London: Routledge, 1994, pp. 66–70; Hall, *Cities*, pp. 314–23.

48 The Vintner's Arms still survived in 1890. For a much less articulate image of it around that date see Elizabeth Edwards, *The Camera as Historian: Amateur Photographers and Historical Imagination, 1885–1918*, Durham, NC: Duke University Press, 2012, p. 53.

49 Engels, *Condition*, p. 88.

50 I am thinking particularly of work by Richard Parkes Bonington, William Wyld and Thomas Shotter Boys: see Marcia Pointon, *The Bonington Circle: English Watercolour and Anglo-French Landscape, 1790–1855*, Brighton: Hendon Press, 1985, pp. 65–6.

51 On this see also Alois Riegl's seminal 1903 essay 'The Modern Cult of Monuments: Its Character and its Origin', republished in *Oppositions* 25 (Fall 1982), pp. 21–51.

52 This use of photography to record older buildings under threat from urban redevelopment can also be found in London at this time: see *Photographic News* 9, no. 375 (10 November 1865). In 1876 the Society for Photographing Relics of Old London was formed, though it was dissolved only ten years later, apparently because its subject had been exhausted: *Photographic News* 20, no. 992 (5 May 1876), p. 205; *Photographic News* 30, no. 1446 (21 May 1886), p. 328. See also Kenneth E. Foote, 'Relics of Old London: Photographs of a Changing Victorian City', *History of Photography* 11, no. 2 (1987), pp. 133–54; and Graham Bush, *Old London Photographed by Henry Dixon and A. & J. Bool*, London: Academy Editions, 1975. In 1889 the Manchester Amateur Photographic Society set up a 'Record and Survey' project that included images of 'business life, habits of the people, and how the poor live', as well as of buildings: see Harry Milligan, 'The Manchester Photographic Survey Record', *Manchester Review* 8 (1958), pp. 193–204; Peter James, 'Evolution of the Photographic Record and Survey Movement, *c.*1890–1910', *History of Photography* 12, no. 3 (1988), pp. 205–18. For the Manchester survey in relation to other surveys of the late nineteenth century see Edwards, *The Camera as Historian*.

53 Shelley Rice, *Parisian Views*, Cambridge, MA: MIT Press, 1997, pp. 85–117.

54 For theorisations of this issue see Doreen Massey, *Space, Place and Gender*, Cambridge: Polity Press, 1994, pp. 2–4 and chapter 11, 'Politics and Space-Time'.

55 Mudd was not beyond repositioning objects in landscape scenes: Mudd, *The Collodio-Albumen Process*, p. 40.

56 Mudd, *The Collodio-Albumen Process*, p. 47.

57 There are other interesting exceptions among Mudd's photographs, such as 'School Mills and Old Footbridge over the River Irk at Mill Brow' (1877), where a gentleman poses proprietorially in front of the mill and 'Men and Women and Delivery Wagons in Front of the John Slater Soda Water Company Manufacturing Plant, Manchester' (no date, Canadian Centre for Architecture). However, neither of these appear in the *Views of Old Manchester and Salford* portfolio.

58 Richard Wright Procter, *Memorials of Manchester Streets*, Manchester: Thomas Sutcliffe, 1874, p. 236.

59 Engels, *Condition*, p. 92.

60 Engels, *Condition*, p. 93.

61 Hayes, *Reminiscences*, p. 1.

62 Hayes, *Reminiscences*, pp. 115–16.

63 Raymond Williams, *The Country and the City*, London: Chatto & Windus, 1973, pp. 9–12.

64 Williams, *The Country and the City*, p. 18.

65 Armstrong, *Scenes in a Library*, p. 296.

66 Armstrong, *Scenes in a Library*, p. 5. Armstrong tends to see the text as illustrative of the image rather than vice versa.

67 Armstrong, *Scenes in a Library*, p. 358. Armstrong's argument seems skewed by implication here because she uses illustrated scientific texts to argue that 'the road toward normalization' of the later nineteenth century had been laid out in the 1870s (chapter 1).

68 Corbett, *River Irwell*, p. vi. Corbett attributes the photograph to George Grundy, another of Mudd's studio assistants.

69 Corbett, *River Irwell*, p. 7.

70 Corbett, *River Irwell*, p. 8.

71 Corbett, *River Irwell*, p. 8.

72 Corbett, *River Irwell*, pp. 121–4. See also John Leigh's appendix to Procter, *Memorials*, p. 371. Even Corbett's father – or Corbett's memory of what his father had said – may be accused of a false pastoralism if we are to believe a 1795 account that describes the Irwell as being 'destitute of fish, the water being poisoned by liquor flowing in from the dye-houses': John Aikin, *A Description of the Country from thirty to forty miles around Manchester*, London: J. Stockdale, 1795, pp. 203–5.

73 'Heterotopias are linked for the most part to bits and pieces of time, i.e., they open up through what we might define as a pure

symmetry of heterochronisms. The heterotopia enters fully into function when men find themselves in a sort of total breach of their traditional time': Michel Foucault, 'Of Other Spaces: Utopias and Heterotopias', in Neil Leach (ed.), *Rethinking Architecture: A Reader in Cultural Theory*, London: Routledge, 1997, p. 354.

74 William Cooke Taylor, *Notes of a Tour in the Manufacturing Districts of Lancashire*, London: Duncan & Malcolm, 1842, p. 155.

75 Procter, *Memorials*, pp. 243–6.

4 · Industrial Greatness: The Town Hall as a Gothic Machine
pages 101–135

1 This was on the Lloyd Street side of the building, but it did not survive later changes to the exterior. It was paired with another, still surviving, roundel on the Princess Street front showing 'a youth of the same period engaged in weaving': *Manchester New Town Hall: General History and Detailed Description of the Building*, Manchester: John Heywood, 1877, p. 5. Both were the work of Thomas Woolner.

2 See the reports, contemporary with the completion of the Town Hall, in *Manchester City News*, 5 January, 12 January and 16 March 1878: Martin Hewitt, *Making Social Knowledge in the Victorian City: The Visiting Mode in Manchester, 1832–1914*, London: Routledge, 2020, p. 94.

3 Eric Hobsbawm, *Labouring Men: Studies in the History of Labour*, London: Weidenfeld & Nicolson, 1964, p. 166.

4 Manchester Council Proceedings 13 (1865–7), 6 February 1866, in Manchester Central Library Archives.

5 'Municipal palace' is John Bright's term, as quoted in William E. A. Axon, *An Architectural and General Description of the Town Hall, Manchester*, Manchester and London: Abel Heywood, 1878, p. 53.

6 Despite Michael T. Saler's *The Avant-Garde in Interwar England: Medieval Modernism and the London Underground*, Oxford: Oxford University Press, 1999, it seems that recent attempts to revive interest in medieval–modern resonances have missed out on an opportunity here. Alexander Nagel's *Medieval Modern: Art Out of Time* (London: Thames & Hudson, 2012), for instance, has no index entries under 'industrial' or even 'machine'.

7 The terms are notable in a book otherwise willing to argue for nuanced complexity: Boyd Hilton, *A Mad, Bad, and Dangerous People? England 1783–1846*, Oxford: Oxford University Press, 2006, pp. 475, 630.

8 John H. G. Archer, 'A Classic of its Age', in John H. G. Archer (ed.), *Art and Architecture in Victorian Manchester*, Manchester: Manchester University Press, 1985, p. 137. On Ruskin's antipathy for Manchester see Francis O'Gorman, 'Sage and City: John Ruskin and Manchester', *Manchester Memoirs* 135 (1996–7), pp. 55–70.

9 This is particularly the case with the French rationalist tradition as conveyed through Eugène Viollet-le-Duc.

10 Quotes from *Manchester New Town Hall*, p. 3; Patrick Joyce, *The Rule of Freedom: Liberalism and the Modern City*, London: Verso, 2003, p. 164. See, similarly, *Builder* 35 (1877), p. 176; Eric Hobsbawm, *The Age of Revolution, 1789–1848* (1962), London: Abacus, 1996, p. 62.

11 Igor Webb, 'The Bradford Wool Exchange: Industrial Capitalism and the Popularity of Gothic', *Victorian Studies* 20, no. 1 (Autumn 1976), p. 45. Webb's article – largely ignored by architectural historians – is one of the few to consider the issue at any length, though it persists in the condescending understanding of the Gothic Revival as a form of nostalgia, a pretence to aristocratic sensibility.

12 Colin Cunningham and Prudence Waterhouse, *Alfred Waterhouse, 1830–1905: Biography of a Practice*, Oxford: Clarendon Press, 1992, p. 51; Charles Dellheim, *The Face of the Past: The Preservation of the Medieval Inheritance in Victorian England*, Cambridge: Cambridge University Press, 1982, p. 133. On the irony of capitalism building medievalist castles see Chris Brooks, *The Gothic Revival*, London: Phaidon, 1999, pp. 170–1.

13 Franco Moretti, *The Bourgeois: Between History and Literature*, London: Verso, 2013, pp. 109, 110 n. 6.

14 Martin J. Weiner, *English Culture and the Decline of the Industrial Spirit, 1850–1950*, Cambridge: Cambridge University Press, 1981, p. 64; Arno Mayer, *The Persistence of the Old Regime: Europe to the Great War*, New York, 1981, pp. 4, 191–2. Surprisingly these are cited approvingly in Moretti, *The Bourgeois*, p. 114; for 'historical screens' see Moretti, *The Bourgeois*, pp. 114, 116.

15 Charles Locke Eastlake, *A History of the Gothic Revival: An Attempt to Show How the Taste for Medieval Architecture, which Lingered in England during the Two Last Centuries Has Since Been Encouraged and Developed*, London: Longmans, Green, 1872, republished Leicester: Leicester University Press, 1970, pp. 27, 372.

16 Heywood, quoted in Dellheim, *Face of the Past*, p. 144. I don't agree with Dellheim's gloss on this, that 'the making of the New Town Hall was a means to transform the cultural image as well as the visual reality of Manchester', as this implies that the industrial – as image and material reality – was to be bypassed or ignored (p. 145).

17 *Manchester New Town Hall*, pp. 3–5. Waterhouse refers here to his own assize courts. Some of the streets immediately facing the Town Hall already had Gothic Revival buildings on them, such as Thomas Worthington's Venetian Gothic Memorial Hall (1863–6) and Clegg & Knowles's Carlton House (1872), which responds directly to the Albert Memorial. At the same time as the town hall competition, a competition for new police courts was launched, and these were eventually built in a Gothic Revival style to designs by Thomas Worthington.

18 Some town halls even had exchanges built into them: Colin Cunningham, *Victorian and Edwardian Town Halls*, London: Routledge & Kegan Paul, 1981, p. 4.

19 For a flavour of just a few of these functions and services: 'The Health department, the building, sanitary and nuisance, the hackney coach, scavenging, markets, paving and highways, and lamps departments, as well as the Court of Record, have each their offices on one or other, or more of the four lower storeys of the building. There are muniment rooms in the basement and in the towers; large cellars for coal in a central position, accessible by the cart entrance, and communicating with the upper floors by hydraulic lifts. Housemaids' closets

have been placed on the different floors, and groups of retiring rooms (in addition with those connected immediately with the principal officers' rooms) are placed in the basement': Alfred Waterhouse, 'Description of the New Town Hall at Manchester', *Sessional Papers Read at the Royal Institute of British Architects* 27 (1876–7), p. 121.

20 Waterhouse, 'Description', p. 120. In some competition designs the public would enter this gallery by an entirely independent staircase from Albert Square, without even having to go into the building: 'Faire Sans Dire', *City of Manchester New Town Hall*, n.p., 1868, p. 4, in Manchester Central Library Archives.

21 For this near-contemporary critique of the council's constitutional make-up and political interests see T. C. Horsfall, 'The Government of Manchester', *Transactions of the Manchester Statistical Society*, 1895–6, pp. 1–28. Horsfall was particularly concerned at the council's inability to do anything about pollution and its lack of interest in the matter.

22 See also Jürgen Osterhammel, *The Transformation of the World*, Princeton: Princeton University Press, 2014, p. 274.

23 The terms are from Harold L. Platt, *Shock Cities: The Environmental Transformation and Reform of Manchester and Chicago*, Chicago: University of Chicago Press, 2005, p. 71.

24 Arthur Redford, *The History of Local Government in Manchester*, vol. 2, London: Longmans, 1940, pp. 253–4; *Guide to the New Town Hall*, Manchester: Tubbs & Brook, 1877. Gas was developing exponentially as an energy source at this time, and the gas department provided an income of some £1.3 million to the city between 1844 and 1887: Peter Thorsheim, *Inventing Pollution: Coal, Smoke, and Culture in Britain since 1800*, Athens: Ohio University Press, 2006, p. 151. There had been a struggle between the Tories and industrialists for the control of gas, until the 1824 Manchester Gas Act made it a public utility and a source of great local pride: Michael J. Turner, *Reform and Respectability: The Making of a Middle-Class Liberalism in Early Nineteenth-Century Manchester*, Manchester: Chetham Society, 1995, pp. 135–42. On private investment, or 'gas and water capitalism', see Anthony Howe, *The Cotton Masters, 1830–1860*, Oxford: Clarendon Press, 1984, pp. 40, 159. On the corporation's profiteering from water supplies see the negative attitude of Ruskin: O'Gorman, 'Sage and City', pp. 57–8.

25 The old Town Hall also had an office for the police and a gaol.

26 William E. A. Axon, *An Architectural and General Description of the Town Hall, Manchester*, Manchester and London: Abel Heywood, 1878, p. xi.

27 As quoted in Redford, *The History of Local Government*, vol. 2, pp. 13–14.

28 Cobden ignored the inconvenient fact that many members of the jury of the Court Leet were industrialists: Roger Lloyd-Jones and M. J. Lewis, *Manchester and the Age of the Factory*, London: Croom Helm, 1988, pp. 135–6.

29 Joseph Aston, *A Picture of Manchester*, Manchester: Aston, 1816.

30 Redford, *The History of Local Government*, vol. 1, pp. 284–6, 317–18; also on the Court Leet see François Vigier, *Change and Apathy: Liverpool and Manchester during the Industrial Revolution*, Cambridge, MA: MIT Press, 1970, chapters 6 and 9.

31 A contemporary description, quoted in Redford, *The History of Local Government*, vol. 1, p. 285; James Wheeler, *Manchester, its Political, Social and Commercial History, Ancient and Modern*, London and Manchester, 1836, pp. 325–8.

32 John Archer, 'A Civic Achievement: The Building of Manchester Town Hall – Part One: The Commissioning', *Transactions of the Lancashire and Cheshire Antiquarian Society* 81 (1988), p. 5.

33 Sven Beckert, *Empire of Cotton: A New History of Global Capitalism*, London: Allen Lane, 2014, p. 246.

34 Quoted in Beckert, *Empire of Cotton*, p. 251; see also p. 272. The survival had largely depended on developing the supply of cotton from India. On Manchester and India see Arthur W. Silver, *Manchester Men and Indian Cotton, 1847–1872*, Manchester: Manchester University Press, 1966.

35 The 'Town's Yard' was an area of disparate municipal uses (stables, workshops, offices, a fire engine house) surrounded by houses and motley industrial buildings: see 'Town Hall Site and Street Improvements', unaccessioned (in October 2016) site plan, in Manchester Central Library Archives. There had been some interest in buying land near the Infirmary but the Town's Yard site had the advantage both of cheapness and of serving the agenda of improvement: Dellheim, *Face of the Past*, p. 141.

36 Cunningham and Waterhouse, *Alfred Waterhouse*, p. 51; Archer, 'A Classic', p. 147.

37 For more on this see Archer, 'A Classic', pp. 127–61.

38 James Kay, *The Moral and Physical Condition of the Working Classes in Manchester* (1832), London: Frank Cass, 1970, p. 27; Raymond Williams, *Politics of Modernism*, London: Verso, 1989, p. 41.

39 Friedrich Engels, *The Condition of the Working Class in England* (1845), Harmondsworth: Penguin, 1987, p. 69.

40 See, for instance, Frederick Lush, 'Remarks on Street Architecture', *Architectural Magazine* 3 (1836), pp. 67–9.

41 *Manchester Faces and Places*, which started in 1889, was a journal with this very theme at its heart. It identifies places, normally streets, with important persons in Manchester's history.

42 By the terms of the Municipal Corporations Act, unelected corporations were replaced by councils elected by adult male direct ratepayers: see John Garrard, *Democratisation in Britain: Elites, Civil Society and Reform since 1800*, Basingstoke: Palgrave Macmillan, 2002. See also Howe, *The Cotton Masters*, pp. 133–61.

43 John Baynes, *The Cotton Trade: Two Lectures*, Blackburn, 1857, p. 68. See also Howe, *The Cotton Masters*, pp. 143–4. In 1853 councillors represented about a fifth of all adult males, some 13,212 people out of a population of 324,000: Councillor Medcalf, 'On the Municipal Institutions of the City of Manchester', *Transactions of the Manchester Statistical Society*, 1854, p. 17. The franchise was based on householders living within seven miles of the city, who paid poor rates on premises situated within the city.

44 Joanna M. Williams, *Manchester's Radical Mayor: Abel Heywood, the Man who Built the Town Hall*, Stroud: History Press, 2017. On Heywood and Thompson see also Dellheim, *Face of the Past*, pp. 142–4.

45 Waterhouse's letters to Joseph Thompson, and Thompson's later commentary on them, are in Manchester Central Library Archives, gb127. Thompson's documents concerning the sculptural and painted decorations are also in Manchester Central Library Archives, M79/1–35. Thompson seems to have collected books along the same lines as John Rylands, which he donated to Owens College (later the University of Manchester): *Manchester Faces and Places* 3 (10 November 1892), pp. 26–7.

46 Waterhouse at one point warned Joseph Thompson, chair of the building committee, that it might be best to cool down the cotton references: 'In [the reception] room it would perhaps be well to introduce illustrations from some poet or some story not necessarily connected with Manchester, so as to take people's thoughts entirely away from cotton and all its works!': Waterhouse to Thompson, 22 May 1876, Manchester Central Library Archives, gb127. For Waterhouse's response to the programme of the Natural History Museum see Carla Yanni, *Nature's Museums: Victorian Science and the Architecture of Display*, London: Athlone Press, 1999, pp. 135–9.

47 Similarly, a system of shafts ventilate the building. See Waterhouse, 'Description', p. 121.

48 Karl Marx, *Capital: A Critique of Political Economy*, vol. 1, trans. Ben Fowkes, Harmondsworth: Penguin, 1976, p. 503. Similarly, in *Grundrisse*, Marx insists on machinery as an integrated system or 'powerful organism' rather than individual machines: David McLellan, *Marx's Grundrisse*, St Albans: Paladin, 1971, pp. 154–5.

49 Archer, 'A Classic', p. 135.

50 *Manchester New Town Hall: Short Description*, four-page printed pamphlet, n.d. but probably *c.*1876, signed by Alfred Waterhouse, in Manchester Central Library Archives.

51 Mike Williams and D. A. Farnie, *Cotton Mills in Greater Manchester*, Preston: Carnegie, 1992, pp. 67–9. The common proximity of architectural aesthetics and engineering aesthetics tends still to be obscured by later assumptions about the Victorian period. A glance through a prominent journal such as the *Civil Engineer and Architect's Journal* immediately demonstrates the intimate promiscuity of the relationship. See, for instance, the image of plate tracery from a village church placed opposite diagrams of fire engines used by the London Fire Brigade: *Civil Engineer and Architect's Journal* 8 (May 1845), pp. 178–9.

52 Carla Yanni, 'On Nature and Nomenclature: William Whewell and the Production of Architectural Knowledge in Early Victorian Britain', *Architectural History* 40 (1997), p. 211.

53 See, for instance, Robert Willis, *Remarks on the Architecture of the Middle Ages especially of Italy*, Cambridge: Deighton, 1835, p. 13.

54 Paul Frankl, *The Gothic: Literary Sources and Interpretations through Eight Centuries*, Princeton: Princeton University Press, 1960, pp. 529–31. See also Robert Mark, 'Robert Willis, Viollet-le-Duc and the Structural Approach to Gothic Architecture', *Architectura* 7, no. 1 (1977), pp. 52–64; and Alex Bremner, review of Alexandrina Buchanan, *Robert Willis and the Foundation of Architectural History*, in *Journal of the Society of Architectural Historians* 73, no. 3 (September 2014), pp. 424–6. Despite the structural rationalism he finds in Willis, Mark also understands the Gothic Revival as backward looking: Mark, 'Robert Willis', p. 64.

55 Jan Rehmann, *Theories of Ideology: The Powers of Alienation and Subjection*, Leiden: Brill, 2013, pp. 5–7.

56 Willis chaired the 'Mechanical Science' section at the Manchester meeting of the British Association in 1842, which was hosted by John Kennedy: *Manchester Guardian*, 22 June 1842.

57 There was little that was new in this. Katie Scott has written of the French rococo that it '[deflected] attention from the technologies of its manufacture and [obscured] the antagonism around which its production was organised': Katie Scott, *The Rococo Interior: Decoration and Social Spaces in Eighteenth-Century Paris*, New Haven: Yale University Press, 1995, p. 7.

58 Most writers have tended to be interested in either the science or the architectural history, though Buchanan's recent biography of Willis deals with both: Alexandrina Buchanan, *Robert Willis and the Foundation of Architectural History*, Woodbridge: Boydell, 2013. There is not much evidence that Willis or Whewell explicitly brought their science and architecture studies together, but Willis did teach an intriguing course at Cambridge titled 'On statics, dynamics and mechanism, with their practical applications to manufacturing processes, to engineering and architecture': T. J. N. Hilken, *Engineering at Cambridge University, 1783–1965*, Cambridge: Cambridge University Press, 1967, p. 53. Recent architectural historical research on Whewell suggests that he used his scientific studies to 'gain authority' for his architectural studies, and emphasises the place of religion and nature in his work: Yanni, 'On Nature and Nomenclature', pp. 204–21. Frankl observed that 'he applied to the study of architecture his method of building up machines from their elements or of reducing them to their elements', but takes the point no further: Frankl, *The Gothic*, p. 529.

59 William Whewell, *On the Philosophy of Discovery*, London: John W. Parker, 1860.

60 William Whewell, *Architectural Notes on German Churches: A New Edition*, Cambridge: Deighton, 1835, p. 220.

61 William Whewell, *Architectural Notes on German Churches with Remarks on the Origin of Gothic Architecture*, Cambridge, 1830. Willis disagreed: see Harvey W. Becher, 'William Whewell's Odyssey: From Mathematics to Moral Philosophy', in Menachem Fisch and Simon Schaffer (eds.), *William Whewell: A Composite Portrait*, New York: Oxford University Press, 1991, p. 6.

62 William Whewell, *History of the Inductive Sciences, from the Earliest to the Present Time*, London: John W. Parker, 1857, vol. 1, p. 262. Whewell acknowledged Willis for this understanding.

63 Whewell, *History*, vol. 1, p. 264.

64 Willis, *Remarks*, p. 107.

65 Willis, *Remarks*, p. 30.

66 Willis, *Remarks*, pp. 34–5.

67 Willis, *Remarks*, p. v.

68 Willis, *Remarks*, p. 25.

69 Robert Willis, *Principles of Mechanism*, London: John W. Parker, 1841, p. 360. Marx attended Willis's lectures at the Government School of Mines in the early 1860s, and his

understanding of machines seems to be based on Willis's definitions: Fumikazu Yoshida, 'Robert Willis' Theory of Mechanism and Karl Marx', *Historia Scientiarum* 25 (1983), pp. 87–92.

70 Robert Willis, *Architectural Nomenclature of the Middle Ages*, Cambridge: Cambridge Antiquarian Society, 1844.

71 Willis separated this into '*Mechanical*, or actual construction' and '*Decorative*, or apparent construction': Willis, *Remarks*, pp. 9, 15. For obsolescence and what Marx called 'moral depreciation' see Daniel M. Abramson, *Obsolescence: An Architectural History*, Chicago: University of Chicago Press, 2016, p. 15. For Whewell on change in architecture see Whewell, *Architectural Notes* (1830), pp. 208–31. This idea of development is also different from the ecclesiological theory of development in architecture: see David B. Brownlee, 'The First High Victorians: British Architectural Theory in the 1840s', *Architectura* 15 (1985), pp. 33–46.

72 See Buchanan, *Robert Willis*, pp. 68, 86–7. Willis planned to write an encyclopedia of British industry: Ben Marsden and Crosbie Smith, *Engineering Empires: A Cultural History of Technology in Nineteenth-Century Britain*, Basingstoke: Palgrave Macmillan, 2005, pp. 229–30. Books on both architectural rationalism and engineering theory were well represented in Willis's library: see *A Catalogue of the Valuable and Extensive Library of Rev Robert Willis*, London: Hodgson, 1872.

73 These are the three parts of his *Principles of Mechanism*.

74 Willis, *Principles of Mechanism*, p. 282. This is to see engineering as being directly comparable to nature, and as such it is distinct from Whewell's idea, coming from comparative anatomy, that the base of a clustered pier was like the bones in a foot because the whole 'anatomy' of the building might be reconstructed from its study: William Whewell, 'Of Certain Analogies between Architecture and the Other Fine Arts', *Royal Institute of British Architects: Sessional Papers*, 1862–3, p. 177.

75 William Blake, *Jerusalem*, chapter 3 (1804–20).

76 Blanqui in 1832, as quoted in David Harvey, *Paris, Capital of Modernity*, New York: Routledge, 2003, p. 66.

77 See, for instance, Evan Leigh, *The Science of Modern Cotton Spinning*, Manchester and London: Palmer and Howe, 1873, vol. 1, p. 122. From 1875 Leigh was president of Manchester's Scientific and Mechanical Society.

78 James White, 'Memoir on a New System of Cog or Toothed Wheels', *Memoirs of the Literary and Philosophical Society of Manchester*, 2nd series 3 (1819), p. 138.

79 Charles F. Foster, *Capital and Innovation: How Britain Became the First Industrial Nation, a Study of the Warrington, Knutsford, Northwich and Frodsham Area, 1500–1780*, Northwich: Arley Hall Press, 2004, pp. 304–5. For a contemporary account of this see John Kennedy, 'Observations on the Rise and Progress of the Cotton Trade in Great Britain', *Memoirs of the Literary and Philosophical Society of Manchester*, 2nd series 3 (1819), p. 124.

80 Richard L. Hills, *Power in the Industrial Revolution*, Manchester: Manchester University Press, 1970, pp. 243–4.

81 William Fairbairn, *Treatise on Mills and Millwork: Part 1*, London: Longmans, 1861, p. 17.

82 Willis, *Principles of Mechanism*, pp. 53–4.

83 Robert Willis, 'On the Teeth of Wheels', *Transactions of the Institution of Civil Engineers* 2 (1838), pp. 104–10.

84 Robert Willis, 'Description of the Cymagraph for Copying Mouldings', *Civil Engineer and Architect's Journal*, July 1842, pp. 219–20.

85 James Nasmyth, *An Autobiography*, London: John Murray, 1885, p. 144. Nasmyth had a notable interest in Norman and Gothic architecture (p. 150).

86 Similarly, the riveting machine designed by William Fairbairn in 1837 in reaction to a boilermakers' strike.

87 Robert Willis, *The Architectural History of Canterbury Cathedral*, London: Longman, Pickering & Bell, 1845, p. vi.

88 Jonathan Crary, *Techniques of the Observer: On Vision and Modernity in the Nineteenth Century*, Cambridge, MA: MIT Press, 1992, pp. 13–14.

89 See, for instance, Willis, *The Architectural History of Canterbury Cathedral*, pp. 76–9, 98. For membrology see Willis, *Remarks*.

90 On the ideology of efficient machinery as found in technical illustrations of machines, see Louise Purbrick, 'Ideologically Technical: Illustration, Automation and Spinning Cotton around the Middle of the Nineteenth Century', *Journal of Design History* 11, no. 4 (1998), pp. 275–93. Whewell and Willis's contemporary at Cambridge, William Farish, professor of chemistry and natural philosophy, should also be mentioned. Farish advocated 120-degree-angled isonometric projection – against both perspectives and orthographic drawings – as a method for drawing new machinery (later in the century this became a standard component of engineering training). What isonometric drawing provided was a way of depicting machines as assemblages of measurable parts. It produced drawings that were both 'impossible' views and efficient vehicles of highly practical information. See William Farish, 'On Isometrical Perspective', *Cambridge Philosophical Transactions* 1, no. 1 (1822), pp. 1–19. As well as industrial machinery, Farish also advocated isometric projection for representing architecture – another example of the traffic between techno-scientific theory and architectural knowledge in Cambridge at this time (pp. 12–13).

91 Ben Marsden, 'The Progeny of These Two "Fellows": Robert Willis, William Whewell and the Sciences of Mechanism, Mechanics and Machinery in Early Victorian Britain', *British Journal for the History of Science* 37, no. 4 (December 2004), p. 423.

92 The juxtaposition of huge cogged wheels and classical elements was common in beam engines, and inspired several Victorians to meditate on the aesthetics of the machine and on applying 'rules for design' to machinery: see Samuel Clegg, *Architecture of Machinery: An Essay on Propriety of Form and Proportion, with a View to Assist and Improve Design*, London: Architectural Library, 1842. Clegg, a prominent engineer, also wrote *Treatise on Eccentric Turning* (1852), and both books were in Willis's library: *A Catalogue*. On the similar rendition of classical forms and machine parts in engineering drawings see Frances Robertson, '"Mere Adventurers

in Drawing": Engineers and Draughtsmen as Visual Technicians in Nineteenth-Century Britain', in Kate Nichols and Rebecca Wade (eds.), *Art versus Industry? New Perspectives on Visual and Industrial Cultures in Nineteenth-Century Britain*, Manchester: Manchester University Press, 2016, p. 124.

93 'The invention of the fly shuttle has made Manchester': Town Hall Committee Minutes, vol. 1, 18 December 1878, Manchester Central Library Archives. Marx was notably sharp on the inadequacies of histories of technology that centred on individual inventors: Marx, *Capital*, p. 493 n. 4.

94 Fredric Jameson, *Marxism and Form*, Princeton: Princeton University Press, 1971, p. 74.

95 There are references in the decoration and in Ford Madox Brown's paintings to pivotal moments in the history of cotton manufacture: to the medieval cotton towns of 'Antwerp ... Bruges and Ghent' and the arrival in the neighbourhood of Manchester in the late sixteenth century of Belgians bearing the trade with them. Tellingly, a third cotton subject was favoured by Brown – the cotton famine – but this was ruled out by his clients in favour of 'The Opening of the Duke of Bridgewater's Canal': Town Hall Committee Minutes, vol. 1, 18 December 1878, Manchester Central Library Archives. That this decision was political rather than because of the overrepresentation of cotton is shown by the rejection of Brown's alternative subject – the Peterloo massacre: Town Hall Committee Minutes, vol. 1, 22 April 1879, Manchester Central Library Archives. See also William Axon's letters and Thompson's replies, Manchester Central Library Archives, M79/9, 10a and M79/9, 11a.

96 Edward Baines, *History of the Cotton Manufacture in Great Britain*, London: Fisher, Fisher & Jackson, 1835, p. 179. See also, Leigh, *The Science of Modern Cotton Spinning*, vol. 2, p. 162.

97 Beckert, *Empire of Cotton*, p. 45.

98 Quoted in William T. Stearn, *The Natural History Museum at South Kensington*, London: Heinemann, 1981, p. 44.

99 See, for instance, Leigh, *The Science*.

100 Willis, *Remarks*, p. 199.

101 There may also be an aspect of prison design here. Waterhouse had designed the Strangeways prison in 1862 and it was completed on its Salford site in 1868. Although this had a radial and not a triangular design, Waterhouse may have come across triangular prisons as part of his process of design: see, for instance, James Elmes, *Hints for the Improvements of Prisons*, London, 1817.

102 Purbrick, 'Ideologically Technical', p. 279. Purbrick points out that the views of machines from above were known as plans (p. 280).

103 Waterhouse, 'Description', p. 123.

104 Cunningham and Waterhouse, *Alfred Waterhouse*, p. 62. These machines had been developed by Alexander MacDonald in the early 1830s in Aberdeen, where there was an extensive granite trade.

105 Archer, 'A Classic', p. 141. For the Dennett system and its concrete see *Building News* 13 (31 August 1866), p. 582.

106 *British Architect* 5 (7 January 1876), p. 2.

107 The phrase is from Jacques Rancière, 'Going to the Expo: The Worker, his Wife and Machines', trans. John Moore, in Adrian Rifkin and Roger Thomas (eds.), *Voices of the People: The Social Life of 'La Sociale' at the End of the Second Empire*, London: Routledge & Kegan Paul, 1988, p. 25.

108 Andrew Ure, *The Philosophy of Manufactures, or, An Exposition of the Scientific, Moral, and Commercial Economy of the Factory System*, London: Charles Knight, 1835, p. 35.

109 Massimiliano Tomba, *Marx's Temporalities*, Leiden: Brill, 2012, p. xiv.

110 Howe, *The Cotton Masters*, pp. 90–132.

111 On the use of local gentry and landowners for ceremonial purposes in the opening of town halls, see Susan O'Connor, 'Architecture, Power and Ritual in Scottish Town Halls, 1833–1973', PhD thesis, University of Bath, 2017. In a satire published by Heywood's press to mark the opening ceremony, one character avers, 'Everybody there met ha' belonged to one party, for I couldno' ha' towd a Tory fro' a Radikil if I hadno' known 'em': *Ab-O'th'-Yate at the Opening of the New Town Hall*, Manchester: Abel Heywood, 1877, p. 12.

112 For this issue in an earlier period see Turner, *Reform and Respectability*, pp. 105–12.

113 The year after the town hall competition saw wages reduced in compensation for the 1866 glut: Marx, *Capital*, pp. 561 n. 28, 584. Diversification of investment was one of the reasons for the manufacturers' relative immunity to the famine: Howe, *The Cotton Masters*, p. 42.

114 Moretti, *The Bourgeois*, pp. 115–16.

115 That such subjects were explicitly excluded from the Town Hall can be seen in the history of the various subjects proposed for Brown's paintings (see n. 95).

116 McLellan, *Marx's Grundrisse*, p. 111.

117 The sculpture hall seems always to have been intended as such, although busts and other sculptures were not added until a few years after the building's completion. Also among those commemorated here are George Wilson (chairman of the Anti-Corn Law League), John Benjamin Smith (first president of the Anti-Corn Law League), William Fairbairn, Thomas Potter (first mayor of Manchester), Thomas Goadsby (mayor from 1861 to 1862) and Henry Patteson (mayor from 1879 to 1880). Bright and Villiers appear in at least two other locations – on the main stairs and in the Great Hall.

118 The entry on machinery in *The Shorter Oxford English Dictionary* dates the first citation of 'machinery of government' to 1855.

119 J. S. Mill, *Considerations on Representative Government* (1861), republished in *On Liberty and Considerations on Representative Government*, Oxford: Basil Blackwell, 1946, pp. 110–11.

120 Mill, *Considerations*, pp. 116–19, 127–9.

121 Crosbie Smith, *The Science of Energy: A Cultural History of Energy Physics in Victorian Britain*, Chicago: University of Chicago Press, 1998, p. 43.

122 Michael Baxandall, *Patterns of Intention: On the Historical Explanation of Pictures*, New Haven: Yale University Press, 1985, p. 107.

123 Michael Baxandall, *Painting and Experience in Fifteenth-Century Italy*, Oxford: Oxford University Press, 1972, pp. 86–8.

124 Baxandall, *Painting and Experience*, p. 37.

125 Baxandall, *Painting and Experience*, pp. 1, 2.

126 Bloch writing in 1937, as quoted in Antoine Picon, *Ornament: The Politics of Architecture and Subjectivity*, Chichester: Wiley, 2013, p. 14.

127 James Nasymth in 1851, as quoted in Marx, *Capital*, p. 563.

128 This was Disraeli's term: Anthony J. Pass, *Thomas Worthington: Victorian Architecture and Social Purpose*, Manchester: Manchester Literary and Philosophical Publications, 1988, p. 115.

129 Marx, *Capital*, p. 564.

130 On the 'maturity' of the cotton industry by the mid-century see David Saul Landes, *The Unbound Prometheus: Technological Change and Industrial Development in Western Europe from 1750 to the Present*, London: Cambridge University Press, 1969; and Michel Aglietta, *A Theory of Capitalist Regulation: The US Experience*, London: Verso, 2015. These converge in a phased chronology that works something like this: emergence (1760s–1770s); diffusion (1790s–1830s); crisis and adaptation (1830s–1840s); maturity – widening of markets, new consumers (1840s–1860s).

131 Walter Benjamin, *The Arcades Project*, trans. Howard Eiland and Kevin McLaughlin, ed. Rolf Tiedemann, Cambridge, MA: Belknap Press, 1999, p. 391.

132 For Ruskin on Gothic as bringing nature into the industrial city see John Ruskin, *The Stones of Venice*, vol. 1, *The Foundations* (1851), New York: Publishers' Plate Renting, 1903, pp. 345–6 (chapter 30, section 6).

133 Brown's dating is off here: Kay patented his invention in 1733 and the protests and resistance it caused took place in the following decade (he fled to France in 1747). For Kay see A. P. Wadsworth and J. De Lacy Mann, *The Cotton Trade and Industrial Lancashire*, Manchester: Manchester University Press, 1931; Michael Andrew Zmolek, *Rethinking the Industrial Revolution: Five Centuries of Transition from Agrarian to Industrial Capitalism in England*, Chicago: Haymarket, 2014, pp. 326–8. As one of the last six panels, the Kay work was done in oil on canvas and then glued to the wall. For Brown see Julian Treuherz, 'Ford Madox Brown and the Manchester Murals', in John H. G. Archer (ed.), *Art and Architecture in Victorian Manchester*, Manchester: Manchester University Press, 1985, pp. 162–207; Paul Barlow, 'Local Disturbances: Ford Madox Brown and the Problem of the Manchester Murals', in Ellen Harding (ed.), *Re-framing the Pre-Raphaelites*, Aldershot: Ashgate, 1996, pp. 81–97; Julie F. Codell, 'Ford Madox Brown, Carlyle, Macaulay, and Bakhtin: The Pratfalls and Penultimates of History', *Art History* 21, no. 3 (September 1998), pp. 324–66; and Elizabeth Prettejohn, 'Ford Madox Brown and History Painting', *Visual Culture in Britain* 15, no. 3 (November 2014), 239–57.

134 The mythology has it that Kay fled to France to escape the weavers, but the real cause of his self-exile was disputes over his patent: Wadsworth and Mann, *The Cotton Trade*, p. 456.

135 This is not to deny the religious resonances of the scene, especially its similarities with the subject of the descent from the cross: Treuherz, 'Ford Madox Brown', p. 203.

136 Brown's descriptions of the murals were republished in Ford Madox Brown, *Mural Paintings in the Large Town Hall Manchester*, Manchester: Manchester Corporation, 1969. Interestingly, Brown emphasises that Kay left for France a ruined man, cheated by the industrialists who exploited his invention.

137 On the gimmick and its status as labour-saving trick in capitalism see Sianne Ngai, *Theory of the Gimmick: Aesthetic Judgement and Capitalist Form*, Cambridge, MA: Belknap Press, 2020.

138 On typology and history in Brown's work see Codell, 'Ford Madox Brown', pp. 336–40.

139 Barlow has also commented on this 'partitioning of the composition', commenting on the relation between Kay's 'attempt to mechanize labour' and this 'space ... bashed into squares': Barlow, 'Local Disturbances', pp. 94–5.

140 This is not quite consistent with a view of the murals that understands them as celebrating 'the refusal of Manchester to emerge as a modern commercial city': Barlow, 'Local Disturbances', p. 83.

141 Treuherz, 'Ford Madox Brown', p. 173.

142 Brown, *Mural Paintings*, p. 19. How far Brown's anti-epic interpretation can be equated with the ideas of his friend William Morris is beyond the scope of this discussion. They had worked together in Morris, Marshall, Faulkner & Co. until a rift in 1874 led to Brown leaving the partnership. Ten years later Morris's visit to Manchester and his viewing of the murals was the occasion for a reconciliation: Julian Treuherz, *Ford Madox Brown: Pre-Raphaelite Pioneer*, Manchester: Manchester Art Gallery, 2011, p. 55. Brown's grandson Ford Madox Ford wrote that 'it would never have entered [Brown's] head to turn one of his frescoes in the Town Hall, Manchester, into a medium for the propaganda of the Social Revolution', but he also claimed that '[Brown] hated the bourgeoisie with a proper hatred': Ford Madox Ford, *Memories and Impressions: A Study in Atmospheres* (1911), New York: Eco, 1985, p. 130.

5 · Devil's Darkness: Industrial Pollution and Culture as Philanthropy *pages 137–163*

1 Quoted in James S. Dearden, *John Ruskin: A Life in Pictures*, Sheffield: Sheffield Academic Press, 1999, p. 166.

2 Quoted in Dearden, *John Ruskin*, p. 167.

3 The scene was not so idyllic in reality: two steam yachts operated on the lake and a steam train, owned by the same company, served the copper mines on the Old Man.

4 Helen Gill Viljoen (ed.), *The Brantwood Diary of John Ruskin*, New Haven: Yale University Press, 1971, p. 11. I find talk of Ruskin's deteriorating mental health in relation to these observations beside the point – they are as little or as much caused by mental illness as any of Ruskin's fears about industry, and the theme of apocalypse was one much mined by him long before this date (see, for instance, *The Queen of the Air: Greek Myths of Cloud and Storm*, 1869). Besides, the final onset of the mental illness that terminated his writing did not take place until 1889.

5 Viljoen (ed.), *The Brantwood Diary*, p. 38.

6 Viljoen (ed.), *The Brantwood Diary*, pp. 191–2.

7 Viljoen (ed.), *The Brantwood Diary*, pp. 216–17.

8 John Ruskin, *The Storm Cloud of the Nineteenth Century*, Orpington: George Allen, 1884, pp. 1, 3, 56.

9 On the 'juddering switch-point' of Ruskin's approach to aesthetic judgement see Caroline Arscott's short, wonderfully suggestive essay 'Cloud Perspective', in Suzanne Fagence Cooper and Richard Johns (eds.), *Ruskin, Turner and the Storm Cloud*, London: Holberton, 2019, pp. 82–5.

10 Coal consumption had increased fivefold over the previous forty years, with a notably larger increase in the north of England: B. R. Mitchell, *Economic Development of the British Coal Industry, 1800–1914*, Cambridge: Cambridge University Press, 1984, pp. 1–9.

11 For the fossil economy see Andreas Malm, *Fossil Capital: The Rise of Steam Power and the Roots of Global Warming*, London: Verso, 2016. On the metabolic rift see John Bellamy Foster, *Marx's Ecology: Materialism and Nature*, New York: Monthly Review Press, 2000, pp. 155–63.

12 This is Fredric Jameson's gloss on Luhmann's argument in his *Differentiation of Society*, trans. Stephen Holmes and Charles Larmore, New York: Columbia University Press, 1982: Fredric Jameson, *The Ancients and the Postmoderns: On the Historicity of Forms*, London: Verso, 2015, p. 24.

13 Georg Lukács, *History and Class Consciousness: Studies in Marxist Dialectics*, trans. Rodney Livingstone, London: Merlin, 1971, p. 102.

14 Fredric Jameson, *The Geopolitical Aesthetic: Cinema and Space in the World System*, Bloomington: Indiana University Press / London: BFI, 1992, p. 79; Jameson, *The Ancients and the Postmoderns*, p. 24. What Jameson calls the 'war on totality' was a feature of academic postmodernism and poststructuralism of the 1980s onwards but its legacies remain structured into our intellectual climate as a form of taboo: Fredric Jameson, *Postmodernism, or, The Cultural Logic of Late Capitalism*, London: Verso, 1991, pp. 400–1. See also Gail Day, *Dialectical Passions: Negation in Postwar Art Theory*, New York: Columbia University Press, 2011.

15 Mark Blackwell (ed.), *The Secret Life of Things*, Lewisburg, PA: Bucknell University Press, 2007; Jonathan Lamb, 'The Implacability of Things', *Public Domain Review*, 3 October 2012, https://publicdomainreview.org/2012/10/03/the-implacability-of-things (accessed 1 March 2018).

16 For just such an account see Adam Trexler, 'Integrating Agency with Climate Critique', *symplokē*, 21 (2013), pp. 226–35. For an excellent critique of this and other new materialist theory as it bears on climate change see Andreas Malm, *The Progress of This Storm: Nature and Society in a Warming World*, London: Verso, 2018, pp. 78–118.

17 Elizabeth Gaskell, *North and South* (1854–5), Harmondsworth: Penguin, 1970, pp. 104–5. A century later Richard Hoggart wrote of a working-class mother's constant battle to keep the home clean in the face of this pollution: 'Everywhere the smoke and soot from the nearby factories and railway lines creep in, and most women "can't abide the thought of dirt getting a hold"': Richard Hoggart, *The Uses of Literacy*, Harmondsworth: Penguin, 1958, p. 39.

18 Quoted in Franco Moretti, *The Bourgeois: Between History and Literature*, London: Verso, 2013, p. 123.

19 Elizabeth Gaskell, *Mary Barton* (1848), Harmondsworth: Penguin, 1970, pp. 351, 333. See also Catherine Gallagher, *The Industrial Reformation of English Fiction, 1832–1867*, Chicago: University of Chicago Press, 1985, pp. 62–87.

20 It-narratives seemed to fade in the nineteenth century, becoming a genre more suitable to children's stories about bubbles and snowflakes, and where they survive their objects become more interrelated with others and more evidently educational. Coal is one such subject: John Plotz, 'Discreet Jewels: Victorian Diamond Narratives and the Problem of Sentimental Value', in Blackwell (ed.), *Secret Life*, p. 336.

21 Jacques Rancière, *Dissensus: On Politics and Aesthetics*, trans. Steven Corcoran, London: Continuum, 2010, p. 143.

22 Reinhold Martin, *The Urban Apparatus: Mediapolitics and the City*, Minneapolis: University of Minnesota Press, 2016, pp. 9–14, 36–7.

23 Rancière, *Dissensus*, p. 119.

24 On the prescriptive potentials of cognitive mapping see Jameson, *Geopolitical Aesthetic*, pp. 188–9.

25 Fredric Jameson, 'Postmodernism, or, The Cultural Logic of Late Capitalism', in Michael Hardt and Kathi Weeks (eds.), *The Jameson Reader*, Oxford: Blackwell, 2000, pp. 228–31.

26 Alberto Toscano and Jeff Kinkle, *Cartographies of the Absolute*, Winchester: Zero Books, 2015, pp. 191–2.

27 Noel Castree, 'The Spatio-temporality of Capitalism', *Time and Society* 18 (2009), pp. 26–61. Alberto Toscano has argued that cognitive mapping has tended to be used as a spatialising of capital without regard to its temporalities: Alberto Toscano, 'The Quantities of the Past: Photography on the Aftermath of Capital', talk given at the Centre for the History and Theory of Photography Centre, Birkbeck, University of London, 13 December 2019.

28 Michael Hardt and Kathi Weeks, 'Introduction', in Hardt and Weeks (eds.), *The Jameson Reader*, p. 22.

29 Kevin Lynch, *The Image of the City*, Cambridge, MA: MIT Press, 1960.

30 Daniel Defoe described the 'Canell or Candle Coal' found around Wigan as 'smooth and slick when the pieces part from one another ... a lady may take them up in a cambric handkerchief and they will not soil it, though they are black as the deepest jet. They are the most pleasant agreeable fuel that can be found': Daniel Defoe, *A Tour thro' the Whole Island of Great Britain, divided into circuits or journies*, as quoted in Alan Davies, *Coal Mining in Lancashire and Cheshire*, Stroud: Amberley, 2010, p. 23.

31 The long-wall system was becoming increasingly used in Lancashire from the 1860s, though pillar and stall layouts still prevailed: Roy Church, with Alan Hall and John Kanefsky, *The History of the British Coal Industry*, vol. 3, *1830–1913: Victorian Pre-eminence*, Oxford: Clarendon Press, 1986, p. 336.

32 Malm, *Fossil Capital*, p. 21.

33 Matthias Dunn, *A Treatise on the Winning and Working of Collieries*, Newcastle upon Tyne: Matthias Dunn, 1848, p. 117; Thomas Farrimond, 'On the Working of Coal Mines, Drainage of Gases, and their Effect on Under and Over-Lying Seams', *Transactions of the Manchester Geological Society* 2, no. 8 (May 1860), pp. 89–94. I've used Dunn and Farrimond as sources for much of what follows, but the account might just as well have come from a book published decades later: see, for instance,

James Tonge, *The Principles and Practice of Coal Mining*, London: Macmillan, 1906, pp. 119–25.

34 Dunn, *A Treatise*, plate 12, fig. 1. Church, *History of the British Coal Industry*, p. 333. However, 'there were as many variations as there were seam characteristics' (p. 328).

35 T. J. Clark, 'From Menzel to Burtynsky: Episodes from an Imagery of Capitalism', in Malcolm Baker and Andrew Hemingway (eds.), *Art as Worldmaking: Critical Essays on Realism and Naturalism*, Manchester: Manchester University Press, 2018, p. 199. The best, and now classic, account of the representation of mines and the coal industries is Allan Sekula, 'Photography between Labour and Capital', in Leslie Shedden (ed.), *Mining Photographs and Other Pictures, 1948–1968*, Halifax, NS: Press of the Nova Scotia College of Art and Design, 1983, pp. 193–268.

36 Sekula, 'Photography between Labour and Capital', p. 217.

37 See the *First Report of the Commissioners (Mines) of the Children's Employment Commission* (1842), this was republished as *Children in the Mines: The Children's Employment Commission of 1842*, Salford: Picks, 1995. For an account that claims to be first hand see John R. Leifchild ('A Traveller Underground'), in *Our Coal and our Coal-Pits: The People in Them, and the Scenes around Them*, London: Longman, 1853, pp. 141–72. John Rylands Library Special Collections, RYL/1/3/1.

38 Children's Employment Commission, *First Report of the Commissioners (Mines)*, Parliamentary Paper, 1842, vol. 15, p. 84.

39 Linda Nochlin, *Misère: The Visual Representation of Misery in the 19th Century*, London: Thames & Hudson, 2018, p. 104.

40 Joseph Dickenson, 'Statistics of the Collieries of Lancashire, Cheshire, and North Wales', *Memoirs of the Literary and Philosophical Society of Manchester* 12 (1855), p. 75.

41 The *Manchester Guardian* was full of reports of fires and fatal accidents in the mines around Wigan. To take just one year: see *Manchester Guardian*, 6 January 1859, 24 August 1859, 24 September 1859 and 28 September 1859.

42 Dunn, *A Treatise*, p. 134.

43 Mokyr calls it 'one of the high-tech sectors of the British economy [in the eighteenth century]': Joel Mokyr, *The Enlightened Economy: Britain and the Industrial Revolution, 1700–1850*, London: Penguin, 2009, p. 105. Sekula, 'Photography between Labour and Capital', p. 204.

44 Raphael Samuel, 'Workshop of the World: Steam Power and Hand Technology in Mid-Victorian Britain', *History Workshop Journal* 3 (Spring 1977), p. 21.

45 Tonge, *Principles and Practice*, p. 121. A more fanciful comparison was made with the city of London: Leifchild, *Our Coal and Our Coal-Pits*, pp. 131–2.

46 The association was quite direct in some drawings, where the layout of seams was superimposed on the pattern of fields: see 'A Plan of Land belonging to Mrs Margaret Garrick situate at Birtley in the County of Durham' (1759), reproduced as fig. 27 in Celina Fox, *The Arts of Industry in the Age of Enlightenment*, New Haven: Yale University Press, 2009.

47 John Rylands Library Special Collections, RYL/1/3/1.

48 A 'leviathan house': John Rylands Library Special Collections, RYL/1/3/1: from a brochure published by Rylands & Sons; D. A. Farnie, 'The Wiener Thesis Vindicated: The Onslaught of 1994 upon the Reputation of John Rylands of Manchester', in David J. Jeremy (ed.), *Religion, Business and Wealth in Modern Britain*, London: Routledge, 1998, p. 96.

49 D. A. Farnie, *John Rylands of Manchester*, Manchester: John Rylands Library, 1993, pp. 14–17, 45; Farnie, 'The Wiener Thesis', pp. 90–5. This prudent diversification is also shown at Gidlow by the coexistence of 'two identical, yet entirely separate, half-mill installations so that the failure of one would not interfere with the other, or completely stop production': John Rylands Library Special Collections, JRLCM 52/1/8/1–11. Rylands & Sons was also known for acquiring already built mills and warehouses, often on the cheap during trade depressions: John Rylands Library Special Collections, RYL/1/5/9; D. A. Farnie, 'John Rylands of Manchester', *Bulletin of the John Rylands Library* 56, no. 1 (Autumn 1973), p. 109. The nearest to favoured architects were Clegg & Knowles, who worked for Rylands & Sons in Portland Street from the 1870s. Farnie's chapter on 'The Wiener Thesis' is a defence of Rylands's reputation as a fair and successful businessman employing thousands in comparatively steady work, which is not the issue I am concerned with here.

50 Rylands had previously rented mines near Bolton: Farnie, *John Rylands*, p. 11. It was not unusual for textile manufacturers to combine cotton with coal: see Anthony Howe, *The Cotton Masters, 1830–1860*, Oxford: Clarendon Press, 1984, p. 39. On the cheapness of coal relative to its proximity see Malm, *Fossil Capital*, 160. See also 'A Captain of Industry', *Manchester Guardian*, 25 December 1886, pp. 497–8.

51 Farrimond, 'On the Working of Coal Mines', p. 91.

52 Evan Leigh, *The Science of Modern Cotton Spinning*, vol. 1, Manchester: Palmer & Howe, 1873; *Manchester City News*, 15 April 1865. Mike Williams and D. A. Farnie, *Cotton Mills in Greater Manchester*, Preston: Carnegie, 1992, p. 98.

53 William Fairbairn, *Treatise on Mills and Millwork*, London, 1863, vol. 2, p. 172.

54 Sven Beckert, *Empire of Cotton: A New History of Global Capitalism*, London: Allen Lane, 2014, chapters 9 and 10; Peter Harnetty, *Imperialism and Free Trade: Lancashire, India, and the Cotton Supply Question*, Manchester: Manchester University Press, 1972.

55 Karl Marx, *Capital: A Critique of Political Economy*, trans. Ben Fowkes, Harmondsworth: Penguin, 1976, vol. 1, p. 494.

56 This description is partly based on Tredgold's own: Thomas Tredgold, *The Steam Engine: Its Invention and Progressive Development*, rev. edn, London: John Weale, 1838, vol. 1, p. 328.

57 Accounts of the relation between architecture and engineering tend to be about the relation between architects and engineers, including their training and professional bodies, rather than about the things (structures, buildings) that define the professions and blur their edges. See, for instance, Andrew Saint, *Architect and Engineer: A Study in Sibling Rivalry*, New Haven: Yale University Press, 2008.

58 Karl Marx, *Capital*, p. 502.

59 Andrew Ure, *The Philosophy of Manufactures, or, An Exposition of the Scientific, Moral, and*

Commercial Economy of the Factory System, London: Charles Knight, 1835, pp. 18, 110.

60 Robert Rawlinson, *Designs for Factory Furnace, and Other Tall Chimney Shafts*, London: Kell, 1858, p. 8.

61 Stephen Mosley, *The Chimney of the World: A History of Smoke Pollution in Victorian and Edwardian Manchester*, London: Routledge, 2008, p. 128.

62 J. W. Graham, principal of Dalton Hall, University of Manchester, as quoted in E. T. Cook, *The Life of John Ruskin*, vol. 2, 1860–1900, London: George Allen, 1911, p. 471.

63 Mosley, *The Chimney of the World*, pp. 18–19.

64 Nicholas Cooke claimed to have observed the phenomenon of melanism in lepidoptera – moths turning black – in the late 1840s in Pettypool Wood, Cheshire. *Tephrosia biundularia* had been creamy white but now 'all are dark, smoky brown, approaching black': Nicholas Cooke, 'On Melanism in Lepidoptera', *Entomologist* 10, no. 167 (April 1877), p. 94. Similarly, *Amphidasis betularia*. This surely disproved natural selection. Manchester and its outlying towns, including Wigan, 'all pouring forth from their tall chimneys chemical fumes and coal smoke', had scattered their deposits on leaves where they had been 'swallowed by the larvae along with their food': Cooke, 'On Melanism', p. 94.

65 Gaskell, *North and South*, p. 96. On smoke abatement societies see Mosley, *The Chimney of the World*. For working-class opposition to environmental pollution see Malm, *Fossil Capital*, p. 244.

66 Both as quoted in Mosley, *The Chimney of the World*, p. 88.

67 T. C. Horsfall, 'The Government of Manchester', *Transactions of the Manchester Statistical Society*, 1895–6, p. 19. Industrial concerns seem to have largely won out in disputes over smoke pollution across the century, but there are interesting examples at the beginning of the century of the Court Leet and police commissioners successfully prosecuting factory owners: Catherine Bowler and Peter Brimblecombe, 'Control of Air Pollution in Manchester Prior to the Public Health Act, 1875', *Environment and History* 6, no. 1 (February 2000), pp. 77–83.

68 Mosley, *The Chimney of the World*, p. 185.

69 The painting was commissioned by Queen Victoria from the artist soon after her trip to the city in 1851: see www.rct.uk/collection/920223/manchester-from-kersal-moor (accessed 17 October 2020).

70 Benjamin Disraeli, *Coningsby* (1844), Harmondsworth: Penguin, 1983, p. 185.

71 Augustus Voelcker, 'On the Injurious Effects of Smoke on Certain Building Stones and on Vegetation', *Journal of the Society of Arts* 12, no. 583 (22 January 1864), p. 153.

72 William Geoffrey Goodacre, *A Scheme for Drawing off and Disposing of all Smoke, Waste Gases, Impure Air, etc*, London: Stationers' Hall, 1891.

73 Peter Spence, *Coal, Smoke, and Sewage, Scientifically and Practically Considered*, Manchester: Cave & Sever, 1857. For 'chimney of the world' see Steven Marcus, *Engels, Manchester and the Working Class*, London: Weidenfeld & Nicolson, 1974, p. 46.

74 *Manchester New Town Hall: General History and Detailed Description of the Building*, Manchester: John Heywood, 1877, p. 5.

75 Timothy Morton, *Hyperobjects: Philosophy and Ecology after the End of the World*, Minneapolis: University of Minnesota Press, 2013, p. 7. Malm argues that this new environmental epoch should be dated not to the moment of James Watt's invention (1784) but, rather, to the 'decisive shift' to steam as a result of the economic and social crisis between 1825 and 1848: Malm, *Fossil Capital*, p. 63.

76 For articles on air pollution in Manchester see *Memoirs of the Manchester Literary and Philosophical Society* 3 (1785–9), pp. 219–33; 15 (1851–2), pp. 207–18; 24 (1867–70), pp. 270–3; and also *Proceedings of the Manchester Literary and Philosophical Society* 7 (1866–7), pp. 157–161; 8 (1868–9), pp. 137–9.

77 Robert Angus Smith, 'On the Air of Towns', *Journal of the Chemical Society* 11 (1859), p. 232.

78 A. H. Davies-Colley, 'Facing Materials for a Smoky Town', *British Architect* 7 (9 February 1877), p. 87. *Manchester New Town Hall: General History and Detailed Description of the Building*, Manchester: John Heywood, 1877, p. 7.

79 'Mr Brooke', 'Stone as a Building Material for Manchester', *British Architect* 7 (2 March 1877), p. 129; Augustus Voelcker, 'On the Injurious Effects of Smoke on Certain Building Stones and on Vegetation', *Journal of the Society of Arts* 12, no. 583 (22 January 1864), pp. 146–53.

80 Voelcker, 'Injurious Effects', p. 149.

81 *Manchester New Town Hall*, p. 3. This source notes that at the moment of its completion the Town Hall was already showing signs of darkening by smoke.

82 There are three accounts of the building science of the library and its relation to environmental issues: John Maddison, 'Basil Champneys and the John Rylands Library', in John H. G. Archer (ed.), *Art and Architecture in Victorian Manchester*, Manchester: Manchester University Press, 1985, pp. 230–49; John Hodgson, '"Carven Stone and Blazoned Pane": The Design and Construction of the John Rylands Library', *Bulletin of the John Rylands Library Manchester* 89, no. 1 (2012–13), pp. 19–81; and Catherine Bowler and Peter Brimblecombe, 'Environmental Pressures on Building Design and Manchester's John Rylands Library', *Journal of Design History* 13, no. 3 (2000), pp. 175–91.

83 James Phillips Kay, *The Moral and Physical Condition of the Working Classes Employed in the Cotton Manufacture in Manchester*, London: Ridgway, 1832, p. 36; Friedrich Engels, *The Condition of the Working Class in England* (1845), Harmondsworth: Penguin, 1987, p. 99.

84 Some associated this with a perceived 'deterioration of the race': John Edward Morgan, *The Danger of Deterioration of Race from the Too Rapid Increase of Great Cities*, London: Longmans, Green, 1866, p. 29.

85 John W. Graham, *The Destruction of Daylight: A Study in the Smoke Problem*, London: George Allen, 1907, p. 5.

86 On Deansgate and municipal improvement in the previous decades see Chris Otter, *The Victorian Eye: A Political History of Light and Vision in Britain, 1800–1910*, Chicago: University of Chicago Press, 2008, pp. 79–82.

87 Alan Kidd, *Manchester*, Keele: Keele University Press, 1993, p. 152.

88 There was some comment on the suitability of the site given the source of Rylands & Sons' wealth: *World*, 29 October 1907.

89 Otter, *Victorian Eye*, p. 81.

90 A link between clerks using pens and hewers using picks is made in Leifchild, *Our Coal and our Coal-Pits*, p. 132.

91 See, for instance, the illustration of a high-pressure boiler that is placed opposite plans and views of buildings in Lincoln's Inn: *Civil Engineer and Architect's Journal* 7 (20 January 1844), pp. 30–1. The journal is full of such juxtapositions.

92 Sekula, 'Photography between Labour and Capital', p. 204.

93 John Rylands Library Special Collections, JRL/5/2/5/13.

94 Bowler and Brimblecombe, 'Environmental Pressures', p. 185.

95 Bowler and Brimblecombe, 'Environmental Pressures', p. 185.

96 John Rylands Library Special Collections, JRL/5/2/1/1/2–3.

97 Although electricity caused pollution from being generated by gas engines. At the library these were situated outside the main building so that their pollution was directed into the surrounding streets: Bowler and Brimblecombe, 'Environmental Pressures', p. 187.

98 It was also intended to have many more screening devices of carved stone in its decoration: Maddison, 'Basil Champneys', p. 241.

99 John Rylands Library Special Collections, JRL/5/2/1/4–5; John Maddison, 'Basil Champneys', pp. 241–3.

100 She 'imbued the library with a liberal but decidedly Nonconformist approach to written culture': Elizabeth Gow and Julianna Simpson, 'Enriqueta Rylands, the John Rylands Library and the Lutheran Legacy', *Bulletin of the John Rylands Library* 93, no. 2 (Autumn 2017), p. 115.

101 Matthew Arnold, *Culture and Anarchy* (1869), Cambridge: Cambridge University Press, 1932, p. 49.

102 Bowler and Brimblecombe, 'Environmental Pressures', p. 181.

103 Mosley, *The Chimney of the World*, p. 103.

104 John Ruskin, 'The Study of Architecture in our Schools', paper delivered at the RIBA, 15 May 1865, published in John Ruskin, *On the Road*, vol. 1, Orpington: George Allen, 1885, p. 378.

105 John Ruskin, *The Stones of Venice*, vol. 3, *The Fall* (1853), New York: Publishers' Plate Renting, 1903, p. 13 (chapter 1, section 14).

106 John Ruskin, *The Stones of Venice*, vol. 2, *The Sea Stories* (1853), New York: Publishers' Plate Renting, 1903, p. 71 (chapter 4, section 14).

107 This might include her upbringing in Havana, Cuba. Enriqueta was the daughter of a marriage between a Yorkshire merchant and a French Cuban woman, whose family wealth was based on slave-owning and trading in sugar. She had a Catholic upbringing but became a Congregationalist under the influence of the Liverpool-based Rev. Thomas Raffles. Sometime in the 1860s she became a companion to John Rylands's first wife Martha; eight months after Martha's death she married the seventy-four-year-old millionaire, when she was thirty-two. Her Cuban background seems to have been little mentioned by her. See Raul Ruiz, 'Mrs Rylands's Cuban Origins', *Bulletin of the John Rylands Library* 85, no. 1 (2003), pp. 121–6; D. A. Farnie, 'Enriqueta Augustina Rylands, 1843–1908', *Bulletin of the John Rylands Library* 71, no. 2 (1989), pp. 3–38.

108 Ruskin, *Stones of Venice*, vol. 3, chapter 1, paragraph 14.

109 Arnold, *Culture and Anarchy*, pp. 6, 51, 105. Many of the fortunes and philanthropic works of Victorians might be looked at in this way. An adjacent example is the library that Lord Lindsay built with the profits accrued by his Wigan coal mines: Stephen J. Milner, 'Manufacturing the Renaissance: Modern Merchant Princes and the Origins of the Manchester Dante Society', in Janet Wolff and Mike Savage (eds.), *Culture in Manchester: Institutions and Urban Change since 1850*, Manchester: Manchester University Press, 2013, pp. 74–5. Beyond this, examples might include the libraries and universities endowed by the Scottish American steel manufacturer Andrew Carnegie and, coming to the present, the Woodlands, an 'ecological' new town paid for by the oil and gas tycoon George Mitchell in Texas, or the eco-town Masdar City, funded by oil wealth, in Abu Dhabi.

110 Much needs to be done here since Mark Girouard's *Sweetness and Light: The Queen Anne Movement, 1860–1900*, Oxford: Clarendon Press, 1977.

111 Ruskin, 'The Study of Architecture', p. 378. Manchester is not explicitly mentioned here but it is likely from other details in this passage that it is the city being referred to. Ruskin had already attacked Free Trade and Manchester's industrial capitalism in 1857 and 1859 in his lectures collected in *Unto This Last* (1860) and *The Two Paths* (1859).

112 John Ruskin, *Fors Clavigera: Letters to the Workmen and Labourers of Great Britain*, vol. 6, Orpington: George Allen, 1876, p. 174 (letter 66). As Fitch has shown, this was a running theme and concern across Ruskin's writing: Raymond E. Fitch, *The Poison Sky: Myth and Apocalypse in Ruskin*, Athens: Ohio University Press, 1982.

113 Ruskin, *The Storm Cloud*, pp. 62, 61, 48.

114 They travelled together in the 1890s and he dedicated poetry to her. She supported his campaigns for the preservation of the Lake District and for setting up the National Trust. I am grateful to Elizabeth Gow, curator at the John Rylands Library, for this information. A graduate of Ruskin's project for overindulged Oxford students, the Hinksey road-mending scheme, Rawnsley represents what has been called 'Romantic ecology', deriving from Wordsworth and Ruskin: Jonathan Bate, *Romantic Ecology: Wordsworth and the Environmental Tradition*, London: Routledge, 1991. He often repeated his master's view of smoke as devil's darkness, the product of an unconstrained industrial world: H. D. Rawnsley, 'Sunlight or Smoke?', *Contemporary Review* 57 (1890), pp. 512–13. See also H. D. Rawnsley, *Ruskin and the English Lakes*, Glasgow: James MacLehose & Sons, 1902.

115 I am grateful to Elizabeth Gow for this information.

116 Walter Benjamin, 'On the Concept of History' (1940), in *Walter Benjamin Selected Writings*, vol. 4, 1938–1940, trans. Edmund Jephcott, Howard Eiland and others, ed. Howard Eiland and Michael W. Jennings, Cambridge, MA: Belknap Press, 2003, p. 392.

6 · The Largest Room: Making a Deal with the Architecture of the Exchange *pages 165–187*

1 There are two women to the right middle ground, both clearly tolerated only as guests (membership was limited to men).

2 The very homogeneity of this mass portrayal places it somewhat at odds with a tradition of describing exchanges as 'exotic' bazaars, where the different lands from which the goods derive are depicted analogously in a motley range of 'peoples' dealing in the exchange: see, for instance, Voltaire's account of the Royal Exchange in London, as discussed in Eric Auerbach, *Mimesis: The Representation of Reality in Western Literature*, trans. Willard R. Trask, Princeton: Princeton University Press, pp. 401–4.

3 'Key to Interior of the Royal Exchange' (1877), Manchester Art Gallery.

4 'Middlemen' is used to indicate what they were doing in the Exchange. Many members were not just merchants, brokers or agents but also manufacturers, engineers, machine makers and so on: *Love and Barton's (Manchester) Exchange Directory of 1848*, Manchester: Love & Barton, 1848. Globalisers might come from any of these groups.

5 Alois Riegl, *The Group Portraiture of Holland* (1902), trans. Evelyn Kain and David Britt, Los Angeles: Getty Research Institute, 1999, p. 62.

6 See Mark Clapson, 'Playing the System: The World of Organised Street Betting in Manchester, Salford and Bolton, c1880 to 1939', in Andrew Davies and Steven Fielding (eds.), *Workers' Worlds: Cultures and Communities in Manchester and Salford, 1880–1939*, Manchester: Manchester University Press, 1992; Ross McKibbon, 'Working-Class Gambling in Britain, 1880–1939', in Ross McKibbin (ed.), *The Ideologies of Class: Social Relations in Britain 1880–1950*, Oxford: Clarendon Press, 1990, pp. 101–38. Walter Benjamin's reflections on the relation between gambling and the automatic actions of the machine are relevant here: Walter Benjamin, 'Some Motifs in Baudelaire' (1939), in Walter Benjamin, *Charles Baudelaire: A Lyric Poet in the Era of High Capitalism*, London: Verso, 1983, pp. 134–6.

7 Riegl has some interesting things to say about attentiveness in group portraiture: Riegl, *Group Portraiture*, pp. 366–7.

8 Theodor Adorno, letter to Walter Benjamin, 1 February 1939, in *Walter Benjamin Selected Writings*, vol. 4, 1938–1940, trans. Edmund Jephcott, Howard Eiland and others, ed. Howard Eiland and Michael W. Jennings, Cambridge, MA: Belknap Press, 2003, p. 203.

9 T. de Courcy Meade, 'Paper Submitted to Improvement and Paving Committees of Manchester City Council', 1908, Chetham's Library.

10 Walter Benjamin, 'Paris, the Capital of the Nineteenth Century', in *Walter Benjamin: Selected Writings*, vol. 3, 1935–1938, trans. Edmund Jephcott, Howard Eiland and others, ed. Howard Eiland and Michael W. Jennings, Cambridge, MA: Belknap Press, 2002, p. 42.

11 In Christopher Wren's plan of London after the Great Fire, the Royal Exchange was envisaged as standing free of other buildings but also as the hub of many 'rays' of roads: Christine Stevenson, *The City and the King: Architecture and Politics in Restoration London*, New Haven: Yale University Press for Paul Mellon Centre for Studies in British Art, 2013, p. 141.

12 This Exchange and exchanges in general are little enough studied, historically or architecturally. Jürgen Osterhammel's otherwise magisterial global history, *The Transformation of the World* (2014), is typical, making no mention at all of commodity or stock exchanges. There is no scholarly account of the history of the Manchester Exchange and its buildings have barely been examined by architectural historians.

13 John Byng in 1790, as extracted in L. D. Bradshaw (ed.), *Visitors to Manchester*, Manchester: Neil Richardson, 1987, p. 19.

14 R. D. H. Scott, *The Biggest Room in the World: A Short History of the Manchester Royal Exchange*, Manchester: Royal Exchange Theatre Trust, 1976, pp. 13–14; Thomas Markus, *Buildings and Power: Freedom and Control in the Origins of Modern Building Types*, London: Routledge, 1993, p. 315.

15 Edwin Simpson, *A Sketch of the History of the Manchester Royal Exchange*, Manchester: Guardian, 1875, p. 3.

16 Daniel Defoe, 'The Anatomy of Exchange Alley' (1719), in *Political and Economic Writings of Daniel Defoe*, vol. 6, *Finance*, ed. W. R. Owens and P. N. Furbank, London: Pickering & Chatto, 2000, p. 144.

17 The manorial rights of the Mosleys over the market were finally bought up only in 1845: George Saintsbury, *Manchester*, London: Longmans, 1887, pp. 176–7.

18 Joseph Aston, *A Picture of Manchester*, Manchester: Aston, 1816, p. 20. See also S. Austin, J. Harwood, G. Pyne and C. Pyne, *Lancashire Illustrated*, London: Fisher & Jackson, 1832, p. 4.

19 Arthur Redford, *The History of Local Government in Manchester*, vol. 1, *Manor and Township*, London: Longmans, Green, 1939, p. 105.

20 Redford, *Manor and Township*, p. 156.

21 Aston, *A Picture*, p. 205.

22 Sven Beckert, *Empire of Cotton: A New History of Global Capitalism*, London: Allen Lane, 2014, p. 73.

23 For war capitalism see Beckert, *Empire of Cotton*, especially chapter 3. The idea has been criticised ('as if war as a means of economic competition ended with the eighteenth century') but seems broadly accurate in terms of slavery and cotton, as well as the long peace after 1815: Mark Harvey, 'Slavery, Indenture and the Development of British Industrial Capitalism', *History Workshop Journal* 88 (2019), p. 67.

24 David Harvey, *Spaces of Global Capitalism*, London: Verso, 2006.

25 Arjan Appadurai, *Modernity at Large*, Minneapolis: University of Minnesota Press, 1996, pp. 34–5.

26 Quoted in Asa Briggs, *Victorian Cities*, Harmondsworth: Penguin, 1968, p. 89.

27 On the Liverpool Cotton Exchange see Beckert, *Empire of Cotton*, chapter 8. On differences between the Manchester and Liverpool exchanges see Scott, *The Biggest Room*, p. 38. For 'coupled nucleii' see John D. Wirth and Robert

L. Jones, *Manchester and São Paulo*, Stanford: Stanford University Press, 1978, p. 133.

28 Simpson, *A Sketch*, p. 5.

29 Elijah Helm, *Chapters in the History of the Manchester Chamber of Commerce*, London: Simpkin, Marshall, 1902, p. 8.

30 Aston, *A Picture*, p. 205.

31 Scott, *The Biggest Room*, p. 17.

32 For Manchester as still a town of small businesses see Hannah Barker, *Family and Business during the Industrial Revolution*, Oxford: Oxford University Press, 2017, pp. 3–4, 78–117.

33 Redford, *Manor and Township*, p. 157.

34 Aston, *A Picture*, pp. 207–8.

35 Aston, *A Picture*, pp. 208–9. This account is also based on Austin and others, *Lancashire Illustrated*, pp. 4–5.

36 The occasion was held at the also newly opened Theatre Royal in King Street, and the line break was accompanied by a change of scene: Scott, *The Biggest Room*, p. 21.

37 For this history see Helm, *Chapters*.

38 Beckert, *Empire of Cotton*, pp. ix–x, 251–4, 328. The combination of aggression and defensiveness, typical of war capitalism, is well represented by the 1794 preamble to the rules of the new body, as well as its determination to work cooperatively with government: Helm, *Chapters*, pp. 1–2; on the work of the chamber during the French wars see especially pp. 2–6.

39 This is probably the portrait now owned by the Manchester Art Gallery and attributed to a follower of Lawrence.

40 On visitors attracted to the London Exchange by the spectacle from its gallery see Natasha Glaisyer, *The Culture of Commerce in England, 1660–1720*, Woodbridge: Boydell, 2006, pp. 48–9. On the Exchange as one of Manchester's tourist attractions see Paul Readman, *Storied Ground: Landscape and the Shaping of English National Identity*, Cambridge: Cambridge University Press, 2018.

41 Pictures and engravings could also be bought in the shops inside the Royal Exchange in London: Glaisyer, *The Culture of Commerce*, p. 29. The gallery ('Mr Ford's Gallery ... universally considered the principal ornament of the building') was the subject of some dispute between Mr Ford, the proprietor of the gallery, and Joseph Aston (Ford was unimpressed by the description in Aston's guidebook): 'Description of the Manchester Exchange by Joseph Aston with notes by W.F.', undated MS in Chetham's Library. Warehouse space could also be found at the Royal Exchange in London: Glaisyer, *The Culture of Commerce*, p. 30.

42 By 1847 the Post Office was removed, its presence in the Exchange regarded as compromising its status as a public utility: Scott, *The Biggest Room*, p. 18.

43 Aston, *A Picture*, p. 209.

44 Glaisyer, *The Culture of Commerce*, pp. 28–9.

45 Léon Faucher, *Manchester in 1844: Its Present Condition and Future Prospects*, Manchester: Heywood, 1844.

46 Markus, *Buildings and Power*, pp. 300–1. On the concept of the network as a nineteenth-century phenomenon see Jürgen Osterhammel, *The Transformation of the World*, Princeton: Princeton University Press, 2014, p. 711.

47 Simon Schaffer, 'A Social History of Plausibility: Country, City and Calculation in Augustan Britain', in A. Wilson (ed.), *Rethinking Social History: English Society, 1570–1920, and its Interpretation*, Manchester: Manchester University Press, 1993.

48 Aston, *A Picture*, p. 207.

49 Christine Stevenson, 'Making Empire Visible at the Second Royal Exchange, London', in Mark Hallett, Nigel Llewellyn and Martin Myrone (eds.), *Court, Country, City: British Art and Architecture, 1660–1735*, New Haven: Yale University Press for Paul Mellon Centre for Studies in British Art, 2016, pp. 53, 65.

50 W. Cooke Taylor, *Notes of a Tour in the Manufacturing Districts of Lancashire*, London: Duncan & Malcolm, 1842, pp. 10–12. For a later account see Joseph Perrin, *The Manchester Hand-Book: An Authentic Account of the Place and its People*, Manchester: Hale & Roworth, 1857, p. 123.

51 John Bright's attempt to address the Exchange as a whole in 1842 was a notorious breach of institutional decorum: *The Centenary of the Manchester Royal Exchange*, Manchester: Manchester Royal Exchange, 1904, p. 15. Bright, like Cobden, was a member of the Exchange.

52 Mills's redesign has sometimes been confused with Harrison's original building: John J. Parkinson-Bailey, *Manchester: An Architectural History*, Manchester: Manchester University Press, 2000, p. 14. Another problem is that the print made to mark Queen Victoria's visit to the building in 1851 seems not to represent the only recently refronted building but to have been based on images of the older frontages, with the temporary structures erected at the apsidal end of the building for the Queen's arrival and entry superimposed: see the reproduction in Scott, *The Biggest Room*, p. 30.

53 *Manchester Guardian*, 11 October 1851, pp. 7–8.

54 Scott, *The Biggest Room*, 31. The appurtenances were quickly auctioned off after the visit: Richard Wright Procter, *Memorials of Manchester Streets*, Manchester: Thomas Sutcliffe, 1874, p. 97.

55 A different exchange was proposed in 1865 on a different site and fostered by a new exchange company. This got as far as purchasing land and obtaining a design by Alfred Waterhouse before the scheme was abandoned. For Waterhouse's design see *Building News*, 12, 1865, pp. 792–3. Another scheme proposed for Albert Square was also abandoned: *The Centenary of the Manchester Royal Exchange*, p. 20.

56 Beckert, *Empire of Cotton*, pp. 320–3.

57 Simpson, *A Sketch*, p. 32.

58 *Directory and Guide to the Manchester Royal Exchange*, Manchester: Richard Collinson, 1905, p. 255 (this was first issued in 1891, when the plan was also printed). Some entries were marked with an asterisk, indicating that they had no fixed place in the Exchange – presumably they could be contacted via their advertised telephone number or address. No such plan existed in Love & Barton's earlier directory, so there must have been some plan or messaging system within the building itself: *Love and Barton's (Manchester) Exchange Directory of 1848*. One member, probably in the mid-century, had his letterhead printed to read 'Manchester 'Change Tuesdays and Fridays from 11½–2½ o'clock and from 4 to 5 o'clock PM opposite No. 8 Pillar Ducie Street side near Window Desk': quoted without a full source in Scott, *The Biggest*

Room, p. 36. Such public advertising of his position was actually against the membership rules.

59 Markus mentions that the mosaic pavement of the Roman square in Ostia was marked with positions for trading merchants: Markus, *Buildings and Power*, p. 310. Plans of the second Royal Exchange in London wrote specialised traders into specific areas of the building's courtyard and surrounding covered 'walks' (see plate on p. 314).

60 W. H. Brindley, *The Soul of Manchester*, Manchester: Manchester University Press, 1929, p. 217. There were industrialists who devised ways of similarly projecting grids onto the factory floor, for proto-Taylorist purposes of monitoring attendance and movement: Beckert, *Empire of Cotton*, p. 193.

61 Mike Davis, *Old Gods, New Enigmas: Marx's Lost Theory*, London: Verso, 2018, pp. 41–2, 46–9, 77–8. 'Concentrating masses of workers in large factories ... [is] *the indispensable precondition* for the emergence of the proletariat as a class': Georg Lukács, *History and Class Consciousness* (1967), trans. Rodney Livingstone, London: Merlin, 1974, p. 173 (italics in original). Engels had made the same argument for the industrial city: Friedrich Engels, *The Condition of the Working Class in England* (1845), Harmondsworth: Penguin, 1987, p. 148.

62 Franco Moretti, *The Bourgeois: Between History and Literature*, London: Verso, 2013, p. 15.

63 A. Marrison, S. Broadberry and T. Leunig, 'Selling English Cotton into the World Market: Implications for the Rationalisation Debate, 1900–1939', in John F. Wilson (ed.), *King Cotton: A Tribute to Douglas A. Farnie*, Lancaster: Crucible, 2009, p. 49.

64 Progress was seriously affected by lack of materials (especially steel) and labour during the Great War: Bradshaw, Gass & Hope archive, Bolton Library and Museums.

65 An alternative solution to this appeared in 1913 with the idea of mirroring Mills & Murgatroyd's portico with another one on the extended east side: 'Proposed Extension of the Manchester Royal Exchange', Parliamentary Bill, 1913, in Manchester Central Library. However, both porticos were now withdrawn to the skin of the building and neither was intended to have an entrance, which was to be on the western side.

66 Brindley, *The Soul of Manchester*, p. 218.

67 'Vision of totality' is from Fredric Jameson, *The Geopolitical Aesthetic: Cinema and Space in the World System*, Bloomington: Indiana University Press / London: BFI, 1995, p. 79.

68 Fredric Jameson, *Brecht and Method*, London: Verso, pp. 151–2.

69 Alberto Toscano and Jeff Kinkle, *Cartographies of the Absolute*, Winchester: Zero Books, 2015, p. 40; Jameson, *The Geopolitical Aesthetic*, p. 79.

70 'Proposed Extension of the Manchester Royal Exchange', Parliamentary Bill, 1913.

71 Meade, 'Paper Submitted', pp. 1–21.

72 Meade, 'Paper Submitted', p. 30.

73 Brindley, *The Soul of Manchester*, p. 203.

74 Meade, 'Paper Submitted', p. 36.

75 Engels, *Condition*, p. 82.

Coda *pages 189–193*

1 It was built in 1870–1. The architect was Edward Salomons; the panel designer was Robert Pollitt; and the panels were executed by T. R. and E. Williams: Clare Hartwell, *Manchester*, London: Penguin, 2001, pp. 167–8.

2 For more on the late flowering of Coburn's work in the service of Manchester industrialists see Mark Crinson, 'Pictorialism and Industry: Alvin Langdon Coburn in Manchester', *History of Photography* 30, no. 2 (2006), pp. 155–72.

3 James McNeill Whistler, 'Ten O'Clock' (1885), in *The Gentle Art of Making Enemies* (1892), New York: Dover, 1967, p. 144. For the Whistler connection see John Taylor, 'Pictorial Photography in Britain 1900–1920', in Arts Council of Great Britain, *Pictorial Photography in Britain, 1900–1920*, London: Arts Council, 1978, p. 19.

4 Arthur Symons, *London: A Book of Aspects*, Minneapolis: Edmund Brooks, 1908, as quoted in Karl Beckson, *Arthur Symons: A Life*, Oxford: Clarendon Press, 1987, p. 242.

5 William H. Mills, *The Manchester Reform Club, 1871–1921*, Manchester: Charles W. Hobson, 1922, p. 89. For more on Manchester's clubs see Simon Gunn, *The Public Culture of the Victorian Middle Class: Ritual and Authority in the English Industrial City, 1840–1914*, Manchester: Manchester University Press, 2000, pp. 84–105.

6 Mills, *The Manchester Reform Club*, p. 89.

7 Mills, *The Manchester Reform Club*, pp. 3–4.

8 Mills, *The Manchester Reform Club*, p. 59.

9 Mills, *The Manchester Reform Club*, p. 85.

10 Mills, *The Manchester Reform Club*, p. 22.

11 Coburn was clearly extending a formula – of empty benches and deserted doorways – that he had developed ten years before: see his illustrations for H. G. Wells, *The Door in the Wall and other Stories*, London: Grant Richards, 1911; and his frontispiece for Henry James, *The Coxson Fund*, New York: Scribners, 1906.

12 Benjamin was notably lukewarm on this as a theory of modern art: Walter Benjamin, 'The Paris of the Second Empire in Baudelaire' (1938), in Walter Benjamin, *Charles Baudelaire: A Lyric Poet in the Era of High Capitalism*, London: Verso, 1983, p. 82.

Photograph Credits

Images have been provided by and are reproduced courtesy of the owners or custodians of the works of art. Images for which additional photographic credit is due are listed below.

Alamy: image on pp. vi–vii, 57, 116

Collection of the author: 1, 5, 29, 30, 169

Wikimedia Commons: 2, 18, 42, 70, 131 (photograph: Stephen Richards), 137 (photograph: Mike Peel), 139 (photograph: Mike Peel), 164 (photograph: David Dixon), 165

© Mark Crinson (photographer): 13, 15, 35, 36, 37, 39, 41, 45, 46, 48, 52, 55, 56, 58, 79, 83, 84, 85, 86, 87, 88, 91 a–c, 98, 99, 108, 109, 110, 111, 129, 130, 133, 140, 143

© Wellcome Images: 35

Bridgeman Images: 38, 145, 156, 158

Royal Collection (in public domain): 60

RIBApix: 133, 138, 141, 142

By permission of the British Library: 153

Index